THE YEARBOOK

OF

OBSTETRICS AND GYNAECOLOGY

VOLUME 8

The Yearbook of
OBSTETRICS
and
GYNAECOLOGY

Volume 8

Edited by
P.M. Shaughn O'Brien

RCOG Press

First published 2000

ISBN 1 900364 30 1

Published by the **RCOG Press** at the
Royal College of Obstetricians and Gynaecologists
27 Sussex Place, Regent's Park
London NW1 4RG
Registered Charity No. 213280

RCOG Press Editor: Jane Moody
Cover designed by Geoffrey Wadsley
Printed by Henry Ling Limited, Dorchester Dorset

Contents

List of contributors

Thomas F. Baskett MB FRCS DHMSA FRCOG
Professor
Department of Obstetrics and Gynaecology
Dalhousie University
5980 University Avenue
Halifax
Nova Scotia B3J 3G9
Canada

S. Anthony Beardsworth MB BS MRCOG
Clinical Research Fellow
Centre for Metabolic Bone Disease
Hull Royal Infirmary
220–236 Anlaby Road
Hull HU3 2RW

John S.G. Biggs MA MD FRCOG
Postgraduate Medical Dean
East Anglian Deanery
Block 3, Ida Darwin site
Fulbourn
Cambridge CB1 5EE

Fiona Broughton Pipkin MA DPhil FRCOG
Professor of Perinatal Physiology
Department of Obstetrics
School of Human Development
Queen's Medical Centre
Nottingham NG7 2UH

Iain T. Cameron MA MD MRACOG MRCOG
Professor of Obstetrics and Gynaecology
University of Southampton
Department of Obstetrics and Gynaecology
The Princess Anne Hospital
Coxford Road
Southampton SO9 4HA

Linda D. Cardozo MD FRCOG
Professor of Urogynaecology
Urogynaecology Unit
Department of Obstetrics and Gynaecology
9th Floor, Ruskin Wing
King's College Hospital
Denmark Hill
London SE5 9RS

Geoffrey Chamberlain MD FRCS FACOG(Hon) FFFP(Hon) FRCOG
Emeritus Professor
Department of Obstetrics and Gynaecology
Singleton Hospital
Swansea SA2 8QA

Allan M.Z. Chang PhD FRACOG FHKAM(O&G) FHKCOG FRCOG
Professor and Chairman
Department of Obstetrics and Gynaecology
Chinese University of Hong Kong
Department of Obstetrics and Gynaecology
1/F, Special Block
Prince of Wales Hospital
Shatin, New Territories
Hong Kong

Tim Chard MD FRCOG
Professor of Obstetrics and Gynaecology
Reproductive Physiology Laboratory
St. Bartholomew's Hospital
London EC1A 7BE

Anna P. Cockell MD MRCOG
Subspecialty Trainee Maternal-Fetal Medicine
Fetal Medicine Unit
Obstetric Hospital
University College Hospital
London WC1E 6AU

Ian D. Cooke MB BS DGO FRCOG
Professor of Obstetrics and Gynaecology
Department of Obstetrics and Gynaecology
Jessop Hospital for Women
Leavygreave Road
Sheffield S3 7RE

William T. Creasman MD FACOG FRCOG
Sims Hester Professor and Chairman
Department of Obstetrics and Gynaecology
Medical University of South Carolina
96 Jonathan Lucas Street
PO Box 250619
Charleston
SC 29425
USA

Howard Cuckle DPhil
Professor of Reproductive Epidemiology
University of Leeds
Reproductive Epidemiology Unit
26 Clarendon Road
Leeds LS2 9NZ

Gustaaf Dekker MD PhD FRACOG FDCOG
Professor in Obstetrics and Gynaecology
Lyell McEwin Health Service
Department of Obstetrics and Gynaecology
Haydown Road
Elizabeth Vale
South Australia 5112
Australia

James Drife MD FRCP(Ed) FRCS(Ed) FRCOG
Professor of Obstetrics and Gynaecology
University of Leeds
Department of Obstetrics
Level D, Clarendon Wing
Belmont Grove
Leeds LS2 9NS

Rachel D'Souza MB BS MRCOG
Clinical Research Fellow
Margaret Pyke Research Institute
73 Charlotte Street
London W1P 1LB

D. Keith Edmonds MB ChB FRACOG FRCOG
Consultant Obstetrician and Gynaecologist
Queen Charlotte's and Chelsea Hospital
Goldhawk Road
London W6 0XG

Mahmoud F. Fathalla MB ChB MCH PhD FACOG FRCOG
Professor of Obstetrics and Gynaecology
Assiut University
PO Box 30
Assiut
Egypt

G. Marcus Filshie DM MFFP FRCOG
Reader/Consultant Obstetrician and Gynaecologist
University of Nottingham
Academic Division of Obstetrics and Gynaecology
Floor D, East Block
Queen's Medical Centre
Clifton Boulevard
Nottingham NG7 2UH

Ian S. Fraser MD CREI FRANZCOG FRCOG
Professor in Reproductive Medicine
Department of Obstetrics and Gynaecology
University of Sydney
NSW 2006
Australia

John Guillebaud MA FRCSE MFFP FRCOG
Professor of Family Planning and Reproductive Health
University College London
Medical Director
Margaret Pyke Centre
73 Charlotte Street
London W1P 1LB

Mark Hamilton MD FRCOG
Consultant Obstetrician and Gynaecologist
Assisted Reproduction Unit
Aberdeen Maternity Hospital
Cornhill Road
Aberdeen AB25 2ZD

Howard S. Jacobs MD FRCP FRCOG
Emeritus Professor of Reproductive Endocrinology
Royal Free and University College Hospital Medical School
The Middlesex Hospital
Mortimer Street
London W1N 8AA

Ian R. Johnson MD FRCOG
Head of School of Human Development
University of Nottingham
Academic Division of Obstetrics and Gynaecology
D floor, East Block, Queen's Medical Centre
Nottingham NG7 2UH

Frank Johnstone MD FRCOG
Consultant/Senior Lecturer
Department of Obstetrics and Gynaecology
Centre for Reproductive Biology
University of Edinburgh
37 Chalmers Street
Edinburgh EH 3 9EW

Joe Jordan MD FRCOG
Medical Director
Birmingham Women's Hospital
Metchley Park Road
Edgbaston, Birmingham B15 2TG

Vik Khullar MB BS MRCOG
Subspecialty Trainee in Urogynaecology
Urogynaecology Unit
Department of Obstetrics and Gynaecology
9th floor, Ruskin Wing
Ruskin Wing
King's College Hospital
Denmark Hill
London SE5 9RS

Matthew F. Kohler MD
Assistant Professor
Department of Obstetrics and Gynaecology
Medical University of South Carolina
96 Jonathan Lucas Street
PO Box 250619
Charleston, SC 29425
USA

Kelvin J.H. Lim MB ChB MRCOG
Specialist Registrar and Clinical Research Fellow
Department of Obstetrics and Gynaecology
Jessop Hospital for Women
Leavygreave Road
Sheffield S3 7RE

Fong Lok MB ChB PhD
Registrar
Department of Obstetrics and Gynaecology
Women's and Children's Hospital
72 King William Street
North Adelaide
South Australia 5006
Australia

Peter W. Nathanielsz MD PhD ScD FRCOG
Director of Laboratory for Pregnancy and Newborn Research
Department of Biomedical Sciences
College of Veterinary Medicine
PO Box 16
Cornell University
Ithaca
NY 14853-6401
USA

Oswald M. Petrucco MB BS CREI RFD FRACOG FRCOG
Senior Lecturer
University of Adelaide
Department of Obstetrics and Gynaecology
1st floor, Queen Victoria Building
Women's and Children's Hospital
72 King William Road
North Adelaide, South Australia 5006
Australia

David W. Purdie MD FRCP(Ed) FRCOG
Head of Clinical Research
Centre for Metabolic Bone Disease
Hull Royal Infirmary
220–236 Anlaby Road
Hull HU3 2RW

Christopher W.G. Redman MA MB BCh FRCP FRCOG
Professor of Obstetric Medicine
Nuffield Department of Obstetrics and Gynaecology
Level 3, Women's Centre
John Radcliffe Hospital
Headington
Oxford OX3 9DU

Jeffrey S. Robinson MB BCh BAO FRACOG FRCOG
Head of Department of Obstetrics and Gynaecology
University of Adelaide
Adelaide
South Australia 5005
Australia

Charles H. Rodeck DSc(Med) FRCPath FMedSci FRCOG
Professor and Head of Department of Obstetrics and Gynaecology
University College London
86–96 Chenies Mews
London WC1E 6HX

Daljit S. Sahota PhD
Assistant Professor
Chinese University of Hong Kong
Department of Obstetrics and Gynaecology
Prince of Wales Hospital
Shatin,
New Territories
Hong Kong

Robert W. Shaw MD FRCS(Ed) FRCOG
Professor of Obstetrics and Gynaecology
University Hospital of Wales
Heath Park
Cardiff CF14 4XW

Gordon C.S. Smith MD MRCOG
Visiting Research Fellow
Laboratory for Pregnancy and Newborn Research
Cornell University
Department of Biomedical Sciences
College of Veterinary Medicine
PO Box 16
Ithaca,
NY 14853-6401
USA

R. William Stones MD MRCOG
Senior Lecturer and Consultant in Obstetrics and Gynaecology
The Princess Anne Hospital
Coxford Road
Southampton SO16 5YA

John Studd DSc MD FRCOG
Consultant Gynaecologist
Chelsea and Westminster Hospital
369 Fulham Road
London SW10 9NH

**E. Malcolm Symonds MD FFPHM FACOG(Hon)
FRANZOG(Hon) FRCOG**
Executive Adviser
Faculty of Medicine
University Putra Malaysia
Department of Obstetrics and Gynaecology
Queen's Medical Centre
Nottingham NG7 2UH

Raewyn Teirney MB ChB MRANZCOG
Fellow in Reproductive Endocrinology
Department of Obstetrics and Gynaecology
Royal Hospital for Women
Randwick
NSW 2031
Australia

Allan Templeton MD FRCOG
Professor and Head of Department of Obstetrics and Gynaecology
University of Aberdeen
Aberdeen Maternity Hospital
Cornhill Road
Aberdeen AB25 2ZD

Eric J. Thomas MD FMedSci MRCOG
Professor of Obstetrics and Gynaecology
The Princess Anne Hospital
Coxford Road
Southampton SO16 5YA

Fred Wadsworth MB BS FRCS(Ed) MRCOG
Research Fellow
Imperial College
Chelsea and Westminster Hospital
369 Fulham Road
London SW10 9NH

James J. Walker MD FRCP(Glas) FRCP(Ed) FRSM FRCOG
Professor of Obstetrics and Gynaecology
St. James's University Hospital
Beckett Street
Leeds LS9 7TF

Charles R. Whitfield MD FRCP(Glas) FRCOG
Emeritus Regius Professor of Midwifery
University of Glasgow
The Queen Mother's Hospital
Yorkhill
Glasgow G3 8SJ

Martin J. Whittle MD FRCP(Glas) FRCOG
Head of Division of Reproductive and Child Health
Department of Fetal Medicine
Birmingham Women's Hospital
Edgbaston
Birmingham B15 2TS

Foreword

The 35 chapters of this volume of the *Yearbook of Obstetrics and Gynaecology* have been specifically commissioned as a special edition to celebrate the new millennium. The content has been devised to record milestones in the specialty of obstetrics and gynaecology which have occurred particularly in the last two decades. The reader will note that each chapter is written, sometimes with co-authors, by a senior author who is an internationally recognised authority on a particular subject. Each author's remit was, where appropriate to the subject, to produce a chapter which summarised the history of the subject, the current status of knowledge and practice and, finally, to predict the future. Perhaps all of this in a single chapter was a tall order but I am sure you will agree that it has worked.

Most of us will recall candidates in the old style MRCOG *viva voce* who were asked about a particular historical figure. The answer was often given as 'an eminent obstetrician and gynaecologist at the turn of the century'. This covered the whole of time because the turn of any century stretches from middle of one to the middle of the next and the particular century need not be identified, thus covering all eventualities. The new MRCOG viva examination (OSCE) prevents us from asking such irrelevant questions. However, we are all interested in who it was that had the original thought and the energy to pursue a new idea to fruition. It is intended that most of the content of this book is written by 'eminent gynaecologists at the turn of the millennium'. It has not been possible to include all those considered to be eminent for editorial reasons, namely the balance of subject matter within the book and the total number of chapters, so I apologise to eminent potential contributors whom I have knowingly or unknowingly omitted.

'Clinical effectiveness', 'evidence-based medicine' and 'critical appraisal of the literature' are fashionable terms devised by people who research and practice their medicine at a desk or via a computer using various search strategies. The contributors to this volume have been chosen because they are all actively involved in research, the development of new ideas and new methods of investigation and treatment, providing the seeds for the reviewers of evidence-based medicine. The authors were, however, asked to construct their chapters as evidence-based reviews wherever possible. One author (Thomas Baskett) pointed out that this was the least appropriate approach and claimed his chapter to be the last bastion of non-evidence based medicine, which is undoubtedly true. Surprisingly, I was able to find only one eponymous procedure whose technique and inventor will live well on into the next millennium.

This book cannot fail to succeed, given the quality of the contributors whom I thank enormously for their time, particularly as they are all extremely busy clinicians and academics who would normally expect to delegate most of the work of preparing such a chapter to a high-flying junior. As well as thanking the contributors, I must also acknowledge Dr Mary Ann Lumsden and Miss Marion Macpherson for their invaluable assistance and constructive help in devising the book's content.

I wish you a successful, productive and happy Millennium.

Shaughn O'Brien
Publications Officer 1996–99

1

Some 20th century milestones in obstetrics and gynaecology

Thomas F. Baskett

INTRODUCTION

The advances in scientific understanding and treatment of disease in the 20th century have exceeded those of all previous centuries. Even for one specialty it is not possible in a short chapter to do justice to the extraordinary changes that have occurred over the last 100 years. I have therefore chosen to highlight four developments that occurred in the 20th century. In doing so, my choices are meant to be representative of the many advances in the physical and social aspects of reproductive health.

Haemolytic disease of the newborn is chosen as it embodies all that is best of the advances in perinatal medicine in this century.

The detection of premalignant disease of the cervix has led, when universally and appropriately applied, to a huge reduction in one of the more unpleasant female genital tract malignancies. Unfortunately, other than trophoblastic disease, advances in the diagnosis and management of other gynaecological malignancies have not been as noteworthy.

The oral contraceptive pill is included for its profound liberating effect on the social and reproductive health of women. Providing, as Sir Dugald Baird (1965) put it, 'freedom from the tyranny of excessive fertility'.

The development of safe and effective oxytocic drugs for the prevention and management of postpartum haemorrhage is representative of the enormous improvement in maternal safety in childbirth.

HAEMOLYTIC DISEASE OF THE NEWBORN

At the start of this century there was no understanding of the pathogenesis of this disease, merely the observation of repetitive and tragic perinatal loss due to 'familial icterus gravis'. In 1932, Louis Diamond described the pathophysiological basis characterised by fetal red cell haemolysis, erythropoiesis and the excessive production of immature nucleated red cells or erythroblasts, for which he coined the term 'erythroblastosis fetalis' (Diamond *et al.* 1932). By 1940, Karl Landsteinder and Alexander Wiener had reported the discovery of the rhesus blood group system. One year later, Philip Levine established the role of isoimmunisation in the pathogenesis of erythroblastosis fetalis (Levine *et al.* 1941).

Thus, by the late 1940s, the pathogenesis of the disease was understood but the perinatal mortality remained at three to four per 1000 births (Tovey 1990). While the maternal anti-D antibody titres tended to reflect the severity of fetal disease, there were many exceptions and accurate prediction was not possible. It was Douglas Bevis (1952), working as a senior registrar in Manchester, who used amniocentesis and analysis of amniotic fluid as a guide to the extent of fetal anaemia. This work was extended by William Liley (1961) of Auckland, who used spectrophotometric analysis of amniotic fluid bilirubin levels, allowing more accurate prediction of the risk of fetal death *in utero*. Based on this prediction, the standard treatment became induction of labour prior to the estimated time of fetal demise; with neonatal exchange transfusion as required. For the fetus with severe disease prior to realistic neonatal viability, Liley (1963) pioneered intrauterine fetal transfusion – the first intrauterine therapeutic procedure.

The evolution of neonatal exchange transfusion for haemolytic disease of the newborn began even before the pathophysiology of the condition was understood. On 18 December 1924, Alfred Hart, a paediatrician at the Toronto Hospital for Sick Children, Ontario, was consulted on a male infant born to a couple who had suffered six previous perinatal deaths due to 'familial icterus gravis'. All of the infants had been born healthy but developed jaundice within the first 48 hours and died after the development of progressive kernicterus. Hart reasoned that 'the condition was due to some unknown toxin circulating in the blood'. To remove the 'circulating toxin' he performed an exchange transfusion with donor blood from 'a healthy male unrelated to the family'. The infant's jaundice subsided and he continued to thrive (Hart 1925). In seeking to remove the 'toxin' Hart had stumbled upon the optimum treatment of exchange transfusion. This report was overlooked and it was not until 1946 that Wallerstein at the Jewish Memorial Hospital in New York successfully used exchange transfusion in three cases of haemolytic disease of the newborn. Both Hart and Wallerstein used the longitudinal sinus through the anterior fontanelle and a peripheral vein to perform the transfusion. Louis Diamond (1947) of Boston later popularised the use of the umbilical vein.

The advent of real-time ultrasound in the 1970s revolutionised the diagnosis and treatment of rhesus (Rh) immunisation, as it has the entire area of fetal diagnosis and treatment. Accurate placental localisation reduced the trauma associated with amniocentesis and intraperitoneal fetal transfusion. Direct intravascular fetal transfusion was developed in the 1980s and improved the outcome, especially for the severely affected or hydropic fetus (Nicolaides *et al.* 1986).

As the understanding of the pathophysiology of the disease led to improved methods of diagnosis and treatment, further basic research delineated the method of its prevention. By the late 1950s it was known that ABO incompatibility between the mother and fetus provided some protection against Rh immunisation, due to naturally occurring anti-A or anti-B eliminating Rh-positive paternal fetal cells before they could stimulate the mother's immune system. Ronald Finn, working in Professor Cyril Clarke's unit in Liverpool, pursued this theory using the Kleihauer–Betke test to detect fetal red cells in maternal blood after delivery. He demonstrated that ABO incompatibility did indeed give a high degree of protection against Rh immunisation. At a symposium in Liverpool in February 1960, Finn postulated that it may be possible to mimic this protection by giving the mother anti-D after delivery, thus destroying any Rh-incompatible fetal cells that cross into the maternal circulation before they could cause sensitisation (Finn 1960). They began work on volunteer Rh-negative male policemen by injecting them with Rh-positive cells followed by anti-D serum. Initially this was unsuccessful as they used the saline (complete) antibody. However, when they changed to the albumin (incomplete) antibody they found it gave significant protection from immunisation (Finn *et al.* 1961). In New York, Freda *et al.* (1964) independently carried out a similar study on 'volunteers' from the local Sing Sing Prison. In 1964, the Liverpool clinical trial on high-risk primiparous women showed conclusively that anti-D gammaglobulin given within 48 hours of delivery protected against immunisation. Studies in other countries confirmed this finding and the dose and its timing were established.

The problem of haemolytic disease of the newborn epitomises the advances in perinatal medicine. Over a period of 30 years, the pathophysiology of this disease was delineated, the diagnosis and treatment successfully refined and the method of its prevention achieved. It represents one of the triumphs of applied basic sciences and clinical investigation contributing, in a sense, to the death of a disease.

CERVICAL CYTOLOGY

Although cytology is a laboratory and morphological method of diagnosis it was only developed and applied through the efforts of clinicians. In 1840, Johannes Müller laid out clear microscopic definitions and criteria to differentiate benign from malignant tumours. He also noted the tendency to non-adherence, or exfoliation, of cancer cells. Julius Vogel of Göttingen, who held the splendid title, 'Extraordinarius of Medicine', examined the secretions from a fistulous connection with a pharyngeal cancer and noted exfoliated cancer cells (Vogel 1843). This was the first diagnosis by exfoliative cytology and was confirmed at the subsequent postmortem examination.

After qualifying in his native Greece, George Nicholas Papanicolaou emigrated to the USA and worked at the New York Hospital and Cornell Medical College. One of his main contributions was a new staining technique for cytological appraisal, which he developed 'after long experimentation' (Papanicolaou 1942). It was not his choice or use of dyes that was so innovative, but the use of alcohol as a counter stain which added transparency and improved cell-type differentiation.

While studying the changes associated with ovulation in vaginal smears at the New York Hospital, he identified tumour cells by chance in a woman with cervical cancer. He reported this finding at the Third Race Betterment Conference in Battle Creek, Michigan, in January 1928 (Papanicolaou 1928). In his conclusion, Papanicolaou said: 'It is not an exaggeration to say that certain cases of cancer of the cervix may be diagnosed by the presence of only one of these cells.'

Unfortunately, this conference was aimed at the wrong audience. The subsequent published proceedings contained photographs of poor quality and many typographical errors. For example, cancerous cells were consistently printed as 'conscious cells'. The publication, therefore, had no impact. Papanicolaou dropped the subject for about ten years but then teamed up with Herbert Trout at the Department of Gynecology in the New York Lying-in Hospital and applied the technique of exfoliative cytology to the diagnosis of precancerous or early cervical cancer. This work was presented at the New York Obstetrical Society on 11 March 1941 and subsequently published in the *American Journal of Obstetrics and Gynecology* (Papanicolaou and Trout 1941). In the conclusion to their paper, the authors expressed the hope that this technique 'because of its simplicity, may eventually be applied widely so that the incipient phases of the disease may come more promptly within the range of our modern modes of treatment which have proved highly effective in early carcinoma'. Papanicolaou and Trout used a glass pipette with bulb suction to aspirate cells from the posterior vaginal fornix. A few years later, James Ernest Ayre, a Canadian gynaecologist, designed his wooden spatula to scrape cells directly from the squamocolumnar junction. He showed that this technique produced fresh cells from the affected area and he likened his technique to a 'surface biopsy' (Ayre 1947). Fifty years later, Ayre's spatula and technique remain in use and the 'pap smear' has been comprehensively vindicated in population studies as a means of detecting premalignant disease of the cervix and reducing the incidence of invasive cancer. When properly applied it has proved to be one of the more effective methods of preventive medicine developed in the 20th century.

ORAL CONTRACEPTION

The oral contraceptive pill, known universally as 'the pill', was anticipated in the early part of the 20th century by Ludwig Haberlandt, Professor of Physiology at the University of Innsbruck. In 1919, he showed that transplanting ovaries from pregnant rabbits to fertile ones rendered them infertile. Haberlandt continued his studies on animals, well aware that the ultimate clinical implication of his work was a method of contraception (Haberlandt 1921). He used the terms 'temporary sterilisation' and 'hormonal sterilis-ation', which he felt would be 'the ideal method for practical medicine and its future task of birth control'. During the 1920s, the hormone-secreting activity of the ovary was studied and assays for oestrogen and progesterone were developed. By 1930, both hormones had been isolated. However, they were inactive when taken by mouth and it was not until the addition of the ethinyl group to oestradiol in 1938 that an orally active oestrogen became available.

Progesterone was only available in minute quantities from animal ovaries. It was Russell Marker, an eccentric American organic chemist, who isolated progesterone from the Mexican black-headed yam in 1943 (Lehmann et al. 1973). Progesterone was now available in large quantities but still not active when taken by mouth. Carl Djerassi was the first to synthesise an orally active progestational agent – norethindrone – in 1951.

The detailed story of the final development of the oral contraceptive pill has been well documented (Goldzieher and Rudel 1974; Gillmer 1997). In essence, Gregory Pincus working at the Worcester Foundation for Experimental Biology in Massachusetts with his research scientist Min Cheuh Chang, in a series of animal studies, demonstrated the effectiveness of progesterone as an inhibitor of ovulation. In 1954, Pincus collaborated with John Rock, a well-known Boston gynaecologist with a special interest in infertility. He used the pill in patients for one to three cycles hoping to achieve 'rebound fertility' after stopping the progestin. Both knew that the ultimate use was as an ovulation-inhibiting birth control agent. However, in the early and mid-1950s, pharmaceutical companies in the USA were as fearful of being linked with contraceptive products as they are of abortifacient medications in the 1990s. For this reason, the first clinical trials of the pill as a birth-control method were carried out in Puerto Rico under the supervision of Celso-Ramon Garcia. The progestin used was found to contain significant amounts of oestrogen, later identified as mestranol, which helped reduce the amount of breakthrough bleeding found with pure progestins. The first oral contraceptive was approved in the USA in May 1960. It was produced by G.D. Searle Co. and was called 'Enovid'. It contained almost 10 mg of progesterone in the form of norethynodrel and 150 µg mestranol.

Less well-known is the background that led to the official position of the Catholic Church on the use of the pill. The social, ethical and moral turmoil engendered by the contraceptive pill was most profoundly felt by those who adhered to Catholic law. In

1958, just before his death, Pope Pius XII decreed that the pill could be used to treat reproductive disorders, but that its use as a contraceptive was unacceptable. His successor, John XXIII, endorsed this mandate in 1963 and established a six-man commission to advise him on population, family and birth control – but died before the commission met. His successor, Paul VI, revised and enlarged this commission in 1964. The commission met several times over the next three years and was eventually expanded to 71 people, including three married couples. Most members of the commission recognised the global need for birth control and argued that the pill, by extending the 'natural' period of rest the ovary underwent each month and postpartum, could therefore be classified as a 'natural' method of birth control. The majority report from the commission, therefore, was to endorse the pill as an acceptable method of birth control for Catholics. However, a small minority of senior and rigid cardinals submitted a minority report to the Pope and their view held sway (Kaiser 1985; Asbell 1995). On 29 July 1968, the long-awaited encyclical *Humanae Vitae* was released. The overwhelming majority view of the commission and the hopes of millions of Catholics throughout the world were dashed, with profound detrimental effects for both world population and the future authority of the Church.

OXYTOCIC DRUGS

Although herbal and animal by-products have been used as putative oxytocic agents for several centuries, the modern era of effective oxytocic drugs really begins with ergot. The name is derived from the French *argot*, a cock's spur, due to the physical resemblance of the spurs of the fungus *Claviceps purpura*. Ergotism, epidemics of which have occurred for at least 1000 years, was caused by eating bread made with rye contaminated with the ergot fungus. During these epidemics it was observed that women would miscarry and midwives, reasoning that ergot must cause uterine contractions, started to use it for cases of prolonged labour with inefficient uterine contractions. It came to be called *pulvis ad partum* – the powder of birth.

John Stearns is credited with making the application of ergot more widespread in the English-speaking world, having learned its use from a midwife in his district of New York State. In 1807, he wrote a letter to a colleague which was subsequently published in the *Medical Repository* of New York (Stearns 1808). In this letter, he pointed out that ergot 'expedites lingering parturition . . . the pains induced by it are peculiarly forcing' and 'in most cases you will be surprised with the suddenness of its operation'. Initially, ergot was used to augment uterine contractions in non-progressive labour. The problem was the unpredictable and occasionally sustained and forceful contractions which could result in asphyxia of the fetus and stillbirth or even rupture of the uterus and death of the mother. In a later publication, Stearns was to emphasise these potential complications and talked of the 'necessity of extreme caution' (Stearns 1822). Unfortunately, others used ergot less thoughtfully and there were many perinatal and maternal deaths associated with its use in labour. Indeed, another prominent New York physician, David Hossack, had condemned the use of ergot during the first and second stages of labour with his pithy quote from a letter he wrote in June 1822 to James Hamilton, the Professor of Obstetrics at the University of Edinburgh. 'The ergot has been called, *pulvis ad partum*; as it regards the child, it may with almost equal truth be denominated the *pulvis ad mortem*.'

Towards the latter half of the 19th century, the use of ergot prior to delivery of the infant was largely abandoned and its use for the treatment of miscarriage and postpartum haemorrhage emphasised. The drawback with the crude ergot preparation was that its oxytocic action was quite variable so that dose and safety margins were impossible to predict. Thus, by the late 19th and early 20th century, many laboratories had started work on the analysis of the alkaloids contained in ergot. In 1932, the Therapeutic Trials Committee of the Medical Research Council, headed by Sir Henry Dale, approached the Professor of Obstetrics, F.J. Browne of University College Hospital, London, to consider clinical trials. Chassar Moir, then a registrar in Browne's department, carried out the studies measuring intrauterine pressure in postpartum patients with a small balloon attached to a recording manometer. Dale appointed his chief research chemist, Harold Dudley, to the daunting task of isolating the dozens of chemical fractions of ergot. Moir then tested each sample for its oxytocic properties on postpartum patients. In 1935, after three years endeavour, ergometrine was isolated (Dudley and Moir 1935). The details of this fascinating discovery have been recorded (Moir 1964).

The first recording of the oxytocic properties of posterior pituitary extract was by Sir Henry Dale in 1906. This observation was contained in a short paragraph within a long paper describing the effects on the blood pressure in cats of various substances, including ergot and endocrine gland extracts (Dale 1906). Dale gave some samples to the obstetrician, William Blair-Bell, who applied posterior pituitary extract in clinical practice and particularly noted the dramatic effect in cases of atonic postpartum haemorrhage (Blair-Bell 1909). He did sound a note of caution about its use before delivery because of the sustained nature of the induced uterine contraction.

Posterior pituitary extract started to be used in obstetrics and, unfortunately, the mistakes of ergot, 100 years before, were repeated. There was a feeling that pituitary extract, being 'physiological' must be safer. However, standardisation of the strength of the early commercial preparations was quite erratic and many cases of fetal asphyxia and uterine rupture occurred.

In 1928, Kamm, working in the Parke-Davis laboratories in the USA (Kamm *et al.* 1928) showed that pituitary extract could be split into two fractions: one oxytocic (oxytocin) and the other vasopressor (vasopressin). These were subsequently marketed under the names Pitocin and Pitressin. However, Pitocin did contain a certain amount of vasopressin and, although much safer than the original extract, it was not devoid of vasopressor side effects.

It was Vincent du Vigneaud of Cornell University who identified the chemical structure of the active principles, oxytocin and vasopressin. In 1953, he achieved synthesis of oxytocin (du Vigneaud *et al.* 1953). Thus, by the 1950s, synthetic preparations of pure oxytocin were widely and commercially available. Pure oxytocin has proved to be the safest of all the oxytocic drugs.

Prostaglandins are a ubiquitous group of substances found in virtually all tissues. The first demonstration that seminal fluid caused contraction of smooth muscle was by Kurzrok in New York and Goldblatt in England (Kurzrok and Lieb 1930; Goldblatt 1933). Von Euler (1934) showed that the effect was due to a lipid fraction, which he named 'prostaglandin'. It was to be 30 years before Sune Bergstrom isolated the crystalline form of prostaglandin (Bergstrom *et al.* 1962). Later, the uterine contraction effect was found to be most predictable and strongest in the prostaglandin $F_{2\alpha}$ series. For postpartum haemorrhage the main advance was the development of the 15-methyl analogue of $PGF_{2\alpha}$ which was found to have a very strong utero-tonic component and much less of the other undesirable smooth muscle stimulation effects (Annathasubramanim *et al.* 1988).

Thus, in the evolution of oxytocic drugs for the management of postpartum haemorrhage, there are really three main epochs, each about 20 years apart. Oxytocin is the cheapest and safest and is now the drug of first choice for this purpose. The first oxytocic, ergometrine, has a long and noble history in the prevention and management of postpartum haemorrhage. However, it does have occasional undesirable vasopressor side effects and is now the drug of second choice. The 15-methyl analogue of $PGF_{2\alpha}$ is more expensive, but is a valuable third-line drug in those rare cases when the uterus is unresponsive to oxytocin or ergometrine.

In the 1980s, randomised controlled trials clearly demonstrated that active management of the third stage of labour with oxytocin and/or ergometrine significantly reduces the risk of postpartum haemorrhage and its sequelae (Prendiville *et al.* 1988). In his retrospective review of the role of ergometrine in the management of postpartum haemorrhage, Chassar Moir (1964) was to say, 'reckoned in the saving of human life, places it among the enduring achievements of medical science'. The accuracy of that appraisal can be judged by the reduction in maternal deaths from haemorrhage in the last half of the 20th century. In the *Confidential Inquiry into Maternal Deaths in England and Wales* for the years 1952–54, there were 188 maternal deaths from haemorrhage. In the last triennium, 1994–96, this had been reduced 20-fold to nine deaths in the whole of the UK (Department of Health 1998). One of the main reasons for this reduction has been the development and correct application of oxytocic drugs. It is for this reason that I include it as one of the major milestones of the 20th century.

However, much remains to be done in the developing world where at least one woman dies in childbirth every minute. A large number of these deaths are due to postpartum haemorrhage, with the lack of available oxytocic drugs being a significant factor. Thus, as is so often the case in modern medicine, we lack the ability and organisation to equitably apply world-wide the simple and effective resources that are available.

The great improvement in maternal safety in pregnancy, largely achieved by the middle of the 20th century, led to a shift in emphasis towards perinatal outcome. As the perinatal results improved, couples gained the security and luxury of concentrating their energy and anxieties on the psychosocial aspects of pregnancy, childbirth and neonatal care. Ironically, as we leave a century in which the safety and success of obstetrical and gynaecological care has improved beyond recognition, in no small part due to medical advances, we find an increasingly critical, dissatisfied and litigious patient population.

References

Annathasubramanim, L., Kuntal, R., Sivariman, R. and Raghaven, K.S. (1988) Management of intractable postpartum haemorrhage secondary to uterine atony with intramuscular 15-methyl $PGF_{2\alpha}$. *Acta Obstet Gynecol Scand Suppl* **145**, 17–19

Asbell, B. (1995) *The Pill: a Biography of the Drug that Changed the World*. New York: Random House

Ayre, J.E. (1947) Selective cytology smear for diagnosis of cancer. *Am J Obstet Gynecol* **53**, 609–17

Baird, D. (1965) A fifth freedom? *BMJ* **ii**, 114–18

Bergstrom, S., Ryhag, E.R., Samuelson, B. and Sjovall, J. (1962) The structure of prostaglandin E, F₁ and F₂. *Acta Chem Scand* **16**, 501–2

Bevis, D.C.A. (1952) The antenatal prediction of haemolytic disease of the newborn. *Lancet* **i**, 395–8

Blair-Bell, W. (1909) The pituitary body and the therapeutic value of the infundibular extract in shock, uterine atony and intestinal paresis. *BMJ* **ii**, 1609–13

Dale, H.H. (1906) On some physiological actions of ergot. *J Physiol* **34**, 163–97

Department of Health (1998) *Why Mothers Die: Report on Confidential Enquiries into Maternal Deaths in the United Kingdom 1994–1996.* London: The Stationery Office

Diamond, L.K. (1947) Erythroblastosis foetalis or haemolytic disease of the newborn. *Proc R Soc Med* **40**, 546–7

Diamond, L.K., Blackfan, K.D. and Batty, J.M. (1932) Erythroblastosis fetalis and its association with universal edema of the fetus, icterus gravis neonatorum and anaemia of the newborn. *J Pediatr* **1**, 269–75

du Vigneaud, V., Ressler, C. and Trippett, S. (1953) The sequence of amino acids in oxytocin, with a proposal for the structure of oxytocin. *J Biol Chem* **205**, 949–57

Dudley, H.W. and Moir, C. (1935) The substance responsible for the traditional clinical effect of ergot. *BMJ* **i**, 520–3

Finn, R. (1960) Erythroblastosis. *Lancet* **i**, 526

Finn, R., Clark C.A. and Donohoe, W.T.A. (1961) Experimental studies on the prevention of Rh haemolytic disease. *BMJ* **i**, 1486–90

Freda, V.J., Gorman, J.C. and Pollack, W. (1964) Successful prevention of experimental Rh sensitization in man with anti-Rh gamma-globulin antibody preparation: a preliminary report. *Transfusion* **4**, 26–32

Gillmer, M.D.G. (1997) The oral contraceptive pill – a product of serendipity. *The Diplomate* **4**, 231–5

Goldblatt, M.W. (1933) Properties of human seminal plasma. *J Physiol* **84**, 208–18

Goldzieher, J.W. and Rudel, H.W. (1974) How the oral contraceptives came to be developed. *JAMA* **230**, 421–5

Haberlandt, L. (1921) Über hormonale sterilisierung des weiblichen tierkoerpers. *Muenchener Medizinische Wochenschrift* **68**, 1577–8

Hart, A.P. (1925) Familial icterus gravis of the newborn and its treatment. *CMAJ* **15**, 1008–11

Kaiser, R.B. (1985) *The Politics of Sex and Religion.* Kansas City: Leaven Press

Kamm, O., Aldrich, T.B., Groute, I.W., Row, L.W. and Bugbee, E.P. (1928) The active principles of the posterior lobe of the pituitary gland. 1. The demonstration of the presence of two active principles. 2. The separation of the two principles and their concentration in the form of potent solid preparations. *Journal of the American Chemical Society* **50**, 573–85

Kurzrok, R. and Lieb, C.C. (1930) Biochemical studies of human semen. *Proc Soc Exp Biol* **26**, 268–72

Landsteiner, K. and Wiener, A.S. (1940) Agglutinable factor in human blood recognized by immune sera for rhesus blood. *Proc Soc Exp Biol NY* **43**, 223–5

Lehmann, P.A., Bolivar, A. and Quintero, R. (1973) Russel E. Marker: pioneer of the Mexican steroid industry. *Journal of Chemical Education* **150**, 195–9

Levine, P., Burnham, L., Katzine, M. and Vogel, P. (1941) The role of isoimmunisation and the pathogenesis of erythroblastosis fetalis. *Am J Obstet Gynecol* **42**, 925–37

Liley, A.W. (1961) Liquor amnii analysis in the management of pregnancy complicated by rhesus sensitisation. *Am J Obstet Gynecol* **82**, 1359–64

Liley, A.W. (1963) Intrauterine transfusion of foetus in haemolytic disease. *BMJ* **ii**, 1107–9

Moir, J.C. (1964) The obstetrician bids, and the uterus contracts. *BMJ* **ii**, 1025–9

Müller, J. (1840) *On the Nature and Structural Characteristics of Cancer and Those Morbid Growths Which May be Confounded With It*. London: Sherwood, Gilbert and Piper

Nicolaides, K.H., Soothill, P.W., Clewell, W., Rodeck, C.H. and Campbell, S. (1986) Rh disease: intravascular fetal blood transfusion by cordocentesis. *Fetal Therapy* **1**, 185–8

Papanicolaou, G.N. (1928) 'New cancer diagnosis' in: *Proceedings of the Third Race Betterment Conference*, pp. 528–34. Battle Creek, MI: Race Betterment Foundation

Papanicolaou, G.N. (1942) A new procedure for staining vaginal smears. *Science* **95**, 438–40

Papanicolaou, G.N. and Trout, H.F. (1941) The diagnostic value of vaginal smears in carcinoma of the uterus. *Am J Obstet Gynecol* **42**, 193–206

Prendiville, W., Elbourne, D. and Chalmers, I. (1988) The effects of routine oxytocic administration in the management of the third stage of labour: an overview of the evidence from controlled trials. *Br J Obstet Gynaecol* **95**, 3–16

Stearns, J. (1808) Account of the pulvis parturiens, a remedy for quickening child-birth. *New York Medical Repository* **11**, 308–9

Stearns, J. (1822) Observations on the secale cornutum or ergot with directions for its use in parturition. *Medical Record* **32**, 90–2

Tovey, L.A.D. (1990) Haemolytic disease of the newborn and its prevention. *BMJ* **300**, 313–16

Vogel, J. (1843) *The Pathology of the Human Body* (translated with additions by G. E. Day). London: H. Ballière

Von Euler, U.S. (1934) An adrenal-like action in extracts from prostatic and related glands. *J Physiol (Lond)* **81**, 102–12

Wallerstein, H. (1946) Treatment of severe erythroblastosis by simultaneous removal and replacement of the blood of the newborn infant. *Science* **103**, 583–4

2

The future of training

John S.G. Biggs

INTRODUCTION

Training is 'the act or process of providing or receiving instruction in or for a particular skill, profession, occupation etc.' (*Shorter Oxford English Dictionary*). This chapter takes up the task of examining training in obstetrics and gynaecology; it reviews the last 50 years, looks at the changes of the last five years and predicts future directions of training in the specialty. The emphasis will inevitably be on training in the UK, with a consciousness that while UK plans and programmes influence those in other countries the reverse is also true.

TRAINING IN THE LAST HALF CENTURY

The Goodenough report of 1944 established the pattern of undergraduate and postgraduate education in Britain for the next 50 years (Biggs 1998). The report quoted the Royal College of Obstetrics and Gynaecology as describing a low standard of midwifery in many parts of the country (Ministry of Health and Department of Health for Scotland 1944). It believed 'additional facilities for the training of students, both graduates and undergraduates, would do much to raise the standard'. At the time, the medical course was expected to include six months' continuous instruction in obstetrics and gynaecology, with two months' residence in a maternity hospital. Experience in the domiciliary midwifery service was part of most training, but even in 1944 this was seen to be in decline.

The Royal Commission chaired by Lord Todd (Department of Health and Social Security 1968) saw a need for major change in postgraduate training 'which seems to us hitherto to have been haphazard and in many respects unsatisfactory'. Todd described 'a notable lack of any attempt to study comprehensively the educational and manpower requirements . . . or to provide a coherent plan for the training and career of the individual doctor'. This was strong stuff.

Todd found young doctors in every field dissatisfied with the absence of information about possible careers, the lack of defined career paths and the uncoordinated provision of adequate and appropriate training. The senior house officer (SHO) years were seen as presenting the most urgent problems because of 'the present disorganised state of training'. Thirty years later, while the needs of higher trainees have been addressed, there is still disorganisation at SHO level.

With reference to obstetrics and gynaecology, Todd noted that College Membership required presentation of case reports and a single examination. His committee felt strongly that a single pass–fail examination had no place and urged the introduction of progressive assessment. The committee hoped for an end to the domination of early postgraduate training by formal exams. These matters have been better addressed in obstetrics and gynaecology than in many other specialties, but much remains to be done.

Moving to the more recent past, the College reviewed programmes of training in 1991 and an editorial on the subject was headed 'What's wrong with the specialty of obstetrics and gynaecology?' (Blunt 1991). There was seen to be little career guidance, a lack of a curriculum and structured training and excessive workloads for trainees. Aims and objectives for trainees were lacking; trainees were likely to be 'over-experienced but under-trained'; there was a lack of training in many of the newly acknowledged requirements of a consultant, especially management, teaching and communication. In a conclusion that reads strangely eight years later, there was said to be an acute shortage of consultant obstetricians; an increase in the numbers of trainees was a pressing need.

Trainees were expressing dissatisfaction in the early 1990s (RCOG National Trainees' Committee 1997). SHOs planning a career in general practice were finding that a six months' post in obstetrics and gynaecology was not well-orientated to their future work and most thought the posts discouraged trainees from subsequently providing intrapartum care (Smith 1991). A booklet describing the features of general-practice training in the specialty was recently reissued (RCGP and RCOG 1997) which lists training objectives for antenatal, postnatal and intranatal care, gynaecology and family planning. It recommends, for example, that after six months the trainee should be able to carry out a low forceps delivery. It was reported that less than 40% of general-practice trainees felt so competent (Smith 1991); questioning of trainees in the last five years suggests that few have instruction or experience in this procedure.

Those trainees wishing to pursue a career in the specialty were likely to be more satisfied with their SHO training, mainly because its longer duration meant growth of confidence in themselves and among senior staff, both medical and midwifery. On graduation to the registrar grade, possibly in a different part of the UK, there would be more responsibility, more experience and the chance to complete College membership examinations. Time as a registrar continued until a senior registrar place was won, often in yet another part of the UK. This would continue for four or more years with gathering of experience and skill until a consultant post was gained. Through the extended training there was no curriculum, no structure and no formal assessment of progress. The next section will demonstrate the scale of the change in training that has ensued following the reforms of higher specialist training introduced by the committee chaired by Calman (Department of Health 1993).

THE CURRENT STATUS OF TRAINING

Higher specialist training in the UK has undergone great change in the last five years following revisions recommended in 1993. A working group chaired by the then Chief Medical Officer for England, Dr, later Sir, Kenneth Calman, had set out to bring specialist training into line with that in the rest of the European Community. An equally important outcome was the modernisation of specialist training in the UK. The changes introduced by Calman addressed deficiencies identified much earlier by Goodenough in 1944 and Todd in 1968 and, in the case of obstetrics and gynaecology, by the College in 1991. The reforms, first described in 1993 (Department of Health 1993) were introduced progressively to all specialties. Obstetrics and gynaecology entered the new specialist registrar (SpR) grade, which merged the former registrar and senior registrar grades, in

April 1996. The new system is described fully in *A Guide to Specialist Registrar Training*, widely known as 'The Orange Book' (Department of Health 1998a).

The elements of the Calman changes are essentially as follows:

(1) Training in a specialty should encompass all training from full registration at the end of the intern year until specialist qualification;

(2) Each College should publish the requirements for entry to the SpR grade for specialties for which it is responsible;

(3) A training curriculum should be published for each specialty by the appropriate College or Colleges;

(4) Higher specialist training should take place in a planned and structured programme;

(5) Progress through higher training should be determined by annual, formal, recorded assessments;

(6) Successful completion of specialist training should result in the award of a certificate leading to specialist registration.

Three years after the start of the Calman system it can be asked how training has changed and how Colleges, especially the RCOG, have responded to the new requirements.

Training in a specialty should encompass all training from full registration until specialist qualification

Specialist training in the Calman system includes training in the SHO grade, called basic specialist or general professional training, as well as higher training in the SpR grade. The case has been made for all specialist training to be within a single grade as in the USA and Canada. While the proposal has not been agreed in the UK, specialties like anaesthesia have moved some distance towards it. The advantage of the dual grade system introduced by Calman is that competitive entry to the higher grade allows redirection of less well-performing trainees at an early stage. Potential advantages of introducing a unified grade include the associated requirement for more rigorous selection, better methods of assessment in the first years and provision of easier transfer of trainees and credit to careers for which they seem better suited.

In conformity with other member states of the European Community, a minimum duration of higher specialist training in the UK was determined for each specialty. These years needed to be added to those spent in basic training and the overall times are shorter than those previously pertaining in many specialties. 'Old hands' continue to regard them as insupportably brief; colleagues in North America see them as surprisingly long. The numbers of years were always meant to be minima that could be exceeded where this would be helpful. Regrettably, many trainees have come to view required extensions as a penalty rather than an advantage in their subsequent careers.

Each College should publish the requirements for entry to the SpR grade for specialties for which it is responsible

In most surgical specialties the key to entry is the surgical Membership (or Associate Fellowship in Scotland) which is based on a reconstituted, four-part examination completed during rotation throughout at least four six-month SHO posts. A basic surgical skills programme must also have been completed. In internal medicine specialties the entry requirement for higher training is possession of the medical Membership, which has seen little recent change. In obstetrics and gynaecology, entry requirements are passing of the first part of the College Membership examination and completion of two years of post-registration training, including one in the specialty. In comparison with other specialties, the barrier to entry is relatively low, leading to large numbers, especially among those coming from abroad, anticipating entry to the higher training grade. Current workforce analysis shows that numbers of higher trainees needed in the specialty will be smaller than formerly. There has been extensive revision of the second part of the College Membership examination; review of the first part is needed within reconsideration of entry requirements to the SpR grade.

A training curriculum should be published for each specialty by the appropriate College or Colleges

The production of College curricula was a drawn-out affair and, as would be expected, changes continue to be made. In anaesthesia, for instance, a year has been added to the training programme and the curriculum changed accordingly. In obstetrics and gynaecology the curriculum took the form of a list of skills a trainee specialist should progressively develop, built into a log book in which competence would be authenticated by a supervising consultant. Within three years the College has undertaken major revision of the list of skills, based on continuing evaluation. Particular attention has been given by the College to the latter part of higher training and curricula have been devised for five nationally recognised sub-specialties. There has also been work in providing outlines of special interest training which the trainee will pursue into a specialist career. Curriculum development has been further advanced in obstetrics and gynaecology than in many other specialties.

Higher specialist training should take place in a planned and structured programme

A single higher specialist training grade gave the opportunity for a plan and structure for the training of each SpR. The arrangements for a programme of training fall to a specialty training committee in each postgraduate dean's area or 'deanery' and to a programme director who matches trainees and their training needs. Most programmes involve rotations every one to two years between teaching and district hospitals. Problems arise when trainees are required to move hospitals, especially when a partner is also in specialist training or children are at school. The reluctance to move house every year or two has led some to accumulate tens of thousands of car miles with the attendant strain and hazard. Higher trainees would have gained if hospital housing of quality had been ensured at the time the new rotations had begun. That having been said, the assurance of a well-balanced programme of training and experience that leads to completion of training has been generally endorsed. At three years from the start of Calman, structured training can be said to have been successfully established.

Progress through higher training should be determined by annual, formal and recorded assessments

Many would contend that determinative assessment was the most important change that came from the Calman report. Prior to the SpR grade there was no formal and recorded measurement of progress in most specialties and no assurance that competence was being progressively attained. The new system requires annual assessment based on written evidence, the outcome of which may be that the trainee moves to the next stage, requires additional training within the next stage, needs more time in the present stage or should discontinue training in the specialty. There is a record of in-training assessment (RITA), which is maintained by the postgraduate dean and copied to the relevant College. Annual assessment at the end of training allows recommendation for award of the certificate of completion. Evaluation of the annual assessment process shows that the mechanics are working well, but the evidence provided of competence may be insufficiently robust in some specialties and more work is needed on this by both Colleges and deaneries.

Successful completion of specialist training should result in award of a certificate leading to specialist registration

The certificate of completion of specialist training, the CCST, is now enshrined in law as almost the only method of entry to the specialist register held by the General Medical Council. This registration is now required for appointment as a consultant in the National Health Service (NHS). While the CCST is a public statement of specialist competence, it gives entry to specialist employment for most people only when an NHS consultant vacancy occurs. The certificate of completion of training, added to a system with published entry standards, structured programmes of training and fairly standard duration of training, required a new approach to medical workforce planning to ensure that those admitted to higher training would be needed as specialists on completion. Workforce planning has affected specialist training in obstetrics and gynaecology more than in any other specialty.

The impact of workforce planning on specialist training

Medical workforce planning in the UK has an undistinguished history but the blame should not all lie with the planners. Training is long; medical practice undergoes change; society alters its work habits and its expectations; medical migration occurs, both in and out; men's and women's roles change; governments change their spending priorities. With the start of the SpR grade a new workforce planning system was introduced. The Specialist Workforce Advisory Group (SWAG) was given the task of matching the numbers entering the SpR grade and the numbers of consultants who would be funded by the NHS when the new trainees finished training, usually five to eight years later. SWAG worked with postgraduate deans to establish a dependable data system based on numbering of higher trainees and quarterly returns. Annual quotas of new trainees were determined from predictions of future need for consultants, based on historical data and existing shortages or excessive numbers of applicants for vacant consultant posts. Quotas were increased, maintained or decreased and deans' recruitment programmes were adjusted accordingly. There has always been a guarded assumption by parties to the planning that funding for consultant expansion would continue and even increase, given the new training duties laid upon consultants and the evidence of increasing clinical loads. The greatest weakness of the SWAG programme is the absence of government policy on consultant expansion and the resulting inability of hospital trusts and health authorities to plan their specialist staffing. It is as though SWAG was required to build a planned medical workforce without the necessary bricks.

Nevertheless, after four years SWAG has achieved balance in numbers of entering trainees and the ability of trusts to employ consultants in most specialties. In obstetrics and gynaecology a balance has not been struck and in July 1999 there were 134 CCST holders without a consultant post in the NHS. This situation will have a significant impact on training in the specialty. Current trainees are seeking ways to prolong training; some are emigrating; some will change career. Of equal consequence, SHOs in the specialty are reviewing the prospects and some are moving to new careers. Evidence from East Anglia suggests that many more of the SHOs in the specialty are those planning a general practice career. The causes of breakdown in planning are legion; one is the appointment by many trusts of non-consultant career grade staff who offer greater service flexibility than consultants. In any case, workforce pressures will have a significant influence on training in obstetrics and gynaecology for some years to come.

FUTURE DIRECTIONS OF TRAINING

Now the 21st century has arrived, the talk in training circles in the UK easily turns to continuing professional development and its place in clinical governance and revalidation of doctors. Staying with postgraduate training, there are four areas of rising priority:

(1) Programmes of training for SHOs;

(2) Assessments that truly measure competence for the job;

(3) Training of trainers;

(4) Making best use of training opportunities.

College committees are conscious of needs in all of them.

Programmes of training for SHOs

The major development of curricula and training programmes in higher specialist training needs to be carried over to the SHO grade. It is likely that every College will be asked to devise a curriculum for the basic years and introduce structured programmes with progressive standards of competence and maximum overlap with other specialties to allow credit should a trainee wish, or be pressed, to seek a different career path. Deans may well be asked to hold a file on each trainee as they do for SpRs; the file would provide objective evidence that could be used in recruitment to the higher grade.

With pending changes in primary care delivery it becomes urgent for the College and its sister College of General Practitioners to identify the current and future training needs for general practitioners and build these into a new curriculum substantially different from that for specialist SHOs. There will be more work with midwives, more training in the community, more office gynaecology, more family planning and much less time in operating theatres. There will be intrapartum care that maximises confidence in examination and a knowledge of the normal, and all this may need to be compacted into a shorter period of time. There is much to be done for the training of future general practitioners.

Assessment of competence

As described above, there is concern that some annual assessments of SpRs are insufficiently based on objective evidence of performance and work is under way to rectify this. At the SHO level there is less confidence in assessments and in some specialties the passing of College examinations is almost the only measure of progress. There are suggestions for objective structured clinical examinations (OSCEs) (Harden and Gleeson 1979) or observations of practice following the model used in summative assessment of GP trainees. GP trainees require confirmation of competence by a supervising consultant at the end of each six months' hospital post and there is a call for stronger evidence for this confirmation.

The College has developed a valuable system of performance measures for SHOs which may be a guide for others, but pressure for improvement in assessments at all grades will grow quickly with government demands for quality in the NHS (Department of Health 1998b).

Training of trainers

There is increasing interest in ensuring that those supervising and instructing junior doctors are trained for the task. The College has a programme for training, as have other Colleges; deans have regional programmes and a call for setting of standards and evaluation of outcomes of this training is to be expected. The UK model for training the trainers is in general practice where a training course is required before assuming the training role. Of equal importance in the GP system, there must be retraining every two or three years in order to maintain a training status. I suspect obstetrics and gynaecology departments will move to having a cadre of trained and certified trainers, perhaps advanced specialist registrars as well as consultants and staff grade doctors, who will play the major parts in the training process. In East Anglia, education and training agreements between the dean and trusts call for all new consultants to undertake training to trainers. I believe the expectation will spread.

Making best use of training opportunities

The permitted working hours of trainees are falling and the need for making best use of every training opportunity becomes greater. A recent review of learning in postgraduate medicine has shown what educators have long known but what is disregarded in construction of much postgraduate training: that the most effective learning takes place not in the class or lecture room but on the job (Hargreaves et al. 1997a,b). The value of this approach, which develops an instinct among both trainees and consultants for learning opportunities within service work and uses only minutes to raise a question or grasp a concept, has been demonstrated (Hargreaves 1996). It should be more widely used.

In their role as major deliverers of service in the NHS, SHOs spend significant parts of their time at night when colleagues, consultants and other potential trainers are least available. As clinical demands grow and working hours fall it must be asked whether ways can be found of reducing SHOs' service commitments outside central hours. Financial and staffing resources may enforce this less-than-ideal arrangement. Careful analysis of the most efficient use of staff has resulted in the reduction in night duty of SHOs (Read et al. 1998). Failure to extend this concept may be due to other priorities or a resigned inertia. The increasing need to make best use of training opportunities demands that all such possibilities are pursued.

References

Biggs, J. (1998) The Goodenough Report and medical education in 50 years of the National Health Service. *Health Trends* **30**, 16–19

Blunt, S.M. (1991) What's wrong with the specialty of obstetrics and gynaecology? *BMJ* **303**, 1416

Department of Health (1993) *Hospital Doctors: Training for the Future* (Chairman, Kenneth Calman). London: Department of Health

Department of Health (1998a) *A Guide to Specialist Registrar Training.* London: Department of Health

Department of Health (1998b) *A First Class Service.* London: Department of Health

Department of Health and Social Security (1968) *Royal Commission on Medical Education 1965–68: Report* (Cm. 3569). London: HMSO

Harden, R.M. and Gleeson, F.A. (1979) Assessment of clinical competence using an objective structured clinical examination. *Med Educ* **13**, 41–54

Hargreaves, D.H. (1996) Training culture in surgery *BMJ* **313**, 1635–9

Hargreaves, D.H., Southworth, G.W., Stanley, P. and Ward, S.J. (1997a) *On-the-Job Training for Physicians.* London: Royal Society of Medicine Press

Hargreaves, D.H., Southworth, G.W., Stanley, P. and Ward, S.J. (1997b) *On-the-Job Training for Surgeons.* London: Royal Society of Medicine Press

Ministry of Health and Department of Health for Scotland (1944) *Report of Interdepartmental Committee on Medical Schools* (Chairman, Sir William Goodenough). London: HMSO

Read, M., Draycott, T. and Beckwith, J. (1998) Night vision. *Health Service Journal* **108**, 24–5

RCGP and RCOG (1997) *General Practitioner Vocational Training in Obstetrics and Gynaecology.* London: Medical Protection Society

RCOG National Trainees' Committee (1997) *Survey of Training 1997. Report by the RCOG National Trainees' Committee.* London: RCOG

Smith, L.F.P. (1991) GP trainees' views on hospital obstetrics vocational training. *BMJ* **303**, 1447–52

3

The future of obstetrics and gynaecology

Robert W. Shaw

INTRODUCTION

There can be no more appropriate time than the start of the next millennium to try and review the future prospects for our specialty of obstetrics and gynaecology. While there are differing reproductive health needs in the countries of the world which affect prioritisation of development in our specialty, the lessons we have and need to learn and the changes occurring in the UK are, or will be, of relevance on a world-wide basis with other healthcare provider systems.

The specialty of obstetrics and gynaecology has seen many rapid changes in the last 50 years. Our future direction and development will depend upon:

(1) Planned changes in healthcare delivery systems;

(2) Changing demands of the public;

(3) Scientific developments in the specialty;

(4) Changing (perhaps restricted) skills of obstetricians and gynaecologists.

CHANGES IN HEALTH SERVICE PROVISION

Development to date

In the UK, the National Health Service (NHS) is a virtual monopoly provider of healthcare. Politically determined changes in its direction and funding levels will clearly have major impacts on any change in our future provision of obstetric and gynaecological services. While the Royal College of Obstetricians and Gynaecologists might have little direct impact on these changes it would be hoped that it can contribute advice to inform and influence central decisions.

The NHS was founded on an inherited system of hospital and general practice. Hospitals had developed in a haphazard way, many emerging from Victorian hospitals and workhouses, some sited because of the legacy of powerful local politicians, all supported by loyal communities often resistant to suggestions of rationalisation or merger. Emergency admissions at the inception of the NHS in 1948 were relatively few in number, nearly always cared for by the resident surgical or medical officer and there were few effective treatments available. Emergency admissions now occupy over 50% of NHS hospital beds. Within the last half century there have been tremendous changes in surgical and medical practices and the introduction of therapies which now offer more effective management and treatment. Many patients lives were lost because of the lack of suitable surgical emergency services. Initial changes were the introduction of recovery rooms to supervise the patient's safe return to consciousness and to monitor physiological stability. Their proven value necessitated a 24-hour availability. As more and more patients with severe conditions survived there became a need to manage patients seriously ill with organ failure. This resulted in the birth of our intensive care units with their multidisciplinary, highly expert teams of specialists. In the 1980s it was recognised that many patients, while not requiring the full support of an intensive care unit, would benefit from increased care and surveillance above that available on general gynaecological or surgical wards. This could be for the administration of sophisticated methods of pain relief, complex fluid replacement or frequent monitoring of vital signs, hence the high-dependency unit evolved. Within obstetrics we have seen increasingly sophisticated monitoring of the mother and fetus in labour where pregnancy complications exist and the introduction of early pregnancy assessment units to monitor and triage patients with potential early pregnancy failure, the latter made possible by the tremendous improvements in ultrasound and rapid enzyme-based assay technology

Implications for the future

These predominantly emergency service improvements have evolved and been organised to fit around elective services. Elective services can be timed and carried out by teams led by consultants, but the emergency services have been less well provided for. The part played by consultants in the emergency service has largely been limited to leadership and management only of the most complicated cases. It is now clear that the treatment and management of services for potentially serious emergencies require timely, prompt and expert direction by consultants. National Confidential Enquiry audits show that the management of the gynaecological patient (Campling et al. 1995), the pregnant mother (Department of Health 1998) and the fetus (Confidential Enquiry into Stillbirths and Deaths in Infancy 1997) all have deficiencies in the service which does not have full cover by consultants. These obvious deficiencies could be met by a requirement for consultant participation in 24-hour cover in the hospital. If introduced now, this desirable development would occur at the same time as a reduction in trainee availability. This has resulted from the shortened postgraduate training scheme introduced following the recommendations of Calman, the reduction in the numbers of trainees needed to address the mismatch of fully trained specialists and consultant job availability and the future reductions in junior doctors working hours as recommended by the European Union Working Hours Directive (NHS Executive Guidance 1998). These issues are further addressed in Chapter 2 on the future of training.

In order to organise teams which cover the most important aspects of emergency care, there needs to be an adequate balance between emergency and elective work to enable the potential of experts to be used efficiently and to retain their interest. This is likely to necessitate the concentration of services within fewer but larger hospitals where complementary services necessary to obstetrics and gynaecology are also available.

Changes in primary care provision

At this time when primary care groups are being formed the role of hospital authorities is changing. Considerable rationalisation of hospital services is occurring, as is centralisation of primary care services. Major obstacles exist preventing the development of primary care to complement hospital services, the foremost of which are lack of time and general practitioner manpower. There is, however, great potential for the expansion of accident and emergency facilities, with treatment for minor ailments and injuries being undertaken in local community hospitals. These hospitals might even provide overnight-stay facilities for those who do not require specific medical supervision and the centralisation of day-case surgery within community hospitals. Provision of more community midwives, with additional special skills training (for example, ultrasound and fetal monitoring) and appropriate equipment, could reduce the frequency of antenatal visits for most women and restrict referrals to those with problems truly requiring specialist consultant obstetrician advice and decision making. Any such changes have major cost implications and the need for agreed specific treatment and diagnostic algorithms to fully and safely use the variety of practitioners and varying skill bases.

LIKELY CHANGES IN ACUTE HOSPITAL SERVICES

The district general hospital and teaching hospital concept has served the NHS well since its inception in the early 1960s (Platt 1962). However, a number of drives for change now exist and these include:

(1) Developments in medical, surgical and clinical practice;

(2) Increasing subspecialisation;

(3) Clinical governance and the quality agenda;

(4) Increasing emergency workload;

(5) Changes in population and age distribution;

(6) A move toward a consultant-provided service;

(7) Multidisciplinary care with interdependence of different medical and nursing specialists;

(8) Anticipated changes in consultant to trainees ratios.

At present, obstetric and gynaecology services are predominantly provided within joint units on district general hospital or teaching hospital sites – although a number of stand-alone units still exist. There are currently 256 obstetric units in the UK which can be subdivided into three main categories in relationship to the number of deliveries they undertake (Table 1) (RCOG 1999a).

Provision of safe obstetric services equipped to deal with all major obstetric emergencies and able to provide adequate facilities for intensive neonatal care already cannot be provided in smaller units (fewer than 1000 deliveries per annum) necessitating the transfer of the mother before or during labour, or the neonate following delivery. There is increasing pressure from paediatricians and others to further rationalise services to larger units where full neonatal intensive care can be provided as well as the full range of anaesthetic, emergency and allied services.

Table 1 *Numbers of obstetric units by deliveries per annum*

Number of deliveries	England	Wales	Scotland	Northern Ireland	Total
Up to 1000	8	1	4	2	15
1001–4000	157	13	16	12	198
More than 4001	36	1	5	–	42
Total	201	15	25	14	255

Breakdown as per returns from 1998 Annual Census (RCOG 1999a)

Suggestions from other groups reviewing acute general hospital service provision (Royal College of Physicians 1996; Royal College of Surgeons 1998) are arguing for a move toward the establishment of acute general hospitals (which would include obstetric, gynaecology and paediatric services) to serve populations of approximately 450 000. This plan would only require about 140 acute general hospitals in the UK with the amalgamation of many hospitals within urban areas, the closure of many hospitals in smaller towns and most within rural areas. It is estimated that 80% of the English population lives within ten miles of the centre of a town and that about 90% could be referred to a hospital with full facilities, covering 500 000 patients or more, within 20 miles of their home (Rosen 1999). This would not be true of Scotland, Wales or Northern Ireland where population distribution and topography of the landscape present particular problems to such an approach without having long transfer times.

While such suggestions, if accepted by the Departments of Health, would clearly have an immense impact on our specialty, the estimated costs to develop such a strategy are immense. It would require 5–12 new hospitals to be built each year for the next ten years at an estimated cost of £5–20 billion (Rosen 1999). Such a capital building programme has never before been undertaken in the NHS and it seems more than likely that some compromise plan will eventually emerge which would involve some rationalisation of the number of obstetric and gynaecology units, particularly within cities which currently have two (or more) units.

CHANGING DEMANDS OF THE PUBLIC

'Every patient who is treated in the NHS wants to know that they can rely on receiving high quality care when they need it' (Department of Health 1997).

'High quality care should be the right for every patient in the NHS' (Department of Health 1998).

Quality issues are high on the Department of Health's agenda, as they have always been within our College and within the guidance the College gives to its Fellows and Members.

Today, the public is better informed than ever before with regard to health problems and needs. Patients receive detailed written handouts and verbal explanations of operations and procedures and have access to extensive literature and advice (although not always appropriate) through the Internet. Consultations are now as much about discussion of their thoughts on management than supply of direct medical advice from the specialist. These new attitudes of the public require new skills from the clinician – the art of listening, of understanding underlying problems and concerns, the art of explaining complications and dealing with complaints and of allowing the patient a major role in determining the treatment to be undertaken.

We are to be held more accountable for outcomes than ever before and will have to justify our results to hospital management (through clinical governance) and to patients. We will need to be aware of the most effective (and cost effective) treatment options and will be more likely to consult and follow evidence-based guidelines in the management of the majority of patients.

This new accountability is already changing our form of practice. It is placing new demands on postgraduate training programmes and teaching and will become a prime mover toward further subspecialisation.

If people are faced with travelling greater distances to be seen in hospital they will wish to see consultants with an in-depth knowledge and training of their specific problem(s) and not trainees. Such expertise may be available within daytime working, but inevitably patients will have to accept that at night they will be initially managed by one of a team of specialists who will have enough core knowledge and skill across the whole specialty to deal with their immediate problems. The maintenance of a high level of core skills and knowledge in obstetrics and gynaecology is thus essential for every specialist and each will have additional special-interest skills to allow the hospital to provide an overall service between a group of colleagues. To split obstetrics entirely from gynaecology would require a doubling of consultants in our specialty and take some 20 years to achieve in terms of training. Such developments are beginning to occur in the larger tertiary teaching hospital centres and would inevitably happen to a greater extent if the plan to proceed towards large district general hospitals occurs (serving populations of more than 450 000). Decisions are required soon to determine long-term manpower planning since it takes eight to nine years to fully train a specialist. However, any changes to manpower numbers must be linked to a guaranteed long-term plan of expansion of consultants, since we cannot allow again the same undesirable situation which is currently affecting the progression of trainees in our specialty.

RESEARCH DEVELOPMENTS AND NEW SKILLS

In the last 20 years alone we have seen an exponential growth in the knowledge and applications of new techniques and treatment options in our specialty. These developments have resulted in the establishment of specific areas of our discipline and the development of the subspecialties. These comprise:

(1) Reproductive medicine (from the study of hormones, genes and the immune system);

(2) Gynaecological oncology (tumour markers, genes and gene mutation, molecular biology of cancer);

(3) Fetomaternal medicine (pathophysiology of the fetus, *in utero* diagnostic techniques and treatment);

(4) Community gynaecology (new methods of fertility regulation, epidemiology of sexually transmitted diseases);

(5) Urogynaecology (physiology, pelvic-floor damage, continence mechanisms).

New advances may well lead to new areas of special interest, of which obstetric maternal disorders might well be next along with the genetics (and potential gene therapy) of reproductive disorders. The increasing numbers of women who are postmenopausal; the potential to alter many long-term disorders such as cardiovascular disease, osteoporosis and cognitive disorders by treatments involving intervention; the move toward human papillo-mavirus immunisation and new strategies to combat sexually transmitted diseases may well lead to the development of effective preventative strategies for some reproductive-associated disorders with potential for a new subspecialty linked with public health medicine. There is no end to the likely special skills and special-interest clinics which will need to be provided. All of these require special skills training programmes and, with the new ethos of proven competence to practice, will no doubt also require specific certification/accreditation schemes to demonstrate acquisition and maintenance of those skills.

CHANGING PRACTICES IN GYNAECOLOGY

Technological advances in instrumentation and optics have seen the potential for many previous open surgical procedures now to be undertaken laparoscopically. Not all gynaecological procedures can be modified in this manner, nor should all gynaecologists expect to be trained to a level to undertake advanced laparoscopic surgical procedures. These advances are, however, already changing practice.

Of even greater implication for future gynaecological practice and training pro-grammes has been the move to an increasing number of operative interventions being performed as day surgical cases or outpatient procedures – perhaps in future in com-munity hospitals. This, together with the potential for current and soon to be introduced 'medical treatments' to replace the need for surgery altogether for many common benign gynaecological problems, will change the emphasis from surgery being the main solution for benign gynaecological disorders and will alter our practice immensely. This raises the likelihood of the development of medical or surgical gynaecology specialists, since not all would have sufficient major surgical cases to maintain their skills or training potential adequately. This would result in a radical change to our current training programmes where all trainees are expected to gain surgical expertise and be competent to perform a wide range of operative procedures.

CHANGES IN THE MEDICAL STAFF WORKFORCE

The current training programmes, while shorter, we hope do provide a more structured approach to training and learning, instil the acceptance of self and peer-group critical appraisal and the need for continuing medical education and professional development. The traditional format of a consultant obstetrician and gynaecologist's post of the past few decades will rapidly disappear. In future, obstetricians and gynaecologists will be involved in hands-on obstetric care on the labour ward with 24-hour commitment as well as being more actively involved in gynaecological emergencies. Job plans will be individualised and will change quite dramatically during the lifetime of an obstetrician and gynaecologist as new skills are learnt to comply with the changing needs of their hospital. There will be a continuum of evolution, initially from a more direct commit-ment to patient care (including acute management in labour, emergencies and on-call), to increasing teaching, trainee evaluation and managerial components with increased tenure in their post and experience (RCOG 1999b).

The increasing proportion of women within our specialty may well mean some will choose to seek part-time appointments (at least initially) as consultants and for both men and women there is likely to be an increased mobility between posts to achieve differing responsibilities and clinical skills, a trend already happening, rather than a lifetime career commitment to one hospital.

CONCLUSIONS

While at present our specialty is overshadowed by issues of training numbers, I believe the future is assured, albeit in a different form of practice. In the future this will be more consultant-provided and can only be achieved by considerable consultant expansion. Advances within our specialty allow for exciting developments in subspecialisation and special skills provision which should enhance job satisfaction. A quality service and maintenance of competence are going to be all important and our posts will continue to evolve throughout our careers. These are opportunities we should strive to achieve. Where and how we work will partly be determined by changes in the NHS as a whole, as both primary care and hospital services undergo major reviews. We must contribute to this process in terms of informing at local level and to central government so that the future of obstetrics and gynaecology remains in our hands, with the well-being of our patients and the attainment of improved standards of care our continuing goals.

References

Campling, E.A., Devlin, H.B., Hoile, R.W. and Lunn, J.N. (1995) *Report of the National Confidential Enquiry into Perioperative Deaths*. London: NCEPOD

Confidential Enquiry into Stillbirths and Deaths in Infancy (1997) *Fourth Annual Report; Concentrating on Intrapartum Deaths 1994–95*. London: Maternal and Child Health Research Consortium

Department of Health (1997) *The New NHS: Modern Dependable*. London: HMSO

Department of Health (1998) *A First Class Service – Quality in the New NHS*. London: HMSO

Department of Health (1998) *Why Mothers Die. Report on Confidential Enquiries into Maternal Deaths in the United Kingdom 1994–96*. London: The Stationery Office

NHS Executive Guidance (1998) *The Working Time Regulations*. London: NHS Executive (Series Number HSC 1998/160)

Platt, H. (1962) *Accident and Emergency Services: Standing Medical Advisory Committee*. London: Department of Health

RCOG (1999a) *Manpower Committee: Annual Staffing Census*. London: RCOG Press

RCOG (1999b) *RCOG Working Party Report: Planning for the Future as Consultants in Obstetrics and Gynaecology*. London: RCOG Press

Rosen, M. (1999) A plan for the NHS for the 21st century. *Anaesthesia* **54**, 483–91

Royal College of Physicians of London (1996) *Patterns of Care by General and Specialist Physicians*. London: RCP

Royal College of Surgeons (1998) *The Provision of Emergency Surgical Services – an Organisational Framework*. London: RCS

4

The consultant in
the millennium

Joe Jordan

HOW MANY CONSULTANT OBSTETRICIANS AND GYNAECOLOGISTS SHOULD THERE BE IN THE UK?

The question has been asked many times over the years and yet the debate continues. Historically, the number of consultants to provide a full service in obstetrics and gynaecology always related to a given number of deliveries and what was described as 'an equivalent gynaecological workload' (RCOG 1983). The traditional pattern was for consultants to do a little of everything – clinical work, teaching, training, supervision, research, management, etc. The first reference to the actual number of consultants required is to be found in the *Report of the Committee on Staffing Structure of Departments of Obstetrics and Gynaecology* (RCOG 1973). This report estimated that the overall need was about one consultant to 1000 deliveries and that this would provide an appropriate gynaecological workload. At that time the number of consultants in England and Wales was 608. They were supported by 101 senior registrars, 421 registrars and 729 senior house officers (SHOs). About 11 of the senior registrars and 281 of the registrars were visitors. The report also suggested that there should be an increase in the number of consultants to meet the need for cover during the absence of colleagues and to provide better input to teaching, but it did not say what that increased number should be.

Ten years later the Royal College advised that the number of consultants required was one for every 500 deliveries per year together with an equivalent gynaecological workload (RCOG 1983). This was based on the Scottish provision of the 1960s, although it is not clear why that number was chosen. It was about twice as generous as that in England and Wales and there was a matching generosity in the number of trainees who outnumbered by twice those in England and Wales. The RCOG felt that one consultant for 500 deliveries was acceptable although, prophetically, it is interesting to note that the consultants in Scotland felt that one consultant for 500 deliveries was not enough.

Since then the duties of a consultant have changed significantly and although extra duties have become the norm, little has ever been discarded. Over the last two decades the UK has seen radical changes in the delivery of health services, in the training of doctors (both at general practitioner level and at specialist training level) and a clear drive towards increasing subspecialisation. Furthermore, development of a primary-care focused health service is recognised as being of crucial significance to the RCOG.

THE CONSULTANT OF TODAY

The Government's 1998 White Paper *A First Class Service: Quality in the New NHS* (Department of Health 1998a) can be summarised in one word 'quality'. Not only is the Government demanding a quality service but there is a public expectation that patients should be seen and managed by consultants, i.e. a move towards a more consultant-based service as compared to the current consultant-led service. The demand for a quality service is also being driven by several other factors:

(1) National Institute for Clinical Excellence (NICE) – will set national standards and a national service framework will detail how services can best be organised for patients with particular conditions. NICE will produce clear guidelines for clinicians about which treatments work best for which patients (Department of Health 1998a);

(2) Commission for Health Improvement (HIMP) – will be a part of the monitoring system for the standards set by NICE. It will provide an independent means of guaranteeing quality throughout the NHS;

(3) Clinical governance – will be a framework through which NHS organisations are accountable for continuously improving the quality of their services and safe-guarding high standards of care by creating an environment in which excellence will flourish. It will involve professional self-regulation and a commitment to life-long learning at the local level (Bloor and Maynard 1998; Scally and Donaldson 1998);

(4) The Confidential Enquiry into Maternal Deaths in the UK recommends more direct consultant input into the management of high-risk pregnancies (Drife and Lewis 1998);

(5) The Confidential Enquiry into Stillbirths and Deaths in Infancy concluded that in almost 80% of such deaths a factor was present during the intrapartum care which may possibly have affected the outcome (CESDI 1997);

(6) Confidential Enquiries into Perioperative Deaths have shown that direct consultant involvement in emergency surgery, particularly out of hours, may have led to an improved outcome for many patients (Scottish Audit of Surgical Mortality 1997; CEPOD 1998);

(7) The clinical negligence scheme for trusts recommends a minimum of 40 hours a week consultant presence in the labour room Currently this is not being provided in the majority of obstetric units (Department of Health 1998b).

The move towards increasing the quality of service being delivered and to a more consultant-based service is to be applauded but it is clearly beginning to add significantly to the working week of the average consultant.

This is compounded by other factors such as the changes in service provision by junior doctors. The Calman report (1993) has resulted in juniors spending less time in service commitment, the resulting shortfall usually made up by consultants. The Calman report also demands more supervised training, which consultants support, but this creates a further demand on consultants' time. The problem is amplified by the reduction in junior doctors' hours of work to 56 hours per week, with a planned reduction to 48 hours to comply with European Commission requirements, resulting in even less junior-doctor time being available in future, creating yet further demands on consultants. The problem is aggravated further as we move into an era in which the numbers of specialist registrars and senior house officers will be reduced, thereby resulting in further strain on the delivery of services in obstetrics and gynaecology.

The drive for a quality service also demands that consultants play an increasing role in the management of their hospital, subject their work to clinical audit, undergo continuing medical education and continuing personal development; factors which impinge even further on the working week of the consultant.

Consultants of today are trying hard to improve the quality of service being delivered. They accept the need for a more consultant-based service and the need to keep up-to-date with new developments. At the same time, they acknowledge the fact that junior doctors need training which is both supervised and structured and that their hours of work must be shorter than in the past. Ironically, those who worked these enormous numbers of hours over the past 25 years are the very same doctors who are now being asked to compensate for the deficiencies created by the current improvement in junior doctors' hours. But, at the end of the day, it is the consultant who bears the brunt of these changes and there seems to be no recognition of the significant increase in the number of consultants required to provide the standards of care required in the year 2000.

THE CONSULTANT OF THE FUTURE

The current situation cannot continue. However, we need to realise that there is no single solution nor will every consultant work in exactly the same way, so let us address the various ways in which our role can be adapted to meet the needs of the patient, the hospital and ourselves.

'Obstetrics and gynaecology' or 'obstetrics or gynaecology'

The debate about splitting obstetrics from gynaecology is intensifying, particularly with the trend towards subspecialisation in teaching hospitals and in larger district general hospitals. However, the current policy of the RCOG is that obstetrics and gynaecology should remain a combined specialty. Specialist registrars during years four and five should receive special interest training allowing them to become a generalist obstetrician and gynaecologist with a special interest in one or two subjects. In addition, there will be some consultants, predominantly the subspecialists, who become either obstetricians or gynaecologists alone and they will tend to work in tertiary referral centres.

Consultant presence in the labour ward

The RCOG and Royal College of Midwives (1999) report, *Towards Safer Childbirth*, advocated a consultant presence in the labour ward for a minimum of 40 hours per week for every unit delivering more than 1000 babies per year. This may not be popular, or even possible, in some hospitals but, nevertheless, the working party felt that a consultant presence in the labour ward was desirable because it would:

(1) Provide clinical leadership;

(2) Establish training and education of staff in a multidisciplinary team;

(3) Develop effective teamwork;

(4) Develop and implement standards of obstetric practice;

(5) Bring experience to clinical diagnosis and opinion;

(6) Audit the effectiveness of practice with a view to modifying it as required.

The RCOG (1999) report *Planning for the Future as Consultants in Obstetrics and Gynaecology* estimated that if units delivering more than 1000 babies per year (239 units out of a total of 256 units in the UK) were to have a consultant presence for 40 hours each week then 215 new consultant posts would be necessary. If all units delivering 1000 babies per year had a 24-hour consultant presence in the labour room (with consultants living in overnight) then 1408 new consultant appointments would be required. Whether or not a 24-hour consultant presence in the labour room will prove more effective is debatable and if more than 40 hours are required then the possibility of 60 hours per week could be considered. This would certainly be more popular with consultants than providing 24-hour residential cover.

How many obstetric units?

Can we sustain the number of units which currently deliver obstetric care? Some smaller units have closed already and consultants have moved to the unit to which the mothers have been referred. The principle of 'cross-trust' working is already practised by some specialties (such as radiotherapy) and this should be considered for certain aspects of obstetric and gynaecological care, i.e. pooling of the specialists in a smaller number of centres. At the present time, development of services is being hampered by the wish of some trusts to provide all medical services and the need for each trust to have a complete range of services and to be financially viable. This situation is neither to the advantage of the patient nor the consultant staff providing the service. Concentrating clinical expertise in specialist centres will provide a larger pool of specialists; at the same time each consultant will receive the support of specialist colleagues working in the same field and be better able to use and develop his or her special expertise. This of course has to be balanced against the need to make services accessible to patients. However, in support of centralising specialist services a recent report by Mullen and Spurgeon (1997) showed that if patients have problems which require the need of specialist services they are prepared to travel, even considerable distances, provided that follow-up and back-up services are available locally.

Delegation of clinical duties

Consultants should also consider the delegation of those tasks which can be done satisfactorily by non-consultant staff. Such opportunities have been discussed in detail in the RCOG (1996) working party report *The Impact of Changing Skill-mix on Clinical Practice*. The midwife is the prime example of delegation of duties. The midwife is the prime example of delegation of duties: she is an independent practitioner in her own right and many now accept the responsibility of establishing intravenous lines and repairing episiotomies. Nurse specialists have also proved effective in aspects of general gynaecology, urogynaecology, reproductive medicine, early pregnancy assessment units, gynaecological oncology and management of pain. Some trusts see staff-grade doctors as an alternative to consultants, but while some doctors will become staff-grade doctors through choice there are many who sadly have no alternative. The RCOG is aware that some doctors are being exploited in these jobs and the significant increase of staff-grade doctors and other unrecognised posts as an alternative to consultants is opposed by the RCOG, as it is counter-productive to the provision of a high-quality consultant-based service.

Should consultants have mentors?

The stress of being a consultant is considerable and newly appointed consultants, in particular, will require advice and support to develop their own skills and to meet their future clinical, managerial and educational responsibilities. The concept of a mentor is beneficial because discussion and confidence between consultants may well be supportive in day-to-day work and might also help towards career and professional development.

Continuing medical education and revalidation

The RCOG has embraced already the concept of continuing medical education (CME) and the first 'white list' was published in January 1999. Although a 'black list' is not a feature of the RCOG CME programme it is just a matter of time before trusts insist that an up-to-date CME portfolio is a prerequisite of employment. Periodic revalidation of doctors is also inevitable and will give recognition to doctors who meet national standards of competence and performance. The risk management agenda will demand this. Responsible consultants will welcome both CME and revalidation; neither should be seen as a threat but rather as a willingness to comply with Government and public demand for a quality service.

Increasing the number of consultants

Reference has been made to the significant increase in the number of consultants required to provide an adequate service in the next century. The RCOG was promised an annual 7% increase in the number of consultants but the number of new consultant posts has fallen significantly short of this. In 1997–98, the increase in consultant numbers was only 0.8%. One short-term solution to increasing the number of consultants is to reduce the number of SHOs and to redirect the money into the provision of a consultant salary. In the past, removal of an SHO meant that the salary returned to the postgraduate dean and the purchasers rather than the hospital but the NHS Executive and the postgraduate deans are now considering providing new consultant posts by using the money saved by a reduction in the number of SHOs. Clearly any reduction in SHO numbers will have a rebound effect. The work currently done by these SHOs will have to be done by others (medical and non-medical). It may also affect the number of young people allowed to train in obstetrics and gynaecology and this, in turn, may affect adversely long-term recruitment to consultant grade. However, it is an interesting concept and one which would increase significantly and quickly the number of consultants available to provide the service. This of course is not the total answer to the problem of consultant numbers. If such a scheme is introduced, we must not lose sight of the fact that the specialty of obstetrics and gynaecology will still require extra funding from the Department of Heath to provide the consultant staffing necessary to provide the service now being demanded by the public, the purchasers and the Government.

Shift of clinical care to primary care

The new Department of Health philosophy is to recommend the increasing shift of clinical care to primary care (Department of Health 1996). General practitioners can manage many common medical conditions that previously were the province of a hospital consultant. Among these are menstrual disorders, basic infertility, pelvic pain, dysmenorrhoea and hormone replacement therapy. This trend will and should continue as general practitioners have increasing access to laboratory and other investigative facilities. In its own way this should be regarded as a form of delegation, from the secondary to the primary care team. This should, in theory, result in the reduction of the outpatient and inpatient workload of the consultant team, but previous experience suggests that more comprehensive general practice actually increases the referral rates for conditions that previously would have been undiagnosed or managed suboptimally (Bowman 1989). Furthermore, such women, when referred eventually by their general practitioner, frequently have problems which require more of the consultant's time.

Consultant job plans

The demands made on the time of the consultant are increasing year by year and yet little attention seems to be given to what consultants can stop doing in order to meet these new demands. Failure to recognise this problem means that many consultants now describe their jobs as intolerable and some as 'impossible'. The consultant job plan is an opportunity to address this situation. The job plan should be reviewed annually and agreed either with the medical or clinical director and with the chief executive. However, many consultants see the annual job plan as a threat to their 'freedom' whereas it should be regarded as an opportunity to agree a pattern of work which uses to the full the special skills and expertise of the consultant, recognises their many non-clinical duties and at the same time leaves the consultant feeling that the agreed weekly commitment is manageable and enjoyable. The job plan should also recognise the commitment of both the consultant and the trust to CME and continuing professional development.

Private practice

Private practice is seen by many as a threat to the provision of a high-quality health service. This is unfortunate because those who 'cheat' are much in the minority. However, it is something of which we need to be conscious and to address. The option to perform private practice within an NHS contract is a right and not a privilege but, as with any right, it should not be abused. Many consultants perceive a full-time contract as allowing time for one private session a week (during normal hours) and a maximum part-time contract as permitting two private sessions a week (during normal working hours). The reality is that time away from the NHS hospital to do private practice is allowed only if it does not conflict with the agreed 'fixed' sessional commitment and that it does not interfere with that NHS work such as teaching, administration and research which has been agreed as 'flexible' work. The contract of a maximum part-time consultant states quite clearly that the consultant is expected to give the equivalent commitment to NHS work as a consultant who is full-time. Conflict is uncommon but when it does occur it can lead to disharmony. Consultants, particularly those with a busy private practice, should be aware of this and ensure that time spent on their private work does not interfere with their fixed or flexible NHS commitments. In the future, perhaps those who have a large private practice should consider a reduced paid sessional commitment to the NHS, for example six to eight sessions only, thereby reducing their stress levels, eliminating any cause for criticism or envy, while at the same time releasing NHS money to provide extra consultant sessions in their hospitals.

As Members and Fellows of the Royal College of Obstetricians and Gynaecologists we agree that the interests of women and their babies must always be our first concern. As consultants we are committed to that. We want to work, we want to use our talents to help women and to teach our successors, we want to be involved in management and administration, we want to initiate audit, we recognise the importance of encouraging and being involved with research and we wish to be involved in the development and introduction of new ideas and technology.

However, we are in some respects like a piece of elastic – we wish to do all of these things but currently we are stretched and there comes a time when the elastic will stretch no more. Most have reached that point and any attempt to stretch the elastic further will cause it to snap.

The NHS needs to be aware of the current problems and to recognise that those problems are genuine. As consultants, we will play our part by changing our pattern of work to meet the needs of the current and developing NHS but we cannot do this without a significant increase in the number of consultants. In the meantime:

(1) Delegate what you can;

(2) Complete and agree an annual job plan which is acceptable to the trust and to yourself;

(3) Support your President and your College in their genuine attempts to maintain the standards of training and service and to increase the number of consultants;

(4) Remember that the original RCOG Charter contained a section (subsequently removed) that obstetricians and gynaecologists should support each other. How prophetic our founders were.

References

Bloor, K. and Maynard, A. (1998) *Clinical Governance: Clinician, Heal Thyself.* York: University of York, Institute of Health Services Management

Bowman, M.A. (1998). The quality of care provided by family physicians. *J Fam Pract* **28**, 346–55

Calman, K.C. (1993) *Hospital Doctors: Training for the Future. Report of the Working Group on Specialist Medical Training.* London: Health Publications Unit

CEPOD (1998) *Report of the National Confidential Enquiry into Peri-operative Deaths 1996/1997.* London: NCEPOD

CESDI (1997) *4th Annual Report 1 January – 31 December 1995.* London: Maternal and Child Health Research Consortium

Department of Health (1996) *Primary Care: Delivering the Future.* London: Department of Health

Department of Health (1998a) *A First Class Service: Quality in the New NHS*. London: Department of Health

Department of Health (1998b) NHS Litigation Authority: clinical negligence scheme for Trust hospitals. *Hospital Doctor* 26 February, 64–5

Drife, J. and Lewis, G. (Eds) (1998) *Why Mothers Die: Report on Confidential Enquiries into Maternal Deaths in the United Kingdom 1994/96*. London: TSO

Mullen, P. and Spurgeon, P. (1998) *Specialist Hospital Services: Exploring Public Attitudes to Travel and Specialist Treatment*. Birmingham: University of Birmingham (Health Services Management Report No. 33)

RCOG (1973) *Report of the Committee on Staffing Structure of Departments of Obstetrics and Gynaecology*. London: RCOG

RCOG (1983) *Report of the Manpower Advisory Sub-committee of the RCOG*. London: RCOG

RCOG (1994) *Minimum Standards of Care in Labour. Report of a Working Party*. London: RCOG

RCOG (1996) *The Impact of Changing Skill-mix on Clinical Practice*. London: RCOG

RCOG (1999) *Planning for the Future as Consultants in Obstetrics and Gynaecology*. London: RCOG

RCOG and Royal College of Midwives (1999) *Towards Safer Childbirth – Minimum Standards for the Organisation of Labour Wards. Report of a Joint Working Party*. London: RCOG

Scally, G. and Donaldson L.J. (1998) Clinical governance and the drive for quality improvement in the new NHS in England. *BMJ* **317**, 61–5

Scottish Audit of Surgical Mortality (1997) *27th SASM Annual Report*. Glasgow: Royal College of Surgeons and Physicians

5

The impact of the courts on obstetric and gynaecological practice

E. Malcolm Symonds

INTRODUCTION

Until the first half of the 1970s, litigation against medical practitioners was a relatively rare event. Annual subscriptions to the Medical Defence Union as late as 1979 were only £80 per annum (Symonds 1990), a figure that had risen to over £1000 by the time that Crown Indemnity was introduced in 1990 and when differential rates were introduced, the annual subscription for obstetricians in the Republic of Ireland has risen to £69,000 per annum.

Under the terms of the House of Lords' decision on 16 July 1998, the multipliers for awards will be substantially increased with settlements to be increased by 20% to 30%, the highest awards going to the youngest claimants with the longest life expectancy. This particularly affects obstetricians and midwives because of the implications for birth-related injuries.

Although the problems are greatest in obstetric claims, the increase in gynaecological claims should not be overlooked. The frequency of claims has risen and the cost of either settlement or defending a claim has also risen substantially.

In the UK, the real cost for the individual practitioner has been hidden by the introduction of Crown Indemnity which guaranteed that health trusts would indemnify their employees for any action leading to litigation arising from the care of patients within their remit. If the trust considers that the performance of the doctor concerned is repeatedly substandard, then his or her work can be reviewed by independent assessors and a judgement made as to whether the doctor is unfit to continue practice, or whether some remedial training should be recommended.

This makes sense and is good practice but the most expensive claims often arise out of birth-related injuries where causation may not be at all clear. Even an isolated clinical misjudgement may lead to a large settlement which would dwarf the claims for a series of errors by a gynaecological surgeon whose practice was substandard.

In a bid to reduce claims arising from poor practice, many trusts have now introduced risk management groups with the specific remit of reviewing all complications in obstetrical and gynaecological management and investigating the standard of care at every level. Such groups have an important role to play in improving the quality of care, but they must not be allowed to become inquisitorial in this function.

It is difficult to quantify what impact all these changes are having on individual practitioners. Certainly they have had an impact on private obstetric practice in the UK on purely financial grounds. Unless an obstetrician has a considerable number of mothers who are prepared to pay large fees which incorporate a loading to cover malpractice costs, private obstetric practice is no longer economically viable.

Caesarean section rates have steadily increased but whether this simply constitutes careful and better practice or proof that the threat of litigation leads to an increase in section rates remains uncertain and unquantifiable.

In gynaecology, the hazards are more clearly defined and less expensive in most instances. Many claims now revolve around issues of consent and there can be little doubt that the quality of information given to patients has improved as a consequence of litigation and the demands of a better-informed public.

CEREBRAL PALSY AND THE OBSTETRICIAN

Major neurodevelopmental handicap occurs in five of every 1000 pregnancies (Paneth and Raymond 1988). All such cases are a potential source of litigation. Given the present popular belief that where there is an adverse outcome there must be fault, it is hardly surprising that most parents will follow all avenues to obtain financial support for the handicapped child and for themselves.

Electronic fetal monitoring was first introduced to prevent intrapartum stillbirth. However, while the use of fetal monitoring did show early evidence of a reduction in the numbers of intrapartum deaths, the technique did not reduce the incidence of cerebral palsy nor indeed was it introduced on that basis.

The general consensus now is that in about 90% of cases, intrapartum hypoxia could not be the cause of cerebral palsy (Yudkin et al. 1995; Nelson 1988). The majority of cases result from developmental and metabolic abnormalities, infections and trauma. Most cases appear to have their origin before the onset of labour or in the neonatal period – particularly in low birth weight infants (Blair and Stanley 1988, 1993). Nevertheless, this does not get the obstetrician off the hook. In those infants where there is indisputable evidence of intrapartum hypoxia and the early onset of severe neonatal encephalopathy, followed by the development of cerebral palsy of the spastic quadriplegia or dyskinetic type, then the causation is most likely to be linked to intrapartum management.

Although there is considerable uncertainty about the ability of electronic monitoring to predict the development of cerebral palsy (Nelson et al. 1996), the fact is that some 70% of all claims are based on the cardiotocograph (CTG) in labour (Symonds and Senior 1991) and on occasions on the antenatal CTG. These authors showed in their series of 110 cases of obstetric brain damage litigation that only 53 infants, all of whom subsequently exhibited cerebral palsy or some other form of brain damage, needed active resuscitation at birth. Only 3% of the infants in this series were of low birth weight (below 1500 g).

In seven cases, there were early heart-rate decelerations present and in five of these cases, delivery was spontaneous. In 24 cases, there were late decelerations and in 46 cases, there were prolonged episodes of bradycardia. Only 14 of the 70 infants with these types of heart-rate abnormalities delivered spontaneously, so clearly the obstetricians recognised the abnormalities and took action to expedite delivery. Unfortunately, in many cases tracings that showed abnormal features with loss of base line variability and late decelerations were simply ignored for long periods of time. Even in the presence of evidence of an alternative causation, such cases are often impossible to defend. This also raises the issue of how long a CTG needs to be abnormal before action is taken. How does a judge interpret the implications of a case where the period of abnormality of a CTG is short followed by a long period up to delivery when it is normal and yet the child develops cerebral palsy?

The problem often faced by a judge is that the causation of cerebral palsy in any individual case may remain undecided, partly because there may be a dispute about the timing of events leading to any cerebral damage and partly because not all causes of cerebral palsy are known. If causation is uncertain, then how is it possible to reach an informed judgement, particularly when the 'experts' for the plaintiff and the defendant may be expressing diametrically opposed views about the nature of the CTG and the management during labour.

Poor intrapartum management, as judged by present day standards, may not be related in any way to adverse outcome but it is impossible to argue in court that poor management was irrelevant unless there is clear evidence of an alternative causation.

What is a reasonable length of time to effect delivery after the recognition of an abnormal CTG? In general terms, a time lapse of about 30 minutes is accepted to allow for the organisation of the theatre and to effect delivery. The fact that staffing rosters, physical facilities and conflicting demands on the staff lengthen that time is not considered to be an excuse for delay.

Faced with all these uncertainties, it is hardly surprising that the obstetrician now tends to intervene sooner than previously and where there are antenatal complications, to resort more readily to elective abdominal delivery. As long as the present adversarial system remains, high section rates are likely to persist.

SHOULDER DYSTOCIA

Shoulder dystocia is one of the most feared complications in obstetric practice. There is only one way to prevent it and that is to deliver the child by caesarean section. However, the difficulty is to decide when to intervene and here the obstetrician is faced with the short-comings of both clinical examination and ultrasonography in estimating fetal weight. The estimation of fetal weight by ultrasound, as based on measurements of various anatomical structures, is not particularly accurate, especially at the upper end of the weight range. With errors ranging from 7% to 10% (Watson et al. 1988), the technique is of least value where it is most needed.

The only really accurate measurement of fetal weight so far reported in the literature is by echo-planar magnetic resonance imaging (Baker et al. 1994) and this is not generally available. Nevertheless, a history of maternal diabetes and the clinical presence of a large fetus suspected to be in excess of 4.5 kg should raise suspicion in the obstetrician of a high risk of shoulder dystocia. Traction injuries often lead to brachial plexus injuries and permanent disabilities and if these injuries are to be avoided, then delivery needs to be by caesarean section. The reality is that these problems often arise in parous women who have had previous successful vaginal deliveries and unless an accurate estimation of fetal weight can be obtained, it is difficult to justify such interventions.

It is, therefore, likely that for the time being cases of shoulder girdle injuries and asphyxial brain damage as a result of delayed and traumatic deliveries associated with shoulder dystocia will continue to appear on the court lists.

ISSUES OF CONSENT IN OBSTETRIC PRACTICE

Obstetricians are frequently faced with issues of non-compliance on one hand and, on the other hand, with the request for elective caesarean section where there appear to be no medical grounds for intervention. Faced with such a situation, the obstetrician can refuse to comply with the request or at least try and persuade the mother that such intervention is not necessary or desirable, or the obstetrician can comply with the request. Given the fact that maternal risk from caesarean section is low, and that if any complications arise after refusal to comply with the woman's request litigation will almost certainly follow, most obstetricians will and probably should comply with the request.

At the other end of the scale, how does one cope with the mother who refuses to comply with treatment or management that constitutes good clinical practice and where all efforts of persuasion fail to convince the mother to comply and therefore to consent. To intervene against the will of the mother constitutes an assault on the person which may lead to criminal charges. However, non-intervention leading to the death of the mother or child may result in allegations that the mother was not of sound mind and was unable to reach a rational decision. Asking the court to intervene before delivery does not necessarily protect the obstetrician from subsequent legal action. The obstetrician may decline to continue to care for the patient but is unlikely to be thanked by any colleague who has to take over. It is important to document all the information given to the mother and attempts made to persuade her to comply with the advice, and then only to intervene when it is clear that the mother is unable to make any decision because she is too ill.

Unfortunately, such cases do come to court where the accusation is made that further steps should have been taken to persuade the mother to accept treatment on the grounds that she was incapable of making a rational decision at the time. The only impact that such a case is likely to have on the obstetrician is to persuade him or her to give up obstetric practice.

FORCEPS DELIVERY

The real acceleration in brain-damage claims in the UK started with the case of *Whitehouse* v. *Jordan* in 1981. This was a case of brain damage which was ascribed to the application of forceps to the fetal head in a woman of small stature, where the attempt at delivery failed and the child was subsequently found to be mentally retarded. The judgement was found in favour of the plaintiff on the basis that the obstetrician had pulled too hard and too long. The Court of Appeal reversed the judgement and the case then went to the House of Lords where the decision of the Court of Appeal was upheld on the basis that an error of clinical judgement did not constitute negligence.

It was hoped at the time that some comfort might be sustained from this judgement but, in the event, this has not proved to be the case. What it has done is to virtually abolish the 'difficult' forceps delivery which, in turn, has been one of the factors increasing the caesarean section rate. That may of course be a significant advance in clinical practice but it may also add to the risks for the mother.

MULTIPLE PREGNANCY

Twin pregnancies pose particular problems in management. It is estimated that twice as many live births in multiple pregnancies have congenital abnormalities (Botting *et al.*

1990) and there is an increased incidence of cerebral palsy, particularly in the second twin, which is not associated in most cases with intrapartum events. There is the additional problem of the higher risk of prematurity. However, litigation commonly arises as a result of:

(1) The failure to diagnose twins and the entrapment of the second twin as a result of the administration of an oxytocic agent after the delivery of the first twin and before the delivery of the second twin;

(2) Abnormal delay between the delivery of the first and second twin resulting in profound hypoxia, often associated with placental separation or cord prolapse. Cases are argued on the basis of what constitutes 'reasonable delay' as commonly it is the second twin that is severely hypoxic and acidotic at birth. Fortunately, with the introduction of routine ultrasound scanning in early pregnancy, it is now rare to see an undiagnosed twin pregnancy at the time of delivery.

However, the reluctance now to perform breech extractions or internal manipulations means that where there is delay in the delivery of the second twin and poor response to oxytocic agents, it is common practice to resort to the delivery of the second twin by caesarean section – a change in practice that is almost certainly the result of the fear of litigation.

GYNAECOLOGICAL PROBLEMS

Common surgical errors such as retained surgical swabs, damage to viscera such as bowel, bladder and ureter and to major blood vessels have always been a source of potential litigation and this has not changed, excepting that the public now tends to seek compensation with greater alacrity and increased frequency. However, no-one has ever believed that forgetting to remove a surgical swab is defensible and therefore this type of mishap carries no new messages and no lessons that have not already been incorporated in to our day-to-day practice.

ISSUES OF CONSENT IN GYNAECOLOGICAL PRACTICE

The nature and demands of informed consent have changed over the last two decades and have had a significant impact on clinical practice. In the Medical Defence Union pamphlet *Consent to Treatment* (1997), the statement is made that:

'The competent adult patient has a fundamental right to give, or withhold, consent to examination, investigation or treatment. This right is founded on the moral principle of respect for autonomy. An autonomous person has the right to decide what may or may not be done to him (or her). Any treatment or investigation or, indeed, even deliberate touching, carried out without consent may amount to battery.'

What was often done in good faith in the past is now no longer acceptable and all gynaecologists would be well advised not to trespass outside these guidelines. Consent must be informed and it is around this issue that many actions have been brought in recent years. The actions are often brought on the basis that although consent was given, it was not informed.

STERILISATION

Nowhere is this matter better demonstrated than in the matter of consent for sterilisation. The issue came to the fore in a landmark judgement in the case of *Gold* v. *Haringey Health Authority* in 1987. The plaintiff underwent a sterilisation operation in 1979 which was performed on the day after delivery of her third child. The procedure was performed on the day after delivery for the purpose of social convenience. She subsequently became pregnant at a time that was consistent with tubal recanalisation and evidence on subsequent histological examination of the fallopian tubes was consistent with this diagnosis. As far as the technical failure of the procedure was concerned, the case was defensible. The allegations were also based on issues of informed consent. Despite the fact that all of the experts agreed that a reasonable body of medical practitioners did not proffer advice on failure rates at that time, the judge found for the plaintiff on the basis that he drew a distinction between advice given in a therapeutic context as distinct from advice given in a contraceptive context, and that the plaintiff should have been advised about the risks of failure.

The judgement was reversed by the Court of Appeal which did not accept this distinction between therapeutic and contraceptive procedures and on the basis that a significant body of medical practitioners did not give advice about failure rates in 1979, and found in favour of the defendants.

However, from that time and as a result of the actions of the courts, gynaecological practice was changed so that now it is standard practice to incorporate information about the possibility of failure into the consent form and to ensure that a verbal explanation is given, with documentation of the fact that this verbal explanation has been given. The only possible benefit to the patient is that early recognition of a pregnancy may allow for early termination if that is requested or required. Despite the claim that is often made that the patient would have continued to use contraception or would have persuaded the husband to have a vasectomy as well, there is little evidence from the experience of gynaecologists and certainly not in the literature, that imparting information about failure rates makes any difference to the acceptance of sterilisation. The decision of the courts has led to a change in practice which is almost entirely of benefit as a defensive and protective practice for the doctors and not for the patients.

FAILURE TO REMOVE THE PRODUCTS OF CONCEPTION

On occasions, attempts at abortion using surgical techniques fail. The failure rate is highest where the gestational age is lowest. It has been demonstrated that the failure rate is 2.47 in 1000 abortions before seven weeks' gestation and 0.38 in 1000 after nine weeks' gestation (Fielding *et al.* 1984).

It may be difficult to identify the products of conception in the early stages of pregnancy, but how far should the gynaecologist act to ensure that a pregnancy has not been missed? Should the patient be warned that in early pregnancy there is a risk that the abortion may not be successful and should all the products of conception be sent for histological confirmation as a routine? At the very least, should all patients be brought back to a clinic for a follow-up visit and subjected to pelvic examination six weeks later to ensure that the pregnancy is not continuing? The answer that most gynaecologists would give to all of these questions is no, both on economic and logistical grounds, but probably the answer from a medico-legal point of view is yes: 'Were you confident, doctor, that you removed the products of conception at the time of the initial procedure and, if so, how can you explain the continuation of the pregnancy?' 'If you were not confident, doctor, that you had terminated the pregnancy, why did you not take further action to ensure that the pregnancy was terminated?'

COMPETENCE IN SURGICAL PROCEDURES

One of the positive benefits of litigation is that it is now generally accepted that no gynaecologist should embark on procedures in which adequate training under supervision has not been received. This has become particularly important in fields such as minimal access surgery. Increasingly, the courts will not accept the occurrence of serious complications as a result of the actions of 'amateur' surgeons and this is of considerable benefit to patients.

CONCLUSIONS

This chapter is not intended to cover the full panoply of issues that contribute to malpractice suits against obstetricians and gynaecologists but rather it is an attempt to address the question of how far the courts have now changed practice in our specialty. In the face of a rising tide of litigation, it is surprising how little impact this has had on recruitment to the discipline as there seem to plenty of young graduates who are prepared to accept the challenges of modern day practice. In the UK this may well be due to the insulating effect of Crown Indemnity.

However, there can be little doubt that the nature of practice has changed to adapt to the present climate. In some situations, that has been of benefit to the standards of clinical care but, weighed against these benefits, there has undoubtedly been an increase in defensive obstetrics, even though it may not be recognised as such. Indeed, it is inevitable that this would be a consequence of increased litigation. What is uncertain and difficult to quantify is how the law and the courts have changed the relationship between doctors and their patients. Consultants now spend a considerable amount of time either answering complaints, many of which are frankly vexatious, or attending case conferences, writing medico-legal reports and appearing in court, either as a defendant or as an expert witness.

Finally, the economic consequences, both in terms of the costs of settlements and legal and expert costs and disbursements, now constitute a serious drain on healthcare resources in all western societies. In litigation, everyone eventually becomes a victim of the system.

References

Baker, P.N., Johnson, I.R., Gowland, P.A. *et al.* (1994) Fetal weight estimation by echo-planar magnetic resonance imaging. *Lancet* **343**, 644–5

Blair, E. and Stanley, F. (1993) When can cerebral palsy be prevented? The generation of causal hypotheses by multivariate analysis of a case control study. *Paediatr Perinat Epidemiol* **7**, 272–301

Blair, E. and Stanley, F.J. (1988) Intrapartum asphyxia: a rare cause of cerebral palsy. *J Pediatr* **112**, 515–19

Botting, B.J., MacFarlane, A.J. and Price, F.V. (Eds) (1990) *Three, Four and More: A Study of Triplet and Higher Order Births.* London: HMSO

Fielding, W.L., Lee, S.Y., Borten, M. and Friedman, E.A. (1984) Continued pregnancy after failed first trimester abortion. *Obstet Gynecol* **63**, 421–4

Gold v. *Haringey Health Authority* [1987] 2 *All England Law Reports* 888

Medical Defence Union (1997) *Consent to Treatment.* London: Medical Defence Union

Nelson, K.B. (1988) What proportion of cerebral palsy is related to birth asphyxia? *J Pediatr* **112,** 572–4

Nelson, K.B., Dambrosia, J.M., Ting, T.Y. *et al.* (1996) Uncertain value of electronic fetal monitoring on predicting cerebral palsy. *N Engl J Med* **334**, 613–18

Paneth, N. and Raymond, S.I. (1988) Cerebral palsy and mental retardation in relation to indicators of perinatal asphyxia. *Am J Obstet Gynecol* **147**, 960–6

Symonds, E.M. (1990) 'Double indemnity and obstetric practice' in: A.A. Templeton and D. Cuisine (Eds) *Reproductive Medicine and the Law*, pp. 85–91. Edinburgh: Churchill Livingstone

Symonds, E.M. and Senior, O.E. (1991) The anatomy of obstetric litigation. *Current Obstetrics and Gynaecology* **1**, 241–3

Watson, W.J., Soisson, A.P. and Harlass, F.E. (1988) Estimated weight of the term fetus. *J Reprod Med* **33**, 369–71

Whitehouse v. *Jordan* [1981] 1 *All England Law Reports* 267

Yudkin, P.L., Johnson, A., Clover, L.M. *et al.* (1995) Assessing the contribution of birth asphyxia to cerebral palsy in term singleton. *Paediatr Perinat Epidemiol* **9**, 156–70

6

Magnetic resonance imaging in obstetrics and gynaecology

Ian R. Johnson

Magnetic resonance imaging (MRI) was first used in the late 1970s in the UK. In 20 years it has developed from a research procedure using prototype machines to a major component of any large imaging department. The full potential of MRI is yet to be realised.

MRI IN OBSTETRICS

In 1983, images were obtained from six pregnant patients in the first trimester who were about to undergo termination of pregnancy (Smith *et al.* 1983). The placenta was demonstrated and some measurements were taken from the fetus. Subsequently, after safety clearance had been given by the National Radiological Protection Board, images were obtained from women in the third trimester of pregnancy with continuing pregnancies (Johnson *et al.* 1984). Although maternal and placental anatomy was displayed, fetal mobility and the long imaging time (two minutes) reduced the fetal detail. At the later gestations more detail could be seen, but even then the internal structure of the fetus was poorly delineated. Further studies (Smith *et al.* 1985; Powell *et al.* 1988) of women in late pregnancy continued to provide images with relatively poor detail because of motion artefacts. Although these workers could identify lungs, liver, heart and bladder, as well as early myelination in parts of the brain, it was clear that the only fetuses which could be seen at all clearly were those in late pregnancy and even then major structures, such as the kidneys, could not be identified.

Reducing motional artefact

Daffos *et al.* (1988) used cordocentesis using curare to immobilise the fetus in order to investigate cerebral abnormalities. Although other groups followed suit, this was clearly only of value if the fetus had already been diagnosed as abnormal by ultrasound. The development of fast scan techniques (Garden *et al.* 1991a) using radio-frequency sequences led to images being obtained in seconds rather than minutes, improving fetal imaging considerably. However, it was the development of echo planar imaging that led to the first detailed pictures of the fetus *in utero* (Johnson *et al.* 1990).

Echo planar images are obtained in a single spin sequence, in milliseconds, allowing acquisition of serial images through the whole of the uterus with no significant motion artefact. Computerised reconstruction of the fetus is then possible, allowing the fetus to be viewed in any plane. Although image resolution is not yet as good as conventional MRI, the speed of acquisition allows much more fetal detail to be seen, even in early pregnancies. More recently, further adaptation of conventional MRI has led to other effective fetal-imaging techniques such as FLASH (Roberts *et al.* 1994) and HASTE (Levene *et al.* 1996).

IMAGING THE FETUS

Fetal anomaly

The success of ultrasound in identifying fetal and congenital anomalies inevitably led to an application of MRI to the same problems. Several groups studied congenital anomalies with MRI using fetal immobilisation (Daffos *et al.* 1988) or fast scan techniques (Stehling *et al.* 1989; Garden *et al.* 1991b). There is no clear evidence of clinical usefulness. In each case the diagnosis was made first by ultrasound and any greater understanding of the problem elucidated by MRI was either not of a major nature or was made too late in pregnancy to make any real difference to the management of the case.

Fetal structure

For many years ultrasound techniques have been employed to estimate fetal weight, but most studies report considerable inaccuracy, with errors of around 10%, often overestimating the low birth weight fetus and underestimating degrees of macrosomia (Benacerraf *et al.* 1988). Using echo planar imaging, Baker *et al.* (1994a) demonstrated, in a small series of women imaged within the week before delivery, that the measured fetal volume correlated with the actual birth weight. The median difference between actual and estimated fetal weight was 3% of the actual birth weight. There was no overestimation of the size of the small fetus nor underestimation of the size of the large fetus.

The size and structure of several fetal organs can readily be identified using fast MRI techniques (Figure 1).

Fetal lungs, brain and particularly liver growth have been investigated (Baker *et al.* 1994b, 1995). A series of single measurements of fetal organ size at different gestations has allowed the establishment of a normal range. Further measurements in fetuses subsequently shown to be growth restricted demonstrated that liver growth was affected early and, in some cases, could be identified several weeks before clinical or ultrasound signs became apparent. Measurement of fetal brain showed a similar trend but, as might be expected, did not correlate with eventual birth weight as well as the liver volume.

These data were derived from cross-sectional studies. A longitudinal study of sufficient size of growth-restricted fetuses *in utero* is still awaited but Duncan *et al.* (1999a) have recently reported a longitudinal study in normal pregnancy. Fetal growth was quantified in 56 pregnancies in terms of fetal volume and volumes of liver, brain and placenta at gestations from 19 weeks to term. A complex relationship exists between the rates of growth of these organs. Further investigation of 38 growth-restricted fetuses (Duncan *et al.* 1999b) showed that reduced growth could be demonstrated in the brain and liver at a time when diagnosis and management would have been altered in 25 of the cases.

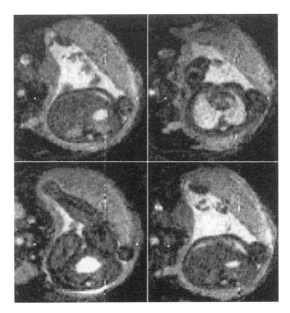

Figure 1   *Four transaxial slices through a fetus at 31 weeks' gestation; the fetus is viewed from below; image 1 (upper right) shows the fluid-filled (white) fan-shaped fetal lungs surrounding the heart; the amniotic fluid appears as a high signal (white) and the medium signal placenta is seen on the right anterolateral aspect of the uterus; image 2 (upper left) is a slice through the fetal liver; the high signal area is fluid in the fetal stomach (viewed from below and so appearing on the right of the picture); the fetal kidneys can be identified posteriorly, either side of the high signal cerebrospinal fluid, immediately below the dark circle of the aorta; image 3 (lower right) again shows mainly fetal liver, with the lower poles of the stomach and kidneys; part of the umbilical cord is seen in the amniotic fluid, with three vessels (dark or lower signal) identifiable; image 4 (lower left) shows the high signal of urine in the fetal bladder and clearly shows a fetal leg, extended within the amniotic fluid*

Clearly, the possibility exists to develop formulae relating the different rates of organ growth in order to facilitate the early detection of growth restriction, both in terms of quantification of the restriction and the timing and rate of progression of the restriction.

Fetal lung volumes increase exponentially with gestation (Baker *et al.* 1994b). The identification of normal lung volumes *in utero* has clear applications in the diagnosis and quantification of lung hypoplasia and has potential use in the study of lung maturity. Attempts have been made to quantify lung volumes using 3D ultrasound (D'Arcy *et al.* 1996; Lee *et al.* 1996), but these may be affected by abnormal amniotic fluid volumes, common in cases involving lung disorders. This is not the case when using MRI, where no such difficulty exists. There is no correlation between amniotic fluid volume and lung volume (Duncan *et al.* 1999c).

Function

Biochemical and physiological changes in fetal organs cause alterations in magnetic resonance properties which can be measured. Spectroscopic analysis of the placenta has been attempted. Garden *et al.* (1991c) generated phosphorus-31 spectra, but only when the placenta was less than 4 cm from the mother's anterior abdominal wall. No clinically useful information has yet been obtained by spectroscopic techniques, although stronger magnets and faster scanning techniques make this possible.

Changes in relaxation times, T_1 and T_2, in fetal lungs with advancing gestation have been investigated (Duncan *et al.* 1999d). Both T_1 and T_2 increased with increasing lung maturity. Preliminary investigations of hepatic function have demonstrated changes in the signal intensity ratio of liver to other organs between 20 and 36 weeks, signifying changes in erythropoiesis (Duncan *et al.* 1997).

Functional MRI has recently been employed to study fetal brain activity *in utero* (Hykin *et al.* 1999). Employing the inherent contrast between diamagnetic oxyhaemo-globin and paramagnetic deoxyhaemoglobin, changes in signal intensity are mapped. When a stimulus is employed that causes brain activation, local blood flow to the cortex increases beyond the rate required for ordinary metabolic demand. Hykin *et al.* (1999) studied five pregnant women near term and demonstrated increased unilateral temporal lobe activity in the fetal brain in response to an auditory stimulus. This technique has the promise of allowing investigation of fetal-brain development in normal and abnormal pregnancies.

Gowland *et al.* (1998) investigated relaxation times in the placentae of 41 normal women and 14 with compromised pregnancies (pre-eclampsia and growth restriction). Both T_1 and T_2 values decreased with gestational age; in the compromised pregnancies, both relaxation times were significantly lower than would be expected at the respective gestations. The authors suggested that pregnancies compromised by pre-eclampsia or growth restriction could be distinguished from normal pregnancies on the basis of placental relaxation times. The usefulness of this technique as a practical clinical tool remains unproven.

Movement of blood within the uterine wall beneath the placenta, in the placenta itself and particularly at the maternal–fetal interface, is not co-ordinated or obviously directional. Assessment of the rate or degree of blood motion is possible, leading to mapping of placental perfusion. In a small series, placental perfusion has been shown to be considerably reduced in growth restriction (Francis *et al.* 1998). Intravoxel incoherent motion, a specialised magnetic resonance technique, has been used to study the motion of blood in the uteroplacental area (Moore *et al.* 1999). Two distinct zones in which different volumes of flow are apparent probably represent the maternal and fetal contri-butions to the uteroplacental blood flow.

SAFETY

MRI has been used for many years to image adults and children without, as yet, reported unwanted effects. In a three-year follow-up of 20 children previously imaged *in utero* using echo planar imaging, it was not possible to link any effects to the use of the technique (Baker *et al.* 1994c). There is no evidence of fetal distress occurring during imaging. Poutamo *et al.* (1998) found no change in fetal cardiotocographic parameters before and after imaging and others have found no change in fetal heart rate patterns actually during the imaging process (B. Strachan, personal communication). One study of the potential of echo planar imaging to cause growth restriction in humans has been reported (Myers *et al.* 1998) in which no effect of MRI was found. No long-term studies of sufficient size have yet been performed to demonstrate the safety of MRI. As yet, no ill effects have been seen, but it will take many years to demonstrate minor or uncommon effects, or to reach a valid conclusion that MRI has been proved to be harmless.

MRI IN GYNAECOLOGY

In gynaecological practice MRI has been most extensively used by oncologists. By varying the spin sequences used, the differing characteristics of normal tissue and gynaecological tumours can be identified. Although specific types of tumour may be recognised, MRI is no substitute for histological diagnosis. Local and metastatic spread can be assessed. MRI is generally superior to computed tomography (CT) in establishing soft tissue contrast in terms of resolution and in tissue characterisation. This is enhanced further by the ability to view the area in multiple planes.

Cervical cancer

Both CT and MRI are used in the staging of cervical cancer to visualise asymmetry and distortion of surrounding tissues but MRI has significant advantages over CT. Using T_2 weighted sequences, cervical cancers display a high signal intensity in relation to normal tissue (Figure 2). Sagittal scans accurately display the relationships between the cervix, vagina, bladder, rectum and the tumour. Parametrial involvement is more clearly seen using the transaxial view. Although early stage II disease is more accurately identified by magnetic resonance than clinical examination, significant superiority is difficult to evaluate. The introduction of surface and endorectal surface coils is likely to improve the accuracy of staging of disease and allow more effective tailoring of treatment (Corn *et al.* 1996; Preidler *et al.* 1996). Identification of lymph node metastases is problematic. The

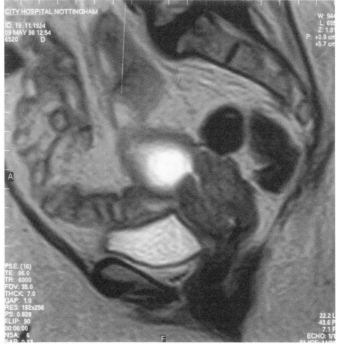

Figure 2 *A cervical cancer involving the upper vagina posteriorly and causing retention of secretions within the uterus; T2 weighting clearly differentiates the tumour from surrounding tissues, particularly the bladder*

signal intensity of nodal tissue and tumour are similar. As with CT, the identification of node involvement depends upon enlargement of the node (Kim *et al.* 1994). Even when nodes are enlarged, the positive predictive value is reduced to 75% because of problems with hyperplasia.

The MRI characteristics of recurrent cervical tumours are similar to those of the primary. In consequence, enhanced definition can be obtained using T_2 weighted sequences. Because of this, the anatomical distortion caused by surgery is less important than when using other imaging modalities. However, after radiotherapy, hyper-vascularity, oedema, inflammation and necrosis all increase the T_2 signal of the tissues and identification of tumour is difficult (Sugimura *et al.* 1990). Fortunately, fibrotic tissue has a low signal on T_2 weighting and, after a period of time, differentiation of tumour and other tissue becomes easier.

Endometrial cancer

MRI is the imaging modality of choice in the assessment of endometrial cancer. The tumour bulk, degree of myometrial invasion, involvement of the cervix and spread to other tissues can all be assessed. T_2 weighted images clearly delineate tumour from normal tissue. Magnetic resonance staging is 85% accurate and in differentiating superficial and deep myometrial invasion (less than or more than one-third of the thickness of the myometrium) MRI has an accuracy of 74% (Hricak *et al.* 1991). MRI has high specificity and positive predictive values in the evaluation of cervical extension of endometrial tumour, particularly in identifying stromal invasion with consequent requirement for more radical surgery (Toki *et al.* 1998). Gadolinium enhancement helps to differentiate tumour from necrotic tissue and fluid. Identification of nodal involvement suffers from the same problems as in cases of cervical carcinoma and here MRI is no better than CT.

Ovarian tumours

Ultrasound is the modality of choice in the imaging of ovarian masses. MRI is of use if ultrasound is inconclusive (Outwater and Dunton 1995). In early disease, the solid and cystic nature of ovarian tumours is easily seen with MRI, as is early breach of the capsule. Accurate identification of bladder and pelvic side-wall involvement is possible, although rectal involvement is more difficult to see. It has been claimed that MRI will detect 95% of surgically proven ovarian masses with a correct characterisation of malignant disease in 100% of cases (Stevens *et al.* 1991). Others are more circumspect, although still claiming around 95% correct characterisation (Ghossain *et al.* 1991; Yamashita *et al.* 1995). Staging is accurate in 70% of cases (Forstner *et al.* 1995). The identification of peritoneal deposits is only reliable when these deposits are greater than 1 cm in size. The actual extent of bowel or omental involvement is difficult to estimate. Recurrent or residual tumour may be identified or even measured, but no advantage over CT has been demonstrated in the management of surgery or chemotherapy.

MRI is particularly reliable in the identification of fat or blood products. Sensitivities and specificities have been claimed (Scoutt *et al.* 1994) for mature cystic teratomas (dermoid cysts) of 100% and 99%, together with 92% and 91% for endometriosis and 96% and 100% for subserosal fibroids. The high specificity in the identification of dermoid cysts and fibroids has been confirmed by others (Gain *et al.* 1993).

FUTURE DEVELOPMENTS

In gynaecology, most MRI work has been in oncology, but the ability of MRI to study physiology and biochemistry is likely to be applied in the study of menstrual function. In particular, the ability to study changes in blood flow will be of major importance. As yet, studies of the structure and function of the bladder and pelvic floor in relation to patients with urinary incontinence are in their infancy.

In obstetrics, MRI creates the possibility of greater understanding of fetal growth, both normal and abnormal, and fetal development. The exciting studies involving activation of the fetal brain lead to the possibility of studying development of brain function and a non-invasive *in utero* technique for evaluating fetal brain normality. Studies currently being undertaken in Nottingham involving blood flow and transfer of oxygen within the uteroplacental unit show considerable promise for evaluating pathophysiological differences between normal and abnormal pregnancy.

Development of the effective use of MRI in obstetrics and gynaecology has been slower than in other medical fields. There has been a natural anxiety about the safety and ethics of using such a technique. In gynaecology, what is required is a series of careful studies to evaluate the clinical effectiveness of the technique, together with an exploration of how this technique can help to solve areas of pathophysiology still shrouded in mystery, the function of the bladder and pelvic floor, dysfunctional uterine bleeding and implantation. In obstetrics, we have a wonderful opportunity to study normal and abnormal fetal development. Clinical applications are still some way off, as is the proper use of MRI spectroscopy, but there is no doubt that the ability to evaluate function in detail is very exciting.

References

Baker, P.N., Johnson, I.R., Gowland, P.A. *et al.* (1994a) Fetal weight estimation using echo planar magnetic resonance imaging. *Lancet* **343**, 644–5

Baker, P.N., Johnson, I.R., Gowland, P.A., Freeman, A., Adams, V. and Mansfield, P. (1994b) Estimation of fetal lung volumes using echo planar magnetic resonance imaging. *Obstet Gynecol* **83**, 951–4

Baker, P.N., Johnson, I.R., Harvey, P.R., Gowland, P.A. and Mansfield, P. (1994c) A three year follow-up of children imaged *in utero* with echo planar magnetic resonance. *Am J Obstet Gynecol* **170**, 32–3

Baker, P.N., Johnson, I.R., Gowland, P.A. *et al.* (1995) Measurement of fetal liver, brain and placental volumes with echo planar magnetic resonance imaging. *Br J Obstet Gynaecol* **102**, 35–9

Benacerraf, B., Gelman, R. and Frigoletts, F. (1988) Sonographically estimated fetal weights: accuracy and limitation. *Am J Obstet Gynecol* **159**, 1118–21

Corn, B.W., Schnall, M.D., Milestone, B., King, S., Hauck, W. and Soln, L.J. (1996) Signal characteristics of tumour shown by high resolution endorectal coil MRI may predict outcome among patients with cervical carcinoma treated with irradiation. A preliminary study. *Cancer* **78**, 2535–42

Daffos, F., Forestier, F., Macaleese, J. *et al.* (1998) Fetal curarisation for prenatal magnetic resonance imaging. *Prenat Diagn* **8**, 311–14

D'Arcy, T.J., Hughes, I.W., Chin, W.S.C. *et al.* (1996) Estimation of fetal lung volumes using enhanced three dimensional ultrasound; a new method and first result. *Br J Obstet Gynaecol* **103**, 1015–20

Duncan, K.R., Baker, P.N., Gowland, P.A. *et al.* (1997) Demonstration of changes in fetal liver erythropoiesis using echo planar magnetic resonance imaging. *Am J Physiol* **273**, 9965–7

Duncan, K.R., Sahota, D.S., Chang, A.M.Z., Gowland, P.A., Johnson, I.R. and Baker, P.N. (1999a) Normal fetal and placental growth defined using echo planar magnetic resonance imaging. *J Soc Gynecol Investig* **6**, 89a

Duncan, K.R., Sahota, D.S., Chang, A.M.Z., Gowland, P.A., Johnson, I.R. and Baker, P.N. (1999b) Asymmetrical fetal organ growth in intrauterine growth restriction first demonstrated using magnetic resonance imaging. *J Soc Gynecol Investig* **6**, 184a–5a

Duncan, K.R., Gowland, P.A., Moore, R.J., Baker, P.N. and Johnson, I.R. (1999c) Assessment of fetal lung growth *in utero* with echo planar magnetic resonance imaging. *Radiology* **210**, 197–200

Duncan, K.R., Gowland, P.A., Freeman, A., Moore, R., Baker, P.N. and Johnson, I.R. (1999d) The changes in magnetic resonance properties of the fetal lungs; a first result and a potential tool for the non-invasive *in utero* demonstration of fetal lung maturation. *Br J Obstet Gynaecol* **106**, 122–5

Forstener, R., Hricak, H., Occhipticti, K.A., Powell, C.B., Frankel, S.D. and Stern, J.L. (1995) Ovarian cancer: staging with CT and MR imaging. *Radiology* **197**, 619–26

Francis, S.T., Duncan, K.R., Moore, R.W., Baker, P.N., Johnson, I.R. and Gowland, P.A. (1998) Non-invasive mapping of placental perfusion. *Lancet* **351**, 1397–400

Gain, K.A., Friedman, D.L., Pettinger, T.W., Alagappan, R., Jeffrey, R.B. and Sommer, F.G. (1993) Adnexal masses; comparison of specificity of endovaginal ultrasound and pelvic magnetic resonance imaging. *Radiology* **186**, 697–704

Garden, A.S., Griffiths, R.D., Weindling, A.M. and Martin, P.A. (1991a) Fast scan magnetic resonance imaging in fetal visualisation. *Am J Obstet Gynecol* **164**, 1190–6

Garden, A.S., Weindling, A.M., Griffiths, R.D. and Martin, P.A. (1991b) Fast scan magnetic resonance imaging of fetal anomalies. *Br J Obstet Gynaecol* **98**, 1217–22

Garden, A.S., Weindling, A.M., Griffiths, R.D. and Martin, P.A. (1991c) Assessment of fetal well-being with magnetic resonance. *J Perinat Med* **19**, 135–48

Ghossain, M.A., Bui, J-N., Ligneres, C. *et al.* (1991) Epithelial tumours of the ovary: comparison of MR and CT findings. *Radiology* **181**, 863–70

Gowland, P.A., Freeman, A., Issa, B. *et al.* (1998) *In vivo* relaxation time measurements in the human placenta using echo planar imaging at 0.5T. *Magn Reson Imaging* **16**, 241–7

Hricak, H., Rubenstein, L.V., Gharman, G.M. and Karstaedt, N. (1991) Magnetic resonance imaging evaluation of endometrial carcinoma; results of an NCI co-operative study. *Radiology* **179**, 829–32

Hykin, J., Moore, R., Duncan, K., Baker, P., Johnson, I. and Gowland, P. (1999) Antenatal demonstration of fetal brain activity using fMRI. *J Soc Gynecol Investig* **6**, 110a–11a

Johnson, I.R., Symonds, E.M., Keane, D.M. *et al.* (1984) Imaging the human pregnant uterus with nuclear magnetic resonance. *Am J Obstet Gynecol* **148**, 1136–9

Johnson, I.R., Stehling, M.K., Blamire, A.M. *et al.* (1990) Study of internal structure of the human fetus *in utero* by echo planar magnetic resonance imaging. *Am J Obstet Gynecol* **163**, 601–7

Kim, S.H., Kim, S.C., Choi, B.I. *et al.* (1994) Uterine cervical carcinoma: evaluation of pelvic node metastases with magnetic resonance imaging. *Radiology* **190**, 807–11

Lee, A., Kratochwic, A., Stumpflan, I., Dentinger, J. and Bernaschek, G. (1996) Fetal lung volume determination by 3 dimensional ultrasonography. *Am J Obstet Gynecol* **175**, 588–92

Levene, D., Hatabu, H., Gaa, J., Atkinson, M.W. and Adelman, R.R. (1996) Fetal anatomy with fast MR sequences. *Am J Radiol* **167**, 905–8

Moore, R., Strachan, B., Baker, P. and Gowland, P. (1999) Utero placental blood movement *in utero* using IVIM echo planar magnetic resonance imaging. *J Soc Gynecol Investig* **6**, 114a

Myers, C., Duncan, K.R., Gowland, P.A., Johnson, I.R. and Baker, P.N. (1998) Failure to detect intrauterine growth restriction following *in utero* exposure to magnetic resonance imaging. *Br J Radiol* **71**, 549–51

Outwater, E.K. and Dunton, C.J. (1995) Imaging the ovary and adenexa: clinical issues and applications of magnetic resonance imaging. *Radiology* **194**, 1–18

Poutamo, J., Partanen, K., Vanninen, R., Vainio, P. and Kirkinen, P. (1998) Magnetic resonance imaging does not change fetal cardiotocograph parameters. *Prenat Diagn* **18**, 1149–54

Powell, M.C., Worthington, B.S., Buckley, J.M. and Symonds, E.M. (1988) Magnetic resonance imaging in obstetrics. Fetal anatomy. *Br J Obstet Gynaecol* **95**, 38–46

Preidler, K.W., Tamussino, K., Szolar, D.M., Ranner, G. and Ebner, F. (1996) Staging of cervical carcinomas. Comparison of body-coil magnetic resonance imaging and endorectal surface coil magnetic resonance imaging with histopathological correlation. *Invest Radiol* **31**, 458–62

Roberts, N., Garden, A.S., Guise, O.L.M., Whitehouse, G.H. and Edwards, R.H.T. (1994) Estimation of fetal volume by magnetic resonance imaging and sterology. *Br J Radiol* **67**, 1067–77

Scoutt, L.M., McCarthy, S.M., Large, R., Bourque, A. and Schwartz, P.E. (1994) Magnetic resonance evaluation of clinical suspected adnexal masses. *J Comput Assist Tomogr* **18**, 609–18

Smith, F.W., Adam, A.H. and Philips, W.D.P. (1983) NMR imaging in pregnancy. *Lancet* **i**, 61–2

Smith, F.W., Kent, C., Abramovich, D.R. and Sutherland, H.W. (1985) Nuclear magnetic resonance imaging – a new look at the fetus. *Br J Obstet Gynaecol* **92**, 1024–33

Stehling, M.K., Mansfield, P., Ordidge, R.J. *et al.* (1989) Echo planar magnetic resonance imaging in abnormal pregnancies, *Lancet* **335**, 157–8

Stevens, S.K., Hricak, H. and Stern, J.L. (1991) Ovarian lesions: detection and characterisation with gadolinium enhanced magnetic resonance imaging at 1.5T. *Radiology* **181**, 481–8

Sugimura, F., Carrington, B.M., Quivey, J.M. *et al.* (1990) Post irradiation changes in the pelvis: assessment with magnetic resonance imaging. *Radiology* **175**, 805–13

Tokai, T., Oka, K., Nakayama, K., Oguchi, O. and Fugit, S. (1998) A comparative study of pre-operative procedures to assess cervical invasion by endometrial carcinoma. *Br J Obstet Gynaecol* **105**, 512–16

Yamashita, Y., Torashima, M., Hatenaka, Y. *et al.* (1995) Adnexal masses: accuracy of characterisation with transvaginal ultrasound and pre-contrast and post-contrast magnetic resonance imaging. *Radiology* **194**, 557–65

7

The development of fetal physiology over the 20th century: contribution to obstetric practice

Fiona Broughton Pipkin

A BRIEF HISTORICAL OVERVIEW

The growth and development of the fetus have fascinated scientist and layman at least since records, pictorial or written, have been kept. One of the larger horses painted on the cave walls at Lascaux in South West France appears to be carrying a foal *in utero*. These paintings are dated some 23 millennia before the birth of Christ. Hippocrates, two and a half millennia ago, published his speculations on the causes of labour and delivery. In the 2nd century AD, Galen described the foramen ovale and the ductus arteriosus, and their closure after birth. From then on anatomists continued to unravel the idiosyncrasies of fetal anatomy. However, it seems not to have been until the work of William Harvey in the 17th century that experimental studies and speculations about fetal physiology really began. His *De Generatione Animalium*, published in 1651, is an absorbing comparative study of the fetus, ranging from chicks through deer to man, with much in between, and although mostly descriptive anatomy, there are also descriptions of physiological experiments (Harvey 1651).

There has been an explosion of interest in fetal physiology in the 20th century with the realisation that the burgeoning sub-speciality of fetomaternal medicine must be strongly based on such work. In the mid-1920s, Huggett, at St Thomas' Hospital Medical School in London, published a series of papers relating to the sensitivity of the respiratory centres of fetal goats and lambs (Huggett 1927, 1929). However, the real flood of interest was mainly initiated in the 1930s by two men, Joseph (later Sir Joseph) Barcroft and Donald Barron in Cambridge. History relates that their collaboration arose by chance from a conversation over afternoon tea. The social side of scientific meetings has always been important! The first paper demonstrating the circulation in the fetal heart and great vessels, using radiography, was published in 1939 (Barclay *et al.* 1939). In the years following the Second World War, knowledge advanced rapidly, but was still confined to studies of terminally-anaesthetised animals, with the consequent uncertainties of interpretation.

Fetal physiology in the UK received a major boost when Geoffrey Dawes was appointed Director of the Nuffield Institute for Medical Research in Oxford in 1948. He was looking for a research area which might afford a closer connection with clinical medicine than the analysis of cardiac and pulmonary reflexes on which he was then engaged. His group began by studying the changes in the fetal circulation at birth and

51

was to be highly productive, not only in output of research papers, but also in the training of younger fetal physiologists. Barron had returned to Yale before the war, and was increasingly determined to study the fetus in as natural a state as possible. In 1965 his group published the first report of studies of chronically-cannulated fetal lambs and goats (Meschia *et al.* 1965). This approach is now almost universally used in the study of 'undisturbed' fetal physiology. The sheep has been widely used as an experimental animal in this context. The fetal lamb near term (approximately 147 days) is comparable in size to the human fetus, and many of its organ systems have been shown to develop functionally similarly. The placental structure is, however, different consisting of multiple (approximately 70) cotyledons. This has the advantage of allowing retrograde cannulation of larger placental or umbilical vessels, but the structural differences must be borne in mind when considering such topics as placental transfer. That, however, is true of almost all animal species used in fetal physiology since the placenta can function efficiently with the most amazing variety of structures. The uterine musculature is much thinner in sheep than in primates, and does not contract nearly as vigorously when it is cut, so that the routine use of tocolytic agents post-operatively is not needed.

In this chapter of the 'Millennium edition' of the *Yearbook of Obstetrics and Gynaecology*, it is particularly pleasant to note that two fetal physiologists have been especially honoured by the College: Sir Joseph Barcroft was made an Honorary Fellow in 1944; the same honour was conferred on Sir Graham (Mont) Liggins, of whom more later, in 1989.

HAS BASIC SCIENTIFIC FETAL PHYSIOLOGY CONTRIBUTED TO CLINICAL PRACTICE?

As an example of the importance of blue skies research, a wide general curiosity and the integration of basic and clinical research, the surfactant story can hardly be bettered. Shepherds have known for as long as there have been shepherds that sheep, unlike pregnant women, usually deliver within a narrow range of gestation (147±1 days) and that if they deliver more than a few days early, the lambs die, apparently because they cannot breathe properly. Aristotle noted that 'Children born before the seventh month cannot possibly live. The seventh month is the earliest possible, yet most of these are weakly and for this reason are swaddled in wool' (Harvey 1651). In the mid-1950s, Pattle, a scientist at Porton Down, was working on the behaviour of bubbles in lung liquids. His observations on their surprising stability led to the discovery of pulmonary surfactant (Pattle 1958). This lipid–protein mixture reduces the surface tension at the air–liquid interface in the lungs, and allows the alveoli to remain expanded during exhalation. Not long after this, it was shown that lung extracts from babies who had died weighing less than 1200 g, or bigger babies who had died from neonatal respiratory distress syndrome (RDS), could not maximally lower the surface tension of a liquid in the same way as lung extracts from larger babies or adults did (Avery and Mead 1959). Mature lung effluent contains high concentrations of phosphatidylcholine (PC) and phosphatidylglycerol (PG). In infants with RDS, PC was low and PG absent. The use of biochemical techniques subsequently showed the pulmonary surfactant to be a complex substance, consisting of lipids, protein, cholesterol and cholesterol esters. About 75% of the lipid fraction is PC. The fully saturated form is 90% dipalmitoyl PC (DPPC) and it is the DPPC and two surfactant proteins, surfactant proteins B (SP-B) and C (SP-C), which lower the surface tension so much. Synthesis occurs in the type II pneumocytes, where the surfactant is stored as lamellar bodies.

An observation of the type made by Avery and Mead (1959) must necessarily lead on to a study of the constituents of the substance of interest; how it is synthesised in the body, what are the control mechanisms for such synthesis and whether such basic scientific knowledge can be used to improve or prevent the clinical problem. The first question can be answered from postmortem studies in human newborns; the remainder move into the realms of fetal physiology and, ultimately, the clinical trial. In the case of surfactant, a valuable prompt was given by the observation that accelerated lung maturity was observed after chronic prenatal 'stress', such as maternal infection, pre-eclampsia, intrauterine growth restriction or fetal surgery.

Liggins et al. (1969) published a report showing that lambs delivered prematurely after having been infused with adrenocorticotrophic hormone or dexamethasone had partly aerated lungs and did survive for a time. Avery was visiting New Zealand at the time the experiments were being done, and Liggins, knowing of her fascinating work, passed on the early results to her while he continued working on the causes of parturition. He also passed on the information to Clements in California. By the next year, Avery's group had published data on the accelerated appearance of surfactant in the fetal lamb following the administration of glucocorticoids (deLemos et al. 1970). A succession of papers began to appear. Rooney et al. (1975) showed that the administration of cortisol to fetal rabbits at 24 days' gestation resulted three days later in a significant increase in the activity of pulmonary glycerolphosphate phosphatidyltransferase, an enzyme involved in the synthesis of PG. The specific effects of low-dose cortisol on surfactant synthesis in lambs at different gestation ages were studied by Brumley et al. (1977) using concentrations of cortisol which gave blood levels approximating to those found in late pregnancy. They showed that, even at 116–121 days (term around 147 days), low-dose cortisol for 72 hours resulted in much greater lung volume on standardised expansion, and a marked rise in the percentage of lung phospholipid which was PC. Antioxidant enzyme activity in lung tissue has also been found to be increased in prematurely-delivered lambs after in utero administration of corticosteroids (Walther et al. 1991).

The animal data had become so compelling, and the fetal outcome for babies delivered prematurely was so poor, that a randomised, placebo-controlled trial was established quite early in the course of these studies. Mothers received 6 mg of betamethasone acetate and 6 mg of betamethasone phosphate or placebo. Data from the trial, which enrolled 282 babies delivered before 37 weeks' gestation, showed a reduction in early neonatal mortality with antepartum treatment from 15.0% to 3.2%. Nine per cent of babies delivered at or before 32 weeks after glucocorticoid treatment developed RDS, compared with 28% of those given placebo. The effects were noted to be greatest in those delivering earliest (Liggins and Howie 1972). Basic science studies had led directly to the introduction of a clinically-valuable prophylactic treatment.

It was becoming apparent that several hormones were involved in stimulating the synthesis and release of surfactant and in structurally preparing the lungs for birth, not only cortisol, but also a thyroid hormone among others. Studies in the early 1970s showed tri-iodothyronine (T3) to stimulate morphologic maturation of the fetal lung. Such studies as those by Rooney et al. (1979), studying the antenatal administration of thyrotropin-releasing hormone (TRH) to rabbit pups and Korda et al. (1984) or Chan et al. (1998) studying the intra-amniotic administration of T3 to fetal lambs, showed the thyroid hormones to stimulate surfactant release and improve anatomical lung maturity and function. T3 rises sharply in late gestation in parallel with cortisol. Therefore there seemed to be a priori evidence suggesting a clinical use for T3 or TRH in enhancing lung maturation when premature delivery was inevitable. However, although the majority of studies suggested some extra benefit when T3 or TRH was given simultaneously with a glucocorticoid, as further animal studies were performed, doubts began to creep in. Studies in rats suggested that although the maternal administration of T3 simultaneously with dexamethasone was associated with an additive effect on fetal lung maturity, the fetuses were smaller and there were increased late intrauterine deaths (Rooney *et al.* 1986). Betamethasone alone, but not betamethasone plus T3, enhanced survival time in prematurely-delivered rabbits (Devaskar *et al.* 1987). Combination treatment of fetal lambs with cortisol and TRH had no greater stimulatory effect on lung function (Ikegami *et al.* 1991) or lung antioxidant synthesis (Walther *et al.* 1991) than treatment with cortisol alone. Indeed, in fetal rats, the antenatal administration of T3 was associated with decreased expression of surfactant protein genes and the genes for the antioxidants copper/zinc superoxide dismutase and catalase (Ramadurai *et al.* 1998).

In spite of these equivocal results, large-scale clinical trials were set up in Australia and the USA, to determine whether the use of TRH in addition to a glucocorticoid conferred extra benefit in terms of lung maturation. TRH was used as there is little placental transfer of T3 or T4 in humans. In the Australian (ACTOBAT) trial, the addition of TRH was associated with greater risk of need for ventilation and respiratory distress syndrome and possibly with small, but consistent, deficits in major milestone achievements at one year postnatal age together with some adverse maternal effects (ACTOBAT 1995). The North American trial concluded that the simultaneous administration of TRH and glucocorticoid 'is no more beneficial than corticoid alone' (Ballard *et al.* 1998).

Another question which had arisen was whether the direct administration of surfactant after birth might also be of benefit. Again, the early experiments were done in animals. Enhorning and Robertson (1972) showed that the administration of concentrated adult surfactant to prematurely-delivered rabbits significantly improved lung inflation characteristics. Other studies followed in a variety of species (e.g. lambs: Adams *et al.* 1978; rhesus monkeys: Enhorning *et al.* 1978) showing that, provided the surfactant was given immediately after birth, there was considerable improvement in lung function. However, the 'foreign' protein content of natural surfactant precluded any possibility of it being used in humans. Biochemical techniques were therefore used to synthesise an artificial surfactant of DPPC and unsaturated PG (7:3). In 1980 a report was published showing that this first synthetic surfactant did indeed improve lung compliance in prematurely-delivered rabbits, although not to as great an extent as natural surfactant (Morley *et al.* 1980). Further development ensued and in the mid-1980s a randomised controlled trial showed that the administration of an artificial surfactant halved the mortality from, and severity of, respiratory distress syndrome (Ten Centre Study Group 1987).

Thus one of the major success stories of perinatal medicine, which has markedly reduced the perinatal mortality and morbidity associated with premature delivery, sprang from basic science, from researchers from different disciplines talking to each other and the ability to evolve hypotheses of causation and hence potential treatment and test them in animal models before moving on to properly-conducted trials in humans. It is possible that the enthusiasm generated by the impact of glucocorticoid administration blinkered researchers to the cautionary notes sounded by some of the animal experiments using T3 or TRH. The information was there.

There just may be a sting in this particular tail. Benediktsson *et al.* (1993) showed that the offspring of rats treated during pregnancy with dexamethasone had lower birth weights and higher blood pressures when adult than did offspring of control rats. More recently, Dodic *et al.* (1998) showed in sheep that even 48 hours maternal treatment with dexamethasone halfway through pregnancy (i.e. considerably earlier than its use in human pregnancy) resulted in the birth of animals which, as adults, had significantly higher blood pressure than controls. Just possibly animal studies are again flagging an area of concern. However, in this instance we will not know for another 20 years or so, and in any event, the early benefit probably outweighs any potential late risk.

An example of a quite different linkage of basic science with clinical practice comes from studies of the fetal renin-angiotensin system (RAS). It was suggested 30 years ago that fetal and newborn animals depend much more on their RAS to maintain cardiovascular homeostasis than do adults (Mott 1969). Subsequently, umbilical venous blood from the normal human baby at vaginal delivery was found to contain much higher plasma angiotensin II (AII) concentrations than are ever encountered in normotensive adult life (Broughton Pipkin and Symonds 1977). Studies were carried out in rabbits and chronically-cannulated fetal lambs and sheep, using angiotensin-converting enzyme inhibitors (ACEIs) such as captopril to block the synthesis of AII, in an attempt to discover what the function of these high circulating AII concentrations was. It quickly became apparent that if fetal lambs were hypoxaemic, hypovolaemic or hypotensive, blockade of the RAS rapidly worsened the lambs' condition, such that intrauterine or intrapartum fetal death was common (Broughton Pipkin *et al.* 1980, 1982; Keith *et al.* 1982). At much the same time, isolated case reports began to appear linking the maternal administration of captopril for hypertension in pregnancy with unexpected fetal death or failure of fetal–neonatal renal function, sometimes prolonged (Broughton Pipkin 1989; Buttar 1997). Similar effects on renal function were being described in sheep (Lumbers *et al.* 1993). Babies of mothers with pre-eclampsia are, by definition, high-risk, and it seemed likely that blockade of the RAS by transplacental passage of maternally-administered ACEIs, was worsening that risk. Pregnancy is now a formal contra-indication to the use of either ACEIs or the more specific angiotensin receptor blockers, such as losartan, which are increasingly used in the treatment of non-pregnant hypertension. Thus a basic science study of fetal physiology led, unexpectedly, to an alteration in clinical practice.

Animals, including humans, lack the enzymes needed to form ω-3 or ω-6 fatty acids (FAs), and must therefore get the precursor 'parent' essential fatty acids (EFAs) from their diet. The daily accumulation of EFAs in the fetus is fastest in the third trimester, so the more prematurely a baby is delivered, the lower its stores of EFAs. Although human milk contains the necessary EFAs, many powdered milk formulas are low in linolenic acid (LNA: 18:3 ω-3), one of the major precursors. Studies in rhesus monkeys showed that when the pregnant mothers, and subsequently the baby monkeys themselves, were fed a diet low in LNA, the plasma and brain docosahexaenoic acid (DHA: 22:6 ω-3) was low, reflecting the fetal and neonatal inability to elongate and desaturate FAs (Neuringer *et al.* 1986). DHA is the major FA in the photoreceptor membranes of the retina. The visual acuity of the baby monkeys, tested at eight weeks, was also significantly reduced (Neuringer *et al.* 1984). Such studies prompted the investigation of formula- and human-milk fed premature babies, which showed similar deficits in visual acuity when unsupplemented formula feeding was given (Hoffman *et al.* 1993). The animal studies also showed how good a correlation there was between brain and red cell membrane FA, allowing subsequent monitoring of the impact of FA supplementation in human premature babies. It is now realised that even term babies do better when formula milk is supplemented with both the precursors and preformed longer-chain FAs, especially DHA (Birch *et al.* 1998).

It is not just the visual development which is affected by maternal FA intake. It was shown some years ago in fetal rabbits that prostaglandin E_1 and prostacyclin, synthesised from arachidonic acid (AA; 20:4 ω-6), stimulate fetal lung adenylate cyclase which is a critical factor for surfactant production (Powell and Solomon 1980). Feeding studies in pregnant rats suggested that supplementation with fish oil (DHA; high in ω-3 FAs) improved fetal lung maturation through an increase in PC synthesis. However, these studies also emphasised the need for caution since too high a ratio of ω-3:ω-6 FAs was associated with growth restriction (Clarke *et al.* 1988). A balance needed to be struck by the addition of both AA and DHA. These experiments, and many others like them, have stimulated the continuing studies of the composition of specialised milks for low-, and very-low birth weight babies.

AND THE FUTURE?

An analysis of 1077 deaths in a Gambian community has recently shown that being born in the hungry season predicts a major excess of premature adult mortality, with infections and pregnancy related maternal deaths as the predominant causes (Ceesay *et al.* 1997; Moore *et al.* 1997). Dietary supplementation for an average of only 82 days in the second half of pregnancy reversed the restriction of fetal growth in the hungry season. This is consistent with findings from the Dutch 'hunger winter' of 1944–1945, and illustrates that fetal growth is most sensitive to nutritional deprivation in the last trimester of pregnancy. A series of epidemiological studies have shown associations of intrauterine exposure to maternal under-nutrition with later hypertension and coronary heart disease in the human population (Barker 1998). Reduced birth weight is associated with higher blood pressure in childhood and adult life and thinness at birth with glucose intolerance and non-insulin dependent diabetes mellitus. Similar studies are being duplicated in animals so that the mechanisms involved may be identified and measures taken to prevent their occurrence. For example, fetal exposure to low-protein diets in rats produces offspring that develop raised systolic blood pressure by the age of weaning. This model of 'programmed' hypertension was used to investigate the role of the RAS in the initiation and maintenance of high blood pressure. By four weeks of age the offspring of low protein-fed dams had systolic blood pressures that were 24–25 mmHg higher than those of rats exposed to a control diet *in utero*. Treatment of pups between two and four weeks postnatal age with an ACE inhibitor completely blocked the development of hypertension in later life (Sherman and Langley-Evans 1998). Studies of the effects of under-nutrition *in utero* on fetal, neonatal and adult health are likely to be of increasing importance in the next millennium.

Another area which fetal physiologists have directly opened up for clinical work is that of surgery *in utero*. It was noticed from the start of chronic preparation of fetal lambs (see above) that the lambs healed amazingly well. The use of 'pig-tail' catheters to relieve pressure on the fetal bladder in the face of ureteric obstruction is now quite widespread. Intrauterine surgery of the human fetus is just beginning to be undertaken on a small-scale. This is never likely to become widespread but some successes are beginning to be reported for spina bifida and facial defects. Stem cell transplantation is another promising area.

I have chosen to concentrate on a few examples and to present them in some detail. For the specialty of fetomaternal medicine to progress there should be a good understanding of the basic science underlying the clinical practice. The rapid development of non-invasive monitoring techniques allows us to make increasingly detailed observational studies of the human fetus but good ethical reasons prevent us from experimental studies. Integrated physiology requires study of the whole animal. The thousands of children and young adults now living who would have died as a result of RDS are an example of the justification for such work.

References

Adams, F.H., Towers, B., Osher, A.B., Ikegami, M., Fujiwara T. and Nozaki, M. (1978) Effects of tracheal instillation of natural surfactant in premature lambs. I: Clinical and autopsy findings. *Pediatr Res* **12,** 841–8

ACTOBAT (1995). Australian collaborative trial of antenatal thyrotropin-releasing hormone (ACTOBAT) for prevention of neonatal respiratory disease. *Lancet* **345**, 877–82

Avery, M.E. and Mead, J. (1959) Surface properties in relation to atelectasis and hyaline membrane disease. *American Journal of Diseases of Children* **97**, 517–23

Ballard, R.A., Ballard, P.L., Cnaan, A. *et al.* (1998) Antenatal thyrotropin-releasing hormone to prevent lung disease in preterm infants. North American Thyrotropin-Releasing Hormone Study Group. *N Engl J Med* **338**, 493–8

Barclay, A.E., Barcroft, J., Barron, D.H. and Franklin, K.J. (1939) A radiographic demonstration of the circulation through the heart in the adult and in the foetus, and the identification of the ductus arteriosus. *Br J Radiol* **12**, 505–18

Barker, D.J. (1998) *In utero* programming of chronic disease. *Clin Sci (Colch)* **95**, 115–28

Benediktsson, R., Lindsay, R.S., Noble, J., Seckl, J.R. and Edwards, C.R. (1993) Glucocorticoid exposure *in utero*: new model for adult hypertension. *Lancet* **341**, 339–41

Birch, E.E., Hoffman, D.R., Uauy, R., Birch, D.G. and Prestidge, C. (1998) Visual acuity and the essentiality of docosahexaenoic acid and arachidonic acid in the diet of term infants. *Pediatr Res* **44**, 201–9

Broughton Pipkin, F. (1989) Are ACE inhibitors safe in pregnancy? *Lancet* **ii**, 482–3

Broughton Pipkin, F. and Symonds, E.M. (1977) Factors affecting angiotensin II concentrations in the human infant at birth. *Clin Sci (Colch)* **52**, 449–56

Broughton Pipkin, F., Turner, S.R. and Symonds, E.M. (1980) Possible risk with captopril in pregnancy: some animal data. *Lancet* **i**, 1256

Broughton Pipkin, F., Symonds, E.M. and Turner, S.R. (1982) The effect of SQ14,225 ('Captopril') upon mother and fetus in the chronically-cannulated ewe and in the pregnant rabbit. *J Physiol (Lond)* **323**, 415–22

Brumley, G.W., Knelson, J.H., Schomberg, D.W. and Crenshaw, C. Jr (1977) Whole and disaturated lung phosphatidylcholine in cortisol-treated, intrauterine growth-retarded and twin control lambs at different gestational ages. *Biol Neonate* **31**, 155–66

Buttar, H.S. (1997) An overview of the influence of ACE inhibitors on fetal-placental circulation and perinatal development. *Mol Cell Biochem* **176**, 61–71

Ceesay, S.M., Prentice, A.M., Cole, T.J. *et al.* (1997) Effects on birth weight and perinatal mortality of maternal dietary supplements in rural Gambia: 5 year randomised controlled trial. *BMJ* **315**, 786–90

Chan, L., Miller, T.F., Yuxin, J. *et al.* (1998) Antenatal triiodothyronine improves neonatal pulmonary function in preterm lambs. *J Soc Gynecol Investig* **5**, 122–6

Clarke, S.D., Benjamin, L., Bell, L. and Phinney, S.D. (1988) Fetal growth and fetal lung phospholipid content in rats fed safflower oil, menhaden oil, or hydrogenated coconut oil. *Am J Clin Nutr* **47**, 828–35

deLemos, R., Shermeta, D.W., Knelson, J., Kotas, R. and Avery, M.E. (1970) Acceleration of appearance of pulmonary surfactant in the fetal lamb by administration of glucocorticoids. *American Review of Respiratory Diseases* **102**, 459–61

Devaskar, U., Church, J.C., Chechani, V. and Sadiq, F. (1987) Effect of simultaneous administration of betamethasone and triiodothyronine (T3) on the development of functional pulmonary maturation in fetal rabbits. *Biochem Biophys Res Commun* **146**, 524–9

Dodic, M., May, C.N., Wintour, E.M. and Coghlan, J.P. (1998) An early prenatal exposure to excess glucocorticoid leads to hypertensive offspring in sheep. *Clin Sci (Colch)* **94**, 149–55

Enhorning, G. and Robertson, B. (1972) Lung expansion in the premature rabbit fetus after tracheal deposition of surfactant. *Pediatrics* **50**, 58–66

Enhorning, G., Hill, D., Sherwood, G., Cutz, E., Robertson, B. and Bryan, C. (1978) Improved ventilation of prematurely delivered primates following tracheal deposition of surfactant. *Am J Obstet Gynecol* **132**, 529–36

Harvey, W. (1651) *De Generatione Animalium*. London: Octavian Pulleyn. (Translation: Whitteridge, G. (1981), p. 397. London: Blackwell Scientific Publications)

Hoffman, D.R., Birch, E.E., Birch, D.G. and Uauy, R.D. (1993) Effects of supplementation with omega-3 long-chain polyunsaturated fatty acids on retinal and cortical development in premature infants. *Am J Clin Nutr* **57** Suppl, 807S–12S

Huggett, A.StG. (1927) Foetal blood-gas tensions and gas transfusion through the placenta of the goat. *J Physiol (Lond)* **62**, 373–84

Huggett, A.StG. (1929) Maternal control of placental glycogen. *J Physiol (Lond)* **67**, 360–71

Ikegami, M., Polk, D., Tabor, B., Lewis, J., Yamada, T. and Jobe, A. (1991) Corticosteroid and thyrotropin-releasing hormone effects on preterm sheep lung function. *Applied Physiology* **70**, 2268–78

Keith, I.M., Wills, J.A. and Weir, E.K. (1982) Captopril: association with fetal death and pulmonary vascular changes in the rabbit. *Proc Soc Exp Biol Med* **170**, 378–83

Korda, A.R., Fleming, S.F., Senior, C. *et al.* (1984) The effect of intra-amniotic injection of triiodothyronine on pulmonary maturity in lambs at 130 days gestation. *Pediatr Res* **18**, 932–5

Liggins, G.C. (1969) Premature delivery of fetal lambs infused with glucocorticoids. *J Endocrinol* **45**, 515–23

Liggins, G.C. and Howie, R.N. (1972) A controlled trial of antepartum glucocorticoid treatment for prevention of the respiratory distress syndrome in premature infants. *Pediatrics* **50**, 515–25

Lumbers, E.R., Burrell, J.H., Menzies, R.I. and Stevens, A.D. (1993) The effects of a converting enzyme inhibitor (captopril) and angiotensin II on fetal renal function. *Br J Pharmacol* **110**, 821–7

Meschia, G., Cotter, J.R., Breathnach, C.S. and Barron, D.H. (1965) The hemoglobin, oxygen, carbon dioxide and hydrogen ion concentrations in the umbilical bloods of sheep and goats as sampled via indwelling plastic cannulas. *Quarterly Journal of Experimental Physiology* **50**, 185–95

Moore, S.E., Cole, T.J., Poskitt, E.M.E. *et al.* (1997) Season of birth predicts mortality in rural Gambia. *Nature* **388**, 434

Morley, C., Robertson, B., Lachmann, B. *et al.* (1980) Artificial surfactant and natural surfactant. Comparative study of the effects on premature rabbit lungs. *Arch Dis Child* **55**, 758–65

Mott, J.C. (1969) The kidneys and arterial pressure in immature and adult rabbits. *J Physiol (Lond)* **202**, 25–44

Neuringer, M., Connor, W.E., Van Petten, C. and Barstad, L. (1984) Dietary omega-3 fatty acid deficiency and visual loss in infant rhesus monkeys. *J Clin Invest* **73**, 272–6

Neuringer, M., Connor, W.E., Lin, D.S., Barstad, L. and Luck, S. (1986) Biochemical and functional effects of prenatal and postnatal omega 3 fatty acid deficiency on retina and brain in rhesus monkeys. *Proc Natl Acad Sci USA* **83**, 4021–5

Pattle, R.E. (1958) Properties, function and origin of the alveolar lining layer. *Proc R Soc Lond B Biol Sci* **148**, 217–40

Powell, W.S. and Solomon, S. (1980) Effects of prostaglandins on the adenylate cyclase activity of lungs from fetal rabbits. *Endocrinology* **107**, 1469–73

Ramadurai, S.M., Nielsen, H.C., Chen, Y., Hatzis, D. and Sosenko, I.R. (1998) Differential effects *in vivo* of thyroid hormone on the expression of surfactant phospholipid, surfactant protein mRNA and antioxidant enzyme mRNA in fetal rat lung. *Exp Lung Res* **24**, 641–57

Rooney, S.A., Gobran, L.I. and Chu, A.J. (1986) Thyroid hormone opposes some glucocorticoid effects on glycogen content and lipid synthesis in developing fetal rat lung. *Pediatr Res* **20**, 545–50

Rooney, S.A., Gross, I., Gassenheimer, L.N. and Motoyama, E.K. (1975) Stimulation of glycerolphosphate phosphatidyltransferase activity in fetal rabbit lung by cortisol administration. *Biochim Biophys Acta* **398**, 433–41

Rooney, S.A., Marino, P.A., Gobran, L.I., Gross, I. and Warshaw, J.B. (1979) Thyrotropin-releasing hormone increases the amount of surfactant in lung lavage from fetal rabbits. *Pediatr Res* **13**, 623–5

Sherman, R.C. and Langley-Evans, S.C. (1998) Early administration of angiotensin-converting enzyme inhibitor captopril, prevents the development of hypertension programmed by intrauterine exposure to a maternal low-protein diet in the rat. *Clin Sci* **94**, 373–81

Ten Centre Study Group (1987) Ten centre trial of artificial surfactant (artificial lung expanding compound) in very premature babies. *BMJ* **294**, 991–6

Walther, F.J., Ikegami, M., Warburton, D. and Polk, D.H. (1991) Corticosteroids, thyrotropin-releasing hormone, and antioxidant enzymes in preterm lamb lungs. *Pediatr Res* **30**, 518–21

8

The placenta as patient

Tim Chard

INTRODUCTION

In a number of cultures the placenta is treated with a high measure of respect, being regarded as an inseparable part of the entire life of an individual and buried with all due ceremony at death (Stirrat 1998). Western society, by contrast, has largely ignored the placenta as a separate life form. Other than providing a source of maternal postnatal nutrition under exiguous circumstances, it is almost always disposed of with no further thought than that usually given to household waste. On rare occasions, it has also been used as a source of pharmaceuticals (serum proteins) and more mundane cosmetic materials. Yet the placenta in many ways qualifies to be considered as a separate individual. It has unique biological activities which are totally distinct from those of the child. It exhibits pathology, including a range of tumours, which are unique to this organ. Finally, some have postulated that the placenta undergoes a process of ageing, quite equivalent to that in the adult and that it is this ageing process which determines many features of a pregnancy, including the all important timing of parturition (Rosso 1976).

Although the placenta is not typically recognised as being a significant part of a modern 'individual', its essential role during gestation is universally recognised. Ballantyne (1902) pointed out that 'the foetus, the membranes, the cord and the placenta form an organic whole, and disease of any part must react upon and affect the others'. For the nine months of a pregnancy it acts for the fetus as kidney, gut and lung. The normal placenta has considerable functional reserves in this respect. During the last half of gestation, growth of the fetus is exponential whereas that of the placenta slows or even ceases. The fact that placental transport capacity can keep pace with fetal growth is accounted for by increases in blood flow on both the fetal and maternal side (Reynolds and Redmer 1995).

There is also a general appreciation that failure of placental function can lead to serious problems for the growing child. But with the focus on the well-being of the fetus itself, it is often forgotten that, with the exception of congenital abnormalities, the origin of most conditions which threaten fetal well-being lie firmly and exclusively within the placenta. The changes in the fetus itself merely reflect the constraints of this nutritional pipeline. Most of the diagnostic tests and proposed therapeutic modalities used in present-day obstetrics have the placenta as their primary target. Indeed, the same also applies to some of the congenital abnormalities.

The importance of the placenta to current management of fetal well-being is such that this organ might properly be deemed as the target of this process: the placenta as the patient.

PLACENTAL FUNCTION

The anatomy and physiology of the human placenta has been reviewed in great detail on numerous occasions. For ease of reference, the key structures involved are shown diagrammatically in Figure 1. Each of these structures may be affected by pathology, with a consequent reduction in placental function and thereby deprivation of the fetus.

The key function of the placenta is transport of nutrients to the fetus and waste products away from the fetus. These transfers occur across a relatively thin tissue consisting of the trophoblast (mostly syncytiotrophoblast), a basement membrane and the endothelium of the fetal capillaries in the chorionic villi. For practical purposes, this tissue is often considered as a rather passive semipermeable membrane, capable of allowing the passage of relatively small molecules but not larger ones such as the plasma proteins. The most notable exception to this is the specific transfer of immunoglobulin G from the mother to the fetus. In reality, this view of the placenta as a semipermeable membrane is greatly simplified. With rare, if any, exceptions, solutes do not move by simple passive diffusion, but rather by a complex set of energy-requiring mechanisms (Bauer *et al.* 1998). It is often not appreciated that the placenta consumes something like one-third of all the nutrients and energy devoted to the fetoplacental unit. The placenta can also be responsible for *de novo* synthesis of essential nutrients for the fetus; for example, a large proportion of the amino acid glycine is derived by placental conversion of serine (Geddie *et al.* 1996).

It is also often not appreciated that the placenta, or certainly the syncytiotrophoblast, has synthetic activities greatly in excess of those of any other tissue in the body at any stage of life. The major sites of synthesis are the so-called 'thick' areas of the syncytiotrophoblast, which are distinct from the 'thin' areas which lie adjacent to fetal capillaries and are considered to be the main site of transfer (Burgos and Rodriguez 1966). The synthetic activities include the production of a wide range of 'specific' proteins and steroids, some with recognised biological activity such as human placental lactogen (hPL) and others without known activity, such as pregnancy-associated plasma protein A

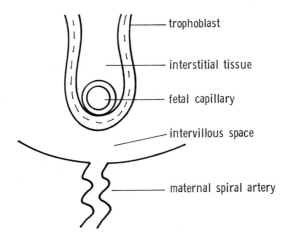

Figure 1 *Diagram of the principal structures involved in placental function; some 100 maternal spiral arteries open into the intervillous space; in a normal placenta at term the flow rate is around 600 ml per minute with a pressure of 70–80 mmHg*

(PAPP-A). The proteins of the growth hormone family provide a good example of specific synthesis. These proteins are coded by five homologous genes at a single locus on chromosome 17. Classic growth hormone is expressed in the pituitary gland, while other members of the gene family, including placental lactogen and the placenta growth hormone variant are expressed specifically in the placenta (Alsat *et al.* 1997). Surprisingly and despite their high levels, the functions of virtually all of the hormonal or other products of the placenta are uncertain. Cases are regularly reported in which one or other material is completely absent due to gene deletion without any apparent adverse effect on the pregnancy (Simon *et al.* 1986). It remains a biological enigma as to why such a substantial resource should be devoted to an apparently pointless system. It has even been suggested that, unlike most classical 'endocrine' systems, the specific products of the placenta in the maternal circulation do not act as effectors, but rather as 'messengers' (Chard 1993). By exiting the placenta, travelling around the maternal circulation and then returning to the placenta where they can combine to cell-surface receptors, these molecules could serve to provide information to the fetoplacental unit about the maternal environment. This hypothetical function, which has been termed 'placental radar' (Chard 1993) has been observed in a number of other biological systems.

In addition to those specific proteins which are produced in substantial amounts, the placenta also produces small quantities of virtually every known protein and peptide produced in the adult organism. This is in contrast to most adult organs in which many genes are 'silent'. Indeed, the placenta appears to reproduce the entire range of synthetic functions associated with antenatal or postnatal life. The major difference is that it does not display any of the tissue or organ distribution which characterises the normal body. Among many examples of the synthesis of 'adult' proteins is the presence in the placenta of a wide range of compounds normally localised in the brain; for example, the hypothalamic releasing factors and the full range of endogenous opioid peptides and their receptors (Ahmed *et al.* 1992). The interactions of placental corticotrophin-releasing hormone with placental pro-opiomelanocortin, adrenocorticotrophin and prostaglandins may have important functions in relation to the paracrine and autocrine regulation of uteroplacental blood flow and in term and preterm labour (Petraglia *et al.* 1987; Challis *et al.* 1995; Cooper *et al.* 1996; Karteris *et al.* 1998; Nodwell *et al.* 1999).

Perhaps surprisingly, there is little evidence for specific control of placental function by the fetus, or vice versa. Suggestions have been made that fetal cortisol may influence the production of placental corticotrophin-releasing hormone (Riley and Challis 1991) and that placental factors may affect the growth and function of the fetal adrenals (Waddell, 1993; Ramsay *et al.* 1985). However, the fact that the placenta can survive the death of the fetus *in utero* (Albrecht and Pepe 1985), while the fetus obviously survives the placenta following delivery, suggests that there would be, at most, limited interdependence within the so-called 'fetoplacental unit'.

The placenta also has a protective role in respect of the fetus. Some of this is a rather obvious barrier function in respect of maternal infections. Other protective functions are more subtle. For example, fetal levels of cortisol are substantially less than those of the mother. The amount of cortisol that crosses the placenta to reach the fetal compartment is determined by the placental enzyme 11β-hydroxysteroid dehydrogenase which inactivates cortisol to the biologically less active cortisone. Failure of this mechanism may expose the fetus to excess glucocorticoid and could, in part, explain some of the long-term sequelae of placental insufficiency for the child and adult (Benediktsson *et al.* 1993;

Edwards *et al.* 1993; Seckl 1997; Seckl and Chapman 1997; Sun *et al.* 1998). The synthetic corticosteroids used therapeutically to enhance fetal lung maturation are largely resistant to placental enzyme inactivation.

THE PLACENTA IN NORMAL AND ABNORMAL PREGNANCY

Early pregnancy

For a surprisingly large number of the diagnostic tests applied during pregnancy the placenta is the primary target. This is particularly the case in early pregnancy. Thus, one of the most commonly used tests in clinical medicine is the qualitative measurement of human chorionic gonadotrophin (hCG) in urine (Chard 1992). The use of this assay to detect early pregnancy extends beyond professionals – it is the most widely used of all over-the-counter diagnostic tests. The woman in the street perceives this as being a test for the presence of a 'baby'; the professional knows that it is the placenta which is detected by this methodology.

The use of a pregnancy test is not merely to satisfy parental curiosity. In the field of gynaecology and emergency medicine it is now universally used to determine whether or not a woman is pregnant in the setting of a clinical situation where this would greatly influence the differential diagnosis. Specifically, any woman of reproductive age presenting with lower abdominal pain should invariably be offered a pregnancy test to exclude the possibility of an abnormal early pregnancy, especially an ectopic pregnancy (Seppala *et al.* 1980). The point made here is that the test is directed specifically at the placenta, rather than the pregnancy as a whole. Positive tests may occur in the absence of a fetus.

Detection of congenital abnormalities

Congenital abnormalities are usually considered as a fetal rather than a placental problem. However, there is abundant evidence that the placenta can exhibit its own abnormalities, which are quite independent from those of the fetus. In particular, the placenta may be a chromosome mosaic in the presence of a normal fetus, the condition known as 'confined placental mosaicism' (Kalousek 1994). This occurs in around 2% of all pregnancies. Confined placental mosaicism is defined as partial or complete dichotomy between the chromosome make-up of the placenta and that of the fetus. Some cases are confined to the trophoblast, others to the stroma of the chorionic villi, while in yet other cases both are involved. Any of these types may be associated with intrauterine growth restriction or intrauterine death, especially those involving both the trophoblast and the stroma (Kalousek 1994). Mosaicism may also play a substantial but ill-defined role in early pregnancy loss. Current advances in cytogenetic analysis suggest that this may be a rich area to explore in the future, the concept being that otherwise unexplained fetal problems might be due to as yet unrecognised placental problems.

As with other pregnancy problems, the placenta may be the diagnostic vehicle even though the intended target is the fetus. The single most effective and widely used screening test for Down syndrome is the measurement of hCG in maternal blood (Macri *et al.* 1994). Other placental proteins also show striking changes but the mechanism is not understood since none of the relevant material is coded on chromosome 21. Nevertheless, the approach illustrates well the concept of 'the placenta as patient' albeit, in this context, as a surrogate for the fetus itself. In the same vein, the placenta is the actual target of one of the most widely used of all 'fetal' biopsies – chorion villus sampling.

There are rare instances in which an identifiable abnormality of the placenta is associated with a specific congenital abnormality in the child. These include placental sulphatase deficiency (associated with congenital ichthyosis) (Rich and Johansen 1993) and PAPP-A deficiency (associated with the Cornelia de Lange syndrome) (Westergaard *et al.* 1983).

Abnormal placentation

Abnormalities in the site or formation of the placenta can lead to haemorrhage from the mother or fetus, or compression of fetal vessels. The most common of such conditions is placenta praevia. Less common but equally or more threatening are the various degrees of placenta accreta.

Premature labour

Preterm labour continues to be one of the most intractable causes of perinatal morbidity and mortality. Despite immense efforts to identify underlying causes, the frequency has remained unchanged almost since records were first kept. Improved survival of premature babies has been solely related to neonatal medicine and not to obstetrics.

Many cases of preterm labour cannot be attributed to a specific cause and are deemed to be 'spontaneous'. In the 1970s and early 1980s a great deal of research effort was directed towards endocrine factors that might be involved. Such factors included products of both the fetus and the placenta. The most commonly used experimental model was the sheep. Here, there emerged an almost unambiguous picture that labour was triggered by the fetal pituitary gland, releasing adrenocorticotrophin, in turn leading to an increase in fetal cortisol which influenced the placenta to cause a substantial increase in oestrogen secretion and fall in progesterone secretion. This altered balance of steroid production by the placenta was believed to play an especially important role in the whole process, triggering the various secondary and tertiary factors (prostaglandin release etc.) involved in uterine contractions.

In the human, evidence for an involvement of the fetal pituitary is limited. Several workers have pointed to changes in placental steroids (oestrogens and progesterone) as preceding the onset of labour, whether term or preterm (Raja *et al.* 1974; Turnbull *et al.* 1974; Darne *et al.* 1987). If true, that would focus attention on the placenta as a prime mover in this particular complication and it might suggest novel therapeutic approaches. However, most workers have been unable to confirm the often quite dramatic changes in placental steroids described by some of the earlier authors (Chew and Ratnam 1976a; Chew and Ratnam 1976b).

Over the past decade much work has addressed the local autocrine or paracrine factors which may be involved in parturition. This work also focuses on the membranes which are, in part, placental. An inflammatory exudate in the myometrium is characteristic of both normal and abnormal labour (Thomson *et al.* 1999). So, too, is an increase in the levels of cytokines and other inflammatory mediators in amniotic fluid (Romero *et al.* 1990; Romero *et al.* 1989). This process can be triggered prematurely by infection and much effort is currently directed towards determining whether the prophylactic use of antibiotics can prevent preterm labour (Brocklehurst 1999). Thus, in the human, attention has shifted from fetal and placental endocrine mechanisms, to local mechanisms some of which are already familiar, while others may be more subtle.

Fetal growth

Postnatal growth of the child is substantially determined by genetic make-up, with nutrition playing a largely permissive role. By contrast, the fetal genome plays only a limited role in growth *in utero*, which is determined by maternal factors including the availability of nutrients, i.e. placental function. Similarly, the hormonal factors (pituitary growth hormone) which are prominent in postnatal life appear to play little if any role in fetal growth *in utero*.

Abnormalities of fetal growth are widely, if sometimes incorrectly (Chard *et al.* 1993), regarded as being a major cause of morbidity and mortality. Substantial resources are devoted towards the identification, during the antenatal period, of the child whose growth is believed to fall at the lower end of a population standard.

Although superficially a fetal problem and identified by direct examination of the fetus (ultrasound etc.), most cases of fetal growth restriction do not appear to have a fetal cause (specific causes such as congenital abnormalities or infections are not considered here).

The only well-recognised pathology, other than smallness, seems to be that in the placenta. This includes several rather non-specific phenomena (fibrin deposition in the intervillous space, placental infarction etc.) (Macpherson 1991; Altshuler 1993) which are probably secondary to a more fundamental cause. The most primary pathology which has been described and which is virtually identical to that associated with many cases of maternal hypertension, is failure of appropriate vascularisation of the placenta at an early stage in the pregnancy. At this time, the decidual spiral arterioles are transformed by invading extravillous cytotrophoblast, leading to a more than ten-fold increase in utero-placental blood flow (Cross *et al.* 1994). This phenomenon was described many years ago (Brosens *et al.* 1967). Adequate blood flow from the maternal arterioles into the inter-villous space depends upon the virtual destruction of the walls of these vessels. Failure of this invasion, leaving the vessel wall intact and thereby capable of constriction, is believed to underlie much of the pathology of both growth restriction and pre-eclampsia (Brosens *et al.* 1977; Pijnenborg *et al.* 1991). Pathologically, the result of this process is acute atherosclerosis and arteriolitis of the maternal spiral arteries. The result of this vascular disease is reduced perfusion of the intervillous space and it is this vascular change which is principally responsible for the situation commonly referred to as 'placental insufficiency'. The reduction in intervillous blood flow resulting from this underlies many of the common adverse perinatal outcomes including growth restriction, fetal hypoxia and perinatal death. Within the placenta itself the most notable effect of a reduction in blood supply is accelerated maturation of the chorionic villi (Macpherson 1991). This is characterised by reduced villous size, an increased number of syncytial knots and an increase in the proportion of vasculosyncytial membranes. There might also be hypo-plasia of the cytotrophoblast and thickening of the trophoblast basement membrane.

Thus, the 'fetal' problem of growth restriction may more properly be regarded as a placental problem in most cases. This is acknowledged by some of the diagnostic procedures which have been applied. At one time the most commonly used test of fetal well-being was the measurement, in maternal blood, of placental products such as oestriol (with a fetal component) or hPL. Levels of these compounds were character-istically low in association with fetal growth restriction. The clinical efficiency of these tests, in terms of predictive value and enabling of therapeutic measures was, however, relatively limited and the so-called 'placental function tests' were largely replaced by biophysical methods during the 1980s (Chard 1987; Arabin *et al.* 1995). In the more recent past attention has again focused on the placenta. It is now generally recognised that the most effective of the biophysical tests and certainly one that is well supported by the known pathology, is measurement of the blood flow in the maternal placental circulation by Doppler ultrasound. Campbell and others (Fay and Ellwood 1991; Bower *et al.* 1993) have shown that persistent bilateral early-diastolic notching of the uterine artery waveform at 24 weeks' gestation can predict the later development of both intra-uterine growth retardation and pre-eclampsia. Although there is little doubt of the validity of this phenomenon in the most severe cases, some reservations have been expressed about the value of this test for screening apparently normal pregnancies (North *et al.* 1994; Kingdom 1998). From the point of view of the argument here it is notable that these tests, like the earlier 'placental function tests', address the placenta itself. In addition, and unsurprisingly, there is evidence that values for blood flow and of placental products may vary in parallel (Bewley *et al.* 1993).

It is generally recognised that, in a developed society, maternal nutrition plays only a small part in the growth of the baby. However, there seems little doubt that it can affect the growth of the placenta; anaemia and iron deficiency during pregnancy are associated with large placental weight and a high ratio of placental weight to birth weight (Godfrey *et al.* 1991).

Maternal hypertensive disease

The fetus suffers most of the consequences of maternal hypertensive disease, with a well-recognised increase in mortality and morbidity. But, as with fetal growth restriction, the primary pathology of this condition lies in the placenta: the earliest event seems to be a failure of adequate vascularisation of the placental bed, leading to constriction of the maternal arterioles (Brosens *et al.* 1977; Pijnenborg *et al.* 1991). Another feature of pre-eclampsia is an increase in the amount of trophoblast tissue which is found in the uterine vein (Chua *et al.* 1991).

Study of placental vascularisation offers promise for the prediction of pre-eclampsia (Fay and Ellwood 1991; Bower *et al.* 1993; Harrington *et al.* 1996) as, indeed, may measurement of biochemical products of the placenta (Simpson *et al.* 1994). Therapeutic approaches to the prevention and treatment of pre-eclampsia have been disappointing, but it is notable that some of the most intensively investigated modalities, such as the administration of aspirin, have the placental circulation as their presumed target.

PLACENTAL TUMOURS

It is often commented that the placenta has many characteristics which, if they were seen in any other tissue, would be considered to be typical of cancer. This applies particularly to the invasive properties of the trophoblast in early pregnancy. Specific features of tumours, such as expression of the p53 protein, are also found in trophoblast (Marzusch *et al.* 1995). However, the fact that in the majority of cases, the rapid invasion of maternal tissues by trophoblast is swiftly constrained within the first few weeks of pregnancy suggests that the analogy with a tumour should not be pursued too far. Instead, the 'invasion' of tissues by the early trophoblast is perhaps more similar to the processes of tissue growth seen in the resolution phase after injury or acute inflammation. The placenta does not display any of the cytogenetic abnormalities which would be considered as typical of tumour growth.

The unique tumours of the trophoblast are choriocarcinoma and hydatidiform mole. A remarkable feature of the complete mole is that it contains only paternally derived chromosomes (Kajii 1977). The maternal chromosome component is lost. The paternal haploid set duplicates but develops successfully only with X-bearing sperm (46,XX; rarely 46,XY is produced by fertilisation of an 'empty egg' by two sperm carrying X and Y chromosomes) (Szulman 1988). These phenomena have led to the interesting hypothesis that the maternal genome is essential for embryonic development, whereas the paternal pronucleus is associated with trophoblast development (Szulman 1988). The fact that the placenta is so biologically distinct may explain why measurement of one of its principal products, hCG, is the perfect tumour marker. Levels in the mother show an almost perfect 1:1 relationship with the tumour mass; disappearance of hCG can be virtually guaranteed to equate with successful treatment.

Another unique feature of placental tumours, especially given the fact that they are highly invasive if unchecked, is their extraordinary sensitivity to chemotherapy. Perhaps this reflects the fact that the placental tumour, having a slightly different genetic composition to its maternal host, is more easily recognised and disposed of as an invader.

The placenta and adult disease

The now classic studies of Barker and colleagues (see O'Brien *et al.* 1999) have shown that low birth weight is a predictive factor for ischaemic heart disease and hypertension in later adult life. Once again, the placenta appears to be the key factor in this situation. The combination of low birth weight and a large placenta is particularly associated with high blood pressure (Martyn *et al.* 1996).

Placental weight

Under most circumstances the weight of the placenta varies in parallel with that of the fetus. However, the placenta may be relatively larger than normal in certain maternal conditions including anaemia, heart disease and pregnancy at high altitudes (Fox and Faulk 1981). Unlike birth weight, placental weight is relatively unaffected by cigarette smoking. Low placental weight may be associated with higher levels of haemoglobin in the newborn. Before 36 weeks' gestation, relatively high placental weight is associated with neonatal asphyxia, death and subsequent neurological abnormality (Naeye 1987).

THE FUTURE

Who owns the placenta?

The 'individuality' of the placenta is perhaps reflected by the lack of dignity in its treatment. The organ is not usually regarded as having any 'rights' and no specific consent is required for its use for either clinical, pathological or experimental processes. At various times it has been deemed to belong either to the child, the mother, the parents, or even the medical staff or unit responsible for the case. With the current concern for what are, after all, human tissues, it is virtually certain that more of this topic will be heard in the future.

Placental treatment

Other than early delivery, there is still virtually no specific and agreed treatment for most of the conditions which threaten fetal well-being. Nevertheless, this is an active area of research and likely to become more so. Evidence for hormonal control of placental function, especially by the insulin-like growth factors, offers hope for the specific enhancement of placental function (Bauer *et al.* 1998). For several decades, researchers have considered the possibility of creating an artificial placenta (Unno *et al.* 1997). The systems so far described are entirely experimental, although some of the techniques used on small babies in present-day neonatal intensive care could be described as creating, at least in part, an 'artificial placenta'.

CONCLUSIONS

No one disputes the critical importance of the placenta to fetal well-being. Equally, the placenta is sometimes not accorded the recognition it deserves as the primary target of most of the diagnostic procedures applied as part of antenatal care. For the future, it may also prove to be an appropriate therapeutic target, thereby amplifying the concept of 'the placenta as patient'.

References

Ahmed, M.S., Cemerikic, B. and Agbas, A. (1992) Properties and functions of human placental opioid system. *Life Sci* **50**, 83–97

Albrecht, E.D. and Pepe, G.J. (1985) The placenta remains functional following fetectomy in baboons. *Endocrinology* **116**, 843–5

Alsat, E., Guibourdenche, J., Luton, D., Frankenne, F. and Evain-Brion, D. (1997) Human placental growth hormone. *Am J Obstet Gynecol* **177**, 1526–34

Altshuler, G. (1993) Some placental considerations related to neurodevelopmental and other disorders. *J Child Neurol* **8**, 78–94

Arabin, B., Ragosch, V. and Mohnhaupt, A. (1995) From biochemical to biophysical placental function tests in fetal surveillance. *Am J Perinatol* **12**, 168–71

Ballantyne, J.W. (1902) *Manual of Antenatal Pathology and Hygiene*. Edinburgh: William Green

Bauer, M.K., Harding, J.E., Bassett, N.S. *et al.* (1998) Fetal growth and placental function. *Mol Cell Endocrinol* **140**, 115–20

Benediktsson, R., Lindsay, R.S., Noble, J., Seckl, J.R. and Edwards, C.R.W. (1993) Glucocorticoid exposure *in utero*: new model for adult hypertension. *Lancet* **341**, 339–41

Bewley, S., Chard, T., Grudzinskas, G. and Campbell, S. (1993) The relationship of uterine and umbilical Doppler resistance to fetal and placental protein synthesis in the second trimester. *Placenta* **14**, 663–70

Bower, S., Bewley, S. and Campbell, S. (1993) Improved prediction of pre-eclampsia by two-stage screening of uterine arteries using the early diastolic notch and color Doppler imaging. *Obstet Gynecol* **82**, 78–83

Brocklehurst, P. (1999) Infection and preterm delivery. *BMJ* **318**, 548–9

Brosens, I., Robertson, W.B. and Dixon, H.G. (1967) The physiological response of the vessels of the placental bed to normal pregnancy. *Journal of Pathology and Bacteriology* **93**, 569–79

Brosens, I., Dixon, H.G. and Robertson, W.B. (1977) Fetal growth retardation and the arteries of the placental bed. *Br J Obstet Gynaecol* **84**, 656–63

Burgos, M.H. and Rodriguez, E.M. (1966) Specialized zones in the trophoblast of the human term placenta. *Am J Obstet Gynecol* **96**, 342–56

Challis, J.R.G., Matthews, S.G., Van Meir, C. and Ramirez, M.M. (1995) The placental corticotrophin-releasing hormone–adrenocorticotrophin axis. *Placenta* **16**, 481–502

Chard, T. (1987) What is happening to placental function tests? *Ann Clin Biochem* **24**, 435–9

Chard, T. (1992) Pregnancy tests: a review. *Hum Reprod* **7**, 701–10

Chard, T. (1993) Placental radar. *J Endocrinol* **138**, 177–9

Chard, T., Yoong, A. and Macintosh, M. (1993) The myth of fetal growth retardation at term. *Br J Obstet Gynaecol* **100**, 1076–81

Chew, P.C.T. and Ratnam, S.S. (1976a) Serial plasma progesterone levels at the approach of labour. *J Endocrinol* **69**, 163–4

Chew, P.C.T. and Ratnam, S.S. (1976b) Serial levels of plasma oestradiol-17β at the approach of labour. *J Endocrinol* **71**, 267–8

Chua, S., Wilkins, T., Sargent, I. and Redman, C. (1991) Trophoblast deportation in pre-eclamptic pregnancy. *Br J Obstet Gynaecol* **98**, 973–9

Cooper, E.S., Geer, I.A. and Brooks, A.N. (1996) Placental proopiomelanocortin gene expression, adrenocorticotropin tissue concentrations, and immunostaining increase throughout gestation and are unaffected by prostaglandins, antiprogestins, or labor. *J Clin Endocrinol Metab* **81**, 4462–9

Cross, J.C., Werb, Z. and Fisher, S.J. (1994) Implantation and the placenta: key pieces of the development puzzle. *Science* **266**, 1508–18

Darne, J., McGarrigle, H.H.G. and Lachelin, G.C.L. (1987) Increased saliva oestriol to progesterone ratio before idiopathic preterm delivery: a possible predictor for preterm labour? *BMJ* **294**, 270–2

Edwards, C.R.W., Benediktsson, R., Lindsay, R.S. and Seckl, J.R. (1993) Dysfunction of placental glucocorticoid barrier: link between fetal environment and adult hypertension? *Lancet* **341**, 355–7

Fay, R.A. and Ellwood, D. (1991) Doppler investigation of uteroplacental blood flow resistance in the second trimester: a screening study for pre-eclampsia and intrauterine growth retardation. *Br J Obstet Gynaecol* **98**, 871–9

Fox, H. and Faulk, W.P. (1981) The placenta as an experimental model. *Clin Endocrinol Metab* **10**, 57–72

Geddie, G., Moores, R., Meschia, G., Fennessey, P., Wilkening, R. and Battaglia, F.C. (1996) Comparison of leucine, serine and glycine transport across the ovine placenta. *Placenta* **17**, 619–27

Godfrey, K.M., Redman, C.W.G., Barker, D.J.P. and Osmond, C. (1991) The effect of maternal anaemia and iron deficiency on the ration of fetal weight to placental weight. *Br J Obstet Gynaecol* **98**, 886–91

Harrington, K., Cooper, D., Lees, C., Hecher, K. and Campbell, S. (1996) Doppler ultrasound of the uterine arteries: the importance of bilateral notching in the prediction of pre-eclampsia, placental abruption or delivery of a small-for-gestational-age baby. *Ultrasound Obstet Gynecol* **7**, 182–8

Kajii, T. (1977) Androgenetic origin of hydatidiform mole. *Nature* **268**, 633–4

Kalousek, D.K. (1994) Current topic: confined placental mosaicism and intrauterine fetal development. *Placenta* **15**, 219–30

Karteris, E., Grammatopoulos, D., Dai, Y. *et al.* (1998) The human placenta and fetal membranes express the corticotropin-releasing hormone receptor 1a (CRH-1a) and the CRH-C variant receptor. *J Clin Endocrinol Metab* **83**, 1376–9

Kingdom, J. (1998) Placental pathology in obstetrics: adaptation or failure of the villous tree? *Placenta* **19**, 347–51

Macpherson, T. (1991) Fact and fancy: what can we really tell from the placenta? *Arch Pathol Lab Med* **115**, 672–81

Macri, J.N., Spencer, K., Garver, L. *et al.* (1994) Maternal serum free β hCG screening: results of studies including 480 cases of Down syndrome. *Prenat Diagn* **14**, 97–103

Martyn, C.N., Barker, D.J.P. and Osmond, C. (1996) Mothers pelvic size, fetal growth and death from stroke in men. *Lancet* **348**, 1264–8

Marzusch, K., Ruck, P., Horny, H-P., Dietl, J. and Kaiserling, E. (1995) Expression of the p53 tumour suppressor gene in human placenta: an immunohistochemical study. *Placenta* **16**, 101–4

Naeye, R.L. (1987) Do placental weights have clinical significance. *Hum Pathol* **18**, 387–91

Nodwell, A., Carmichael, L., Fraser, M., Challis, J. and Richardson, B. (1999) Placental release of corticotrophin-releasing hormone across the umbilical circulation of the human newborn. *Placenta* **20**, 197–202

North, R.A., Ferrier, C., Long, D., Townend, K. and Kincaid-Smith, P. (1994) Uterine artery Doppler flow velocity waveforms in the second trimester for the prediction of pre-eclampsia and fetal growth retardation. *Obstet Gynecol* **83**, 378–86

O'Brien, P.M.S., Wheeler, T. and Barker, D.J.P. (Eds) (1999) *Fetal Programming: Influences on Development and Disease in Adult Life.* London: RCOG Press

Petraglia, F., Sawchenko, P.E., Rivier, J. and Vale, W. (1987) Evidence for local stimulation of ACTH secretion by cortico-releasing factor in human placenta. *Nature* **328**, 717–19

Pijnenborg, R., Anthony, J., Davey, D.A. *et al.* (1991) Placental bed spiral arteries in the hypertensive disorders of pregnancy. *Br J Obstet Gynaecol* **98**, 648–55

Raja, R.L.T., Anderson, A.B.M. and Turnbull, A.C. (1974) Endocrine changes in premature labour. *BMJ* **ii**, 67–71

Ramsay, T.G., Sheahan, J.A., Hausman, G.J. and Martin, R.J. (1985) Effects of fetal decapitation upon porcine placental metabolism: evidence for a fetal influence in placental metabolism. *Biol Neonate* **47**, 42–53

Reynolds, L.P. and Redmer, D.A. (1995) Utero-placental vascular development and placental function. *J Anim Sci* **73**, 1839–51

Rich, D.E.E. and Johansen, K.A. (1993) Placental sulfatase deficiency and congenital ichthyosis with intrauterine fetal death: case report. *Am J Obstet Gynecol* **168**, 570–1

Riley, S.C. and Challis, J.R.G. (1991) Corticotrophin-releasing hormone production by the placenta and fetal membranes. *Placenta* **12**, 105–19

Romero, R., Manogue, K.R., Mitchell, M.D. *et al.* (1989) Infection and labor. IV. Cachectin-tumor necrosis factor in the amniotic fluid of women with intraamniotic infection and preterm labor. *Am J Obstet Gynecol* **161**, 336–41

Romero, R., Avila, C., Santhanam, U. and Sehgal, P.B. (1990) Amniotic fluid interleukin 6 in preterm labor: association with infection. *J Clin Invest* **85**, 1392–400

Rosso, P. (1976) Placenta as an ageing organ. *Current Concepts in Nutrition* **4**, 23–41

Seckl, J.R. (1997) Glucocorticoids, feto-placental 11β-hydroxysteroid dehydrogenase type 2, and the early life origins of adult disease. *Steroids* **62**, 89–94

Seckl, J.R. and Chapman, K.E. (1997) The 11β-hydroxysteroid dehydrogenase system, a determinant of glucocorticoid and mineralcorticoid action. *Eur J Biochem* **249**, 361–4

Seppala, M., Ranta, T., Tontti, K., Stenman, U.H. and Chard, T. (1980) Use of a rapid hCG-β subunit radioimmunoassay in acute gynaecological emergencies. *Lancet* **i**, 165–6

Simon, P., Decoster, C., Brocas, H., Schwers, J. and Vassart, G. (1986) Absence of human chorionic somatomammotropin during pregnancy associated with two types of gene deletion. *Hum Genet* **74**, 235–8

Simpson, J.L., Shulman, L., Dungan, J., Phillips, O. and Elias, S. (1994) 'Mid-trimester biochemistry in prediction of third trimester complications' in: J.G. Grudzinskas, T. Chard, M. Chapman and H. Cuckle (Eds) *Screening for Down's Syndrome*, pp. 325–38. Cambridge: Cambridge University Press

Stirrat, G.M. (1998) 'The bundle of life – the placenta in ancient history and modern science' in: P.M.S. O'Brien (Ed.) *Yearbook of Obstetrics and Gynaecology* **6**, pp. 1–14. London: RCOG Press

Sun, K., Yang, K. and Challis, J.R.G. (1998) Glucocorticoid actions and metabolism in pregnancy: implications for placental function and fetal cardiovascular activity. *Placenta* **19**, 353–60

Szulman, A.E. (1988) Trophoblastic disease: clinical pathology of hydatidiform moles. *Obstet Gynecol Clin North Am* **15**, 443–56

Thomson, A.J., Telfer, J.F., Young, A. *et al.* (1999) Leucocytes infiltrate the myometrium during human parturition: further evidence that labour is an inflammatory process. *Hum Reprod* **14**, 229–36

Turnbull, A.C., Flint, A.P.F., Jeremy, J.Y., Patten, P.T., Keirse, M.J.N.C. and Anderson, A.B.M. (1974) Significant fall in progesterone and rise in oestradiol levels in human peripheral plasma before onset of labour. *Lancet* **i**, 101–4

Unno, N., Baba, K., Kozuma, S. *et al.* (1997) An evaluation of the system to control blood flow in maintaining goat fetuses on arterio-venous extracorporeal membrane oxygenation: a novel approach to the development of an artificial placenta. *Artif Organs* **21**, 1239–46

Waddell, B.J. (1993) The placenta as hypothalamus and pituitary: possible impact on maternal and fetal adrenal function. *Reprod Fertil Dev* **5**, 479–97

Westergaard, J.G., Chemnitz, J. and Teisner, B. (1983) PAPP-A: a possible marker in the classification and diagnosis of Cornelia de Lange syndrome. *Prenat Diagn* **2**, 225–8

9

Antenatal screening for chromosomal and genetic abnormalities

Howard Cuckle

HISTORICAL PERSPECTIVE

Routine antenatal screening for serious congenital abnormalities was first introduced in the 1970s – maternal serum α-fetoprotein (AFP) screening at 16–18 weeks' gestation and ultrasound anomaly screening at 18–20 weeks. In the UK uptake was high and led to a marked fall in the birth prevalence of structural abnormalities, particularly neural tube defects (NTDs). Consequently, by the early 1980s chromosomal and genetic disorders had become the main preventable causes of severe abnormality at birth.

Chromosomal disorders

Aneuploidy and other chromosomal anomalies are common in pregnancy but screening is targeted at those fetuses that are sufficiently viable to survive to term in relatively large numbers but are associated with a severe phenotype. By far the most frequent is Down syndrome, with a birth prevalence in the absence of prenatal diagnosis and therapeutic abortion of about 1.6 per 1000 in the UK. Edwards syndrome is severe and has one-tenth the birth prevalence, whereas sex chromosome aneuploidies are common but relatively benign.

In the past, the only way to identify women at high enough risk of Down syndrome to warrant an offer of invasive prenatal diagnosis was on the basis of advanced reproductive age or a previous affected pregnancy. However, epidemiological risk factors alone are inadequate in screening for this disorder. Despite the eight-fold increase in risk between 30 and 40 years of age, most cases occur in young women because most pregnancies are in women aged under 30 years and less than 1% of cases occur in couples with a previous affected pregnancy.

The last 15 years have seen a substantial change in screening practice. The current norm is to identify high-risk pregnancies by routinely measuring multiple markers in maternal serum. Centres implementing this approach have experienced a substantial decline in birth prevalence.

Genetic disorders

Serious disorders caused by genetic mutations are much rarer than those with a chromosomal aetiology. Cystic fibrosis (CF) is the most common single gene disorder in white

74

European populations with a prevalence in the UK of 0.4 per 1000 births. CF is inherited as a simple Mendelian autosomal recessive condition with a carrier frequency of one in 24. Thus, one in 600 couples are both carriers and have a one in four chance of CF in every pregnancy. There are other recessive conditions at least as common as this but in the UK they are only in ethnic minority populations (for example, haemoglobinopathies and Tay-Sachs disease). Severe dominant, X-linked and non-Mendelian genetic conditions are much less common than CF.

In the past, antenatal screening for genetic disorders was only feasible in affected families with informative genetic markers. Even in these cases testing was of limited value since, for recessive conditions, simply knowing that one of the parents may be a carrier does not greatly increase the risk of an affected infant. Advances in molecular biology have opened up the possibility of routine DNA testing in all pregnancies in order to identify individual carriers and, for recessive conditions, carrier couples. In 1989, the gene responsible for CF was cloned. While there are over 700 different disease-causing mutations, in most white European populations a large proportion of carriers are accounted for by 10–20 mutations. The laboratory techniques for simultaneously detecting multiple mutations are straightforward and can be performed in a blood, mouthwash or buccal-smear sample.

SCREENING FOR CHROMOSOMAL DISORDERS TODAY

Multiple-marker screening for Down syndrome is established practice in the UK. Most centres use two or three maternal-serum markers in the second trimester but some use a fourth serum marker and, increasingly, centres are moving towards first-trimester screening with both maternal-serum and ultrasound markers. The same markers can be used to screen for other chromosomal disorders.

Second-trimester serum markers

Many analytes have been shown to be increased or decreased on average in the serum of women with affected pregnancies. However, only four are in widespread use – human chorionic gonadotrophin (hCG), the free-β subunit of hCG, AFP and unconjugated oestriol (uE$_3$). At present hCG or free β-hCG is the marker of first choice, with AFP as the second marker and uE$_3$ the third. Levels are usually expressed as multiples of the normal median (MoM) for the relevant gestation, in order to standardise for both gestational and laboratory differences. Table 1 shows the average level for each marker in Down-syndrome pregnancies, based on a meta-analysis of 47 published series.

Test interpretation

The average levels in Table 1 can be considered as a 'typical' marker profile for a Down-syndrome pregnancy, while 1 MoM for each marker is a typical profile for unaffected pregnancies. However, variability due to assay error, gestational error, within-person fluctuation and large inter-person differences mean that few results are typical. The statistically optimal way of interpreting an individual's profile is to estimate the risk of Down syndrome from the maternal age and marker levels and compare it with a fixed cut-off risk. If the risk is greater than the cut-off the result is regarded as 'screen-positive', otherwise it is 'screen-negative'.

Table 1 *Second-trimester maternal serum markers of Down syndrome*

Marker	Down syndrome	Average (MoM)	95% CI
hCG	850	2.02	1.91–2.13
Free β-hCG	477	2.30	2.13–2.49
AFP	1140	0.73	0.71–0.75
uE$_3$	613	0.73	0.70–0.76

Based on the meta-analyses in Cuckle (1995)

The most widely used method of deriving the risk is to fit a multivariate Gaussian model to the overlapping frequency distributions of marker levels in affected and unaffected pregnancies. From the model, a likelihood ratio is calculated and applied to a curve relating the risk of Down syndrome to maternal age. The likelihood ratio is a measure of how much closer the individual's profile is to a typical Down syndrome rather than unaffected profile. The parameters of the maternal age curve are obtained by regression analysis on the combined results of several published age-specific birth prevalence series (Cuckle *et al.* 1987). Similarly, the parameters of the marker distributions are best derived by meta-analysis of all the published results on Down-syndrome pregnancies and tailored to fit the unaffected pregnancies from the local screened population (Cuckle 1995).

Predicted and observed performance

The same statistical modelling technique can be used to predict the outcome of a screening programme (Royston and Thompson 1992). Table 2 shows the predicted detection rate for a 5% false-positive rate using different marker combinations, and the predicted detection and false-positive rates for different risk cut-off points.

So far the detailed results of nineteen large prospective second-trimester multimarker intervention studies have been published and the combined results confirm the model predictions. The precise screening protocol differed between studies – all used hCG or free β-hCG together with uE$_3$ (1), AFP (7) or both (11); most screened all women but five were restricted to those under 35 or 38 years of age and there were twelve different risk cut-off points. Table 3 summarises the combined performance and, for comparison, that which would be predicted from the protocols used. Prospective studies tend to exaggerate the detection rate since non-viable true-positives are terminated whereas the corresponding non-viable true-negatives are not discovered. Even taking account of this non-viability bias the observed performance was at least as good as the prediction. The prospective studies also demonstrate the acceptability of screening – overall there was an 80% uptake rate and, of those with screen-positive results, 79% accepted invasive prenatal diagnosis.

Inhibin as a fourth marker

Fourteen studies have been reported showing that second trimester maternal serum inhibin levels are raised on average in Down-syndrome pregnancies. The studies used

Table 2 *Predicted Down syndrome detection rate (DR) and false-positive rate (FPR) according to second-trimester maternal serum marker combination*

Combination	DR for 5% FPR	Cut-off risk (at term)					
		1 in 200		1 in 250		1 in 300	
		DR	FPR	DR	FPR	DR	FPR
hCG alone	48.4	47.1	4.6	51.6	6.1	55.7	7.7
hCG and uE$_3$	56.3	53.6	4.2	57.6	5.5	60.9	6.8
hCG and AFP	58.9	56.7	4.3	60.7	5.6	63.7	6.8
hCG, AFP and uE$_3$	62.4	59.1	4.0	62.7	5.1	65.6	6.2
Free β-hCG alone	53.6	51.6	4.5	55.4	5.7	58.8	7.1
Free β-hCG and uE$_3$	60.7	58.0	4.2	61.7	5.4	64.7	6.5
Free β-hCG and AFP	62.9	61.3	4.5	65.0	5.7	68.2	7.0
Free β-hCG, AFP and uE$_3$	66.6	63.5	4.1	67.0	5.2	69.8	6.3

Based on affected parameters in Cuckle (1995) and unaffected parameters from 18 000 women screened at 14–19 weeks' gestation in Leeds and assuming the maternal age distribution for England and Wales in 1990–95 (OPCS 1993, 1994, 1995, 1996, 1997)

Table 3 *Observed and predicted screening performance in 19 large second-trimester prospective intervention studies*

Performance indicator	Observed	Predicted
Detection rate	67%	65%
False-positive rate	4.5%	4.3%
Risk if screen-positive	1:47	1:46
Risk if screen-negative	1:1900	1:1900

323 000 women were screened including 473 with Down syndrome (Cuckle 1996; Benn 1998; Lam *et al.* 1998); the predicted results are based on the screening protocol in each study when applied to the maternal age distribution for England and Wales in 1990–95 (OPCS 1993, 1994, 1995, 1996, 1997); to allow for non-viability bias the expected number of detected cases was increased by one-third

either an 'immunoreactive' assay which detects several inhibin species or one specific for inhibin A, the dimer comprising the α and β$_A$ subunits. Those comparing the different assays in the same samples found inhibin A to be the better marker. The ten series measuring inhibin A included a total of 525 affected pregnancies with an average value of 1.86 MoM (95% CI 1.74–1.98) (Cuckle *et al.* 1996; Westrom *et al.* 1997; D'Antona *et al.* 1998; Haddow *et al.* 1998; Renier *et al.* 1998). The model-predicted increase in detection rate for a fixed 5%, when inhibin A is added to two or three marker combinations, is 7%.

Maternal urine instead of serum

Several markers of Down syndrome have been discovered in maternal urine. The β-core fragment is the major metabolic product of hCG in maternal urine and second-trimester levels are increased on average in Down-syndrome pregnancies to a greater extent than maternal serum hCG and free β-hCG. To date there have been eight published series including a total of 253 cases and the overall average value is 3.75 MoM (95% CI 3.21–4.37) (Cuckle *et al.* 1999; Hsu *et al.* 1999). However, this does not mean that urinary β-core hCG can replace the maternal serum hCG assays for Down-syndrome screening. Firstly, the standard deviation of the urine marker is wide, partly because only a random urine sample is available and, as a result, discriminatory power is no better than in serum. Secondly, there is significant heterogeneity between the published studies and so the overall average value may be misleading. This is possibly due to differences in assay method, study design and the integrity of urine samples during transport and storage.

Other urinary hCG species – free β-hCG and hyperglycosylated hCG – are elevated on average in affected pregnancies, although fewer cases have been tested than for β-core hCG. In contrast, maternal urine total oestrogen and total oestriol levels are reduced on average in Down-syndrome pregnancies.

Urine is a safer medium than blood and may be more acceptable to women since not only is venepuncture avoided but the test can be performed without seeing a doctor. However, more research is needed before it can be considered as an alternative to current practice.

First trimester serum markers

At present, most centres perform serum screening for Down syndrome at 15–19 weeks' gestation so that the same sample can be used in AFP screening for NTDs. Moving the test to earlier in pregnancy has the obvious advantages of earlier reassurance and, if a therapeutic abortion is necessary, this could be completed before fetal movements are felt and therefore less traumatically. The only disadvantage is that NTD detection would require either a separate AFP test after 15 weeks' gestation (it is invalid earlier) or reliance on the ultrasound anomaly scan at 18–20 weeks' gestation.

Three of the established second-trimester markers are of value in early pregnancy, namely free β-hCG, AFP and uE$_3$; in the first trimester hCG is a much poorer marker than free β-hCG. In addition, another placental product, pregnancy associated plasma protein A (PAPP-A), has consistently yielded reduced levels on average in first-trimester Down-syndrome pregnancies, although the reduction is greatest in the early first trimester. Table 4 shows the average level for each marker in Down-syndrome pregnancies based on a meta-analysis of 44 published series.

Table 4 *First-trimester maternal serum markers of Down syndrome*

Marker	Down syndrome	Average (MoM)	95% CI
Free β-hCG	579	1.98	1.83–2.10
AFP	542	0.79	0.75–0.84
uE$_3$	226	0.74	0.67–0.82
PAPP-A			
6–8 weeks	31	0.35	0.25–0.49
9–11 weeks	197	0.40	0.35–0.46
12–14 weeks	113	0.62	0.52–0.74

Based on the meta-analyses in Cuckle and van Lith (1999)

Ultrasound markers

Several second-trimester ultrasound markers of Down syndrome have been reported but they have low discriminatory power. In contrast, nuchal translucency (NT) is a highly predictive first trimester ultrasound marker. Early studies reported the NT in millimetres rather than in gestation-standardised terms, resulting in lack of comparability between centres. This has now been overcome with more recent studies expressing results in MoM. The most reliable information on the average NT in affected pregnancies is from the massive multicentre prospective intervention study organised by the Fetal Medicine Foundation (Snijders *et al.* 1998). Unlike other studies it is based on routine scanning among low-risk women in non-specialist units. Among the first 326 Down-syndrome pregnancies in the study the median NT was 2.27 MoM. Because of non-viability bias, which is even stronger in the first trimester than the second, the observed distribution of NT values is positively skewed. A 'potentially viable' subset, comprising all third-trimester survivors together with a random sample comprising half of those terminated in the first trimester and two-thirds terminated in the second, had a median of 2.02 MoM (Nicolaides *et al.* 1998).

Predicted and observed first trimester performance

Table 5 shows the predicted performance of serum screening at 9–11 weeks' gestation with and without NT determination at 11–13 weeks. A Gaussian model was used with serum parameters from the meta-analysis and NT parameters from the above potential viable subset. The estimated detection rate for a 5% recall rate using PAPP-A and free β-hCG is similar to two-to-three-marker second-trimester screening. The addition of further serum markers yielded an increase comparable with inhibin A in the second trimester. NT alone had a predicted detection rate of the same magnitude and the addition of serum markers increased this to a maximum of 88%.

Among almost 100 000 completed singleton pregnancies screened in the Fetal Medicine Foundation study, the recall rate was 8% and the observed detection rate was 82% (Snijders *et al.* 1998). To allow for non-viability bias a further estimate of the detection rate was made by comparing the observed number of Down-syndrome births in the screened population with the number expected from the maternal age distribution. This yielded a rate of 78%, which is similar to the rate of 77% predicted for an 8% recall rate using the above model.

Maternal serum screening has a poorer performance in twin than in singleton pregnancies because the normal co-twin masks the abnormal marker production associated

Table 5 *Predicted Down syndrome detection rate for a 5% false-positive rate according to second-trimester maternal marker combination*

Serum markers	Serum only	Serum and NT
None	–	72.7
Free β-hCG	41.8	77.7
PAPP-A	52.2	81.2
PAPP-A and free β-hCG	64.6	86.4
PAPP-A, free β-hCG, AFP and uE$_3$	70.1	88.3

Based on parameters in Cuckle and van Lith (1999); NT=nuchal translucency with the affected twin. Thus, even with four second-trimester markers the predicted detection rate for a 5% recall rate is only 47% (Cuckle 1998). Since the NT distribution does not differ materially in singleton and twin pregnancies, first-trimester screening is the method of choice.

Other chromosomal disorders

In Edwards syndrome the average maternal serum hCG or free β-hCG, AFP and uE$_3$ are about 0.30 MoM, 0.65 MoM and 0.45 MoM, respectively. Some centres have extended the second-trimester Down-syndrome screening test to routinely test for Edwards syndrome. On the basis of published parameters using a one in 50 risk cut-off point the predicted detection rate is 45% and the false-positive rate under 0.1%. On average, PAPP-A and NT levels are similar to those in Down syndrome so that first-trimester screening with four serum markers and NT yields a 54% predicted detection rate. Other disorders are not formally screened but triploidy and Turner syndrome have their own marker profiles and are sometimes detected through screening.

SCREENING FOR GENETIC DISORDERS TODAY

Cystic fibrosis

Current commercial multiple-mutation DNA tests can detect about 86% of CF carriers in Scotland, Wales and the north, or 80% elsewhere; this yields a detection rate of 74% and 64%, respectively. There are two types of screening strategy. With a sequential or stepwise method, DNA testing is offered to the mother and a sample is only requested from the father if she is found to be a carrier. In about 0.1% a carrier couple would be identified; a further 3% would be discordant, with only one partner identified as a carrier and a one in 460–660 CF risk. With a pairwise or couple approach, testing is offered to couples and samples are obtained from both parents at the outset. DNA testing is done sequentially and carrier females are not informed of their results until that of their partner becomes available, thus avoiding unnecessary anxiety. There are then two ways of reporting the results: either to disclose the carrier status of each partner or a non-disclosure approach whereby the result is reported as screen-positive for carrier couples, otherwise as screen-negative. Non-disclosure is aimed at avoiding anxiety in discordant couples but it leads to increased costs due to the necessary re-testing of couples who have changed partners in subsequent pregnancies.

To date 11 prospective intervention studies have been reported, five in the UK, four in the USA and one each in Germany and Denmark. These demonstrate that screening is both feasible and acceptable (Table 6) and that concerns about discordant couples are unfounded.

Haemoglobinopathies

Thalassaemia and sickle-cell disease are the most common genetic disorders world-wide but in the UK they are largely confined to high-risk ethnic populations. Among those with origins in Cyprus, the Indian sub-continent, South-east Asia, Africa or the Caribbean and the Middle East, β-thalassaemia is common. Prevalence ranges from 0.1 per 1000 births in Afro-Caribbeans to six per 1000 in Cypriots. The risk of

Table 6 *Antenatal cystic fibrosis (CF) screening results from 11 prospective studies*

Offer	Denominator	Acceptance rate
Screening	Woman or couple	74% (38 964 of 52 801)
Screening	Partner of carrier[a]	92% (651 of 704)
Prenatal diagnosis	Carrier couple	89% (51 of 57)
Termination	CF diagnosis	94% (17 of 18)

[a]Studies using a sequential testing protocol; based on the meta-analysis of Murray *et al.* (1999)

α-thalassaemia is mainly in Cypriots and South-east Asians with a prevalence of about 0.1 per 1000. The same ethnic groups, apart from South-east Asians, are at risk of sickle-cell disease, but the high prevalence is in West Africans (15 per 1000) and Afro-Caribbeans (three per 1000).

Carriers are detected by cytometry and haemoglobin separation. In some countries, general population screening has led to the identification of a large proportion of carrier couples prior to pregnancy and the birth prevalence has fallen markedly. In the UK, a relatively small proportion of carriers has been detected and antenatal screening represents an important opportunity. The recommended policy is to offer screening to all pregnant women in units where at least 15% are from the high-risk groups and otherwise to screen selectively when one of the partners is at high risk (Standing Medical Advisory Committee on Sickle Cell Disease, Thalassaemia and other Haemoglobin-opathies 1993). In carrier couples, prenatal diagnosis appears to be generally acceptable, although uptake is higher in some groups when the test is offered in the first trimester rather than the second.

Tay-Sachs disease

Tay-Sachs disease is caused by deficient activity of β-hexosaminidase (Hex A) and in 1985 the gene for the α-subunit of the enzyme was cloned. To date, more than 70 disease causing mutations have been identified in the gene. Among Ashkenazi Jews the prevalence is 0.25 per 1000 births, some 100 times higher than in the general population and just three mutations account for about 97% of carriers.

Before the discovery of the gene, carriers could only be identified by blood Hex A testing. However, this is technically difficult during pregnancy and the biochemical test does not identify carriers with certainty. In a study of 1364 samples tested by both bio-chemical and DNA methods, no mutations were found in all 43 with biochemically inconclusive results and 15 of the 67 with positive screening results (DeMarchi *et al.* 1996).

In some countries a high proportion of Ashkenazi carriers have been identified through testing outside pregnancy. In the UK there is some prenuptial testing among Orthodox Jews but there is no concerted population screening programme and antenatal screening is an option. DNA screening for carrier couples during pregnancy would have a 94% detection rate among Ashkenazi Jews.

Fragile X syndrome

Fragile X syndrome is a non-Mendelian condition and the second most common cause of learning disability after Down syndrome, with a birth prevalence of 0.25 per 1000 males and 0.12 per 1000 females. It results from a mutation in a gene on the X chromosome which is characterised by a repeat sequence of the trinucleotide cytosine–guanine–guanine interspersed with adenine–guanine–guanine. The sequence is polymorphic with respect to the number of repeats. In males an allele with more than 200 repeats, termed a full mutation, is always associated with the affected phenotype, whereas in females only half are affected. Those with fewer repeats are unaffected but among females an allele in the range 55–199, termed a premutation, confers a high risk of expansion to a full mutation in the offspring. There is no direct expansion from a normal allele to a full mutation, only through a premutation.

Antenatal screening could be carried out to detect women with either a full mutation or premutation. Those with a full mutation will have a one in three chance of an affected infant and for carriers of a premutation the risk is about one in 25. Models predict that the detection rate would approach 100% with a false-positive rate of 0.4% (Murray *et al.* 1997).

When antenatal screening is performed in affected families, the acceptability of invasive prenatal diagnosis is high among carriers. Moreover, in such families termination of pregnancy appears to be acceptable when a full mutation is detected, even for female fetuses, where there is at present no reliable way of predicting the phenotype. However, this uncertainty may be a major impediment to general population screening. One option is to restrict screening to those with *a priori* evidence of a male fetus, based on ultrasound or DNA amplification of Y-chromosome sequences in maternal blood. Large-scale population screening programmes are under way but the results have not yet been published.

FUTURE DEVELOPMENTS

Technical developments leading to cheaper, quicker and safer prenatal diagnosis may have an important influence on screening policy in the future. However, in the UK the greatest challenge is not technical, but rather to improve the quality of existing screening services.

Chromosomal analysis by DNA methods

The labour intensive nature of cytogenetics means that the cost of karyotyping is high and the need to culture amniocytes prior to analysis means a two-to-three-week turn-round time. Fluorescence *in situ* hybridisation has been shown to be a feasible alternative approach and now the polymerase chain reaction (PCR) of uncultured amniocytes has been successfully evaluated in a large series (Verma *et al.* 1998). Small tandem repeat markers on chromosome 21 were amplified and detected by fluorescent methods using a gene scanner. Informative results were obtained for all but nine clear and 28 visibly blood-stained samples out of a total of 2139 samples. All 30 Down-syndrome pregnancies with informative samples were correctly diagnosed and there were no false-positives. Results were available the same day as the amniocentesis and the cost was low.

Fetal DNA in maternal blood

Fetal nucleated red cells and trophoblasts are known to circulate in small numbers in maternal blood and also cell-free DNA of fetal origin. The existence of circulating fetal

DNA in most pregnancies can be demonstrated using PCR to amplify Y-chromosome specific sequences when the fetus is male. In principle, the DNA could be used to diagnose aneuploidy and several techniques are being developed to do this. The first stage of the process is to increase the relative concentration of fetal cells in the blood sample. Magnetic and fluorescent antibodies have been used to do this while other researchers use the physical properties of the different cell types. The next step is to find a few fetal cells, prove that they are fetal and determine in each the number of copies of chromosome 21, 18, 13 and possibly X and Y. The results so far are not sufficiently reliable to replace established diagnostic techniques and the cost is high. However, the approach could eventually be used in screening rather than diagnosis. One strategy would be to refer to invasive diagnosis women identified as being at high risk by biochemical screening and to apply the fetal-cell test to those with borderline risks. Those with positive or equivocal results could go on to have invasive prenatal diagnosis.

Improved information and equity

The most difficult aspect of antenatal screening is how to provide sufficient information to allow informed choice and how to help support women while they make their choice. In the UK, screening services are grossly under-resourced; with more funds high-quality information materials could be provided to ease and supplement face-to-face contact. Glossy leaflets, free videos, designated telephone helplines and, for some, Internet sites should be available to women offered screening and not just those tested in the private sector or within a research programme.

In the past, the decision whether or not to establish an antenatal screening programme was made at the level of the individual maternity unit. Local enthusiasm or proximity to a teaching hospital with a research interest in the field has determined who was the first to benefit from a new screening technique. Gradually the test then spreads to other centres and it can take ten years or more before there is anything like national coverage. This is clearly inequitable.

The establishment of a National Screening Committee in the Department of Health is likely to lead to better resourced, more evidence-based services with equality of access.

References

Benn, P.A. (1998) Preliminary evidence for associations between second-trimester human chorionic gonadotropin and unconjugated oestriol levels with pregnancy outcome in Down syndrome pregnancies. *Prenat Diagn* **18**, 319–24

Cuckle, H.S. (1995) Improved parameters for risk estimation in Down syndrome screening. *Prenat Diagn* **15**, 1057–65

Cuckle, H.S. (1996) Established markers in second trimester maternal serum. *Early Hum Dev* **47** Suppl, 27–9

Cuckle, H.S. (1998) Down syndrome screening in twins. *J Med Screen* **5**, 3–4

Cuckle, H.S. and van Lith, J.M.M. (1999) Appropriate biochemical parameters in first trimester screening for Down syndrome. *Prenat Diagn* **19**, 505–12

Cuckle, H.S., Wald, N.J. and Thompson, S.G. (1987) Estimating a woman's risk of having a pregnancy associated with Down syndrome using her age and serum alpha-fetoprotein level. *Br J Obstet Gynaecol* **94**, 387–402

Cuckle, H.S., Holding, S., Jones, R., Groome, N.P. and Wallace, E.M. (1996) Combining inhibin A with existing second-trimester markers in maternal serum screening for Down syndrome. *Prenat Diagn* **16**, 1095–100

Cuckle, H.S., Canick, J.A. and Kellner, L.H. (1999) Collaborative study of maternal urine β-core human chorionic gonadotropin screening for Down syndrome. *Prenat Diagn* **19**, 911–17

D'Antona, D.F., Wallace, E.M., Shearing, C., Ashby, J.P. and Groome, N.P. (1998) Inhibin A and pro-αC inhibin in Down syndrome and normal pregnancies. *Prenat Diagn* **18**, 1122–6

DeMarchi, J.M., Caskey, C.T. and Richards, C.S. (1996) Population-specific screening by mutation analysis for diseases frequent in Ashkenazi Jews. *Hum Mutat* **8**, 116–25

Haddow, J.E., Palomaki, G.E., Knight, G.J., Foster, D.L. and Neveux, L.M. (1998) Second trimester screening for Down syndrome using maternal serum dimeric inhibin A. *J Med Screen* **5**, 115–19

Hsu, J-J., Spencer, K., Aitken, D.A. *et al.* (1999) Urinary free beta hCH, beta core fragment and total oestriol as markers of Down syndrome in the second trimester of pregnancy. *Prenat Diagn* **19**, 146–58

Lam, Y.H., Ghosh, A., Tang, M.H.Y. *et al.* (1998) Second-trimester maternal serum alpha-fetoprotein and human chorionic gonadotropin screening for Down syndrome in Hong Kong. *Prenat Diagn* **18**, 585–9

Murray, J., Cuckle, H., Taylor, G. and Hewison, J. (1997) Screening for fragile X syndrome; information needs for health planners. *J Med Screen* **4**, 60–94

Murray, J., Cuckle, H., Taylor, G., Littlewood, J. and Hewison, J. (1999) Screening for cystic fibrosis. *Health Technol Assess* **3**, 1–97

Nicolaides, K.H., Snijders, R.J.M. and Cuckle, H.S. (1998) Correct estimation of parameters for ultrasound nuchal translucency screening. *Prenat Diagn* **18**, 519–21

OPCS (Office of Population Censuses and Surveys) (1993) *Birth Statistics: Review of the Registrar General on Births and Patterns of Family Building in England and Wales, 1991.* London: HMSO (Series FM1, no. 20)

OPCS (Office of Population Censuses and Surveys) (1994) *Birth Statistics: Review of the Registrar General on Births and Patterns of Family Building in England and Wales, 1992.* London: HMSO (Series FM1, no. 21)

OPCS (Office of Population Censuses and Surveys) (1995) *Birth Statistics: Review of the Registrar General on Births and Patterns of Family Building in England and Wales, 1993.* London: HMSO (Series FM1, no. 22)

OPCS (Office of Population Censuses and Surveys) (1996) *Birth Statistics: Review of the Registrar General on Births and Patterns of Family Building in England and Wales, 1994.* London: HMSO (Series FM1, no. 23)

OPCS (Office of Population Censuses and Surveys) (1997) *Birth Statistics: Review of the Registrar General on Births and Patterns of Family Building in England and Wales, 1995.* London: HMSO (Series FM1, no. 24)

Renier, M.A., Vereecken, A., van Herck, E., Straetmans, D., Ramaeckers, P. and Buytaert, P. (1998) Second trimester maternal dimeric inhibin-A in the multiple-marker screening test for Down syndrome. *Hum Reprod* **13**, 744–8

Royston, P. and Thompson, S.G. (1992) Model-based screening by risk with application to Down syndrome. *Stats Med* **11**, 257–68

Snijders, R.J.M., Noble, P., Sebire, N., Souka, A. and Nicolaides, K.H. (1998) UK multi-centre project on assessment of risk of trisomy 21 by maternal age and fetal nuchal-translucency thickness at 10–14 weeks of gestation. *Lancet* **352**, 343–6

Standing Medical Advisory Committee on Sickle Cell Disease, Thalassaemia and other Haemoglobinopathies (1993) *Report of a Working Party.* London: HMSO

Verma, L., Macdonald, F., Leedham, P., McConachie, M., Dhanjal, S. and Hulten, M. (1998) Rapid and simple prenatal DNA diagnosis of Down syndrome. *Lancet* **352**, 9–12

Wenstrom, K.D., Owen, J., Chu, D.C. and Boots, L. (1997) α-fetoprotein, free β-human chorionic gonadotropin, and dimeric inhibin A produce the best results in a three analyte, multiple marker screening test for fetal Down syndrome. *Am J Obstet Gynecol* **177**, 987–91

10

Maternal mortality: national and international perspectives

James Drife

SUMMARY

Of all indicators of public health, the maternal mortality rate (MMR) provides the clearest illustration of the gap between rich and poor countries. The MMR is the number of deaths of women during pregnancy and the puerperium per 100 000 live and stillbirths. At present it varies from 4.6 in Hong Kong to 1238 in rural Zambia.

In the UK in 1994–96, the MMR was 12.2. It had fallen from around 400 in 1935 to 9.9 in 1985. This fall (which was not interrupted by the Second World War) was due to improved health care, with factors as diverse as the introduction of antibiotics in the 1930s and the Abortion Act in 1967. Better practice in hospitals has played a large part – for example, deaths due to anaesthesia fell from 50 in 1967–69 to one in 1994–96.

Britain's Confidential Enquiry into Maternal Deaths (CEMD) began in 1952 and is the world's longest running self-audit by health professionals. In 1952–54 the leading cause of maternal death was hypertensive disease, which caused 246 deaths. By 1994–96 this number had fallen to 20. The leading cause now is thromboembolism, which caused 48 deaths in 1994–96. Since 1985, indirect deaths have steadily increased and are now equal in number to direct deaths, the most common causes being cardiac disease (39 deaths) and epilepsy (19 deaths). Greater attention is being paid to previously ignored causes such as violence and psychiatric illness.

Because of the CEMD, identification of cases in the UK is particularly good. This makes comparison with other developed countries difficult because in many countries, including the USA, maternal deaths are underestimated. Nevertheless, shared trends can be seen. In both the UK and the USA, the MMR has not fallen since the mid-1980s in spite of the identification of substandard care and lip service paid to the idea of improvement. In developed countries, the MMR among black women is higher than among other ethnic groups.

Globally, the annual number of maternal deaths is about 585 000, of which 99% occur in developing countries. In many developing countries, complications of pregnancy and childbirth are the leading causes of death among women of reproductive age. The most important is haemorrhage, which causes 25% of maternal deaths world-wide. The others are infection (15%), unsafe abortion (13%), eclampsia (12%) and obstructed labour (8%).

In 1987 the Safe Motherhood Initiative was launched by international organisations including the World Health Organization (WHO). Its goal of halving the global MMR by the year 2000 has not been achieved but lessons have been learned. Most maternal deaths and many infant deaths could be prevented by routine care for all pregnancies (including a skilled attendant at birth), by emergency treatment of complications and by basic neonatal care and postpartum family planning. This would cost about US$3 per person per year in low-income countries. What is lacking is not knowledge or money but the political will to save women's lives.

INTRODUCTION

The reduction in maternal mortality in developed countries during this century has been one of medicine's major achievements. Concern is growing, however, that MMRs in the developed countries have ceased to fall despite the continuing identification of substandard care. MMRs in the developing world, by contrast, remain high. Increasing attention is now being paid to this problem. This has led to a recent increase in research on maternal mortality in both rich and poor countries. This chapter reviews evidence published during the 1990s.

UK PERSPECTIVE

The MMR in the UK in 1994–96 was 12.2 (Department of Health 1998). This is higher than in some other developed countries, probably because of better reporting, but is very different from the rate 70 years ago.

History

The MMR in Britain remained virtually unchanged from 1847 (when accurate records began) until 1935. It was around 400, or one in 250 births. Other indicators, such as infant mortality, began to fall well before 1935 and the MMR may have been kept artificially high through neglect of asepsis and inexpert GP obstetrics (Loudon 1992; Pini 1996).

Between 1935 and 1985 a dramatic fall occurred. The introduction of sulphonamides in 1937 rapidly reduced the numbers of deaths from puerperal sepsis. This was followed by safe blood transfusion, ergometrine for postpartum haemorrhage, smaller family size and the Abortion Act of 1967. It was specific factors such as these, not general improvements in public health, that reduced the MMR. Better training of professionals contributed: the Royal College of Obstetricians and Gynaecologists (RCOG) was founded in 1929 and the Midwives Act was passed in 1936.

It is impossible to say which improvements were most important, as none was introduced as part of a controlled clinical trial. Writing about maternity care initiatives in developing countries, Sloan (1998) suggested that innovations can be evaluated only if control groups are available and that 'the progress of safe motherhood can only be hindered by avoiding the difficult but necessary controlled evaluations of safe motherhood interventions'. This was not the experience in Britain, where safe motherhood was achieved with rapidity in historical terms.

Since 1985 in the UK, however, there has been no improvement. The overall MMR is around ten and the figure for direct deaths is five to six. This does not mean that maternal deaths have reached an irreducible minimum. Substandard care is being identified and improvements could still be made. During the 1980s, however, the priority in maternity care shifted from 'safety at all costs' to a balance between safety and the wish to make childbirth a pleasant and fulfilling experience. Nevertheless, public expectations regarding safety are higher than ever. It is the professionals who have lost their enthusiasm for further reducing the MMR.

The Confidential Enquiry

In 1928 the British Government set up a committee on maternal mortality and morbidity, which introduced the concept of a 'primary avoidable factor' in its reports. The CEMD was launched in 1952 (Godber 1994) and has remained essentially unchanged since. Detailed enquiries are conducted in private by clinicians – doctors and, nowadays, midwives – and the results are made public in a national report which draws attention to areas of 'substandard care'. Uptake of its recommendations is now being audited (Hibbard and Milner 1995). The foresight of its founders is shown by the extension of their method in the 1990s to other areas (for example, Confidential Enquiry into Stillbirths and Deaths in Infancy 1998).

Causes of maternal mortality

In the triennium 1994–96 there were 376 maternal deaths, of which 134 were direct and 134 indirect. The remainder were fortuitous or late deaths. The changes over a 40-year period are shown in Table 1. Maternal deaths from abortion and from anaesthesia have been almost eliminated. This did not happen overnight – a fact which should be noted by those who expect changes to produce instant results. Deaths from criminal abortion continued for 15 years after the 1967 Abortion Act. Anaesthesia was made safe through painstaking attention to detail by anaesthetists (May 1994) and by a steady move towards a consultant-based service. As obstetricians respond to calls to do the same (Confidential Enquiry into Stillbirths and Deaths in Infancy 1997; Royal College of Obstetricians and Gynaecologists 1999) we should note the success of our trainee-based service in reducing deaths from haemorrhage, which is still the leading cause of maternal death world-wide.

We must also recognise areas that need improvement. Deaths from thromboembolism increased by over 50% between 1991–93 and 1994–96. This was partly due to better case ascertainment, but there were also increases in thromboembolic deaths after vaginal delivery, abortion and ectopic pregnancy. Improvement can be achieved by recognising risk factors, better prophylaxis (Greer 1997) and raising awareness among GPs and other specialists.

Indirect deaths have steadily increased over the last 12 years and are now equal in number to direct deaths. This is a higher proportion than in other countries, again

Table 1 *Numbers of direct deaths reported to the CEMD*

Cause	England and Wales 1952–55	UK 1994–96
Hypertensive disease	246	20
Haemorrhage	188	12
Abortion	153	1
Thrombosis and thromboembolism	148	48
Anaesthesia	49	1
Sepsis	42	14

suggesting that case reporting is good in the UK. The leading cause is cardiac disease (39 cases). Nineteen deaths were due to epilepsy, suggesting that women with this condition are not receiving optimal advice in pregnancy. Other emerging topics, such as psychiatric disorders, are discussed below.

OTHER DEVELOPED COUNTRIES

The MMR in most developed countries is around five to ten (Hibbard and Milner 1994). Small differences between countries are probably due to variations in reporting (Gissler *et al.* 1997; Salanave *et al.* 1999). For example, in the UK in 1994–96, the MMR according to the Registrar General's figures was 7.2, but according to the CEMD's reports was 9.9. When a new computer program was used to link the two, the figure became 12.2 – an apparent 'rise' from the previous triennium (Department of Health 1998).

Even before this program, the CEMD was recognised internationally as obtaining 'as close to complete ascertainment of maternal deaths as is possible' (Atrash *et al.* 1995). There is, however, strong evidence that maternal mortality is still seriously under-estimated in developed countries including the USA (Atrash *et al.* 1995; Salanave *et al.* 1999). In Taiwan, under-reporting of maternal mortality is estimated at 58% and misclassification at 53% (Kao *et al.* 1997). Under-reporting has been documented in developing countries (Mungra *et al.* 1998).

Under-reporting might explain differences in the causes of death in neighbouring countries. Thromboembolism, the leading cause in England and Wales in 1976–79, accounted for only a small proportion of deaths in the Nordic countries in the 1970s (Bergsjo 1997), and for only 15% of direct deaths in the Netherlands from 1983 to 1992, while pre-eclampsia accounted for 35% (Schuitemaker *et al.* 1998; Onrust *et al.* 1999). By contrast in Hong Kong, where the MMR is now only four, the most common cause between 1986 and 1990 was pulmonary embolism, which accounted for over 50% of maternal deaths (Duthie *et al.* 1994).

Risk factors

Some recently identified risk factors are common to many developed countries.

Ethnic origin

The MMR is higher in some ethnic groups than in others. For example in Australia, which has an MMR of nine, of approximately 25 maternal deaths a year about 30% are of women of Aboriginal or Torres Strait Islander descent, a group that comprises only 3% of the population. The MMR in this group is 40 compared with two to three among non-Aboriginal women (O'Loughlin 1997).

In the Netherlands, where 3.8% of the population is non-Dutch, a Confidential Enquiry examined 154 of the 192 direct and indirect deaths from 1983 to 1992. Of these, 23.4% occurred in non-Dutch women and 21% of the women were non-white (Schuitemaker *et al.* 1998).

In the USA there is a four-fold excess risk in black women (Centers for Disease Control and Prevention 1995; Berg *et al.* 1996). In 1996, the MMR was 20.3 in black women and 5.1 in white women (Centers for Disease Control and Prevention 1998a,b). The greatest differential by race was for direct obstetric causes, for which the MMR was 18 in black women and 4.4 in white women. In Tennessee, non-white women were 6.9

times more likely to experience a postdelivery pregnancy-related death than white women (Jocums *et al.* 1998).

In the UK, the most recent report of the CEMD showed a similar trend, with an increased risk among black women compared to other ethnic groups. The relative risk was estimated at around three. The increased numbers of deaths among black women were not due to a single specific cause. It is not yet possible to say what the reason for this difference is, but further research is urgently needed.

Immigrant women in the UK have an increased risk of maternal death. An analysis of death registrations from 1970 to 1985 showed that women born in southern Asia and 'Europe and the USSR' had a slightly increased relative risk of around 1.6. Among women born in West Africa, however, the relative risk was 10.3 and among those born in the Caribbean it was 4.6 (Ibison *et al.* 1996). It is of great concern that this differential seems to persist into the next generation.

Age and parity

High parity has long been recognised as a risk factor but maternal age may be more important. In the Nordic countries in the 1970s, the MMR for women aged under 20 was 4.1 and for those over 40 it was 74.2 (Bergsjo 1997). In the UK the corresponding figures for 1985–96 were 7.6 and 30.3 (Department of Health 1998). The difference is not due to a single cause. Possibly younger women can survive a 'near miss' which in an older woman would result in death.

The 'grande multipara' may be at less risk as far as mortality is concerned than the older mother. In the UK, the MMR for women of parity four or more was 25.6 in 1991–93 and 10.8 in 1994–96 (Department of Health 1998). 'Grande multiparity' is now uncommon in the UK but more women are delaying childbearing until their late thirties or even their forties (Gibert *et al.* 1999).

Multiple pregnancy

Estimates from the Concerted European Investigation have concluded that the MMR for singleton births in Europe was 5.2 and for multiple pregnancies was 14.9 (Senat *et al.* 1998). Similar conclusions have been reached elsewhere (Blickstein 1997).

Causes of maternal death

Two specific causes are briefly covered.

Violence

In Britain and the Americas, violent death is becoming prominent as other causes become less common (Rizzi *et al.* 1998). In Utah between 1982 and 1994, trauma caused the same number of maternal deaths (ten) as pulmonary embolism. Eight were due to road traffic accidents and two to homicide (Jacob *et al.* 1998). Of 61 violent postdelivery deaths in Tennessee, 35 were accidental, 19 were due to homicide and seven to suicide (Jocums *et al.* 1998). In North Carolina, injury is the most common cause of maternal death and homicide is the most common cause of fatal injury (Harper and Parsons 1997).

In the UK in 1994–96, 13 maternal deaths were due to road traffic accidents and three to murder (all by the woman's partner). The CEMD report now includes a chapter on psychiatric disorder. The 1994–96 report discusses 28 cases, including five suicides during pregnancy, four in the puerperium and 14 classified as late indirect deaths and five deaths from substance abuse. The histories make disturbing reading, and suggest that care is not reaching vulnerable women.

Abortion

Safe abortion is important in both developed and developing countries. When St Petersburg entered the Europe's Healthy Cities Project in 1991, the city's MMR was approximately 70, and 40.6% of maternal deaths were due to abortion. Top priority was given to preventing death from illegal abortion. Contraceptive services were improved, though surveys showed that these did not reach poor women. In 1995 the MMR had fallen to 31 but abortion still caused over half the maternal deaths (Stephenson *et al.* 1997). Abortion is discussed again below.

DEVELOPING COUNTRIES

Of all health statistics monitored by the WHO, maternal mortality is the one with the largest discrepancy between developed and developing countries (Kirwin 1998). The WHO has revised its estimates upwards (Court 1996) – about 1600 maternal deaths occur each day world-wide and the total is around 585 000 a year, of which 99% are in developing countries (WHO and UNICEF 1996).

The Safe Motherhood Initiative

In 1985 the WHO held the first international meeting devoted to maternal mortality and in 1987 the Safe Motherhood Initiative was launched (Rosenfield 1997). It is co-sponsored by several organisations including the WHO, UNICEF, the World Bank, the International Planned Parenthood Federation and the Population Council. Further information is available on its website at http://www.safemotherhood.org/.

The Initiative had the ambitious target of halving the world's maternal deaths by the year 2000. This has not happened, but a deeper understanding of the problems has developed (Kasonde and Kamal 1998; Konteh 1998) and some progress has been made. Across the world there has been an increase in the proportion of births with a skilled attendant, although in Africa the figure is only 42%. Globally, the leading cause of maternal death is haemorrhage, which is estimated to account for 25% of all deaths from direct and indirect causes. The others are infection (15%), unsafe abortion (13%), eclampsia (12%), obstructed labour (8%) and other direct causes (8%). Indirect causes account for 20%.

Prevention of Maternal Mortality Network

Also in 1987, Columbia University and the Carnegie Corporation, New York, launched the Prevention of Maternal Mortality Network. Multidisciplinary teams were formed in Nigeria, Ghana and Sierra Leone (Kamara 1997). A major focus was on improving the availability, quality and use of emergency obstetric care. The programme ended in 1997 and one of the lessons was that emergency obstetric care need not be costly because in many areas facilities exist and staff are already in place (Maine 1997).

Attempts have been made to combine emergency obstetric care and antenatal care in community-based maternity care programmes. When one such programme in Bangladesh was monitored a decrease in obstetric mortality was observed, but a similar decrease occurred in a control area, making conclusions difficult to draw (Ronsmans *et al.* 1997).

Causes of maternal mortality

The relative importance of different causes varies from country to country. In some areas adolescent marriage is a major factor. In many countries, unsafe abortion is of great importance (Kulczycki *et al.* 1996; Le Coeur *et al.* 1998). World-wide, 20 million unsafe abortions take place each year. Of all women in the world, 40% now have a right to choose but 25% still have no access to legal abortion (Singh and Ratnam 1998).

Transport factors

In some areas the accessibility of care is important. In a remote area of Zambia the MMR has been estimated at 1238 – that is, over 1% of pregnancies – ten times higher than in an urban area of the same country. The major causes of direct maternal death in the rural area were obstructed labour and sepsis (Vork *et al.* 1997).

In Pakistan the MMR varies from 281 in Karachi to 673 in Balochistan, which includes areas with a poor transport system. Over 50% of the deaths in this survey were caused by haemorrhage, the other leading causes being sepsis (16%) and eclampsia (14%). Training birth attendants to use oxytocics should reduce avoidable deaths (Fikree *et al.* 1997).

Social factors

Kerala, a state in south-west India, has a strong participatory democracy movement. Despite a *per capita* income lower than the Indian average, it has high rates of female literacy, contraceptive use is high and the MMR is 200, compared to 580 for the whole of India (O'Loughlin 1997). Nevertheless, suggestions that social change is needed to reduce maternal mortality can demotivate healthcare workers. Good emergency obstetric care is also necessary and need not await increased female literacy.

National resources

Developing countries lack the resources of industrialised countries (Kale 1996) but saving mothers' lives depends more on political will than on money. Visitors to medical congresses in both developed (Fiander and van den Broek 1995) and developing (Drife 1996) countries are often troubled by the emphasis on technology and the menopause, compared to maternal mortality. According to the Safe Motherhood Initiative most maternal deaths and many infant deaths could be prevented by simple measures – routine care for all pregnancies, including a skilled attendant at birth (Kwast 1996), emergency treatment of complications and basic neonatal care and postpartum family planning – and this would cost about US$3 per person per year in low-income countries.

THE FUTURE

The needs of developed and developing countries appear widely different but they have some themes in common. In both, the MMR is a sensitive measure of a nation's attitude to women's health and in both, a major bar to improvement is complacency.

The UK

In the UK the pressing need is to reduce deaths from thromboembolism. Women at risk should be identified before pregnancy. Better targeted prophylaxis is needed and warning symptoms must be taken seriously.

'Near miss' enquiries

As maternal deaths decline, attention is turning to 'near misses' – incidents which might have resulted in death but for prompt and effective treatment (Yoong *et al.* 1996). Near misses have been examined on a local basis, using criteria such as admission to an intensive care unit (Bewley and Creighton 1997; Baskett and Sternadel 1998). Mantel *et al.* (1998) described a system for defining severe acute maternal morbidity in South Africa. This identified nearly five times as many cases as maternal death and allowed for an effective audit system of maternal care. Haemorrhage is much more common among 'near misses' than in mortality enquiries. 'Near miss' enquiries will probably become incorporated into clinical governance in the UK. Hospital-based 'near miss' enquiries have also been proposed for developing countries (Filippi *et al.* 1998).

Other developed countries

Under-reporting of maternal deaths should be addressed and the CEMD model can be recommended. Research is needed to determine the reasons for the high MMR among black women compared to other groups.

Developing countries

The challenge in the developing world is daunting (Pittrof 1996). The Safe Motherhood Initiative has produced useful lessons. The social status of women is an important factor, but maternal mortality has a stronger relationship with health-service input than with social factors (Bouvier-Colle *et al.* 1995). The message that lives can be saved at low cost needs to be repeated to politicians and the public.

Another lesson from the Safe Motherhood Initiative is that effort needs to be focused. A district focus has been suggested (Tarimo 1996). Work needs to be targeted on maternal mortality, not diffused on other aspects of women's health. The most effective way of preventing death is to provide effective, accessible emergency obstetric care, although collaborative initiatives to reduce maternal mortality and HIV may be worthwhile (Graham and Newell 1999).

People in developed countries want to help developing countries but this can create resentment (Kale 1996). Short-term initiatives are of limited value and each country has to help itself. The RCOG, with more than 50% of its membership overseas, represents a world-wide network of key professionals. With improved communication, particularly through the internet, the RCOG is well placed to use expertise gained in the UK for the benefit of women throughout the world (Hussain 1995).

References

Atrash, H.K., Alexander, S. and Berg, C.J. (1995) Maternal mortality in developed countries: not just a concern of the past. *Obstet Gynecol* **86**, 700–5

Baskett, T.F. and Sternadel, J. (1998) Maternal intensive care and near-miss mortality in obstetrics. *Br J Obstet Gynaecol* **105**, 981–4

Berg, C.J., Atrash, H.K., Koonin, L.M. and Tucker, M. (1996) Pregnancy-related mortality in the United States, 1987–1990. *Obstet Gynecol* **88**, 161–7

Bergsjo, P. (1997) Recent evolution within obstetrics. *Acta Obstet Gynecol Scand* **76**, 613–18

Bewley, S. and Creighton, S. (1997) 'Near-miss' obstetric enquiry. *Journal of Obstetrics and Gynaecology* **17**, 26–9

Blickstein, I. (1997) Maternal mortality in twin gestations. *J Reprod Med* **42**, 680–4

Bouvier-Colle, M.H., Varnoux, N., Breart, G. and Medical Experts Committee (1995) Maternal deaths and substandard care: the results of a confidential survey in France. *Eur J Obstet Gynecol Reprod Biol* **58**, 3–7

Centers for Disease Control and Prevention (1995) Differences in maternal mortality among black and white women – United States, 1990. *JAMA* **273**, 370–1

Centers for Disease Control and Prevention (1998a) Deaths: final data for 1996. *Natl Vital Stat Rep* **47**, 13

Centers for Disease Control and Prevention (1998b) Maternal mortality – United States, 1982–1996. *JAMA* **280**, 1042–3

Confidential Enquiry into Stillbirths and Deaths in Infancy (1997) *Fourth Annual Report: Concentrating on Intrapartum Deaths 1994–95*. London: Maternal and Child Health Research Consortium

Confidential Enquiry into Stillbirths and Deaths in Infancy (1998) *Fifth Annual Report*. London: Maternal and Child Health Research Consortium

Court, C. (1996) WHO claims maternal mortality has been underestimated. *BMJ* **312**, 398

Department of Health (1998) *Why Mothers Die. Report on Confidential Enquiries into Maternal Deaths in the UK 1994–96*. London: The Stationery Office

Drife, J.O. (1996) We know why they die. *BMJ* **312**, 1044

Duthie, S.J., Lee, C.P. and Ma, H.K. (1994) Maternal mortality in Hong Kong 1986–1990. *Br J Obstet Gynaecol* **101**, 906–7

Fiander, A. and van den Broek, N. (1995) 27th British Congress of Obstetrics and Gynaecology. *Br J Obstet Gynaecol* **102**, 1017

Fikree, F.F., Midhet, F. Sadruddin, S. and Berendes, H.W. (1997) Maternal mortality in different Pakistani sites: ratios, clinical causes and determinants. *Acta Obstet Gynecol Scand* **76**, 637–45

Filippi, V., Alihonou, E., Mukantaganda, S., Graham, W.J. and Ronsmans, C. (1998) Near misses; maternal morbidity and mortality. *Lancet* **351**, 145–6

Gilbert, W.M., Nesbitt, T.S. and Danielson, B. (1999) Childbearing beyond age 40: pregnancy outcome in 24 032 cases. *Obstet Gynecol* **93**, 9–14

Gissler, M., Kauppila, R., Merilainen, J., Toukomaa, H. and Hemminki, E. (1997) Pregnancy-associated deaths in Finland 1987–1994 – definition, problems and benefits of record linkage. *Acta Obstet Gynecol Scand* **76**, 651–7

Godber, G. (1994) The origin and inception of the confidential enquiry into maternal deaths. *Br J Obstet Gynaecol* **101**, 946–7

Graham, W.J. and Newell, M.L. (1999) Seizing the opportunity: collaborative initiatives to reduce HIV and maternal mortality. *Lancet* **353**, 836–9

Greer, I. (1997) Epidemiology, risk factors and prophylaxis of venous thrombo-embolism in obstetrics and gynaecology. *Baillières Clin Obstet Gynaecol* **11**, 403–30

Harper, M. and Parsons, A.L. (1997) Maternal deaths due to homicide and other injuries in North Carolina: 1992–1994. *Obstet Gynecol* **90**, 920–3

Hibbard, B.M and Milner, D. (1994) Maternal mortality in Europe. *Eur J Obstet Gynecol Reprod Biol* **56**, 37–41

Hibbard, B. and Milner, D. (1995) Auditing the audit – the way forward for the Confidential Enquiries into Maternal Deaths in the United Kingdom. *Contemporary Review of Obstetrics and Gynaecology* **7**, 97–100

Hussain, J. (1995) Maternal health in the developing world: how can the RCOG contribute? *Br J Obstet Gynaecol* **102**, 1017

Ibison, J.M., Swerdlow, A.J., Head, J.A. and Marmot, M. (1996) Maternal mortality in England and Wales 1970–85: an analysis by country of birth. *Br J Obstet Gynaecol* **103**, 973–80

Jacob, S., Bloebaum, L., Shah, G. and Varner, M.W. (1998) Maternal mortality in Utah. *Obstet Gynecol* **91**, 187–91

Jocums, S.B., Berg, C.J., Entman, S.S. and Mitchell, E.F. (1998) Postdelivery mortality in Tennessee, 1989–91. *Obstet Gynecol* **91**, 766–70

Kale, R. (1996) Maternal mortality in India. *BMJ* **313**, 304

Kao, S., Chen, L.M., Shi, L. and Weinrich, M.C. (1997) Underreporting and misclassification of maternal mortality in Taiwan. *Acta Obstet Gynecol Scand* **76**, 629–36

Kamara, A. (1997) Lessons learned from the PMM Network experience. *Int J Gynaecol Obstet* **59** Suppl 2, S253–8

Kasonde, J.M. and Kamal, I. (1998) Safe motherhood: the message from Colombo. *Int J Gynaecol Obstet* **63** Suppl 1, S103–5

Kirwin, S. (1998) WHO reaffirms commitment to women's health. *BMJ* **316**, 1113

Konteh, R. (1998) Saving mothers' lives: things can go wrong. *World Health Forum* **19**, 136–9

Kulczycki, A., Potts, M. and Rosenfield, A. (1996) Abortion and fertility regulation. *Lancet* **347**, 1663–8

Kwast, B.E. (1996) Reduction of maternal and perinatal mortality in rural and peri-urban settings: what works? *Eur J Obstet Gynecol Reprod Biol* **69**, 47–53

Le Coeur, S., Pictet, G., M'Pele, P. and Lallemant, M. (1998) Direct estimation of maternal mortality in Africa. *Lancet* **352**, 1525–6

Loudon, I. (1992) *Death in Childbirth: An International Study of Maternal Care and Maternal Mortality 1800–1950.* Oxford: Clarendon Press

Maine, D. (1997) Lessons for program design from the PMM projects. *Int J Gynaecol Obstet* **59** Suppl 2, S259–65

Mantel, G.D., Buchmann, E., Rees, H. and Pattinson, R.C. (1998) Severe acute maternal morbidity: a pilot study for a definition of a near-miss. *Br J Obstet Gynaecol* **105**, 985–90

May, A.E. (1994) The confidential enquiry into maternal deaths 1988–90. *Br J Anaesth* **73**, 129–31

Mungra, A., van Bokhoven, S.C., Florie, J., van Kanten, R.W., van Roosmalen, J. and Kanhai, H.H.H. (1998) Reproductive age mortality survey to study under-reporting of maternal mortality in Surinam. *Eur J Obstet Gynecol Reprod Biol* **77**, 37–9

O'Loughlin, J. (1997) Safe motherhood: impossible dream or achievable reality? *Med J Aust* **167**, 622–5

Onrust, S., Santema, J.G. and Aarnoudse, J.G. (1999) Pre-eclampsia and the HELLP syndrome still cause maternal mortality in the Netherlands and other developed countries; can we reduce it? *Eur J Obstet Gynecol Reprod Biol* **82**, 41–6

Pini, P. (1996) Doctors should have left well alone. *Lancet* **347**, 1174

Pittrof, R. (1996) The sorry state of reproductive health of women: a global overview. *Contemp Rev Obstet Gynaecol* **8**, 93–7

Rizzi, R.G., Cordoba, R.R. and Maguna, J.J. (1998) Maternal mortality due to violence. *Int J Gynaecol Obstet* **63** Suppl 1, S19–24

Ronsmans, C., Vanneste, A.M., Chakraborty, J. and van Ginneken, J. (1997) Decline in maternal mortaltiy in Matlab, Bangladesh: a cautionary tale. *Lancet* **350**, 1810–14

Rosenfield, A. (1997) The history of the Safe Motherhood Initiative. *Int J Gynaecol Obstet* **59** Suppl 2, S7–9

Royal College of Obstetricians and Gynaecologists (1999) *Towards Safer Childbirth: Minimum Standards for Organisation of Labour Wards. Report of a Working Party*. London: RCOG

Salanave, B., Bouvier-Colle, M.H., Varnoux, N., Alexander, S., Macfarlane, A. and the MOMS Group (1999) Classification differences and maternal mortality: a European study. *Int J Epidemiol* **28**, 64–9

Schuitemaker, N., van Roosmalen, J., Dekker, G., van Donger, P., van Geijn, H. and Gravenhorst, J.B. (1998) Confidential enquiry into maternal deaths in the Netherlands 1983–1992. *Eur J Obstet Gynecol Reprod Biol* **79**, 57–62

Senat, M.V., Ancel, P.Y., Bouvier-Colle, M.H. and Breart, G. (1998) How does multiple pregnancy affect maternal mortality and mobidity? *Clin Obstet Gynecol* **41**, 79–83

Singh, K. and Ratnam, S.S. (1998) The influence of abortion legislation on maternal mortality. *Int J Gynaecol Obstet* **63** Suppl 1, S123–9

Sloan, N.L. (1998) Maternal mortality. *Lancet* **351**, 992

Stephenson, P., Chalmers, B., Kirchenko, V.F., Repina, M.A. and Wagner, M. (1997) Reducing maternal mortality in St Petersburg. *World Health Forum* **18**, 189–93

Tarimo, E. (1996) Safe motherhood and district health systems. *Eur J Obstet Gynecol Reprod Biol* **69**, 5–10

Vork, F.C., Kyanamina, S. and Van Roosmalen, J. (1997) Maternal mortality in rural Zambia. *Acta Obstet Gynecol Scand* **76**, 646–50

WHO and UNICEF (1996) *Revised 1990 Estimates of Maternal Mortality. A New Approach by WHO and UNICEF*. Geneva: WHO

Yoong, A., Nunns, D. and Raychaudhuri, K. (1996) The use of near-miss maternal morbidity to improve the quality of obstetric care. *Contemp Rev Obstet Gynaecol* **8**, 143–6

11

Pre-eclampsia

Christopher W.G. Redman

INTRODUCTION

Eclampsia was recognised as an illness of pregnant or puerperal women by the ancient Greeks. The concept of pre-eclampsia, the prodromal state, that may culminate in the *grand mal* convulsions of eclampsia, evolved over the last 100 years. Hyperuricaemia as a prominent laboratory feature was identified before the Second World War. Clotting disturbances were noted a little later and the concept of disseminated intravascular coagulation began to evolve after 1950 (McKay *et al.* 1953). It was not until 1982 that the acronym HELLP (haemolysis, elevated liver enzymes and low platelet count) syndrome was coined to describe the concurrence of liver and clotting dysfunction with haemolysis (Weinstein 1982). But even now, at the start of the new millennium, the definition and causation of pre-eclampsia are uncertain. It cannot be predicted or prevented effectively. The only sure knowledge is that it resolves after delivery, which remains the mainstay of management.

The idea that pre-eclampsia is a placental disease arose when eclampsia was associated, at postmortem, with deported fragments of trophoblast lodged in the pulmonary capillaries (Schmorl 1893). The concept was consolidated when eclampsia in women with molar pregnancies was recognised (Holland 1909). There followed ideas of placental toxins and the term 'toxaemia of pregnancy', now obsolete. The discovery that placental ischaemia might be important (Page 1948) led to more intensive study of the pathology of the spiral arteries, with the discovery of the obstructive lesions called acute atherosis (Zeek and Assali 1950) and the maladaptation related to deficient placentation (Robertson *et al.* 1975). Placental infarction and other ischaemic lesions were found to be more common (Little 1960).

The original clinical perception was that pre-eclampsia was an appallingly dangerous condition for the mother. The fate of the fetus was a secondary consideration. It was known that perinatal mortality was high but not why. Only in the 1960s was the concept of intrauterine growth restriction developed (Gruenwald 1966) and since then the full perinatal toll of pre-eclampsia in terms of prematurity, impaired growth and intrauterine asphyxia has been defined.

Clinical management improved with the increasing sophistication of induced delivery and management of preterm infants. Before the introduction of oxytocin in the mid-1960s labour could only be induced, unreliably, by amniotomy. Under these conditions it was mandatory to prevent eclampsia and two mainstreams evolved – heavy sedation evolving out of the Stroganoff regimen and the use of parenteral magnesium sulphate, developed empirically in the USA. To treat or prevent pre-eclampsia, diuretics were tested in the 1960s and antihypertensive agents in the 1970s and 1980s. Antiplatelet therapy for the prevention of pre-eclampsia has been tested in the 1980s and 1990s. None has conferred easily discernible benefits.

CURRENT STATUS

Inheritance

It has long been recognised that pre-eclampsia has genetic components. The current issue is whether it is a single causative gene or multiple susceptibility genes that are relevant. The fact that identical twin sisters show low concordance for pre-eclampsia (Thornton and Onwude 1991) makes a single gene unlikely but not impossible. Multiple genes (including those predisposing to thrombophilia) have been associated with an increased risk of pre-eclampsia (Morgan and Ward 1999). Fetal (including paternal) genes may be important. Certain unrelated fetal genotypes confer an increased susceptibility to maternal pre-eclampsia including trisomy 13 (Boyd *et al.* 1987), long-chain 3-hydroxyacyl coenzyme A dehydrogenase deficiency (Wilcken *et al.* 1993) and possibly the male gender (James 1995). There is new evidence that certain men confer an added risk of pre-eclampsia which can be detected when women change partners (Lie *et al.* 1998).

Pathogenesis

Prior exposure to paternal antigens may protect against pre-eclampsia. For example, the risk of pre-eclampsia decreases the longer the duration of pre-conceptual cohabitation (Robillard *et al.* 1994) or with artificial insemination by partner rather than by a third-party donor (Smith *et al.* 1997). These observations might explain the well-known first pregnancy preponderance of pre-eclampsia. They suggest some form of partner-specific maternal immune adaptation.

It is likely that this affects placentation, which is deficient in pre-eclampsia. During the first half of pregnancy cytotrophoblast invades the placental bed, at which time the spiral arteries, the end arteries of the uteroplacental circulation, dilate and lose their musculo-elastic structure. Because the arteries are invaded by the cytotrophoblast, which adopts an endothelial phenotype forming a pseudoendothelial lining (Zhou *et al.* 1997), it is considered that they directly induce the morphological changes. In pre-eclampsia, trophoblast invasion is restricted and the spiral arteries remain unadapted to the needs of pregnancy. Cytotrophoblast does not express the classical transplantation antigens HLA-A, HLA-B and HLA-D but only HLA-C and a unique non-polymorphic antigen, HLA-G. Nevertheless, invasive cytotrophoblast may interact directly with abundant maternal decidual immune cells, which largely constitute a specialised form of large granular lymphocyte (King *et al.* 1998). Experimental evidence suggests that these lymphocytes may in addition play a more direct role in the arterial remodelling than has been previously been realised (Guimond *et al.* 1998).

How the underperfused placenta generates the maternal signs of pre-eclampsia is unclear. Until the end of the 1980s it was not possible to explain the polymorphic features of pre-eclampsia and its crises by a single pathogenic process. Then it was realised that the maternal endothelium was a target tissue for pre-eclampsia (Roberts *et al.* 1989) and that many, if not all, of the features of pre-eclampsia can be explained by generalised maternal endothelial activation. This could include endothelial-induced vasoconstriction causing hypertension, abnormal endothelial permeability causing oedema and a diffuse endothelium-dependent pro-coagulant drive to account for the clotting dysfunction of the disorder. Subsequent work has confirmed these suppositions.

Recently, the concept has been generalised by showing that the endothelial dysfunction is one part of a maternal systemic inflammatory response to pregnancy, which also involves circulating leucocytes (Redman *et al.* 1999). A systemic inflammatory response is already well established in normal pregnancy, albeit exaggerated in pre-eclampsia (Sacks *et al.* 1998). Thus, pre-eclampsia appears to be the extreme end of a spectrum of inflammatory responses universally induced by all pregnancies. If true, this would imply that pre-eclampsia is unlikely to have a single cause, be predicted by a single test, or prevented by a single measure (Redman *et al.* 1999). Current knowledge is consistent with these predictions.

It has also been proposed that poor placentation is not the same as pre-eclampsia (which is considered to be the maternal syndrome of hypertension, proteinuria and other features such as activation of the clotting system) (Redman *et al.* 1999).

It is not clear what placental factors drive this inflammatory response. At present there are two likely theories which are not mutually exclusive. The first is that placental hypoxia causes release into the maternal circulation of products of oxidative stress (Walsh and Wang 1993), which in turn provokes endothelial dysfunction. The second is that there are one or more circulating factors derived from the syncytiotrophoblast surface that specifically stimulate endothelial dysfunction (Smarason *et al.* 1993) and inflammatory responses. Circulating antioxidant activity is reduced in pre-eclampsia (Davidge *et al.* 1992) and most (e.g. Hubel *et al.* 1996), but not all, authors (Morris *et al.* 1998) find increased circulating products of oxidative stress relative to normal pregnancy. These concepts are summarised in Figure 1.

Risk

Risk factors may be specific to the mother or to the pregnancy. They are listed in Table 1. Some, such as primigravidity or a past history of pre-eclampsia, are well known. The concept of primigravidity may be better considered as one of primipaternity, which can account for the increased likelihood of pre-eclampsia with a new partner or sperm donor. The protective effect of a longer duration of cohabitation (Robillard and Hulsey 1996) could explain at least part of the special predisposition of teenagers to the condition. Some risk factors are so obvious that they are taken for granted as a primary feature of the disease; in this category is advancing gestational age. If it is considered that poor placentation is a separate condition that may or may not be associated with pre-eclampsia, then this pathology arising in the first trimester must be judged to be a powerful predisposing factor (Redman *et al.* 1999).

Obese women are particularly susceptible (many authors, e.g. Sibai *et al.* 1997). Obesity is associated with non-insulin-dependent diabetes, hypertension and polycystic ovarian syndrome. All have been separately identified as risk factors. The importance of renal disease increases with the degree of renal and hypertension. Recently, asthma has also been identified as a risk factor (Demissie *et al.* 1998) although there is evidence that this may be more associated with corticosteroid therapy than with the disease itself (Schatz *et al.* 1997).

Of the placental and fetal factors some give larger than average placentas, for example in association with multiple pregnancy, placental hydrops or hydatidiform mole. This has led to the old concept of hyperplacentosis (Jeffcoate and Scott 1959) as a predisposing factor.

It is a surprising but consistent observation that cigarette smokers suffer less pre-eclampsia but at the expense of increased risks of other problems such as abruption (Cnattingius *et al.* 1997).

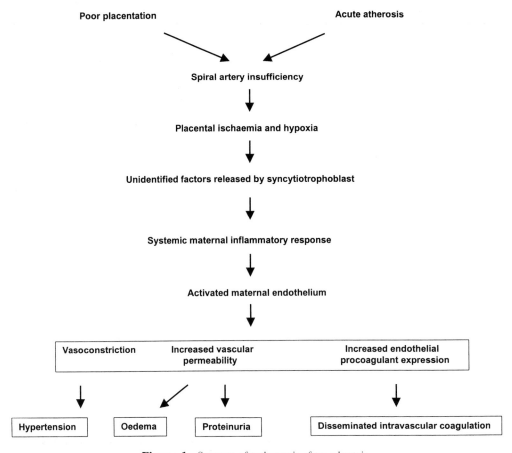

Figure 1 *Summary of pathogenesis of pre-eclampsia*

Prediction

It is inherently unlikely that the wide range of different time courses over which pre-eclampsia can develop, ranging from early in the second half of pregnancy to a fulminating postpartum illness, at term, without prodromal signs (Douglas and Redman 1994) will all be predicted by a single test. An extraordinary range of changes around mid-pregnancy, or earlier, have been associated with later pre-eclampsia. These include:

(1) Elevated mid-trimester blood pressure (Ales *et al.* 1989) or 24-hour blood-pressure profile as early as the first trimester (Hermida *et al.* 1998);

(2) Increased pressor sensitivity to infused angiotensin (Gant *et al.* 1973);

(3) Increased urinary microalbuminuria (Rodriguez *et al.* 1988);

(4) Calcium creatinine ratio (Suarez *et al.* 1996) or kallikrein creatinine ratio (Millar *et al.* 1996);

(5) Increased maternal blood β-hCG (Muller *et al.* 1996);

Table 1 *Risk factors for pre-eclampsia*

Factors	References
Maternal-specific	
Primigravidity	Many authors
Primipaternity	Robillard and Hulsey 1996
Short period of cohabitation	Robillard and Hulsey 1996
Increasing maternal age	Many authors
Previous pre-eclampsia	Many authors
Obesity	Many authors
Polycystic ovarian syndrome	Diamant *et al.* 1982
Family history of pre-eclampsia	Cincotta and Brennecke 1998
Medical disorders	
Diabetes	Many authors
Chronic hypertension	Many authors
Chronic renal disease	Many authors
Antiphospholipid antibody syndromes	Branch *et al.* 1989
Migraines	Marcoux *et al.* 1992
Asthma	Demissie *et al.* 1998
Stressful employment	Klonoff Cohen *et al.* 1996
Pregnancy-specific	
Advancing gestational age	Many authors
Poor placentation	Robertson *et al.* 1975
Multiple pregnancy	Many authors
Hydatidiform mole	Chun *et al.* 1964
Triploidy	Rijhsinghani *et al.* 1997
Trisomy 13	Boyd *et al.* 1987
Trisomy 16 mosaic	Brandenburg et al. 1996
Placental hydrops	Jeffcoate and Scott 1959
?Male fetus	James 1995

(6) Plasma fibronectin (Lockwood and Peters 1990) or fasting free fatty acids (Lorentzen *et al.* 1995);

(7) High-resistance flow patterns detected by Doppler ultrasound in the uterine arteries (Bower *et al.* 1993).

For almost all procedures, other studies refute their potential usefulness; for example, measurement of angiotensin sensitivity (Kyle *et al.* 1995) or uterine artery flow velocity waveforms (Mires *et al.* 1998) has not proved as effective as claimed. These findings are concordant with the inflammatory hypothesis that predicts that one effective predictive test for pre-eclampsia will not be found.

Prevention

If pre-eclampsia and normal pregnancy are merely different aspects of the range of maternal responses to pregnancy, a single effective preventive measure is also unlikely to be available for all types of pre-eclampsia. A wide range of measures has been tested and none is of proven general effectiveness, although some trials suggest that benefit may be restricted to subgroups. The subject and its disappointing story has been recently reviewed (Sibai 1998). This is demonstrated with the testing of low-dose aspirin, where the extraordinary promise of earlier small trials (e.g. Beaufils *et al.* 1985) could not be confirmed in a series of large trials (Sibai *et al.* 1993; CLASP 1994; ECCPA 1996; Rotchell *et al.* 1998). There could be a number of reasons of which the most obvious (that accepted by the majority) is that low-dose aspirin is ineffective (Darling 1998). It is also possible that low-dose aspirin benefits only a subgroup, with unusually active platelets and clotting, that comprises a small minority of all the cases at risk. If true, then the large trials would be expected to show little or no benefit because they are designed to answer the wrong question. Even so, a large trial targeted at 'high-risk' women also showed no benefit from active treatment (Caritis *et al.* 1998), although the at-risk groups were broadly selected and undoubtedly heterogeneous. In addition, treatment was started at an average time of 20.2 weeks, which may be too late if the action of aspirin influences placentation (which is essentially completed by this time) rather than the maternal syndrome itself. These points are raised merely to indicate that trials of treatment to prevent processes that are not clearly understood are likely to be hit-or-miss affairs. A positive result is informative, a negative result may not be. Other measures such as diuretics, salt restriction, antihypertensive drugs, calcium supplements, or dietary supplements seem not to prevent pre-eclampsia either. Anti-oxidants attract much interest at the time of writing but well-designed trials have not yet been reported.

Definition and diagnosis

Definitions are the reference point for diagnosis and there are various similar accepted versions, such as that of the American College of Obstetricians and Gynecologists (1996) or that adopted by the International Society for the Study of Hypertension in Pregnancy (Davey and MacGillivray 1988). These permit consistency in considering what is not understood but are arbitrary, and not based on any 'gold standard' because there is none. The definitions emphasise pregnancy-induced hypertension (PIH) and pregnancy-induced proteinuria. They are useful, particularly for research purposes or epidemiology, but can be misleading for clinical practice because the disease is extraordinarily variable and presentations that fall outside accepted criteria are not uncommon. For example, 10% of cases of eclampsia are totally unheralded and a further 30% incompletely heralded either by PIH or pregnancy-induced proteinuria alone (Douglas and Redman 1994). Now that clotting and hepatic complications are not only recognised but easily measurable there is no reason why they cannot be included to define severe variants. Such measures, not universally available, are not useful for epidemiological studies but could be applied to clinical practice. At some point in the next decade the problem of whether or not hypertension should be an essential part of the syndrome complex needs to be addressed. The decision to make it such is arbitrary and depends more on the fact that a high blood pressure is easy to demonstrate and not that it is the most fundamental part of the disorder. Diagnosis depends on demonstrating the concurrence of typical signs. Hence, although the definitions demand that these are new hypertension and proteinuria, the range of signs could be expanded to include other features such as gestational thrombocytopenia or hyperuricaemia.

Management

The key aspect of clinical management is the need to know that symptomless women are developing pre-eclamptic signs. This demands regular screening that constitutes the main burden of the repetitive visits in antenatal clinics – testing the urine and measuring the blood pressure. The tests are cheap and non-invasive with an answer available on the spot. They are also imprecise. For example, it has been claimed that dipstick testing of urine has too high a false positive and false negative rate to be a valid screening test (Kuo *et al.* 1992; Brown and Buddle 1995). A separate problem is how often it is necessary to screen. The longer the screening interval the more likely it is that cases will be missed until they have evolved to a dangerous degree. If plans to reduce antenatal care (Department of Health 1993) are implemented the screening intervals will be longer and the likelihood of missing women who are developing pre-eclampsia will be increased. Trials that purport to demonstrate that this does not happen are much too small to exclude this possibility (Khan *et al.* 1998). In short, these proposals for huge changes in obstetric care are not evidence-based.

The most important recent advance in the management of pre-eclampsia in the UK has been the acceptance of the US practice of administering magnesium sulphate parenterally to prevent eclamptic convulsion. A large and definitive trial confirmed with reasonable certainty that magnesium sulphate was superior to either diazepam or phenytoin in preventing recurrent convulsions in eclamptic women (Collaborative Eclampsia Trial 1995). The mode of action of magnesium sulphate is uncertain. Of the possible mechanisms cerebral vasodilation (Kemp *et al.* 1993; Perales *et al.* 1997) is the most plausible, especially as cerebral vasoconstriction and focal ischaemia is probably the underlying pathology of eclampsia (e.g. Duncan *et al.* 1989; Kanayama *et al.* 1993; Qureshi *et al.* 1996). The trial evidence does not yet justify the practice of giving magnesium sulphate prophylactically. This is not because there is much doubt that convulsions can be prevented, albeit incompletely. The problem is one of predicting which women are likely to get eclampsia. Nearly one-third of the cases of eclampsia in the UK are not completely heralded by prodromal signs of pre-eclampsia (Douglas and Redman 1994). With present knowledge they are essentially not preventable. Of the rest, the evidence is that 100 women would need to be treated to prevent one case (Lucas *et al.* 1995) even with severe disease (Chua and Redman 1991). This would imply that 30 000 women, namely nearly 5% of all pregnant women who have pre-eclampsia, would be treated every year in the UK to prevent heralded eclampsia. At this level side effects, even if rare, could become a major issue. By far the most critical is the risk of maternal cardiorespiratory arrest through accidental overdose which can cause maternal death. This is most likely in the context of acute renal failure, which is a common complication of severe pre-eclampsia, when magnesium ion can accumulate rapidly in the blood to reach toxic concentrations. Other adverse effects include hypocalcaemia, profound hypotension and reduced fetal heart rate variation. Individuals with disordered neuromuscular function are particularly sensitive to paralysis by magnesium sulphate. There are no data to indicate how maternal mortality changes if eclampsia is prevented. It is worth remembering that as many as half the maternal deaths from the disease occur without eclamptic convulsions (Department of Health 1998). Other aspects are equally dangerous.

THE PERSPECTIVE FOR THE NEXT DECADE

A better understanding of the possible forces that drive the syndrome of pre-eclampsia is emerging. It is likely that poor placentation will come to be seen as only one of a number of different causes and there is a strong case for considering it as a separate condition. As the pathogenesis becomes more clearly defined, better diagnostic and preventive strategies will emerge, but they are unlikely ever to be applicable to all women with all varieties of pre-eclampsia. Rather, different categories will need to be targeted to particular subgroups.

References

American College of Obstetricians and Gynecologists (1996) *Hypertension in Pregnancy*. Washington, DC: ACOG (ACOG Technical Bulletin No. 219)

Ales, K.L., Norton, M.E. and Druzin, M.L. (1989) Early prediction of antepartum hypertension. *Obstet Gynecol* **73**, 928–33

Beaufils, M., Uzan, S., Donsimoni, R. and Colau, J.C. (1985) Prevention of pre-eclampsia by early antiplatelet therapy. *Lancet* **i**, 840–2

Bower, S., Bewley, S. and Campbell, S. (1993) Improved prediction of pre-eclampsia by two-stage screening of uterine arteries using the early diastolic notch and color Doppler imaging. *Obstet Gynecol* **82**, 78–83

Boyd, P.A., Lindenbaum, R.H. and Redman, C.W.G. (1987) Pre-eclampsia and trisomy 13: a possible association. *Lancet* **ii**, 425–7

Branch, D.W., Andres, R., Digre, K.B. *et al.* (1989) The association of antiphospholipid antibodies with severe pre-eclampsia. *Obstet Gynecol* **73**, 541–5

Brandenburg, H., Los, F.J. and In't Veld, P. (1996) Clinical significance of placenta-confined nonmosaic trisomy 16. *Am J Obstet Gynecol* **174**, 1663–4

Brown, M.A. and Buddle, M.L. (1995) Inadequacy of dipstick proteinuria in hypertensive pregnancy. *Aust N Z J Obstet Gynaecol* **35**, 366–9

Caritis, S., Sibai, B., Hauth, J. *et al.* (1998) Low-dose aspirin to prevent pre-eclampsia in women at high risk. National Institute of Child Health and Human Development Network of Maternal-Fetal Medicine Units. *N Engl J Med* **338**, 701–5

Chua, S. and Redman, C.W.G. (1991) Are prophylactic anticonvulsants required in severe pre-eclampsia? *Lancet* **337**, 250–1

Chun, D., Braga, C., Chow, C. and Lok, L. (1964) Clinical observations on some aspects of hydatidiform moles. *J Obstet Gynaecol Br Cwlth* **71**, 180–4

Cincotta, R.B. and Brennecke, S.P. (1998) Family history of pre-eclampsia as a predictor for pre-eclampsia in primigravidas. *Int J Gynaecol Obstet* **60**, 23–7

CLASP (1994) A randomised trial of low-dose aspirin for the prevention and treatment of pre-eclampsia among 9364 pregnant women. *Lancet* **343**, 619–29

Cnattingius, S., Mills, J.L., Yuen, J. *et al.* (1997) The paradoxical effect of smoking in pre-eclamptic pregnancies, smoking reduces the incidence but increases the rates of perinatal mortality, abruptio placentae, and intrauterine growth restriction. *Am J Obstet Gynecol* **177**, 156–61

Collaborative Eclampsia Trial (1995) Which anticonvulsant for women with eclampsia? Evidence from the Collaborative Eclampsia Trial. *Lancet* **345**, 1455–63

Darling, M. (1998) Low-dose aspirin not for pre-eclampsia. *Lancet* **352**, 342

Davey, D.A. and MacGillivray, I. (1988) The classification and definition of the hypertensive disorders of pregnancy. *Am J Obstet Gynecol* **158**, 892–8

Davidge, S.T., Hubel, C.A., Brayden, R.D., Capeless, E.C. and McLaughlin, M.K. (1992) Sera antioxidant activity in uncomplicated and pre-eclamptic pregnancies. *Obstet Gynecol* **79**, 897–901

Demissie, K., Breckenridge, M.B. and Rhoads, G.G. (1998) Infant and maternal outcomes in the pregnancies of asthmatic women. *Am J Respir Crit Care Med* **158**, 1091–5

Department of Health (1993) *Changing Childbirth. Report of the Expert Maternity Group.* London: HMSO

Department of Health (1998) *Why Mothers Die. Report on Confidential Enquiries into Maternal Deaths in the United Kingdom 1994–1996*, pp. 36–46. London: The Stationery Office

Douglas, K.A. and Redman, C.W.G. (1994) Eclampsia in the United Kingdom. *BMJ* **309**, 1395–400

Duncan, R., Hadley, D., Bone, I., Symonds, E.M., Worthington, B.S. and Rubin, P.C. (1989) Blindness in eclampsia, CT and MR imaging. *J Neurol Neurosurg Psychiatry* **52**, 899–902

ECPPA (1996) Randomised trial of low dose aspirin for the prevention of maternal and fetal complications in high risk pregnant women. ECPPA (Estudo Colaborativo para Prevencao da Preeclampsia corn Aspirina) Collaborative Group. *Br J Obstet Gynaecol* **103**, 39–47

Gant, N.F., Daley, G.L., Chand, S., Whalley, P.J. and MacDonald, P.C. (1973) A study of angiotensin 11 pressure response throughout primigravid pregnancy. *J Clin Invest* **52**, 2682–9

Gruenwald, P. (1966) Growth of the human fetus. II. Abnormal growth in twins and infants of mothers with diabetes, hypertension or isoimmunisation. *Am J Obstet Gynecol* **94**, 1120–32

Guimond, M.J., Wang, B. and Croy, B.A. (1998) Engraftment of bone marrow from severe combined immunodeficient (SCID) mice reverses the reproductive deficits in natural killer cell-deficient tg epsilon 26 mice. *J Exp Med* **187**, 217–23

Hermida, R.C., Ayala, D.E., Mojon, A. *et al.* (1998) Blood pressure excess for the early identification of gestational hypertension and pre-eclampsia. *Hypertension* **31**, 83–9

Holland, E. (1909) Recent work on the aetiology of eclampsia. *J Obstet Gynaecol Br Emp* **16**, 255–73

Hubel, C.A., McLaughlin, M.K., Evans, R.W., Hauth, B.A., Sims, C.J. and Roberts, J.M. (1996) Fasting serum triglycerides, free fatty acids, and malondialdehyde are increased in pre-eclampsia, are positively correlated, and decrease within 48 hours post partum. *Am J Obstet Gynecol* **174**, 975–82

James, W.H. (1995) Sex ratios of offspring and the causes of placental pathology. *Hum Reprod* **10**, 1403–6

Jeffcoate, T.N.A. and Scott, J.S. (1959) Some observations on the placental factor in pregnancy toxemia. *Am J Obstet Gynecol* **77**, 475–89

Kanayama, N., Nakajima, A., Maehara, K. *et al.* (1993) Magnetic resonance imaging angiography in a case of eclampsia. *Gynecol Obstet Invest* **36**, 56–8

Kemp, P.A., Gardiner, S.M., Bennett, T. and Rubin, P.C. (1993) Magnesium sulphate reverses the carotid vasoconstriction caused by endothelin-1, angiotensin 11 and neuropeptide-Y, but not that caused by NG-nitro-L-arginine methyl ester, in conscious rats. *Clin Sci (Colch)* **85**, 175–81

Khan, N.D., Gulmezoglu, M. and Villar, J. (1998) Who should provide routine antenatal care for low-risk women, and how often? A systematic review of randomised controlled trials. WHO Antenatal Care Trial Research Group. *Paediatr Perinat Epidemiol* **12** Suppl 2, 7–26

King, A., Burrows, T., Verma, S., Hiby, S. and Loke, Y.W. (1998) Human uterine lymphocytes. *Hum Reprod Update* **4**, 480–5

Klonoff Cohen, H., Cross, J.L. and Pieper, C.F. (1996) Job stress and pre-eclampsia. *Epidemiology* **7**, 245–9

Kuo, V.S., Koumantakis, G. and Gallery, E.D. (1992) Proteinuria and its assessment in normal and hypertensive pregnancy. *Am J Obstet Gynecol* **167**, 723–8

Kyle, P.M., Buckley, D., Kissane, J., de Swiet, M. and Redman, C.W.G. (1995) The angiotensin sensitivity test and low-dose aspirin are ineffective methods to predict and prevent hypertensive disorders in nulliparous pregnancy. *Am J Obstet Gynecol* **173**, 865–72

Lie, R.T., Rasmussen, S., Brunborg, H., Gjessing, H.K., Lie, N.E. and Irgens, L.M. (1998) Fetal and maternal contributions to risk of pre-eclampsia, population based study. *BMJ* **316**, 1343–7

Little, W.A. (1960) Placental infarction. *Obstet Gynecol* **15**, 109–30

Lockwood, C.J. and Peters, J.H. (1990) Increased plasma levels of ED 1+ cellular fibronectin precede the clinical signs of pre-eclampsia. *Am J Obstet Gynecol* **162**, 358–62

Lorentzen, B., Drevon, C.A., Endresen, M.J. and Henriksen, T. (1995) Fatty acid pattern of esterified and free fatty acids in sera of women with normal and pre-eclamptic pregnancy. *Br J Obstet Gynaecol* **102**, 530–7

Lucas, M.J., Leveno, K.J. and Cunningham, F.G. (1995) A comparison of magnesium sulfate with phenytoin for the prevention of eclampsia. *N Engl J Med* **333**, 201–5

McKay, D.G., Merrill, S.J., Weiner, A.E., Hertig, A.T. and Reid, D.E. (1953) The pathologic anatomy of eclampsia, bilateral renal cortical necrosis, pituitary necrosis, and other acute fatal complications of pregnancy, and its possible relationship to the generalised Shwartzman phenomenon. *Am J Obstet Gynecol* **66**, 507–39

Marcoux, S., Berube, S., Brisson, J. and Fabia, J. (1992) History of migraine and risk of pregnancy-induced hypertension. *Epidemiology* **3**, 53–6

Millar, J.G., Campbell, S.K., Albano, J.D., Higgins, B.R. and Clark, A.D. (1996) Early prediction of preeclampsia by measurement of kallikrein and creatinine on a random urine sample. *Br J Obstet Gynaecol* **103**, 421–6

Mires, G.J., Williams, F.L., Leslie, J. and Howie, P.W. (1998) Assessment of uterine arterial notching as a screening test for adverse pregnancy outcome. *Am J Obstet Gynecol* **179**, 1317–23

Morgan, T. and Ward, K. (1999) New insights into the genetics of pre-eclampsia. *Semin Perinatol* **23**, 14–23

Morris, J.M., Gopaul, N.K., Endresen, M.J. *et al.* (1998) Circulating markers of oxidative stress are raised in normal pregnancy and pre-eclampsia. *Br J Obstet Gynaecol* **105**, 1195–9

Muller, F., Savey, L., Le Fiblec, B. *et al.* (1996) Maternal serum human chorionic gonadotropin level at fifteen weeks is a predictor for pre-eclampsia. *Am J Obstet Gynecol* **175**, 37–40

Page, E.W. (1948) Placental dysfunction in eclamptogenic toxemias. *Obstet Gynecol Surv* **3**, 615–28

Perales, A.J., Torregrosa, G., Salom, J.B., Barbera, M.D., Jover, T. and Alborch, E. (1997) Effects of magnesium sulphate on the noradrenaline-induced cerebral vasoconstrictor and pressor responses in the goat. *Br J Obstet Gynaecol* **104**, 898–903

Qureshi, A.I., Frankel, M R., Ottenlips, J R. and Stem, B.J. (1996) Cerebral hemodynamics in preeclampsia and eclampsia. *Arch Neurol* **53**, 1226–31

Redman, C.W.G., Sacks, G.P. and Sargent, I.L. (1999) Pre-eclampsia, an excessive maternal inflammatory response to pregnancy. *Am J Obstet Gynecol* **180**, 499–506

Rijhsinghani, A., Yankowitz, J., Strauss, R.A., Kuller, J.A., Patil, S. and Williamson, R.A. (1997) Risk of pre-eclampsia in second-trimester triploid pregnancies. *Obstet Gynecol* **90**, 884–8

Roberts, J.M., Taylor, R.N., Musci, T.J., Rodgers, G.M., Hubel, C.A. and McLaughlin, M.K. (1989) Pre-eclampsia, an endothelial cell disorder. *Am J Obstet Gynecol* **161**, 1200–4

Robertson, W.B., Brosens, I. and Dixon, G. (1975) Uteroplacental vascular pathology. *Eur J Obstet Gynecol Reprod Biol* **5**, 47–65

Robillard, P.Y. and Hulsey, T.C. (1996) Association of pregnancy-induced-hypertension, pre-eclampsia, and eclampsia with duration of sexual cohabitation before conception. *Lancet* **347**, 619

Robillard, P.Y., Hulsey, T.C., Perianin, J. *et al.* (1994) Association of pregnancy-induced hypertension with duration of sexual cohabitation before conception. *Lancet* **344**, 973–5

Rodriguez, M.H., Masaki, D.I., Mestman, J., Kumar, D. and Rude, R. (1988) Calcium/creatinine ratio and microalbuminuria in the prediction of pre-eclampsia. *Am J Obstet Gynecol* **159**, 1452–5

Rotchell, Y.E., Cruickshank, J.K., Gay, M.P. *et al.* (1998) Barbados Low Dose Aspirin Study in Pregnancy (BLASP), a randomised trial for the prevention of pre-eclampsia and its complications. *Br J Obstet Gynaecol* **105,** 286–92

Sacks, G.P., Studena, K., Sargent, I.L. and Redman, C.W.G. (1998) Normal pregnancy and pre-eclampsia both produce inflammatory changes in peripheral blood leukocytes akin to sepsis. *Am J Obstet Gynecol* **179**, 80–6

Schatz, M., Zeiger, R.S., Harden, K., Hoffman, C.C., Chilingar, L. and Petitti, D. (1997) The safety of asthma and allergy medications during pregnancy. *J Allergy Clin Immunol* **100**, 301–6

Schmorl, G. (1893). Quoted in: Chesley, L.C. (1978) *Hypertensive Disorders of Pregnancy*, p. 582. New York: Appleton-Century-Crofts

Sibai, B.M. (1998) Prevention of pre-eclampsia, a big disappointment. *Am J Obstet Gynecol* **179**, 1275–8

Sibai, B.M., Caritis, S.N., Thom, E. *et al.* (1993) Prevention of pre-eclampsia with low-dose aspirin in healthy, nulliparous pregnant women. The National Institute of Child Health and Human Development Network of Maternal–Fetal Medicine Units. *N Engl J Med* **329**, 1213–18

Sibai, B.M, Ewell, M., Levine, R.J. *et al.* (1997) Risk factors associated with pre-eclampsia in healthy nulliparous women. The Calcium for Pre-eclampsia Prevention (CPEP) Study Group. *Am J Obstet Gynecol* **177**, 1003–10

Smarason, A.K., Sargent, I.L., Starkey, P.M. and Redman, C.W.G. (1993) The effect of placental syncytiotrophoblast microvillous membranes from normal and pre-eclamptic women: growth of endothelial cells *in vitro*. *Br J Obstet Gynaecol* **100**, 943–9

Smith, G.N., Walker, M., Tessier, J.L. and Millar, K.G. (1997) Increased incidence of pre-eclampsia in women conceiving by intrauterine insemination with donor versus partner sperm for treatment of primary infertility. *Am J Obstet Gynecol* **177**, 455–8

Suarez, V.R., Trelles, J.G. and Miyahira, J.M. (1996) Urinary calcium in asymptomatic primigravidas who later developed pre-eclampsia. *Obstet Gynecol* **87**, 79–82

Thornton, J.G. and Onwude, J.L. (1991) Pre-eclampsia, discordance among identical twins. *BMJ* **303**, 1241–2

Walsh, S.W. and Wang, Y. (1993) Deficient glutathione peroxidase activity in pre-eclampsia is associated with increased placental production of thromboxane and lipid peroxides. *Am J Obstet Gynecol* **169**, 1456–61

Weinstein, L. (1982) Syndrome of hemolysis, elevated liver enzymes, and low platelet count, a severe consequence of hypertension in pregnancy. *Am J Obstet Gynecol* **142**, 159–67

Wilcken, B., Leung, K.C., Hammond, J., Kamath, R. and Leonard, J.V. (1993) Pregnancy and fetal longchain 3-hydroxyacyl coenzyme A dehydrogenase deficiency. *Lancet* **341**, 407–8

Zeek, P.M. and Assali, N.S. (1950) Vascular changes with eclamptogenic toxemia of pregnancy. *Am J Clin Pathol* **20**, 1099–109

Zhou, Y., Damsky, C.H. and Fisher, S.J. (1997) Pre-eclampsia is associated with failure of human cytotrophoblasts to mimic a vascular adhesion phenotype. One cause of defective endovascular invasion in this syndrome? *J Clin Invest* **99**, 2152–64

12

Intrauterine growth restriction

Jeffrey S. Robinson, Fong Lok and Gustaaf Dekker

INTRODUCTION

A century ago it was clearly recognised that there were babies who were small but vigorous survivors. Sir Isaac Newton was born on Christmas Day in 1642 and it has been noted that 'he was so small that he could have been put into a quart pot' (Simpson 1907). It is likely that Sir Isaac was both premature and small-for-dates. In the mid-20th century precedence was given to birth weight to define prematurity (World Health Organization 1961) even though it was recognised many years earlier that 'some born prematurely have quite considerable weight, mainly accounted for by the presence of fat in their tissues. These infants as a rule do not live long; their pulmonary apparatus functions imperfectly. . . . On the other hand, there are tiny, puny infants with great vitality. They never seem to rest. Their movements are untiring and their crying lusty, for their organs are quite capable of performing their allotted functions. These infants will live, for although their weight is inferior to those we have just mentioned, they have great power of resistance, for their sojourn in the womb is longer' (Budin 1907). It would be hard to improve on this description of the growth-restricted baby although it could equally describe a healthy small baby that has grown to its environmental and genetic potential. This highlights a continuing dilemma of recognition of the fetus whose growth is abnormally constrained from the slowly growing healthy fetus. The role of a small placenta, which fails to adequately supply the fetus resulting in a light, undernourished baby at term was recognised by McBurney (1947) who noted that this undernourishment may be severe enough to result in intrauterine death before the onset of labour.

Accurate weighing of the baby at birth was only introduced during the late 18th and early 19th centuries. About the same time it was recognised that the male larger fetus requires greater nourishment than the female fetus for its survival. The high death rate of twins (approaching 50%) was attributed to 'scanty nutrition, by which they are oftener blighted *in utero* than single children' (Clarke 1787). These are also both excellent descriptions of the condition currently known as intrauterine growth restriction. The percentage of babies who are of low birth weight (<2500 g) remained between 5% and 20% in British, European and North American cities throughout the 19th and early 20th centuries. Stillbirth rates were high and fluctuated between 5% and 15% (Steckel 1998).

The advent of ultrasound examination in the second half of the 20th century has dramatically improved the estimation of gestational age. Ultrasound also allowed clear definition of the normal pattern of fetal growth for the first time. In the final years of the

20th century, patterns of fetal growth have been linked to the metabolic and endocrine state of the fetus (Soothill *et al.* 1987). However, relatively few and small studies have linked these to longer-term outcomes for offspring (Soothill *et al.* 1992; Ley *et al.* 1996). The final years of the century have linked poor fetal growth with the early onset of common adult diseases including hypertension, cardiovascular deaths and non-insulin-dependent diabetes mellitus; components of the insulin resistance or metabolic syndrome (Barker 1998). This has placed a new urgency on the definition of advice to the woman before and during pregnancy to improve both short- and long-term outcomes.

CURRENT UNDERSTANDING OF INTRAUTERINE GROWTH RESTRICTION

Consumer pressure in the last decade of the 20th century led to the introduction of the term, 'intrauterine growth restriction' (Bastian 1992). This replaced 'intrauterine growth retardation' which generated too many adverse views of poor neurological outcome among parents. However, intrauterine growth restriction/retardation has only been accepted in the second half of the century. Even now, there are those who consider that growth restriction does not really exist as a definable entity as it cannot be separated from a normal distribution of birth weight (McIntosh and Chard 1995).

DEFINITION OF INTRAUTERINE GROWTH RESTRICTION

Intrauterine growth was originally assessed using the birth-weight-for-gestational-age charts which were initially promulgated by Lubchenko *et al.* (1963). Others have attempted to provide a generic chart derived from a range of populations (Dunn 1985). However, these have to be reviewed periodically, especially if there is evidence of a secular trend in the distribution of birth weight (Arbuckle *et al.* 1993; Power 1994). Part of this change may be due to a reduction in the induction of labour and maternal smoking (Bonellie and Raab 1997; Cnattingius and Haglund 1997).

A useful clinical definition that encompasses restriction of growth across the range of birth weight is still elusive. Clinicians wisely retreat into the simple and pragmatic definition of growth restriction as birth weight below the tenth centile for gestational age or a similar definition (below the third centile or two standard deviations below mean weight for age). However, this is really a definition of small-for-dates. It is even more problematical when preterm delivery occurs, since growth restriction is more common in babies born early compared to those who remain *in utero* until term (Persson 1992). Correction for maternal size and parity by Thomson *et al.* (1968) showed that many babies were not really small-for-dates: a recent phenomenon has revised this concept in the 'customised growth charts' (Gardosi *et al.* 1992). The latter is a useful concept for the clinician as it provides diagnostic information at any stage of pregnancy.

CAUSES OF GROWTH RESTRICTION

Intrauterine growth restriction implies that growth has been constrained by extrinsic or intrinsic mechanisms. The restricting factor may only be present for a part of pregnancy and may affect the embryo or fetus differently depending on the time of exposure. For example, poorly controlled maternal diabetes with high glucose concentrations inhibits growth of the early embryo but accelerates growth of the fetus in the second half of pregnancy. More commonly, growth rate may be set higher and later events slow growth. Inhibition of growth in each stage of pregnancy induces specific birth phenotypes with their own short- and long-term consequences.

On most occasions it is not possible to define a cause for growth restriction. Small mothers and primiparity are inescapable biological factors reducing growth of the fetus. Spontaneous multiple pregnancy may also be unavoidable but, unfortunately, ovulation induction and advanced reproductive technologies have greatly increased the rate of multiple pregnancy in many communities. It remains a challenge to reduce the rate of twinning in these pregnancies to the population norm as is currently happening for higher-order multiple pregnancies. Selective reduction to reduce higher-order multiple pregnancies is a poor solution since growth restriction may occur more often in the surviving fetuses.

Maternal size may be an inescapable factor within one generation, although there is good evidence that maternal height is increasing in many communities (Forsen et al. 1997). This has been attributed to a long-term improvement in nutrition of the community. Unfortunately, there is also evidence that obesity is increasing in many communities and this may carry an adverse reproductive consequence for primigravidae (Cnattingius et al. 1998).

It is not the purpose of this brief review to list the potential causes of growth restriction as these can readily be found elsewhere (Peters et al. 1983; Kramer 1987; Meis et al. 1997; Kramer 1998). World-wide, adverse maternal nutrition is still a major factor restricting growth of the fetus. Somewhat surprisingly, this may also be true for growth restriction at term in a developed society (Conti et al. 1998). If this is generally true, there may be significant opportunities to reduce the prevalence of growth restriction by simple means. Maternal cigarette smoking has been recognised as a cause of fetal growth restriction and there is now evidence that its effect in some communities may be declining (Cnattingius et al. 1998). Intervention studies have shown that smoking may be further reduced (Lumley et al. 1999). There has been a dramatic increase in the number of babies of low-birth weight in New York City and this has been attributed to increased drug abuse (Joyce 1990).

Pre-eclampsia remains a major cause of growth restriction. The mechanism causing restriction of fetal growth is likely to be a reduced supply of nutrients and oxygen in the second half of pregnancy. However, its origins arise much earlier with failure of the physiological change in the spiral arterioles (Khong et al. 1986). The last third of the 20th century has seen the rise and fall of aspirin as a panacea to prevent growth restriction, pre-eclampsia and preterm birth. A more rigorous definition of thrombophilic states and their effects on pregnancy outcome will encourage a selective use of anticoagulants, including the use of aspirin.

DIAGNOSIS OF THE COMPROMISED GROWTH-RESTRICTED FETUS

Diagnosis of small-for-dates by clinical methods is notoriously inaccurate, with only a quarter of those with birth weight below the tenth centile detected in antenatal care (Hepburn and Rosenberg 1986; Kean and Liu 1996). Measurement of symphysial–fundal height, although attractive for its cost and simplicity in application, is not supported by the only randomised trial of its use (Lindhard et al. 1990). First trimester growth restriction may signal aneuploidy (Kuhn et al. 1995).

Ultrasound

A two-stage ultrasound scanning protocol with scans in mid-pregnancy and in the early third trimester is the most successful way of detecting the slowly growing fetus (Neilson *et al.* 1984). This has been compared with birth-weight-for-age charts. However, ultrasound has clearly demonstrated that preterm delivery, particularly in the early third trimester, is accompanied by fetal growth restriction compared with those remaining *in utero* until term (Persson 1992). Preterm babies that fail to meet normal growth as estimated by ultrasound and who are above birth-weight-for-age standards are more likely to be admitted to a nursery, but may have no greater risk of adverse perinatal sequelae than normally grown fetuses (Stratton *et al.* 1995). As noted earlier, customised fetal-growth charts are being introduced to reduce the risk of false-positive diagnosis of growth restriction (Gardosi *et al.* 1992). The fetal size is 'customised' for gestational age, sex, maternal height, weight at first visit, ethnic group and parity (Gardosi *et al.* 1995). Fetuses that are reclassified as normally grown by this technique have a good perinatal outcome. This is a little surprising given that primiparity and obesity may adversely affect perinatal outcomes in large population-based cohorts. The customised growth charts also identify growth-restricted fetuses that would be considered normally grown by other means. These fetuses have significantly more adverse perinatal outcomes than normally grown fetuses (de Jong *et al.* 1998).

Ultrasound should also be used to measure placental size. Remarkably little emphasis has been given to the assessment of placental volume in early pregnancy even though it may be a better predictor of size at birth than measurements of the size of the fetus in mid-pregnancy (Howe 1994).

Detection of the fetus at risk requires more than an estimate of size or growth rate of the fetus from serial ultrasound examinations. Reduction in amniotic fluid volume frequently accompanies growth restriction. Charting maternal counts of fetal movements was not beneficial (Grant *et al.* 1989). Doppler ultrasound is a useful method of assessing the health of the fetus in a high-risk pregnancy, however, this does not provide a firm guide to the timing of delivery (Neilson and Alfirevic 1999).

Fetal heart rate

Fetal heart rate decelerations are not uncommon when the fetus is growth restricted. Short-term variability of the fetal heart rate is also reduced. Both of these may be present for days or weeks before fetal demise or delivery. Early randomised controlled trials of antenatal fetal heart-rate monitoring failed to show that this technique is of benefit in high-risk populations including women with growth-restricted fetuses (Pattison and McCowan 1999).

Fetal blood sampling

The role of fetal blood sampling in evaluating the acid-base status of the growth-restricted fetus is limited owing to its invasive nature and associated risks (Nicolini *et al.* 1990; Shalev *et al.* 1995).

All these emphasise the need for a systematic approach of assessment of new techniques before their widespread adoption into clinical practice. It is hardly surprising that there are wide areas of disagreement about the correct timing of delivery at different gestational ages. The growth restriction intervention trial should help to resolve this uncertainty (GRIT Study Group 1996).

TREATMENT TO ALLEVIATE GROWTH RESTRICTION

Maternal malnutrition is a major contributor to growth restriction. However, nutritional supplementation of the mother's diet during pregnancy has not always had the intended outcome. High-density protein supplements have even reduced mean birth weights. Overall, a small increase in birth weight has been achieved with protein calorie supplements (Rush 1989). Birth weight may not be the most suitable primary end-point and it has been suggested that birth length or later height may detect beneficial effects of supplementation (Kusin *et al.* 1992). Protein energy supplementation in the large randomised trial of women in the Gambia exposed to seasonal famine increased maternal weight gain during pregnancy, birth weight and head circumference. Birth length was not affected in this study. The odds ratios for a low birth weight baby, still-birth or a neonatal death in the first week were all reduced, demonstrating the benefits of supplementation of an at-risk population (Ceesay *et al.* 1997).

Recent meta-analysis of interventions to prevent or treat impaired fetal growth found that relatively few improve perinatal outcomes (Gulmezoglu *et al.* 1997). This analysis noted that smoking cessation, antimalarial chemoprophylaxis in primigravidae and balanced protein energy supplementation are likely to be beneficial. Other interventions, which were identified as suitable topics for further study, included zinc, folate and magnesium supplementation. A major conclusion of this review is that the importance given to impaired fetal growth in the epidemiological and clinical literature is not matched by the size or quality of the trials of intervention strategies to alleviate this important clinical problem.

The recent identification of thrombophilic states as causes of recurrent miscarriage, intrauterine growth restriction and pre-eclampsia should lead to well-designed studies to assess treatments to overcome the particular thrombophilic state. In this context aspirin may find a resurgence of interest and a validated clinical indication. Aspirin has been used to improve the outcome of pregnancy in the presence of antiphospholipid antibodies in women with recurrent miscarriage but it may not prevent growth restriction (Rai *et al.* 1997). A recent meta-analysis of 13 clinical trials has shown that early prophylactic use of aspirin reduces the incidence of growth restriction in at-risk women (Leitich *et al.* 1997).

Maternal hyperhomocysteinaemia identifies another group of women at risk of carrying a growth-restricted fetus or of severe early onset pre-eclampsia. A preliminary study suggests that administration of folate and pyridoxine normalises the maternal homocysteine concentrations and when combined with low-dose aspirin reduces the risk for recurrent severe pre-eclampsia and increases birth weight (Leeda *et al.* 1998). The effect on fetal growth requires further study in a prospective randomised trial, which will have to be multicentre, given the comparative rareness of this abnormality. However, hyperhomocysteinaemia is an excellent example of the trend towards recognition of the effects of single-gene mutations on perinatal outcome. It is still unusual to have a readily identified intervention of a new genetic defect as is available with folate with or without pyridoxine supplements for the common mutation, thermolabile methylenetetrahydro-folate reductase. Other causes of mild hyperhomocysteinaemia include heterozygous cystathione-β synthase, folate, pyridoxine or vitamin B_{12} deficiencies.

OUTCOMES OF GROWTH RESTRICTION

The evidence that growth-restricted fetuses carry an increased risk of an adverse perinatal outcome is overwhelming and will not be detailed here. However, as perinatal mortality rates decline, the proportion of perinatal deaths due to unexplained stillbirths, many of which are growth restricted, indicates that this should be given research priority. Indeed, unexplained stillbirths are now more common than sudden infant death, which receives more funding and publicity. New strategies need to be evolved to explore potential causes of these tragedies, some of which may be preventable.

Adverse neurological outcomes are more common when growth restriction has been identified. Neonatal encephalopathy is an immediate risk after birth (Badawi *et al.* 1998). The type of neurological outcome detected depends on the age of the offspring when follow-up examinations are undertaken. For example, cerebral palsy may not be identified until the child is a few years old and learning difficulties and attention span may not be identified until later. Intriguingly, pre-eclampsia associated with fetal growth restriction is under-represented as an antecedent factor for cerebral palsy (Palmer *et al.* 1995). Restriction of fetal growth has been identified as one of the perinatal risk factors for schizophrenia in the offspring (Brown *et al.* 1996).

There is now compelling evidence that life-long follow-up is required to identify adverse outcomes of poor or restricted fetal growth. A remarkable series of epidemiological studies has linked poor fetal growth with common adult diseases (for review see Barker 1998). However, these studies relate indices of fetal growth across the normal spectrum with diseases including hypertension, ischaemic heart disease, stroke and non-insulin-dependent diabetes. Our studies in Adelaide (Moore *et al.* 1999) confirm that blood pressure increases with decreasing birth weight and that this effect is amplified between eight and 20 years of age more in those who were light at birth. Those who were light at birth are insulin resistant and maintain normal glucose tolerance at 20 years of age by increasing insulin secretion and by other means. Body shape at birth also predicts fasting plasma lipid concentrations. Many of the set points of endocrine systems are different in those who were light compared to normal or heavier at birth. The recognition that maternal body habitus may confer additional risks on the long-term health of the offspring imposes a transgenerational dimension to follow-up studies (Forsen *et al.* 1997). It is hard to dismiss these associations as a simple expression of a genetic background of the mother or the conceptus since many of these changes can be induced in experimental animals by changing maternal nutrition or by limiting placental function (Robinson *et al.* 1999).

THE IMPERATIVES FOR THE NEW MILLENNIUM

Attempting to predict future trends in the care of the woman with a growth-restricted fetus requires several additions to current clinical practice. Lifestyle factors that adversely impact on growth of the fetus are well known in many communities, but changing these is a slow process and more successful strategies need to be developed. Cigarette smoking was identified as a factor reducing growth and even survival of the fetus more than 40 years ago. Currently, there is marginal evidence that women are changing this habit.

Defining the optimal diet before and during pregnancy for women of different body habitus is still a goal for the future in developed societies. Simply providing sufficient protein energy intake for all is an unmet goal in both developing and developed societies. Folate supplementation, in addition to preventing neural tube defects, may also prevent fetal growth restriction in some women. Providing supplements that reduce pre-eclampsia or preterm birth may also reduce growth restriction, for example calcium supplements (Crowther *et al.* 1999).

Our diagnostic acumen combined with present technology is inadequate to detect and define the at-risk growth-restricted fetus. Ultrasound can detect the small fetus and Doppler helps in recognition of the at-risk fetus. However, we are only at the beginning of testing the timing of delivery in well-designed trials. These studies will initially concentrate on immediate perinatal outcomes. New systems will need to be defined to enable long-term follow-up studies of these randomised trials.

The new century will bring increasing use of large databases to define factors that impinge on the growth of the fetus. These will pose problems for communities which give priority to the privacy of the individual. Linking sufficiently large, or national, databases is already providing new insights into the factors affecting the growth and welfare of the fetus (Cnattingius and Haglund 1997; Herman *et al.* 1997). Communities without this facility can only assume that the same weightings will apply for their population. Countries such as Australia where detailed databases may exist at single institutions, but with progressively less information available at regional, state or national level, may not be in a position to define circumstances for optimal pregnancy outcome.

The race to sequence the human genome will define new genetic syndromes associated with growth restriction. However, it is more likely that defining the interaction of the internal and external environments of the mother and the genetic composition of the mother and her fetus will provide new avenues for improving the outcome of pregnancy and for reducing the impact of growth restriction. The recent observations that slow fetal growth is associated with altered programming of cardiovascular and endocrine systems and thus predisposes an individual to common adult diseases (Barker 1998; O'Brien *et al.* 1999), challenges our traditional management of growth restriction, most of which are based on short-term perinatal outcomes. New studies will have to integrate these new findings into obstetric and preventive strategies to reduce the life-long impact of intrauterine growth restriction.

Acknowledgments

Professor Robinson gratefully acknowledges financial support from the National Health and Medical Research Council and from the Women's and Children's Hospital Foundation for studies noted in this review.

References

Arbuckle, T.E., Wilkins, R. and Sherman, G.J. (1993) Birth weight percentiles by gestational age in Canada. *Obstet Gynecol* **81**, 39–48

Badawi, N., Kurinczuk, J.J., Keogh, J.M. *et al.* (1998) Antepartum risk factors for newborn encephalopathy: the Western Australian case–control study. *BMJ* **317**, 1549–53

Barker, D.J.P. (1998) *Mothers, Babies and Health in Later Life*. Edinburgh: Churchill Livingstone

Bastian, H. (1992) Confined, managed and delivered: the language of obstetrics. *Br J Obstet Gynaecol* **99**, 92–3

Bonellie, S.R. and Raab, G.M. (1997) Why are babies getting heavier? Comparison of Scottish births from 1980 to 1992. *BMJ* **315**, 1205

Brown, A.S., Susser, E.S., Butler, P.D., Andrews, R.R., Kaufmann, C.A. and Gorman, J.M. (1996) Neurological plausibility of prenatal nutritional deprivation as a risk factor for schizophrenia. *J Nerv Ment Dis* **184**, 71–85

Budin, P. (1907) *The Nursling*. London: Caxton Publishing

Ceesay, S.M., Prentice, A.M., Cole, T.J. *et al.* (1997) Effects on birth weight and perinatal mortality of maternal dietary supplements in rural Gambia: 5 year randomised controlled trial. *BMJ* **315**, 786–90

Clarke, J. (1787) Observations on the causes of the excess of the mortality of males above females. *Proc R Soc Lond* **77**, 349–64

Cnattingius, S. and Haglund, B. (1997) Decreasing smoking prevalence during pregnancy in Sweden: the effect on small-for-gestational-age births. *Am J Public Health* **87**, 410–13

Cnattingius, S., Bergstrom, R., Lipworth, L. and Kramer, M. (1998) Prepregnancy weight and the risk of adverse pregnancy outcomes. *N Engl J Med* **338**, 147–52

Conti, J., Suzanne, A. and Taylor, A. (1998) Eating behaviour and pregnancy outcome. *J Psychosom Res* **44**, 465–77

Crowther, C.A., Hiller, J.E., Bryce, R. *et al.* (1999) Calcium supplementation in nulliparous women for the prevention of hypertension, preeclampsia and preterm birth: an Australian randomised trial. *Aust N Z J Obstet Gynaecol* **39**, 12–18

de Jong, C.L., Gardosi, J., Dekker, G.A., Colenbrander, G.J. and van Geijn, H.P. (1998) Application of customised birth weight standard in the assessment of perinatal outcome in a high risk population. *Br J Obstet Gynaecol* **105**, 531–5

Dunn, P.M. (1985) A perinatal growth chart for international reference. *Acta Paediatr Suppl* **319**, 180–7

Forsen, T., Eriksson, J.G., Tuomilehto, J., Teramo, K., Osmond, C. and Barker, D.J.P. (1997) Mother's weight in pregnancy and coronary heart disease in a cohort of Finnish men: follow-up study. *BMJ* **315**, 837–40

Gardosi, J., Chang, A., Kaylan, B., Sahota, D. and Symonds, E.M. (1992) Customised antenatal growth charts. *Lancet* **339**, 283–7

Gardosi, J., Mongelli, M., Wilcox, M. and Chang, A. (1995) An adjustable fetal weight standard. *Ultrasound Obstet Gynecol* **6**, 168–74

Grant, A., Elbourne, D., Valentin, L. and Alexander, S. (1989) Routine formal fetal movement counting and risk of late antepartum late deaths in normally formed singletons. *Lancet* **ii**, 345–9

GRIT Study Group (1996) When do obstetricians recommend delivery for a high-risk preterm growth retarded fetus? *Eur J Obstet Gynecol Reprod Biol* **67**, 121–6

Gulmezoglu, M., de Onis, M. and Villar, J. (1997) Effectiveness of interventions to prevent or treat impaired fetal growth. *Obstet Gynecol Surv* **52**, 139–49

Hepburn, M. and Rosenberg, K. (1986) An audit of the detection and management of small-for-gestational-age babies. *Br J Obstet Gynaecol* **93**, 212–16

Herman, A.A., McCarthy, B.J., Bakewell, J.M. *et al.* (1997) Data linkage methods used in maternity-linked data birth and infant death surveillance data sets from the United States (Georgia, Missouri, Utah and Washington), Israel, Norway, Scotland and Western Australia. *Paediatr Perinat Epidemiol* **11** Suppl 1, 5–22

Howe, D.T. (1994) 'Maternal factors, fetal size and placental ratio at 18 weeks: their relationship to final size' in: R.H.T. Ward, S.K. Smith and D. Donnai (Eds) *Early Fetal Growth and Development*, pp. 345–54. London: RCOG Press

Joyce, T. (1990) The dramatic increase in the rate of low birth weight in New York City: an aggregate time-series analysis. *Am J Public Health* **80**, 682–4

Kean, L.H. and Liu, D.T. (1996) Antenatal care as a screening tool for the detection of small-for-gestational-age babies in the low-risk population. *Journal of Obstetrics and Gynaecology* **16**, 77–82

Khong, T.Y., DeWolf, F., Robertson, W.B. and Brosen, I. (1986) Inadequte maternal vascular response to placentation in pregnancies complicated by pre-eclampsia and by small for gestational age infants. *Br J Obstet Gynaecol* **93**, 1049–59

Kramer, M.S. (1987) Determinants of low birth weight: methodological assessment and meta-analysis. *Bull World Health Organ* **65**, 663–737

Kramer, M.S. (1998) Socio-economic determinants of intrauterine growth retardation. *Eur J Clin Nutr* **52** Suppl 1, S29–33

Kuhn, P., Brizot, M.L., Pandya, P.P., Snijders, R.J. and Nicolaides, K.H. (1995) Crown–rump length in chromosomally abnormal fetuses at 10–13 weeks gestation. *Am J Obstet Gynecol* **172**, 32–5

Kusin, J.A., Kardjati, S., Houtkooper, J.M. and Renqvist, U.H. (1992) Energy supplementation and postnatal growth. *Lancet* **340**, 623–6

Leeda, M., Riyazi, N., de Vries, J.I., Jakobs, C., van Geijn, H.P. and Dekker, G.A. (1998) Effects of folic acid and vitamin B$_6$ supplementation on women with hyperhomocysteinemia and a history of preeclampsia or fetal growth restriction. *Am J Obstet Gynecol* **179**, 135–9

Leitich, H., Egarter, C., Husslein, P., Kaider, A. and Schemper, M. (1997) A meta-analysis of low dose aspirin for the prevention of intrauterine growth retardation. *Br J Obstet Gynaecol* **104**, 450–9

Ley, D., Tideman, E., Laurin, J., Bjerre, I. and Maršál, K. (1996) Abnormal fetal aortic velocity waveform and intellectual function at 7 years of age. *Ultrasound Obstet Gynecol* **8**, 160–5

Lindhard, A., Nielsen, P.V., Mouritsen, L.A., Zachariassen, A., Sorensen, H.U. and Roseno, H. (1990) The implications of introducing the symphyseal–fundal height-measurement. A prospective randomized controlled trial. *Br J Obstet Gynaecol* **97**, 675–80

Lubchenko, L.O., Hansman, C., Dressler, M. and Boyd, B. (1963) Intrauterine growth as estimated by birtweight data from 24–42 weeks of gestation. *Pediatrics* **32**, 793–800

Lumley, J., Oliver, S. and Waters, E. (1999) 'Smoking cessation programs implemented during pregnancy' in: *The Cochrane Library*, Issue 1. Oxford: Update Software

McBurney, R.D. (1947) The undernourished full term infant. A case report. *The Western Journal of Surgery, Obstetrics and Gynaecology* **55**, 363–70

McIntosh, J.E.A. and Chard, T. (1995) The influence on a 'normal' birth weight distribution of a minor population of growth retarded infants: a Monte Carlo simulation. *Eur J Obstet Gynecol Reprod Biol* **60**, 41–4

Meis, P.J., Michielutte, R., Peters, T.J. *et al.* (1997) Factors associated with term low birth weight in Cardiff, Wales. *Paediatr Perinat Epidemiol* **11**, 287–97

Moore, V.M., Cockington, R.A., Ryan, P. and Robinson, J.S. (1999) The relationship between birth weight and blood pressure amplifies from childhood to adulthood. *J Hypertens* **17**, 883–8

Neilson, J.P. and Alfirevic, Z. (1999) 'Doppler ultrasound in high risk pregnancies' in: *The Cochrane Library*, Issue 1. Oxford: Update Software

Neilson, J.P., Munjanja, S.P. and Whitfield, C.R. (1984) Screening for small-for-dates fetuses: a controlled trial. *BMJ* **289**, 1179–82

Nicolini, U., Nicolaides, P., Fisk, N.M. *et al.* (1990) Limited role of fetal blood sampling in prediction of outcome in intrauterine growth retardation. *Lancet* **336**, 768–72

O'Brien, P.M.S., Wheeler, T. and Barker, D.J.P. (Eds) (1999) *Fetal Programming: Influences on Development and Disease in Later Life*. London: RCOG Press

Palmer, L., Blair, E., Petterson, B. and Burton, P. (1995) Antenatal antecedents of moderate and severe cerebral palsy. *Paediatr Perinat Epidemiol* **9**, 171–84

Pattison, N. and McCowan, L. (1999) 'Cardiotocography for antepartum fetal assessment' in: *The Cochrane Library*, Issue 1. Oxford: Update Software

Persson, P-H. (1992) 'Fetal growth curves' in: F. Sharp, R.B. Fraser and R.D.G. Milner (Eds) *Fetal Growth*, pp. 13–25. London: RCOG Press

Peters, T.J., Butler, N.R., Fryer, J.G. and Chamberlain, G.V.P. (1983) *Plus ça change*: predictors of birth weight in two national studies. *Br J Obstet Gynaecol* **90**, 1040–5

Power, C. (1994) National trends in birth weight: implications for future adult disease. *BMJ* **308**, 1270–1

Rai, R., Cohen, H., Dave, M. and Regan, L. (1997) Randomised controlled trial of aspirin and aspirin plus heparin in pregnant women with recurrent miscarriage associated with phospholipid antibodies (or antiphospholipid antibodies). *BMJ* **314**, 253–7

Robinson, J.S., McMillen, C., Edwards, L. *et al.* (1999) 'The effect of maternal nutrition on growth and development before and after birth' in: P.M.S. O'Brien, T. Wheeler and D.J.P. Barker (Eds) *Fetal Programming: Influences on Development and Disease in Later Life*, pp. 217–30. London: RCOG Press

Rush, D. (1989) 'Effect of change in protein and calorie intake during pregnancy on growth of the human fetus' in: I. Chalmers, M. Enkin and M.J.N.C. Keirse (Eds) *Effective Care in Pregnancy and Childbirth*, pp. 255–80. Oxford: Oxford University Press

Shalev, E., Blondheim, O. and Peleg, D. (1995) Use of cordocentesis in the management of preterm and growth-restricted fetuses with abnormal monitoring. *Obstet Gynecol Surv* **50**, 839–44

Simpson, A.R. (1907) *Introduction to The Nursling by Pierre Budin*. London: Caxton

Soothill, P.W., Nicolaides, K.H. and Campbell, S. (1987) Prenatal asphxia, hyperlacticaemia, hypoglycaemia, and erythroblastosis in growth retarded fetuses. *BMJ* **294**, 1051–6

Soothill, P.W., Ajayi, R.A., Campbell, S. *et al.* (1992) Relationship between fetal acidemia at cordocentesis and subsequent neurodevelopment. *Ultrasound Obstet Gynecol* **2**, 80–3

Steckel, R.H. (1998) Birth weights and still births in historical perspective. *Eur J Clin Nutr* **52** Suppl 1, S16–20

Stratton, J.F., Ni Scanaill, S., Stuart, B. and Turner, M.J. (1995) Are babies of normal birth weight who fail to reach their growth potential as diagnosed by ultrasound at increased risk? *Ultrasound Obstet Gynecol* **5**, 114–18

Thomson, A.M., Billewicz, W.Z. and Hytten, F.E. (1968) The assessment of fetal growth. *J Obstet Gynaecol Br Cwlth* **75**, 903–16

World Health Organization (1961) *Public Health Aspects of Low Birth Weight*. Geneva: WHO (Technical Report Series no. 217)

13

Prenatal diagnosis

Charles H. Rodeck and Anna P. Cockell

THE HISTORY OF PRENATAL DIAGNOSIS

The prevalence of congenital abnormalities, from major to minor, is in the region of 2% (Baird et al. 1988). Prenatal diagnosis of certain congenital birth defects has, in some guise or other, been rapidly incorporated into routine antenatal care since it was initiated in the 1960s. Prenatal diagnosis plays an important role in determining fetal normality for potential parents but also allows them the widest options after diagnosis of an abnormality. This may be to prepare the mother and family prior to delivery, allowing optimisation of antenatal management and providing treatment that may limit intrauterine progression of disease, or allow her to opt for termination and prevent handicap.

Diseases such as haemophilia, following X-linked inheritance, were the first group of severe inherited disorders that became amenable to prenatal diagnosis in 1960 (Riis and Fuchs 1960). In families at high risk of these diseases, fetal sex was determined by identifying the Barr body in amniocytes of female fetuses. Fetal karyotype was diagnosed from amniocyte culture in 1965 (Steele and Breg 1965) and then the first report of cytogenetic prenatal diagnosis of Down syndrome by amniocentesis followed in 1968 (Valenti et al. 1968). The finding of elevated levels of amniotic fluid α-fetoprotein (α-FP) in anencephalic fetuses was made in 1972 (Brock and Sutcliffe 1972). Although transcervical endoscopic chorionic villus sampling (CVS) had been described as early as 1968 (Mohr 1968), CVS was only introduced into routine clinical practice in the 1980s. The initial attempts to culture villi obtained by CVS had been disappointing and, coincident with the emerging evidence of the safety of second trimester amniocentesis, CVS was initially ignored. However, as gene analysis using recombinant DNA technology developed, interest in CVS returned. Prenatal diagnosis of fetal haemoglobinopathies by direct gene analysis from chorionic villi was reported in 1982 (Old et al. 1982). Fetal karyotyping was then reported from culture of mesenchymal trophoblast cells (Niazi et al. 1981) and from direct analysis on cytotrophoblast in 1983 (Simoni et al. 1983). Fetoscopy and fetal blood sampling then emerged as the next stage in prenatal diagnosis.

The first attempts to obtain fetal blood directly were by blind placental aspiration causing bleeding from the chorionic plate into the amniotic cavity and then aspiration of blood stained amniotic fluid (Valenti 1973). Not surprisingly, the maternal contamination and fetal loss rate were unacceptable. Fetoscopy-guided needling of the umbilical cord was the first satisfactory method of fetal blood sampling (Rodeck and Campbell 1978). Development of ultrasound allowed non-invasive visualisation of the fetus and its rapid evolution led to its widespread use as both a screening and diagnostic tool for prenatal diagnosis. Ultrasound-guided needling of the fetus and its circulation has now replaced the fetoscopic approach (Daffos *et al.* 1983). Significant developments have been made in the areas of cytogenetics, biochemistry and molecular biology, allowing many disorders to be amenable to prenatal diagnosis by amniocentesis or CVS. Fetal blood sampling, with its inherently higher fetal loss rate, is now only indicated in certain disorders or gestations when the less invasive methods are unable to give a reliable diagnosis.

Screening of low-risk populations for genetic defects is now integral to antenatal care in the developed world. Screening policies have been widely introduced for prenatal diagnosis of both Down syndrome and neural tube defects. This has led to the widespread introduction of maternal serum screening using various serological parameters, and also to the routine use of ultrasound in both the first and second trimesters of pregnancy. Aneuploidy may be screened for using the first trimester scan (including the nuchal translucency measurement) and also by the use of sonographic markers and structural anomalies in the second trimester.

Prenatal diagnosis has been rapidly accepted within antenatal care in accordance with modern society's changing attitudes to childbearing, congenital defects and religious beliefs. In this changing climate, with the reluctance to accept physical handicap, the ethical issues implicit in prenatal diagnosis should not be ignored. Furthermore, economic constraints will be increasingly important as medical resources are challenged by the rapid growth of these technologies and choices.

INVASIVE TESTING – INDICATIONS AND COMPLICATIONS

Invasive tests in pregnancy are used to obtain fetal cells, fluids or tissues for prenatal diagnosis (Table 1). These may be indicated when fetal karyotype, DNA, infection or a biochemical assay is being investigated. The choice of invasive test (Table 2) is determined by the indication and fetal gestation, balanced against the safety of the procedure (for review see Jauniaux and Rodeck 1995).

Amniocentesis

The risk of miscarriage following amniocentesis is approximately 1 in 100, based on the only randomised controlled trial (Tabor *et al.* 1986). The amniotic membrane may fail to seal and this may lead to persistent amniotic fluid leakage or chorioamnionitis. There is a small risk of fetal injury but is this is minimised by ultrasound guidance. The risks to the pregnancy are increased if the procedure is performed as early as 11–13 weeks' gestation, as shown by two recent studies. The first study compared early with conventional (at least 15 weeks' gestation) amniocentesis (CEMAT Group1998) while the second compared early amniocentesis with CVS (Sundberg *et al.* 1997). In both studies, fetal loss

Table 1 *Prenatal diagnostic tests*

Non-invasive diagnosis	*Invasive diagnosis*
Ultrasound	Amniocentesis Chorionic villus sampling Fetal blood sampling Fetal tissue sampling

Table 2 *Fetal invasive tests and common current indications*

Invasive test	Indications
Amniocentesis	Karyotype Biochemical assay OD 450 (rhesus disease) Blood grouping (e.g. rhesus, platelets)
Chorionic villus sampling	Karyotype Single gene defects (e.g. haemoglobinopathies)
Fetal blood sampling	Anaemia Infection Alloimmune thrombocytopenia Karyotype

and talipes equinovarus was found to be increased in the early amniocentesis group. Longer-term complications may include respiratory problems in the neonate (Tabor *et al.* 1986). Amniocentesis is now recommended from 15 weeks' gestation. High resolution ultrasound has replaced its use in the diagnosis of neural tube defects.

Chorionic villus sampling

The indications for CVS are similar to those for amniocentesis, although it has not been used as frequently for fetal karyotyping. It can be performed transcervically or transabdominally. The preferred route and technique is determined by the placental localisation, gestation, safety of the procedure and operator experience. The transcervical approach to the placenta is limited to 10–13 weeks' gestation, by the distance to, and localisation of, the placenta. The transabdominal approach can be performed at any gestation after 11 weeks and is only limited by the accessibility of the placenta. Slight vaginal bleeding may occur after transcervical sampling (1–4%) (Rhoads *et al.* 1989), but this is normally from the cervix. Intrauterine infection and chorioamnionitis are rare but serious complications (less than 0.1%) (Jauniaux and Rodeck 1995). Reports have associated CVS with a higher incidence of transverse limb-reduction defects and oromandibular limb hypogenesis than the background frequency of limb-reduction defects in the general population (0.03–0.06%). However, this is now recognised to be closely related to the gestation at the time of the CVS. A much higher incidence of limb-reduction defects occurs in pregnancies when a CVS is performed before nine weeks' gestation compared with sampling after nine and a half weeks' gestation, suggesting a gestational age relationship (Brambati *et al.* 1992; Rodeck 1993). Trauma to the placenta is also an important factor and it has been shown that single-needle transabdominal CVS by aspiration causes more placental disruption and fetomaternal haemorrhage than transcervical biopsy forceps (Rodeck *et al.* 1993).

Fetal blood sampling

Fetal blood sampling is performed for rapid determination of fetal karyotype later in pregnancy, for prenatal diagnosis of haemoglobinopathies, coagulopathies and immunodeficiencies. It is also used in the assessment of fetal infection, the alloimmunised fetus and non-immune hydrops. Assessment of fetal well-being from blood acid-base parameters in the growth-restricted fetus has no longer been found to be helpful. The site for sampling is determined by the fetal and placental position, the placental insertion of the umbilical vein being the most commonly used site. The intrahepatic vein yields a pure fetal venous sample, minimising risks of arterial spasm, cord tamponade and feto-maternal haemorrhage. Published fetal-loss rates following fetal blood sampling are between 0% (Pielet *et al*. 1988) and 24.7% (Maxwell *et al*. 1991). However, fetal loss rates are related to the indication for the procedure, with losses of up to 12.7% in severe growth restriction and 0.99% for diagnosis of haemoglobinopathies (Antsaklis *et al*. 1998). Other complications include fetomaternal alloimmunisation, chorioamnionitis, preterm delivery and abruption. The complication rate falls as both fetal gestation and operator experience increase.

Fetal tissue or body fluid sampling

Many disorders do not have a chromosomal abnormality or an enzyme defect expressed in chorion, fetal blood or cultured amniocytes or, alternatively, a DNA probe may not be available. Prenatal diagnosis is then achieved by direct fetal tissue sampling. In inherited skin disorders (for example, epidermolysis bullosa letalis) histology, immunofluorescent and ultrastructural studies on fetal skin are used (Rodeck *et al*. 1980). In a few rare and lethal inborn errors of metabolism where protein expression is localised to hepatocytes (for example, ornithine carbamyl transferase deficiency) liver biopsy is used (Rodeck *et al*. 1982). For the assessment of renal function in fetuses with renal pathology, aspiration of the bladder or of a hydronephrosis can be performed. Urine biochemistry can be compared to the reference ranges for gestational age, to confirm normal renal function (Nicolini *et al*. 1992). The risk of fetal loss secondary to ultrasound-guided invasive procedures for fetal tissue or body fluid sampling is 1–2%, probably no higher than the risks associated with fetal blood sampling.

Cytogenetics and prenatal diagnosis

The rapid development of cytogenetics over the last 30 years has increased the armamentarium of options in prenatal diagnosis. Fetal cells in amniotic fluid require one to three weeks' culture to provide sufficient dividing cells (metaphase nuclei) for karyotype analysis. Between 15 and 20 weeks' gestation, the viable cell to amniotic fluid ratio optimises culture yield. Chorionic villi from CVS consist of an inner mesenchymal core and an outer cytotrophoblast, the latter in particular containing dividing cells. The cytotrophoblast will yield metaphases suitable for direct analysis and short-term culture (48 hours) and results can be backed up by long-term culture of the mesenchymal core. Fetal blood provides lymphocytes which grow well. With any technique there is a risk of cell-culture failure, a risk quoted as approximately 1%. Maternal cell contamination is a recognised complication, although rare, and particularly important in the long-term culture of chorionic villi. Results from chorionic villi may be mosaic, a recognised cause of failed diagnosis, although it may be placentally confined, and have arisen from non-disjunction in the actively dividing cytotrophoblast cells. Culture of the mesenchyme may solve the problem but an amniocentesis may be required to determine fetal karyotype.

Fluorescence *in situ* hybridisation (FISH) can now be used to accurately and rapidly exclude the major trisomies (13, 18, 21) and sex chromosome anomalies (XO, XXY, XYY) by using specific DNA probes. It has been shown to provide a quick accurate result (24–48 hours) in a large pilot study of 904 cases (Eiben *et al.* 1998). Non-dividing cells (interphase nuclei) can be used in this technique. Double-stranded DNA is treated to become single-stranded and mixed, to allow hybridisation, with fluorescent labelled single-stranded probes. This can, in the first instance, be used in the investigation of ultrasound-detected anomalies. FISH on amniocytes is now often used in preference to direct preparations from CVS, avoiding the detection of placentally confined mosaicism.

Choice of invasive test in prenatal diagnosis

The choice of test for prenatal diagnosis involves balancing the risk to the fetus and the appropriate test for diagnosis; potential parents seek an early and safe test. However, invasive testing in the first trimester has a higher fetal loss rate than in the second, and many pregnancies complicated with serious abnormalities will spontaneously abort in the first or early second trimester. Any benefit attributed to early first-trimester diagnosis must be carefully weighed against the potential harm which may result from making parents choose to terminate a wanted pregnancy which might have been lost spontaneously (Chitty *et al.* 1998). The role of fetal blood sampling in prenatal diagnosis has declined, particularly for rapid fetal karyotyping. FISH analysis of amniocytes (see above) and an increased use of 'late' CVS with advances in the molecular techniques for genetic diagnosis, fetal genotyping and fetal infection have led to this decline. There has also been an increase in the use of non-invasive assessment of the fetus for rhesus iso-immunisation and intrauterine growth restriction (Doppler velocimetry waveform assessment and fetal liver and spleen measurements).

SCREENING VERSUS DIAGNOSTIC TESTS IN PRENATAL DIAGNOSIS

Standard screening policies to detect Down syndrome initially relied on the maternal age-related risk (Hook 1981), offering fetal karyotyping to women over the age of 35 years. However, this failed to reduce the incidence significantly, as the majority of affected babies are born to women under the age of 35 years (Walker and Howard 1986). This stimulated the development of screening tests to identify pregnancies at high risk of aneuploidy. In the prenatal diagnosis of Down syndrome, the maternal age-related risk may be altered by results of maternal serum screening and/or nuchal translucency measurements (see below). Alternatively, ultrasound screening in the second trimester may be used to identify structural defects that are known to be associated with aneuploidy, for example a cardiac abnormality. An invasive diagnostic test for karyotyping may then be considered in these pregnancies. Screening tests should have a high sensitivity (detection rate) and high specificity (low false-positive rate). Diagnostic tests must be as safe and accurate as possible.

ULTRASOUND IN PRENATAL DIAGNOSIS

Second trimester ultrasonography

Routine ultrasound screening is recommended in the UK (RCOG 1984) and performed at 18–20 weeks' gestation when the fetal heart and kidney structures become more discernible. This anomaly scan includes a series of pre-defined images to obtain standardised measurements. An evaluation is made of the key structures, for example intracranial structures, fetal spine, kidneys, heart and extremities. This detects 60–80% of major and 35% of minor congenital malformations (Chitty *et al.* 1991; Luck 1992). An increased sensitivity for ultrasound diagnosis is achieved in high-risk pregnancies where a specific fetal part is surveyed, for example following a high maternal serum α-FP (MS α-FP) suggestive of a neural tube defect or a family history of a cardiac abnormality. The diagnosis of neural tube defects has now been reported to be almost 100% with the combined use of MS α-FP and high-resolution ultrasound scan (Chan *et al.* 1993). The cranial signs of neural tube defects have been well reported and now play an important part in screening for these anomalies (Nicolaides *et al.* 1986). The detection rates for open spina bifida are 80–100% using ultrasound alone without MS α-FP (Hill 1999), although small defects may only be detected in a referral setting in the presence of cranial signs. Most units are now relying on high-resolution ultrasound alone. A standard four-chamber view of the heart is included in the anomaly scan. This view demonstrates the four cardiac chambers, the ventricular and atrial septa and valves of the chambers (De Vore 1985) and will detect 25% of fetal cardiac abnormalities, which includes the majority of the most serious cardiac anomalies.

Subtle features of aneuploidy may be detected by ultrasound (for review see Nesbit and Chitty 1999), which otherwise have no consequence to the pregnancy outcome in the longer term. They include the identification of pyelectasis (mild renal pelvic dilatation), hyperechogenic bowel, bilateral mild ventriculomegaly and clinodactyly. These can be readily identified within the routine second-trimester anomaly scan. Identification of these 'markers' may modify risk estimates of aneuploidy initially determined by maternal age and serum screening. However, the majority of studies reporting the associations of markers with aneuploidy have been based on selected populations and extrapolation of the associated risks to a low-risk population may be inappropriate.

First-trimester ultrasonography

With improved technology, particularly with the use of transvaginal probes (Achiron and Tadmor 1991), it has become possible to assess fetal anatomy in the late first and early second trimester (Timor-Tritsch *et al.* 1988; Cullen *et al.* 1989). First-trimester sonographic assessment of fetal anatomy has become an important component of prenatal diagnosis. It requires a good understanding of embryological development and diagnostic criteria and limitations for specific anomalies must be clearly established before first-trimester ultrasound screening can be introduced universally (Green and Hobbins 1988). A normal sonographic assessment at 12 weeks' gestation can be reassuring, yet such reassurances must be guarded in view of the failure to detect some anomalies that are sonographically gestation-dependent, for example duodenal atresia and hydrocephalus. The natural history of some conditions detected in the first trimester remains unclear, for example bright echogenic kidneys and choroid plexus cysts. Furthermore, some findings resolve spontaneously with no long-term consequences, e.g. cystic hygroma.

An increased nuchal translucency thickness in the first trimester was reported to have an association with aneuploidy by Bronshtein *et al.* (1989) and with Down syndrome by Szabo and Gellen (1990). The nuchal translucency is the maximum thickness of the subcutaneous translucency between the skin and the soft tissue overlying the cervical spine of the fetus (normal nuchal translucency measurement <3 mm) and can be conveniently assessed at the dating scan between 11 and 12 weeks' gestation (for review see Chitty and Pandya 1995; Pandya *et al.* 1995). The sensitivity of this test has been variously described from 0–88% for a false-positive rate of 2.7–9.9%, based initially on high-risk or selected populations. More recently Snijders *et al.* (1998), in a multicentre audit of 96 000 low-risk pregnancies, reported a sensitivity of 82.2% with a false-positive rate of 8.3% in the detection of aneuploidy, with a high negative predictive value (99.9%). Increased nuchal translucency is also recognised to be associated with structural defects of the cardiovascular or skeletal systems, not necessarily amenable to prenatal diagnosis in the first trimester. Brady *et al.* (1998) reported abnormalities of these systems in 10.1% (nine of 89 cases) of patients with increased nuchal translucency (>3.5 mm), compared with 2% (five of 302) in those with a nuchal translucency of less than 3.5 mm. This highlights the need to perform a detailed second-trimester scan following the identification of increased nuchal translucency in a karyotypically normal fetus.

MATERNAL SERUM SCREENING IN PRENATAL DIAGNOSIS

The analysis of specific biochemical markers in the maternal serum, derived from the fetoplacental unit, is a non-invasive technique to identify pregnancies at high risk of certain birth defects. An accurate assessment of fetal age, by first trimester fetal crown–rump measurement, is paramount to interpret these values. Currently, serum maternal biochemistry is performed at 15–19 weeks' gestation for screening for neural tube defects and Down syndrome, although there are many studies evaluating a spectrum of serological markers which may be useful at earlier gestations for the detection of Down syndrome. However, the demand for earlier screening must be supported by a safe diagnostic test that can be offered at a comparable gestation.

α-FP is produced primarily from the fetal liver and levels in the fetal blood are high. Therefore any interruption in the fetal skin integrity or functional performance of the feto-placental unit will alter amniotic and therefore maternal serum levels of α-FP. A number of fetal structural abnormalities will elevate MS α-FP, such as abdominal wall defects (gastroschisis, exomphalos) and open neural tube defects. Falsely elevated MS α-FP can be due to an underestimation of fetal age, multiple pregnancy or fetal demise, thus emphasising the standard practice of performing an ultrasound scan before interpretation of serum biochemistry. A maternal serum threshold of 2.5 MoM (multiples of the median) will correctly identify 79% of the fetuses with open spina bifida (UK Collaborative Study 1982). Recent reports suggest that the detection of open spina bifida can be as high as 80–100% with ultrasound alone when using sonographic features as discussed earlier. Some units have now abandoned the use of MS α-FP screening for the detection of neural tube defects, although they may have continued its use in association with serum screening for Down syndrome.

The first maternal serum biochemical marker to be associated with Down syndrome was α-FP which was found to be 0.7–0.8 MoM in affected pregnancies. High levels of human chorionic gonadotrophin (hCG), particularly the free β-subunit, and low levels of unconjugated oestriol have been used, in combination with maternal age, to increase the sensitivity of serum screening to detect Down syndrome. The use of different combinations of markers are known as the 'double' test (α-FP and free β-hCG) and 'triple' test (α-FP, hCG and oestriol), balancing an increased sensitivity against cost effectiveness as more markers are used in combination. (Kellner *et al.* 1995). For first-trimester Down syndrome screening, maternal serum pregnancy-associated plasma protein-A (which is reduced) and free β-hCG (which is raised) may be useful (Brambati *et al.* 1993). Serum screening in the second trimester has also been reported to be useful in the detection of Edwards syndrome (trisomy 18). These pregnancies tend to have low maternal serum hCG, α-FP and unconjugated oestriol.

Developments in serum screening for prenatal diagnosis of aneuploidy continue to be made. Options include a 'two-stop' or serial screening process (a first-trimester scan followed by maternal serology at 16 weeks' gestation) or a single assessment with ultrasound and serology at 12–14 weeks' gestation. The effectiveness of these prenatal screening regimes have yet to be fully evaluated.

FUTURE DEVELOPMENTS IN PRENATAL DIAGNOSIS

There is an increasing use of both magnetic resonance imaging and 3-D sonography in prenatal diagnosis and their role will become evident in the next few years. Non-invasive techniques of obtaining fetal cells for cytogenetic diagnosis are being developed, minimising the risks to the fetus and ideally providing an early diagnosis. Nucleated fetal haemopoietic cells and fragments of syncytiotrophoblast are shed into the maternal blood stream during pregnancy and can provide cells for karyotypic analysis (Price *et al.* 1991). These cells carry specific antigens and can be separated from maternal cells by immunological methods but, currently, this provides a poor yield with low sensitivity for prenatal diagnosis. Fetal cells have also been obtained non-invasively from cervical mucus prior to transcervical CVS (Adinolfi *et al.* 1995). However, again the yield of fetal cells is disappointing for reliable fetal diagnosis.

Newer laboratory techniques are developing to more rapidly process cytogenetic material obtained invasively. Polymerase chain reaction (PCR) on amniotic fluid samples, with amplification of chromosome-specific DNA markers, can provide a rapid result. A recent study by Verma *et al.* (1998) reported informative results in 99.6% of non-blood stained samples and correctly classified 32 cases of Down syndrome using this technique. Quantitative fluorescent multiplex PCR amplifies polymorphic small tandem repeats specific for two loci on each chromosome and this has also been reported to be effective in the rapid detection of chromosome anomalies (Pertl *et al.* 1996). Comparative genomic hybridisation, another relatively new cytogenetic technique, is based on a combination of fluorescein microscopy and digital image analysis. Hybridisation of a mixture of fluorescein-labelled test DNA and reference DNA on normal metaphase chromosomes is performed. Comparative analysis allows identification of all unbalanced chromosome aberrations of test DNA in a single experimental step.

CONCLUSIONS

Prenatal diagnosis has been rapidly expanding over the last 30 years. It has become incorporated into routine antenatal care in the guise of routine ultrasonography for major structural abnormalities and maternal serum screening for aneuploidy. As ultrasonographic equipment, cytogenetic technology and molecular biology have improved, it has become possible to perform prenatal diagnosis for an increasing number of fetal conditions and earlier in gestation.

References

Achiron, R. and Tadmor, O. (1991) Screening for fetal anomalies during the first trimester of pregnancy: transvaginal versus transabdominal sonography. *Ultrasound Obstet Gynecol* **1**, 186–91

Adinolfi, M., Sherlock, J., Soothill, P. and Rodeck, C. (1995) Molecular evidence of fetal derived chromosome 21 markers (STRs) in transcervical samples. *Prenat Diagn* **15**, 35–9

Antsaklis, A., Daskalakis, G., Papantoniou, N. and Michalas, S. (1998) Fetal blood sampling – indication related losses. *Prenat Diagn* **18**, 934–40

Baird, P.A., Anderson, T.W., Newcombe, H.B. and Lowry, R.B. (1988) Genetic disorders in children and young adults: a population study. *Am J Hum Genet* **4**, 677–93

Brady, A.F., Pandya, P.P., Yuksel, B., Greenough, A., Patton, M.A. and Nicolaides, K.H. (1998) Outcome of chromosomally normal livebirths with increased fetal nuchal translucency at 10–14 weeks' gestation. *J Med Genet* **35**, 222–4

Brambati, B., Simoni, G., Travi, M. *et al.* (1992) Genetic diagnosis by chorionic villus sampling before 8 gestational weeks: efficiency, reliability, and risks on 317 completed pregnancies. *Prenat Diagn* **12**, 789–99

Brambati, B., MacIntosh, M.C.M. and Teisner, B. (1993) Low maternal serum levels of pregnancy associated plasma protein A (PAPP-A) in the first trimester in association with abnormal fetal karyotype. *Br J Obstet Gynaecol* **100**, 324–6

Brock, D.J.H. and Sutcliffe, R.G. (1972) Alpha-fetoprotein in the antenatal diagnosis of anencephaly and spina bifida. *Lancet* **ii**, 197–9

Bronshtein, M., Rottem, S., Yoffe, N. and Blumenfeld, Z. (1989) First trimester diagnosis of nuchal cystic hygroma by transvaginal sonography: diverse prognosis of the septated and nonseptated lesion. *Am J Obstet Gynecol* **161**, 78–82

CEMAT (The Canadian Early and Mid-trimester Amniocentesis Trial) Group (1998) Randomised trial to assess safety and fetal outcome of early and midtrimester amniocentesis. *Lancet* **351**, 242–7

Chan, A., Robertson, E.F., Haan, A., Keane, R.J., Ranieri, E. and Carney, A. (1993) Prevalence of neural tube defects in South Australia, 1966–1991. Effectiveness and impact of prenatal diagnosis. *BMJ* **307**, 703–6

Chitty, L.S. and Pandya, P.P. (1995) Ultrasound screening for fetal abnormalities in the first trimester. *Prenat Diagn* **17**, 1269–81

Chitty, L.S., Hunt, L.S., Moore, J. and Lobb, M.O. (1991) Effectiveness of routine ultrasonography in detecting fetal structural abnormalites in a low risk population. *BMJ* **303**, 1165–9

Chitty, L.S., Statham, H., Solomu, W., Dimavicis, J. and Green, J. (1998) Grief after termination for fetal abnormality – is there a gestational effect? *Ultrasound Obstet Gynecol* **12**, 1 (abstract)

Cullen, M.T., Green, J.J., Reece, E.A. and Hobbins, J.C. (1989) Evaluation of the first trimester embryo. A comparison of transvaginal and abdominal sonography. *J Ultrasound Med* **8**, 565–9

Daffos, F., Capella-Pavlovsky, M. and Foriester, F. (1983) A new procedure for fetal blood sampling *in utero. Prenat Diagn* **3**, 271–4

De Vore, G.R. (1985) Prenatal diagnosis of congenital heart disease: a practical approach for the fetal ultrasonographer. *J Clin Ultrasound* **13**, 229–35

Eiben, B., Trawaki, W., Hammans, W. *et al.* (1998) A prospective comparative study on fluorescence *in situ* hybridization (FISH) of uncultured amniocytes and standard karyotype analysis. *Prenat Diagn* **18**, 901–6

Green, J.J. and Hobbins, J.C. (1988) Abdominal ultrasound examination of the first-trimester fetus. *Am J Obstet Gynecol* **159**, 165–75

Hill, L. (1999) 'Detection of neural tube defects' in: C.H. Rodeck and M.J. Whittle (Eds) *Fetal Medicine: Basic Science and Clinical Practice*, pp. 599–640. London: Harcourt Brace

Hook, E.M. (1981) Rates of chromosome abnormalities at different maternal ages. *Obstet Gynecol* **58**, 282–5

Jauniaux, E. and Rodeck, C.H. (1995) Use, risks and complications of amniocentesis and chorionic villus sampling for prenatal diagnosis. *Early Pregnancy* **1**, 245–52

Kellner, L.H., Weiner, Z., Weiss, R.R. *et al.* (1995) Triple marker (alpha-fetoprotein, unconjugated estriol, human chorionic gonadotrophin) versus alpha-fetoprotein plus free β-subunit in second trimester maternal serum screening for fetal Down syndrome: a prospective comparison study. *Am J Obstet Gynecol* **173**, 1306–9

Luck, C.A. (1992) Value of routine ultrasound scanning at 19 weeks: a four year study of 8894 deliveries. *BMJ* **304**, 1474–8

Maxwell, D., Johnson, P., Hurley, P., Kneales, K., Allan, L. and Knott, P. (1991) Fetal blood sampling and pregnancy loss in relation to indication. *Br J Obstet Gynaecol* **98**, 892–7

Mohr, J. (1968) Foetal genetic diagnosis: development of techniques for early sampling of foetal cells. *APMIS* **73**, 73–7

Nesbit, D. and Chitty, L.S. (1999) 'Second trimester ultrasound markers of aneuploidy' in: P.M.S. O'Brien (Ed.) *Yearbook of Obstetrics and Gynaecology* **7**, 263–86. London: RCOG Press

Niazi, M., Coleman, D.V. and Loeffler, F.E. (1981) Trophoblast sampling in early pregnancy. Culture of rapidly dividing cells from immature placental villi. *Br J Obstet Gynaecol* **88**, 1081–5

Nicolaides, K.H., Campbell, S., Gabbe, S.G. and Guidetti, R. (1986) Ultrasound screening for spina bifida: cranial and cerebellar signs. *Lancet* **ii**, 72–4

Nicolini, U., Fisk, N.M., Rodeck, C.H. and Beacham, J. (1992) Fetal urine biochemistry: an index of renal maturation and dysfunction. *Br J Obstet Gynaecol* **99**, 46–50

Old, J.M., Ward, R.H.T., Petrou, M., Karagozlu, F., Modell, B. and Weatherall, D.J. (1982) First trimester diagnosis of haemoglobinopathies: three cases. *Lancet* **ii**, 1413–16

Pandya, P.P., Snijders, R.J.M., Johnson, S.J., Brizot, M. and Nicolaides, K.H. (1995) Screening for fetal trisomies by maternal age and fetal nuchal translucency thickness at 10 to 14 weeks of gestation. *Br J Obstet Gynaecol* **102**, 957–62

Pertl, B., Weitgasser, U., Kopp, S., Kroisel, P.M., Sherlock, J. and Adinolfi, M. (1996) Rapid detection of trisomies 21 and 18 and sexing by quantitive fluorescent multiplex PCR. *Hum Genet* **98**, 55–9

Pielet, B.W., Socol, M.L. and MacGregor, S.N. (1988) Cordocentesis: an appraisal of risks. *Am J Obstet Gynecol* **159**, 1497–500

Price, J.O., Elias, S., Wachtel, S.S. *et al.* (1991) Prenatal diagnosis with fetal cells isolated from maternal blood by multiparameter flow cytometry. *Am J Obstet Gynecol* **165**, 1731–7

RCOG (Royal College of Obstetricians and Gynaecologists) (1984) *Report of the RCOG Working Party on Routine Ultrasound Examination in Pregnancy*. London: RCOG Press

Rhoads, G.C., Jackson, L.G., Schlesselman, S.A. *et al.* (1989) The safety and efficacy of chorionic villus sampling for early prenatal diagnosis of cytogenetic abnormalities. *N Engl J Med* **320**, 609–17

Riis, P. and Fuchs, F. (1960) Antenatal determination of foetal sex in prevention of hereditary diseases. *Lancet* **ii**, 180–2

Rodeck, C.H. (1993) Fetal development after chorionic villus sampling. *Lancet* **341**, 468–9

Rodeck, C.H. and Campbell, S. (1978) Sampling pure fetal blood by fetoscopy in second trimester of pregnancy. *BMJ* **ii**, 728–34

Rodeck, C.H., Eady, R.A. and Gosden, C.M. (1980) Prenatal diagnosis of epidermolysis bullosa letalis. *Lancet* **i**, 949–52

Rodeck, C.H., Patrick, A.D., Pembrey, M.E., Tzannotos, C. and Whitfield, A.E. (1982) Fetal liver biopsy for prenatal diagnosis of ornithine carbamyl transferase. *Lancet* **ii**, 297–300

Rodeck, C.H., Sheldrake, A., Beattie, B. and Whittle, M.J. (1993) Maternal serum alpha-protein after placental damage in chorionic villus sampling. *Lancet* **341**, 500

Simoni, G., Brambati, B., Danesino, C. *et al.* (1983) Efficient direct chromosome analysis and enzyme determinations from chorionic villi samples in the first trimester of pregnancy. *Hum Genet* **63**, 349–57

Snijders, R.J.M., Noble, P. and Souka, A.P. (1998) UK multicentre project on assessment of risk of trisomy 21 by maternal age and fetal nuchal-translucency thickness at 10–14 weeks of gestation. *Lancet* **351**, 343–6

Steele, M.W. and Breg, W.T. (1965) Chromosome analysis of human amniotic fluid cells. *Lancet* **i**, 383–5

Sundberg, K., Bang, J., Smidt-Jensen, S. *et al.* (1997) Randomised study of fetal loss related to early amniocentesis versus chorionic villus sampling. *Lancet* **350**, 697–703

Szabo, J. and Gellen, J. (1990) Nuchal fluid accumulation in trisomy 21 detected by vaginosonography in the first trimester. *Lancet* **336**, 1133

Tabor, A., Philip, J., Madson, M., Bang, J., Obel, E.B. and Norgaard-Pedersen, B. (1986) Randomised controlled trial of genetic amniocentesis in 4606 low-risk women. *Lancet* **i**, 1287–93

Timor-Tritsch, I.E., Farine, D. and Rosen, M. (1988) A close look at early embryonic development with the high-frequency transvaginal transducer. *Am J Obstet Gynecol* **159**, 676–81

UK Collaborative Study (1982) UK collaborative study on alpha-fetoprotein in relation to neural tube defects – fourth report 1982. Estimating an individuals chance of having an open spina bifida and the value of repeat AFP testing. *J Epidemiol Community Health* **36**, 87–92

Valenti, C. (1973) Antenatal detection of haemoglobinopathies. A preliminary report. *Am J Obstet Gynecol* **115**, 851–3

Valenti, C., Schutta, E.J. and Kehaty, T. (1968) Prenatal diagnosis of Down syndrome. *Lancet* **ii**, 220

Verma, L., MacDonald, F., Leedham, P., McConachie, M. and Hulten, M. (1998) Rapid and simple prenatal diagnosis of Down syndrome. *Lancet* **352**, 9–12

Walker, S. and Howard, P.J. (1986) Cytogenetic prenatal diagnosis and its relative effectiveness in the Mersey region and North Wales. *Prenat Diagn* **6**, 12–23

14

Community obstetrics and gynaecology: inpatient management on an outpatient basis

James J. Walker

HISTORY OF CARE PROVISION IN OBSTETRICS AND GYNAECOLOGY

Healthcare provision in the UK in the last century has been dominated by the introduction of the National Health Service in 1948 under the guidance of Aneurin Bevan of the then Labour government. Prior to this, most hospitals in the UK had been run by local authorities or voluntary organisations. After the NHS Act (1948), all hospitals were compulsorily acquired and all treatments became universally available and free at the point of access. All hospital doctors, nurses and ancillary staff became salaried employees of the state.

At the same time, community-based services such as district nursing, midwifery, ambulance and school health services remained the responsibility of the local councils under the supervision of the local medical officer of health. General practitioners remained outside the system and were separately contracted by the state as private businesses. This meant that, although the state is the monopoly employer of GPs, they are classified as self-employed and contracted on an 'item of service' basis. Each GP has a minimum list of general medical services that they agree to provide as a contractual obligation and it is an offence not to provide them. There is also a list of optional services that GPs may choose to provide, for which additional remuneration is received. These lists have changed over the years and some of the optional services cover areas of concern to the obstetrician and gynaecologist, such as cervical screening, family planning and obstetric care.

The original ethos behind the NHS was the belief that, with the provision of a complete healthcare service which was free at the point of access, major diseases would be eliminated and the NHS would no longer be needed. The community-based services would provide family-orientated health care, with the focus on preventative medicine, and would refer all patients with more significant conditions to hospital-based services. The problem with modern day medical practice is that, far from not being needed, the NHS has expanded and even more options for health care are available. This has inevitably increased the cost to the taxpayer. The dramatic fall in maternal and perinatal morbidity and mortality over the last 50 years and the general improvement in the health of the nation has led to a change of focus for reproductive health care, away from disease towards the screening and supportive care of a healthy population. There is also an increase in the need to manage what could be called 'softer' diseases, such as menorrhagia and pelvic pain. There has been increasing pressure to provide care outside the hospital and in an environment more focused on women themselves rather than on healthcare providers.

The natural barriers between hospitals and the community do not lend themselves to such changes, however. Recent changes to the service have aggravated the problem, with the development of hospital trusts, fundholding GPs and competition between community and acute services increasing the barriers. Despite this, there have been various developments in community-based health care. With further reorganisation of the health service into larger multihospital trusts and primary care groups which incorporate many GP practices within a geographical area, opportunities now exist to develop health-care provision with a blurring of the edges between acute services and the community, to the long-term benefit of women themselves. This can be seen as an extension of the accepted practice of shared-care between the hospital and community which has been successfully implemented for antenatal services.

CURRENT STATUS

Obstetrics

Our specialty is advanced in some areas of community-based services, particularly in obstetrics, where there is a well-established community-based obstetric service in which GPs and midwives are mutually involved in antenatal care. Initially, shared care was a concept developed to share antenatal care between the GP and the hospital consultant. Midwives were largely removed from this system to become clinic assistants rather than lead clinicians in their own right. This led to large antenatal clinics with women visiting hospital at least ten times during the antenatal period and as many as another ten visits to their GP. The move towards hospital-based antenatal care was based on an attempt to develop a comprehensive screening system to prevent high maternal and fetal morbidity and mortality. Similarly, the reductions in maternal mortality over the 1950s led to a relaxing of this attitude and a move towards returning much of antenatal care into a community-based setting.

In the 1980s, the structure of antenatal care was questioned (Hall *et al.* 1980). Various pilot schemes and trials were set up to consider how antenatal care could be changed to benefit woman and children without detriment to their care (Tucker *et al.* 1994; Turnbull *et al.* 1996). This led to the increased involvement of midwives, both in hospital clinics and in the community (Cheyne *et al.* 1995). The community midwives were, in most circumstances, organised from the local maternity unit and, although based in and working in the community, there was a blurring of the division between hospital practice and the community base, allowing easy transfer of patients in and out of the two systems. Peripheral clinics were set up, often in GP's surgeries or health clinics (Turnbull *et al.* 1996). Midwives would be the lead clinicians, working in close collaboration with GPs and with direct access to hospital consultants (Cheyne *et al.* 1995). The majority of antenatal care was based in the community and women would only go to hospital if there was need for access to technology or specific clinical skills. Various systems were set up demonstrating that there was no correct way to provide antenatal care, but showing that it could be tailored to both the woman and the environment. It did not matter who provided the antenatal care as long as people were willing to work in teams and refer women to the necessary level of skill and knowledge as the need arose. Investigations comparing community-based services to traditional hospital-based services demonstrated that there was little difference in the number of visits that a woman made during her antenatal period. There was also little difference in overall morbidity, although there might have been slight reductions in the diagnoses of mild problems within the midwife-led groups (Tucker *et al.* 1994; Ratcliffe *et al.* 1996; Turnbull *et al.* 1996; Hundley *et al.* 1997; Khan-Neelofur *et al.* 1998; Shields *et al.* 1998; Waldenstrom and Turnbull 1998).

During this time, the main loser from these developments was the GP, who felt that these changes were largely midwife-driven, often to the exclusion of the GP, who was responsible for the patient prior to and following the pregnancy. Gradually, much of this conflict has been eliminated and antenatal care in most of the country is now based on a few targeted hospital-based visits, largely related to visits for ultrasound or when medical decisions are required. Problems that have arisen are more related to the fact that in many areas the drive for change was to remove patients from hospital practice, secondary to the *Changing Childbirth* report (Department of Health 1993), rather than setting up an infrastructure within the community to run antenatal care services.

The main reason for the success of these ventures is the direct access to hospital services for those practising in the community. This has been greatly facilitated by developments begun in Glasgow in the early 1980s. The first antenatal day unit was started at the Glasgow Royal Maternity Hospital in 1981, initially targeted towards the care of women with hypertension in pregnancy, but then expanded to investigate women presenting with small-for-date fetuses, lack of fetal movements or other concerns which can be identified through the antenatal care system (Walker 1994). Day units provided an ambulatory outpatient service to which women could be referred from any antenatal care system in the community without the need for referral through a consultant clinic. The woman could be seen on the day of referral or a day suitable to them and they would have access to full inpatient monitoring on an outpatient basis. This arrangement provided community-based clinics with full hospital-based medical backup providing three levels of service provision:

(1) Within the community, with close collaboration between the midwife and the GP;

(2) An easy-referral outpatient monitoring facility providing full inpatient facilities on an ambulatory basis, supervised by senior medical staff skilled in the area;

(3) Hospital admission, which may still be required for a small number of women with specific problems.

The effect of this system on the Glasgow Royal Maternity Hospital was a dramatic fall both in the number of patients admitted per year and in average bed occupancy over the years following the introduction of the day unit and community-based clinics (Table 1). These findings have been confirmed by randomised trial (Tuffnell *et al.* 1992) and shown to be economically beneficial (Twaddle and Harper 1992). The main advantages of these structures are the levels of trust between the various care providers and the ease with which women can be transferred from the community to the day unit and back (depending on the level of risk and assessment). Common ownership of the day unit facilities by people within the community avoids the feeling that women are being referred to a separate consultant-based environment.

This model has become widely copied throughout the country and has led to a dramatic change in the way we provide antenatal care (Table 2). Much routine antenatal

Table 1 *The effects on the numbers of hypertensive patients monitored and admitted, the total number of inpatient days and the overnight antenatal bed occupancy since the opening of the antenatal daycare unit in August 1981 in the Glasgow Royal Maternity Hospital*

Year	1980	1981	1982	1983	1984	1985	1986	1987	1988	1989
Total deliveries	3817	3733	3585	3937	3991	4233	4301	4388	4109	3989
Total hypertension diagnosed	563	551	534	584	604	682	691	676	643	634
Admitted	352	343	256		146	134	121	135	120	115
Inpatient days	1065	1197	921	770	790	736	370	423	372	352
Average bed occupancy		57	55	46	34	27	24	27	22	20
Day-care referrals	0	25	75	245	423	456	485	492	482	473
Attendances	0	45	110	331	779	957	1134	1059	1102	1092

Table 2 *Current and future practice of antenatal care in Leeds*

Event	Current practice	Future practice
Booking	Mixed	Community
Booking ultrasound	Hospital	Community
Triple testing	Mixed	Community
Detailed scanning	Hospital	Mixed
Early pregnancy bleeding	Mixed	Community
Routine antenatal care	Mixed	Community
High-risk antenatal care	Hospital	Mixed
Maternal/fetal assessment	Hospital	Mixed
Post-dates assessment	Hospital	Community
Delivery	Mixed	Mixed
Postnatal care	Mixed	Mixed

care, such as booking, screening tests, counselling and parentcraft teaching, can be provided in the community setting. Attendance at hospital is only required for access to ultrasound equipment or specialised services for special needs, such as diabetes, hypertension, small-for-date fetuses or past obstetric history. The concept of shared care is now two-way, in that hospital-based services are a shared resource that community-based midwives and GPs can use, which have simple referral methods, without need of consultant approval. This practice can be made robust with consensus guidelines developed by health professionals and by the removal of the conflict encouraged by *Changing Childbirth* concerning who is the lead clinician. There is still work needed before the system is developed fully and, with changing demands and expectations, the system needs to be flexible. However, there is an acceptance of the concept that all facilities that are potentially available to the pregnant woman should be available to all, if required, without need for the care to be based within the hospital setting. At any given contact point, the individual providing the care may not have all the skills necessary to deal with all the problems with which women might present, but they should always be able to refer the woman to a clinician with the necessary expertise.

Other specialties

These developments in the antenatal care system were possible because of existing community-based services and the links that already existed between these services and hospital-based services. This is also true in other specialties, such as psychiatry (Weal 1979; Hoge *et al.* 1992) and paediatrics (Giebink 1993), where community-based services and the development of day-care units is widely established. In these situations, not only is money saved but there are other benefits in keeping patients out of hospital and in the community. Other services include access to monitoring specific problems such as drug abuse (Alterman *et al.* 1994), infectious disease (Atkins and Kohn 1992) and pelvic inflammatory disease (Cacciatore *et al.* 1992).

Good co-ordination between hospital services and the community has helped to develop services which have reduced the overall incidence of chlamydial infection, reduced ectopic pregnancy and potentially reduced long-term morbidity of infection (Egger *et al.* 1998). This is the result of close collaboration between hospital-based services that see the sequelae of these problems and the community where the initial events take place. Therefore, community-based services could not only improve access to facilities for women in need but may also reduce the long-term morbidity from complications.

The current system produces a barrier between community services and acute trusts which interferes with this concept of sharing care, not only with community-based health providers but also with family carers. However, this cannot be solved simply by transferring the current practice into outpatient or community services. Many studies into outpatient surgery have suggested that the costs and the problems are simply transferred to the community carers (Gui *et al.* 1999)

Those services that have developed successful community-based services have existing community-based facilities and some, like the psychiatric services, are currently based within community trusts. This is not the case in gynaecology, where there is still a definite demarcation between community-based and acute service care. The development of the specialty of community gynaecology is mostly isolated within the community-based services rather than closely linked with hospital-based services. This does not encourage the development of community-based gynaecological practice supported from hospital trusts nor the blurring of edges between community and hospital practice. If the development of community-based gynaecology is to progress, there must be close co-operation between acute services and community-based physicians now under the direction of the primary care groups, which can allow the development of shared-care similar to that already existing in obstetrics.

Gynaecology

Much work has already been done in developing outpatient gynaecology and the majority of gynaecological practice is now performed in an outpatient setting (Table 3). Outpatient endometrial biopsy can be carried out using ultrasound and Pipelle biopsy techniques and even more invasive techniques, such as hysteroscopy, can be provided successfully on an outpatient basis, requiring transient access for the patient to currently hospital-based facilities (Quinn and Ludkin 1997; Kremer *et al.* 1998). With the proper provision of skills and equipment, many of these services could be provided within the community (Campo *et al.* 1999), in many instances by hospital-based practitioners travelling into the community (Milne *et al.* 1992). The nurse practitioner could also develop a role modelled on the midwifery service.

Table 3 *The move from inpatient gynaecology practice to outpatient care and the overall decrease in procedures done in St James Hospital, Leeds*

Year	1992–93	1993–94	1994–95	1995–96
Total elective	7597	8069	9803	8546
Inpatient	3719	2338	2476	2218
Day cases	3878	5731	7327	6328
Percentage day cases	51	71	75	74
Acute admissions	1684	1749	1751	2740
Total admissions	9281	9818	11554	11286

Similarly, there is increasing development of gynaecological expertise within the community, both within general practice and also within the family planning structure, which now includes community gynaecology.

Colposcopy has been provided in community-based services for many years (Pfenninger 1992; Cherry *et al.* 1996) and as long as there is adequate training and good communication to hospital-based backup services, there is no reason why this provision cannot be extended. The provision of a colposcopy service within family planning clinics has a long history (Kitchener *et al.* 1987). The advantages are similar to the development of community-based obstetric care in that access to these facilities for women most at need is increased without the need for attendance at a hospital-based clinic. This means that opportunistic screening and treatment are easier to apply. Contrary to diluting the skill base, this can actually give wider access to skilled facilities.

Equipment is now smaller and more portable and easier to use by less skilled personnel, making it more easily transferred into the community. Outpatient hysteroscopy performed without general anaesthetic is well tolerated by the majority of women (Kremer *et al.* 1998). There is no reason why these facilities need to be provided within a hospital theatre as long as adequate equipment and backup facilities are available at the site of provision (Campo *et al.* 1999).

Changing practice away from hospital-based facilities into community-based services has been developed by many using educational packages and consensus guidelines (Fender *et al.* 1999). A similar approach is being made in the management of menopausal problems, for example with the development of consensus guidelines within Yorkshire increasing the confidence of GPs to provide menopause advice and care without needing to refer to specialist services. There is, however, a need to provide information to women themselves (Lee 1989) and the development of roving facilities available within health centres or even within shopping areas to provide opportunistic drop-in advice has been tried and found to be successful in pilot schemes (Campbell and Macdonald 1996; Smart 1996; Pastore and Nelson 1997).

Any development of community-based services not only requires facilities to be provided but also education of both the public and medical practitioners (Lee 1989; Fender *et al.* 1999). The expectation of what can be provided by community-based services needs to be changed, as many women feel that referral to hospital specialists will provide them with the best care. Similarly, community-based services need to be provided with the equipment and training to provide these services and need to be trusted by the hospital-based practice (Quinn and Ludkin 1997). There is a need to work closely with acute trusts to adequately develop facilities and referral systems. Development of nurse practitioner services based away from the hospital and working in the community is important in this respect. Rather than providing an area of conflict with medical practitioners, this would increase the ability of community-based physicians to provide care for their patients and would also spread the influence of hospital-based practice into the community, through working in a team environment.

Potentially, this is most easily achieved in the area of family planning, where women may require referral to hospital practice for sterilisation or termination of pregnancy. At present, these services are often performed through the GP rather than directly from community-based family planning services. Many clinics also provide other healthcare services such as smear testing, colposcopy and menopause advice. This could be far better developed to full community gynaecology provision linking closely with and blurring the edges between community-based and hospital-based practice. Women requesting contraceptive advice with a need for sterilisation or termination presenting to community-based services would have direct access to hospital-based clinics and theatres without need for separate referral. This would streamline the services provided and reduce the overall cost but maintain and improve the provision of care. The problem at the current time is that family planning services have an uncertain future, since they were previously under the control of the community trusts, which have largely disappeared with the advent of primary care groups.

There is much evidence to suggest that systems developed for day-care management within the community are of great benefit to those who use the services and are not developed just to appear modern or to save costs. Community-based services should aim to at least maintain the level of care provided and also reduce the need for hospital attendance or admission, which are expensive and inconvenient to the patient. Adequate guidelines are important, with everyone understanding their role and to whom to refer if they need help.

THE FUTURE

Future aims should be to develop facilities that provide a hub-and-spoke structure of health care (Figure 1). All women should be provided with general widespread gynaecological and obstetric practices within the community. These can provide a community-based service centred round each primary care group with facilities for the assessment and investigation of pregnancy complications and gynaecological complaints (Table 4). Further development of consensus guidelines is required.

In obstetrics, care for early pregnancy problems and day unit facilities for the later pregnancy assessment (Table 2) could be provided. Hospital-based practices, such as ultrasound and fetal monitoring, could be provided in these units with outreach services from the hospital providing support and backup. Women in early labour could be assessed within the community and in their home by community-based midwives centred in each of these area units, with admission to hospital when labour is established or if any other need arises. Similarly, after delivery women can be referred back into the community where full support facilities could be provided, including close follow-up for mother and baby. This would reduce the need for women to remain in hospital after delivery and increase the continuity of care. Many of these facilities are already in existence or could be provided relatively simply.

It is in gynaecology where most development is required. The structure should be similar. Menorrhagia, postmenopausal bleeding, pelvic pain, incontinence and abnormal

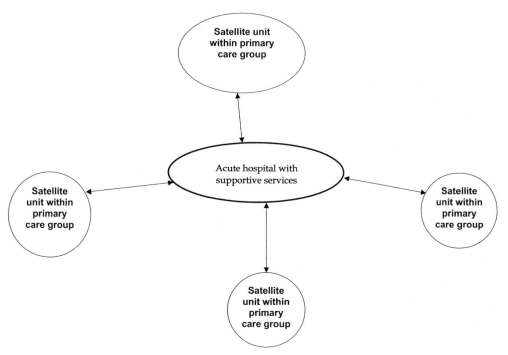

Figure 1 *The hub-and-spoke structure of health care*

Table 4 *The additional requirements of a community-based facility*

Staff	Daily attendance (hours)
Community midwife	24
Gynaecological nurse practitioner with family-planning training	24
Community-based physicians	
General practitioner	24
Community gynaecologist	12
Hospital-based visiting radiographer	4
Hospital-based visiting gynaecologist	4
Hospital-based visiting obstetrician	4

Equipment	Hours of use
Ultrasound machine	12
Colposcopy equipment	4
Hysteroscopy equipment	4
Three or four examination/consulting rooms	24
Pregnancy testing/family-planning facilities	24

Table 5 *Current and future practice of gynaecological care in Leeds*

Event	Current practice	Future practice
Endometrial biopsy	Mixed	Mixed
Colposcopy	Hospital	Mixed
Hysteroscopy	Hospital	Mixed
Gynaecological scanning	Hospital	Mixed
Urogynaecology	Hospital	Mixed
Pelvic infection	Hospital	Mixed
Pelvic pain	Mixed	Mixed
Menorrhagia	Mixed	Mixed

cervical smears could all be managed initially in the community setting with adequate ultrasound, Pipelle, hysteroscopy and colposcopy facilities being provided by people adequately trained, equipped and following accepted guidelines (Table 5). Similar facilities are required for the provision of colposcopy and hysteroscopy and could be shared. Hospital-based practitioners could go out to these units on a regular basis to provide support and backup and ensure the maintenance of standards. Close linking with existing community services, such as family planning, and hospital-based services, such as genito-urinary medicine, would help provide a wide range of reproductive health care for the women most at need, preventing multiple clinic attendances and the chance of default. Other women's healthcare provisions, such as mammography, could be provided on the same basis. The idea of short hospital stay in obstetrics can also be extended to gynaecology, where pre-operative assessments and much postoperative care could be provided within the woman's home by community-based outreach nurse practitioners. This would shorten the length of expensive hospital stays.

As we move into the next millennium we should be thinking of innovative methods of caring for the needs of women in our community and not along divisive lines of specialty and subspecialty. It is important that women are provided with the best possible care and facilities available but, as far as possible, care should be brought to them unless that is not the most efficient and best way of providing it. Many other specialties have models of people working within the hospital and also within the community setting. These changes should be a mutual development between the community and the hospital base and not complicated by purchasing and provision. Ownership should not be an issue but provision of care within the community connecting into hospital-based services as required and referral back into the community should be seamless. These developments could be linked to 24-hour community health facilities where there is a permanent presence of a midwife and reproductive health nurse with back-up from community-based physicians. These developments would mean that the siting of hospitals is less critical. The sites of provision of community-based services would be of more importance and these can be provided within the communities at most need. The poor infrastructure of our many old and decaying hospitals could be replaced by fewer hospital facilities providing 'state of the art' 24-hour medical services linked to 'state of the art' satellite services providing 24-hour support in the community in a hub-and-spoke fashion (Figure 1).

References

Alterman, A.I., O'Brien, C.P., McLellan, A.T. *et al.* (1994) Effectiveness and costs of inpatient versus day hospital cocaine rehabilitation. *J Nerv Ment Dis* **182**, 157–63

Atkins, B.L. and Kohn, P. (1992) An infectious disease day-care unit – the first year. *J Infect* **25**, 191–6

Cacciatore, B., Leminen, A., Ingman-Friberg, S., Ylostalo, P. and Paavonen, J. (1992) Transvaginal sonographic findings in ambulatory patients with suspected pelvic inflammatory disease. *Obstet Gynecol* **80**, 912–16

Campbell, H. and Macdonald, S. (1996) Evaluation of the woman's drop-in service in Benarty, Fife. *J Public Health Med* **18**, 143–51

Campo, R., Van Belle, Y., Rombauts, L., Brosens, I. and Gordts, S. (1999) Office mini-hysteroscopy. *Hum Reprod Update* **5**, 73–81

Cherry, S., Blackledge, D. and Russell, R. (1996) Colposcopy in general practice. *Aust Fam Physician* **25**, 1737–42

Cheyne, H., Turnbull, D., Lunan, C.B., Reid, M. and Greer, I.A. (1995) Working alongside a midwife-led care unit: what do obstetricians think? *Br J Obstet Gynaecol* **102**, 485–7

Department of Health (1993) *Changing Childbirth*. London: HMSO

Egger, M., Low, N., Smith, G.D., Lindblom, B. and Herrmann, B. (1998) Screening for chlamydial infections and the risk of ectopic pregnancy in a county in Sweden: ecological analysis. *BMJ* **316**, 1776–80

Fender, G.R., Prentice, A., Gorst, T. *et al.* (1999) Randomised controlled trial of educational package on management of menorrhagia in primary care: the Anglia menorrhagia education study. *BMJ* **318**, 1246–50

Giebink, G.S. (1993) Care of the ill child in day-care settings. *Pediatrics* **91**, 229–33

Gui, G.P., Cheruvu, C.V., Subak-Sharpe, I., Shiew, M., Bidlake, L. and Fiennes, A.G. (1999) Communication between hospital and general practitioners after day-case surgery: a patient safety issue. *Ann R Coll Surg Engl* **81**, 8–9, 12

Hall, M., Chang, P.K. and MacGillivray, I. (1980) Is routine antenatal care worthwhile? *Lancet* **ii**, 78–80

Hoge, M.A., Davidson, L., Hill, W.L., Turner, V.E. and Ameli, R. (1992) The promise of partial hospitalization: a reassessment. *Hospital Community Psychiatry* **43**, 345–54

Hundley, V.A., Milne, J.M., Glazener, C.M. and Mollison, J. (1997) Satisfaction and the three C's: continuity, choice and control. Women's views from a randomised controlled trial of midwife-led care. *Br J Obstet Gynaecol* **104**, 1273–80

Khan-Neelofur, D., Gulmezoglu, M. and Villar, J. (1998) Who should provide routine antenatal care for low-risk women, and how often? A systematic review of randomised controlled trials. WHO Antenatal Care Trial Research Group. *Paediatr Perinat Epidemiol* **12** Suppl 2, 7–26

Kitchener, H.C., Burnett, R.A., Wilson, E.S. and Cordiner, J.W. (1987) Colposcopy in a family planning clinic: a future model? *BMJ* **294**, 1313–15

Kremer, C., Barik, S. and Duffy, S. (1998) Flexible outpatient hysteroscopy without anaesthesia: a safe, successful and well tolerated procedure. *Br J Obstet Gynaecol* **105**, 672–6

Lee, T. (1989) Patient information: the key to increased automony. *Professional Nurse* **5**, 43–4

Milne, R.G., Torsney, B. and Watson, J. (1992) The chief scientist reports. Consultant outpatient services: provision at health centres in Scotland. *Health Bull (Edinb)* **50**, 457–67

Pastore, M.T. and Nelson, A. (1997) A breastfeeding drop-in center survey evaluation. *Journal of Human Lactation* **13**, 291–8

Pfenninger, J.L. (1992) Colposcopy in a family practice residency. The first 200 cases. *J Fam Pract* **34**, 67–72

Quinn, P. and Ludkin, H. (1997) 3M NATN Joint Award 1996. Bradford's direct access hysteroscopy service. *Br J Theatre Nursing* **6**, 8–10

Ratcliffe, J., Ryan, M. and Tucker, J. (1996) The costs of alternative types of routine antenatal care for low-risk women: shared care vs care by general practitioners and community midwives. *J Health Serv Res Policy* **1**, 135–40

Shields, N., Turnbull, D., Reid, M., Holmes, A., McGinley, M. and Smith, L.N. (1998) Satisfaction with midwife-managed care in different time periods: a randomised controlled trial of 1299 women. *Midwifery* **14**, 85–93

Smart, S. (1996) Addressing the health needs of teenagers with a drop-in clinic. *Nursing Standard* **10**, 43–5

Tucker, J., Du, V.F., Howie, P., McIlwaine, G. and Hall, M. (1994) Is antenatal care apportioned according to obstetric risk? The Scottish antenatal care study. *J Public Health Med* **16**, 60–70

Tuffnell, D.J., Lilford, R.J., Buchan, P.C. *et al.* (1992) Randomised controlled trial of day-care for hypertension in pregnancy. *Lancet* **339**, 224–7

Turnbull, D., Holmes, A., Shields, N. *et al.* (1996) Randomised, controlled trial of efficacy of midwife-managed care. *Lancet* **348**, 213–18

Twaddle, S. and Harper, V. (1992) An economic-evaluation of day-care in the management of hypertension in pregnancy. *Br J Obstet Gynaecol* **99**, 459–63

Waldenstrom, U. and Turnbull, D. (1998) A systematic review comparing continuity of midwifery care with standard maternity services. *Br J Obstet Gynaecol* **105**, 1160–70

Walker, J.J. (1994) Daycare assessment and hypertensive disorders of pregnancy. *Fetal Maternal Med Rev* **6**, 57–70

Weal, E. (1979) Not hospital, not home: partial care fills a gap. *Innovations* **6**, 25–9

15

HIV and pregnancy: national and international perspectives

Frank Johnstone

HISTORY

HIV is a global pandemic, which has dominated public and scientific attention in the late twentieth century. The particular resonance from the conjunction of sex, travel, young adulthood, death and a new virus has defined it in the public mind as the archetypal modern-day plague. In many countries, deaths from HIV disease are significantly reducing life expectancy for women and children. How have we reached this point?

HIV type 1, the main cause of AIDS, probably crossed to humans from a single sub-species of chimpanzee (Gao *et al.* 1999). The chimpanzee immunodeficiency virus may have been present for hundreds of thousands of years but phylogenetic analysis suggests that the inter-species jump occurred (at least three times) as recently as 50–60 years ago (Zhu *et al.* 1998). Microbial cross-species transmission is relatively frequent (Weiss and Wrangham 1999) but setting up a long transmission chain is rare. What propelled HIV spread in the initial, silent epidemic is uncertain. Altered patterns of sexual behaviour, urbanisation, migration, increasing population density and much easier access to transport were all probably important.

From the initial epicentre, the relentless spread of HIV and AIDS as a predominantly sexually transmitted disease has continued. Indeed the pandemic is increasingly out of control, with 1% of all sexually active adults now infected and 16 000 more people becoming infected each day (Editorial 1998). The greatest impact has been in sub-Saharan Africa, where ten million women of childbearing age are currently infected and prevalence rates of 35% or higher are reported in antenatal clinic attendees in some urban areas. Mortality has risen dramatically and tragically. Although the numbers of infected people in Africa are at least stabilising and in other parts of the world (Europe, North America, Latin America) stabilising or falling, it is the explosive exponential increase in South-east Asia which is defining the scale of the pandemic for the next century. By 1990, HIV was the third leading cause of death in adults in their prime years in the developing world (Carael *et al.* 1998). There have been reversals of many of the hard-won improvements in child survival.

There has been an enormous and unparalleled research effort. The first report of disease was in 1981, following deaths in gay men from rare opportunistic infections. Two years later HIV-1 was identified. It was cultured the next year and a serological test was made generally available in 1985. Since then, our knowledge of HIV has far superseded that for any other virus. There have also been profound advances in understanding of the immune system (Pantaleo 1999). The scientific effort on pregnancy has been particularly impressive. The early establishment of cohorts such as the European Collaborative Study Group meant that data were collected systematically and many prevailing uncertainties were resolved. A number of important randomised controlled trials make this one of the most clearly evidence-based subjects in pregnancy management. Perinatal transmission can now be substantially reduced.

In recent years, the availability of quantitative measurements of plasma viraemia and the fast tracking of new, effective antiviral drugs has transformed treatment. Highly active antiretroviral therapy (HAART) using several drugs (for example one protease inhibitor and at least two nucleoside analogue reverse transcriptase inhibitors will reduce plasma viraemia to undetectable levels in over 50% of patients (Carpenter *et al.* 1998). HAART prolongs life, reduces morbidity and has been so effective that AIDS wards have been closed.

But not all the news is good. There are serious adverse effects with some drugs, adherence is difficult to maintain with complex drug regimes and there are increasing reports of drug resistance. Underlying the scientific advance is the reality that over 90% of those infected by HIV are in developing countries. For women in many developing countries these interventions will not be affordable. Indeed, many women do not even have access to HIV testing and information. HIV has emphasised the global inequity of resources, the inadequacies in infrastructure and the limitations in access to care. It has also highlighted many examples of the discrimination and exploitation of women.

CURRENT STATUS OF HIV IN PREGNANCY

Context of care

The history and circumstances of HIV infection gives added significance to a number of care issues. Instead of sympathy, help and support from their community, infected individuals have often faced antagonism and discrimination. Because of this, HIV has focused particular attention on confidentiality, empowerment and shared partnership of decision making. Sharing accurate, up-to-date information and discussing choices make up a large component of management. Useful sources include conferences, study groups and contact with those involved in research studies. There is also a useful web site: http://hivinsite.ucsf.edu. Advice on other issues can be obtained through the Terence Higgins Trust.[1]

Interaction of HIV and pregnancy

Two systematic reviews conclude that HIV adversely affects pregnancy outcome and that pregnancy increases the rate of progression of HIV disease. The authors point out that the associations are not strong and could be due to bias (Brocklehurst and French 1998; French and Brocklehurst 1998). These reviews are useful, but of limited clinical value because they do not disentangle the key variables of place and illness.

In Africa, many women have an increased load of other infectious disease (particularly malaria and tuberculosis), may enter pregnancy in a vulnerable nutritional state and, if they have advancing disease, will most commonly present with weight loss. It is not

---

[1] Terence Higgins Trust, 52–54 Gray's Inn Road, London WC1X 8JU; telephone +44 (0) 207 831 0330.

surprising that all reports from Africa conclude that birth weight is reduced. Several suggest that perinatal outcome is adversely affected. The additional demands of pregnancy could increase the subsequent rate of progression of maternal disease (Johnstone 1995).

However, in the different circumstances of the developed world and in women who are immunocompetent, there is no evidence that pregnancy affects surrogates of progression of disease (Brettle et al. 1995; Hocke et al. 1995). Birth weight may be slightly reduced (Johnstone et al. 1996) and there could be an association with chorioamnionitis. These effects appear small, but important. In particular, women who are severely immunocompromised are more likely to deliver prematurely than those infected women who are not and this effect is seen also with increased viral load (O'Shea et al. 1998).

Women should be given information based on context.

Vertical transmission

Before specific treatment, the estimated rate of vertical transmission varied from 15% to 20% in Europe, 15% to 30% in the USA and 25% to 35% in Africa (Newell and Peckham 1993). However, most of this infection is now preventable.

Timing and mechanisms have been comprehensively discussed (Newell 1998). The baby can be infected before, during or after birth. However, transmission in early pregnancy is rare and in non-breastfeeding populations it is estimated that approximately two-thirds of transmission occurs around delivery. This is based on timing of first polymerase chain reaction positivity (Kalish et al. 1997). In breastfeeding populations the proportion of babies becoming infected at delivery may be nearer to 50%.

Intuitively, it is easy to understand how infants could become infected by exposure to maternal contaminated blood or cervical discharge during labour and delivery. Gastric, ocular or pulmonary surfaces are all possible sites of entry of the virus (Baba et al. 1995). Where twins are discordant for infection, the first twin is much more likely than the second twin to be the one affected (Duliège et al. 1995). Furthermore, chorioamnionitis may be the major obstetric risk factor for transmission of HIV (Goldenberg et al. 1998). This would explain the increased risk associated with preterm birth and prolonged rupture of the membranes. There is also a plausible mechanism. Bacterial invasion of the uterus initiates massive cytokine response, cytokines attract a large number of leucocytes into the amniotic fluid and viral transmission has been shown to be feasible by this route in monkeys. This hypothesis can be tested and is important because antibiotic treatment is relatively cheap and, together with a late pregnancy, short-course antiretroviral strategy, might be cost effective in developing countries where more elaborate anti-retroviral regimes are not affordable (Goldenberg et al. 1998).

It is difficult to separate transmission during delivery from transmission in early neonatal life through breastfeeding, but breastfeeding may double the risk of transmission (Dunn et al. 1992) and infants should be fed on breastmilk substitutes in settings where this is a safer alternative. Late postnatal transmission of HIV infection through breastfeeding (greater than three months after delivery) is substantial (Leroy et al. 1998). This has initiated discussions about the advisability of earlier weaning in women for whom refraining completely from breastfeeding is not an option.

Zidovudine

ACTG076 was a landmark, randomised, placebo-controlled, double-blind trial carried out in 43 centres in the USA and France (Connor et al. 1994; Sperling et al. 1996).

Treatment with zidovudine (ZDV) 500 mg daily or placebo was started at a median of 26 weeks. Women also received ZDV or placebo intravenously during labour (2 mg per kg body weight over a one-hour period, followed by a continuous infusion of 1 mg per kg per hour until delivery) and their infants received ZDV syrup (2 mg per kg four times daily for six weeks, beginning 8–12 hours after birth). There was a 68% reduction in the frequency of transmission, from 25.5% in the placebo group to 8.3% in the ZDV group.

There has been ample confirmation that this intervention is effective in the real world, with reduced vertical transmission in the USA and France (Fiscus *et al.* 1996; Mayaux *et al.* 1997).

In two hospitals in Bangkok, Thailand, a double-blind, placebo-controlled, randomised controlled trial examined a much simpler regime. ZDV was given to the mother only from 36 weeks' gestation, with a twice-daily regime, and was given orally in labour (every three hours). Mother-to-child transmission was reduced by 51%, being 18.9% in the placebo arm and 9.4% in the ZDV arm (Shaffer *et al.* 1999). This extended the possible use of the drug considerably.

Two other similarly designed trials examined the effect of short-course oral ZDV in breastfeeding populations. Both showed that ZDV was well accepted, well tolerated and still effective. The study in Côte d'Ivoire and Burkina Faso (Dabis *et al.* 1999) analysed infection rates in 400 liveborn infants at six months of age, with a reduction from 27.5% in the placebo group to 18.0% in the ZDV group. In the other study, from Abidjan, Côte d'Ivoire, infection rates were examined in 230 babies at three months of age, with a similar reduction from 26.1% to 16.5% (Wiktor *et al.* 1999). These reductions were somewhat less than seen in the Bangkok trial, which in turn showed less effect than the ACTG076 trial, but they are still substantial.

How does ZDV work? In the Bangkok study, reduction in viral load explained 80% of the effect and this may perhaps be the most important mechanism. In ACTG076, the effect was not due simply to reduction in viral load because, by the time of delivery, this reduction was only 0.3 log and was calculated to account for only 17% of the effect (Sperling *et al.* 1996). Perhaps there was selection of less fit virus and there may be an effect from pre-exposure prophylaxis, similar to the post-exposure prophylaxis used in healthcare workers (Cardo *et al.* 1997). An effect through reduction in incidence of preterm delivery has been suggested (Bailey *et al.* 1999).

Although prospective studies have shown no serious short-term risks of ZDV for the baby, concerns remain about the long term. One study, giving ZDV in high doses to pregnant mice and monkeys, showed genotoxic and tumour-inducing effects but other animal studies have been largely reassuring (Centers for Disease Control and Prevention 1998). In addition, follow-up has shown no difference in any parameters between infants who were exposed to the ZDV regime compared with placebo (Culnane *et al.* 1998). There were no malignancies in 734 infants with *in utero* ZDV exposure up to six years of age (Hanson *et al.* 1997). Nevertheless, the report of mitochondrial toxicity in four children where there had been exposure to zidovudine monotherapy, and the plausible mechanism, is concerning (Blanche *et al.* 1999).

The current position is that zidovudine monotherapy has not been proven to be causally related to mitochondrial toxicity, but there is uncontestable evidence that it does greatly reduce HIV vertical transmission. Present evidence is therefore strongly in favour of use of ZDV. Careful follow-up of the children is essential.

Other antiretroviral therapy

Nevirapine is a non-nucleoside reverse transcriptase inhibitor, with several theoretical advantages for short-term prophylaxis around the time of delivery. Now there is evidence of effectiveness. A randomised study from Kampala, Uganda, compared nevirapine and zidovudine given around the time of delivery (Guay *et al.* 1999). The risk of infection by age 14–16 weeks was 25.1% in the zidovudine group and 13.1% in the nevirapine group, a reduction in risk of nearly 50%. Compared with some other study populations, these pregnancies were at high risk for transmission. Nearly all the babies were breastfed. The mothers had a median plasma viral load that was five times higher than those women in the ACTG076 study.

Although short-term nevirapine prophylaxis may have an important place in less developed countries, and as an adjunct in the developed world, zidovudine therapy remains the standard drug method of reducing the rate of vertical transmission. However, monotherapy conflicts with contemporary standards of treatment of HIV (because drug resistance rapidly develops). The use of combination antivirals, by further lowering plasma viraemia, might further reduce the risk of transmission. Trying to balance optimal therapy for mother and child is fraught with difficulty and uncertainty.

At present, there is no antiretroviral with either definite positive evidence of human risk or with adequate data to demonstrate safety (Centers for Disease Control and Prevention 1998). According to the USA Food and Drug Administration classification ddC, d4T, 3TC, indinavir, nevirapine and delaverdine are in category C (animal studies have either not been done or have shown abnormalities); and ddI, saquinavir, ritonavir and nelfinavir are in category B (animal studies fail to show a risk to the fetus) (Tovo *et al.* 1999).

One study reported a cluster of unusual and serious adverse effects in sixteen pregnancies where the women took combination therapy including a protease inhibitor (Lorenzi *et al.* 1998). A high proportion of preterm births was reported in this study, but these are high-risk pregnancies for preterm delivery. Data on short-term safety will accumulate quite quickly. But what should be done in the meantime?

Where a woman is ill and requiring therapy in pregnancy the current standard of care is combination antiretroviral therapy. Similarly, if a woman enters pregnancy on HAART, and after consideration of all the risks plans to continue, the choice is between maintaining HAART throughout pregnancy, or stopping all drugs when pregnancy is diagnosed and restarting them at twelve weeks.

More contentious is the situation where the woman is clinically well and antiretroviral naïve. Current consensus is that for women with a relatively low viral load, ZDV monotherapy for the third trimester is appropriate. On theoretical grounds, the development of resistance should be minimised by the limited viral replication and the time-limited exposure to ZDV. In one study, patients with less than twelve months' exposure to ZDV responded as well to combination therapy as did those without prior ZDV (Saravolatz *et al.* 1996). A follow-up study of the ACTG076 trial did not show a high risk of acquired ZDV resistance (Eastman *et al.* 1998). Importantly, monotherapy removes the risk of possible adverse effects from other antiviral drugs. Such adverse effects could have far-reaching consequences, not just for the individuals harmed, but also in reduced public acceptance of all antiretroviral regimes during pregnancy.

Where women have a high viral load the correct management is uncertain. ZDV and lamivudine have satisfactory clinical tolerance data but there are concerns about this combination, both about drug resistance and possible neonatal mitochondrial toxicity (Blanche *et al.* 1999; Johnstone 2000). Current recommendations in the USA are that antiretroviral therapy should be selected according to the indications for treatment of the woman herself. Thus, it is suggested that monotherapy should not be used, as it is considered substandard therapy for HIV-infected individuals. Only time will tell whether HAART, being increasingly used, will be safe for the children.

Caesarean section

A randomised trial of about 300 HIV infected women has shown that caesarean section was associated with a significant reduction in transmission (European Mode of Delivery Collaboration 1999). This is the first time that a randomised mode-of-delivery trial has actually reached a definite conclusion. The finding has been supported by a large meta-analysis of nearly 12 000 mother-and-child pairs. The odds ratio for that data set was 0.45 (International Perinatal HIV Group 1999). In women taking ZDV the scope for further reduction is limited. Nevertheless, all the studies show that the extra intervention of caesarean section has an independent effect in these women (Kind et al. 1998; Mandelbrot et al. 1998; European Mode of Delivery Collaboration 1999; International Perinatal HIV Group 1999). Caesarean sections are protective only when performed before labour or soon after rupture of the membranes. On general principles, attempts should be made to minimise contact of the baby with maternal fluids and one method of 'bloodless caesarean section' has been described (Towers et al. 1998). The above studies show that the combination of prophylactic ZDV and elective caesarean section reduce the risk of transmission to less than 2%.

Issues in the developing world

The 'developing world' is of course not one entity and there are large differences in resources, infrastructure and prevalence of HIV. However, many countries cannot afford the interventions described above. Even in relatively rich South Africa the short course ZDV regimen would consume a substantial proportion of the health budget (Wilkinson et al. 1998).

One of the most problematic issues is breastfeeding. This has been estimated to double the risk of vertical transmission (Dunn et al. 1992) and even after three months the risk of infection is substantial (Leroy et al. 1998; Newell 1998). Yet in many countries, high rates of infant morbidity and mortality are associated with alternative feeding methods. In addition, formula feeding is expensive and could be stigmatising.

WHO, UNICEF and UNAIDS recommend that women in developing countries should have access to voluntary counselling and testing and that HIV-positive women should have access to short-course antiretroviral therapy and breastmilk substitutes wherever possible. For many women this will not be possible, even allowing for a negotiated reduction in the price of ZDV and international aid initiatives. Furthermore, drug therapy is only one part of a comprehensive package of care (UK NGO AIDS Consortium 1998). An interesting review of cost-effectiveness and cost–benefit models presents the issues for developing countries (Newell et al. 1998). The research agenda is not only still open (Wilkinson et al. 1999), but is becoming more complex all the time.

THE FUTURE

At the millennium, forty million people will be living with HIV or AIDS. By 2010 AIDS will double child mortality in some countries and there will be more than forty million children under the age of five years who have lost one or both parents (WHO 1998). By 2020 HIV will be the second leading cause of death in adults in their prime years in the developing world (Carael *et al.* 1998) which will result in serious demographic distortions. Those women dying of HIV are in their economic prime of life, have important skills and experience, are responsible for much of the hard physical work, much of the food production and preparation and for the care of the young, the old and the sick.

In the developed world there will be a decline in new infections. Drug development will focus on better tolerated, once-daily drugs to overcome the problems of adherence and toxicity. In the short term this will become a manageable illness, a chronic rather than a fatal disease. In the longer term it may be possible to achieve a cure (i.e. eradicate latently infected cells). In pregnancy, HIV testing will be normalised and accepted in all areas which have significant prevalence. Information about the efficiency and safety of antiviral drugs will accumulate rapidly. Vertical transmission rates should be reduced to 2% or less. Thus, it seems likely that the epidemic will be contained and that the outlook for women and children will be greatly improved.

In the developing world, problems of resources and infrastructure will limit the application of possible treatments. Different countries will define their own strategies in the light of available resources and HIV prevalence. Every effort must be made to limit new infections. The priorities will be improved access to treatment for sexually transmitted diseases, public education, condom distribution and safe blood transfusion; in pregnancy, strategies based around short courses of antiretrovirals and, perhaps, breastmilk substitutes will become widespread. There will be major international initiatives with reduction in the price of ZDV and further international steps to remove the debt burden from some countries. It is to be hoped that there will be trends towards lessening the destabilising social effects of enforced migration of the male workforce and the exploitation of women.

One major uncertainty for the future is the long-term safety of antiviral drugs for the exposed uninfected offspring. If there were serious consequences, such as widespread premature ageing or a high rate of early malignancies this would cast a shadow over the impressive gains in the prevention of transmission. Only time will tell.

Immunisation holds the long-term future, but this is far away. Live attenuated virus is fraught with worry about possible pathogenicity. The subtype chosen for most vaccine development is Clade B which dominates infection in Europe and North America. Clade C is more common in the developing world where most infection is present (Editorial 1998). Only two phase III vaccine trials are under way and results are not due until 2003 (Editorial 1998). Even if these results are favourable there will remain substantial obstacles to be overcome.

HIV may not be the last new global infection. The ecological effects of population growth, climatic and environmental change, global migration and selective pressures from widespread use of microbial agents are causing changing patterns in other infectious diseases (Decosas *et al.* 1995; Wilson 1995). Despite notable successes, a hostile microbial world is currently seen as the greatest threat to our future (Culliton 1995). The lessons learned from HIV may help in other global problems of infection.

With human ingenuity, co-operation and resilience, HIV disease may at least be controlled and the world can benefit from the important lessons learned. Management of sexually transmitted diseases and maternity care will continue to play key roles in the amelioration of the impact of the pandemic.

Acknowledgements

This chapter was written with help from Laurent Mandelbrot and Marie-Louise Newell.

References

Baba, T.W., Jeong, Y.S., Penninck, D., Bronson, R., Greene, M.F. and Ruprecht, R.M. (1995) Pathogenicity of live attenuated SIV after mucosal infection of neonatal macaques. *Science* **267**, 1820–5

Bailey, A.J., Newell, M-L., Peckham, C.S. for the European Collaborative Study (1998) Is zidovudine therapy in pregnant HIV-infected women associated with gestational age and birthweight ? *AIDS* **13**, 119–24

Blanche, S., Tardieu, M., Rustin, P. *et al.* (1999) Persistant mitochondrial dysfunction and perinatal exposure to antiretrovirol nucleoside analogues. *Lancet* **354**, 1084–9

Brettle, R.P., Raab, G.M. and Ross, A. (1995) HIV infection in women: immunological markers and the influence of pregnancy. *AIDS* **9**, 1177–84

Brocklehurst, P. and French, R. (1998) The association between maternal HIV infection and perinatal outcome: a systematic review of the literature and meta-analysis. *Br J Obstet Gynaecol* **105**, 836–48

Carael, M., Schwartlander, B. and Zewdie, D. (1998). Preface. *AIDS* **12** Suppl, S1–2

Cardo, D.M., Culver, D.H., Ciesielski, C.A. *et al.* (1997) A case–control study of HIV seroconversion in health care workers after percutaneous exposure. *N Engl J Med* **337**, 1485–90

Carpenter, C.C., Fischl, M.A., Hammer, S.M. *et al.* (1998) Antiretroviral therapy for HIV infection in 1998: updated recommendations of the International AIDS Society USA Panel. *JAMA* **280**, 78–86

Centers for Disease Control and Prevention (1998) Public Health Service Task Force recommendations for the use of antiretroviral drugs in pregnant women for maternal health and for reducing perinatal HIV-1 transmission in the United States. *MMWR Morb Mortal Wkly Rep* **47**, 1–30

Connor, E.M., Sperling, R.S., Gelber, R. *et al.* (1994) Reduction of maternal–infant transmission of human immunodeficiency virus type-1 with zidovudine treatment. *N Engl J Med* **331**, 1173–80

Culliton, B.J. (1995) The greatest threat of all. *Nat Med* **1**, 1221

Culnane, M., Fowler, M. and Lee, S.S. (1999) Lack of long-term effects of *in utero* exposure to zidovudine among uninfected children born to HIV-infected women. *JAMA* **281**, 151–7

Dabis, F., Msellati, P., Meda, N. *et al.* (1999) 6-month efficacy, tolerance, and acceptability of a short regimen of oral zidovudine to reduce vertical transmission of HIV in breastfed children in Côte d'Ivoire and Burkina Faso: a double-blind placebo-controlled multicentre trial. *Lancet* **353**, 786–92

Decosas, J., Kane, F., Anarfi, J.K. *et al.* (1995) Migration and AIDS. *Lancet* **346**, 826–8

Duliège, A-M., Amos, C.I., Felton, S., Biggar, R.J. and Goedert, J.J. (1995) The international registry of HIV-exposed twins. Birth order, delivery route and concordance in the transmission of human immunodeficiency virus type 1 from mothers to twins. *J Pediatr* **126**, 625–32

Dunn, D.T., Newell, M.L., Aden, A.E. and Peckham, C.S. (1992) Risk of human immunodeficiency virus type 1 transmission through breastfeeding. *Lancet* **340**, 585–8

Eastman, P.S., Shapiro, D.E., Coombs, R.W. *et al.* (1998) Maternal viral genotypic zidovudine resistance and infrequent failure of zidovudine therapy to prevent perinatal transmission of human immunodeficiency virus type 1 in paediatric AIDS Clinical Trials Group Protocol 076. *J Infect Dis* **177**, 557–64

Editorial (1998) An HIV vaccine: how long must we wait? *Lancet* **352**, 1323

European Collaborative Study (1998) Is zidovudine therapy in pregnant HIV-infected women associated with gestational age and birth weight? *AIDS* **13**, 119–24

European Mode of Delivery Collaboration (1999) Elective caesarean section versus vaginal delivery in prevention of vertical HIV-1 transmission: a randomised clinical trial. *Lancet* **353**, 1035–9

Fiscus, S.A., Adimora, A.A., Schoenbach, V.J. *et al.* (1996) HIV infection and the effect of zidovudine therapy on transmission in rural and urban counties. *JAMA* **27**, 1483–8

French, R. and Brocklehurst, P. (1998) The effect of pregnancy on survival in women infected with HIV: systematic review of the literature and meta-analysis. *Br J Obstet Gynaecol* **105**, 827–35

Gao, F., Bailes, E., Robertson, D.C. *et al.* (1999) Origins of HIV-1 in the chimpanzee *Pan troglodytes*. *Nature* **397**, 436–41

Goldenberg, R.L., Vermund, S.H., Goepfert, A.R. and Andrews, W.W. (1998) Choriodecidual inflammation: a potentially preventable cause of perinatal HIV-1 transmission? *Lancet* **352**, 1927–30

Guay, L.A., Musoke, P., Fleming, T. *et al.* (1999) Intrapartum and neonatal single-dose nevirapine compared with zidovudine for prevention of mother-to-child transmission of HIV-1 in Kampala, Uganda: HIV NET 012 randomised trial. *Lancet* **354**, 795–802

Hanson, C., Cooper, E., Antonelli, T. *et al.* (1997) 'Lack of tumours in infants with perinatal HIV exposure and fetal/neonatal exposure to zidovudine' in: *Proceedings of National Conference on Women and HIV, May 4–7, Pasadena, California*. Abstract 304.3

Hocke, C., Morlat, P. and Chene, G. (1995) Groupe d'Epidemologie Clinique des SIDA en Aquitaine: prospective cohort study of the effect of pregnancy on the progression of human immunodeficiency virus infection. *Obstet Gynecol* **86**, 886–91

International Perinatal HIV Group (1999) The mode of delivery and the risk of vertical transmission of HIV-1: a meta-analysis from fifteen prospective cohort studies (the International Perinatal HIV Group). *N Engl J Med* **340**, 977–87

Johnstone, F.D. (1995) 'Pregnancy outcome and management in HIV infected women' in: M. de Swiet (Ed.) *Medical Disorders in Obstetric Practice*, pp. 568–99. London: Blackwell Science

Johnstone, F.D. (2000) HIV, pregnancy and antiretrovirals: what went right? *Contemporary Reviews in Obstetrics and Gynaecology* 229–34

Johnstone, F.D., Raab, G.M. and Hamilton, B.A. (1996) The effect of human immuno-deficiency virus infection on birth characteristics. *Obstet Gynecol* **88**, 321–6

Kalish, L.A., Pitt, J., Lew, J. *et al.* (1997) Defining the time of fetal or perinatal acquis-ition of human immunodeficiency virus type 1 infection on the basis of age at first positive culture. *J Infect Dis* **175**, 712–15

Kind, C., Rudin, C., Siegrist, C.A. *et al.* (1998) Prevention of vertical HIV transmission: additive protective effect of elective caesarean section and zidovudine prophylaxis. *AIDS* **12**, 205–10

Leroy, V., Newell, M-L., Dabis, F. *et al.* (1998) International multicentre pooled analysis of late postnatal mother-to-child transmission of HIV-1 infection. *Lancet* **352**, 597–600

Lorenzi, P., Masserey Spicher, V., Laubereau, B. *et al.* and the Swiss HIV Cohort Study, the Swiss Collaborative HIV and Pregnancy Study and the Swiss Neonatal HIV Study (1998) Antiretroviral therapies in pregnancy: maternal, fetal and neonatal effects. *AIDS* **12**, F214–47

Mandelbrot, L., Le Chenadec, J., Berrebi, A. *et al.* (1998) Perinatal HIV-1 transmission: interaction between zidovudine prophylaxis and mode of delivery in the French Perinatal Cohort. *JAMA* **280**, 55–60

Mayaux, M.J., Teglas, J.P., Mandelbrot, L. *et al.* (1997) Acceptability and impact of zido-vudine prevention on mother-to-child HIV-1 transmission in France. *J Pediatr* **131**, 857–62

Newell, M.L. (1998) Mechanisms and timing of mother-to-child transmission of HIV-1. *AIDS* **12**, 831–7

Newell, M.L. and Peckham, C.S. (1993) Risk factors for vertical transmission of HIV-1 and early markers of HIV infection in children. *AIDS* **7** Suppl 1, S91–7

Newell, M.L., Dabis, F., Tolley, K. and Whynes, D. (1998) Cost effectiveness and cost benefit in the prevention of mother-to-child transmission of HIV in developing countries. *AIDS* **12**, 1571–80

Pantaleo, G. (1999) Unravelling the strands of HIV's web. *Nat Med* **5**, 27–8

Saravolatz, L.D., Winslow, D.L., Collins, G. *et al.* (1996) Zidovudine alone or in combination with didanosine or zalcitabine in HIV-infected patients with acquired immunodeficiency syndrome or fewer than 200 CD4 cells per cubic millimeter. *N Engl J Med* **335**, 1099–106

Shaffer, N., Chuachoowong, R., Mock, P.A. *et al.* (1999) Short course zidovudine for perinatal HIV-1 transmission in Bangkok, Thailand: a randomised controlled trial. *Lancet* **353**, 773–80

Sperling, R., Shapiro, D.E., Coombs, R.W. *et al.* (1996) Maternal viral load, zidovudine treatment, and the risk of transmission of human immunodeficiency virus type 1 from mother to infant. *N Engl J Med* **335**, 1621–9

Tovo, P-A., Newell, M-L., Mandelbrot, L., Semprini, E. and Giaquinto, C. (1999) Recommendations for the management of HIV-infected women and their infants – a European consensus. *Prenatal and Neonatal Medicine* **4**, 3–17

Towers, C.V., Deveikis, A., Asrat, T., Major, C. and Nageotte, M.P. (1998) A 'bloodless caesarean section' and perinatal transmission of the human immunodeficiency virus. *Am J Obstet Gynecol* **179**, 708–14

UK NGO Aids Consortium (1998) Working group on access to treatment for HIV in developing countries; statement from international seminar on access to treatment for HIV in developing countries, London June 5 and 6, 1998. *Lancet* **352**, 1379–80

Weiss, R.A. and Wrangham, R.W. (1999) From Pan to pandemic. *Nature* **397**, 385–6

WHO (1995) *The World Health Report 1995: Bridging the Gaps.* Geneva: World Health Organization

Wiktor, S.Z., Ekpini, E., Karon, J.M. *et al.* (1999) Short course oral zidovudine for prevention of mother-to-child transmission of HIV-1 in Abidjan, Côte d'Ivoire: a randomised trial. *Lancet* **353**, 781–5

Wilkinson, D., Floyd, K. and Gilks, C.F. (1998) Antiretroviral drugs as a public health intervention for pregnant HIV infected women in rural South Africa: an issue of cost-effectiveness and capacity. *AIDS* **12**, 1675–82

Wilkinson, D., Karim, S.S.A. and Coovadia, H.M. (1999) Short course antiretroviral regimens to reduce maternal transmission of HIV. *BMJ* **318**, 479–80

Wilson, M.E. (1995) Infectious diseases: an ecological perspective. *BMJ* **311**, 1681–4

Zhu, T., Korber, B.T., Nahmias, A.J., Hooper, E., Sharp, P.M. and Ho, D.D. (1998) An African HIV-1 sequence from 1959 and implications for the origin of the epidemic. *Nature* 391, 594–7

16

Making labour safer: staffing levels at the turn of the century

Martin J. Whittle

INTRODUCTION

The labour ward is a place which must fulfil a number of functions, not all of which are necessarily compatible with one another. It should be a place of tranquillity in which couples can experience one of life's more important experiences, namely the birth of their baby. Usually this event is without complication but occasionally things go wrong, leading to the development of a real medical emergency. Sometimes the labour ward will contain seriously ill mothers and must function much like an intensive-care ward.

These potentially competing factors make the organisation and running of the labour ward a complex business requiring the development of an effective multidisciplinary team of midwives, obstetricians, anaesthetists, paediatricians and other ancillary personnel. Such teams are not developed by accident and their existence should not be a foregone conclusion; indeed, it would seem likely that they are less, rather than more, likely to exist.

Why should this be of concern? Over the last 20 years both perinatal and maternal mortality rates have fallen steadily (Figures 1 and 2). Since these improvements have occurred in the face of a tradition of minimal consultant input to the labour ward, it begs the question about whether changes are now appropriate.

Certainly, at the beginning of the 20th century, the problems of traumatic delivery were significant and the reluctance to perform a caesarean section led to the need for high forceps, difficult breech deliveries and prolonged labours. The disappearance of these types of complications, which occurred from the necessity to avoid caesarean section if possible because of the lack of availability of safe anaesthesia, has led to an improved outcome, but undoubtedly the greatest contribution to reduced perinatal mortality has come from better neonatal care. A more detailed analysis of the causes of loss followed the establishment, in 1993, of the Confidential Enquiry into Stillbirths and Deaths in Infancy (CESDI). Interestingly, little change in intrapartum causes appears to have occurred in the last 10–15 years (Figure 1). The fourth annual report (CESDI 1997) attempted to determine whether some losses arose from care which fell below acceptable standards. Of concern was the finding that, in 78% of cases in which there was perinatal loss, a different course of action might have resulted in a better outcome. This observation involved midwives in about 27% of cases, obstetricians in about 63% and paediatricians in 57.5%. Poor communication between professionals underlay about 25% of the adverse outcomes. The method by which these cases were collected and assessed was a potential source of criticism, but a further analysis which appeared in the CESDI

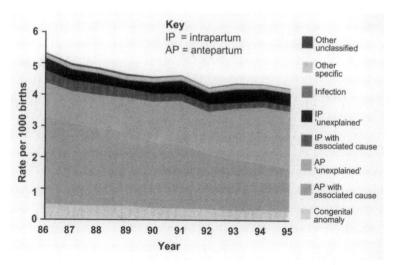

Figure 1 *Perinatal mortality 1986–95 (Wigglesworth classification) (reproduced with permission from the Fourth CESDI Annual Report)*

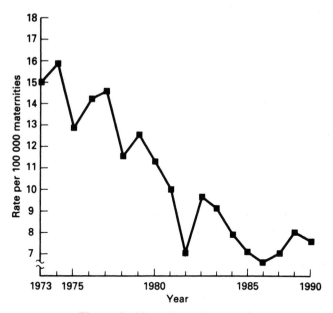

Figure 2 *Maternal mortality 1973–90*

fifth annual report suggested that agreement between observers in the most troublesome cases was nearly 80% (CESDI 1998).

The most recent triennial (1994–96) report on confidential enquiries into maternal deaths in the UK (Department of Health 1998) indicates an overall maternal death rate of 9.9 per 100 000 maternities, similar to the previous triennial report. However, lack of consultant involvement in some maternal deaths remained a criticism. In addition, the availability of written guidelines for the management of major obstetric complications was not universal. For example, only 66% of units had guidelines for thromboembolic disorders, although around 90% had them for severe hypertension, eclampsia and major haemorrhage. On the other hand, only 20% had guidelines for severe genital tract infection. Even when maternal death is rare, there seems to be room for improvement not only in terms of personnel but also of organisation.

In 1994, the College published a report (Royal College of Obstetricians and Gynaecologists 1994) which attempted to define the requirements for a satisfactory level of care for women in labour and for their babies. It outlined staffing levels for midwives, obstetricians, anaesthetists and paediatricians and indicated necessary infrastructure support. It even recommended the appropriate environment, in terms of suitable rooms for labour and for the delivery itself.

There is no evidence that the report particularly influenced how labour wards were managed or organised and certainly little progress has been made in increasing the involvement of consultant obstetricians in labour.

A new report was published in 1999 by the Royal College of Obstetricians and Gynaecologists. There were several reasons for a new report. The two confidential enquiries into perinatal and maternal deaths discussed above suggested that better care on the labour ward might lead to improvements in losses. Major changes in staff availability and the demands upon staff means that the whole issue of staffing levels needs to be reviewed. For example, the reduction in junior doctors' hours and the increased need for them to leave the hospital to attend teaching and instruction has meant that the burden of labour-ward care has fallen increasingly on consultants. This applies not only during the day but increasingly at night, a phenomenon which has arisen as the level of experience of junior staff falls. This process will lead inevitably to a consultant-based service, but without the support that such a situation requires. For example, to staff a labour ward for 24 hours using consultant staff would require about 16 doctors. This sounds excessive but takes account of the other duties of consultants such as clinics, gynaecological operating and committee work. In addition, it is important that a consultant living in at night has the next 24 hours without duties.

Midwives are, to some extent, in no better a situation. The responsibilities of the midwife have increased and the mothers they care for have greater expectations. The benefits of one midwife to one mother in labour is clear; evidence would suggest that there is a lower intervention rate when there is continual professional care in labour (Oakley 1988). The midwife has the central responsibility for the mother with an uncomplicated pregnancy and labour. There has been concern that the increased presence of the consultant in the labour ward might lead to a medical take-over, but this is definitely not the intention. However, doctors and midwives must work together for the benefit of all women, something which requires trust and respect for one another's professional skills and abilities. The crucial fact is that there needs to be an organisational structure which will provide women with care appropriate to their needs.

LABOUR WARD ORGANISATION

Although labour wards have generally been run by midwives, it is often the medical staff who set the protocols, if they exist, for the induction, augmentation and general management of labour. The imposition of new ideas and plans without consultation has been the cause of considerable discontent. More enlightened departments may have encouraged midwifery and anaesthetic input but often only on an *ad hoc* basis. More recently, there may be influence from audit and from risk-assessment studies. Thus, there are a number of potential sources of input into the management of the labour ward but these need to be co-ordinated if they are to be effective.

The organisational core of the labour ward should be the labour-ward forum. This group would comprise a lead obstetrician and midwife together with representatives of anaesthetists, paediatricians, junior medical and midwifery staff, risk managers, administrative staff and consumers. This may sound unwieldy but it provides a number of interested parties with a degree of ownership of the labour-ward arrangements.

The role of the labour-ward forum would be to agree staffing levels, monitor training, establish protocols and guidelines and organise educational and up-dating meetings. Of particular importance would be the need to ensure that the labour ward was appropriately staffed both at senior and junior levels. It is important to establish the principle that senior involvement in the labour ward has become a requirement not an option. Thus, at least 40 hours of consultant cover is required from Monday to Friday, with consultants actually present in the ward. The problem with this idea is that it only provides active cover between 9 a.m. and 5 p.m., whereas most data would suggest that problems tend to occur outside these hours. Clearly, more prolonged contact with consultants is desirable but the 40 hours should be seen as the start of a process which ultimately results in consultants in the labour ward on a regular basis in exactly the same way as in clinics and operating sessions. At what point consultants decided to leave the running of the labour ward to their junior colleagues and ceased to see it as part of their job is lost in history. In any case there are undoubtedly regional differences. The availability of experienced senior registrars meant that consultants were infrequently required in the first place and therefore staying was considered unnecessary and a waste of their time. The new 'Calman' training has, to some extent changed that, because juniors do not now have the experience to deal with some of the labour-ward complications and increasingly seek the experienced help of consultants. In addition, concerns over medicolegal implications have created a culture of ensuring that the most senior staff available are present if there are complications.

LABOUR WARD STAFFING

It has become clear that a new approach to the staffing structure on the labour ward is required. As far as midwives are concerned, a standard has been suggested by the Audit Commission that at least 60% of the time there should be a staffing level of 1.15 midwives to one woman in labour (Garcia *et al.* 1998). The eventual aim would be that 75% of women should have the same midwife throughout their labour. This requires some ingenuity to achieve since midwives may have responsibilities to attend operating theatres, monitor the condition of ill obstetric patients and also have a teaching role, not only for midwives but also for medical students and senior house officers. The Audit Commission suggested that some improvements in the availability of midwives to support women in labour could be achieved through flexible working practice and, while this may be desirable, a national shortage of trained midwives creates difficulties with this concept.

Medical staffing levels have become an issue because of the loss of junior support which has followed the introduction of the Calman training programme and, as discussed, above the Government's New Deal. The difficulties with junior staffing and availability have made it imperative that the role and activity of consultants on the labour ward be reviewed. It is proposed that in units delivering between 1000 and 4000 babies a year there should be at least 40 hours of consultant activity in the labour ward from Monday to Friday and between 9 a.m. and 5 p.m. What would this achieve? This principle should draw consultants back into the labour ward and instil the view that they are required there in much the same way as they are for their clinics and operating lists. The labour ward should not be regarded as an optional extra and labour-ward activity should appear as part of the consultant's defined job and not as an extra duty.

It seems odd to have to define the duties of a consultant on the labour ward, but since the main perceived responsibility for many has been to provide cover rather than do anything active it may be helpful to indicate some of the roles. One concern which has been expressed is that an overburdening consultant presence may cramp trainees' opportunities to make decisions and manage the labour ward as well as gaining experience in the training and instruction of more junior staff, all of which is within the ambit of the senior trainee's own role. There is, therefore, a fine dividing line between support and interference but this is not a problem unique to the labour ward. The consultant's role in training senior trainees' surgical skills, or even clinical decision making, is to allow sufficient freedom for the individual to experience the emotion of making difficult decisions and yet for them to be secure in the knowledge that more senior help is at hand if required. It is at this point that labour ward activity seems to differ from more recognised consultant responsibilities and yet it is just as important that the trainee feels that help and advice are available if required.

Consultants have extremely important roles on the labour ward, including the provision of leadership, the training and education of staff as part of a multidisciplinary team and bringing experience to clinical diagnosis and opinion. In addition, consultants have an important responsibility to monitor and audit activity on the labour ward as fastidiously as they would for other areas of practice.

Not all consultants will want major involvement on the labour ward but in any one labour ward there should be at least one consultant with a particular interest who will take absolute responsibility for its organisational aspects. The number of consultants having a major role will depend on the amount of activity in the ward. The possibility of 24-hour cover has been proposed for those units delivering more than 4000 babies a year and certainly if they deliver more than 6000 babies a year. This would be a major step but it seems possible that there will eventually be a move in this direction.

The reasons for this are simple. The number of problems generated on busy units frequently demand the consultant's presence. This is not just during the period covered by the 40-hour proposals as many problems occur out of hours. Thus, unless sufficient numbers of consultants can be employed, life for consultants in the busiest units will become intolerable. A properly organised 24-hour rota means that consultants gain control of their on-call commitments and can develop an organisation which should be satisfactory. Labour units in the USA are staffed by specialist staff on a 24-hour basis and rota difficulties are solved by having large numbers of staff available.

The implications of these changes include the possibility that obstetrics and gynaecology may develop as separate specialties, something which has been generally resisted. Most doctors enter obstetrics and gynaecology because of the two components, but the exigencies of the service make it probably inevitable that a split will occur. The out-of-hours work for obstetrics is greater than for gynaecology and so more obstetricians than gynaecologists are required. The nature of gynaecology has changed and common conditions, such as dysfunctional bleeding, are as amenable to hormonal treatment as to surgery and so the number of hysterectomies performed, for example, appears to be falling. Indeed, gynaecology could and, perhaps, has become a more medically based subject.

This potential change raises some serious issues about career pathways. It is possible that, even if newly appointed consultants concentrate initially on obstetrics, many eventually spend increasing time on gynaecological matters as their careers unfold. This pattern would make it imperative that gynaecological skills were maintained. However, that may no longer be the credo. This being the case, what does a young obstetric consultant do with his career after, say, ten years of obstetrics and no gynaecology?

What has this to do with standards on the labour ward? The role of consultants must be seen as crucial, but their involvement demands some major changes in their pattern of work and in their career structure. The imposition of these changes without adequate planning or consideration of these important issues could result in the collapse of support from obstetricians for the proposed improvements in labour-ward care that most regard as desirable.

OTHER MANPOWER ISSUES

The involvement of other specialists in the labour ward seems less contentious; something which could be regarded as an indictment as far as obstetricians are concerned. Thus, anaesthetists have had staffing guidelines for some time. Their view is that one consultant session for between 500 and 3000 deliveries a year up to 3000 deliveries a year is acceptable, but full cover, that is a full day of two sessions, per 500 deliveries thereafter, is appropriate. The need for consultant anaesthetist involvement has been recognised for some time, not only to provide an epidural service but also for the management of serious obstetric conditions such as pre-eclampsia and haemorrhage.

Paediatricians also have standards for consultant staffing which are based on workload and case mix. Obviously the requirements for units which do not take tertiary referrals will be much less than for those that do, but even small units must have personnel capable of resuscitating the newborn baby. One problem which paediatric staff face is the difficulty of adequate staffing, especially in intensive care units. This may produce some interesting results, one of which may be the amalgamation of obstetric units into larger units which would make more efficient use of available staff. Thus, paediatrics could be the engine for change in obstetrics.

TRAINING AND EDUCATION

One standard which has not previously been defined for the labour ward is systematic training in issues such as the management of labour and, in particular, the interpretation of cardiotocograms. The latter are a particular problem and a lack of understanding of their use has probably led not only to poor decision making in terms of a failure to identify fetal distress, but also the over-eager tendency to intervene in labour and deliver by caesarean section.

There is a requirement to ensure that staff are well trained in the use of cardiotocography and also have a sound knowledge of the management of labour. It is vital that both midwives and obstetric staff work together and have an understanding of each others' various responsibilities and an ability for both groups to communicate satisfactorily. This will not be possible unless individuals are taught in the same way and, ideally, at the same time.

CONCLUSIONS

The labour ward has been a neglected area as far as consultant obstetricians are concerned. While the care of low-risk cases has been, and should be, the preserve of the midwife, the development of complications during labour involves the obstetrician. The condition of the mother and her baby can deteriorate rapidly and when this happens a system must exist which allows a quick and appropriate response. Until now this has largely been at junior doctor level and although this has worked tolerably well, current circumstances, which include falling junior support and experience, increasing litigation, increasing patient expectations and adverse comments from both maternal and perinatal mortality reports, demand change. Such change will have profound effects on how obstetricians work and organise their professional lives and their careers, all of which will have implications for staffing levels, conditions of service and, almost certainly, remuneration.

References

CESDI (Confidential Enquiry into Stillbirths and Deaths in Infancy) (1997) *Fourth Annual Report.* London: Maternal and Child Health Research Consortium

CESDI (Confidential Enquiry into Stillbirths and Deaths in Infancy) (1998) *Fifth Annual Report.* London: Maternal and Child Health Research Consortium

Department of Health (1998) *Why Mothers Die? Report on Confidential Enquiries into Maternal Deaths in the UK 1994–96.* London: The Stationery Office

Garcia J., Redshaw, M., Fitzsimmons, B. and Keene J. (1998) *First Class Delivery.* Abingdon, Oxon: Audit Commission Publications

Oakley, A. (1988) Is support good for mothers and babies? *Journal of Reproductive and Infant Psychology* **6**, 3–21

Royal College of Obstetricians and Gynaecologists (1994) *Minimum Standards of Care in Labour. Report of a Working Party.* London: RCOG

Royal College of Obstetricians and Gynaecologists (1999) *Towards Safer Childbirth: Minimum Standards for Organisation of Labour Wards. Report of a Working Party.* London: RCOG.

17

Rhesus disease: success but unfinished business

Charles R. Whitfield

HISTORICAL BACKGROUND

The main features of rhesus (Rh) disease were first described by Louise Bourgeois (1609), midwife to the French royal family, following the birth of twins to a multipara, one of which was grossly oedematous and died immediately, the other dying deeply jaundiced after four days.

Almost 270 years later, Orth (1875) in Germany described kernicterus, eventually shown by Claireaux *et al.* (1953) to be due to indirect bilirubin staining of the basal ganglia; and Jakesch (1878) in Prague reported a hydropic stillborn with bloated placenta, intensely yellow amniotic fluid, marked splenomegaly and a 'leukaemic diathesis' in the blood, liver and spleen, the preceding pregnancy having led to neonatal death. This complex was described in more detail by Ballantyne (1892) who distinguished it from congenital syphilis. He added an occasional association of 'general dropsy of the fetus' with maternal hypertension and oedema, soon confirmed by Dienst (1905) – were these the first reports of so-called 'maternal syndrome'? Ballantyne also reported a familial incidence, confirmed later by Hellman and Hertig (1938) who noted the rarity in firstborns and the often increasing severity in subsequent infants. Also, in Edinburgh, Buchan and Comrie (1909) described a family with a syndrome of congenital anaemia, jaundice, splenomegaly and overproduction of nucleated red cells. Schridde (1910) postulated abnormal haemopoiesis as the cause of hydrops fetalis (HF) and Rautman (1912) recognised Jakesch's leukaemic diathesis to be excessive primitive red cells, including megaloblasts, which he termed 'erythroblastosis fetalis' (EBF). Later, in Boston, USA, Diamond *et al.* (1932) made their first major contribution by linking congenital anaemia, icterus gravis and HF as a single disease, namely haemolytic disease of the newborn (HDN).

Understanding the pathophysiology

The first step towards revealing the role of red cell antibodies was made by the Austrian Nobel Prize winner Landsteiner (1901), who distinguished four varieties of human blood according to the presence or absence of two agglutinogens (A and B) in the erythrocytes. Next, Dienst (1905) reported enhanced anti-A and anti-B titres after the birth of group A or B babies to group O mothers, postulating transplacental bleeding from the fetus which he also thought might cause eclampsia.

161

Hirszfeld (1928) made the first suggestion that EBF might result from fetomaternal blood group incompatibility following stillbirths or abortions and soon there were reports of transfusion reactions not involving the ABO system with the father often being the blood donor (for example, Stetson 1933). From a review of aetiological theories, Darrow (1938) deduced correctly that EBF and HDN were caused by a maternal antibody reaction to some constituent of fetal blood, speculating however that this was fetal haemoglobin.

There followed in close succession a series of important clinical and laboratory observations. Investigating a severe transfusion reaction after stillbirth, Levine and Stetson (1939) found maternal antibodies which agglutinated red cells from the father and from most group-O subjects, suggesting that the mother had been immunised to a paternally derived fetal antigen which she lacked. Next, Landsteiner and Wiener (1940) described how the serum of rabbits, in which immune antibodies had been produced by injection of rhesus monkey blood, had caused agglutination in 87% of human blood samples they tested and they designated these antibodies as anti-Rh. Wiener and Peters (1940) found these antibodies in three more transfusion reactions, noting that most such reactions after pregnancy followed stillbirths or abortions. They concluded that the antibodies arose in response to leakage of red cells from the placental circulation of a Rh-positive fetus into the circulation of a Rh-negative mother, confirming the inspired suggestion by Dienst (1905) 35 years earlier. Finally, Levine *et al.* (1941) went back to the blood of the father of the stillborn reported in 1939 to confirm him as Rh-positive.

By 1943, research in the USA (particularly by Alexander Wiener at the Rockefeller Institute) and in the UK (under the Medical Research Council) had defined a series of interrelated Rh factors. Inheritance of the triple-antigen complexes, determined by three allelic genes closely located on the same chromosome, follows Mendelian principles. Individuals are either homozygous or heterozygous for each antigen in their genotypes. Each gene has two main variables designated by the system of Fisher and Race (1946) as C or c, D or d and E or e, some of which have unusual but important variants, for example C^w and D^u. It is remarkable that Fisher reasoned his solution to the Rh system between two consecutive evenings in a Cambridge public house.

It was also at about this time and in equally unusual circumstances – a dimly lit wartime train journey – that Coombs was inspired to devise his antiglobulin test which remains in routine use to detect red cell antibodies in maternal serum (indirect test) or coating of red cells by antibody (direct test) (Coombs *et al.* 1945).

The final proof that fetal red cells could cross the placental barrier was reported by Chown (1954) and Gunson (1957) using differential agglutination to confirm large transplacental bleeds (>100 ml) resulting in severe neonatal anaemia and subsequent maternal immunisation. Fetomaternal haemorrhage (FMH), exceptionally of such magnitude, became well recognised when the Kleihauer–Betke test (Kleihauer *et al.* 1957) became generally available, an incidence in one-fifth of postpartum blood samples being reported by Zipursky *et al.* (1959).

Exchange transfusion

The first major clinical milestone was neonatal exchange transfusion, first used in recognised Rh HDN by Wallerstein (1946) in New York. He used the sagittal sinus and a peripheral vein, as had Hart (1925) in Toronto, when faced with the challenge of an initially healthy baby whose six preceding siblings had all died with developing jaundice soon after birth. In the year after Wallerstein's report, Diamond (1947) advocated cannulating the umbilical vein for access. Largely as a result of this new procedure, OPCS-registered infant deaths from HDN were halved from about 0.8 to 0.4 per 100 births in England and Wales between 1950 and 1965 (Clarke 1982), since when intrauterine fetal transfusion also began to make its impact.

Toward immunoprophylaxis

The rarity of ABO incompatibility in parents of infants with HDN was noted by Levine (1943); its protection against subsequent Rh sensitisation was shown in Finland by Nevanlinna and Vainio (1956) and its effect against fetal blood persisting in the mother's circulation by Finn et al. (1961) in Liverpool. The last group reported a significant association between 'large' FMH and Rh antibody forming within three months, and also that in several male volunteers anti-D serum given intravenously eliminated half of previously injected D-positive red cells and 'coated' some of those still circulating. These findings supported the original contention by Finn (1960) that natural (ABO) protection could be mimicked by injecting anti-D to give a temporary passive immunity which should neutralise circulating D-positive fetal erythrocytes, and a series of experimental studies was carried out, aiming to establish a safe and effective method of Rh immunoprophylaxis (Clarke et al. 1963; Clarke 1967, 1972).

Similar research had started independently in New York (Freda et al. 1964), the two instigators being still in residency training (Freda in obstetrics and gynaecology, Gorman in pathology). In both programmes experiments on male volunteers (convicts in New York and policemen in Liverpool) led to clinical trials starting in 1964 (April in New York and May in Liverpool). These provided convincing evidence of the efficacy of anti-D immunoglobulin G (IgG) given postpartum to non-immunised D-negative mothers delivered of D-positive ABO-compatible babies (Combined Study from Centres in England and Baltimore 1966, 1971; Freda 1967; Woodrow et al. 1971). Trials of high titre anti-D serum (instead of IgG) had already started in 1962 in St Louis, USA (Hamilton 1967) and in 1963 in Germany (Schneider and Preisler 1965).

In 1970, a World Health Organization Scientific Group reviewed the remarkably uniform success of postpartum anti-D prevention in controlled trials, despite differences in design and dosage (WHO 1971). Only 0.5% of at-risk mothers had detectable anti-D antibodies six months later and another 1–2% in a further D-positive pregnancy (compared with 8.5% in controls at each stage, a combined rate of 17% without prophylaxis).

ROUTINE ANTI-D PROPHYLAXIS

Once enough IgG had been harvested, by plasmapheresis from donors whose anti-D had been 'boosted', prophylaxis was introduced in most countries with significant (mainly Caucasian) Rh D-negative populations. In the USA, a commercial product (Rho GAM®, Ortho Diagnostics) in doses of 300 µg (1500 iu) became widely available in 1968. In the UK in 1969 supplies were sufficient to begin step-by-step implementation, using unpaid volunteer donors, in initially 200 µg (1000 iu) doses restricted to non-immunised D-negative primiparas and other non-immunised D-negative mothers with only unsuccessful previous pregnancies and delivered of D-positive ABO-compatible babies. As supplies improved in 1971, postpartum prophylaxis was extended to all D-negative mothers delivering D-positive infants, the standard dose was halved to 500 iu, and a 250-iu dose was provided for all D-negative women having induced abortions up to 20 weeks' gestation, beyond which the full standard dose was used. The Medical Research Council Anti-D Working Party (1974) confirmed 500 iu as the 'lowest effective dose', but advised that a Kleihauer test always be performed to warn if additional anti-D is needed to 'cover' an unusually large FMH (giving 500 iu for every 4 ml or fraction of 4 ml of fetal red cells estimated to have entered the mother's blood).

The higher routine dosage of 1000–1500 iu of anti-D IgG, without a test for FMH, as more recently advised by the European Commission, has already caused some confusion and would probably prove both wasteful and unreliable in protecting against occasional considerable FMH which could prompt strong immunisation (Committee for Proprietary Medicinal Products for the European Community 1994).

The British Health Departments' 'green handbook', *Haemolytic Disease of the Newborn* (Standing Medical Advisory Committee 1976) warned that in Rh D-negative women placental damage might cause FMH at amniocentesis, abdominal injury or external fetal manipulation (for example, version), or at threatened, spontaneous or induced abortion, which should be covered by anti-D IgG. In an addendum (Standing Medical Advisory Committee 1981), antepartum haemorrhage and chorion villus sampling were added, as should be fetoscopy and transabdominal fetal blood sampling (FBS). The guidelines for giving anti-D IgG at abortions were reviewed in 1991. It should be given for induced abortion at any gestational age and for spontaneous complete or threatened abortions after 12 weeks, or if there had been instrumentation to remove products of conception. When a pregnancy remains viable after early threatened abortion and vaginal bleeding continues intermittently in a woman shown to be D-negative, the injection should be repeated about every six weeks. Because it was now clear that some women had been D-immunised by ectopic pregnancy the need for anti-D should be considered if this condition is present or suspected.

The impact of anti-D prophylaxis soon became apparent. In Connecticut, USA, where uptake was remarkably good, increasing from 93% to 99% after delivery and to 98% after abortion, the number of mothers with anti-D antibodies at delivery and the number of perinatal deaths from Rh HDN both fell by about two-thirds (Nusbacher and Bove 1980). Despite less satisfactory uptake, a similar reduction in registered perinatal deaths from all causes of HDN was achieved in England and Wales.

Nevertheless, it soon became clear that antepartum transplacental bleeding from the fetus often occurs in the absence of overt potentially sensitising events and that D-immunisation may occur during pregnancy, so that with only postpartum prophylaxis up to 0.5% of D-negative women will have anti-D antibodies within six months after confinement (Contreras 1998).

Antenatal anti-D prophylaxis: the McMaster Conference

In 1977 in Hamilton, Canada, the McMaster Conference on Prevention of Rhesus Immunization reviewed the results of prophylactic programmes and considered how to reduce further the incidence of Rh isoimmunisation and HDN (Davey and Zipursky 1979). Evidence showed that, with postpartum prophylaxis, the overall incidence of anti-D antibodies appearing within six months after delivery was 0.25% in 75 000 D-negative primiparas in 11 countries. During a further D-positive pregnancy in 11 000 women in eight countries it was 0.9%. In almost one-quarter of D-immunisations the antibodies had appeared during pregnancy. Considering only first pregnancies, isoimmunisation occurred without overt antepartum incidents in 0.87% of them and in 80% of them the antibodies were detected at or after 28 weeks, suggesting this as the optimal time to initiate antepartum prophylaxis. Most of the babies had mild HDN or were unaffected, but some subsequent babies born to these women needed intrauterine or exchange transfusion (Bowman *et al.* 1978).

The efficacy of antepartum prophylaxis was confirmed at the McMaster Conference. In 3017 D-negative 'primigravidas' at three centres (mostly in Winnipeg), tested at delivery and six weeks later, only two active immunisations occurred (0.07%) compared with 59 in 3615 controls (1.63%). Some multigravidas were included, having had both antepartum and postpartum anti-D IgG in their previous pregnancies and, although there was not a uniform treatment protocol (1500 iu at 28 weeks and/or at 34 weeks), these variations do not detract seriously from the 24-fold benefit from antepartum prevention.

Other trials

The results of other trials were in agreement. In Yorkshire, Tovey *et al.* (1983) reported that only two of 1238 D-negative primigravidas receiving 500 iu of anti-D IgG at 28 and 34 weeks and giving birth to D-positive infants, developed immune anti-D by delivery (0.16%) compared with 18 of 2000 historical, but otherwise comparable, controls (0.9%). Three hundred and twenty-five of the trial group had a further D-positive pregnancy, in two of which (0.6%) anti-D appeared for the first time, compared with 11 of 528 subsequent D-positive pregnancies in the control group (2.1%) as well as 18 in whom antibody had already developed in the first pregnancy; a combined total of 29 (5.5%).

In Paris, Huchet *et al.* (1987) gave 500 iu of anti-D at 28 and 34 weeks to 599 D-negative primigravidas subsequently giving birth to D-positive babies; immune anti-D was found after delivery in only one of them (0.17%) compared with seven of 590 controls (1.19%). This study included Kleihauer tests in the control group at 28 and 34 weeks, the results of which reflected incidences of FMH of 5.5 and 7.0% at these gestational ages.

Recently, Mayne *et al.* (1997) reported a trial in Derby in which, using the same dosage and timing as in the Yorkshire and Paris studies (above) anti-D IgG was given to an increasing proportion of at-risk D-negative mothers (mostly primigravid). Overall sensitisation fell from the previous rate of 1.2% to 0.28%, which applied to only four secundigravidas, only one of whom was known to have had anti-D IgG after her first confinement. Routine Kleihauer estimations identified FMH in excess of 4 ml in 1.5% of almost 5000 patients.

Despite such evidence and the successful implementation of programmes for routine antepartum prophylaxis elsewhere, there has been reluctance to adopt this policy in the UK, largely because of logistics and economics. It has been estimated that routine two-dose (500 iu each) proplylaxis for non-immunised D-negative primigravidas would almost double the requirement for anti-D doses and if all D-negative multigravidas were to be included there would be a more than three-fold increase (Lee 1991). Additionally, there has not been a vigorous demand from the obstetric specialty for this step to be taken, probably mainly because the success of postpartum protection and the increasing concentration of cases at *de facto* referral centres means that many obstetricians no longer have close familiarity with the effects of Rh disease and some have been able to rely on recently licensed imported, but expensive, commercial anti-D IgG for antepartum use. The general relative unawareness of the residual Rh problem is increased by the under reporting of wastage from Rh disease (Whitfield *et al.* 1997).

It was in the hope of reducing the requirement for immunoglobulin that a randomised half-dose trial (250 iu at 28 and 34 weeks) was undertaken in England and Scotland (Lee and Rawlinson 1995). However, when it became clear that the hoped-for difference in immune anti-D rates between the control and treatment groups of D-negative primigravidas having D-positive babies was not emerging, recruitment was discontinued. At six months postpartum, four of 513 patients in the treatment group (0.78%) but nine of 595 controls (1.5%) had developed immune anti-D and it was considered that, although two doses of 250 iu of anti-D may reduce active immunisation, they are not as effective as two standard 500 iu doses.

The Edinburgh Consensus Conference on Anti-D Prophylaxis

In Edinburgh in 1997, 20 years after the McMaster Conference, the Royal College of Physicians of Edinburgh and the Royal College of Obstetricians and Gynaecologists convened a joint consensus conference on anti-D prophylaxis. The cases for and against routine antenatal prophylaxis were presented, discussed and then considered, with other published evidence, by an expert panel required to make a definitive statement on this specific issue.

In its final consensus statement, published in full in a supplement to the *British Journal of Obstetrics and Gynaecology* (Consensus Conference on Anti-D Prophylaxis 1998), the panel stated the following:

'routine antenatal anti-D prophylaxis is of proven benefit and this would significantly reduce levels of RhD alloimmunisation';

'because all Rh D-negative pregnant women are at risk from hidden bleeds, they should be given anti-D IgG prophylactically';

'antenatal prophylaxis has the potential over time to save more resources than it costs if restricted to primigravidas' (and multigravidas without living children), but 'there is no effective argument and no ethical' or economic justification 'against protecting all Rh D-negative women';

'it was expected that UK blood transfusion centres could supply enough high titre plasma for making polyclonal anti-D at least for primigravidas', and in the long term for all Rh D-negative women when 'the cost per life year is still likely to compare favourably with other NHS interventions'.

Although the conference was aware that difficulties in recruiting donors had forced postponement of routine antepartum prophylaxis in Australia, a presentation from one English centre had shown how procurement of hyperimmune anti-D plasma for making anti-D IgG can be stepped up substantially (de Silva 1998).

The consensus panel supported current guidelines on anti-D prophylaxis, both during pregnancy and postpartum and was reassured that these recommendations (particularly in relation to the first trimester) will remain under review. However, there was concern that 'there is abundant evidence that the recommendations are not being fully applied', especially regarding potentially sensitising antepartum events and estimation of the size of

FMH, and that in initiating routine antenatal prophylaxis 'health authorities should first check on compliance with current guidelines'.

Other matters considered at the conference included continued development of a safe and effective monoclonal anti-D IgG to supplement and eventually replace polyclonal anti-D and the possible place of anti-D IgG in the treatment of immune-mediated thrombocytopenia.

MANAGEMENT

Haematological surveillance

At booking, as well as routine grouping and Rh-typing, all pregnant women should be screened for Rh and other atypical red-cell antibodies which may cause HDN (most often anti-Kell, occasionally anti-Duffy or anti-Kidd, rarely others such as anti-S). Screening should be repeated monthly from 24 weeks in Rh D-negative women and in all others at 34 weeks to detect late onset antibodies or those present but undetectable earlier. Previous blood transfusion calls for an extra test at 28 weeks (Bowell et al. 1986). Positive screens require confirmation, specification of the atypical antibody or antibodies and measurement by automated quantitation rather than by imprecise titration. In the case of anti-D, quantitations should be against the national anti-D standard (National Blood Transfusion Immunoglobulin Working Party 1991). Once detected, quantitation should be repeated monthly from 20 weeks.

When a maternal antibody that may cause HDN is present, the appropriate paternal genotype should be determined to help predicting the likelihood of HDN and, taken with the history, its possible severity. It will also assist counselling about further pregnancies.

The level and trend of maternal antibody, with the previous history, should guide the timing of amniocentesis or FBS to predict severity. If no previous baby has been affected, maternal antibody concentrations remaining at or below 2.5 iu/ml on continued four-weekly testing should allow term delivery without invasive diagnosis. Levels exceeding 20 iu/ml, especially in a first affected pregnancy, warn that severe haemolysis may occur. A sharp rise over four weeks (e.g. <5–20 iu/ml, or <15–40 iu/ml) indicates that an acute haemolytic crisis may have begun or is impending and requires urgent amniocentesis or FBS, or delivery if near term.

Assays to measure *in vitro* the binding and lytic activity of blood group antibodies, including the antibody-dependent cell-mediated cytotoxicity (ADCC) test (Urbaniak et al. 1984) have not found general favour in the UK or the USA and there is no evidence that they are better predictors than repeated measurement of anti-D IgG against the national standard.

Regarding Rh antibodies other than anti-D, anti-c may cause as severe HDN, but anti-C and anti-E much less often. Rh D^u-positive subjects do not form immune anti-D.

These guidelines are broadly consistent with those of the British Committee for Standards in Haematology (1996) intended mainly for haematology departments, with the advice that 'because most practitioners do not see many cases of HDN it is essential that patients with antibodies of clinical significance should be referred for advice to a specialist at the earliest opportunity'. For the same reason, the booking obstetrician should transfer the responsibility for making an individualised management plan to a tertiary centre providing specialised multidisciplinary care for these mothers and their babies.

Kleihauer (or rosette or flow cytometry) tests to estimate FMH are indicated when any potentially sensitising events occur that require anti-D prophylaxis, including unexplained abdominal pain suggesting possible placental separation, or elevation of maternal serum α-fetoprotein which may reflect FMH. Because of lack of uniformity of technique and poor reproducibility, Bromilow *et al.* (1996) proposed relegating Kleihauer tests to a screening role followed, if a possibly large FMH (>4 ml) is revealed, by flow cytometry to count Rh D-positive red cells in the mother's D-negative blood. The need for additional anti-D IgG would be confirmed or avoided. This practice could obviously apply to late abortions, in which the fetus is often not Rh-typed yet a substantial FMH may occur.

While there is good compliance with the need to obtain cord blood samples at delivery (for Coombs test, haemoglobin and bilirubin measurements), frequently no attempt is made to obtain fetal blood after stillbirth or late abortion, although this may provide a reminder of the need for anti-D prophylaxis and a guide for counselling. Also, maternal blood is not always obtained at delivery of Rh D-negative mothers not already known to have developed antibodies, although a Kleihauer test will occasionally show that extra anti-D IgG is needed. A first detection of antibodies at this stage will show that sensitisation occurred during the pregnancy, not postpartum as is too often assumed.

Biophysical surveillance

Fetal measurements by ultrasound are used to confirm gestational age as a reliable reference for timing amniocentesis and interpreting its results, and for deciding the optimal times for transfusion and delivery. Frequent imaging enables early detection of ascites or hydrothorax as a warning that deterioration has begun, or of developing generalised hydrops when its reversal may still be possible by immediate intravascular intrauterine transfusion (IUT). The practical value of measuring vascular diameters (e.g., of the descending aorta or intrahepatic segment of the umbilical vein), liver size or Doppler flow velocities has yet to be accepted generally.

Regular fetal heart rate recordings should be part of surveillance from mid-pregnancy onward whenever severe Rh disease seems possible, a sustained or recurrent sinusoidal pattern being evidence of critical anaemia which, if confirmed by FBS, requires delivery (or exceptionally IUT).

Obstetric intervention

Once the pathophysiology of EBF and HDN was understood, especially the progressive course *in utero* as well as after birth, some obstetricians were persuaded of the logic of inducing labour near term to avoid continuing deterioration, but this had to be balanced against the complications of induction and of prematurity, particularly in babies already compromised by severe haemolytic disease. In a trial of routine induction three to five weeks before estimated term compared with awaiting spontaneous labour, mortality was higher with the active policy (36% against 24%; Mollison and Walker 1952) and kernicterus was more likely (Armitage and Mollison 1953). However, with oxytocic infusions to supplement induction and improving neonatal care, selective early induction when previous infants were stillborn or there were high antibody titres, while taking account of paternal genotype, carried a lower mortality than non-intervention in Belfast (16% against 29%; Fisher 1957) and in Western Australia (Kelsall *et al.* 1958). From Newcastle, UK, Walker and Murray (1956) reported that, in more than 1000 affected families, 'if a previous baby was stillborn from haemolytic disease there is about an 80% chance that the next baby if allowed to go to a spontaneous delivery will also be stillborn'. This gave strong support for early delivery in such cases, but implied letting the first stillbirth happen.

Unfortunately, when a previous baby has been affected, especially if severely and the paternal Rh genotype is probably heterozygous, maternal antibody levels are often unhelpful. Therefore, a new approach was needed to predict the severity of haemolysis in the current fetus and its likely further course in order to anticipate fetal death, or nearing term to deliver a less severely affected baby.

Amniocentesis and amniotic fluid analysis

The way ahead had, in fact, already been pointed out in Manchester, where Bevis (1950, 1956) showed a correlation between the concentration of bilirubin (and other haemoglobin breakdown products) in the amniotic fluid and the baby's haemoglobin at birth, but no practical system to manage individual patients was devised until Liley's breakthrough studies in New Zealand.

Liley (1961) validated his spectrophotometric measurement of the optical density 'peak' at 450 nm (ΔOD450) caused by bilirubin in amniotic fluid and showed that predicting the severity of HDN is improved by allowing for the normal gradual decline in ΔOD450 during the third trimester, hence the downward slope of his three prediction zones in which ΔOD450 values are plotted against gestational age. Liley also showed that in Rh disease the trend between measurements usually follows this decline, but sometimes an abnormal trend reaches a different zone and corrects an initial incorrect prediction. Therefore, two measurements, about three weeks apart, are usually made to reveal the trend clearly. Selective early induction based on this system reduced perinatal mortality from Rh disease from 22% to 9% during the five years to 1962 (Liley 1963).

Liley's methods, sometimes with modified zones, were soon adopted widely and successfully and his 9% 'wastage' was matched in at least two large series – in New York, repeated ΔOD450 estimations were graded to show how long pregnancies might continue without risk of fetal death (Freda 1965); and in Belfast, extrapolation of the ΔOD450 trend to an 'action line' indicating the optimal time for intervention, by delivery or IUT, became the main basis of managing 1372 pregnancies in six years (Whitfield 1970, 1976).

Other uses of amniotic fluid included measuring fetal pulmonary surfactant, but the need for this has been reduced by advances in neonatal intensive care and improved fetal condition achieved by IUTs. DNA Rh testing, using the polymerase chain reaction can be used on amniocytes in the second trimester (Bennett et al. 1993) but at present may still carry a 1% error rate (Lighten et al. 1995).

Fetal blood sampling

FBS by ultrasound-guided percutaneous umbilical puncture (cordocentesis) was introduced by Daffos et al. (1985) in Paris. They reported haematological indices for normal fetuses, including haemoglobin and haematocrit values rising from 11.5 g/dl and 37% at 20 weeks to 13.5 g/dl and 42% at 30 weeks (Forrestier et al. 1986).

FBS may be used in early pregnancy to determine the fetal Rh or other (e.g. Kell) type and for a direct Coombs test, when there has been previous severe disease or the father is probably heterozygous for the antigen concerned.

When the history suggests fetal death is likely or ominous warning signs develop, for example on ultrasound imaging or a sustained or recurrent sinusoidal heart rate pattern, FBS should be arranged as a confirmatory first step to proceeding to immediate intravascular IUT. In the third trimester, without such warning signs or history, amniocenteses for ΔOD450 estimation usually suffice.

The availability of FBS and the inapplicability of Liley's prediction zones before week 27 has prompted the question 'have Liley charts outlived their usefulness?' (Nicolaides *et al.* 1986). This reveals a lack of awareness of how to exploit the plateau normally followed by bilirubin in the amniotic fluid from before mid-pregnancy until Liley's zones apply. ΔOD 450 measurements and their trend can be used at this stage to indicate if and when FBS is needed (Ananth and Queenan 1989). Otherwise, amniocentesis is a simpler and safer procedure, it can almost always be directed by ultrasound to avoid an anteriorly sited placenta and consequent FMH which, by boosting immunisation, may exacerbate the condition of the fetus or a future one. The Winnipeg group also found serial ΔOD450 values in the second trimester to be often highly informative without FBS (Albar *et al.* 1993).

Integrated prediction

In deciding when intervention is called for, these various methods should be regarded as complementary. Queenan *et al.* (1993) based their practical four-zone scheme on 789 ΔOD450 measurements in 539 pregnancies between 14 and 40 weeks, integrated with antibody titres and the results of ultrasound and FBS. Their scheme is also cost-effective, mainly through early identification of D-negative fetuses, for which invasive procedures can be avoided, and now DNA Rh testing on amniotic fluid cells can have a useful place in such management systems (Bowman 1997).

Intrauterine transfusion

Having achieved many fewer perinatal losses, it was once again Liley (1963) who took the next stride by tackling the problem of hydropic change and fetal death occurring before early rescue to neonatal care becomes an option. Having on occasions at intended amniocentesis needled and withdrawn ascitic fluid from the distended abdomen of severely affected fetuses and, emboldened by a visitor's evidence that Nigerian babies with sickle-cell disease readily absorb normal red cells injected intraperitoneally, Liley decided to exploit this knowledge by transfusing Rh D-negative blood into the fetal abdomen in the hope of gaining time for the fetus to mature sufficiently for delivery. The fourth fetus on which this was attempted, at 32 weeks and again ten days later, became the first ever survivor of such a procedure which, late in 1963, made fetal medicine a therapeutic as well as a diagnostic discipline.

Using x-rays with radio-opaque contrast injected into the amniotic cavity and swallowed by the fetus to 'mark' its gut in the target area, Liley inserted a Tuohy needle through which he threaded a plastic epidural catheter to transfuse packed Rh D-negative cells fully compatible with the mother. Later, it would become standard practice to irradiate the donor blood and test it for the cytomegalovirus. IUT soon became used widely and, before anti-D prophylaxis had made a substantial impact on case numbers, some centres achieved survival rates after IUT of about 30%, including 34% in a survey of more than 1000 pregnancies at 15 centres in the USA (Queenan 1969) which included some transfusions performed via hysterotomy, an approach that has not become an established option because of few survivals. In the centralised regional Rh service in Winnipeg, an initial similar survival rate of 30% rose steadily to 59% and then to 70% (79 out of 113) in the eight years to 1978 (Bowman 1978), attributable mainly to the growing experience of a small multidisciplinary team.

Refinements in technique have been made, including fluoroscopy with image intensification, instead of several x-ray exposures, to give continuous imaging with less radiation. A major advance was guidance by high resolution real-time ultrasound, introduced by Hobbins *et al.* (1976).

The most important advance was direct transfusion into the fetal circulation via an umbilical vessel (usually vein) at fetoscopy, first reported by Rodeck *et al.* (1981). Better survival rates were soon achievable by this technique, Nicolaides and Rodeck (1985) reporting 29 of 34 (84%) severely affected fetuses surviving, including 13 of 15 (87%) with hydrops first transfused before 25 weeks, representing a milestone in the attempted treatment of HF. Fetoscopic guidance gave way to the much less cumbersome procedure of ultrasound-guided intravascular IUT and survival rates better than 90% were soon declared from Winnipeg (Harman *et al.* 1990) and Iowa (Weiner *et al.* 1991) and are now achieved by other experienced teams. Some preferred to give exchange, rather than 'straight', transfusions (Poissonier *et al.* 1989; Grannum 1993), but this has not become usual practice because the capacitance of the fetoplacental circulation seems to guard against vascular overload.

Helen Liley, a neonatologist in Christchurch, New Zealand, writing 34 years after her father performed the first IUTs, summarised the advantages of intravascular over intraperitoneal IUT as follows: enabling larger volumes to be given, transfusion earlier in pregnancy if necessary, prolongation of gestation for longer and achieving lower failure and operative mortality rates, especially when HF is present (Liley 1997).

Nevertheless, while agreeing that the intravascular route is usually the one of choice, the Winnipeg team believes that their considerable experience with both techniques 'has demonstrated a clear, although limited, need to continue familiarity with the intraperitoneal approach' (Harman and Bowman 1993). It is only for non-hydropic fetuses and if the placenta lies posteriorly, if the cord insertion in inaccessible or abnormal (e.g., velamentous), if the umbilical vein is too narrow (<4 mm) or if an intravascular attempt has failed or resulted in a cord haematoma or thrombus.

Other therapies

Of other treatments that have been tried, repeated maternal plasma exchange from early pregnancy (Fraser *et al.* 1976; Robinson 1984) has had its advocates and some sustained interest, but has not been generally accepted and there has been no firm evidence that it can contribute to the survival rates achievable by experienced Rh teams without resort to such demanding and expensive therapy.

So far, benefit from attempted suppression of immunisation by drugs (including promezathine and corticosteroids), by high-dose non-specific IgG, or by ingestion of material from D-positive red cell membranes is unproven or disproven.

Neonatal management

It is not the purpose here to include a review of neonatal management, except to recognise wholeheartedly that our paediatric colleagues deserve at least equal credit for the great advances made since Rh disease was understood. They have shared the clinical excitement of successful treatment. No hospital providing a Rh referral service should exist without neonatologists having particular expertise in HDN.

THE UNFINISHED BUSINESS

Incidence and future implications

Without prophylaxis, about one in six Rh D-negative women with D-positive babies will develop anti-D antibodies. In the UK, despite postpartum prophylaxis since 1969, the sensitisation rate remains 'unacceptably high at around 1.5%', and more than 1000 Rh D-negative women delivering D-positive babies become actively immunised each year (Letsky and de Silva 1994). In hospitals served by the Liverpool Blood Centre during 1994, Howard *et al.* (1997) found that there was 95% compliance with postpartum prevention, but antenatal guidelines were less well implemented, especially for abdominal trauma and antepartum bleeding (for example, inadequate doses of anti-D after 20 weeks) and the purpose of Kleihauer tests was sometimes misunderstood.

The incidences of different circumstances in which the sensitising FMH occurs indicate where attention is now needed. Table 1 categorises 463 pregnancies in D-immunised women at The Queen Mother's Hospital, Glasgow, during the 20 years 1977 to 1996, as:

(1) *Preprophylaxis*, where immunisation occurred before there was immunoprophylaxis or before the woman qualified for it according to the guidelines applying at the time and where she was under care;

(2) *Administrative*, when she qualified for prophylaxis but did not receive it;

(3) *Therapeutic*, when immunisation occurred despite correctly given anti-D IgG;

(4) *Antepartum*, when there was clear evidence, gathered when necessary from many sources including overseas, that sensitisation had occurred either during the current or a previous pregnancy;

Table 1 *Causes of RhD immunisation in all pregnancies managed in the Rh referral service at the Queen Mother's Hospital, Glasgow, between 1977 and 1996, subdivided into four quinquennia*

Category	1977–81	1982–86	1987–91	1992–96	Total (1977–96)
Preprophylaxis	41 (41%)	11	3	–	55
Transfusion	1	–	–	1	2
Administrative	11	9	19	6	45 (10%)
Therapeutic	6	18	20	20	64 (14.5%)
Antepartum					
Current pregnancy	25	26	21	15	87
Previous pregnancy	16	36	64	71	187
Total antepartum	41 (40%)			86 (69%)[a]	274 (59%)[b]
Uncertain	3	6	4	10	23
Total	103	106	131	123	463

[a]76% and [b]62% if uncertain category is excluded

(5) *Uncertain*, when, despite thorough investigation, it remained unclear how immunisation had occurred.

The main point of interest is that, as the number of women in the preprophylaxis category declined, from a rate of 41% during 1977–81 to none in 1992–96, the proportion with definite evidence of antepartum sensitisation increased to a rate of 69%, or 76% if the uncertain category is excluded. It is a matter of concern that administrative failures have accounted for about one-tenth of the immunisations during the whole period and that in about one-third of the therapeutic failures there was no evidence that a Kleihauer sample was submitted or the result documented; an inappropriate dose of anti-D was given in less than 5%.

Because this hospital deals with few early spontaneous abortions and almost no therapeutic abortions, the role of abortion is under-emphasised by these data. Otherwise, they lend strong support to the final statement of the Edinburgh Consensus Conference on Anti-D Prophylaxis (1998) that, while every effort is required to ensure compliance with current and future guidelines, a substantial further impact will be made only if routine antepartum prophylaxis is introduced.

Continued vigilance regarding Kleihauer (or alternative) testing is called for. It is hoped that the revised guidelines on prophylaxis for abortions will be understood and implemented by hospitals, family practitioners and casualty departments. It seems certain that, in the past, guidelines and other important notices did not always succeed in negotiating the bureaucratic channels of communication. It is therefore hoped that in future such important information will be sent promptly and directly to the practitioners and clinicians concerned.

The present delay in obtaining imported anti-D IgG to replace UK supplies at hypothetical risk of transmitting new-variant Creutzfeldt–Jakob disease and the consequent standstill in approving routine antepartum prophylaxis is unfortunate. One hopes that antepartum prophylaxis will not be 'rationed out' for false economy. Eventually, supplies of monoclonal anti-D will solve the problem, but it seems this is not likely to occur soon.

Total rhesus mortality

This is defined as including all abortions following fetal death, stillbirths and neonatal deaths attributed primarily to Rh disease or its treatment and also any postneonatal deaths in which Rh disease or its treatment was the primary cause. It is a much more inclusive definition than perinatal mortality, which excludes abortions (until recently, defined as occurring before 28 weeks) and also excludes deaths after seven days of life. The valuable running audit since 1977 by Sir Cyril Clarke and his colleagues continues to illustrate the downward trend of registered stillbirths and deaths certified as due or partly due to haemolytic disease in England and Wales, highlighting where attention should be directed and the relatively increasing importance of antibodies other than anti-D (Clarke and Mollison 1989; Hussey and Clarke 1991, 1992; Clarke and Hussey 1994). However, it excludes the late abortions which make up about one-half of all Rh mortality (Tovey 1992; Murphy and Whitfield 1994). While inspection of case notes showed that around 30% of deaths notified to the England and Wales audit were wrongly certified due to HDN, actual and anecdotal evidence suggests that as many or more Rh losses are also miscoded.

In five years in Scotland there was considerable under-reporting of Rh mortality, five times as many confirmed Rh deaths occurring as were known to the General Register Office (Whitfield *et al.* 1997). Extrapolating these data to the UK suggests that there may still be as many as 50 annual losses due to Rh HDN (or six per 100 000 live births) compared with an average of 15.4 per year notified to and accepted by the continuing Clarke audit during the same five years. The recent reduction to 24 weeks of the lower limit for registering stillbirths will allow more, but not all, the losses previously designated as late abortions to be included in the hoped for continued audit of deaths from haemolytic disease in England and Wales.

The small, but persisting, wastage represents the 'peak of the iceberg' of severe Rh disease with its human and economic costs and its demands on high-quality staff and facilities. It reinforces the case for more concentration of patients and the specialised care needed. It will often be possible to organise an efficient shared care system between referring and referral centres, with the latter having prime responsibility for deciding clinical management.

Non-D antibodies

The England and Wales audit shows that there has been no real change in the number of deaths registered due to HDN caused by antibodies other than anti-D, but their relative importance has been increasing. In the five years of the survey between 1988 and 1992 they account for one-quarter of all the deaths correctly certified due to HDN.

The management of pregnant women with non-Rh antibodies that can cross the placenta should follow the same system as for those with Rh antibodies, with the exception that many will have been immunised by previous blood transfusions with antigens which their partners do not carry, particularly in the case of anti-Kell, as the majority of the population is Kell-negative. The partner's genotype for the factor concerned should therefore be determined. DNA typing for Kell or other significant atypical antigen would be particularly useful. It is also often stated that amniotic fluid ΔOD450 values under-predict the severity of Kell haemolytic disease (Caine and Mueller-Heubach 1986) but this has not been a universal experience.

References

Albar, H., Harman, C.R., Pollock, J. *et al.* (1993) Amniotic fluid spectrophotometry for evaluation of alloimmune disease in mid-trimester. *Br J Obstet Gynaecol* **100**, 772

Ananth, V. and Queenan, J.T. (1989) Does midtrimester OD 450 of amniotic fluid reflect severity of RH disease? *Am J Obstet Gynecol* **161**, 47–9

Armitage, P. and Mollison, P.L. (1953) Further analysis of controlled trials of treatment of haemolytic disease of the newborn. *J Obstet Gynaecol Br Empire* **60**, 605–20

Ballantyne, J.W. (1892) *The Diseases and Deformaties of the Foetus.* Edinburgh: Oliver and Boyd

Bennett, P.R., Le Kim, C.V., Colin, Y. *et al.* (1993) Prenatal determination of fetal RhD type by DNA amplification. *N Engl J Med* **329**, 607–10

Bevis, D.C.A. (1950) Composition of liquor amnii in haemolytic disease of newborn. *Lancet* **ii**, 443

Bevis, D.C.A. (1956) Blood pigments in haemolytic disease of the newborn. *J Obstet Gynaecol Br Empire* **63**, 68–75

Bourgeois, L. (1609) *Observations Diverses, sur la Stérilité, Perte de Fruict, Foecondité, Accouchements, et Maladie des Femmes et Enfants Nouveaus-naiz.* Paris: Saugrain

Bowell, P.J., Allen, D.L. and Entwistle, C.C. (1986) Blood group antibody screening tests during pregnancy. *Br J Obstet Gynaecol* **93**, 1038–43

Bowman, J. (1997) The management of hemolytic disease of the fetus and newborn. *Semin Perinatol* **21**, 39–44

Bowman, J.M. (1978) The management of Rh-isoimmunisation. *Obstet Gynecol* **52**, 1–16

Bowman, J.M., Chown, B. and Lewis, M. (1978) Rh-isoimmunization during pregnancy: antenatal prophylaxis. *CMAJ* **118**, 623–7

British Committee for Standards in Haematology (1996) Guidelines for blood grouping and red cell antibody testing during pregnancy. *Trans Med Soc Lond* **6**, 71–4

Bromilow, I., Dugald, J.K.M. and Walkinshaw, S. (1996) Importance of accurate assessment of fetomaternal haemorrhage after late abortions. *BMJ* **313**, 1200–1

Buchan, A.H. and Comrie, J.D. (1909) Four cases of congenital anaemia with jaundice and enlargement of the spleen. *J Pathol Bacteriol* **13**, 398–413

Caine, M.E. and Mueller-Heubach, E. (1986) Kell sensitization in pregnancy. *Am J Obstet Gynecol* **154**, 85–90

Chown, B. (1954) Anaemia from bleeding of the fetus into mother's circulation. *Lancet* **i**, 1213–15

Claireaux, A.E., Cole, P.G. and Lathe, G.H. (1953) Icterus of the brain in the newborn. *Lancet* **ii**, 1226–30

Clarke, C.A. (1967) Prevention of Rh-haemolytic disease. *BMJ* **ii**, 7–12

Clarke, C.A. (1972) Practical effects of blood group incompatibility between mother and fetus. *BMJ* **i**, 90–5

Clarke, C.A. (1982) The present mortality of Rhesus haemolytic disease. *Maternal and Child Health* January, 4–11

Clarke, C.A. and Hussey, R.M. (1994) Decline in deaths from Rhesus haemolytic disease of the fetus and newborn, 1977–87. *J R Coll Physicians Lond* **23**, 181–4

Clarke C.A. and Mollison, P.L. (1989) Deaths from Rh haemolytic disease of the fetus and newborn. *Lancet* **ii**, 1226–30

Clarke, C.A., Donohoe, W.T.A., McConnell, R.B. *et al.* (1963) Further experimental studies in the prevention of Rh haemolytic disease. *BMJ* **i**, 979–84

Combined Study from Centres in England and Baltimore (1966) Prevention of Rh haemolytic disease: results of the clinical trial. *BMJ* **ii**, 907–14

Combined Study from Centres in England and Baltimore (1971) Prevention of Rh haemolytic disease: final results of the 'high risk' clinical trial. *BMJ* **ii**, 607–9

Committee for Proprietary Medicinal Products for the European Community (1994) Note for guidance: core summary of product characteristics for human anti-D immunoglobulin im. Brussels: *CEC* 111/34463/92E

Consensus Conference on Anti-D Prophylaxis (1998) *Br J Obstet Gynaecol* **105** Suppl 18, 1–44

Contreras, M. (1998) The prevention of Rh haemolytic disease of the fetus and newborn – general background. *Br J Obstet Gynaecol* **105** Suppl 18, 7–10

Coombs, R.R.A., Mourant, A.E. and Race, R. (1945) A new test for the detection of weak and 'incomplete' Rh agglutinins. *British Journal of Experimental Pathology* **26**, 255–66

Daffos, F., Capella-Paviovsky, M. and Forrestier, F. (1985) Fetal blood sampling during pregnancy with use of a needle guided by ultrasound: a study of 606 cases. *Am J Obstet Gynecol* **153**, 655–60

Darrow, R.R. (1938) Icterus gravis (erythroblastosis) neonatorum: examination of aetiologic considerations. *Arch Pathol* **25**, 378–417

Davey, M.G. and Zipursky, A.M. (1979) McMaster Conference on prevention of Rh immunization. *Vox Sang* **36**, 50–64

de Silva, M. (1998) The procurement of hyperimmune anti-D plasma for anti-D Ig manufacture in England. *Br J Obstet Gynaecol* **105** Suppl 18, 28

Diamond, L.K. (1947) Erythroblastosis foetalis or haemolytic disease of the newborn. *Proc R Soc Med* **40**, 546–9

Diamond, L.K., Blackfan, K.D. and Baty, J.M. (1932) Erythroblastosis fetalis and its association with universal oedema of the fetus, icterus gravis neonatorum and anemia of the newborn. *J Pediatr* **1**, 269–309

Dienst, A. (1905) Eclampsia: further studies. *Zentralbl Gynakol* **20**, 253–364

Finn, R. (1960) Erythroblastosis. *Lancet* **i**, 526–7

Finn, R., Clarke, C.A. and Donohue, W.T.A. (1961) Experimental studies on the prevention of Rh haemolytic disease. *BMJ* **i**, 1486–90

Fisher, O.D. (1957) Influence of elective induction of labour on mortality in haemolytic disease of the newborn. *BMJ* **i**, 615–17

Fisher, R.A. and Race, R.R. (1946) Rh gene frequencies in Britain. *Nature* **157**, 48–9

Forrestier, F., Galacteras, F. and Bardakjian, J. (1986) Haematological values in 163 normal fetuses between 18 and 30 weeks' gestation. *Pediatr Res* **20**, 342–6

Fraser, I.D., Bothamley, J.A., Bennet, M.O. *et al.* (1976) Intensive antenatal plasmapheresis in severe rhesus isoimmunisation. *Lancet* **i**, 6–9

Freda, V.J. (1965) The Rh problem in obstetrics and a concept of its management using amniocentesis and spectrophotometric scanning of amniotic fluid. *Am J Obstet Gynecol* **92**, 341–74

Freda, V.J. (1967) Prevention of Rh isoimmunization: progress report of the clinical trial in mothers. *JAMA* **199**, 390–4

Freda, V.J., Gorman, J.G. and Pollack, W. (1964) Successful prevention of experimental sensitization in man with an anti-Rh gamma globulin preparation. *Transfusion* **4**, 26–32

Grannum, P.A.T. (1993) '*In utero* intravascular exchange transfusion of severe erythroblastosis fetalis' in: F.A. Chervanek (Ed.) *Ultrasound in Obstetrics and Gynecology* **2**, pp. 1321–6. Boston: Little, Brown

Gunson, H.H. (1957) Neonatal anaemia due to fetal haemorrhage into the maternal circulation. *Am J Clin Pathol* **20**, 3–8

Hamilton, E.G. (1967) Prevention of Rh isoimmunization by injection of anti-D antibody *Obstet Gynecol* **30**, 812–15

Harman, C.R. and Bowman, J.M. (1993) 'Intrapartum fetal transfusion' in: F.A. Chervanek (Ed.) *Ultrasound in Obstetrics and Gynaecology* **2**, pp. 1293–313. Boston: Little, Brown

Harman, C.R., Bowman, J.M., Manning, F.A. *et al.* (1990) Intrauterine transfusion – intraperitoneal versus intravascular. *Am J Obstet Gynecol* **162**, 1053–9

Hart, A.P. (1925) Familial icterus gravis of the newborn and its treatment. *CMAJ* **15**, 1008–11

Hellman, L.M. and Hertig, A.T. (1938) Pathological changes in the placenta associated with erythroblastosis of the fetus. *Am J Pathol* **14**, 111–20

Hirszfeld, L. (1928) Uber die konstitutionsserologie im Zussammenhang mit der blut-grosspanforschung. *Klinische Wochenschrift* **6**, 1881

Hobbins, J.C., Davis, C.D. and Webster, J. (1976) A new technique utilising ultrasound to aid intrauterine transfusion. *J Clin Ultrasound* **4**, 135–7

Howard, H.L., Martlew, V.J., McFadyen, I.R. *et al.* (1997) Preventing Rhesus D haemolytic disease of the newborn by giving anti-D immunoglobulin: are the guidelines being adequately followed? *Br J Obstet Gynaecol* **104**, 37–41

Huchet, J., Dallemagne, S., Huchet, C. *et al.* (1987) Application ante-partum du traitement préventif d'immunisation chez les femmes Rhésus negatif. *J Gynecol Obstet Biol Reprod (Paris)* **16**, 101–11

Hussey, R.M. and Clarke, C.A. (1991) Deaths from Rh haemolytic disease in England and Wales in 1988 and 1989. *BMJ* **303**, 445–6

Hussey, R.M. and Clarke, C.A. (1992) Deaths from haemolytic disease of the newborn in 1990. *BMJ* **304**, 444

Jakesch, W. (1878) A case of hydrops universalis of the foetus and hydrops placentae. *Centrälbl Gynäkol* **26**, 619–24

Kelsall, G.A., Vos, G.H. and Kirk, R.L. (1958) Case for induction of labour in treatment of haemolytic disease of the newborn. *BMJ* **ii**, 468–73

Kleihauer, E., Braun, H. and Betke, K. (1957) Demonstration of fetal haemoglobin in the circulating erythrocytes. *Klinische Wochenschrift* **35,** 637–42

Landsteiner, K. (1901) Über agglutinationserscheinungen normalen menschlichen Blutes. *Wien Klinische Wochenshrift* **14**, 1132–4

Landsteiner, K. and Wiener, A.S. (1940) An agglutinable factor in human blood recognised by immune sera for rhesus blood. *Proc Soc Exp Biol Med* **43**, 223–5

Lee, D. (1991) Anti-D immunoglobulin. *Prescribers' Journal* **31**, 135–7

Lee, D. and Rawlinson, V.I. (1995) Multicentre trial of antepartum low-dose anti-D immunoglobulin. *Trans Med Soc Lond* **5**, 15–19

Letsky, E.A. and de Silva, M. (1994) Preventing Rh immunisation: much scope for improvement. *BMJ* **309**, 213–14

Levine, P. (1943) Serological factors as possible causes of spontaneous abortion. *J Hered* **34**, 71–5

Levine, P. and Stetson, R.E. (1939) Unusual cases of intra group agglutination. *JAMA* **113**, 126–7

Levine, P., Burnham, L. Katzin, E.M. *et al.* (1941) The role of isoimmunization in the pathogenesis of erythroblastosis fetalis. *Am J Obstet Gynecol* **42**, 925–37

Lighten, A.D., Overton, T.G., Sepulveda, W. *et al.* (1995) Accuracy of prenatal determination of RhD type status by polymerase chain reaction in amniotic cells. *Am J Obstet Gynecol* **173**, 1182–5

Liley, A.W. (1961) Liquor amnii analysis in the management of the pregnancy complicated by rhesus sensitisation. *Am J Obstet Gynecol* **82**, 1359–70

Liley, A.W. (1963) Intrauterine transfusion of foetus in haemolytic disease. *BMJ* **ii**, 1107–9

Liley, H.G. (1997) Rescue in inner space: management of Rh hemolytic disease. *J Pediatr* **131**, 340–2

Mayne, S., Parker, J.S., Harden, T.A. *et al.* (1997) Rate of RhD sensitisation before and after implementation of a community based antenatal prophylaxis programme. *BMJ* **315**, 1588

Medical Research Council Anti-D Working Party (1974) Controlled trial of various anti-D dosages in suppression of Rh sensitization following pregnancy. *BMJ* **ii**, 175–80

Mollison, P.L. and Walker, W. (1952) Controlled trials of the treatment of haemolytic disease of the newborn. *Lancet* **i**, 429–33

Murphy, K.W. and Whitfield C.R. (1994) Rhesus disease in this decade. *Contemporary Reviews in Obstetrics and Gynaecology* **6**, 61–7

National Blood Transfusion Immunoglobulin Working Party (1991) Recommendations for the use of anti-D immunoglobulin. *Prescribers' Journal* **31**, 137–45

Nevanlinna, H.R. and Vainio, T. (1956) The influence of mother-child ABO-incompatibility. *Vox Sang* **1**, 26–36

Nicolaides, K.H. and Rodeck, C.H. (1985) 'Fetal therapy' in: J. Studd (Ed.) *Progress in Obstetrics and Gynaecology* **5**, pp. 48–51. Edinburgh: Churchill Livingstone

Nicolaides, K.H., Rodeck, C.H. and Mibashan, R.S. (1986) Have Liley charts outlived their usefulness? *Am J Obstet Gynecol* **155**, 90–4

Nusbacher, J. and Bove, J.R. (1980) Rh immunoprophylaxis: is antepartum therapy desirable? *N Engl J Med* **303**, 935–7

Orth, J. (1875) Über das Vorkommen von bilirubinkrystallen beinengeborenen kindern. *Virchow's Archives of Pathological Anatomy* **63**, 647

Poissonier, M-H., Brossard, Y., Demedeiros, N. *et al.* (1989) Two hundred intrauterine exchange transfusions in severe blood incompatibilities. *Am J Obstet Gynecol* **161**, 709–13

Queenan, J.T. (1969) Intrauterine transfusion: a co-operative survey. *Am J Obstet Gynecol* **168**, 1370–6

Queenan, J.T., Tomai, T.P., Serdar, H.V. *et al.* (1993) Deviation in amniotic fluid optical density at a wavelength of 450 nm in Rh-immunized pregnancies from 14 to 40 weeks gestation: a proposal for clinical management. *Am J Obstet Gynecol* **168**, 1370–6

Rautman, H. (1912) Über blutbildung bei totales allgeneiner wasserucht. *Beitrage zur Pathologischen Anatomie* **54**, 322–49

Robinson, E.A.E. (1984) Principles and practice of plasma exchange in the management of Rh haemolytic disease of the newborn. *Plasma Therapy and Transfusion Technology* **5**, 7–14

Rodeck, C.H., Holman, C.A., Karnicki, J. *et al.* (1981) Direct intravascular fetal blood transfusion by fetoscopy in severe rhesus isoimmunisation. *Lancet* **i**, 625–7

Schneider, G. and Preisler, O. (1965) Untersuchungen zur serologischen prophylaxe de Rh-sensibilisierung. *Blut* **12**, 4

Schridde, H. (1910) Die angerborene allgemeine Wasserucht. *Muenchener Medizinische Wochenschrift* **57**, 397–8

Standing Medical Advisory Committee (1976) *Haemolytic Disease of the Newborn.* London: HMSO

Standing Medical Advisory Committee (1981) *Addendum to Haemolytic Disease of the Newborn.* London: HMSO

Stetson, R.E. (1933) Causes and prevention of post-transfusion reactions. *Surg Clin North Am* **13**, 319–45

Tovey, L.A.D. (1992) Towards the conquest of Rh haemolytic disease: Britain's contribution and the role of serendipity. *Trans Med Soc Lond* **2**, 99–109

Tovey, L.A.D., Townley, A. and Stevenson, B.J. (1983) The Yorkshire antenatal anti-D immunoglobulin trial in primigravidae. *Lancet* **ii**, 244–6

Urbaniak, S.J., Ayoub Greiss, M., Crawford, R.J. *et al.* (1984) Prediction of the outcome of Rh haemolytic disease of the newborn: additional information using an ADCC assay. *Vox Sang* **46**, 323–9

Walker, W. and Murray, S. (1956) Haemolytic disease of the newborn as a family problem. *BMJ* **i**, 187–93

Wallerstein, H. (1946) Treatment of severe erythroblastosis by simultaneous removal and replacement of the blood of the newborn infant. *Science* **103**, 583–4

Weiner, C.P., Williamson, R.G., Wenstrom, K.D. *et al.* (1991) Management of fetal hemolytic disease by cordocentesis: II, outcome of treatment. *Am J Obstet Gynecol* **165**, 1302–7

WHO Scientific Group (1971) *Prevention of Rh Sensitization*, p. 23. Geneva: World Health Organization (Technical Report Series No. 468)

Whitfield, C.R. (1970) A three year assessment of an Action Line method of timing intervention in rhesus isoimmunization. *Am J Obstet Gynecol* **108**, 1239–44

Whitfield, C.R. (1976) Rhesus haemolytic disease. *J Clin Pathol* **29** Suppl 103, 54–62

Whitfield, C.R., Raafat, A. and Urbaniak, S.J. (1997) Underreporting of mortality from Rh haemolytic disease in Scotland and its implications: retrospective review. *BMJ* **315**, 1504–5

Wiener, A.S. and Peters, H.R. (1940) Hemolytic reactions following transfusion of blood of the husband's group with three cases in which the same agglutinogen was responsible. *Ann Intern Med* **13**, 2306–22

Woodrow, J.C., Clarke, C.A., McConnell, R.B. *et al.* (1971) Prevention of Rh-haemolytic disease: results of the 'low risk' trial. *BMJ* **ii**, 610–12

Zipursky, A., Hull, A., White, F.D. *et al.* (1959) Foetal erythrocytes in the maternal circulation. *Lancet* **i**, 451–2

18

Regulation of the myometrium: term and preterm labour

Peter W. Nathanielsz and Gordon C.S. Smith

INTRODUCTION

However far removed the world of clinical obstetrics seems from the world of basic science, drugs routinely employed in obstetrics, such as oxytocin, prostaglandin gel and corticosteroids, have their origins in the experimental science of the last 50 years. Clinical trials of these drugs were necessarily preceded by the identification of the native hormone (or local regulator), elucidation of its chemical structure and chemical synthesis of the molecule (or a derivative), pharmacological characterisation of its effects in animal models and *in vitro* experiments with human tissue. Effective clinical practices of the future will increasingly have as their bases current and future basic biomedical research. The aim of this chapter is to summarise key areas in uterine physiology and outline the potential for these systems to yield novel and improved therapies to alter function of key intrauterine tissues.

CLINICAL AIMS OF DRUG THERAPY

Treatment of premature labour

The ultimate goal of treating preterm labour is the stated aim of many basic studies of myometrial physiology and pharmacology. However, of the three principal clinical goals discussed (treatment of preterm labour, induction of labour and treatment of postpartum haemorrhage), management of premature labour is perhaps the one with the most ambiguous indication. Preterm labour is undoubtedly a major source of morbidity and mortality. While the administration of steroids to pregnant women in premature labour between one and seven days prior to preterm delivery accelerates fetal lung maturation and reduces perinatal morbidity and mortality (Creasy and Iams 1999), the evidence that inhibiting uterine contractility with drugs has any effect on fetal and neonatal survival is sparse. Tocolytic therapy concurrent with steroid administration is largely justified on the grounds that it might delay delivery to allow steroids to have their maximum effect on fetal lung maturation. There is no direct evidence from a large-scale randomised controlled trial that steroids and tocolytics are associated with a significantly better outcome than steroids alone. The lack of a clear beneficial effect of tocolysis may be related to the pathophysiology of premature labour. In some cases it is thought that premature labour may be induced by the fetus in response to a hostile intrauterine environment, which may have its origins in early pregnancy (Smith *et al.* 1998a).

181

Artificially prolonging fetal exposure to an adverse intrauterine environment is potentially harmful. In other cases, labour is associated with intrauterine infection and delaying delivery is also potentially harmful in this context (Creasy and Iams 1999). However, premature labour is simply a descriptive term, not a disease, and it is the end-point of diverse pathological processes. It is likely that pharmacological inhibition of premature delivery confers a differing degree of benefit or harm depending on the nature of the pathophysiological process.

Induction of labour

In contrast to the treatment of premature delivery, induction of labour has been shown, in the context of post-dates pregnancy, to reduce both maternal morbidity (caesarean section) (Hannah *et al.* 1992) and may also reduce perinatal mortality (Grant 1994). The apparent protective effect of induction of labour post-term on the risk of caesarean section is likely to be due to the increased risk of caesarean section associated with advancing gestational age post-term (Saunders and Paterson 1991). However, at a given gestational age, a woman whose labour has been induced is more likely to require a caesarean section than a woman in spontaneous labour (Saunders and Paterson 1991). The challenge is how to induce labour in a manner that does not increase the risk of operative delivery.

Contraction of the postpartum uterus

Failure of contraction of the uterus postpartum with consequent primary postpartum haemorrhage kills approximately 125 000 women in the world each year (Drife 1997). In this case there is no ambiguity in the purpose of treatment; it is to contract the uterus and maintain it in a contracted state. An effective, tonic constrictor of the pregnant human uterus that has long-term stability at tropical room temperatures would have considerable potential to reduce global maternal mortality. However, this aspect of the control of the uterus is relatively ignored in the context of myometrial pharmacology.

TARGET TISSUES FOR DRUG THERAPY

Research on factors controlling parturition has naturally tended to focus on the factors which control myometrial contractility. However, in both premature labour and induction of labour, other systems are also important. The tendency to focus on the myometrium led to studies in which nitric oxide donors were administered as a treatment for premature labour (Lees *et al.* 1994). Subsequently, this class of drug was found to be an effective agent for priming the cervix (Thomson *et al.* 1997, 1998). Non-myometrial intrauterine tissues are potentially both a source of unwanted adverse effects and an ignored target for novel therapeutic agents; 30% of cases of premature delivery follow prelabour rupture of the fetal membranes (Garite 1999).

Myometrium

All currently employed treatments for premature labour are inhibitors of myometrial contractility. A wide range of drugs has been evaluated, such as calcium channel blockers (Papatsonis *et al.* 1997), potassium channel activators, such as diazoxide (Caritis *et al.*

1979), β-2 adrenoceptor agonists (Caritis *et al.* 1988), prostaglandin H synthase (PGHS) inhibitors (Van den Veyver and Moise 1993) and nitric oxide (NO) donors (Lees *et al.* 1994). All these drugs affect other maternal systems, particularly other smooth muscles. It seems that the best prospect of discovering drugs with true specificity for the myometrium lies in a better understanding of the physiological and pathological factors which stimulate myometrial contraction in term and preterm labour. It is of particular importance to determine those systems that are unique to the myometrium or are more fundamentally involved in control of myometrial smooth muscle than in the common sites of adverse effects, such as vascular smooth muscle.

Cervix

No drug currently used in the treatment of premature labour has the cervix as its principal target. This unfortunate deficiency may reflect the fact that it is technically less straightforward to determine the effect of drugs on non-myometrial tissues. Drugs used for induction of labour are, however, given with the primary intention of altering the cervix, notably synthetic prostaglandins (Greer 1992). These drugs have considerably simplified the management of women presenting with an unfavourable cervix at term and post-term who require to have labour induced. The principal adverse effect of prostaglandins in this context is unwanted contraction of the uterus that can be sufficiently severe as to cause fetal distress. Excessive and inappropriate myometrial contraction in turn may necessitate tocolytic therapy or caesarean section.

Decidua

Activation of the decidua is considered to play an important role in the physiological control of labour (Casey and MacDonald 1988). Oxytocin is synthesised in the human choriodecidua and levels are increased during spontaneous labour and *in vitro* treatment with oestrogen (Chibbar *et al.* 1995). The oxytocin released may have a paracrine role by stimulating the myometrium which expresses oxytocin receptors (Fuchs *et al.* 1984) or an autocrine role, since the choriodecidua also expresses oxytocin receptor (Takemura *et al.* 1994). It seems likely, therefore, that exogenous oxytocin given to induce uterine contraction acts in part through decidual activation and, conversely, oxytocin receptor antagonists may have an inhibitory effect on the decidua. Similarly both PGHS (Fuentes *et al.* 1996) and prostaglandin receptors (Smith *et al.* 1998b) are expressed in the decidua. It seems likely that the decidua has a key role in the processes leading to term and preterm labour.

Fetal membranes

Prelabour rupture of the fetal membranes has a role in approximately 30% of preterm deliveries (Garite 1999). Consequently, the factors that control the membranes are potentially important in the control of premature labour. The fetal membranes are sources of prostaglandins (Mijovic *et al.* 1997) and the chorion of the non-human primate expresses the number of genes encoding prostaglandin receptors (Smith *et al.* 1998b). It is possible, therefore, that the beneficial effect of prostaglandin synthesis inhibitors in the treatment and prophylaxis of preterm labour (Van den Veyver and Moise 1993) and the use of exogenous synthetic prostaglandins to induce labour are mediated in part through the fetal membranes. Many other systems are known to have direct and indirect effects on the fetal membranes (French and McGregor 1996).

PATTERNS OF PHARMACOLOGICAL ACTIVITY

Enzyme inhibition

Many drugs act by inhibiting enzyme activity. An enzyme inhibitor will have the opposite effect on the system to the net product of the enzyme's activity. For example the net effect of prostaglandins on the myometrium is stimulatory and, consequently, PGHS inhibitors act as uterine tocolytics (Van den Veyver and Moise 1993). Conversely, inhibiting the synthesis of a product that has an inhibitory effect results in activation. An example of this would be the reversal of endotoxin-induced hypotension elicited by NO synthase inhibitors (Wolkow 1998). A number of important enzymes in the control of labour have multiple products, for example PGHS (Smith 1992) and lipoxygenase (Goetzl *et al.* 1995). It follows, therefore, that loss of some products may have effects that are opposed to the desired therapeutic result, for example the profound inhibitory effect of EP_2 receptor activation (Senior *et al.* 1993; Garcia-Villar *et al.* 1995), will be lost following prostaglandin synthesis inhibition.

Interaction with receptors

Since many readily available drugs can either activate or block receptors and receptors can either stimulate or inhibit systems, it follows that there are at least four possible ways in which drugs with selective activity at receptors might have effects; these are summarised in Table 1. In addition, the magnitude of the predicted effect of an antagonist is dependent on the levels of the endogenous agonist. If there is no endogenous agonist and the receptor lacks intrinsic (tonic) activity, the antagonist will have no effect. The converse is true of an agonist. The higher the concentration of the endogenous agonist, the higher the concentration of exogenous agonist required to exert a given effect (Smith and McGrath 1994). Some drugs are partial agonists of receptors, that is they stimulate the receptor, but their maximal effect is less than the maximal effect of a full agonist. In the presence of low concentrations of the endogenous agonist these drugs act as weak agonists and in the presence of high concentrations of the endogenous agonist, they act as weak antagonists.

Table 1 *Potential effects of agonists and antagonists, related to the physiological role of the endogenous hormone*

Effect of drug at receptor	Effect of endogenous hormone	
	Stimulatory	*Inhibitory*
Agonist	+ (e.g. oxytocin to induce labour)	− (e.g. ritodrine to inhibit uterine contraction)
Antagonist	− (e.g. labetalol to lower blood pressure)	+ (e.g. tamoxifen to induce ovulation)

Interaction with intracellular signal transduction systems

It is possible for drugs to bypass the proximal portion of the signal transduction system and interact directly with post-receptor events. Some enzyme inhibitors act in this way, for example phosphodiesterase inhibitors, which increase levels of cyclic adenosine monophosphate (cAMP) or cyclic guanosine monophosphate (cGMP) by inhibiting their metabolism (Polson and Strada 1996). Some bacterial toxins interact directly with G-proteins (Barritt and Gregory 1997), which are the protein link between many receptors and their second messenger (Sanborn et al. 1998). The NO produced by NO donors interacts directly with the enzyme (soluble guanylate cyclase) to generate the second messenger cGMP (Wink and Mitchell 1998). As knowledge of the intracellular events increases, it is likely that many drugs will be developed which act at post-receptor events. However, at the present time, the ease of study and enormous diversity of receptors makes them both convenient and more specific targets. However, a similar diversity is present in many of the post-receptor events, such as multiple forms of G-protein (Sanborn et al. 1998) and isoforms of enzymes of phosphodiesterase (Polson and Strada 1996). This heterogeneity also promises the potential for drugs with highly tissue-specific effects acting at a post-receptor system. The isoform selective phosphodiesterase inhibitor, sildenafil (Viagra,® Pfizer) used for the treatment of erectile dysfunction, is an example of such a drug (Goldstein et al. 1998).

Interaction with ion channels

Many drugs modulate ion channel activity and alter the intracellular concentration of calcium. Smooth muscle activation increases as intracellular calcium increases (Karaki et al. 1997). Drugs can act directly on calcium channels; for example, nifedipine, which inhibits calcium influx, reduces intracellular calcium and is, therefore, tocolytic (Ray and Dyson 1995). Alternatively, drugs can interact with channels that control membrane potential, such as potassium channels. Since potassium is a cation and is present in higher concentration inside the cell than outside, increasing the permeability of the cell membrane to potassium results in hyperpolarisation (that is it makes the membrane potential more negative) and decreasing the permeability of the cell membrane to potassium causes depolarisation. Changes in membrane potential alter the activity of voltage-operated calcium channels such that depolarisation promotes calcium influx and hyperpolarisation inhibits calcium influx. Therefore, drugs that activate potassium channels, such as diazoxide, cause smooth muscle relaxation and drugs that inhibit potassium channels, such as glibenclamide, may contract smooth muscle (Kuriyama et al. 1995). The effect of such drugs clearly depends on the type of ion channels present on the tissues and their degree of endogenous activation or inhibition.

SPECIFIC BIOLOGICAL TARGETS FOR DRUG THERAPY

Prostaglandin H synthase

Prostaglandins have long been known to have a key role in human parturition (Challis et al. 1997) and indomethacin, a non-selective PGHS inhibitor, is currently widely employed as a tocolytic (Van den Veyver and Moise 1993). There are two isoforms of the enzyme, PGHS-1 and PGHS-2 (Vane et al. 1998). Increased expression of PGHS-2 may be the major source of increased levels of prostaglandins associated with human labour (Fuentes *et al.* 1996; Mijovic *et al.* 1997). Currently, treatment with indomethacin is dose-limited by its adverse effects on the fetus, specifically contraction of the fetal ductus arteriosus and reduced fetal urine output (Van den Veyver and Moise 1993). Selective PGHS-2 inhibitors do not contract the human ductus arteriosus (Sawdy *et al.* 1997). These properties mean that the critical sources of prostaglandins involved in labour might be more effectively inhibited with a lower exposure to adverse fetal effects. These drugs must be regarded as some of the most promising novel uterine tocolytics.

Prostanoid receptors

The effects of prostaglandins are mediated by a family of prostanoid receptors (Coleman *et al.* 1994). There are at least four subtypes of receptor for prostaglandin E_2 (PGE$_2$), which is probably the most important prostaglandin in the control of labour (both physiological and therapeutic) and there is expression of a number of these subtypes in key tissues in the human and non-human primate uterus (Senior *et al.* 1993; Smith *et al.* 1998b). The existence of multiple subtypes of receptor for PGE$_2$ raises the possibility that novel drugs with selective activity at a given receptor subtype might modulate some of the effects of PGE$_2$, but not others. A drug that primed the cervix without contracting the uterus would clearly be desirable in the induction of labour. A drug which blocked the contractile effect of PGE$_2$ on the uterus, but maintained its inhibitory effect, through the EP$_2$ receptor, would have advantages over even isoform-selective PGHS inhibitors and would not be expected to contract the ductus arteriosus (Smith *et al.* 1994; Smith 1998).

It had been proposed that high levels of expression of EP$_2$ receptor in the baboon cervix suggested that an EP$_2$ receptor agonist might prime the cervix (Smith *et al.* 1998b). However, it has recently been shown that labour is associated with reduced expression of the EP$_2$ receptor gene in baboon myometrium, cervix and decidua (Smith *et al.* 1999), suggesting that the EP$_2$ receptor may have a key inhibitory role in maintaining gestation. It follows that an EP$_2$ receptor agonist may have a role in the treatment of premature labour (although this depends on whether EP$_2$ receptor expression is maintained in premature labour) and that an EP$_2$ receptor antagonist may be able to induce labour by blocking the inhibitory effect of endogenous prostaglandin on the EP$_2$ receptor. Selective prostaglandin receptor agonists and antagonists are not as close to immediate clinical applications as selective PGHS-2 inhibitors. Ultimately, however, prostanoid receptor blockers may replace PGHS synthesis inhibitors and selective agonists may ultimately replace the clinical use of native PGE$_2$ and prostaglandin $F_{2\alpha}$.

Oxytocin receptor

Synthetic oxytocin has been widely used for many years in the induction of labour and management of postpartum haemorrhage. More recently, selective blockers of the oxytocin receptor have been developed as uterine tocolytics (Shubert 1995). These agents have resolved some of the debate about the role of oxytocin in late gestation. It has been suggested that endogenous oxytocin did not have a role in physiological labour, since circulating levels of oxytocin did not rise during labour (Thornton *et al.* 1992). However, studies on non-human primates have shown that the oxytocin receptor antagonist atosiban inhibits the switch from low-amplitude, low-frequency contractures to the high-amplitude, high-frequency contractions of labour at term (Honnebier *et al.* 1989) and a randomised controlled clinical trial demonstrated that the antagonist atosiban had similar tocolytic efficacy to ritodrine (Goodwin *et al.* 1996). The discrepancy between the effectiveness of atosiban and the lack of any rise in circulating concentrations of oxytocin during the conditions where atosiban is effective may be explained by the drug blocking the autocrine and paracrine effects of decidual oxytocin (Chibbar *et al.* 1993, 1995; Takemura *et al.* 1994) or by an increase in the number or affinity of oxytocin receptors in key tissues during labour.

Adrenoceptors

Drugs with activity at the β-2 adrenoceptor have been employed for many years as uterine tocolytics. The principal drawback of these drugs is the high frequency of maternal adverse effects that necessitate discontinuation in up to 10% of women. Adverse effects may be severe (such as cardiac arrhythmia in 1–5%) and have been associated with maternal mortality (Creasy and Iams 1999). Given the lack of an unambiguous benefit of any tocolytic drug in premature labour, drugs that have a significant potential to cause maternal morbidity and mortality should be used with extreme caution. Since current drugs are already highly selective for the known receptor, there is little potential for their modification.

Steroids

Studies in the non-human primate have implied a key role for oestrogen in the normal process of term labour. Thus, administration of exogenous androstenedione induced labour in rhesus monkeys (Mecenas *et al.* 1996) and this effect is blocked by administration of an aromatase inhibitor (Nathanielsz *et al.* 1998), which prevents the formation of oestrogen from androgen. Oestrogen formation in late gestation depends on androgen precursors synthesised in the fetal adrenal cortex. Recent work has identified multiple oestrogen receptors encoded by separate genes (MacGregor and Jordan 1998). The multiple roles of oestrogen, especially its effects on uterine blood flow, renders it unlikely that blocking the oestrogen receptor or its biosynthetic pathway will represent safe strategies in the treatment of preterm labour. Conversely, however, there may be a role for oestrogen or its precursors in the induction of labour. Topical oestradiol gel has been used to prime the cervix (Magann *et al.* 1995). It may be that topical androstenedione may be a better option, given the results of experiments in non-human primates.

Nitric oxide

The discovery of NO led to considerable interest in its potential as a uterine tocolytic. It is perhaps humbling to the would-be perinatal pharmacologist that the most likely future role for these drugs may be to induce labour. The effects of NO donors on myometrial contractility were found to be less effective than either calcium channel or potassium channel blockers *in vitro* (Norman *et al.* 1997) and a randomised controlled clinical trial demonstrated that high-dose intravenous glyceryl trinitrate was a less effective tocolytic than intravenous magnesium sulphate (El-Sayed *et al.* 1999). However, recent randomised controlled trials have demonstrated that NO donors are more effective than placebo in priming the cervix prior to first-trimester termination of pregnancy (Thomson *et al.* 1997) and that they induce less uterine contraction than prostaglandin analogues (Thomson *et al.* 1998). They clearly have real potential, therefore, as improved agents for priming the cervix at term. Most current protocols using effective doses of PGE₂ to prime the cervix at term involve admission to hospital to allow for fetal monitoring and ready access to caesarean delivery, both of which follow from the unpredictable extent to which prostaglandins may stimulate uterine activity (Greer 1992). A drug that does not have this effect would have the potential for outpatient administration and repeated dosing, with implications for both cost and convenience of the delivery of care.

Drugs with activity at ion channels

Calcium channel blockers are currently in widespread clinical use as tocolytics (Ray and Dyson 1995). There are fewer adverse effects on the mother associated with these agents than with β-2 agonists and no major known adverse effects on the human fetus, although animal studies have suggested the possibility of adverse fetal effects (Ducsay *et al.* 1985). The principal adverse effects of these drugs relate to dilation of maternal vascular smooth muscle, resulting in hypotension and headache. These adverse effects relate to the widespread role of dihydropyridine-sensitive calcium channels in the control of smooth muscle. Some studies have suggested that potassium channel activators may have greater promise in having selective effects on myometrial activity compared with vascular smooth muscle (Morrison *et al.* 1993). However, the adenosine triphosphate (ATP)-sensitive potassium channel activator, diazoxide, was investigated as a potential tocolytic years before its mechanism of action was understood (Caritis *et al.* 1979). The drug was found also to lack specificity for the uterus and caused hypoglycaemia in the neonate (insulin release is also controlled by ATP-sensitive potassium channels). However, as knowledge of potassium channels increases, it may be that a uterus-specific channel will be identified.

DRUG DEVELOPMENT: THE FUTURE

Many other systems exist which may have roles in the control of human labour and which may be targets for novel therapies; for example, corticotrophin-releasing hormone (Challis *et al.* 1995), endothelin (Wolff *et al.* 1996) and parathyroid hormone-related poly-peptide (Pitera *et al.* 1998). The list of known endogenous agents which can affect uterine smooth muscle is vast and well beyond that described above. Furthermore, it is certain that there are other systems, as yet undiscovered, which will ultimately be proved to have important physiological and potential therapeutic roles in the control of labour. The vast number of potentially important systems, known and unknown, raises the question of how the best targets for novel therapies might be identified from the multitude of potential candidate systems.

Currently, there is a perfectly natural tendency among scientists to focus on subjects that are fashionable, and NO must be the prime example of this. A Medline search of myometrium and NO generates 54 citations, myometrium and leukotrienes generate 14 citations. Does this reflect the true relative contribution of NO and leukotrienes to the control of myometrial contractility? The answer is almost certainly 'no'.

The fundamental need is to focus studies on the factors that are actually important in the control of the uterus rather than simply study molecules that have been recently identified. Novel techniques in molecular biology are likely to provide the solution. By subtracting cDNA libraries obtained from labouring and non-labouring myometrium, the genes differentially expressed during labour can be identified. The specificity of this technique has been refined using the polymerase chain reaction (suppression subtractive hybridisation) and has recently revealed the previously unknown increase in thrombo-spondin-1 mRNA in myometrium associated with parturition (Wu *et al.* 1999). With the cloning of the human genome to be completed within the next few years, tissue-specific characterisation of the process of labour in terms of genetic expression should be achievable within the next decade. Furthermore, instead of sequencing individual clones from the subtracted cDNA libraries and screening for their expression by Northern blot, the technique may be combined with the recently developed gene chip technology, which allows expression of thousands of genes to be assessed in a single experiment (Johnston 1998). Having identified genes of interest, their recombinant products can be studied in mammalian cells, which allows characterisation of their function (Kenakin 1996). The identification of drugs with specificity at the gene product can be determined using the technology of the high-throughput screen utilising systems expressing the recombinant protein (Young *et al.* 1998). The investigation of the control of the uterus and the development of novel drugs to manipulate the process is poised to enter a more rational, efficient and effective phase and a possible model for future drug development is outlined in Figure 1. Ultimately, however, the novel therapeutic agents identified will have to be related to the function of the whole organism, first in animal studies and then by randomised controlled comparisons with existing therapies in clinical trials.

Synthesis of cDNA libraries from tissues of interest, taken from women both in labour and not in labour

↓

Suppression subtractive hybridisation to identify genes selectively expressed in tissues associated with parturition (Wu *et al.* 1999)

↓

Screen of thousands of genes using gene chip technology (Johnston 1998)

↓

Transfection of appropriate cells with gene of interest to characterise function (Kenakin 1996)

↓

High-throughput screen of systems expressing recombinant product to identify drugs with selective activity (Young *et al.* 1998)

↓

Tests of drugs *in vitro*

↓

Tests of drugs in animal models (especially non-human primate)

↓

Evaluation of drug in randomised controlled trials

Figure 1 *Model for future drug development using novel molecular techniques*

References

Barritt, G.J. and Gregory, R.B. (1997) An evaluation of strategies available for the identification of GTP-binding proteins required in intracellular signalling pathways. *Cell Signal* **9**, 207–18

Caritis, S.N., Edelstone, D.I. and Mueller-Heubach, E. (1979) Pharmacologic inhibition of preterm labor. *Am J Obstet Gynecol* **133**, 557–78

Caritis, S.N., Darby, M.J. and Chan, L. (1988) Pharmacologic treatment of preterm labor. *Clin Obstet Gynecol* **31**, 635–51

Casey, M.L. and MacDonald, P.C. (1988) Biomolecular processes in the initiation of parturition: decidual activation. *Clin Obstet Gynecol* **31**, 533–52

Challis, J.R., Matthews, S.G., Van, M.C. and Ramirez, M.M. (1995) Current topic: the placental corticotrophin-releasing hormone–adrenocorticotrophin axis. *Placenta* **16**, 481–502

Challis, J.R.G., Lye, S.J. and Gibb, W. (1997) Prostaglandins and parturition. *Ann N Y Acad Sci* **828**, 254–67

Chibbar, R., Miller, F.D. and Mitchell, B.F. (1993) Synthesis of oxytocin in amnion, chorion, and decidua may influence the timing of human parturition. *J Clin Invest* **91**, 185–92

Chibbar, R., Wong, S., Miller, F.D. and Mitchell, B.F. (1995) Estrogen stimulates oxytocin gene expression in human chorio-decidua. *J Clin Endocrinol Metab* **80**, 567–72

Coleman, R.A., Smith, W.L. and Narumiya, S. (1994) VIII International Union of Pharmacology classification of prostanoid receptors: properties, distribution and structure of the receptors and their subtypes. *Pharmacol Rev* **46**, 205–29

Creasy, R.K. and Iams, J.D. (1999) 'Preterm labor and delivery' in: R.K. Creasy and R. Resnik (Eds) *Maternal–Fetal Medicine*, pp. 498–531. Philadelphia: W.B. Saunders

Drife, J. (1997) Management of primary postpartum haemorrhage. *Br J Obstet Gynaecol* **104**, 275–7

Ducsay, C.A., Cook, M.J., Veille, J.C. and Novy, M.J. (1985) 'Cardiorespiratory effects of calcium channel-blocker tocolysis in pregnant rhesus monkeys' in: C.T. Jones and P.W. Nathanielsz (Eds) *The Physiological Development of the Fetus and Newborn*, pp. 423–8. London: Academic Press

El-Sayed, Y.Y., Riley, E.T., Holbrook, R.H.J., Cohen, S.E., Chitkara, U. and Druzin, M.L. (1999) Randomized comparison of intravenous nitroglycerin and magnesium sulfate for treatment of preterm labor. *Obstet Gynecol* **93**, 79–83

French, J.I. and McGregor, J.A. (1996) The pathobiology of premature rupture of membranes. *Semin Perinatol* **20**, 344–68

Fuchs, A.R., Fuchs, F., Husslein, P. and Soloff, M. (1984) Oxytocin receptors in the human uterus during pregnancy and parturition. *Am J Obstet Gynecol* **150**, 734–41

Fuentes, A., Spaziani, E.P. and O'Brien, W.F. (1996) The expression of cyclooxygenase-2 (COX-2) in amnion and decidua following spontaneous labor. *Prostaglandins* **52**, 261–7

Garcia-Villar, R., Green, L.R., Jenkins, S.L., Wentworth, R.A., Coleman, R.A. and Nathanielsz, P.W. (1995) Evidence for the presence of AH13205–sensitive EP_2 prostanoid receptors in the pregnant baboon but not in the pregnant sheep myometrium near term. *J Soc Gynecol Investig* **2**, 6–12

Garite, T.J. (1999) 'Premature rupture of the membranes' in: R.K. Creasy and R. Resnik (Eds) *Maternal–Fetal Medicine*, pp. 659–724. Philadelphia: W.B. Saunders

Goetzl, E.J., An, S. and Smith, W.L. (1995) Specificity of expression and effects of eicosanoid mediators in normal physiology and human diseases. *FASEB J* **9**, 1051–8

Goldstein, I., Lue, T.F., Padma-Nathan, H., Rosen, R.C., Steers, W.D. and Wicker, P.A. (1998) Oral sildenafil in the treatment of erectile dysfunction. Sildenafil Study Group. *N Engl J Med* **338**, 1397–404

Goodwin, T.M., Valenzuela, G.J., Silver, H. and Creasy, G. (1996) Dose ranging study of the oxytocin antagonist atosiban in the treatment of preterm labor. Atosiban Study Group. *Obstet Gynecol* **88**, 331–6

Grant, J.M. (1994) Induction of labour confers benefits in prolonged pregnancy. *Br J Obstet Gynaecol* **101**, 99–102

Greer, I.A. (1992) 'Cervical ripening' in: J.O. Drife and A.A. Calder (Eds) *Prostaglandins and the Uterus*, pp. 191–209. London: Springer-Verlag

Hannah, M.E., Hannah, W.J., Hellmann, J., Hewson, S., Milner, R. and Willan, A. (1992) Induction of labor as compared with serial antenatal monitoring in post-term pregnancy: a randomized controlled trial. The Canadian Multicenter Post-term Pregnancy Trial Group. *N Engl J Med* **326**, 1587–92

Honnebier, M.B., Figueroa, J.P., Rivier, J., Vale, W. and Nathanielsz, P.W. (1989) Studies on the role of oxytocin in late pregnancy in the pregnant rhesus monkey: plasma concentrations of oxytocin in the maternal circulation throughout the 24-h day and the effect of the synthetic oxytocin antagonist [1-β-Mpa(β-(CH2)5)1,(Me(Tyr2, Orn8] oxytocin on spontaneous nocturnal myometrial contractions. *Journal of Developmental Physiology* **12**, 225–32

Johnston, M. (1998) Gene chips: array of hope for understanding gene regulation. *Curr Biol* **8**, R171–4

Karaki, H., Ozaki, H., Hori, M. *et al.* (1997) Calcium movements, distribution, and functions in smooth muscle. *Pharmacol Rev* **49**, 157–230

Kenakin, T. (1996) The classification of seven transmembrane receptors in recombinant expression systems. *Pharmacol Rev* **48**, 413–63

Kuriyama, H., Kitamura, K. and Nabata, H. (1995) Pharmacological and physiological significance of ion channels and factors that modulate them in vascular tissues. *Pharmacol Rev* **47**, 387–573

Lees, C., Campbell, S., Jauniaux, E. *et al.* (1994) Arrest of preterm labour and prolongation of gestation with glyceryl trinitrate, a nitric oxide donor. *Lancet* **343**, 1325–6

MacGregor, J.I. and Jordan, V.C. (1998) Basic guide to the mechanisms of antiestrogen action. *Pharmacol Rev* **50**, 151–96

Magann, E.F., Perry, K.G.J., Dockery, J.R.J., Bass, J.D., Chauhan, S.P. and Morrison, J.C. (1995) Cervical ripening before medical induction of labor: a comparison of prostaglandin E₂, estradiol, and oxytocin. *Am J Obstet Gynecol* **172**, 1702–6

Mecenas, C.A., Giussani, D.A., Owiny, J.R. *et al.* (1996) Production of premature delivery in pregnant rhesus monkeys by androstenedione infusion. *Nat Med* **2**, 443–8

Mijovic, J.E., Zakar, T., Nairn, T.K. and Olson, D.M. (1997) Prostaglandin-endoperoxide H synthase-2 expression and activity increases with term labor in human chorion. *Am J Physiol* **272**, E832–40

Morrison, J.J., Ashford, M.L., Khan, R.N. and Smith, S.K. (1993) The effects of potassium channel openers on isolated pregnant human myometrium before and after the onset of labor: potential for tocolysis. *Am J Obstet Gynecol* **169**, 1277–85

Nathanielsz, P.W., Jenkins, S.L., Tame, J.D., Winter, J.A., Guller, S. and Giussani, D.A. (1998) Local paracrine effects of estradiol are central to parturition in the rhesus monkey. *Nat Med* **4**, 456–9

Norman, J.E., Ward, L.M., Martin, W. *et al.* (1997) Effects of cGMP and the nitric oxide donors glyceryl trinitrate and sodium nitroprusside on contractions *in vitro* of isolated myometrial tissue from pregnant women. *J Reprod Fertil* **110**, 249–54

Papatsonis, D.N., Van, G.H., Ader, H.J., Lange, F.M., Bleker, O.P. and Dekker, G.A. (1997) Nifedipine and ritodrine in the management of preterm labor: a randomized multicenter trial. *Obstet Gynecol* **90**, 230–4

Pitera, A.E., Smith, G.C., Wentworth, R.A. and Nathanielsz, P.W. (1998) Parathyroid hormone-related peptide (1 to 34) inhibits *in vitro* oxytocin-stimulated activity of pregnant baboon myometrium. *Am J Obstet Gynecol* **179**, 492–6

Polson, J.B. and Strada, S.J. (1996) Cyclic nucleotide phosphodiesterases and vascular smooth muscle. *Annu Rev Pharmacol Toxicol* **36**, 403–27

Ray, D. and Dyson, D. (1995) Calcium channel blockers. *Clin Obstet Gynecol* **38**, 713–21

Sanborn, B.M., Yue, C., Wang, W. and Dodge, K.L. (1998) G protein signalling pathways in myometrium: affecting the balance between contraction and relaxation. *Rev Reprod* **3**, 196–205

Saunders, N. and Paterson, C. (1991) Effect of gestational age on obstetric performance: when is 'term' over? *Lancet* **338**, 1190–2

Sawdy, R., Slater, D., Fisk, N., Edmonds, D.K. and Bennett, P. (1997) Use of a cyclo-oxygenase type-2–selective non-steroidal anti-inflammatory agent to prevent preterm delivery. *Lancet* **350**, 265–6

Senior, J., Marshall, K., Sangha, R. and Clayton, J.K. (1993) *In-vitro* characterization of prostanoid receptors on human myometrium at term pregnancy. *Br J Pharmacol* **108**, 501–6

Shubert, P.J. (1995) Atosiban. *Clin Obstet Gynecol* **38**, 722–4

Smith, G.C.S. (1998) The pharmacology of the ductus arteriosus. *Pharmacol Rev* **50**, 35–58

Smith, G.C.S. and McGrath, J.C. (1994) Interactions between indomethacin, noradrenaline and vasodilators in the fetal rabbit ductus arteriosus. *Br J Pharmacol* **111**, 1245–51

Smith, G.C.S., Coleman, R.A. and McGrath, J.C. (1994) Characterization of dilator prostanoid receptors in the fetal rabbit ductus arteriosus. *J Pharmacol Exp Ther* **271**, 390–6

Smith, G.C.S., Smith, M.F., Mcnay, M.B. and Fleming, J.E. (1998a) First-trimester growth and the risk of low birth weight. *N Engl J Med* **339**, 1817–22

Smith, G.C.S., Baguma-Nibasheka, M., Wu, W.X. and Nathanielsz, P.W. (1998b) Regional variations in contractile responses to prostaglandins and prostanoid receptor messenger ribonucleic acid in pregnant baboon uterus. *Am J Obstet Gynecol* **179**, 1545–52

Smith, G.C.S., Wu, W.X. and Nathanielsz, P.W. (1999) Baboon labor is associated with decreased uterine prostanoid EP_2 receptor expression. *J Soc Gynecol Investig* **6**, 128A–9A

Smith, W.L. (1992) Prostanoid biosynthesis and mechanisms of action. *Am J Physiol* **263**, F181–91

Takemura, M., Kimura, T., Nomura, S. *et al.* (1994) Expression and localization of human oxytocin receptor mRNA and its protein in chorion and decidua during parturition. *J Clin Invest* **93**, 2319–23

Thomson, A.J., Lunan, C.B., Cameron, A.D., Cameron, I.T., Greer, I.A. and Norman, J.E. (1997) Nitric oxide donors induce ripening of the human uterine cervix: a randomised controlled trial. *Br J Obstet Gynaecol* **104,** 1054–7

Thomson, A.J., Lunan, C.B., Ledingham, M. *et al.* (1998) Randomised trial of nitric oxide donor versus prostaglandin for cervical ripening before first-trimester termination of pregnancy. *Lancet* **352**, 1093–6

Thornton, S., Davison, J.M. and Baylis, P.H. (1992) Plasma oxytocin during the first and second stages of spontaneous human labour. *Acta Endocrinologica (Copenhagen)* **126**, 425–9

Van den Veyver, I.B. and Moise, K.J. (1993) Prostaglandin synthetase inhibitors in pregnancy. *Obstet Gynecol Surv* **48**, 493–502

Vane, J.R., Bakhle, Y.S. and Botting, R.M. (1998) Cyclooxygenases 1 and 2. *Annu Rev Pharmacol Toxicol* **38**, 97–120

Wink, D.A. and Mitchell, J.B. (1998) Chemical biology of nitric oxide: insights into regulatory, cytotoxic, and cytoprotective mechanisms of nitric oxide. *Free Radic Biol Med* **25**, 434–56

Wolff, K., Faxen, M., Lunell, N.O., Nisell, H. and Lindblom, B. (1996) Endothelin receptor type A and B gene expression in human nonpregnant, term pregnant, and pre-eclamptic uterus. *Am J Obstet Gynecol* **175**, 1295–300

Wolkow, P.P. (1998) Involvement and dual effects of nitric oxide in septic shock. *Inflamm Res* **47**, 152–66

Wu, W.X., Ma, X.H., Zhang, Q., Unno, N. and Nathanielsz, P.W. (1999) Suppression subtractive hybridization identified a marked increase in thrombospondin-1 associated with parturition in pregnant sheep myometrium. *Endocrinology* **140**, 2364–71

Young, K., Lin, S., Sun, L. *et al.* (1998) Identification of a calcium channel modulator using a high throughput yeast two-hybrid screen. *Nat Biotechnol* **16**, 946–50

19

Maternity care 2000

Geoffrey Chamberlain

At the end of the 20th century the Royal College of Obstetricians and Gynaecologists is over 70 years old. Much in the modern maternity services in the UK and Commonwealth owes its origin and evolution to the RCOG and its sister college, the Royal College of Midwives. In these 70 years, research has developed and practice improved in an exponential way. This chapter traces the progress of the many facets of modern maternity care.

BACKGROUND

Population

The general fertility rate for this country was declining at the beginning of the century and has, with minor variations, stayed much the same throughout the past hundred years (Figure 1) with a small rise after each World War and a more sustained rise in the 1960s.

Maternal mortality

The rate of death of mothers in relation to childbirth (the maternal mortality rate or MMR) was persistently high in the early days of the century and did not reduce until the late 1930s (Figure 2). A major factor in this abrupt reduction was the introduction of antibiotics, which prevented deaths from puerperal sepsis. Other important medical changes at about this time were the introduction of a national blood transfusion service and better training of both midwives and doctors by their respective Colleges. More gradual was the realisation that good antenatal care could prevent problems in labour. Data on MMR were collected and, from 1953, published in the triennial Confidential Enquiries into Maternal Deaths, a continuing peer-reviewed audit.

Perinatal mortality

The concept of perinatal deaths (composed of stillbirth and first-week deaths) was introduced in the UK just after the Second World War. It was adjudged that baby deaths at this time were most likely to include obstetric factors. Recently, better neonatal care is keeping babies alive beyond the first week into the second, third and fourth weeks of life; so data on neonatal death rates for the first 28 days need to be examined as well as those of the perinatal period.

Perinatal deaths are more sensitive to socio-economic influences than maternal deaths and their value as a measure of maternity care quality is diminished in a developed country

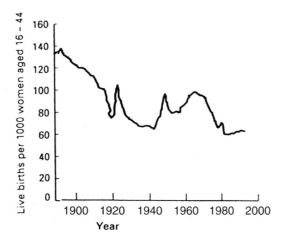

Figure 1 *General fertility rate in England and Wales (1900–95)*

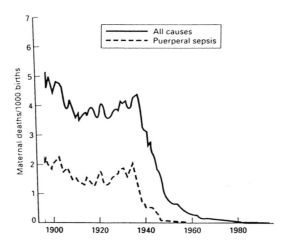

Figure 2 *Maternal mortality ratios (MMR) in England and Wales (1900–95)*

where the numbers are small and the social and economic influences are great. Figure 3 shows perinatal deaths since the foundation of the RCOG. First-week deaths reduced at a faster rate than stillbirths from the 1950s to the 1980s, much of this reflecting better neonatal facilities (Harvey 2000). The biggest problem with perinatal deaths at the millennium is low birth weight, particularly of those babies who are small for gestational age. Research is directed at preventing preterm labour and so allowing the fetus to mature further before birth.

In the last decade a new enquiry, the Confidential Enquiry into Stillbirths and Deaths in Infancy in the United Kingdom, was introduced to examine deaths from the twentieth week of gestation to the end of the first year of life. Regional panels of relevant medical

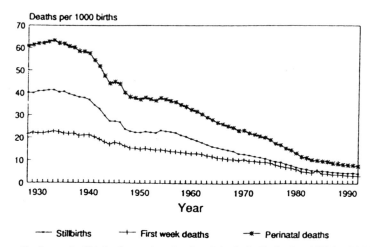

Figure 3 *Rates of stillbirths, first-week and perinatal deaths in England and Wales (1928–95)*

and midwifery staff assess the records of babies confidentially and produce reports which draw attention to factors contributing to deaths (Maternal and Childhealth Research Consortium 1998).

Attitudes towards childbirth

The more passive acceptance by women of the events of childbirth in the earlier part of the century has been replaced in later years by the wish for an active involvement of women in the birth. While the feminist movement has been one of the leaders in this, it is not entirely so motivated. Women, quite rightly, want to have a say in their management. The mean number of children in a family in the UK has reduced from six to two during the course of this century and most couples want to ensure a perfect child each time. This leads sometimes to illogical results but the basic premise is understandable (Craig 1998). We have moved into the era of birth plans, when the woman writes down her wishes in detail during pregnancy about how she would prefer labour to be conducted. This sounds reasonable and provides grounds for discussion but in some cases this is spilling over into difficult attitudes, such as the wish to have no medical students present at delivery, despite reassurances that they are the doctors of the future. These attitudes have been given a boost in the last few years by the various superficial patient charters produced by the Department of Health which often lead to unrealistic expectations (Department of Health 1994).

Obstetricians themselves are looking at their practices more carefully. Few innovations have previously been subject to controlled trials to assess their effectiveness. Now obstetricians realise that they have to convince women of the value of many modern practices. What some call 'high technology' must be shown to be helpful for those women and infants who are at high risk. It then becomes 'appropriate technology'. Interventions must be explained and consent must be properly informed. More women have their partner present at the birth and he can help to act as her advocate when stress makes critical thinking difficult. All this can achieve better co-operation between the woman and her attendants.

The midwife

Midwives are independent practitioners in their own right. They have been especially trained and can deal independently with normal labour while also detecting variations which may lead to problems. They are not just nurses and are the only branch of the nursing profession which can diagnose and act on their diagnoses as well as prescribing scheduled drugs on their own initiative. The midwife has been the backbone of maternity care this century and midwives perform three-quarters of all deliveries (Garcia 1997). In the 1960s, there was a decline in their influence which paralleled the increase in technology and operative-style deliveries. This seems to have reduced and midwives are coming back into their own, partly catalysed by more efficient regulation of midwives by their own College. The Department of Health enhanced their role in the report *Changing Childbirth* (Department of Health 1993). One of the report's recommendations was the concept of a lead professional, who would nearly always be a midwife, to co-ordinate care and see that the woman received appropriately timed advice and investigations in pregnancy. While not necessarily delivering the baby, the lead professional would be in contact with the delivery team. Regulation of midwives' working hours has taken something away from the individualisation of care, but the idea of team midwifery means that the woman is looked after in labour by someone she has met in the antenatal period.

ANTENATAL CARE

Antenatal clinics

The concept of antenatal clinics took off in the mid-1920s after Janet Campbell of the Ministry of Health devised a formal programme of antenatal visits for women, who were often grand multiparae with poor nutrition. From this stemmed the framework of about 10–15 visits during pregnancy, monthly at first and weekly at the end. This programme has become sacrosanct to professionals and women alike. Attempts have been made in the last two decades to reduce the number of visits for women who are not at high risk. This must be done with care for, although the outcome remains the same, women may feel resentment that they are not given as much antenatal care as their mothers or sisters (Sikorski *et al.* 1996). Antenatal programmes have never been scrutinised rigorously with randomised controlled trials but this is badly needed to see if we are now being overprotective of pregnant women (Hall 1992).

Multiphased screening

The demedicalisation of antenatal care and delegation to midwives should be used as a time of re-examination and putting to one side the less useful clinical assessments and laboratory tests.

Antenatal care now is returning from the hospitals to the GP's surgery where the practice midwife may well carry out the hands-on care. It is a multiphased screening service and should be performed by those who have been appropriately trained. Any abnormal results arising from the screening tests should be passed to professionals who have the skills to deal with these data.

At the latter end of pregnancy, clinical skills of palpation are needed for the clinical detection of cephalopelvic disproportion or malpresentations; this has been the same for the last

50 years. In earlier pregnancy, however, new techniques have made big differences. Ultrasound is probably the major advance in investigations used in antenatal care. Devised by Ian Donald in Glasgow, ultrasound was refined by a series of his pupils, notably Stuart Campbell, in London. Now virtually every woman in the UK has at least one ultrasound visit in the first half of pregnancy to measure fetal size and from it extrapolate a more precise idea of fetal maturity and expected date of delivery. Later, expected growth rates of the fetus can be quantified by further measurements. The number of fetuses may be checked in early pregnancy and structural congenital abnormalities can be detected. More recently, chromosomal abnormalities have been shown to produce physical markers which are easily and precisely localised on ultrasound; for example the increased nuchal pad thickness in Down syndrome. Clustering of these soft markers leads to the assessment of more precise risk levels.

A useful test is the measurement of afferent blood flow to the placental bed or fetal blood flow in the umbilical arteries. Each can be done non-invasively with Doppler ultrasound and provides valuable warning of the quality of survival as well as a prognosis for survival itself (Alfirevic and Neilson 1995). Such antenatal testing is probably of much more value than antenatal external cardiotocography (CTG). Perhaps in the next century the antenatal CTG machine will give way to Doppler equipment in fetal assessments.

Many tests were added in the antenatal period often with more enthusiasm than scientific justification. Thanks to the impetus of the National Perinatal Epidemiology Unit in Oxford, these tests are now being examined for their usefulness in predicting fetal and maternal hazards. Those that have low prediction rates are being rejected. Among this latter group were many of the biochemical tests measuring hormone and enzyme profiles which were widely used in the 1960s. Their predictive values were low while their ranges of accepted normality were wide. Antenatal testing for various abnormalities still depends too much upon the whims of individual obstetricians. Only when evidence-based medicine guides us logically will we have a universal antenatal screening service in this country.

The antenatal detection of fetal abnormalities will often lead a couple to request a termination of pregnancy, available under the 1990 modification of the Abortion Act 1967. The earlier termination is performed the easier it is for the woman and her professionals; hence, attempts are being made to use early tests for abnormalities so as to have earlier results and action. Early detection of anomalies is not the only reason for abnormality testing. Some conditions will require surgery promptly after birth. If these conditions are diagnosed antenatally, the woman should be booked into a unit with neonatal paediatric surgeons available to provide immediate care. Other women may wish to know about the anomaly in order to have time to prepare themselves, their partners and other children in the family, because the forthcoming baby will certainly affect the lives of the whole family.

Mother's health

With the greater necessity for a double income in the family, many women are working in pregnancy and others are working for longer. Maternity pay and benefits are at a low level in the UK compared with the rest of Europe. Beyond the teratogenic hazards of certain chemical and physical agents which have been well documented (Paul 1993) there does not seem to be any great harm in a woman working during pregnancy. It is now becoming normal to continue non-strenuous work until 34–38 weeks of gestation.

Some pregnancy-related conditions are detected by clinical screening, allowing prompt and early treatment. For example, in later pregnancy many of the traditional antenatal examinations such as weighing, urine testing, checking uterine size and listening to the fetal heart are of doubtful value (Steer 1993). Conditions such as pregnancy-induced hypertension and pre-eclampsia are detected by repeated blood pressure and urine testing. The older practice of treating these conditions with heavy sedation has been replaced in the UK by the prescription of magnesium sulphate 40 years after it was used in many other western countries. Symptomatic diseases of pregnancy are diagnosed in the antenatal period by clinical and ultrasound tests.

The scourge of antepartum haemorrhage is now better managed. There is wider use of conservative therapy in placenta praevia with appropriate caesarean section at correct fetal maturity. The earlier resort to caesarean section and the correct blood volume replacement has considerably reduced the risks of abruptio placentae in the UK.

More women with clinical diseases are having successful pregnancies. For example, insulin-dependent diabetic women did not become pregnant earlier in the century. Such women can now be controlled before pregnancy and, with frequent and repeated consultations at combined diabetic–antenatal clinics, can be brought safely to late gestation and delivery. Similarly, women with heart disease can be coaxed through pregnancy, providing the appropriate physicians and obstetricians work together. The new scourge of HIV in the UK is often the result of syringe-sharing by drug addicts. Transmission to the fetus can be reduced by treatment with antiretroviral agents such as zidovudine in late pregnancy and labour while the wider use of caesarean section seems to avoid passage of the fetus through the high-risk infected area of the cervix and vagina.

The prevention of preterm labour and premature rupture of membranes has not advanced greatly. The hope for the wider use of cervical cerclage in the middle of the century has not been fulfilled (Chalmers et al. 1989). The use of tocolytic drugs has not been shown to be useful beyond the short term (RCOG 1997). The major use of tocolytic drugs is to postpone labour for 48 hours to allow antenatal steroids to be given to the mother to help the maturation of the fetal lungs. Attempts to prevent preterm labour by education programmes and bed rest do not seem to have succeeded (Weston et al. 1995).

Multiple pregnancy rates are increasing following the wider use of assisted fertility programmes so that several eggs may be fertilised at one coitus or cycle of in vitro fertilisation. Advice to reduce the number of eggs fertilised from the Human Fertility and Embryology Authority has been partly successful. Babies resulting from multiple pregnancies are always smaller than singletons and are usually born earlier. Hence, they produce a greater strain on the neonatal care services.

The combination of the swinging moods and hormone fluxes of pregnancy can lead to extremes of psychological behaviour. These are now more widely recognised by professionals and better treatments are being offered, because it is accepted that such pharmacy need not affect the fetus or newborn baby and does alleviate problems for the mother. Regional mother-and-baby units have been opened in psychiatric units where, after delivery, both can be looked after in safety. Separation of the baby from the mother in this instance is not wise or necessary.

LABOUR CARE

Delivery is the high point of pregnancy. In folk lore and in modern thought, childbirth is the all important moment. This is the time of fulfilment for the woman and her control of it must be enhanced and respected by professionals.

Birth place

Before this century virtually all deliveries took place at home. Gradually, as the decades passed, women came into hospital for delivery (Chamberlain *et al.* 1997). This was partly of their own volition as they realised that, with fewer babies, they wanted to make sure each one was safe. They considered that better facilities and staff for dealing with emergencies were present in hospitals and thought it wise to be there. This was partly reinforced by doctors who confused the increasing technology needed to monitor abnormal labour with that needed for normal deliveries; they forgot that the latter could be dealt with differently. Pressure groups were formed to counter this drift towards hospital deliveries but these mostly started too late to reverse the trend (Figure 4). In consequence, home deliveries became less frequent. The decline in popularity of home deliveries owed more to fashion rather than to any strong medical direction. Doctors followed the trend rather than led it and tried retrospectively to justify the move on medical grounds.

Probably about 10–15% of women in the UK would like to give birth at home. They have the legal right to this choice, however much doctors and midwives may advise it to be unwise. There has been a small increase in home deliveries in the last ten years and, if this trend was to be extrapolated into the next century, could rise to a level of about 5% in ten years. A prospective control study by intent to deliver at home was performed by the National Birthday Trust (Chamberlain *et al.* 1997). This showed that low-risk women who are selected and properly screened throughout pregnancy, with planned good delivery care in the home, were no more putting themselves or their babies at risk than were similar low-risk women delivering in hospital. Facilities for any changes will have to be provided if the increasing demand continues.

Deliveries are now being concentrated in fewer hospitals with each hospital performing more. The optimum size for a unit is now 3000 deliveries a year, allowing the employment of adequate numbers of consultants and resident staff. With a smaller

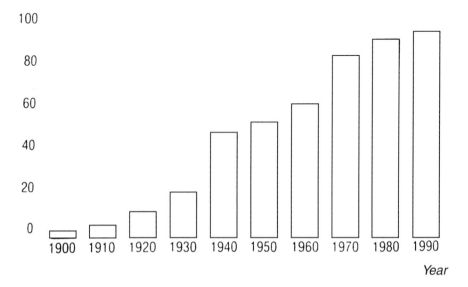

Figure 4 *Percentage of deliveries in institutions in England and Wales (1900–90)*

clinical load, it is difficult to run rotas for senior house officers in obstetrics, anaesthesia and paediatrics; Colleges are planning to remove recognition from such posts for training. In consequence, career trainees are not moving to these units. Trust administrators are fast realising that a unit without College recognition can be run with staff-grade doctors with the appointment of other locally contracted doctors. After years of building up the tradition of people entering the subject through the RCOG and being overseen by that College, this is a retrograde and dangerous step which may lead to a diminution in the high standards of obstetrics that have been built up in the UK.

District general hospitals are tending to take on more deliveries at the expense of GP isolated units (Table 1). The number of deliveries in free-standing GP units in the last quarter of this century has been reduced from 44 000 to 9000 and more GPs are unwilling to take part in intrapartum care. This is due to a perceived lack of expertise, fear of litigation, unacceptable encroachment on off-duty and surgery hours and inadequate remuneration (Zander and Chamberlain 1999). Free-standing midwife-led units arose in the last decade of the century. Here, with no resident doctors on call, midwives care for preselected women and are responsible for seeking specialist obstetric and neonatal help if necessary.

Induction of labour

The indications for inducing labour when the obstetrician thinks the baby would be better out of the uterus have increased during the century. Earlier methods of sweeping or rupturing the membranes carried risks of infection. Now, most labours start from induction by local prostaglandin preparations, possibly augmented by rupturing the membranes once labour starts. Intravenous oxytocin was used heavily in the 1980s but its use is now reducing. In the UK, induction rates rose to 40% in the 1970s; they now range from 10% to 20% depending on the unit, the type of women seen and the women's own opinions.

Method of delivery

Three-quarters of births in the UK are normal vaginal deliveries, mostly cephalic occipito-anterior or directly posterior. The number of vaginal breech deliveries has diminished greatly in the last years of the century because of the rush to perform caesarean sections on babies in such a presentation. There is no evidence that caesarean

Table 1 *Percentage of women delivering in various sites in England (1994–95) (Department of Health 1997)*

Site of delivery	Deliveries (%)
Consultant ward	56
Combined consultant/GP ward	38
Isolated GP unit	3
Home	2
Other including isolated midwifery unit or in transit	<1
Total	100

section improves the outcome for a normal baby of mature gestation who is presenting by the breech but the attitudes of both the profession and the public do not recognise this (Hofmeyr and Hannah 1998).

Caesarean section rates in the UK increased to about 17% by the end of the century (Figure 5). Some of this increase is due to better management of fetuses who are at hypoxic risk but much is due to fear of medicolegal retribution if things do not go well with a vaginal delivery (Savage and Francome 1993). The idea seems rooted in the courts that the safest way to deliver a baby is by caesarean section and it is difficult to disabuse the judiciary of this. Recent work showing the damage done to the pelvic floor by delivery is being used as a justification of more choice for women for elective caesarean section (Paterson-Brown and Fisk 1997).

The rates of assisted operative vaginal deliveries have diminished in parallel with the rise in caesarean sections. Forceps are still used in about 8% of deliveries but rotation of occipital transverse with straight forceps is a reducing art and vacuum extraction or caesarean section are used instead (Table 2). Vacuum extraction has increased in the second half of the century to about 5% of deliveries. It is not an alternative to forceps as a method of delivery but is a parallel method of assistance. In the UK, vacuum extractor usage is midway in the range of almost universal use in north-west Europe and almost complete rejection in the USA.

All these operative deliveries are performed by doctors of various grades, while nearly all the normal deliveries are now performed by midwives. Few doctors, excepting those in training, look after women in labour. The exception is in the private sector in the UK, although delivery rates there are small (less than 2%); here private medical practitioners deliver babies in all types of delivery.

Pain relief

From the beginning of this century the changes in methods of relief for labour pain have been enormous. Chloroform and twilight sleep with morphine and scopolamine have

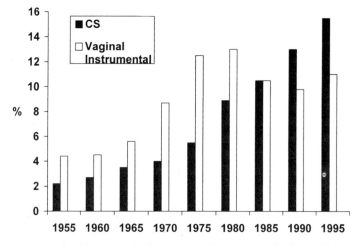

Figure 5 *Operative delivery rates in England and Wales to 1985 (England only from 1990)*

Table 2 *Percentage of women by method of delivery in England (1994–95) (Department of Health 1997)*

Method of delivery	Deliveries (%)
Natural vaginal delivery	75
Assisted vaginal delivery:	
Forceps	6
Vacuum extraction	4
Caesarean section:	
Elective	8
Emergency	7
Total	100

gone. Nitrous oxide, a well-known gaseous analgesic, was introduced in the 1930s and various equipment was devised to provide a safe dosage to enable its use by midwives and without a medical presence. This continues into 2000 when half the women in labour make use of nitrous oxide. Other agents came and went, such as trichlorethylene. Pethidine was widely used in the 1950s and 1960s as an analgesic but, because of the depression of neonatal respiration in some cases and the woman's control of labour in others, usage has dropped to about one-third of women by the end of the century.

Continuous epidurals were introduced in the 1970s and are now popular. They undoubtedly give good pain relief and concerns about post-delivery backache are being resolved by careful choice of women for epidural analgesia and aftercare. It is probably the best method of pain relief and at present about 25% of women have an epidural to cover labour and 50% to cover caesarean section, more for elective than emergency operations. Spinal anaesthetic is also useful for operative delivery as it can be given quickly and works immediately. The limitation on epidural and spinal analgesia is not the woman's request but the number of skilled anaesthetists available for obstetric units.

CARE IN THE PUERPERIUM

After delivery women are attended in their homes mostly by midwives and GPs. Although 95% of them deliver in a hospital unit, half leave hospital within 48 hours. A few who have had caesarean sections may stay until the fifth day. This has followed the faster mobilisation of women after delivery because of the risks of deep vein thrombosis and a need in the 1980s for obstetric beds in hospitals. In the 1930s, women often stayed in bed for five days after normal delivery and in hospital for two weeks. Both these figures have been greatly reduced.

Breastfeeding, the best method of feeding the young human, is still waning in popularity, although there was a slight increase in the 1970s. Today, only about 40% of women will breastfeed for six weeks, despite the great advantages of breast milk for the child: its biochemical composition, immunological components and other health benefits. The manufacturers of milk formulae strongly encouraged the use of their products in the 1950s and 1960s. This has now been somewhat reduced, due to restrictions on advertising and public pressure.

NEONATAL SERVICES

Paediatricians have developed neonatal services greatly in the last quarter of the century. Special neonatal intensive care units now exist in tertiary-level hospitals with neonatal nurseries at secondary level. Much more is known of the physiology of the newborn and basic care has progressed following this knowledge. While in the 1950s it was unusual for a paediatrician to attend delivery units, it is now normal for them to be present for any potentially difficult case and they should be available to be called within minutes of any unexpected neonatal problems. Their principal use in this instance has been in the rapid resuscitation of the baby. Intubation of the trachea, which used to be performed by obstetricians and midwives, has now passed to paediatricians (Hamilton 1999). However, there are not enough paediatricians and some units do not have good paediatric cover. This is being redressed rapidly by the concentration of women into larger centres, where there is a greater likelihood of a neonatal paediatrician covering the full 24 hours.

CONCLUSIONS

At the end of this millennium the maternal mortality, stillbirth and neonatal mortality rates are the lowest they have ever been. There must be no complacency over these rates. They could be reduced further by at least 50% by better use of existing practices. The old concept that there is an irreducible minimum of deaths is not sustainable and all must work to reduce these figures. In parallel with death rates, morbidity in the mother and baby is reducing. More small babies are now surviving and long-term follow-up studies indicate that those who live through the first month of life are usually healthy. Family size is reducing and contraception is increasing but there are still concerns with certain social groups, such as the under-sixteens and social class V. Cigarette smoking is still a cause for concern in some groups and carbohydrate intolerance rates seem to be rising.

Quite rightly, the midwife is taking her place in the front-line of care, being recognised as a practitioner in her own right. The Department of Health's wish for a consultant-led service is held back by a lack of consultant obstetricians which, in turn, is due to the wrong priorities in the use of finance in National Health Trusts and a lack of direction in the Department of Health. A backlog of trained obstetricians exists at the upper end of senior training grades, yet there is a deficiency in consultant levels. This must be redressed urgently in the next few years.

Practices in obstetrics are changing; difficult vaginal deliveries are being replaced by caesarean sections in the UK. The older members of the profession may shake their heads at this but should remember that an elective caesarean section performed by a senior doctor in the afternoon is likely to have much better results than an emergency section by a less experienced junior doctor in the middle of the night. While there are still increased risks for caesarean section over vaginal birth, these are being reduced. With a smaller family size in 2000 and the preferences of women, rates of caesarean section may rise to 20%. To wring one's hands and cry back to the old days might not be the best policy for all the women of the UK in the next century.

References

Alfirevic, Z. and Neilson, J. (1995) Doppler ultrasonography in high risk pregnancies: systematic review with meta-analysis. *Am J Obstet Gynecol* **172**, 1379–87

Chalmers, I., Enkin, M. and Keirse, M. (1989) *Effective Care in Pregnancy and Childbirth*, pp. 633–45. Oxford: Oxford University Press

Chamberlain, G., Wraight, A. and Crowley, P. (1997) *Homebirths*. Carnforth: Parthenon

Craig, R. (1998) *Women's Views Count: Building Responsive Maternity Services*. London: College of Health

Department of Health (1993) *Changing Childbirth*. London: HMSO

Department of Health (1994) *The Patient's Charter – Maternity Services*. London: HMSO

Department of Health (1997) *Statistical Bulletin*. London: HMSO

Garcia, J. (1997) *Changing Midwifery Care: the Scope for Evaluation*. Oxford: National Perinatal Epidemiology Unit

Hall, M. (1992) 'The content and progress of antenatal care' in: G. Chamberlain and L. Zander (Eds) *Pregnancy Care in the 1990s*. Carnforth: Parthenon

Hamilton, P. (1999) ABC of labour care: care of the newborn in the delivery room. *BMJ* **318**, 1403–6

Harvey, D. (2000) *Practical Perinatal Care: the Baby Under 1000 g*. Oxford: Butterworth-Heinemann

Hofmeyr, G. and Hannah, M.E. (1998) Planned caesarean section for term breech delivery (Cochrane Review). In: *The Cochrane Library*, Issue 2. Oxford: Update Software

Maternal and Childhealth Research Consortium (1998) *Fifth Annual Report of the Confidential Enquiry into Stillbirths and Deaths in Infancy*. London: MCHRC

Paterson Brown, C. and Fisk, N. (1997) Caesarean section: every woman's right to choose. *Curr Opin Obstet Gynecol* **9**, 351–5

Paul, M. (1993) *Occupational and Environmental Reproductive Hazards: a Guide for Clinicians*. Baltimore: Williams and Wilkins

RCOG (1997) *Beta-agonists for the Care of Women in Preterm Labour*. London: RCOG (Guideline no. 1R)

Savage, W. and Francome, C. (1993) Why caesarean section? *Br J Obstet Gynaecol* **100**, 493–6

Sikorski, J., Wilson, J., Clement, S. *et al.* (1996) Randomised trial comparing two schedules of antenatal visits: the antenatal care project. *BMJ* **312**, 546–53

Steer, P. (1993) Rituals in antenatal care – do we need them? *BMJ* **307**, 697–8

Weston, W., Knox, M., Eilers, G., Pauwels, J. and Lundsdorff, D. (1995) The effectiveness of preterm birth prevention educational programmes for high-risk women: a meta-analysis. *Obstet Gynecol* **86**, 705–12

Zander, L. and Chamberlain, G. (1999) Place of birth. *BMJ* **318**, 721–3

20

Implantation

Ian D. Cooke and Kelvin J. H. Lim

INTRODUCTION

Successful human reproduction remains an enigma, limiting our understanding of its various pathological manifestations. Progress in unravelling this mystery may come from greater understanding of the molecular factors involved in mediation of successful implantation, a crucial step in ensuring the success or failure of human reproduction. However, as ethical considerations are paramount in studies on human implantation, the currently available information has been derived mainly from *in vivo* murine or *in vitro* human models. This unavoidable limitation has contributed to the relatively slow progress of knowledge concerning human implantation.

Successful implantation is a complex process and in humans appears to be confined to an 'implantation window' occurring seven to ten days after the mid-cycle luteinising hormone (LH) surge (days LH +7 to +10) (Bergh and Navot 1992). A multitude of progressive steps is necessary to ensure its success, with the most important steps represented by apposition, adhesion and invasion (Bischof and Campana 1996). Apposition describes the close contact between the conceptus and endometrium prior to the establishment of physical connections. When physical connections are established the adhesion phase is entered. This proceeds to invasion when the conceptus starts to insinuate its way into the maternal endometrium. It is during this period that the semi-allograft human conceptus initially encounters maternal immune cells and coexists with them throughout its gestation, giving rise to an immunological paradox that has remained since its first description 47 years ago by the Nobel Laureate Sir Peter Medawar (1953).

The recent advent of molecular biology and advances in immunology may prove to be the most significant steps in understanding implantation. This has led to the discovery of three main groups of molecular factors involved in mediation of successful implantation, comprising adhesion molecules, proteases (also known as proteinases) and cytokines. A summary of the major characteristics of each molecular group is first presented prior to detailed discussions on their role in implantation.

CHARACTERISTICS OF MOLECULAR FACTORS IMPLICATED IN IMPLANTATION

Adhesion molecules

Adhesion molecules are proteins involved in cell-surface interactions essential for normal morphogenesis and maintenance of tissue integrity in multicellular organisms. Several subgroups of adhesion molecules exist, although current evidence implicates primarily integrins in implantation. Integrins are membrane glycoproteins composed of two subunits (α and β) forming homologous groups with only 40–50% similarity in amino acid sequence (Ruoslahti 1991a). As integrins are cell-surface proteins, they have an extracellular domain, as well as a transmembrane and cytoplasmic segment, allowing integrins to function as a link between the cytoskeleton and extracellular matrix (Hynes 1987, 1992; Sastry and Horwitz 1993). The α subunit functions as the receptor binding site (Hynes 1992) and is able to pair with a multitude of β subunits, creating diversity in recognition of different adhesive substrates. There are currently a total of 15 α and eight β subunits, known as α_{1-9}, IIb, E, M, L, V, X and β_{1-8}, expression of which may be modulated by cytokines (Dedhar 1989; Ignotz et al. 1989).

Fibronectin is recognised by several integrins, comprising $\alpha_3\beta_1$, $\alpha_4\beta_1$ (Wayner and Carter 1987; Hemler 1990), $\alpha_4\beta_7$ (Ruegg et al. 1992), $\alpha_5\beta_1$ (Pytela et al. 1985), $\alpha_V\beta_1$ (Vogel et al. 1990), $\alpha_V\beta_3$ (Ruoslahti 1991b), $\alpha_V\beta_6$ (Ruoslahti et al. 1994) and $\alpha_V\beta_8$ (Weinacker et al. 1994). The integrins binding to collagen are $\alpha_1\beta_1$, $\alpha_2\beta_1$ and $\alpha_3\beta_1$ (Wayner and Carter 1987; Languino et al. 1989; Kirchhofer et al. 1990), while intercellular adhesion molecules (ICAM) are recognised by $\alpha_M\beta_2$, $\alpha_L\beta_2$, vascular cell adhesion molecules (VCAM) by $\alpha_4\beta_1$, $\alpha_4\beta_7$ (Ruoslahti et al. 1994) and laminin primarily by $\alpha_6\beta_1$ as well as $\alpha_1\beta_1$, $\alpha_2\beta_1$, $\alpha_3\beta_1$, $\alpha_7\beta_1$ and $\alpha_6\beta_4$ (Lotz et al. 1990).

Proteases

Proteases are enzymes responsible for mediating the degradation and dissolution of extracellular matrixes. While several classes of proteases exist, the current evidence for a possible role in implantation primarily implicates serine proteases and matrix metalloproteases. Serine proteases such as urokinase (uPA) and tissue (tPA) plasminogen activators function mainly to catalyse the conversion of plasminogen to plasmin, although they are also capable of a wide range of proteolytic activity (Dano et al. 1985). The additional properties of uPA involve cell adhesion and migration whereas tPA is involved in fibrinolysis (Hart and Rehemtulla 1988). In common with other enzymes, uPA and tPA are synthesised and stored as proenzymes and are inhibited by complexing with plasminogen activator inhibitors 1 (PAI-1) and 2 (PAI-2) (Schleef et al. 1988).

Matrix metalloproteases (MMP) form a family of homologous enzymes secreted as inactive proenzymes and incorporate a zinc atom on their active site (Matrisian 1990). Partial hydrolysis results in loss of a propeptide and activation. Three subgroups of MMP exist, representing the only enzymes known to digest the endometrial extracellular matrix (Bischof and Martelli 1992) and comprise gelatinases (MMP-2, MMP-9), collagenases (MMP-1, MMP-8, MMP-13) and stromelysins (MMP-3, MMP-7, MMP-10, MMP-11). The functions of each MMP are as suggested by their subgroup nomenclature, with gelatinases responsible for digestion of gelatine (denatured collagen) and type IV collagen (major constituent of basement membranes) whereas collagenases digest collagen types I–III, VII and X, the main collagen found in the interstitium of extracellular matrix. In contrast, stromelysins exhibit a broad range of activity and are capable of digesting type IV collagen and gelatine (as per gelatinases) as well as type VII collagen (as per collagenases), laminin, fibronectin and proteoglycans (Bischof and Campana 1996).

Plasmin has been shown to be a potent activator of several MMPs (Murphy et al. 1992), together with similar evidence for cytokines (Edwards et al. 1987; Ito et al. 1990; McNaul et al. 1990; Overall et al. 1991). Once activated, the control of MMP activity is modulated by specific local tissue inhibitors, three of which have been described. Tissue inhibitors of MMP are known as TIMP-1, TIMP-2 and TIMP-3, a family of homologous, cysteine-rich proteins that exert their activity by binding to the MMP. TIMP-1 and TIMP-2 appear to interact preferentially with gelatinases and stromelysins to inhibit the digestion of type IV collagen (Goldberg et al. 1989; Howard et al. 1991a,b). Activators of TIMP include MMP and cytokines (Roeb et al. 1994).

Cytokines

The nomenclature 'cytokine' is relatively recent (Cohen et al. 1974), although these substances were first recognised in 1966 by demonstration of normal macrophage migration being inhibited by materials released from sensitised lymphocytes upon exposure to antigen (Bloom and Bennett 1966). Cytokines are polypeptide proteins involved in the control of local and systemic events of the immune response, healing, haemopoeisis and cellular functions. They are produced mainly by immune cells, although virtually every nucleated cell type in the body is capable of cytokine production. They are pleiotropic, expressing features of 'redundancy' or 'overlap', where the effects of each cytokine are not exclusive but may be reproduced by other cytokines with over-lapping functions; 'synergism/antagonism', where exposure of cells to two or more cytokines at a time may lead to different responses and 'receptor transmodulation', where a cytokine may increase or decrease the expression of receptors for another cytokine (Le and Vilcek 1994). The number of cytokines discovered has been increasing steadily and includes interleukins (IL-1 to IL-18), tumour necrosis factors α (TNF-α) and β (TNF-β), colony-stimulating factors (M-CSF, G-CSF, GM-CSF), transforming growth factors (TGF-α, β) and interferon γ (IFN-γ).

The potential roles of cytokines in implantation are extensive, as cytokines have been implicated in the apposition, adhesion and invasion phases. The main cytokines involved are IL-1, leukaemia inhibitory factor (LIF), macrophage colony-stimulating factor (M-CSF), as well as the T-helper 1 immune response cytokines IFN-γ, IL-2, IL-12, TNF-β and T-helper 2 immune response cytokines IL-4, 6, 10 and 13. It is during apposition and adhesion that IL-1, LIF and M-CSF appear to exert their effects, whereas the T-helper 1 and 2 immune response cytokines potentially influence events later on at the invasion phase.

APPOSITION AND ADHESION PHASE OF IMPLANTATION

Apposition or orientation of the blastocyst within the lumen of the uterus starts on day LH +6 when the human conceptus measures 300–400 mm in diameter and the uterine lumen is minimal, due to suction of endometrial fluid by pinopods. This progresses to adhesion, when the conceptus physically encounters maternal endometrium, and repre-sents the primary event in mammals initiating invasion (Enders 1981). Current evidence suggests that adhesion molecules and cytokines (IL-1, LIF, M-CSF) may play an important role during this period, whereas MMP may not.

The expression of α_1, α_2, α_3, α_4, α_5, α_6, α_V, β_1, β_3, β_4 integrins has been demonstrated in secretory endometrium (Lessey and Castelbaum 1995), allowing recognition and adhesion of fibronectin ($\alpha_3\beta_1$, $\alpha_4\beta_1$, $\alpha_5\beta_1$, $\alpha_V\beta_1$, $\alpha_V\beta_3$), collagen ($\alpha_1\beta_1$, $\alpha_2\beta_1$, $\alpha_3\beta_1$) VCAM ($\alpha_4\beta_1$) and laminin ($\alpha_6\beta_1$, $\alpha_1\beta_1$, $\alpha_2\beta_1$, $\alpha_3\beta_1$, $\alpha_6\beta_4$). It is therefore interesting to note that the murine embryo expresses laminin during the two-to-four-cell stage (Cooper and MacQueen 1983) and fibronectin during blastocyst formation (Thorsteinsdottir 1992), whereas the human embryo produces laminin at the morula stage (Turpeenniemi-Hujanen *et al.* 1992). The discovery that murine embryos are also capable of producing α_1, α_2, α_3, α_5, α_6, α_V, α_7, β_1, β_3 integrins (Sutherland *et al.* 1993) further clarifies the situation, as the potential exists for the murine embryo to recognise and bind to fibronectin, collagen and laminin, thus providing the necessary physical tools to ensure conceptus adhesion to maternal endometrium (Figure 1).

In contrast to the physical nature of adhesion molecule involvement in apposition and adhesion during implantation, cytokines appear to act through regulation of cell function, including adhesion molecule expression (Dedhar 1989; Ignotz *et al.* 1989). The expression of M-CSF prior to murine implantation appears to be confined to uterine epithelium and undergoes a five-fold increase during implantation (Arcecei *et al.* 1989). Moreover, studies on implantation utilising the osteopetrotic (op/op) mouse, a genetically modified species characterised by osteopetrosis and complete absence of M-CSF production, yielded some interesting observations. These mice were noted to be infertile, due to the inability to initiate adhesion and hence implantation, despite normal fertilisation and blastocyst formation. However, the administration of exogeneous M-CSF appears to result in normal implantation (Pollard *et al.* 1991). Studies in humans have shown a similar pattern of M-CSF expression in the endometrium (Daiter *et al.* 1992), although the importance of M-CSF in human conceptus adhesion remains to be proven.

The importance of LIF was also derived from murine models, with expression detected in both the endometrium and blastocyst during the peri-implantation period (Bhatt *et al.* 1991). This expression of endometrial LIF appears to be under maternal control as it is still expressed in artificially induced pseudopregnant states and absent in cases of delayed implantation by either ovariectomy or the sucking stimulus when blastocysts are floating in the endometrial cavity (Bhatt *et al.* 1991). Moreover, deletion of the LIF gene in mice resulted in the inability of the blastocyst to implant, although

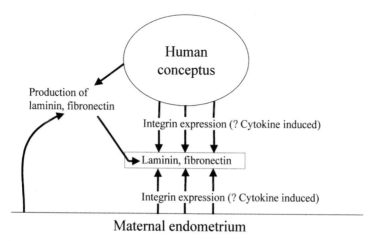

Figure 1 *Potential role of integrins and cytokines during apposition and adhesion phases of implantation; integrins expressed by human conceptus and maternal endometrium functions as the 'sticky' physical surface for laminin and fibronectin adherence; the resulting complex provides the necessary physical links to allow initiation of invasion*

fertilisation was unaffected and the blastocysts were able to be successfully implanted in surrogate normal female mice with LIF expression (Stewart *et al.* 1992). The ability to initiate implantation was also restored by exogenous administration of LIF. Human data on LIF have demonstrated its expression to be mostly confined to the epithelial fraction of the endometrium. It is maximal during the implantation period (Charnock-Jones *et al.* 1994; Kojima *et al.* 1994). This expression of LIF appears to be independent of hormonal influences (oestradiol and progesterone), although other cytokines exert a modulatory effect (Arici *et al.* 1995). The presence of LIF receptor in human blastocysts further supports a role for LIF in apposition or adhesion of the conceptus to maternal endometrium (Charnock-Jones *et al.* 1994).

IL-1 comprises two distinct cytokines, IL-1α and IL-1β, which act on the same receptor (IL-1R). Murine endometrium is known to express IL-1α and IL-1β, reaching a peak during the peri-implantation period, regardless of the absence or presence of the conceptus (Choudhuri and Wood 1993; De *et al.* 1993). More importantly, IL-1α and IL-1β are also produced by the conceptus prior to implantation (Zolti *et al.* 1991). This corresponds to the presence of IL-1R within the endometrium in the peri-implantation period which, when functionally blocked by the administration of an IL-1R antagonist, prevents blastocyst adhesion to maternal endometrium and leaves it floating free within the uterine cavity (Simon *et al.* 1994). The human endometrium expression of IL-1α, IL-1β and IL-1R has been shown to have a similar pattern to murine models (Kauma *et al.* 1990; Simon *et al.* 1993a,b). In addition, IL-1R antagonist expression has also been demonstrated within the human endometrium, with production declining as implantation approaches (Simon *et al.* 1995). However, the human embryo was not consistently shown to be producing IL-1α and IL-1β, as contradictory results were available from different authors using different *in vitro* models (Hardy *et al.* 1993; Seifer *et al.* 1993; Tarlatzis *et al.* 1994; Austgulen *et al.* 1995). The results from a recent *in vitro* study appear to clarify the observed anomalies, as differential IL-1α and IL-1β production was observed depending on the culture media. Human embryos cultured under routine *in vitro* fertilisation conditions or co-cultured with human endometrial stromal cells fail to produce IL-1α or IL-1β, whereas co-culture with endometrial epithelial cells or endometrial epithelial cell conditioned media resulted in IL-1α and IL-1β production (De los Santos *et al.* 1996). These results suggest that IL-1α and IL-1β production by the human conceptus may be regulated by an epithelial factor yet to be identified. What it also illustrates clearly are the technical limitations of using *in vitro* models to study molecular factors involved in human implantation.

INVASION PHASE OF IMPLANTATION

The process of invasion is probably the most critical step of implantation. A fine balance of regulatory activity is a prerequisite to ensure its smooth progression, as overactivity during invasion may result in pathological conditions such as placenta accreta, increta and percreta, while underactivity may represent the basis for miscarriage, pre-eclampsia and intrauterine growth restriction. As invasion is chronologically the longest step involved in implantation, the subsequent discussions are divided into 'early invasion', which represents the activities up until the conceptus encounters maternal immune cells and 'late invasion', when the conceptus is in direct contact with maternal immune cells.

Early invasion

Early invasion is initiated when maternal tissues are digested to allow the conceptus to start burrowing into the extracellular matrix of the endometrium. The role of MMPs comes to the fore during this period, as they are capable of disrupting the basement membrane, the first physical barrier to intrusion of the conceptus into the endometrial milieu. This is supported by the observation that the developing human conceptus, via its trophoblastic component, secretes a variety of MMPs, especially MMP-2 and MMP-9, the gelatinases responsible for digestion of type IV collagen (Puistola *et al.* 1989; Bischof 1991). The importance of gelatinase secretion by the human conceptus is clear as the main constituent of endometrial basement membrane, the first physical barrier to invasion, is type IV collagen (Turpeenniemi-Hujanen *et al.* 1992). Moreover, type IV collagen also represents a major component of the uterine extracellular matrix at the fetomaternal interface barrier (Emonard *et al.* 1990; Alexander and Werb 1991), the environment which the conceptus encounters after successfully breaching the endometrial basement membrane. However, as discussed earlier, MMPs are secreted as inactive pro-enzymes and, therefore, are dependent on other molecular factors such as plasmin and cytokines for conversion to the active state (Figure 2).

The conversion of plasminogen to plasmin is dependent on uPA and tPA, which have been demonstrated to be produced by the developing murine blastocyst during implantation (Strickland *et al.* 1976; Sappino *et al.* 1989). In addition, under *in vitro* culture conditions, human trophoblast cells are known to produce uPA mainly within the first 24 hours, suggesting that its production is a transient phenomenon coinciding with the moment of early invasion (Queenan *et al.* 1987). The activity of uPA and tPA may itself be regulated by the endometrial production of its inhibitor PAI under the influence of cytokines (Emmeis and Kooistra 1986; Lockwood *et al.* 1994). This may represent one facet of the mechanisms involved in the control of MMP activity. Once activated, MMPs require strict regulation to prevent over-activity and, hence, over-invasion, which is achieved by the presence of the MMP inhibitors, TIMP.

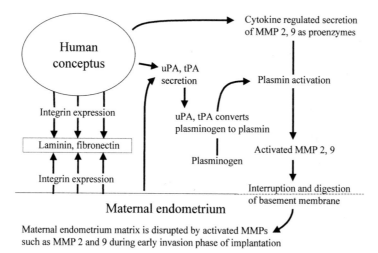

Figure 2 *Proposed interactions during early invasion phase of implantation; MMP = matrix metalloproteases; tPA = tissue plasminogen activator; uPA = urokinase plasminogen activator*

Cytokines are important regulators of MMP activity, as they are capable of activating MMP as well as TIMP. The regulatory role of cytokines may be evident from the observation that TNF-α acts to increase TIMP expression in humans, therefore limiting the activity of MMP (Ito *et al.* 1990). In addition, murine TIMP production has been shown to be upregulated by IL-1β and IL-6 (Roeb *et al.* 1994), although the cytokine most implicated in human regulation of MMP and TIMP is TGF-β. The human endometrium is known to produce TGF-β (Graham *et al.* 1992), which possesses the ability to stimulate TIMP expression in fibroblasts within the extracellular matrix, as well as inhibition of stromelysin (such as MMP-3, MMP-7, MMP-10 and MMP-11) production (Matrisian 1990). This combination of roles seems to implicate TGF-β as a major determinant in the control of conceptus intrusion during the early stages of invasion (Figure 3).

Late invasion

This represents the most crucial step of implantation, as the equilibrium achieved during this period must be maintained throughout the normal intrauterine gestation of the human conceptus. It is also during this period that the conceptus is fully exposed to the maternal environment as encountered through maternal peripheral blood circulation. Inevitably, the fetomaternal interaction is then propelled into a new dimension, as this phase of implantation encompasses the maiden encounter of maternal immune-system cells by the conceptus. The immunological paradox that arises in normal pregnancy, whereby the semi-allograft human conceptus, which is immunologically foreign to the mother due to its paternal genetic contribution, evades immune rejection, was first described over 45 years ago (Medawar 1953). However, it is only recently that inroads have been made into understanding this enigma with the advances in immunology and molecular biology. Despite this, human data on the events unfolding during this crucial period remain sparse because of ethical considerations. Instead, the prerogative derives from work done in murine models.

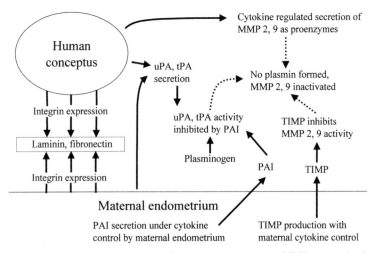

Figure 3 *Proposed control mechanisms for modulating matrix metalloproteases (MMP) action by tissue inhibitors of MMP (TIMP), plasminogen activator inhibitors (PAI) and cytokines*

The primary function of the human immune response is to differentiate between self and non-self, leading to attack and rejection of non-self foreign bodies or antigens, known as immunogens. Evolution has resulted in the development of two distinct immune responses in vertebrates, the innate response and adaptive response, whereas invertebrates only possess an innate immune response (Janeway 1992; Rinkevich 1998). The human innate immune response represents a more primitive, non-specific first line of defence against immunogens, mediated by neutrophils and natural killer cells.

In contrast, the human adaptive immune response is a specific, targeted, second-line response against particular immunogens mediated by T lymphocytes (T-helper cells which express cluster of differentiation-4 (CD4), and T-cytotoxic cells expressing cluster of differentiation-8 (CD8) on their cell surface), B lymphocytes and macrophages. The adaptive immune response is initiated when an immunogen encounters antigen presenting cells (APC) such as macrophages, which process the immunogen to ensure recognition by T-helper cells. These then initiate the adaptive immune response, which comprises a T-helper 1 (TH-1) cytotoxic response and a T-helper 2 (TH-2) humoral response depending on the type of cytokines present. The cytokines responsible for inducing a TH-1 response in humans include IFN-γ, IL-2, IL-12, TNF-β while TH-2 cytokines include IL-4, 6, 10 and 13 (Romagnani 1992, 1995). Studies on murine models have shown that the TH-1 cytokines and hence immune responses are responsible for fetal rejection, whereas TH-2 cytokines mediate a humoral response, which may be necessary to ensure normal reproduction (Wegmann et al. 1993).

However, confirmation of the *status quo* in humans is awaited, despite the available evidence showing the human endometrium to be a rich source of cytokine production and to host a variety of immune cells, which vary throughout the menstrual cycle (Klentzeris et al. 1992; Tabibzadeh and Sun 1992; Bulmer 1995). A different approach to that of murine models may be necessary to overcome the ethical constraints inherent within studies on human implantation. Progress in understanding fetomaternal interactions during implantation and subsequent human reproduction may derive from studies on women who suffer from recurrent miscarriage, as they represent one extreme of human reproduction outcome (Lim et al. 1996).

The first study exploring the role of a dichotomous T-helper response in human reproduction was an *in vitro* model, using peripheral lymphocytes extracted from women who suffered unexplained recurrent miscarriage and exposing them to choriocarcinoma cells in culture (Hill 1995). It was noted that the recurrent miscarriage lymphocytes produced almost no TH-2 cytokines (IL-4, IL-10) but copious amounts of TH-1 cytokines (IFN-γ, IL-2, TNF-β), whereas the converse was true for controls consisting of men and fertile women. However, as the endometrial and peripheral immune cell populations may be inherently different (Klentzeris et al. 1992), a more reserved interpretation of the results is necessary. An attempt to overcome this limitation was made in a recent study, which utilised immune cells extracted from the decidua of four women with unexplained recurrent miscarriage. The small sample source necessitated *in vitro* expansion of the immune cells, prior to chemical rather than biological stimulation to determine the profile of cytokine production (Piccinni et al. 1998). In contrast to the previous study, no difference in TH-1 cytokine (IFN-γ, TNF-β) production by these women was observed, although the TH-2 cytokine (LIF, IL-4, IL-10) production was lower compared to decidual lymphocytes from women undergoing termination of pregnancy. An additional finding relating to progesterone was that TH-2 cytokine expression was induced *in vitro*, but only at non-physiological levels exceeding 4770 nmol/l.

Our studies analysing the *in vivo* profile of TH-1 and TH-2 cytokine expression within peri-implantation endometrium of ten normal and 25 women who suffered recurrent miscarriage may provide clarification of the conflicting *in vitro* human results. Due to ethical considerations, the endometrial specimens were collected during perceived implantation (days LH +7 to +10) of a non-conception cycle. They were then analysed by reverse transcriptase-polymerase chain reaction (RT-PCR) and enzyme-linked immunosorbent assay (ELISA) for the respective presence of mRNA and protein secretion of TH-1 (IFN-γ, IL-2, IL-12, TNF-β) and TH-2 cytokines (IL-4, 6, 10, 13). In addition, the influence of systemic hormones (FSH, LH, oestradiol, progesterone, testosterone and dehydroepiandrosterone sulphate on TH-1 and TH-2 cytokine expression *in vivo* was investigated.

The results yielded some interesting observations. Normal women, defined as those with no previous miscarriage history and at least one successful vaginal livebirth delivery, exhibited a major paucity of TH-1 cytokine expression (Lim *et al.* 1998), especially of IL-12, the key cytokine involved in initiation of a TH-1 response (Hsieh *et al.* 1993) and IFN-γ, the corresponding cytokine involved in perpetuation of a TH-1 response (Romagnani 1994). The converse was observed for the TH-2 cytokines IL-4, critical for the establishment of a TH-2 response (Seder *et al.* 1992; Piccotti *et al.* 1996) and IL-6, which perpetuates the TH-2 response. However, there was no dominant expression of the cytokines implicated in antibody production, IL-10 and IL-13 (Punnonen *et al.* 1993), perhaps explaining why studies in normally fertile women consistently fail to detect allograft protective 'blocking antibodies' (Neppert *et al.* 1989; Coulam 1992) (Figure 4).

The opposite situation was observed in women with recurrent miscarriage, the results of which were similar regardless of the underlying recurrent aetiology of miscarriage as currently recognised (Lim *et al.* 2000). This represents a potentially important point as it suggests that the findings are not confined to unexplained recurrent miscarriage and may be applicable to other pathological manifestations of human reproduction. It is noteworthy that all the TH-1 cytokines studied (IFN-γ, IL-2, IL-12, TNF-β) had significantly greater expression in women with recurrent miscarriage compared with

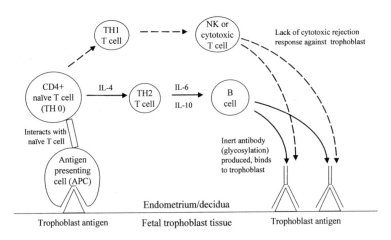

Figure 4 *Proposed maternal immune response during late invasion phase of normal implantation; CD = cluster of differentiation; NK = natural killer; TH = T-helper; → present; – – → absent*

controls. The resulting environment would not be conducive to maternal immune tolerance of the human conceptus, indeed, it would facilitate a TH-1 rejection response, manifest clinically by the repeated miscarriages. Analysis of the TH-2 cytokine results supported this, as a paucity of IL-4 and IL-6 secretion was observed, contributing further to the TH-1 dominance. This may be interpreted as supporting the *in vivo* presence of a predominant TH-2 response mediating successful implantation and a predominant TH-1 response mediating rejection of the human conceptus (Figure 5).

It is tempting to postulate a potential interaction between the endocrine and immune systems via progesterone-induced modulation of cytokine production, as this would correlate with the various observations showing the importance of progesterone in human reproduction. The discovery that progesterone was indeed able to induce TH-2 cytokine (IL-4) production *in vitro* appears to provide the missing link, but this effect was only observed at progesterone levels exceeding 4770 nmol/l (Piccinni *et al.* 1995, 1998). However, as the serum progesterone level in early through to late pregnancy ranges from 100 to 500 nmol/l (Turnbull *et al.* 1974), it becomes evident that the *in vitro* and *in vivo* differences are of an order of magnitude, tempering the initial excitement. Furthermore, no correlation was evident *in vivo* between serum hormone levels (FSH, LH, oestradiol, progesterone, testosterone, DHEAs) and endometrial TH-1, TH-2 cytokine expression from our study (Lim *et al.* 2000).

CURRENT KNOWLEDGE OF IMPLANTATION

Slowly but surely, inroads are being made into understanding the enigma of human reproduction through our greater understanding of the molecular events involved in mediating successful implantation. The importance of molecular factors is only just beginning to be understood, with cytokines forming the common thread throughout the processes encountered during implantation. Cytokines are regulators of cellular function

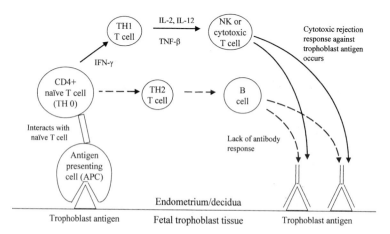

Figure 5 *Proposed maternal immune response during late invasion phase of RM implantation; CD = cluster of differentiation; NK = natural killer; TH = T-helper; → present; − − → absent*

and have been shown to control the production and activities of adhesion molecules, proteases as well as having a pivotal role in initiating and perpetuating the different arms of the maternal immune response. The role of adhesion molecules appears to be maximal during the apposition and adhesion phases of implantation, by forming the necessary physical link, while proteases appear to be necessary to initiate the invasion phase of implantation by disrupting the basement membrane through enzymatic action. This preliminary understanding concerning the myriad events associated with implantation represents the foundation to build on, as the major limiting factor affecting current attempts to improve human reproduction outcome is unsuccessful implantation. The implantation failure rate in normally fertile women has been demonstrated to be 17–22% (Wilcox *et al.* 1988; Ellish *et al.* 1996), whereas infertile women undergoing assisted conception have an implantation failure rate of 85% (Edwards 1995). It is evident that successful human reproduction remains an inefficient process, while the currently available treatments appear to have a low therapeutic value.

FUTURE DIRECTIONS FOR IMPLANTATION RESEARCH IN THE NEW MILLENNIUM

Why is it necessary to invest in research aimed at unravelling the mysteries of implantation when a variety of clinical treatments is currently available for the pathological manifestations of deficient implantation such as pre-eclampsia, miscarriage and intrauterine growth restriction? The answer becomes clear when the underlying basis for the available treatments is explored, as the current therapies can only delay or minimise the after effects but not reverse the natural progression of pre-eclampsia, miscarriage and intrauterine growth restriction. If the events and control mechanisms involved in implantation are understood, it will then be possible to modulate them. This will result in more efficient treatments and prevention of embryo wastage as currently experienced during *in vitro* fertilisation, leading to an improved reproductive outlook for unexplained infertility, recurrent miscarriage and other clinical manifestations of deficient implantation.

A multitude of future research pathways is to be traversed for this to become reality in the new millennium. These include:

(1) The development of a new *in vitro* matrix system which replicates as much as possible the complex endometrial milieu and hence overcomes the current limitations of Matrigel™ (Collaborative Research Inc., Bedford, MA, USA) in studying implantation (Bentin-Ley *et al.* 1994, 1995);

(2) A novel method of delivering cytokines to the uterine cavity that improves on the current liposome technology (Smith *et al.* 1997);

(3) Continuation of implantation research using murine models;

(4) The advent of cytokine immunomodulation to alter maternal T-helper immune response as tried successfully in animal models to prevent repeated miscarriages (Chaouat *et al.* 1990, 1994);

(5) Gene therapy, to selectively inhibit or induce cytokine production *in vivo* to achieve an environment conducive to successful implantation.

References

Alexander, C.M. and Werb, Z. (1991) 'Extracellular matrix degradation' in: E.D. Hay (Ed.) *Cell Biology of Extracellular Matrix*, pp. 255–302. New York: Plenum Press

Arcecei, R.J., Shanahan, F., Stanley, E.R. *et al.* (1989) The temporal expression and location of colony stimulating factor-1 (CSF-1) and the receptor in the female reproductive tract are consistent with CSF-1 regulated placental development. *Proc Natl Acad Sci U S A* **86**, 8818–22

Arici, A., Engin, O., Attar, E. *et al.* (1995) Modulation of leukaemia inhibitory factor gene expression and protein biosynthesis in human endometrium. *J Clin Endocrinol Metab* **80**, 1908–15

Austgulen, R., Arntzen, K.J., Vatten, L.J. *et al.* (1995) Detection of cytokines (interleukin-1, interleukin-6, transforming growth factor-β) and soluble tumour necrosis factor receptors in embryo culture fluids during *in vitro* fertilization. *Hum Reprod* **10**, 171–6

Bentin-Ley, U., Pedersen, B., Lindenberg, S., Larsen, J.F., Hamberger, L. and Horn, T. (1994) Isolation and culture of human endometrial cells in a three-dimensional culture system. *J Reprod Fertil* **101**, 327–32

Bentin-Ley, U., Lindenberg, S., Horn, T. and Larsen, J.F. (1995) Ultrastructure of endometrial epithelial cells in a three-dimensional culture system for human implantation studies. *J Assist Reprod Genet* **12**, 632–8

Bergh, P.A. and Navot, D. (1992) The impact of embryonic development and endometrial maturity on the timing of implantation. *Fertil Steril* **58**, 537–42

Bhatt, H., Brunet, L.J. and Stewart, C.L. (1991) Uterine expression of leukaemia inhibitory factor coincides with the onset of blastocyst implantation. *Proc Natl Acad Sci U S A* **88**, 11408–12

Bischof, P. (1991) 'Blastocyst implantation from the physiology to the experimental model' in: K. Yoshinaga, A.J. Rao and P.R. Adiga (Eds) *Perspectives in Primate Reproductive Biology*, pp. 62–76. New Delhi: Wiley Eastern

Bischof, P. and Campana, A. (1996) A model for implantation of the human blastocyst and early placentation. *Hum Reprod Update* **3**, 262–70

Bischof, P. and Martelli, M. (1992) Proteolysis in the penetration phase of the implantation process. *Placenta* **13**, 17–24

Bloom B.R. and Bennett, B. (1966) Mechanism of a reaction *in vitro* associated with delayed-type hypersensitivity. *Science* **153**, 80–2

Bulmer, J. (1995) 'Immune cells in decidua' in: M. Kurpisz and N. Fernandez (Eds) *Immunology of Human Reproduction*, pp. 313–34. London: Bios Scientific Publishing

Chaouat, G., Menu, E., Clark, D.A., Dy, M., Minkowski, M. and Wegmann, T.G. (1990) Control of fetal survival in CBA/JxDBA/2 mice by lymphokine therapy. *J Reprod Fertil* **89**, 447–58

Chaouat ,G., Menu, E., Assal-Meliani, A. *et al.* (1994) Allopregnancy is a TH 2 like phenomenon: IL 10 can prevent CBAxDBA/2 fetal wastage and TH 2 cytokine can be induced *in vivo* by tau interferons. *Colloque Foundation Marcel Merieux*. Annecy: Foundation Marcel Merieux

Charnock-Jones, D., Sharkey, A., Fenwick, P. *et al.* (1994) Leukaemia inhibitory factor mRNA concentration peaks in human endometrium at the time of implantation and the blastocyst contains mRNA for the receptor at this time. *J Reprod Fertil* **101**, 421–6

Choudhuri, R. and Wood, G.W. (1993) Production of interleukin-1, interleukin-6 and tumour necrosis factor alpha in the uterus of pseudopregnant mice. *Biol Reprod* **49**, 596–603

Cohen, S., Bigazzi, P.E. and Yoshida, T. (1974) Similarities of T cell function in cell-mediated immunity and antibody production. *Cell Immunol* **12**, 150–9

Cooper, A.R. and MacQueen, H.A. (1983) Subunits of laminin are differentially synthesized in mouse eggs and early embryos. *Dev Biol* **96**, 467–71

Coulam, C.B. (1992) Immunologic tests in the evaluation of reproductive disorders: a critical review. *Am J Obstet Gynecol* **167**, 1844–51

Daiter, E., Pampfer, S., Teung, Y.G. *et al.* (1992) Expression of colony stimulating factor-1 (CSF-1) in the human uterus and placenta. *J Clin Endocrinol Metab* **74**, 850–8

Dano, K., Abdreasen, P.A., Grondahl-Hansen, J. *et al.* (1985) Plasminogen activators, tissue degradation and cancer. *Adv Cancer Res* **44**, 139–266

De, M., Sanford, T.R. and Wood, G.W. (1993) Expression of interleukin-1, interleukin-6 and tumour necrosis factor alpha in mouse uterus during the peri-implantation period of pregnancy. *J Reprod Fertil* **97**, 83–9

De los Santos, M.J., Mercader, A., Frances, A. *et al.* (1996) Immunoreactive human embryonic interleukin-1 system and endometrial factors regulating their secretion during embryonic development. *Biol Reprod* **54**, 563–74

Dedhar, S. (1989) Regulation of expression of the cell adhesion receptors, integrins, by recombinant human interleukin-1β in human osteosarcoma cells: inhibition of cell proliferation and stimulation of alkaline phophatase activity. *J Cell Physiol* **138**, 291–9

Edwards, R.G. (1995) Clinical approaches to increasing uterine receptivity during human implantation. *Hum Reprod* **10** Suppl 2, 60–6

Edwards, D.R., Murphy, G., Reynolds, J.J. *et al.* (1987) Transforming growth factor beta modulates the expression of collagenase and metalloproteinase inhibitor. *EMBO J* **6**, 1899–1904

Ellish, N.J., Saboda, K., O'Connor, J., Nasca, P.C., Stanek, E.J. and Boyle, C. (1996) A prospective study of early pregnancy loss. *Hum Reprod* **11**, 406–12

Emmeis, J.J. and Kooistra, T. (1986) IL-1 and lipopolysaccharide induce an inhibitor of tissue-type plasminogen activator *in vivo* and in cultured endothelial cells. *J Exp Med* **163**, 11260–4

Emonard, H.P., Christiane, Y., Smet, M., Grimaud, J.A. and Foidart, J.M. (1990) Type IV and interstitial collagenolytic activities in normal and malignant trophoblast cells are specifically regulated by the extracellular matrix. *Invasion Metastasis* **10**, 170–7

Enders, A. (1981) Embryo implantation with emphasis on the rhesus monkey and the human. *Reproduction* **5**, 163–7

Goldberg, G.I., Marmer, B.L., Grant, G.A. *et al.* (1989) Human 72 kDa type IV collagenase forms a complex with a tissue inhibitor of metalloproteases designated TIMP-2. *Proc Natl Acad Sci U S A* **86**, 8207–11

Graham, C.H., Lysiak, J.J., McCrae, K.R. *et al.* (1992) Location of transforming growth factor beta at the human fetal-maternal interface: role in trophoblast growth and differentiation. *Biol Reprod* **46**, 561–72

Hardy, R.I., Anderson, D.J. and Hill, J.A. (1993) Lack of correlation between IL-1α in pre-implantation culture media and pregnancy outcome *Fertil Steril* **61** Suppl, 1–139

Hart, D.A. and Rehemtulla, A. (1988) Plasminogen activators and their inhibitors: regulators of extracellular proteolysis and cell function. *Comp Biochem Physiol B Biochem Mol Biol* **90**, 691–708

Hemler, M.E. (1990) VLA proteins in the integrin family: structures, functions and their role on leucocytes. *Annu Rev Immunol* **8**, 365–400

Hill, J.A. (1995) T helper 1 type immunity to trophoblast: evidence for a new immunological mechanism for recurrent abortion in women. *Hum Reprod* **10** Suppl 2, 114–20

Howard, E.W., Bullen, E.C. and Banda, M.J. (1991a) Preferential inhibition of 72 and 92 kDa gelatinases by tissue inhibitor of metalloproteinases-2. *J Biol Chem* **266**, 13070–5

Howard, E.W., Bullen, E.C. and Banda, M.J. (1991b) Regulation of the autoactivation of human 72 kDa progelatinase by tissue inhibitor of metalloproteinases. *J Biol Chem* **266**, 13064–9

Hsieh, C.S., Macatonia, S.E., Tripp, C.S., Wolf, S.F., O'Garra, A. and Murphy, K.M. (1993) Development of TH1 CD4+ T cells through IL-12 produced by listeria-induced macrophages. *Science* **260**, 547–9

Hynes, R.O. (1987) Integrins: a family of cell surface receptors. *Cell* **48**, 549–54

Hynes, R.O. (1992) Integrins: versatility, modulation and signalling in cell adhesion. *Cell* **69**, 11–25

Ignotz, R.A., Heino, J. and Massague, J. (1989) Regulation of cell adhesion receptors by transforming growth factor: regulation of vitronectin receptor and LFA-1. *J Biol Chem* **264**, 389–92

Ito, A., Sato, T., Iga, T. *et al.* (1990) Tumour necrosis factor bifunctionally regulates matrix metalloproteinases and tissue inhibitor of metalloproteinases production by human fibroblasts. *FEBS Lett* **269**, 93–5

Janeway, C.A. (1992) The immune system evolved to discriminate infectious nonself from noninfectious self. *Immunol Today* **13**, 11–16

Kauma, S., Matt, D. and Strom, S. *et al.* (1990) Interleukin 1 β, human leucocyte antigen HLA-DR α and transforming growth factor β expression in endometrium, placenta and placental membranes. *Am J Obstet Gynecol* **163**, 1430–7

Kirchhofer, D., Languino, L.R., Rouslahti, E. *et al.* (1990) α₂β₁ integrins from different cell types show different binding specificities. *J Biol Chem* **265**, 615–18

Klentzeris, L.D., Bulmer, J.N., Warren, M.A., Morrison, L., Li, T.C. and Cooke, I.D. (1992) Endometrial lymphoid tissue in the timed endometrial biopsy: morphometric and immunohistochemical aspects. *Am J Obstet Gynecol* **167**, 667–74

Kojima, K., Kanzaki, H., Iwai, M. *et al.* (1994) Expression of leukaemia inhibitory factor in human endometrium and placenta. *Biol Reprod* **50**, 882–7

Languino, L.R., Gehlsen, K.R., Wayner, E. *et al.* (1989) Endothelial cells use α₂β₁ integrin as a laminin receptor. *J Cell Biol* **109**, 2455–62

Le, J. and Vilcek, J. (1994) 'Immunology of cytokines: an introduction' in: A. Thompson (Ed.) *The Cytokine Handbook*, 2nd edn, pp. 1–20. London: Academic Press

Lessey, B.A. and Castelbaum, A.J. (1995) Integrins in the endometrium. *Reprod Med Rev* **4**, 43–58

Lim, K.J.H., Odukoya, O.A., Li, T.C. and Cooke, I.D. (1996) Cytokines and immuno-endocrine factors in recurrent miscarriage. *Hum Reprod Update* **2**, 469–81

Lim, K.J.H., Odukoya, O.A., Ajjan, R., Li, T.C., Weetman, A.P. and Cooke, I.D. (1998) The profile of cytokine mRNA expression in peri-implantation human endometrium. *Mol Hum Reprod* **4**, 77–81

Lim, K.J.H., Odukoya, O.A., Ajjan, R., Li, T.C., Weetman, A.P. and Cooke, I.D. (2000) The role of T-helper cytokines in human reproduction. *Fertil Steril* **73**, 136–42

Lockwood, C.J., Krikun, G., Papp, C. *et al.* (1994) The role of progestationally regulated stromal cell tissue factor and type 1 plasminogen activator inhibitor (PAI-1) in endometrial haemostasis and menstruation. *Ann N Y Acad Sci* **734**, 57–79

Lotz, M.M., Korzelius, C.A. and Mercurio, A.M. (1990) Human colon carcinoma cells use multiple receptors to adhere to laminin: Involvement of $\alpha_6\beta_4$ and $\alpha_2\beta_1$ integrins. *Cellular Research* **1**, 249–57

Matrisian, L.M. (1990) Metalloproteinases and their inhibitors in matrix remodelling. *Trends Genet* **6**, 121–5

McNaul, K.L., Chartrain, N., Lark, M. *et al.* (1990) Disco-ordinate expression of strome-lysin, collagenase and tissue inhibitor of metalloproteinases-1 in rheumatoid human synovial fibroblasts. *J Biol Chem* **265**, 17238–45

Medawar, P.B. (1953) Some immunological and endocrinological problems raised by evolution of viviparity in vertebrates. *Symp Soc Exp Biol* **7**, 320–38

Murphy, G., Atkinson, S., Ward, R., Gavrilovic, J. and Reynolds, J.J. (1992) The role of plasminogen activators in the regulation of connective tissue metalloproteinases. *Ann N Y Acad Sci* **667**, 1–12

Neppert, J., Mueller-Eckhardt, G., Neumeyer, H. *et al.* (1989) Pregnancy maintaining antibodies: workshop report (Giessen 1988). *J Reprod Immunol* **15**, 159–67

Overall, C.M., Wrana, J.L. and Sodek, J. (1991) Transcriptional and post-transcriptional regulation of 72 kDa gelatinase/type IV collagenase by transforming growth factor β 1 in human fibroblast. *J Biol Chem* **266**, 14064–71

Piccinni, M.P., Giudizi, M.G., Biagiotti, R. *et al.* (1995) Progesterone favors the development of human T-helper cells producing TH-2 type cytokines and promotes both IL-4 production and membrane CD30 expression in established TH-1 cell clones. *J Immunol* **155**, 128–33

Piccinni, M.P., Beloni, L., Livi, C., Maggi, E., Scarselli, G. and Romagnani, S. (1998) Defective production of both leukaemia inhibitory factor and type 2 T-helper cytokines by decidual T cells in unexplained recurrent abortions. *Nat Med* **4**, 1020–4

Piccotti, J.R., Chan, S.Y., Goodman, R.E., Magram, J., Eichwald, E.J. and Bishop, D.K. (1996) IL-12 antagonism induces T-helper 2 responses, yet exacerbates cardiac allograft rejection. *J Immunol* **157**, 1951–7

Pollard, J.W., Hunt, J.S., Wiktor-Jedrzejczak, W. *et al.* (1991) A pregnancy defect in the osteopetrotic (op/op) mouse demonstrates the requirement for CSF-1 in female fertility. *Dev Biol* **148**, 273–83

Puistola, U., Ronnberg, L., Martikainen, H. and Turpeenniemi-Hujanen, T. (1989) The human embryo produces basement membrane collagen (type IV collagen) degrading protease activity. *Hum Reprod* **4**, 309–11

Punnonen, J., Aversa, G., Cocks, B.G. *et al.* (1993) Interleukin 13 induces interleukin 4 independent IgG4 and IgE synthesis and CD23 expression by human B cells. *Proc Natl Acad Sci U S A* **90**, 3730–4

Pytela, R., Pierschbacher, M.D. and Ruoslahti, E. (1985) Identification and isolation of a 140 kDa cell surface glycoprotein with properties of a fibronectin receptor. *Cell* **40**, 191–8

Queenan, J.T., Kao, L.C., Arboleda, C.E. *et al.* (1987) Regulation of urokinase type plasminogen activator production by cultured human cytotrophoblast. *J Biol Chem* **262**, 10903–6

Rinkevich, B. (1998) Immunology of human implantation: from the invertebrate's point of view. *Hum Reprod* **13**, 455–9

Roeb, E., Graeve, L., Mullberg, J. *et al.* (1994) TIMP-1 protein expression is stimulated by IL-1beta and Il-6 in primary rat hepatocytes. *FEBS Lett* **349**, 45–9

Romagnani, S. (1992) Human TH1 and TH2 subsets: regulation of differentiation and role in protection and immunopathology. *Int Arch Allergy Immunol* **98**, 279–85

Romagnani, S. (1995) Biology of human TH 1 and TH 2 cells. *J Clin Immunol* **15**, 121–9

Ruegg, C., Postigo, A.A., Sikorski, E.E. *et al.* (1992) Role of integrin $\alpha_4\beta_7/\alpha_4\beta_p$ in lymphocyte adherence for fibronectin and VCAM-1 in homotypic cell clustering. *J Cell Biol* **117**, 179–89

Ruoslahti, E. (1991a) 'Integrins as receptors for extracellular matrix' in: E.D. Hay (Ed.) *Cell Biology of Extracellular Matrix*, pp. 343–8. New York: Plenum Press

Ruoslahti, E. (1991b) Integrins. *J Clin Invest* **87**, 1–5

Ruoslahti, E., Noble, N.A., Kagami, S. *et al.* (1994) Integrins. *Kidney Int* **45** Suppl 44, S17–22

Sappino, A.P., Huarte, J., Belin, D. *et al.* (1989) Plasminogen activators in tissue remodelling and invasion: mRNA localization in mouse ovaries and implanting embryos. *J Cell Biol* **109**, 2471–9

Sastry, S.K. and Horwitz, A.F. (1993) Integrin cytoplasmic domains: mediators of cytoskeletal linkages and extra and intracellular initiated transmembrane signalling. *Curr Opin Cell Biol* **5**, 819–31

Schleef, R.R., Wagner, N.V. and Loskutoff, D.J. (1988) Detection of both type 1 and 2 plasminogen activator inhibitors in human cells. *J Cell Physiol* **134**, 269–74

Seder, R.A., Paul, W.E., Davis, M.M. and Fazekas de St, G.F. (1992) The presence of IL-4 during *in vitro* priming determines the lymphokine producing potential of CD4+ T cells from T cell receptor transgenic mice. *J Exp Med* **176**, 1091–8

Seifer, D.B., Romero, R., Berlinsky, D. *et al.* (1993) Absence of immunoreactive cytokines in supernatants of individual pre-implantation human embryos. *Am J Reprod Immunol* **30**, 105–7

Simon, C., Piquette, G.N., Frances, A. *et al.* (1993a) Localisation of interleukin-1 type receptor and interleukin-1 β in human endometrium throughout the menstrual cycle. *J Clin Endocrinol Metab* **77**, 549–55

Simon, C., Piquette, G.N., Frances, A. *et al.* (1993b) Interleukin-1 type receptor messenger ribonucleic acid (mRNA) expression in human endometrium throughout the menstrual cycle. *Fertil Steril* **59**, 791–6

Simon, C., Frances, A., Piquette, G.N. *et al.* (1994) Embryonic implantation in mice is blocked by interleukin-1 receptor antagonist (IL-1Ra). *Endocrinology* **134**, 521–8

Simon, C., Frances, A., Yon Lee, B. *et al.* (1995) Immunohistochemical localization, identification and regulation of the interleukin-1 receptor antagonist in the human endometrium. *Mol Hum Reprod* **1** (*Hum Reprod* **10**, 2472–7)

Smith, S.K., Sharkey, A. and Charnock-Jones, D.S. (1997) Cytokines in the implantation site. *Acta Obstet Gynecol Scand* **76** Suppl 167, 6

Stewart, C.L., Kaspar, P., Brunet, L.J. *et al.* (1992) Blastocyst implantation depends on maternal expression of leukaemia inhibitory factor. *Nature* **359**, 76–9

Strickland, S., Reich, E. and Sherman, M.I. (1976) Plasminogen activator in early embryogenesis: enzyme production by trophoblast and parietal endoderm. *Cell* **9**, 231–40

Sutherland, A.E., Calarco, P.G. and Damsky, C.H. (1993) Developmental regulation of integrin expression at the time of implantation in the mouse embryo. *Development* **119**, 1175–86

Tabibzadeh, S. and Sun, X.Z. (1992) Cytokine expression in human endometrium throughout the menstrual cycle. *Hum Reprod* **7**, 1214–21

Tarlatzis, B.C., Bili, H., Daniilidis, M. *et al.* (1994) Interleukin production by human pre-implantation embryos *Fertil Steril* **63** Suppl, 1–165

Thorsteinsdottir, S. (1992) Basement membrane and fibronectin matrix are distinct entities in the developing mouse blastocyst. *Anatomy Research* **232**, 141–9

Turnbull, A.C., Patten, P.T., Flint, A.P.F., Keirse, M.J.N.C., Jeremy, J.Y. and Anderson, A.B.M. (1974) Significant fall in progesterone and rise in oestradiol levels in human peripheral plasma before the onset of labour. *Lancet* **i**, 101–4

Turpeenniemi-Hujanen, T., Ronnberg, L., Kauppiila, A. and Puistola. U. (1992) Laminin in the human embryo implantation: analogy to the invasion by malignant cells. *Fertil Steril* **58**, 105–13

Vogel, B.E., Tarone, G., Giancotti, F.G. *et al.* (1990) A novel fibrin receptor with an unexpected subunit composition ($\alpha_v\beta_1$). *J Biol Chem* **265**, 5934–7

Wayner, E.A. and Carter, W.G. (1987) Identification of multiple cell adhesion receptors for lagen and fibronectin in human fibrosarcoma cells possessing unique α and β common units. *J Cell Biol* **195**, 1873–84

Wegmann, T.G., Lin, H., Guilbert, L. and Mosmann, T.R. (1993). Bidirectional cytokine interactions in the maternal-fetal relationship: is successful pregnancy a TH 2 phenomenon? *Immunol Today* **14**, 353–6

Weinacker, A., Chen, A., Agrez, M. *et al.* (1994) Role of the integrin avb6 in cell attachment to fibronectin. Heterologous expression of intact and secreted forms of the receptor. *J Biol Chem* **269**, 6940–8

Wilcox, A.J., Weinberg, C.R., O'Connor, J.F. *et al.* (1988) Incidence of early loss of pregnancy. *N Engl J Med* **319**, 189–94

Zolti, M., Ben-Rafael, Z., Meirom, R. *et al.* (1991) Cytokines involvement in oocytes and early embryos. *Fertil Steril* **56**, 265–72

21

Women, the profession and the reproductive revolution

Mahmoud F. Fathalla

IN THE BEGINNING

When God blessed them and said unto them, be fruitful and multiply and replenish the Earth, it was not an easy undertaking. They needed thousands of years to reach the first billion. Recently, they have been very good at it. While it has taken 123 years for world population to increase from one billion to two billion, succeeding increments of one billion took 33 years, 14 years and 13 years, respectively (United Nations 1994a). World population reached five billion in 1987; 16th June 1999 was set as the day the world population would reach the six billion mark (UNFPA 1998). There are legitimate reasons to worry that our species may have overdone it, possibly compromising the health of the planet and threatening its biological diversity.

Homo sapiens, an ever-evolving animal, is now adapting its reproductive behaviour to the new dramatic realities, by the increasing adoption of a small family norm, with consequent decline in total fertility. A reproductive revolution has been sweeping the globe. It began in the 19th century in the North. During the second half of the 20th century, the change has been spreading fast in the South. Fertility has been declining at an unprecedentedly steep rate and is continuing to decline.

In this reproductive upheaval, there is one clear winner to emerge: women. Women's potential has long been suppressed to serve the survival needs of humanity, with millions of women sacrificing their lives in the process. From now on, childbearing is becoming *a* function of women and not *the* function of women. Women are becoming producers, not just reproducers. With the adoption of the small family norm and with the empowerment of women to regulate and control their fertility, the woman is finally emerging from behind the mother.

Throughout the major part of human history, the role of the woman has been defined in terms of her reproductive potential. This is also how our profession of obstetrics and gynaecology has been shaped in the past. Our profession is facing a challenge and has to adapt to the new role of women if we want to continue to be relevant to the health needs of women and responsive to women's perspectives (Fathalla 1997).

SETTING THE STAGE FOR THE 21ST CENTURY

Fertility decline

Fertility level is measured by demographers as the total fertility rate, which reflects the average total number of children that a woman would have by the end of her reproductive life if current fertility patterns remain unchanged. The total fertility rate has continued to decline in all regions of the world in recent decades. The pace of fertility decline has been very steep in developing countries. Between the mid-1960s and the 1990s, 17 countries have experienced fertility declines of more than 50% and an additional 31 countries have experienced declines exceeding 25% (Ross *et al.* 1992).

In the more recent period between 1980 and 1996, the total fertility rate declined from 3.7 to 2.8 in the world at large (World Bank 1998). For high-income countries, the rate declined from 1.9 to 1.7 (already below the replacement level needed to keep the size of population stable). For low- and middle-income countries, as a whole, fertility declined from 4.1 to 3.0, with wide differences between regions but with a consistent downward trend. In East Asia and the Pacific, it declined from 3.1 to 2.2, in Europe and Central Asia from 2.5 to 1.8, in Latin America and the Caribbean from 4.1 to 2.8, in the Middle East and North Africa from 6.1 to 4.0, in South Asia from 5.3 to 3.4 and in Sub-Saharan Africa from 6.6 to 5.6 (Figure 1).

Fertility decline should not be viewed only in demographic terms. Fertility by choice, not by chance, is a basic requirement for women's health, well-being and quality of life (Fathalla 1993). A woman who does not have the means or the power to regulate and control her fertility cannot be considered in a 'state of complete physical, mental and social well-being', the definition of health in the constitution of the World Health Organization. She cannot have the joy of a pregnancy that is wanted, avoid the distress of a pregnancy that is unwanted, plan her life, pursue her education, undertake a productive career or plan her births to take place at optimal times for childbearing, ensuring more safety for herself and better chances for her child's survival and healthy growth and development.

Contraceptive use

Homo sapiens has to accomplish the reproductive revolution while retaining a reproductive system geared to high fertility. Women, or their partners, have to use contraception. Women have a span of about 30 reproductive years, during which they were meant by Nature to become pregnant. If women are to bear only one or two children, they will spend only one to three years in childbearing. For the remaining years, they, or their partners, will have to lead a 'contraceptive life' if they are to remain sexually active.

Levels of contraceptive use are estimated as percentages of currently married women of reproductive age (15–49 years) including, where possible, those in consensual unions. According to the latest available United Nations estimates, of the 899 million currently married women of reproductive age in the world, 57% are using contraception at any one time (United Nations 1994b). The prevalence among developing countries as a whole is 53% and in the more developed countries 72% (Table 1). Regional differences in levels of use remain large. While there remain many countries in Africa and several in other regions where the level of contraceptive use is still low, most developing countries that have available data on trends have experienced a substantial increase in the level of contraceptive use.

Contraceptive technology

A scientific revolution in contraceptive technology in the past few decades has helped these hundreds of millions of people to achieve their aspirations to regulate and control

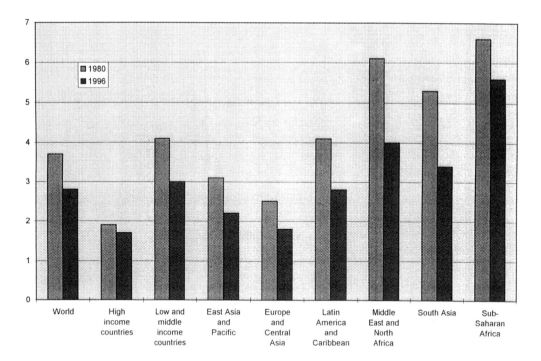

Figure 1   *Total fertility rate 1980–96*

their fertility. The fruits of science have been enjoyed by people living in the most varied circumstances: in the skyscrapers of Manhattan; in peri-urban slums in Latin America; in rural communities of the Indian subcontinent; people in all socio-economic strata; people with different cultures, religious beliefs and value systems; and people postponing a first pregnancy, spacing their children or putting the limit on childbearing.

Until the middle of the 20th century, contraceptive choice was limited to either coitally related methods, which lacked effectiveness, or permanent methods. Contraceptive choices have now been broadened (Fathalla 1994a). Contraception was moved outside the bedroom by the development of systemic methods such as 'the pill'. People no longer had to make the choice between a method to be used at every coitus or a permanent method; long-acting reversible methods now offer protection ranging from one month to several years. Also, highly effective but reversible methods became an available option. Technical developments have allowed sterilisation to be performed as an outpatient procedure and without the need for general anaesthesia.

But perhaps the most significant development, brought about by the contraceptive technology revolution, has been the empowerment of women. For the first time, women had at their disposal effective methods that *they* could use to regulate and control their fertility, without being too dependent on the co-operation of their male partner.

Methods of contraceptive use are shown in Table 2 for different regions of the world. Methods used by women now make up about two-thirds of contraceptive practice worldwide, and such methods have been increasing their share in total contraceptive use. The most widely used methods are female sterilisation, intrauterine devices and oral pills. The main male methods are still the condom and vasectomy. Other supply methods include

Table 1   *Contraceptive use in the world*

	Couples of reproductive age, 1990 (millions)	Level of contraceptive use (%)
World	899	57
Less developed regions	710	53
Africa	97	18
Asia and Oceania		58
Eastern Asia	236	79
Other countries	309	42
Latin America and the		
Caribbean	67	58
More developed regions	189	72

Source: United Nations (1994b)

injectables, diaphragms, cervical caps and spermicides. Non-supply methods include periodic abstinence, withdrawal and folk methods.

Contraceptive safety

As with any drug, increasing the effectiveness of contraceptives commonly has a trade-off in decreasing the margin of safety. From a public-health point of view, contraceptive drugs and devices have an excellent record of safety. They have been used by hundreds of millions of women over extended periods of time and under varied circumstances. Few drugs have been, and continue to be, subjected to such scientific scrutiny as regards safety (Beral *et al.* 1999). This scrutiny is particularly important because, unlike those who use drugs to cure illness, people who use contraceptives are undertaking preventive action.

Fertility control by women and fertility control of women

Women have more at stake in fertility control than anyone else. Contraceptives are meant to be used by women to empower them, to maximise their choices, to give them control of their fertility and thus their lives. The convenience of long-acting and permanent methods is welcomed by many women. These methods, however, can be used and have been used by governments and others to control rather than to empower women (Fathalla 1995). Some governments are short-sighted, not to see that when women are given a real choice, and the information and means to implement their choice, they will make the most rational decision for themselves, for their communities and ultimately for the world at large.

The Programme of Action of the International Conference on Population and Development, Cairo, 1994, emphasised that 'The aim of family-planning programs must be to enable couples and individuals to decide freely and responsibly the number and spacing of their children and to have the information and means to do so and to ensure informed choices and make available a full range of safe and effective methods' and that 'Demographic goals, while legitimately the subject of government development strategies, should not be imposed on family-planning providers in the form of targets or quotas for the recruitment of clients' and that 'Advancing gender equality and equity and the

Table 2   *World contraceptive method prevalence*

	World	*Less developed regions*	*More developed regions*
Female sterilisation	17	20	8
Male sterilisation	5	5	4
Pill	8	6	16
IUD	12	14	6
Condom	5	3	14
Other supply methods	2	1	2
Non-supply methods	8	5	22
Total	57	53	72

Source: United Nations (1994b)

empowerment of women, and the elimination of all kinds of violence against women, and ensuring women's ability to control their own fertility, are cornerstones of population and development-related programs' (United Nations 1994a).

The unmet need

In spite of all the rhetoric about population and family planning, recent estimates by the United Nations Population Fund suggest that 120–150 million women who want to limit or space their pregnancies are still without the means to do so effectively. Altogether 350 million couples lack information about contraception and access to a range of contraceptive services (UNFPA 1997).

The Cairo consensus

At the Cairo International Conference on Population and Development (ICPD) in 1994, a great transition was made from 'counting the people' to 'the people count'. Representatives of 180 countries reached a new consensus that responding to the needs of individuals is the way to address the aggregate problem of rapid population growth. Population policies should address social development beyond family planning, with particular emphasis on advancement of the status and empowerment of women, and family planning should be provided in the context of reproductive healthcare (Sinding and Fathalla 1995).

Family planning is a basic reproductive right. It does not, however, include all the aspirations of people, and particularly women, in the reproductive process. The concept of reproductive health has evolved to provide a more comprehensive approach to meeting the health needs related to reproduction. Reproductive health implies that, apart from the absence of disease or infirmity, people have the ability to reproduce, to regulate their fertility and to practice and enjoy sexual relationships. It further implies that reproduction is carried to a successful outcome through infant and child survival, growth and healthy development. It finally implies that women can go safely through pregnancy and childbirth, that fertility regulation can be achieved without health hazards and that people are safe in having sex (Fathalla 1991). The commitment was made in the Programme of Action of the Cairo ICPD that 'All countries should strive to make accessible through the primary healthcare system, reproductive health to all individuals of appropriate ages as soon as possible and no later than the year 2015' (United Nations 1994a).

Five years after Cairo, the United Nations undertook an ICPD+5 review process, submitted to the United Nations General Assembly on 30 June to 2 July 1999. The review showed that the broad-based definition of reproductive health is being accepted by an increasing number of countries and steps are being taken to provide comprehensive services in many countries, with increasing emphasis being given to quality of care. However, for some countries and regions, progress has been limited and in some cases setbacks have occurred (United Nations 1999).

CHALLENGES FOR THE 21ST CENTURY

A changing role for women

Although progress in building women's capabilities has been significant, the human-development achievements of women still fall below those of men in every country (United Nations Development Programme 1998). Women still have an uphill struggle, but women are 'not for turning'. We, as health professionals entrusted with the health of women, cannot be neutral in the social struggle of women. We have to stand beside women and behind women. We have to speak for women's rights, because we know more than others that the powerlessness of women is a serious health hazard (Fathalla 1994b).

Quality versus quantity

With the adoption of a small family norm, demand for quality of births has substituted for quantity of births. This places a heavier burden on our profession. Aldous Huxley's vision in his famous novel of a 'Brave New World', where people get the embryos they ask for, is not too far away. New frontiers of science have opened the way for hitherto unimaginable reproductive technologies, with vast ethical implications.

Contraception-21

Current contraceptive 'hardware' (methods) used with improved software (service delivery approaches) together with a few developments now at the end of the research pipeline, has carried us through the end of this century but will fall far short in meeting the agenda for the 21st century. According to current population projections, the next few decades will witness the entry of more new contraceptive users than in any comparable time in human history, past or future.

The need for new contraceptive methods is not because currently available methods are not good, but because they are not adequate to meet the widely diverse needs of all the hundreds of millions of people using contraception now and in the future. There is not, and there probably will never be, an ideal method of contraception for all users, but there can be a variety of 'ideal methods' for the needs of different users.

Science is ripe for a 'Contraception-21' initiative (Fathalla 1994c). While advances in cell and molecular biology and in biotechnology have opened new frontiers for medical and biological sciences, the field of contraceptive research and development has yet to benefit from the opportunities provided by these new advances, A recent US Institute of

Medicine study addressed the question of whether there are possibilities that have been generated through the insights and mechanisms unfolding in contemporary science that would offer fresh, exciting and plausible leads for a new generation of contraceptives (Harrison and Rosenfield 1996). The study concluded that, even with the uncertainties of science, there are indeed good prospects in the science. Some of this promise could be realised in the nearer term; some, as is always the case early in the discovery process, must be seen as more distant possibilities. There is, however, no dearth of ideas, no lack of potential targets.

Apart from a general need to expand contraceptive choice and to develop safer and more user-controlled methods, the field of contraceptive research and development should be oriented to meeting needs of women that are currently unmet by existing methods.

There is a need for more participation by men in fertility regulation. Men have not benefited that much from the new developments in contraceptive technology. There is still a remarkable gap between the need and demand for novel male contraceptives on the one hand, and the state of development or even the state of basic knowledge about the function of the male reproductive system on the other. A sustained research effort is needed if men are to have broader contraceptive choices to enable them to share effectively in the responsibility for fertility regulation.

The need for a contraceptive method which a woman can use and control to protect herself against sexually transmitted infections has become urgent. According to a World Bank study quantifying the burden of disease, sexually-transmitted diseases (STDs) rank as the second major cause of the disease burden in young adult women in developing countries, accounting for 8.9% of the total disease burden in that age group (World Bank 1993). Among males of the same age group, STDs are not among the first ten causes and account only for 1.5% of the disease burden. For a mix of biological and social reasons, women are more likely to be infected, are less likely to seek care, are more difficult to diagnose, are at more risk for severe disease sequelae and are more subject to social discrimination and consequences. The most effective method available for protection against STDs, the condom, is controlled by men.

The global drama of unsafe abortion has reached a dimension that can no longer be neglected. Approximately 26 million legal and 20 million illegal abortions were estimated to have been performed world-wide in 1995, resulting in a world-wide abortion rate of 35 per 1000 women aged 15–44 years (Henshaw *et al.* 1999). Partly because of the reality of present gender power relationships, women are often exposed to unprotected sexual intercourse. There is a need for more back-up methods which women can use in such instances, before a pregnancy is established, to decrease or eliminate the need for induced abortion. This retroactive contraception would be suited to the particular needs of adolescents where the decision to use contraception is often made postcoitally.

References

Beral, V., Hermon, C., Kay, C., Hannaford, P., Darby, S. and Reeves, G. (1999) Mortality associated with oral contraceptive use: 25-year follow-up of cohort of 46 000 women from Royal College of General Practitioners' oral contraceptive study. *BMJ* **318**, 96–100

Fathalla, M.F. (1991) Reproductive health: a global overview. Frontiers in human reproduction. *Ann N Y Acad Sci* **626**, 1–10

Fathalla, M.F. (1993) Contraception and women's health. *Br Med Bull* **49**, 245–51

Fathalla, M.F. (1994a) 'Family planning and reproductive health – a global overview' in: F. Graham-Smith (Ed.) *Population – The Complex Reality: A Report of the Population Summit of the World's Scientific Academies*, pp. 251–70. London: Royal Society and Colorado: North American Press

Fathalla, M.F. (1994b) Women's health: an overview. *Int J Gynaecol Obstet* **46**, 105–18

Fathalla, M.F. (1994c) 'Mobilization of resources for a second contraceptive technology revolution' in: P.F.A. Van Look and G. Peres-Palacios (Eds) *Contraceptive Research and Development 1984 to 1994. The Road from Mexico City to Cairo and Beyond*, pp. 527–524. Oxford: Oxford University Press

Fathalla, M.F. (1995) The impact of reproductive subordination on women's health: family planning services. *The American University Law Review* **44**, 1179–90

Fathalla, M.F. (1997) *From Obstetrics and Gynaecology to Women's Health: The Road Ahead.* Carnforth: Parthenon

Harrison, P.F. and Rosenfield, A. (Eds) (1996) *Contraceptive Research and Development: Looking to the Future.* Washington DC: National Academy Press

Henshaw, S.K., Singh, S. and Haas, T. (1999) The incidence of abortion world-wide. *International Family Planning Perspectives* **25**, S30–8

Ross, J.A., Mauldin, W.P., Green, S.R. and Cooke, E.R. (1992) *Family Planning and Child Survival Programs as Assessed in 1991.* New York: The Population Council

Sinding, W.S. and Fathalla, M.F. (1995) The great transition. *Populi* December, 18–21

UNFPA (1997) *The Right to Choose: Reproductive Rights and Reproductive Health.* New York: United Nations Population Fund

UNFPA (1998) *The State of World Population 1998 – The New Generations.* New York: United Nations Population Fund

United Nations (1994a) *Population and Development. Volume 1. Programme of Action Adopted at the International Conference on Population and Development, Cairo, 5–13 September 1994*, pp. 9, 24, 31, 32. New York: UN Department for Economic and Social Information and Policy Analysis (ST/ESA/SER.A/149)

United Nations (1994b) *World Contraceptive Use 1994.* New York: UN Department for Economic and Social Information and Policy Analysis. Population Division (ST/ESA/SER.A/143)

United Nations (1999) *Overall Review and Appraisal of the Implementation of the Programme of Action of the International Conference on Population and Development.* New York: UN General Assembly Twenty-first Special Session (A/s-21/5Add.1)

United Nations Development Programme (1998) *Human Development Report 1998.* Oxford and New York: Oxford University Press

World Bank (1993) *World Development Report – Investing in Health.* New York: Oxford University Press

World Bank (1998) *World Development Report – Knowledge for Development.* New York: Oxford University Press

22

Adolescent gynaecology

D. Keith Edmonds

HISTORY

Recognition of adolescent gynaecology as a specialty came only recently. The first European clinic was set up in 1940 in Prague, Czechoslovakia, by Professor Peter and the first textbook on the subject, written by Dr Goodrich Shauffler, was published in the USA in 1941. The ensuing 30 years brought contributions to the literature, both in North America and in the UK and, here, Professor Sir John Dewhurst became recognised as the first gynaecologist with a special interest in paediatric and adolescent gynaecology. It was only beginning to be recognised that children with intersex problems needed special gynaecological attention, that problems around puberty and its development were complex and required multidisciplinary input and that the management of congenital malformations of the genital tract themselves required specialist attention. Throughout Europe individuals began to develop special interests and to set up clinics and gradually a network of clinicians formed the Fédération Internationale de Gynécologie Infantile et Juvenile (FIGIJ) in 1971. As knowledge of reproductive neurophysiology, endocrinology and genetics has grown during the last 30 years our understanding of the special needs of paediatric and adolescent patients has become increasingly apparent. The multidisciplinary approach by paediatricians, paediatric surgeons and gynaecologists has led to a vastly improved understanding and management of various problems facing the paediatric and adolescent patient. In 1997, the first national centre for reconstructive surgery of congenital malformations of the genital tract was established and recognised at Queen Charlotte's and Chelsea Hospital, London, under the directorship of the author. Specialist clinics for puberty and growth disorders are well established by paediatricians in specialist centres in the UK and now the patient with specific problems relating to adolescence can seek help from specially trained medical personnel. In the USA and Canada there is now a recognised subspecialty of paediatric and adolescent gynaecology with a specialist training programme available in three centres. The recognition that these patients require specialist attention from all healthcare workers has now been achieved and future development will mean continuing co-operation and involvement in a multidisciplinary approach.

CURRENT STATUS

Paediatric and adolescent gynaecology has now evolved into primarily adolescent gynaecology. The paediatric component is now managed by paediatric endocrinologists and paediatric urological surgeons. Thus, problems of intersex, while of interest to the gynaecologist, will not remain the realm of the gynaecologist in the future. However, there are a number of aspects of adolescent gynaecology which have become the recognised areas of interest for this subject.

PUBERTY

The current understanding of the control of onset of puberty has advanced considerably. The nuclei of the neurones that are responsible for the production of gonadotrophin-releasing hormone (GnRH) lie in the arcuate nucleus of the hypothalamus (Lee 1988). These neurones develop during fetal life and are functional by 12 weeks' gestation. By 20 weeks' gestation pulsatile release of gonadotrophins is well described and the suppression of follicle-stimulating hormone (FSH) and luteinising hormone by circulating oestriol, whose origin lies in the placenta, is apparent and therefore the feedback mechanism is intact (Asa *et al.* 1986). At birth, the withdrawal of this oestrogen suppression by detachment of the female fetus from the placenta leads to vastly elevated levels of gonadotrophin equivalent to menopausal levels of FSH (Grumbach *et al.* 1975). These levels remain elevated for some six to twelve months before undergoing suppression. As FSH release is governed entirely by GnRH secretion, the suppression of FSH must result from decreased activity in the GnRH cell nucleus. Therefore, the genes that determine the production of GnRH must themselves be suppressed (Knobil 1990) and current knowledge suggests that the mechanism involved in that process probably involves corticotrophin-releasing factor and leptin. Leptin is a peptide release from adiposites and, of interest, most infants' body fat content is relatively high until they are about one year of age. They then become lean and leptin production is decreased. At around eight to ten years of age, body fat content increases, leptin levels rise and the association with the onset of GnRH pulses and puberty is apparent (Clayton *et al.* 1997). Certainly, puberty can be induced in rats using infusions of leptin (Chehab *et al.* 1997), but the direct association with puberty in humans remains to be defined. Pulsatile release of FSH begins at around eight or nine years of age and is nocturnal initially; pulse frequency and amplitude then increase throughout the nocturnal hours and eventually at around 11 or 12 years of age, nocturnal pulses are no longer unique. The daytime pattern of pulsatile gonadotrophin release becomes established. During this time, secondary sexual characteristics begin to develop and eventually, when ovarian function begins to produce oestradiol levels that are significant, the possibility of menarche arises. Breast development also occurs at a similar time. Menarche is established in the UK at around $12^{1}/_{2}$ years of age, but the range is considerable, being between 11 and 16 years of age (Wyshak 1983) and the establishment of the ovulatory reproductive menstrual cycle may take many years beyond this point. A number of studies have established that it may take up to eight years from menarche for regular ovulatory cycles to occur (Dewhurst *et al.* 1971; Vollman 1977; Vihko and Aptar 1984). During these menstrual years menstruation may be erratic and dysfunctional as it is in the latter years of menstrual life.

Some patients fail to establish pubertal features. In patients with Turner syndrome the genetic problem of 45XO leads to streak ovaries which contain no oocytes, and no activity from the ovaries in the production of oestradiol. Once this diagnosis has been made it is necessary to induce secondary sexual characteristics using exogenous oestrogen and a number of regimes for this have been suggested (Albanese and Stanhope 1995). It is of paramount importance that the rate at which puberty is induced should be the same as would happen naturally, thus ensuring that various somatic growth patterns are mimicked in the normal way.

With the advent of ovulatory cycles, primary dysmenorrhoea becomes an apparent symptom in most girls. The aetiology of this problem has been clearly defined as secondary to prostaglandin production and the pain that is experienced by these teenagers is due to a combination of a direct effect of prostaglandins on pain fibres and also ischaemia due to inhibition of uterine blood flow during uterine contraction. While some degree of dysmenorrhoea is extremely common, excessive dysmenorrhoea is less frequent. The understanding of the pathophysiology of this situation has allowed a greater ability to manage these girls. It was previously thought that most teenage girls complaining of severe dysmenorrhoea had psychological problems, but studies on prostaglandin production have clearly demonstrated that prostaglandin production is excessive in these girls, leading to increased pain, which is way above the average. While some teenage girls may well have a psychological input into their pain perception, it has been accepted that this is much less than previously estimated.

Strategies for the management of dysfunctional uterine bleeding and dysmenorrhoea have changed. The management of menstrual dysfunction depends entirely upon evidence of anaemia and whether or not there is an associated problem with dysmenorrhoea (Edmonds 1999). If the patient does not suffer with anaemia then it is generally thought to be unnecessary to administer any medication. If anaemia does result then it is apparent that blood loss is greater than normal and some strategy to prevent this excessive blood loss must be put in place. The choice of medication will either be progestogens or the combined oral contraceptive pill and if dysmenorrhoea is a feature the combined oral contraceptive pill is by far the best therapy. It is sometimes difficult to convince parents that their young daughters need such therapy, but it is incumbent upon the physician to explain the situation and encourage the right therapy to be taken. In those girls in whom dysmenorrhoea is the sole symptom, then either antiprostaglandins of various formulations or the oral contraceptive pill are the therapies of first choice. However, in any teenage girl in whom standard antidysmenorrhoea therapy fails, it is important to exclude the possibility of a uterine anomaly, particularly rudimentary uterine horns, and it is imperative that ultrasound imaging of the pelvis is carried out. The possibility of endometriosis must also be borne in mind. Our awareness of the possibility of endometriosis occurring in teenage years has been a recent development and clinicians must take this into account when dealing with what seems to be unresolved pelvic pain in teenagers (Edmonds 1999).

Some teenagers will develop menstrual dysfunction leading to secondary amenorrhoea. This has become an increasingly common problem over the last 15 years, in association with dieting and anorexia nervosa. There can be little doubt that teenage role models, as presented by the media and the fashion industry, lead these girls to focus on icons who are underweight. As they progress through puberty they make many efforts to mimic their idols in all sorts of walks of life and those who feel the need to fit the model that is their image will end up with dietary dysfunction and, in some cases, anorexia nervosa and bulimia. This loss of body weight may well lead to arrest of menstruation and it may well be that leptin production falls so dramatically that if the mechanism that controls menstrual function at a hypothalamic level is shut off it would result in amenorrhoea. The subtleties of weight loss may be difficult to detect, but clinicians must bear this in mind in all teenagers in whom this situation occurs. Secondary amenorrhoea may be due to polycystic ovarian syndrome but again we must be careful in our diagnosis of this condition. Ultrasound of the ovaries during puberty and in the early menstrual years will often show pictures of the multicystic ovary, as opposed to the polycystic ovary. The multicystic ovary is a normal phenomenon. It is therefore imperative that we do not wrongly label patients based on ultrasound alone. While polycystic ovaries are a common feature, polycystic ovarian syndrome is less common. Its diagnosis and management are important. Currently, the control over this condition is brought about by the oral contraceptive pill which regulates menstrual cycles, but also controls the endocrine dysfunction in association with this condition. However, it does not impact on insulin resistance and careful counselling of teenage girls with this condition who are about to take the oral contraceptive pill is important. If their weight is to be controlled during the years that follow, their eventual fertility and long-term health may well be governed by adequate advice at this stage in their life.

CONGENITAL MALFORMATIONS OF THE GENITAL TRACT

Absence of the vagina and uterus is the second most common cause of primary amenorrhoea, second only to Turner syndrome. It is without doubt the most common cause of primary amenorrhoea with secondary sexual characteristics being present. It is important that we realise the diagnosis as a possibility. Changes that have occurred in the last 20 years have at last influenced doctors to consider more frequently congenital abnormalities as an aetiology for amenorrhoea. All too often in the past, the idea that amenorrhoea should not be investigated until 16 years of age was standard practice. This resulted in many teenagers who had a congenital abnormality being told that they were normal, only subsequently to discover at the age of 16 years that they had no uterus or vagina. Our knowledge and information about these congenital abnormalities has led to a much greater awareness of these problems. Fortunately, an holistic approach is now being adopted to the management of teenage girls with these disorders. Congenital abnormalities of the genital tract fall primarily into two types: those that are obstructive and those that are due to congenital absence. The obstructive disorders include those due to transverse vaginal septae and those due to longitudinal vaginal septae. The longitudinal vaginal septum is present when a duplex uterine system develops and subsequently two vaginas are destined to develop. However, on some occasions there is failure of complete cannulisation of one of the vaginas leading to a blind hemivagina. When menstruation ensues this hemisystem fills up with menstrual blood and causes pain and this outflow-tract obstruction can be treated effectively by removal of the septum. Obstetric outcome in these patients is usually extremely good and requires no further surgical or obstetric intervention and they should be managed as any duplex system. Those disorders that are due to transverse vaginal septae fall into four categories. The intact hymen is a simple outflow tract obstruction due to a thin membrane, which clinically is easy to diagnose with a blue bulging structure at the introitus. Its removal is simple and results in subsequently completely normal function. Transverse septae within the vagina however occur at three levels. The junction between the middle and lower third, at the middle third and in the upper third of the vagina. Obstruction of the lower third is the most common and probably results from failure of cannulisation at the junction between the origin of the vagina in the urogenital sinus and the vaginal portion that derives from the cervix. The upper part of the vagina beyond the septum is usually capacious and able to contain large volumes of menstrual blood. This means that the clinical presentation of these girls is usually of a pelvic mass in association with cyclical abdominal pain. However, as the vagina is a distensible organ, there is little retrograde menstruation in association with this and the pelvis usually remains entirely normal. Removal of the septum needs to be performed expertly to ensure that no vaginal stricture remains in the long term and the outcome of obstetric performance is excellent. The problems of middle and upper third obstructions are much more complex and here the surgical management of removal of the septae is difficult. The amount of vagina that can distend with menstrual blood is limited and retrograde menstruation is common. Pelvic endometriosis is an almost universal feature in these circumstances. Occasionally, endometriomata have been described, but the architecture of the pelvis may be severely damaged and fertility is impaired. The surgical removal of these septae can commonly lead to vaginal strictures and again surgical expertise in these areas of congenital malformations should be sought (Edmonds 1994).

In congenital absence of the uterus and vagina, known as the Mayer-Rokitansky-Kuster-Hauser (MRKH) syndrome, the genes responsible for development of the uterus seem to be non-functional. The basis for this genetic defect remains to be delineated, but it would seem that the genes are likely to be co-located with those responsible for renal development, as the association between renal abnormalities and uterine abnormalities is common. The management of young women with this condition has changed vastly in the last 20 years. The approach has changed from being primarily surgical to a non-surgical approach and the results of this type of transition have been excellent. The use of graduated dilators has led to 85% of patients with MRKH syndrome avoiding surgery. Their vaginas are functional and do not contain any scar tissue and sexual satisfaction rates are considerably higher. In those patients requiring a surgical approach various operations still are performed. In the USA and Canada the approach tends to be based on the use of skin grafting and in Europe the Vecchetti technique; in the UK the use of amnion. It would seem that each type of approach brings almost universally equal success and of those patients requiring surgery, 20% of them will have sexual function difficulties, in spite of their surgery. While the anatomical correction of their problem is important, it is also imperative that these girls receive a psychological support mechanism, because failure to establish this support means any attempt at anatomical restoration and subsequent sexual function will be compromised (Edmonds 1994).

The malformations that result from congenital adrenal hyperplasia have undergone a revolution in management in the last 30 years. In the early part of this period the approach was, without question, one of anatomical correction of the phallus if it was enlarged and the subsequent surgery for the genital tract being carried out in teenage years. However, during the 1970s and 1980s, paediatric urological surgeons have taken the approach of trying to correct the anatomical abnormality of the introitus as early as possible and many girls world-wide now have their surgery performed between the age of two and five years. This is proven to be an extremely sensible approach. In those girls with simple anatomical problems (Prada 1–3) there is little doubt that the surgical outcome is best performed in early years. However, the more severe problems are probably still better left until teenage years and, here, major reconstruction of the genital tract and the urological tract is required if a good result is to be attained in the end. This anatomical result has a direct impact on whether or not these women will subsequently go on and attempt conception. There is no doubt, from studies reported in the past, that the more severe the form of congenital adrenal hyperplasia (CAH) the less is the likelihood of an obstetric outcome (Mulkaikal et al. 1987). This did not just relate to the severity of the CAH, but to the skill of the surgeon in reconstructing the anatomy so that intercourse can occur normally and the skill of the endocrinologist in controlling the CAH so that normal endocrine function will ensue. This latter problem is difficult to attain, but is paramount if fertility is to be achieved.

CONTRACEPTION

In the UK we have had little impact on unwanted pregnancy in the last 30 years. In 1972 the abortion rate in girls under 15 years of age was 2.3 per 1000 residents and in girls aged 16–19 years it was 17.4 per 1000. At the end of 1997 the figures were 3.3 and 24.5 per 1000, respectively (Office for National Statistics 1997). Our failure to have any impact on the abortion rates is a sad indictment of all the strategies that have been adopted to try to overcome this problem. For 20 years, between the early 1970s and the middle 1990s, the overwhelming strategy has been sexual health education. This has been advocated widely with the concept that sex education has to begin before puberty if teenagers are going to be aware of the need for contraception. However, although we have introduced didactic information, we have failed to accept the discussion that needs to be embarked upon if the facts are to be translated into actions. The amount of resources spent every year in the USA on the abortion service is sufficient to offer private health care to the whole nation's needy, were unwanted pregnancies avoided. The social and psychological problems which ensue from the necessity of teenage girls having to choose to have an abortion cannot be understated. It is therefore imperative that we look at the issue of unwanted pregnancy as an urgent requirement, not only in the UK but world-wide. The population of the world is expanding in a way that can only be described as frightening and unless we control unwanted pregnancy and introduce contraceptive techniques which control family size then we can expect a population crisis in the next millennium.

The teenage girl will rely primarily on two methods of contraception. Firstly, the condom and secondly, the oral contraceptive pill. In a study from the USA which looked at the reasons why teenagers seeking abortion had failed to take contraceptives, the most common reply was that they did not have any contraception available at the time intercourse occurred. As a society we must come to terms with the fact that intercourse is going to occur in teenagers and that 40% of teenagers will have had sexual intercourse by 16 years of age. It is still socially unacceptable for a teenage girl to have a condom in her handbag. She fears her parents discovering it and, therefore, will not embark on this type of protective mechanism. However, the advent of a number of sexually transmitted diseases, including HIV, means that barrier methods of contraception have an enormous attraction for teenagers. We must, therefore, change our attitude if we are to encourage teenage girls not to become pregnant. While it would be ideal for teenage girls to be encouraged to merely say 'no' when approached to have intercourse, idealism and realism do not equate in these circumstances. The use of the oral contraceptive pill tends to fluctuate with the latest press reports and subsequent requests for termination of pregnancy are mirrored three months later. Again, there is a responsibility in society to ensure that any press reporting must carefully represent the best interests of women and must not be misleading or misinterpreted, or we risk increasing the problem of unwanted pregnancy, rather than making our teenagers responsible.

The change in our social structure in the latter part of this century has meant that the unwanted pregnancy rate has risen. In the first half of this century many women would conceive and have their first babies before they were 21 years of age. By 1970, the average age of a woman having her first baby was 21 years of age. By 1990 this had risen to 28 years of age. Thus, it was previously socially accepted that most women would conceive and have their children early in life and pregnancies were accepted and became wanted. Our attitude towards families and the age at which women have their families has changed dramatically and while our contraceptive results in women in their twenties have improved, they have not for teenagers. The fact that we have not impacted on this abortion rate means that a percentage of these girls will subsequently not be able to have the families they desire because they have chosen to have an abortion and have subsequently had complications that have damaged their fertility. This cannot be best social practice and some radical changes are needed if we are to impact on this extremely difficult area of paediatric and adolescent gynaecology.

THE FUTURE

Looking forward to the next millennium one can really only hope to look a short time ahead, based on the current knowledge and advances that are being made. In addressing the various areas that have changed in the last 30 years and looking into the future, it is likely that the genetic basis of the control of onset of puberty will be fully understood and the genes involved in this process will be clearly defined. It may then be possible that abnormalities in the way puberty develops could be controlled by controlling the genes, particularly in those teenagers in whom menstrual dysfunction is a major problem. Other than this, there is little benefit in terms of therapeutics for the discovery of this genetic mechanism. The mechanism involved in prostaglandin physiology is important and the interaction between prostaglandins and endometrial cell growth and the apoptosis of the menstrual cycle will probably lead to new therapeutic modalities to control this. This may well lead to medications which could obliterate the problem of dysmenorrhoea, which would be a major advance for many teenagers. It may be that these advances come through a greater understanding of angiogenic growth factors and matrix metalloproteinase physiology and our understanding of local intracellular interaction will open up new therapeutic areas. This in itself may also lead to new and novel approaches to contraception whereby implantation may become impossible in the presence of these medications. A delivery system will need to be devised that is acceptable to women and particularly to teenagers and were this to be envisaged in the future the problem of unwanted pregnancy may begin to be addressed. The advent in the last three years of the progesterone-impregnated intrauterine contraceptive device may make some further advances in the next century. It may become useful in teenagers for both contraceptive and menstrual dysfunction. The social attitude towards intrauterine contraceptive devices needs to be greatly changed if this type of approach is to be successful and the bad publicity of the 1970s and the associated risk of infection need to be refuted for these modern devices. However, the potential is enormous and this approach to menstrual dysfunction and menstruation generally may be the greatest gynaecological advance of the next 20–30 years. Not only will teenagers benefit, but adult women during their reproductive years and women with menstrual disorders in their forties will also benefit. Amenorrhoea, other than at those times when women wish to conceive, may well become the norm. As menstruation is an unnecessary physiological function unless conception is required, this change in therapeutics may have major benefits.

In the realm of congenital abnormalities it is likely that tissue engineering is going to lead to organ growth. As a result of these novel technological advances two particular possibilities arise for the woman who has been born without a uterus and vagina. Firstly, the possibility of uterine transplantation will become a possibility. However, the immune-complex difficulties in association with this, as well as the vascular changes that are necessary were the uterus to become pregnant need to be overcome, but this is likely to be possible in the next few years. However, the idea that donor organs will be available for this particular therapy seems doubtful and, inevitably, the idea of a uterine transplant being performed following a tissue engineered organ is more likely to be feasible. Early advances in this area have already led to the development of epithelia, myometrial cells and other simple structures. It is only a matter of time before we are able to grow organs for transplantation. Here, the use of these organs to replace the missing vagina and uterus becomes feasible. This would be a major advance for current sufferers of MRKH syndrome or women who have lost their uterus for a variety of other reasons. The replacement organs would then function normally, thereby returning these psychologically harmed people to some degree of normality.

Our understanding of the genetic basis of CAH is now clear and it will be increasingly possible to screen the population at risk to discover whether or not the genes exist within a particular couple. It might then be possible to either select embryos that do not contain the genetic defect or to manage a pregnancy such that the offspring are not affected in an anatomical way. It might even be possible to introduce the missing genes into fetuses *in utero* and thereby correct the endocrine problem. Again, this type of technology is a long way from being a reality at the present time. In the interim, the management of women with CAH needs a different outlook. As much of their physical and genital development and subsequent fertility is dependent on their endocrine control and endocrine control is so difficult with their adrenal *in situ*, there is a case to be argued as to whether or not these girls should have their adrenal glands removed soon after birth and a replacement endocrine regime introduced to try to ensure that they have normal development. This novel and somewhat radical approach to the management of this disorder may lead to much better outcome statistics and an improved quality of life. While a wish list for the future could be endless, one must not forget the advances of the last 30 years which have provided a platform of novel approaches to enable us to even consider the developments of the future.

References

Albanese, A. and Stanhope, R. (1995) Investigation of delayed puberty. *Clin Endocrinol (Oxf)* **43**, 105–10

Asa, A.L., Kovacs, K., Lazlo, F.A., Domokos, I. and Ezrin, C. (1986) The human fetal adenohypophysis. *Neuroendocrinology* **43**, 308–16

Chehab, F.F., Mounzih, K., Lu, R. and Lim, M.E. (1997) Early onset of reproductive function in normal female mice, treated with leptin. *Science* **275**, 88–90

Clayton, P., Gill, M., Hall, C., Tillman, V., Whatmore, A. and Price, D. (1997) Serum leptin through childhood and adolescence. *Clin Endocrinol (Oxf)* **46**, 727–34

Dewhurst, C.J., Cowell, C.A. and Barrie, L.C. (1971) The regularity of the early menstrual cycles. *J Obstet Gynaecol Br Cwlth* **78**, 1093–5

Edmonds, D.K. (1994) 'Sexual developmental anomalies and their reconstruction' in: J. Sanfilippo, D. Muram and C.J. Dewhurst (Eds) *Pediatric and Adolescent Gynaecology*, pp. 535–66. Philadelphia: W.B. Saunders

Edmonds, D.K. (1999) Dysfunctional uterine bleeding in adolescence *Clin Obstet Gynecol* **13**, 239–49

Grumbach, M.M., Grave, G.D. and Mayer, F.E. (1975) *The Control of the Onset of Puberty.* New York: John Wiley

Knobil, E. (1990) The GnRH pulse generator. *Am J Obstet Gynecol* **153**, 1721–6

Lee, P.A. (1988) The neuroendocrinology of puberty. *Seminars in Reproductive Medicine* **6**, 13–20

Mulkaikal, R.M., Migeon, C.J. and Rock, J.A. (1987) Fertility rates in female patients with congenital adrenal hyperplasia *N Engl J Med* **316**, 178–80

Office for National Statistics (1997) *Abortion Statistics.* London: HMSO

Vihko, R. and Aptar, D. (1984) Endocrine characteristics of adolescent menstrual cycles. *J Steroid Biochem* **20**, 231–6

Vollman, R.F. (1977) *The Menstrual Cycle*, pp. 19–72. Philadelphia: W.B. Saunders

Wyshak, G. (1983) Secular changes in age at menarche. *Ann Hum Biol* **10**, 75–7

23

Surgical contraception

G. Marcus Filshie

INTRODUCTION

By the time of the millennium, over 328 million couples throughout the world will be protected from pregnancy by female sterilisation (Mumford and Kesel 1992). In the UK, over 70 000 women have been sterilised per annum, most operations being performed laparoscopically. In the USA, over 600 000 procedures are performed per annum, probably half of these being undertaken during the postpartum period, mainly at the time of a caesarean section. In the less developed world where sophisticated laparoscopic techniques are less widespread the postpartum mini-laparotomy is popular.

FEMALE STERILISATION – HISTORICAL OVERVIEW

James Blundell first reported a case of female sterilisation in a textbook over 160 years ago, when tubectomy was recommended at the time of caesarean section in patients with contracted pelvis. Fifty years later, in 1880, in Ohio, USA, Lungren ligated the fallopian tube, also at caesarean section, in a woman with a similar problem. Since then, a multitude of different methods of occlusion of the fallopian tubes has been developed, the most notable being the Madlena procedure of 1910 and the techniques of Irving (1924), Pomeroy (1930), Aldridge (1934), Kroener (1935) and Uchida (1946). These have been ably summarised by Rioux (1991). In 1965, Sir Dugall Baird delivered his famous lecture – The Fifth Freedom (from the fear of unwanted pregnancy) – and highlighted the role of sterilisation.

The traditional indications for sterilisation, either male or female, were for medical reasons or for grand multiparity. Procedures were performed at the time of caesarean section or immediately postpartum. Female sterilisation was not performed frequently until the advent of laparoscopy, which enabled the procedure to be performed safely on a day-care basis. Although crude laparoscopy was originally performed in 1910 by Kelling in dogs, Jacobeus from Sweden first introduced a laparoscope into humans in 1911 and it was he who coined the phrase 'laparoscopy'. The use of the laparoscope to perform female sterilisation was first recorded by Ruddock in 1934. Anderson (1937), from the USA, first designed a purpose-built electrode for tubal fulguration. Powers and Barnes described laparoscopic tubal fulguration techniques in 1941 but it was not until 20 years later, in 1960, that Palmer gave a huge impetus to laparoscopic tubal fulguration and popularised the method in France. In 1964, Frangenheim from Germany, and in 1965, Steptoe in the UK, popularised these methods in their respective countries. The laparoscope was substantially improved by the addition of the Hopkins–Ron lens

241

system and the advent of the cold light source. Laparoscopic tubal ligation was later adopted by Cohen and Wheeless in the USA. Laparoscopic tubal ligation became so popular that it was used for sterilising women for social reasons as well as for medical reasons. As large numbers of patients underwent the operation, complications and fatalities relating to bowel burns came to light from unipolar diathermy, these burns often being found at a site distant from the operating field. To reduce these complications bipolar cautery was introduced by Rioux (Canada), Kleppinger (USA) and Hirsch (Germany). Despite bipolar cautery, thermal injuries continued and so a number of mechanical methods of tubal occlusion emerged. These included the Falope ring in 1975 (Yoon and King 1975), the Hulka clip in 1973 (Hulka *et al.* 1973) and the Filshie clip in 1981 (Filshie *et al.* 1981). Tupla and Bleier plastic clips also emerged. Today only the Falope ring and Hulka and Filshie clips are being used on a regular basis (Figure 1).

SURGICAL APPROACHES

Laparoscopy

The laparoscopic technique is widely used and preferred. Its use is popular both in developed and developing countries. The procedure may be performed under local or general anaesthetic. The patient is placed on the operating table, usually in the lithotomy position and, following catheterisation, a pneumoperitoneum is created by instilling, through a Veress needle just below the umbilicus, 2–3 l of carbon dioxide, or nitrous oxide if local anaesthetic is employed. A trocar and cannula are inserted just below the

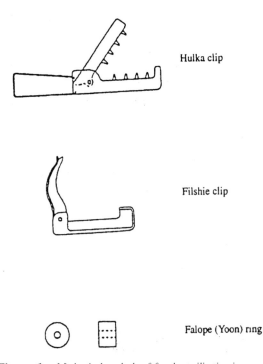

Hulka clip

Filshie clip

Falope (Yoon) ring

Figure 1 *Mechanical methods of female sterilisation in current use*

umbilicus to allow the insertion of a standard laparoscope. The patient is placed in the Trendelenberg position and the pelvic organs, including the fallopian tubes, are visualised. Using a suprapubic second puncture a further trocar and cannula are inserted to allow the introduction of the appropriate operating instrument, for example a clip applicator, a ring applicator or cautery forceps. The tubes may be anaesthetised by dropping local anaesthetic (2 ml 4% lignocaine or 10 ml 0.5% marcaine) to reduce the peri- and postoperative discomfort (Ezoh *et al.* 1995; Alexander *et al.* 1997), whether the procedure is performed using local or general anaesthesia. There are single puncture techniques for all these methods and their use depends on the surgeon's preference. As a rule, a single puncture technique is more difficult to perform but may be more acceptable for certain patients.

Mini-laparotomy

In countries or locations where laparoscopy is not available, mini-laparotomy, performed under local or general anaesthetic, is available. This method is perfectly acceptable and has minimal extra morbidity when performed by skilled surgeons. It is especially suitable for puerperal sterilisation. A transverse incision 2–3 cm above the pubic symphysis allows access to the tubes, provided the uterine fundus is elevated using vaginal manipulation. For puerperal sterilisation a subumbilical incision is best.

METHODS OF FEMALE STERILISATION

Non-laparoscopic methods (mini-laparotomy or laparotomy)

The Pomeroy operation

This is probably one of the most popular methods world-wide. A loop of the isthmic portion of the fallopian tube is pulled up and ligated with an absorbable suture and the isolated loop of the tube is excised. When the suture is absorbed, the divided ends of the tube should not only be occluded but also fall apart and separate (Bishop and Nelms 1930). Histological examination of the excised part of the uterine tube provides evidence that the operation has been carried out on the correct structure.

Fimbriectomy

This is claimed to be a reliable technique but as the remaining tubal stump has been shown to regenerate microfimbria, giving rise to an unacceptable failure rate, it is not recommended (Oskowitz *et al.* 1982).

The Uchida method

This involves injecting the fallopian tube with saline and excising a portion of the endo-salpinx. One end is ligated outside the mesosalpinx and one end is buried within the mesosalpinx.

The Irving technique

This involves burying the proximal stump of the fallopian tube into the muscular layer of the uterus. There is an increased morbidity which is not offset by a significant increase in effectiveness.

The Parkland technique

This technique involves cutting the fallopian tube and placing a ligature on each cut end of the tube.

Hysterectomy

Hysterectomy, either by the abdominal route or the vaginal route, is used as a method of sterilisation. It is particularly acceptable when gynaecological symptoms such as menorrhagia or fibroids are present. It is also used in Catholic countries where sterilisation is not acceptable but where hysterectomy is acceptable as a cure for gynaecological symptoms. It is of interest to note that, following hysterectomy, 23 cases of abdominal pregnancies (Jackson *et al.* 1980) and 43 cases of ectopic pregnancy (Isaacs *et al.* 1996) have been reported. Removal of the ovaries, although effective, is not an acceptable method of sterilisation since it precipitates the menopause.

Laparoscopic methods

Laparoscopy requires great skill and experience in order to provide a safe and effective technique (Chamberlain and Brown 1978). Four main techniques of tubal occlusion are currently employed:

(1) Diathermy coagulation;
(2) Bipolar diathermy;
(3) Hulka and Filshie clips;
(4) Falope ring.

Diathermy coagulation

Unipolar coagulation was first used laparoscopically and substantially increased the popularity of sterilisation. However, inadvertent damage to organs other than the uterine tubes, as well as the high failure rate associated with inadequate coagulation, has put the method into disrepute. The mortality rate is up to ten per 100 000 operations (Chamberlain and Brown 1978) and this was attributed to either life-threatening internal haemorrhage from direct puncture of blood vessels or to bowel burns causing faeculent peritonitis. Unipolar diathermy generates temperatures of 200–300°C and the heat may spread to sites distant from the application of the forceps so that injuries may not be noticed at the time of the operation.

Bipolar diathermy

This has been introduced as a safer modality. The temperature generated is the same as that with unipolar diathermy, but it significantly reduces (although does not eliminate) the risk of thermal injury. This is because the electric current only passes between the jaws of the coagulation forceps and not outward from a single point (as with unipolar diathermy) through the patient's body to a negative plate applied either to the thigh or the back.

Clips

The Hulka clip (Hulka *et al.* 1973) and the Filshie clip (Filshie *et al.* 1981) (Figure 1) have been safely and acceptably used. The clip should normally be placed over the isthmic part of the fallopian tubes as this is the thinnest part. Application over the ampulla is not recommended as it is possible not to completely occlude the whole tube. Most failures associated with the application of clips are due to faulty technique, either because the wrong structure has been clipped or because the tube has not been completely occluded.

The Falope ring

The Falope ring (Yoon and King 1975) (Figure 1) is made of silicone rubber and is easy to place over the tubes but, if an attempt is made to place the ring too near the uterus, or if the tube is too thick, the tube may be transected leading to haemorrhage.

Anaesthesia

Short-acting general anaesthetic agents are usually employed, together with intubation and administration of a muscle relaxant. There is, however, no statistical evidence that there is any increased morbidity when intubation is not used (Chamberlain and Brown 1978).

Local anaesthesia

For safety reasons this could, and possibly should, be used more often, and ideally patients should be given the choice. Its use for both the application of clips and rings and cautery is well documented (MacKenzie *et al.* 1987; Lipscomb *et al.* 1992; Green-Thompson *et al.* 1993). Essentially, 10 ml of 1% lignocaine with 1:200 000 epinephrine (5 µg per ml) is injected into the skin and underlying fascia to the peritoneum where the puncture sites are to be. A pneumoperitoneum with nitrous oxide is produced using a standard technique. Nitrous oxide produces less shoulder discomfort than carbon dioxide; 1 ml of 2–4% lignocaine or 0.5% bupivacaine is slowly dropped onto each fallopian tube – the Veress needle is extremely useful for this step. In a recent study, patients were given 800 mg ibuprofen 30 minutes preoperatively and midazolam 3 mg, alfentanil 1 mg and atrophine 0.6 mg intravenously immediately preoperatively, to allay anxiety and for further analgesia (Lipscomb *et al.* 1992), which gave satisfactory results. Postoperatively, ibuprofen 800 mg may be given eight-hourly for postoperative discomfort. If tubal cautery is used, CO_2 should be used as the insufflation gas.

OPERATIVE MORTALITY

All operations have risks, particularly of sepsis and haemorrhage. The laparoscopic approach, when performed correctly, has remarkably few immediate complications, particularly of wound sepsis. In one of the largest mortality survey series published involving 29 deaths (Peterson *et al.* 1983), 38% were related to anaesthetic problems and 24% due to sepsis – most of which related to bowel injury, including bowel burns. Haemorrhage was associated with 14% of cases. The remainder were due to a miscellaneous group including myocardial infarction, pulmonary embolus and gas embolus. The present estimated mortality from female sterilisation is 3.6 per 100 000 (Peterson *et al.* 1997), which is considerably lower than the mortality of childbearing which is 5.5 per 100 000. This benefit is particularly important in developing countries where the maternal mortality can be in excess of one per 1000.

EFFECT ON MENSTRUATION

The effect of sterilisation on menstruation has always been open to debate. Fowkes and Chamberlain (1985), Rulin et al. (1985) and Shain et al. (1989) have reported an increase in menstrual loss and spotting. Rulin (1985, 1989) and Shain et al. (1989) have reported an increase in pelvic pain. An absence of pain, however, has been recorded by Lieberman et al. (1978), Bhiwandiwala et al. (1982) and Fortney et al. (1983) and in some studies over 10 000 subjects have been studied. Wilcox et al. (1992) have reported, in a prospective study of over 5000 patients followed for five years, an increased number of menstrual disturbances including pain, bleeding and spotting and that these symptoms were not associated with the degree of tissue destruction at the time of surgery. Menstrual disturbances did increase with the passage of time. Hysterectomy has been reported to be increased following sterilisation (Goldhaber et al. 1993). It would seem, however, that women who have been sterilised have a greater willingness to seek advice about menstrual problems and to have a hysterectomy than women who have not been sterilised.

ECTOPIC PREGNANCIES

Sterilisation failure may result in an intrauterine or ectopic pregnancy. The latter is a potentially life-threatening complication which is of particular significance in developing countries or to patients who do not have immediate access to medical care. Ectopic pregnancies occur as a result of a fistula which may be:

(1) A direct tuboperitoneal fistula, which could occur from the stump of the proximal tube. This could occur with any method of female sterilisation;
(2) As a result of endosalpingosis following tubal ligation;
(3) A tubo-tubal fistula.

Mechanical methods produce a low incidence of ectopic pregnancies, whereas the incidence following electrocautery may be as high as 67% (FDA Advisory Panel meeting, February 1996) (Table 1). Ectopic pregnancy accounts for 6–8% of maternal deaths.

Table 1 *Ectopic pregnancies by method*[a]

| Method | Ectopic pregnancies | | Total pregnancies | Ectopic pregnancies per 1000 pregnancies |
	n	per 1000 procedures		
Filshie[b]				
n=5454	1	0.2	24	4
Falope ring				
n=1480	1	0.7	5	20
Hulka clip				
n=1062	0	–	9	–
Pomeroy				
n=722	0	–	2	–
Bipolar				
n=471	2	4.3	3	67

[a]Data presented by Professor Theodore King at the FDA Advisory Panel meeting, 26 February 1996;
[b]pooled interval and postpartum data

REGRET

Post-sterilisation regret occurs, and at least 5% of patients and between 1% and 2% of these will regret sterilisation sufficiently to warrant a request for a reversal procedure. Factors that contribute to regret, apart from complications and failure, are patients under 25 years of age and when the procedure is associated with pregnancy, for example postpartum or postabortum (Chi and Jones 1994). Low parity regret is usually in association with a culture that expects high parity. Patients sterilised when they have no children seem to regret the procedure least because they are often polarised into that decision at an early age.

STERILISATION FAILURES

Sadly, there is always a possibility that a sterilisation procedure may fail. As pregnancies have occurred following hysterectomy, it is not surprising that a small operative procedure on the fallopian tubes is not 100% effective. A sterilisation procedure may fail because of fistula formation, as previously described. Failure may also occur if only part of a tube is occluded by a clamp or because the whole tube has not been pulled into the ring and only part of the tube has been ringed. Anecdotal cases have been reported of the rings wriggling off the tube by vigorous peristalsis. Yoon and King (1975) recommend that sexual intercourse and even pelvic examination should be avoided in the first month after placement of the rings. If any doubt occurs as to the correct application of the ring, then a second one should be applied close to the first. Should there be a large gap between the two rings, then a hydrosalpinx may occur. This applies equally to the placement of clips.

Each method has an intrinsic failure rate in addition to operator error rate, which also depends on a number of variables. Important variables include the age of the patient, whether the operation was postpartum or postabortum and whether there was associated tubal pathology, for example the presence of adhesions. Operator experience and laparoscopic equipment condition can affect the ease and accuracy of the procedure. Failure rates quoted in the literature will inevitably have a range of values. The ideal figure to quote would be the surgeon's own figures. Many studies have been retrospective. The largest prospective study comes from the Centers for Disease Control and Prevention which is known as the 'CREST study' (Collaborative Review of Sterilisation) (Peterson et al. 1996). As this is a US study, Filshie clip data were not included. A long-term study of the Filshie clip is presently being conducted. Long-term follow-up data for unipolar coagulation, bipolar coagulation, Falope rings and Hulka clips are now available. In the CREST collaborative study, 10 863 patients were enrolled and 10 685 patients were followed up. Data were collected at one, three, five, eight and 14 years following the procedure. The cumulative ten-year pregnancy rate was highest in the Hulka clip method (36.5 per 1000) and the bipolar method (24.8 per 1000). The ten-year failure rate for postpartum patients having partial salpingectomy was 7.5 per 1000, which challenges the view that postpartum failures are higher than in interval procedures.

The failure rate was highest in young women and this included 53.3 per 1000 with bipolar coagulation and 51.2 per 1000 with Hulka clip application. Pregnancies occurred fairly evenly throughout successive years following the operation. The results of the CREST study are shown in Table 2.

A long-term prospective study of the Filshie clip system is currently being conducted. Patients were recruited from 1982 to 1992. Over 400 women were operated on using

Table 2   *The cumulative failure rate per 1000 patients of the common methods of female sterilisation over ten years*

Method	Rate per 1000
Unipolar coagulation[a]	7.5
Postpartum Pomeroy[a]	7.5
Silicon band (Falope ring)[a]	17.7
Bipolar coagulation[a]	24.8
Spring clip (Hulka)[a]	36.5
Filshie clip[b]	5

[a]CREST study (Peterson *et al.* 1996); [b]Filshie *et al.* (1998)

local anaesthetic and an initial follow-up report of 200 patients has been published (Filshie *et al.* 1998). Only one failure was reported in this study and is also shown in Table 2.

OTHER LONG-TERM SEQUALAE

Clip migration

The Filshie clip is the preferred method of female sterilisation in a number of countries. Over 3.5 million pairs have been estimated to have been applied. Innocent migration of the clips off a closed tube is common and the estimated incidence is over 30%. The pathophysiology is related to the speed at which peritoneal-like tissue forms over the clip, anchoring it to the fallopian tube. If the peritonealisation is quick, the clip remains *in situ*; if it is slow, the tube may become transected with both ends of the tube healed over to form a cul-de-sac. The clip will then have no covering tissue to maintain its position and will fall off and migrate.

The clip usually migrates to the omentum but, less commonly, may remain in the pouch of Douglas, paracolic gutters or at any other site. In a prospective study involving over 6000 patients, presented to the FDA Advisory Panel hearing in 1996, three clips were noted to have been expelled from the body via the vagina, urethra and rectum but in no case was any morbidity observed on examination. If a pelvic abscess occurs then the clip may be expelled abdominally when the abscess bursts or is incised (Robson and Kerin 1993). Both Filshie clips and Hulka clips have been known to migrate (Gooden *et al.* 1993).

If a migrated clip is noted incidentally, for example when x-rays have been taken because of urinary or skeletal problems, reassurance is normally all that is warranted. To inform the patient to use another method of contraception, or to resort to laparoscopy or indeed laparotomy, is not indicated in the overwhelming majority of cases, as the morbidity of such procedures is significantly in excess of leaving the clip in place, whether it be open or closed.

A case presentation relating to a clip migrating to the umbilicus and a full review was conducted by Amu and Husemeyer in 1999. They concluded that 'the remarkable absence of serious sequalae from the migration of either type of sterilisation clip is reassuring'.

COUNSELLING

Counselling is the process of giving information to a couple so that they can understand the nature of the operation and its consequences sufficiently well to be able to give informed consent. The following checklist is useful to follow:

(1) Alternative methods of contraception;
(2) Type of operative procedure;
(3) Permanency;
(4) Risks; for example, conversion to a laparotomy, puncture of visceral organs, anaesthetic problems;
(5) Medical condition of the patient;
(6) Alternative procedure;
(7) Procedure performed at the time of a pregnancy;
(8) Possible regret;
(9) Contraception prior to the procedure.

SPECIAL CONSIDERATION

Extra care and time should be taken when the patients are young (under 25 years of age) and of low parity, as regret is more common in these circumstances. If poor financial circumstances are present clients should be made aware of potential improvements which may occur. Psychosexual problems or marital disharmony are only rarely improved by a sterilisation procedure. Marital guidance or psychosexual counselling should be considered first. Proximity to the menopause is not as cost effective as traditional contraceptive methods, particularly as fertility is usually low at this age. However, there are some couples who would not accept an abortion under any circumstances.

REVERSAL OF STERILISATION

Marital breakdown and the formation of a new partnership is the most common reason for women seeking a reversal of the operation. Other reasons include loss of spouse or child, change in financial circumstances, regret when the procedure has been associated with a termination of pregnancy and coexisting loss of libido. In 1979, the Association of Voluntary Surgical Contraception suggested that 'the patients should think of the operation as irreversible, but the surgeon should perform the operation as if it was reversible'. As clips and rings are more reversible than cautery or the Pomeroy technique, they should be used, especially in high-risk circumstances. Success after a reversal operation procedure is approximately 72% for the Falope ring, in comparison with 84–87% for the spring clip and 90% for the Filshie clip (Owen 1984). A reversal procedure involves a mini-laparotomy with excision of the clip or ring and excision of the closed end of the tube. Healthy tissue is usually identified 1–2 mm from the site of the operation. For the muscle and serosa, six and eight non-absorbable sutures may be used, respectively. Stents are optional. Laparoscopic procedures have been developed, but success rates at present are only 50%.

MEDICO-LEGAL CONSIDERATIONS

A failure of a sterilisation procedure is the most common cause of medico-legal complaints. The UK Medical Protection Society reports that this is responsible for 29% of claims in obstetrics and gynaecology (Orr 1985). The four areas of litigation involve:

(1) Failure to warn patients that there is a failure or complication rate;
(2) Negligence in performing the sterilisation;
(3) Inadvertent injury during the course of the procedure;
(4) Failure to recognise a coexisting pregnancy.

Careful and meticulous attention to surgical techniques should reduce (2) and (3). To reduce (1), careful counselling should be adopted by the GP, the counsellor and the surgeon. It is helpful if full documentation can be made of the counselling checklist. To avoid (4) a careful menstrual history must always be obtained immediately prior to the operation and a pregnancy test should always be performed if there is any doubt. It is the author's view that patients should take full responsibility for any pregnancy which co-exists at the time of the procedure, but this is not the legal view, which places the onus on the surgeon to exclude pregnancy.

MALE STERILISATION – HISTORICAL OVERVIEW

Prior to 1970, vasectomy was only rarely performed. However, following publication from the Margaret Pyke Centre, London, of 1000 vasectomies followed up for one year after the operation, it gained widespread support (Margaret Pyke Centre 1973). When family planning services became freely available in 1974, many local authorities included vasectomy among their services. This was further enhanced when vasectomy became an item of service for family planning.

Vasectomy is becoming increasingly popular. A total of 42 million couples world-wide rely on vasectomy and it has been estimated that some 70 000 procedures are performed annually in the UK. In the developed world there are approximately equal numbers of vasectomies and female sterilisations. However, vasectomy is less popular and may be culturally unacceptable or illegal in some developing countries.

METHODS

A vasectomy may be performed under general or local anaesthesia. At present, most patients have a local anaesthetic procedure as it is quicker and safer. Traditionally, the local anaesthetic is administered to the skin and vas either in the midline or in preparation for a lateral incision. An incision (1–2 cm long) is made to the skin down to the spermatic sheath. The sheath and vas is then grasped through the incision by special forceps, for example Soonawalla, and the sheath is incised until the vas is encountered. The vas is picked out from the sheath (a No.1 needle is helpful here) and the vas is freed from the surrounding tissue. A portion of the vas is removed and both ends of the vas are ligated. Ideally, a needle-point diathermy is then inserted down each vas to cauterise the lumen. The testicular end is sometimes tied back on itself. This helps to keep one end out of the sheath while the other end falls into the sheath. Bleeding points are cauterised and the procedure is repeated on the other side. A dissolvable skin suture is usually placed in the skin incision.

The no-scalpel technique

This procedure was developed in China and involves the use of two special instruments (Li et al. 1991). These are ring-grasping forceps and a sharp pair of pointed dissecting forceps. A local anaesthetic is injected into the skin and to the vas 2–3 cm away from the testicular end to affect a proximal block. Both vasa are anaesthetised. The oedema generated by the local anaesthetic is therefore 2–3 cm away from the operating site so that the vas can be easily palpated. The vas, and anaesthetised overlying skin, is grasped in the ring forceps. The skin is punctured by one blade of the sharp dissecting forceps and, through this puncture site, both blades are inserted down to the vas. The forceps blades are then opened to spread the tissue. The vas can therefore be seen immediately and exteriorised by the dissecting forceps. The vas is stripped clear of any tissue and ligated as before. The placing of fascia between the two ends has been advocated to reduce the failure rate, although this stage has been regarded as optional. No suture is usually required.

In a study from Bangkok, Thailand, at the King's Birthday Festival in December 1987, 1203 patients were operated on (Niraphpongporn *et al.* 1990) and a comparison was made between a standard vasectomy technique and the no-scalpel technique. The following results were recorded. Twenty-eight physicians operated on 1203 patients. Twelve physicians used the no-scalpel technique and 16 physicians used a standard technique. The mean number of procedures was 57 (SD=12) for the no-scalpel technique compared with 33 (SD=13) for the standard procedure. Nineteen complications were reported during the two weeks following the operations. Sixteen occurred in the standard technique (3.1 per 100 procedures) and three occurred following the no-scalpel technique (0.4 per 100 procedures). Haemorrhage was the most common complication and two patients required surgical drainage. Nine of eleven haemorrhages (including those requiring drainage) resulted from the standard procedure. Eight patients had an infection diagnosed, seven of those resulting from the standard technique and one following the no-scalpel technique.

The advantages of the no-scalpel technique are:

(1) Shorter time required;
(2) Less pain and oedema (0.09%);
(3) Lower risk of infection (0.9%);
(4) More acceptable to men;
(5) Vasal nerve block ensures painless procedure;
(6) Quicker resumption of sexual intercourse.

MORBIDITY

Vasectomy has a very low mortality (Giovannucci *et al.* 1992) but has a relatively high morbidity. Approximately 4–5% of cases will develop a small haematoma or experience sepsis. Large haematomas may need evacuation as would an abscess. However, such interventions are required only once or twice per 1000 cases. Long-term problems are rare; sperm granulomas and neuromas have been noted. There is no evidence that either testicular cancer or cardiovascular disease are increased with vasectomy. However, there may be a small increase in prostatic cancers, but this is regarded as being so small as to be insignificant relative to the advantages of a vasectomy (Schwing and Guess 1996).

COUNSELLING

The principles of counselling are the same as those adopted for female sterilisation. However, there are extra facts to be understood and accepted by the patient. There is a short-term failure rate of three to five per 1000. These can be identified by performing two sperm counts following the procedure. This may take between ten and 20 weeks postoperatively and is said to require an average of 20 ejaculations. Patients are therefore advised to continue other forms of contraception until these two counts have proved negative. There is evidence of long-term intermittent presence of sperm in the ejaculate, which could rarely result in a pregnancy (Philip *et al.* 1984). Complications of the procedure should be mentioned and also accepted by the patient. It is wise to ensure that the client seeks immediate advice should any complications occur. A leaflet describing the procedure and its complications should be available for the couple to read.

The Royal College of Obstetricians and Gynaecologists provides a comprehensive evidence-based clinical guideline for both male and female sterilisation (RCOG 1999).

References

Alexander, C.D., Wetchler, B.V. and Thompson, R.E. (1987) Bupivacaine infiltration of the mesosalpinx in ambulatory surgical laparoscopic tubal sterilisation. *Can J Anaesth* **34**, 362–5

Amu, O. and Husemeyer, R.P. (1999) Migration of sterilisation clips: case report and review. *Br J Fam Plann* **25**, 27–8

Bhiwandiwala, P.P., Mumford, S.D. and Feldblum, P.J. (1982) A comparison of different laparoscopic sterilisation occlusion techniques in 24 439 procedures. *Am J Obstet Gynecol* **144**, 319–31

Bishop, E. and Nelms, W.F. (1930) A simple method of tubal sterilisation. *New York State Journal of Medicine* **30**, 214–16

Chamberlain, G. and Brown, J.C. (Eds) (1978) *Gynaecological Laparoscopy. Report of the Working Party of the Confidential Enquiry into Gynaecological Laparoscopy.* London: RCOG

Chi, I.C. and Jones, D.B. (1994) Incidence, risk factors, and prevention of poststerilisation regret in women: an updated international review from an epidemiological perspective. *Obstet Gynecol Surv* **49**, 722–32

Ezoh, U.O., Shoulder, V.S., Martin, J.L., Breeson, A.J., Lamb, M.D. and Vellacott, I.D. (1995) Local anaesthetic on Filshie clips for pain relief after tubal sterilisation: a randomised double-blind controlled trial. *Lancet* **346**, 82–5

Filshie, G.M., Casey, D., Pogmore, J.R. *et al.* (1981) The titanium/silicone rubber clip for female sterilisation. *Br J Obstet Gynaecol* **88**, 655–62

Filshie, G.M., Helson, K. and Teper, S. (1998) 'Day-case sterilisation with the Filshie clip in Nottingham. Ten-year follow-up study: the first 200 cases' in: *Seventh Annual Meeting of the International Society for Gynecological Endoscopy (ISGE), Sun City, South Africa*, pp. 145–59. Bologna: Monduzzie Editore SpA

Fortney, J.A., Cole, L.P. and Kennedy, K.I. (1983) A new approach to measuring menstrual pattern change after tubal sterilisation. *Am J Obstet Gynecol* **147**, 830–6

Fowkes, J. and Chamberlain, G. (1985) Effects of sterilisation on menstruation. *South Med J* **78**, 544–7

Giovannucci, E., Ibsteson, T.D., Speizer, F.E. *et al.* (1992) A long-term study of mortality in men who have undergone vasectomy. *N Engl J Med* **326**, 1392–8

Goldhaber, M.K., Armstrong, M.A., Golditch, I.M. *et al.* (1993) Long-term risk of hysterectomy among 80 007 sterilised and comparison women at Kaiser Permanente 1971–87. *Am J Epidemiol* **138**, 508–21

Gooden, M.D., Hulka, J.F. and Christman, G.M. (1993) Spontaneous vaginal expulsion of Hulka clips. *Obstet Gynecol* **81**, 884–6

Green-Thompson, R.W., Popis, M. and Cairncross, N.W.A. (1993) Outpatient laparoscopic tubal sterilisation under local anaesthesia. *Obstetrics and Gynaecology Forum*, pp. 4–14 [Available from: Private Bag X14, Parklands 212, Cape Town, South Africa]

Hulka, J.F., Fishbourne, J., Mercer, J.P. *et al.* (1973) Laparoscopic sterilisation with a spring clip. A report of the first fifty cases. *Am J Obstet Gynecol* **116**, 715–18

Isaacs, J.D., Cesare, C.D. and Cowan, B.D. (1996) Ectopic pregnancy following hysterectomy: an update for the 1990s. *Obstet Gynecol* **88**, 732

Jackson, P., Barrowclough, I.W., France, J. and Phillips, L.I. (1980) A successful pregnancy following total hysterectomy. *Br J Obstet Gynaecol* **87**, 353–5

Li, S., Goldstein, M., Zhu, J. *et al.* (1991) The no-scalpel vasectomy. *J Urol* **145**, 341–4

Lieberman, B.A., Belsey, E., Gordon, A.G. *et al.* (1978) Menstrual patterns after laparoscopic sterilisation using a spring-loaded clip. *Br J Obstet Gynaecol* **85**, 376–80

Lipscomb, G.H., Stovall, T.G., Ramanathan, J.A. and Ling, F.W. (1992) Comparison of Silastic rings and electrocoagulation for laparoscopic tubal ligation under local anaesthesia. *Obstet Gynecol* **80**, 645–9

MacKenzie, I.Z., Turner, E., O'Sullivan, G.M. and Guillebaud, J. (1987) Two hundred outpatient laparoscopic clip sterilisations using local anaesthesia. *Br J Obstet Gynaecol* **94**, 449–53

Margaret Pyke Centre (1973) One thousand vasectomies. *BMJ* **4**, 216–21

Mumford, S.D. and Kessel, E. (1992). Sterilisation needs in the 1990s: the case for quinacrine nonsurgical female sterilisation. *Am J Obstet Gynecol* **167**, 1203–7

Niraphpongporn, A., Huber, D. and Krieger, J.N. (1990) No scalpel vasectomy at the King's birthday vasectomy festival. *Lancet* **335**, 894–5

Orr, C.J.B. (1985) 'Female sterilisation – the medico-legal aspects' in: G.V.P. Chamberlain, C.J.B. Orr and F. Sharp (Eds) *Litigation and Obstetrics and Gynaecology*, pp. 177–83. London: RCOG

Oskowitz, S., Havercamp, A.D. and Freedman, W.L. (1982) 'Experience in series of fimbriectomies' in: *Year Book of Obstetrics and Gynecology*, pp. 267–8. Chicago: Year Book Medical Publishers

Owen, E. (1984) Reversal of female sterilisation. Review of 252 microsurgical salpingosalpingostomies. *Med J Aust* **25**, 276–80

Peterson, H.B., DeStephano, F., Rubin, G.L. *et al.* (1983) Deaths attributed to tubal sterilisation in the United States 1977–1981. *Am J Obstet Gynecol* **140**, 131–6

Peterson, H.B., Zhisen, X., Hughes, J.M. *et al.* (1996) The risk of pregnancy after tubal sterilisation: findings from the US Collaborative Review of Sterilisation. *Am J Obstet Gynecol* **174**, 1161–70

Peterson, H.B., Pollack, A.E. and Warshaw, J.S. (1997) 'Tubal sterilisation' in: J.A. Rock and J.D. Thompson (Eds) *Te Linde's Operative Gynecology*, 8th edn, pp. 529–47. Philadelphia: Lippincott-Raven

Philip, T., Guillebaud, J. and Budd, D. (1984) Late failure of vasectomy after two documented analysis showing azoospermic semen. *BMJ* **289**, 77–9

RCOG (1999) *Male and Female Sterilisation.* London: RCOG Press (Evidence-based Clinical Guidelines No. 4)

Rioux, J.E. (1991) 'Female sterilisation' in: G.M. Filshie and J. Guillebaud (Eds) *Contraception, Science and Practice.* Sevenoaks: Butterworth

Robson, S. and Kerin, J. (1993) Recurrence of pelvic abscess associated with a detached Filshie clip. *N Z J Obstet Gynaecol* **33**, 446–8

Rulin, M.C., Turner, J.H., Dunworth, R. and Thompson, D.S. (1985) Post tubal ligation syndrome – a misnomer. *Am J Obstet Gynecol* **151**, 13–19

Rulin, M.C., Davidson, A.R., Philliber, S.G. *et al.* (1989) Changes in menstrual symptoms among sterilised and comparison women: a prospective study. *Obstet Gynecol* **74**, 149–54

Schwing, P.J. and Guess, H.A. (1996) Vasectomy and cancer: an update. *Gynaecological Forum* **1**, 24–8

Shain, R.N., Miller, W.B., Mitchell, G.W. *et al.* (1989) Menstrual pattern change one year after sterilisation: results of a controlled prospective study. *Fertil Steril* **52**, 192–203

Wilcox, L.S., Martinez-Schnell, B., Peterson, H.B. *et al.* (1992) Menstrual function after sterilisation. *Am J Epidemiol* **135**, 1368–81

Yoon, I.B. and King, T.M. (1975) A preliminary and immediate report on a new laparoscopic tubal ring procedure. *J Reprod Med* **15**, 54–7

24

Contraception: past, present and future

John Guillebaud and Rachel D'Souza

INTRODUCTION

The passage into a new millennium is a great opportunity: to reminisce, observing how the gradual understanding of reproductive anatomy and physiology has enabled progress in the field of contraception; to assess our current practice (with its achievements and deficiencies); and to take action to limit unwanted conception and impact upon the current exponential population growth. Methods of sterilisation are not included here.

HISTORY OF CONTRACEPTION

Historically, most people have deduced that coitus and conception are associated, yet further understanding has been limited. Contraceptive methods used have been numerous and varied; some with effect, others superstitious. Aristotle believed the 'male essence' to contain all the elements needed for reproduction, the female being the reservoir only (Robertson 1990).

Many of the earliest recorded methods modify the sexual act and are still used today: coitus interruptus, coitus reservatus and coitus saxonicus (pressure on the male perineum at ejaculation causing reflux of sperm into the bladder). Advice to a woman wishing to avoid conception has included spitting three times into the mouth of a frog, refraining from orgasm; or early postcoital methods: sneezing violently, swallowing a cold drink or jumping backwards seven times. Unfortunately, attempts at abstaining during the 'unsafe' time of the menstrual cycle were hampered by a belief that this was during menstruation.

Ancient 'oral contraceptives' have included myrrh and white pepper, bees, tadpoles, camel sweat, beans on an empty stomach, even boiled mules' testicles (the mule being a sterile animal) (Cayley 1983). More effective may have been potions using the Mexican wild yam (containing progesterone), ergot (oestrogenic) and cottonseed oil (containing gossypol, the first male anti-fertility drug).

Possibly the earliest reference to the male condom is a cave painting in the Dordogne, dated 10,000 BC (Hicks and Bradley 1995). Through the centuries, condoms have been made of a variety of materials, including tortoiseshell and oiled silk paper, goat bladder, sheep appendices, made-to-size linen tied with silk ribbon and soaked in herbal brews and inorganic salts and even membranous tissue of the Romans' enemies' long muscles. Purposes have included decoration, denotion of rank, infection control (particularly of syphilis in the 16th century) and (perhaps later) contraception. The invention in 1844 of

255

vulcanisation enabled mass marketing of stretchable rubber condoms and, hence, availability to the poor. Latex superseded rubber in the 1930s and, with automated production, different sizes, flavours, colours and textures have been created.

Vaginal barriers, douches and spermicides are also far from new. From crocodile dung, honey and resin pessaries, pine bark and cabbage leaves to sponge or wool soaked in oil, lemon juice, quinine or rock salt or even half a lemon, most will have had a physical barrier and some also a spermicidal effect. Wilde developed the first rubber cap in 1823 and Mensinga a rubber diaphragm, requiring expert fitting, in 1882. Even a female rubber condom was available by the 1920s.

The contraceptive effect of an intrauterine foreign body has long been known and was recommended by Casanova in the form of a gold ball. The 'stem' pessary of 1868, initially intended for prolapse correction, was superseded by Richter's silkworm-gut ring; Gräfenberg's 'silver ring' of coiled tin/copper alloy; inert polythene rings and coils; in the 1970s copper-bearing devices; and in 1976 a hormone-releasing system (Figure 1). Efficacy has gradually improved and infection risk declined.

Discovery over the past century of hormonal influences on ovulation led to the use of artificial hormones in contraception. Yet the oldest natural method of birth control involves female hormones: the inhibitory effects of breastfeeding on ovulation. In 1960, the first contraceptive pill 'Enovid®', was licensed (the 'Pincus Pill') containing 150 µg mestranol and 10 mg norethynodrel. The initial intent was to use a pure progestogen,

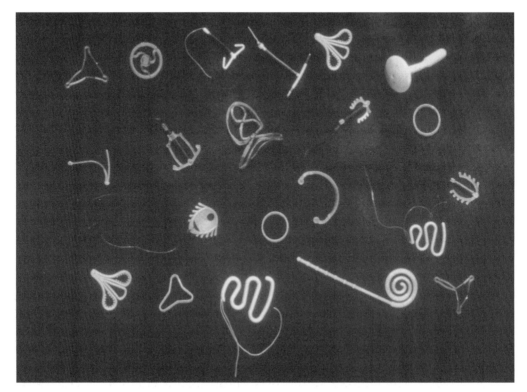

Figure 1 *A collection of old and newer framed IUDs (courtesy of Professor Thiery, Department of Obs/Gyn, University Hospital, Ghent, Belgium)*

but oestrogen contamination was found by serendipity to enhance the contraceptive effect (Gillmer 1997). As adverse cardiovascular effects have emerged, the oestrogen dose has been considerably lowered and new progestogens introduced. By 1966, progestogens alone were found to be better tolerated and yet contraceptive if given continuously in low dosage. Junkman, in 1966, produced a long-acting progestogen for injection, depot medroxyprogesterone acetate.

CURRENT METHODS OF CONTRACEPTION

This section is far from exhaustive, but highlights some current controversies (Figures 2, 3 and 4).

The combined oral contraceptive pill

This is the most extensively studied medicine ever prescribed. It is a reversible, convenient and highly effective contraceptive, with just 0.4% failure per year with perfect consistent and correct use, although up to 8% with typical use. It also has numerous non-contraceptive health benefits: light, regular and usually painless withdrawal bleeds and reduction in pelvic inflammatory disease, ovarian cysts, rheumatoid arthritis and benign breast disease (Guillebaud 1997). However, while it is available over-the-counter in many countries, with over 200 million ever-users world-wide, its use in Japan was only licensed in 1999.

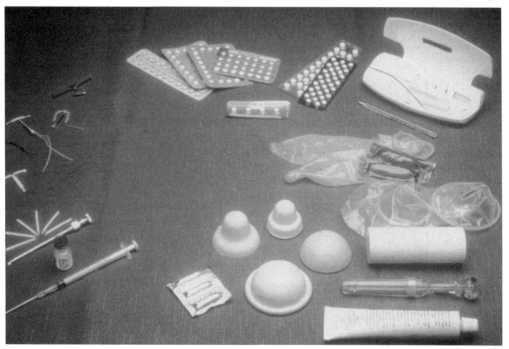

Figure 2   *Currently available contraceptive methods in the UK (courtesy of Walli Bounds, Research Co-ordinator, Margaret Pyke Memorial Trust)*

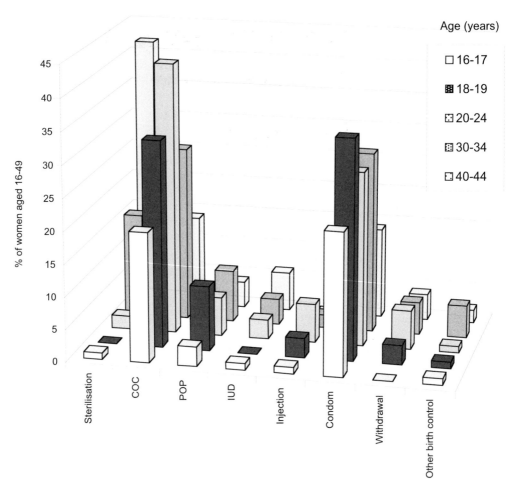

Figure 3 *Current use of contraception by age in the UK (from the ONS Omnibus Survey, Department of Health 1997); no method of contraception was used for some, ranging from 67% of those 16–17 years to 21% of those 40–44 years; reasons given included no sexual relationship, pregnancy and hysterectomy*

With current low ethinyloestradiol levels the combined oral contraceptive pill is safe in the healthy woman, as emphasised by the Royal College of General Practitioners study (Beral *et al.* 1999). This study followed 46 000 women for 25 years, half of whom were pill users at recruitment. It found that none of the adverse effects of the combined oral contraceptive persists beyond ten years after stopping use, with no detectable difference in mortality between ever-users and never-users.

Yet the combined oral contraceptive is clearly not risk-free. The Collaborative Group on Hormonal Factors in Breast Cancer (1996) combined data from 54 studies with over 53 000 women with breast cancer. They found a 24% increased risk among current combined oral contraceptive users, but the tumours in pill users were clinically less advanced and less aggressive. This risk was not related to dose, type or duration of combined oral contraceptive and had disappeared ten years after stopping. Thus, the relationship does not seem to be by initiation of the disease but rather due to either

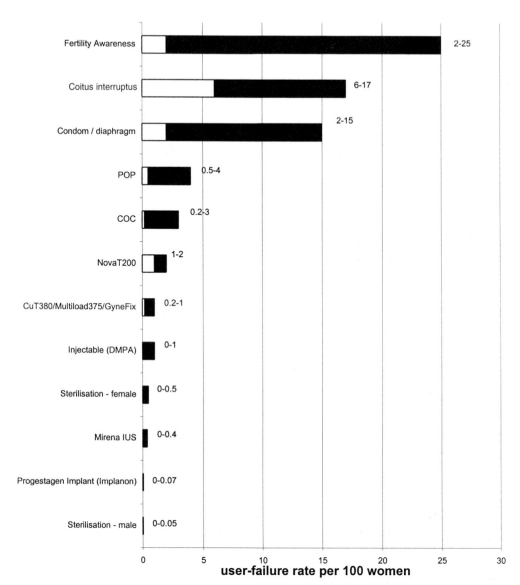

Figure 4   *User failure rate of contraceptive methods (range in world literature; excludes atypical studies giving particularly poor results and all extended-use studies); results depend on age and other fertility factors such as breastfeeding; using no method has a 'failure rate' (i.e. pregnancy rate) of 80–90 per 100 young women and 10–12 per 100 at age 45 years*

increased detection or late-stage promotion of malignant change. Obviously, this increased risk means more attributable cases where the individual background risk is larger, whether because of increased age or a family history.

The combined oral contraceptive may also act as a weak cofactor for cervical cancer, possibly speeding transition through pre-invasive stages. A doubling of cervical neoplasia in long-term users of the combined oral contraceptive pill versus the intrauterine device was found in a prospective study by Vessey *et al.* (1983) and later studies are congruent with this, although the findings have been challenged because of the problems in controlling for sexual activity. Benign liver tumours, although rare, do occur more frequently in combined oral contraceptive users, unlike hepatocellular carcinoma where there is no clear evidence of causation. In contrast, numerous studies have shown the risk of ovarian and of endometrial cancer to be reduced – to around half among all users and to one-third in long-term users, the effect lasting 10–15 years in ex-users.

The most recent 'pill scare' on 18 October 1995, unique to the UK, was based on three studies incriminating desogestrel/gestodene (DSG/GSD) products as doubling the risk of venous thromboembolism for users in comparison with those containing levonorgestrel (LNG) or norethisterone (NET). This difference has some measure of biological plausibility: DSG/GSD pills are more 'oestrogenic' than LNG/NET pills, as shown by their effects on acne and high-density lipoprotein-cholesterol, and prothrombotic coagulation changes are oestrogen-related. Yet the venous thromboembolism finding may in part be explained by prescriber bias (leading to diagnostic bias) and to the healthy-user effect in long-term users of LNG/NET products. In April 1999, the UK Committee on Safety of Medicines concluded that the excess risk of venous thromboembolism through using DSG/GSD rather than LNG/NET brands is smaller than originally quoted: about ten rather than 15 per 100 000 women years, which equates to just two deaths per annum per million users. The Committee removed the 1995 restriction on prescribing, leaving it to clinical judgement coupled with patient preference (Glasier 1999).

Conversely, DSG/GSD pills might yet prove to have relative advantages for arterial wall disease in higher-risk women. A lower risk of myocardial infarction was found for users of DSG/GSD pills compared with NET/LNG pills in the Transnational study (1997) but not confirmed in the larger MICA study (O'Brien 1999).

Hypertensive pill users have a three-fold greater risk of myocardial infarction than normotensive users and smoking pill users a ten-fold greater risk than non-smoking users. Yet there is no significant excess risk of myocardial infarction or stroke among healthy, non-smoking normotensive women with either current or past use of any of the modern low-oestrogen brands, as confirmed by several large studies (Ory 1998). Although theoretically advantageous, there is no evidence to date that 20 µg ethinyloestradiol preparations further reduce cardiovascular risk.

'Current scientific evidence suggests only two prerequisites for the safe provision of combined oral contraceptives:

(1) A careful personal and family medical history with particular attention to cardiovascular risk factors;
(2) An accurate blood pressure measurement' (Hannaford and Webb 1996).

Risk factors should in future be separately assessed according to whether they relate to risk of venous or arterial disease. The established contraindications are described in standard texts (Guillebaud 1998).

The progestogen-only pill

This is an under-used and under-researched yet effective method, particularly for the woman who is lactating or is aged over 35 years. Contraindications are few, with no significant increase in risk of acute myocardial infarction, stroke or venous thromboembolism found in a multinational study (WHO 1998). Hence, the progestogen-only pill is useful for women with diabetes, hypertension and migraine. Adverse effects, if any, are troublesome (irregular bleeding, functional ovarian cysts and breast tenderness) rather than life-threatening.

The progestogen-only pill requires diligent daily pill consumption, with a delay as little as three hours interfering with its efficacy. Its inhibition of cervical mucus penetrability seems to be adequately restored within 48 hours of renewed pill-taking. However, current Family Planning Association advice is to take extra precautions for seven days, partly because its anti-ovulatory effect (in about 60% of cycles) may, by analogy with the combined oral contraceptive, take seven days for restoration. Of the six varieties available in the UK, none as yet contain the newer progestogens, although the arrival is imminent of Cerazette® (Organon), containing 75 µg desogestrel, which inhibits ovulation to a far greater degree than existing progestogen-only pills. Some authorities advocate doubling the daily dose to women over 70 kg, as efficacy may be reduced. This is suggested by research of progestogen rings and a non-marketed version of Norplant® (Hoechst Marion Roussel) (McCann and Potter 1994).

Injectables

The only injectable currently licensed for long-term use in the UK is Depo-Provera® (Pharmacia & Upjohn), 150 mg of medroxyprogesterone acetate given intramuscularly every 12 weeks. High efficacy is achieved by inhibition of ovulation and contraindications are few. Non-contraceptive benefits include a reduction in the frequency of both sickle-cell crises and epileptic seizures in the respective sufferers. Weight gain and irregular bleeding can be problematic; the latter may resolve by giving the next injection early or adding oestrogen. Return of fertility may be delayed (median nine months after the last injection), but there is no evidence that Depo-Provera® causes permanent infertility (Lande 1995).

Anxiety about cancer risk, based on animal research, has been refuted by World Health Organization (WHO) data which show no overall increased risk of cancers of the ovary or cervix and a five-fold reduction in risk of endometrial carcinoma. The small possible weak cofactor effect on breast cancer could be due to surveillance bias. Any risk of teratogenicity (including reduced fetal growth) is small.

With 45% of Depo-Provera® users amenorrhoeic after one year, the debate continues over long-term risk of osteoporosis or arterial wall disease. Hypo-oestrogenism is present in the majority because of sustained ovarian inhibition. A case–control study found the bone density of long-term depot medroxyprogesterone acetate (DMPA) users to be intermediate between those of normal premenopausal and postmenopausal controls (Cundy 1991). Two studies in 1998 did not confirm this adverse effect: a cross-sectional study of 185 users (Gbolade et al. 1998) and a New Zealand study comparing past- with never-users (Glasier 1999). The World Health Organization Scientific Group (1998) reassures regarding cardiovascular risk but the study is short-term and lacks statistical power. Until more prospective data are available, current practice at the Margaret Pyke Family Planning Centre is to discuss the uncertainty after five years of use (sooner in smokers or if there are symptoms of hypo-oestrogenism) and then usually to check a plasma oestradiol level prior to the next dose. If two measurements are less than 100 pmol/l, we consider switching method or adding-back oestrogen.

Subcutaneous implants

Norplant® (Hoechst Marion Roussel), with levonorgestrel in six Silastic® capsules, has received much adverse publicity, chiefly because of removal difficulties – mostly where

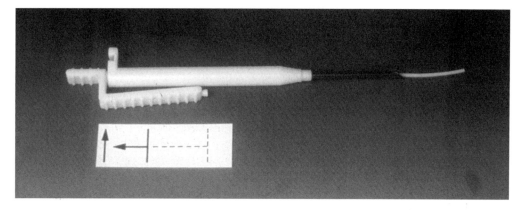

Figure 5 *Implanon (courtesy of Organon Laboratories Ltd)*

insertion has been too deep. This problem is less unlikely with the newer uni-rod implant Implanon® (Organon). This contains 68 mg etonogestrel within a flexible polyethyl-enevinylacetate membrane, released steadily over three years and is individually packed in the needle of a sterile, disposable inserter (Figure 5).

Like Norplant®, Implanon® is highly effective, with no pregnancies yet being reported after 70 000 cycles of use in 2300 women (Edwards and Moore 1999). It acts primarily by inhibiting ovulation and also reduces cervical mucus sperm penetrability. Comparative studies of Implanon® with Norplant® show that frequent and prolonged bleeding (occurring in approximately one in four women) remains the chief reason for requesting removal, although amenorrhoea is more likely with Implanon® (30–40% versus 20–30%, respectively, at one year). On removal of Implanon®, which took an average of 2.6 minutes in the trials, about 80% of women return to their normal ovulatory cycling within three months (70% with Norplant®).

Postcoital contraception

Three methods are currently used in the UK:

(1) The combined hormonal method – Schering PC4® (Schering Health) – two tablets each containing 50 μg oestrogen plus 250 μg levonorgestrel, two tablets repeated after 12 hours;

(2) The progestogen-only method (POEC) – 750 μg levonorgestrel, repeated after 12 hours;

(3) Insertion of a copper IUD.

A World Health Organization Scientific Group randomised controlled trial of 1998 women found POEC to prevent 85% (95% CI 74–93%) of pregnancies expected without treatment, compared with 57% (95% CI 39–71%) for Schering PC4®, with significantly less vomiting (6% versus 19%) and nausea (23% versus 51%). The efficacy of both treatments declined linearly with increasing time since unprotected coitus. Additionally, POEC is safe when Schering PC4® is contraindicated. These two facts add support to the argument for non-medical provision of emergency contraception. Marketing of a single 750 μg tablet is expected by 2000.

Insertion of a copper IUD before implantation, assumed to be up to five days after the calculated ovulation day, is effective emergency conception in almost 100% of women, even where multiple exposure has occurred. The Mirena® (Schering Health) intrauterine system is not recommended for this indication since its action appears to be slower than the effects of copper on sperm and blastocysts.

Intrauterine devices

Copper IUDs are used by just 4% of women of reproductive age, yet by more than 106 million women world-wide. Action is mainly by preventing fertilisation since, in studies, fertilised ova are almost never retrievable from the genital tract of copper IUD-users. However, their effectiveness when inserted postcoitally indicates they can also act to block implantation, such that they should be avoided by those who accept only prefertilisation methods (Treiman et al. 1995).

Comparing the framed devices, combining data from two studies suggests that the copper T380 – in either GynaeT380slimline (withdrawn in 1999 for commercial reasons) or Tcu380A form – is at least twice as effective as the NovaT200® (Schering) in the first year of use (failure rate 0.4 per 100 women) and five times as effective cumulatively over five years (failure rate 1.3 per 100 women), with no pregnancies detected after 5–12 years (Guillebaud 1998) – hence the 1998 UK approval of ten-years' use. Marketed in 1999, the NovaT380® (Schering) (with a failure rate of 0.5 and 1.6 per 100 women at one and two years) appears an improvement on the NovaT200®, although there is no comparative evidence to refute the impression that the copper T380 is still more effective (Batar et al. 1999). The Multiload 375® (Organon), another option for multiparae, also performs less well than the copper T380 in comparative studies. Less frequent replacement reduces the risks of IUDs, most of which are insertion-related: infection, perforation and expulsion. Any copper device which has been fitted above the age of 40 years may be that woman's last device and may never need to be changed.

GyneFix® (Contrel) (Figure 6), licensed in the UK since 1997, is a frameless device with six copper bands on a knotted polypropylene thread, embedded by a stylet-introducer 9–10 mm into the fundal endometrium. It is similar in efficacy to Cu T380, as confirmed in a continuing Chinese multicentre study, with approximately 600 parous women randomised to either the GyneFix or the CuT380A. At three years, fewer expulsions had occurred with GyneFix (3.0%) compared with CuT380A (7.4%) and rates of removal for medical reasons were lower (8.3% compared with 14.1%) (Wildemeersch et al. 1999 and unpublished data). Malpositioning is also less likely. More, longer-term comparative data are needed.

The Mirena® intrauterine system offers contraception which is reversible and yet as effective as female sterilisation, the latter being less effective than once believed (Peterson et al. 1996). This framed device releases 20 µg/24 hours of levonorgestrel from its polydimethylsiloxane reservoir over at least five years. The progestogen mainly acts locally causing endometrial suppression (leading to amenorrhoea in 20% at one year) and, by action on the cervical mucus and uterotubal fluid, sperm migration is impaired. Systemic adverse effects such as mastalgia, acne and depression are minimal. It is licensed for menorrhagia whenever this coincides with a contraceptive need, but so far in the UK it is not licensed for progestogenic protection of the endometrium during oestrogen therapy. Initially, erratic/prolonged uterine bleeding can be problematic, but this usually resolves within one to six months. In amenorrhoeic women adequate oestrogen production appears to continue.

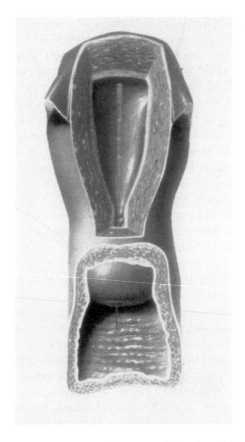

Figure 6 *GyneFix (courtesy of Dirk Wildermeersch, Department of Obs/Gyn, University Hospital, Ghent, Belgium)*

A common concern with IUDs is the risk of infection. This is a legacy from the disaster of the Dalkon Shield, whose polyfilament thread facilitated transfer of potential pathogens from the lower to the upper genital tract and some fatal cases of pelvic inflammatory disease occurred. Modern copper devices have a monofilament thread and do not themselves cause infection. This was shown in the WHO report by Farley *et al.* (1992) of over 23 000 IUD insertions world-wide. The infection rate was increased for the first 20 days following IUD insertion (probably due to interference with protective mechanisms allowing pre-existing sexually transmitted organisms to ascend) but then returned to the pre-insertion risk for each population studied. Thus, unless prevalence is low, prescreening at least for *Chlamydia trachomatis* is advisable, with prophylactic antibiotics where time does not allow for awaiting the result. There should also be counselling about sexually transmitted disease and concurrent use of condoms if appropriate.

Barrier methods

Barrier methods are back 'in fashion', often together with another contraceptive because of their protective effect against sexually transmitted infections. The thinner and wider

Avanti® (London Rubber Company) substitutes polyurethane for latex, eliminating potential damage by oil-based lubricants and enhancing shelf life and acceptability.

For the woman, the rubber diaphragm remains a good option for dedicated couples who accept a failure rate of 4–8% in the first year. Some women may prefer the fit of a cervical cap, particularly if cystitis occurs. All require concomitant spermicide use, the most widely used being nonoxynol '9', as a cream, jelly, pessary or pressurised foam. For those who are allergic to this, benzalkonium chloride (marketed as Pharmatex® by Innothera Laboratoire) is an alternative (Bounds 1999). Femidom® (Chartex International), a polyurethane sac with an outer ring at the introitus and a loose inner ring, has variable acceptability but theoretically better protection against infection than a diaphragm (Bounds 1999).

The marketing of Persona® (Unipath Ltd) in 1996 has increased the scope of 'natural' regulation of fertility. A small computerised monitor optically measures urine levels of oestrone-3-glucuronide and luteinising hormone and signals 'safe' times, also based on stored information from the user's last six menstrual cycles. The failure rate of about 6% at one year can be improved by relying only on the post-ovulatory infertile phase.

THE FUTURE

We are still some way from the ideal contraceptive, combining reversibility, efficacy, convenience (not coitus-related), acceptability (no adverse effects, aesthetically pleasing and no cost), 'forgetability' (no maintenance) and protection against infection. Despite the scientific opportunities, contraceptive research and development is hampered by negative publicity, legal threats and ethical and indemnity dilemmas such that the pharmaceutical companies see it as a 'high-risk venture'.

Oral hormonal methods

The combined oral contraceptive pill is likely to remain popular well into the 21st century. Attempts to improve its safety by substituting natural oestrogen for the synthetic ethinyloestradiol have so far failed because of unpredictable absorption, resulting in breakthrough ovulation and breakthrough bleeding. There is hope that selective modulators of hormone receptors may eventually replace currently available oestrogens and progestogens with the aim of avoiding their risks (particularly venous thromboembolism), while also reducing the incidence of common diseases such as breast cancer (Baird and Glasier 1999).

Mifepristone, a progesterone antagonist, currently used in termination of pregnancy, is also highly effective at preventing implantation used within 72 (or more) hours of coital exposure, even at a low dose of 10 mg (which causes less delay of the next menses). It appears effective used either 'once a month' in the early luteal phase or 2–5 mg daily, at preventing both ovulation and the formation of a secretory endometrium. Of concern is its potential non-legal use as an abortifacient.

Topical hormonal methods

Numerous self-fitting progestogen-releasing vaginal rings are under investigation for contraceptive use, releasing either progestogen alone or in combination with oestrogen or orally inactive natural progesterone. Transdermal contraceptive patches (progestogen-only and combined with oestrogen) are in phase III trials, with marketing of a combined patch likely in 2001 as Evra® (Jansen Cilag).

Injectables and implants

Improvements are focusing on better delivery systems to achieve steadier plasma hormonal levels while avoiding initial excessively high levels, new long-acting progestogens, and the combination with oestrogen to improve bleeding patterns. The latter includes the monthly Cyclofem® (25 mg medroxyprogesterone acetate plus 5 mg oestradiol cypionate; Pharmacia and Upjohn) and Mesigyna® (norethisterone acetate plus oestradiol valerate; Schering). Endorsed by the World Health Organization, both are highly effective and popular in South America. Hormonal release is steady from a microcrystalline aqueous suspension. A self-applicator appears to be acceptable and would ease service provision. Biodegradable rods have been under development for over 15 years; difficulties include retrievability and slow *in-situ* absorption.

Gonadotrophin hormone releasing hormone (GnRH) analogues show great contraceptive potential by ablating the menstrual cycle and blocking spermatogenesis in men. Currently they are expensive, not available orally and require add-back gonadal steroid replacement, then endometrial protection in the woman.

Looking further ahead, long-acting antagonists to follicle-stimulating hormone (FSH) and human chorionic gonadotrophin (hCG) receptors might be developed to prevent follicular development or to block implantation respectively. The action of peptides involved in sperm–oocyte fusion might also be blocked by similar technology.

Intrauterine devices

Development is concentrating on using smaller, more flexible devices and on improving anchoring methods and allowing immediate post-placental insertion. A hybrid of the Mirena® intrauterine system and the GyneFix®, with intrauterine Silastic® cylinders or threads releasing progestogen, is under development, combining the benefits of each. Intracervical devices, releasing either copper or steroid hormones, attached mechanically or by post-insertion expansion of a stent, avoid blind insertion, and an intrauterine foreign body and potentially reduce bleeding and pain complications, but no product is imminent.

Barrier methods

New options, designed for over-the-counter use, have limited efficacy data despite recent attainment of marketing permission in Europe (CE marking): Lea's Shield® (Yama Inc.), a silicone 'one size fits all' vaginal cap; Femcap® (Femcap Inc.), in two sizes, with a curved circumferential rim designed to locate in the fornices; and the disposable Oves® cap (Veos Ltd) with its soft polyurethane dome (Figure 7) (Bounds 1999). Acceptability studies to date have given mixed results. However, the loose-fit bidirectional male polyurethane condom Ez-on® (Mayer Laboratories Inc.) shows promise.

With the increasing prevalence of sexually transmitted infections, the search continues for spermicides with virucidal and microbiocidal activity, but which avoid the vaginal irritation associated with heavy use of nonoxynol '9'. Chlorhexidine and dextrin sulphate are currently being evaluated and also additives that enhance vaginal-wall coating of

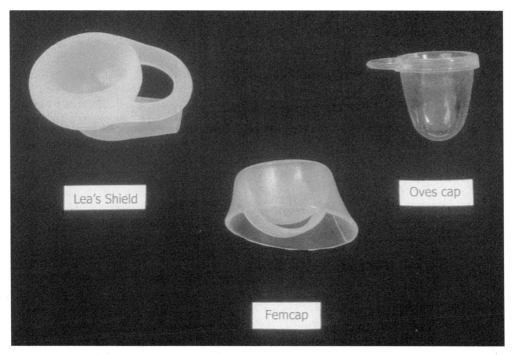

Figure 7 *New cervical caps*

candidate compounds. 'User-friendly' delivery systems, such as sponges or vaginal rings are important to increase acceptability.

Immune approaches

Immune approaches (with vaccines to hCG, GnRH, the zona pellucida or various sperm antigens) are still developmental despite over 25 years of research. Difficulties include individual variation, reversibility and avoidance of (auto)-immune disorders.

Male hormonal methods

Numerous trials are in progress world-wide, with the possibility of a commercially available product by 2010. Gonadotrophin production, and hence spermatogenesis, can be suppressed using supraphysiological doses of testosterone esters, but with resultant unfavourable changes in plasma lipids, prostatic hypertrophy and aggression. Suppression is also possible using a progestogen or GnRH analogue but this requires combining with physiological doses of testosterone to maintain libido and potency. Administration is possible by injection or implant, transdermally and orally.

CONCLUSION

With all the above recent and likely prospective developments in contraception, we look forward to a time in which unintended pregnancy is seen as a mystery of the past.

References

Baird, D.T. and Glasier, A.F. (1999) Science, medicine and the future: contraception. *BMJ* **319**, 969–72

Batar, I., Kuukankorpi, A., Rauramo, I. and Siljander, M. (1999) Two-year clinical experience with NovaT380, a novel copper–silver IUD. *Advances in Contraception* **15**, 37–48

Beral, V., Hermon, C., Kay C., Hannaford, P., Darby, S. and Reeves, G. (1999) Mortality associated with oral contraceptive use: 25-year follow-up of cohort of 46 000 women from Royal College of General Practitioners' oral contraception study. *BMJ* **318**, 96–100

Bounds, W. (1999) 'Non-hormonal methods' in: J. Ferguson and M. Upsdell (Eds) *Key Advances in the Effective Management of Contraception*, pp. 61–3. London: RSM Press

Cayley, J.A. (1983) A brief history of contraception. *British Journal of Sexual Medicine* Jan, 20–6; Feb, 27–35

Collaborative Group on Hormonal Factors in Breast Cancer (1996) Breast cancer and hormonal contraceptives: collaborative reanalysis of individual data of 53 297 women with breast cancer and 100 239 women without breast cancer from 54 epidemiological studies. *Lancet* **347**, 1713–27

Cundy, T., Cornish, J., Roberts, H., Elder, H. and Reid, I. (1998) Spinal bone density in women using depot medroxyprogesterone contraception. *Obstet Gynecol* **92**, 569–73

Edwards, J. and Moore A. (1999) Implanon – a review of clinical studies. *Br J Fam Plann* **24**, 3–16

Farley, T.M., Rosenberg, M.J., Rowe, P. *et al.* (1992). Intrauterine devices and pelvic inflammatory disease: an international perspective. *Lancet* **339**, 785–8

Gabelnick, H. (1998) 'Future methods' in: R.A. Hatcher *et al.* (Eds) *Contraceptive Technology* (17th Edn), pp. 615–22. USA: Contraceptive Technology Communications

Gbolade, B., Ellis, S., Murby, B., Randall, S. and Kirkman, R. (1998) Bone density in long-term users of depot medroxyprogesterone acetate. *Br J Obstet Gynaecol* **105**, 790–4

Gillmer, M.D.G. (1997) The oral contraceptive pill – a product of serendipity. *The Diplomate* **4**, 231–5

Glasier, A. (1999) 'Hormonal contraception' in: J. Ferguson and M. Upsdell (Eds) *Key Advances in the Effective Management of Contraception*, pp.41–4. London: RSM Press

Guillebaud, J. (1997) 'Contraception' in: A. McPherson and D. Waller (Eds) *Women's Health*, pp. 128–216. Oxford: Oxford University Press (General Practice Series)

Guillebaud, J. (1998) *Contraception Today: A Pocket Book for General Practitioners* (3rd Edn). London: Martin Dunitz

Hannaford, P. and Webb, A. (1996) Evidence-guided prescribing of combined oral contraceptives: consensus statement. *Contraception* **54**, 125–9

Hicks, D. and Bradley, K. (1995) The history of the condom. *British Journal of Sexual Medicine* March/April, 21–2

Lande, R.E. (1995) *New Era for Injectables*. Baltimore: Johns Hopkins School of Public Health, Population Information Program (Population Reports K5)

McCann, M. and Potter, L. (1994) Progestin-only oral contraception: a comprehensive review. *Contraception* **50** Suppl, 1–189

O'Brien, P.A. (1999) The third generation oral contraceptive controversy. *BMJ* **319**, 795–6

Ory, H.W. (1998) Cardiovascular safety of oral contraceptives. *Contraception* **58** Suppl, 9-13S

Peterson, H.B., Xia, Z., Hughes, J.M. *et al.* (1996) The risk of pregnancy after tubal sterilisation: findings from the US collaborative review of sterilisation. *Am J Obstet Gynecol* **174**, 1161–70

Robertson, W. (1990) *An Illustrated History of Contraception*. Carnforth: Parthenon

Treiman, K., Liskin, L., Kols, A. and Rinehart, W. (1995) *IUDs – An Update*. Baltimore: Johns Hopkins School of Public Health, Population Information Program (Population Reports B6)

Vessey, M.P., Lawless, M., McPherson, K. and Yeates, D. (1983) Neoplasia of the cervix uteri and contraception: a possible adverse effect of the pill. *Lancet* **ii**, 930–4

Wildemeersch, D. Batar, I., Webb, A. *et al.* (1999) GyneFix. The frameless intrauterine contraceptive implant – an update. *Br J Fam Plann* **24**, 149–59

World Health Organization Scientific Group (1998) *Cardiovascular Disease and Steroid Hormone Contraception*. Geneva: WHO (Technical Report Series 877)

25

Polycystic ovary syndrome

Howard S. Jacobs

HISTORY

Polycystic ovary syndrome (PCOS) became a realistic clinical entity with the description by Stein and Leventhal (1935) of seven patients with menstrual irregularities, obesity and hirsutism. At operation, their ovaries were larger than normal and had capsular thickening. Following wedge biopsy the menstrual cycles became more regular. Histology confirmed thickening of the capsule, showed multiple small cysts and follicles and a great increase in interstitial cells.

The clinical triad of menstrual disturbance, dermal hyperandrogenism (hirsutism, seborrhoea and acne, alopecia) and obesity, known as the Stein–Leventhal syndrome, featured in gynaecological practice predominantly as a surgically treatable cause of anovulatory infertility. Owing to the inaccessibility of the ovaries (several-fold enlargement has to occur for them to be clinically identified as larger than normal) attention turned to endocrine investigation. The pattern of development of radioimmunoassay meant that the first disturbance identified was hypersecretion of luteinising hormone (LH) (Shoham *et al.* 1993). Demonstration of increased secretion of androgens was bedevilled for years by the complexities of androgen secretion and metabolism, together with methodological problems of the measurement of steroids in blood. Moreover, it was not until it was realised that the hyperinsulinism of obesity inhibited synthesis of sex hormone binding globulin by the liver (Plymate *et al.* 1988) that measurements of total serum testosterone concentrations in women with PCOS could be adequately interpreted.

Following introduction of pelvic ultrasonography in the 1980s, the ultrasound features of the polycystic ovary were characterised (Adams *et al.* 1985) and then identified in around 20% of volunteer adult women (Polson *et al.* 1988). This prevalence was initially startling but has been confirmed in numerous studies, performed with increasing ingenuity to avoid surveillance bias. It is now safe to accept that the characteristic ultrasound finding (ovaries that are larger than normal, with an echodense central stroma and peripherally arranged follicles or cysts) does indeed occur in a fifth of adult women and in an increasing proportion of children (around 6% of six-year-olds and about 10% of ten-year-olds) (Bridges *et al.* 1993). These morphological features run in families (Hague *et al.* 1988) and, in the author's experience, it is unusual to see a patient with ovaries that are polycystic on ultrasound who does not have a first-degree relative with the same findings. We will return to the question of what is being inherited; here it is important to note that not all women who have polycystic ovaries have PCOS – that is, the association of polycystic ovaries with characteristic symptomatology. As will be emphasised, the most important factor that results in evolution of the syndrome is the development of insulin resistance in a woman with polycystic ovaries.

CURRENT STATUS

PCOS usually presents during adolescence with a menstrual disturbance, or the results of hyperandrogenism; that is to say, with seborrhoea, acne, hirsutism or androgenic alopecia (Balen *et al.* 1995). The menstrual disturbance is usually oligomenorrhoea but may be amenorrhoea or polymenorrhoea. About 25% have a regular ovulatory menstrual cycle. A reduction in the rate of ovulation obviously reduces the rate of conception. The impairment of fertility is, however, usually greater than can be explained solely by fewer ovulations per unit of time. Unpredictability of the time of ovulation in an irregular cycle is important but adverse effects of obesity (Norman and Clark 1998) and elevated LH secretion may also be implicated.

The endocrine features of PCOS include a raised serum LH concentration in about 40% of cases, together with an increase in the rate of testosterone secretion. The latter may not be reflected in an increase in the serum total testosterone concentration if the sex hormone binding globulin concentration is suppressed, as is the case in obesity (Nestler *et al.* 1991). An increase in the total serum testosterone concentration in obese women with PCOS therefore implies a prodigious increase in testosterone production and clearance rates. The major clinical value of measuring the serum total testosterone concentration in a hirsute patient is that a level below 6 nmol/l makes an androgen-secreting tumour extremely unlikely .

The proportion of cases with particular symptoms and biochemical and endocrine findings is influenced by two demographic features. The first is referral bias, since the proportion complaining of infertility or menstrual problems will be greater in gynaecology than in reproductive endocrine clinics; the reverse is true of the complaint of hirsutism or alopecia. The second is the background prevalence of obesity. Obesity is an important cause of insulin resistance, which is the major determinant of the expression of PCOS.

Polycystic ovaries, PCOS and insulin resistance

In women with PCOS, resistance to the action of insulin is specific to the extra splanchnic disposal of glucose (Dunaif *et al.* 1992). As a consequence of this peripheral insulin resistance, euglycaemia can only be maintained through compensatory hypersecretion of insulin. The insulin resistance spares the liver – the fasting glucose concentration is normal, serum sex hormone binding globulin (Nestler *et al.* 1991) and high-density lipoprotein concentrations (Conway *et al.* 1992) are suppressed – perhaps the skin and the ovary. Ovarian dysfunction results, in direct proportion to the intensity of compensatory hyperinsulinism (Conway *et al.* 1990). Reduction of insulin levels by diet, exercise or drugs improves menstrual cyclicity and lowers serum androgen levels.

Insulin resistance in PCOS has been extensively reviewed (Holte 1996; Dunaif 1997; Nestler 1997; Poretsky *et al.* 1999). Dunaif *et al.* (1995) have described a specific defect in transduction of the insulin signal which is considered to be an inherited feature of the fibroblasts of women with PCOS. In addition, insulin resistance develops as children enter puberty in response to the increase of growth hormone secretion that underlies the acceleration in growth at this age (Amiel *et al.* 1991). To give an idea of the dimensions of this effect, in children with diabetes insulin requirements typically double during the adolescent growth spurt. In girls with polycystic ovaries, these two forms of insulin resistance contribute to the development of obesity and of the symptoms of PCOS. Obesity itself, present in some 40% of women with PCOS (Balen *et al.* 1995), worsens insulin resistance and so causes further deterioration of ovarian function. Should the patient come from a family with diabetes mellitus, there is the added risk of developing the insulin resistance of non-insulin-dependent diabetes mellitus. Finally, as will be discussed, serum leptin concentrations rise with increasing obesity and there is evidence that leptin can impair the action of insulin in hepatocytes (Cohen *et al.* 1996).

Leptin and obesity: implications for PCOS

Leptin, a cytokine of the tumour necrosis factor group, was originally identified in obese mice as the product of the *ob* gene (Halaas and Friedman 1997). In humans, expression of this gene in white fat cells is stimulated by insulin, glucocorticoids, noradrenaline and nutrients (Rohner-Jeanrenaud and Jeanrenaud 1996). Serum leptin concentrations and *ob* gene expression in adipose tissue are increased in obesity (Considine *et al.* 1996) and are three times higher in women than in men, a difference which persists after correction for fat mass. Oestrogen is not responsible (Havel *et al.* 1996; Rosenbaum *et al.* 1996) but part of the difference may be explained by the effect of androgens (Wabitsch *et al.* 1997). On the other hand, since expression of leptin messenger RNA is higher in subcutaneous than visceral fat (Hube *et al.* 1996), the difference may be related to the higher ratio of subcutaneous to visceral adipose mass in women compared with men (Kotani *et al.* 1994).

In women with PCOS, serum leptin concentrations have been reported to be higher (Brzechffa *et al.* 1996) or not different (Chapman *et al.* 1997; Laughlin *et al.* 1997; Mantzoros *et al.* 1997; Rouru *et al.* 1997) from those in weight-matched controls. The relationship of leptin secretion to insulin resistance was investigated by Laughlin *et al.* 1997). Among several factors studied, they found that only the 24-hour mean insulin concentration contributed significantly to leptin levels independently of body mass index and percentage of body fat. Despite this relationship and the two-fold higher mean insulin concentration in the patients with PCOS compared with controls, the expected increase of serum leptin concentrations was not observed. The authors considered their results were most readily explained by the presence of a PCOS-specific form of insulin resistance in adipocytes, which impairs the stimulatory effect of insulin on leptin secretion (Ciaraldi *et al.* 1997). Finally, obesity in PCOS is characterised by a disproportionate increase in visceral fat (Bjorntorp 1996) which increases the ratio of the circumference of the waist to that of the hip, i.e. an increase in the type of fat that undersecretes leptin compared with subcutaneous fat.

It remains to consider the possibility of an impact of leptin directly on the ovary. Karlsson *et al.* (1997) found that leptin inhibited LH-stimulated oestradiol production by granulosa cells but had no effect on cells incubated in the absence of LH. This finding, together with the impairment by leptin of the augmentation by insulin-like growth factor-I of follicle stimulating hormone stimulated oestradiol production by rat granulosa cells (Zachow and Magoffin 1997), indicates inhibition by leptin of the ovarian response to gonadotrophins. Perhaps the effect on the ovary of high-circulating concentrations of leptin in obese patients with PCOS explains their otherwise surprisingly impaired response to gonadotrophin stimulation (White *et al.* 1996). Presumably, the response of the ovaries of such patients represents a balance between the stimulatory effects of insulin and the inhibitory effects of leptin.

Long-term implications of insulin resistance in women with PCOS

Clinical expression of PCOS correlates with the degree of compensatory hyperinsulinism, both in terms of hypersecretion of androgens and menstrual cyclicity. Hyperinsulinism is also associated with the development of a number of cardiovascular risk factors, such as depression of high-density lipoprotein and elevation of low-density lipoprotein cholesterol, an increased risk of hypertension, non-insulin-dependent diabetes and atherosclerosis. Based on assessment of these risk factors in a long-term follow-up of patients with surgically proven PCOS (Dahlgren *et al.* 1992a), Dahlgren *et al.* (1992b) postulated a six-fold increase in the lifetime risk of a myocardial infarction in women with PCOS. To test this hypothesis, Pierpoint *et al.* (1998) followed up 786 women who had been diagnosed at wedge resection as having PCOS an average of 30 years earlier. While there was a significant increase in the number of deaths attributed to diabetes mellitus, based on death certification, there was no difference in the risk of death from a heart attack in women with PCOS compared with age-matched controls. There was, however, a statistically significant reduced risk of death from stroke. More recently, we have analysed the cardiovascular morbidity in the surviving cohort of this study. Despite finding an increase in the prevalence of diabetes, we found no increase in the risk of cardiovascular disease (S.H. Wild *et al.*, unpublished data).

How can one explain the paradox of an increase in cardiovascular risk factors but no increase in cardiovascular events? The first point to note is that, while there was a strong association of dyslipidaemia and impaired carbohydrate metabolism with body weight, overall the women in this cohort were not obese, the mean body mass index at follow-up being 27 kg/m^2. It seems likely, therefore, that the risk of cardiovascular disease in women with PCOS is more related to body weight and composition than to ovarian status. The second consideration is that women with PCOS tend to have higher oestrogen levels than women with normal ovaries, and perhaps endogenous oestrogens provide cardioprotective benefits similar to those of exogenous hormones. Finally, there is the possibility that the increased serum levels of vascular endothelial growth factor that have been observed in women with PCOS (Agrawal *et al.* 1998) protect the heart from the effects of ischaemia caused by atherosclerosis.

MANAGEMENT OF PCOS

Infertility

Three factors contribute to infertility in women with PCOS. The first is compensatory hyperinsulinism, the intensity of which determines the rate of ovulation. The second is hypersecretion of LH, which may have an adverse effect on fertility and pregnancy outcome independent of ovulation (Balen *et al.* 1993). The third is the intrinsic tendency of the polycystic ovary to over-respond to gonadotrophin stimulation, which places the patient at particular risk of ovarian hyperstimulation and multiple pregnancy.

The earlier discussion of the pathophysiology of insulin secretion emphasises the centrality of enhancing insulin sensitivity in the management of all aspects of PCOS. In overweight patients aerobic exercise should be increased and calorie consumption reduced (particularly in the form of fat). The change in weight required to obtain a return of ovulation cycles, or at least to regain an ovulatory response to clomiphene, may be quite small – of the order of a 5% fall in total body weight (Kiddy *et al.* 1992) – perhaps because the important change is in the metabolically active visceral rather than peripheral fat. At present there is much interest in insulin-sensitising drugs. While encouraging small-scale trials with troglitazone (Dunaif *et al.* 1996) and D-chiro-inositol (Nestler *et al.* 1999) have been published, neither drug is presently available in the UK. Metformin is presently being intensively promoted on several polycystic ovary Internet sites. Used for many years to reduce hyperglycaemia in patients with non-insulin-dependent diabetes, metformin reduces hepatic glucose output (Christiansen and Hellerstein 1998) (normal in women with PCOS) but does also increase peripheral sensitivity to insulin (Bailey and Turner 1996). Several short-term trials in non-diabetic women with PCOS have been published, with conflicting results (Wyne and Bradshaw 1998). It remains unclear how much of the benefit observed should be attributed to the medication and how much to concomitant weight loss. Now that a simple method for assessing insulin resistance, at least in obese patents, has been described (Legro *et al.* 1998) (the ratio of the fasting glucose to insulin concentration), it should be easy to select patients for prospective randomised controlled trials of insulin-sensitising drugs. It will also be important to incorporate analyses of the effects of diet and exercise. Until such studies are complete, it is not possible to advise patients with PCOS about the value of treatment with metformin.

For women who remain anovulatory despite attempts to enhance insulin sensitivity, induction of ovulation with clomiphene is the treatment of choice. For reasons elaborated elsewhere (Balen and Jacobs 1997), we recommend that the dose does not exceed 100 mg/day for five days per cycle and that the duration does not exceed six cycles. For women who do not conceive with clomiphene, we next consider treatment with gonadotrophins or by laparoscopic ovarian diathermy (Armar *et al.* 1990). The most favourable results with the latter procedure have been obtained in women with anovulatory infertility, a raised serum LH concentration and a normal body weight (Donesky and Adashi 1995). Administration of gonadotrophin injections to women with polycystic ovaries remains a difficult form of therapy because of the inherent tendency of polycystic ovaries to over-respond, with the development of multiple small- and medium-sized follicles. This exuberant response puts the patient at special risk of ovarian hyperstimulation and multiple pregnancy. We therefore consider it wrong to treat patients with polycystic ovaries with gonadotrophins without the appropriate ultrasound resources and skills in surveillance. We also insist that the patient is able to commit herself to frequent scanning.

Using an algorithm based on the above treatments, the cumulative pregnancy rate at one year in women with PCOS with anovulatory infertility is of the order of 80%, with a multiple pregnancy rate (predominantly twins) of around 6% and the occasional case of ovarian hyperstimulation syndrome (Balen *et al.* 1994).

Hyperandrogenism

Three principles guide the treatment of hirsutism (Conn and Jacobs 1998). The first is that medication with anti-androgens complements, but does not replace, reduction of insulin drive to the ovary. Treatments that worsen insulin resistance are to be avoided. Treatment with glucocorticoids makes no sense and even women with late-onset 21 hydroxylase deficiency (isolated or coexisting, as it does, with some 10% of cases of PCOS) (Hague *et al.* 1989) fare better with anti-androgens than with prednisolone or dexamethasone. The second is that efforts to reduce androgen drive to the skin should be combined with depilatory treatment. The roles are complementary because, while the latter is required to remove hair from the skin, the former is needed to reduce the rate of hair (re)growth. The third principle is that secure contraception is required during treatment with anti-androgens because of the risk of the medication crossing into the fetal circulation and feminising a male child.

Presently available medications include those which suppress androgen secretion (combined oral contraceptive pill, gonadotrophin-releasing hormone analogues) and those which impair its action. The latter may act on androgen receptors, such as cyproterone acetate, spironolactone and flutamide, or inhibit 5α reduction of testosterone to the more virilising dihydrotestosterone (e.g. finasteride). Details of treatment have been recently reviewed (Diamanti-Kandarakis *et al*. 1995; Conn and Jacobs 1997). Clinical efficacy is similar with all the drugs so the choice is mainly guided by the profile of adverse reactions – for example, Dianette® (Schering Health) is avoided in women with contraindications to the contraceptive pill, spironolactone is avoided in women with excessive menstrual bleeding. The patient needs to be counselled about the slowness of the response to treatment, its probable duration and the need to decide between the immediate priorities of dealing with hirsutism or starting treatment to enhance fertility.

FUTURE DEVELOPMENTS

Future research into PCOS will surely focus on unravelling its molecular genetics. Progress will, however, require agreed definitions of the phenotype. The most obvious explanations for discrepant findings centre around whether the syndrome is defined endocrinologically, as is the case in North America, or by reference to the presence of morphological changes in the ovaries, as happens in Europe. An important recent study assessed 37 candidate genes for linkage and association with PCOS or hyperandrogenaemia in data obtained from 150 families (Urbanek *et al*. 1999). The genes studied were involved in a variety of metabolic and endocrine pathways thought to be implicated in the pathophysiology of PCOS. Evidence of linkage was found for two genes only, CYP11A and follistatin. The former encodes side-chain cleavage enzyme, which converts cholesterol to pregnenolone, a rate-limiting step in steroidogenesis. Presumably, a mutation causing up-regulation of this enzyme could result in an increase in androgen secretion, a cardinal feature of the syndrome. The most striking linkage was, however, found with follistatin. This protein binds and neutralises activin, a widely distributed paracrine hormone which promotes follicular development, inhibits androgen production by theca cells and increases secretion of follicle-stimulating hormone and insulin. Reversal of these activities because of a mutation causing overexpression of the gene encoding activin's inhibitor, that is, follistatin, might plausibly reproduce many of the features of PCOS. No doubt the rapid advances in modern genetics will soon permit refutation or confirmation of these fascinating observations (Odunsi and Kidd 1999).

Clinically, we may anticipate developments in drug therapy in two spheres. The first is in new insulin-sensitising drugs, most likely thiazolidineiones (for example, troglitazone, rosiglitazone and pioglitazone). These compounds, which are high-affinity ligands for novel nuclear receptors called peroxisome proliferator-activated receptors, enhance insulin sensitivity through mechanisms that are not understood at present (Reginato and Lazar 1999). The second is in new anti-androgens, particularly the development of inhibitors of the type-15α reductase which are anticipated to be especially active in the scalp, thus providing a remedy for androgenic alopecia.

References

Adams, J., Franks, S., Polson, D.W. *et al.* (1985) Multifollicular ovaries: clinical and endocrine features and response to pulsatile gonadotropin releasing hormone. *Lancet* **ii**, 1375–9

Agrawal, R., Sladkevicius, P., Engmann, L. *et al.* (1998) Serum vascular endothelial growth factor concentrations and ovarian stromal blood flow are increased in women with polycystic ovaries. *Hum Reprod* **13**, 651–5

Amiel, S.A., Caprio, S., Sherwin, R.S., Plewe, G., Haymond, M.W. and Tamborlane, W.V. (1991) Insulin resistance of puberty: a defect restricted to peripheral glucose metabolism. *J Clin Endocrinol Metab* **72**, 277–82

Armar, N.A., McGarrigle, H.H., Honour, J., Holownia, P., Jacobs, H.S. and Lachelin, G.C. (1990) Laparoscopic ovarian diathermy in the management of anovulatory infertility in women with polycystic ovaries: endocrine changes and clinical outcome. *Fertil Steril* **53**, 45–9

Bailey, C.J. and Turner, R.C. (1996) Metformin. *N Engl J Med* **334**, 574–9

Balen, A.H. (1995) Hypersecretion of luteinizing hormone in the polycystic ovary syndrome and a novel hormone 'gonadotrophin surge attenuating factor'. *J R Soc Med* **88**, 339P–41P

Balen, A.H. and Jacobs, H.S. (1997) *Infertility in Practice.* Edinburgh: Churchill Livingstone

Balen, A.H., Tan, S.L. and Jacobs, H.S. (1993) Hypersecretion of luteinising hormone: a significant cause of infertility and miscarriage. *Br J Obstet Gynaecol* **100**, 1082–9

Balen, A.H., Braat, D.D., West, C., Patel, A. and Jacobs, H.S. (1994) Cumulative conception and live birth rates after the treatment of anovulatory infertility: safety and efficacy of ovulation induction in 200 patients. *Hum Reprod* **9**, 1563–70

Balen, A.H., Conway, G.S., Kaltsas, G. *et al.* (1995) Polycystic ovary syndrome: the spectrum of the disorder in 1741 patients. *Hum Reprod* **10**, 2107–11

Bjorntorp, P. (1996) The android woman – a risky condition. *J Intern Med* **239**, 105–10

Bridges, N.A., Cooke, A., Healy, M.J., Hindmarsh, P.C. and Brook, C.G. (1993) Standards for ovarian volume in childhood and puberty. *Fertil Steril* **60**, 456–60

Brzechffa, P.R., Jakimiuk, A.J., Agarwal, S.K., Weitsman, S.R., Buyalos, R.P. and Magoffin, D.A. (1996) Serum immunoreactive leptin concentrations in women with polycystic ovary syndrome. *J Clin Endocrinol Metab* **81**, 4166–9

Chapman, I.M., Wittert, G.A. and Norman, R.J. (1997) Circulating leptin concentrations in polycystic ovary syndrome: relation to anthropometric and metabolic parameters. *Clin Endocrinol (Oxf)* **46**, 175–81

Christiansen, M.P. and Hellerstein, M.K. (1998) Effects of metformin on hepatic glucose metabolism. *Current Opinion in Endocrinology and Diabetes* **5**, 252–5

Ciaraldi, T.P., Morales, A.J., Hickman, M.G., Odom-Ford, R., Olefsky, J.M. and Yen, S.S. (1997) Cellular insulin resistance in adipocytes from obese polycystic ovary syndrome subjects involves adenosine modulation of insulin sensitivity. *J Clin Endocrinol Metab* **82**, 1421–5

Cohen, B., Novick, D. and Rubenstein, M. (1996) Modulation of insulin activities by leptin. *Science* **274**, 1185–8

Conn, J.J. and Jacobs, H.S. (1997) The clinical management of hirsutism. *Eur J Endocrinol* **136**, 339–48

Conn, J.J. and Jacobs, H.S. (1998) Managing hirsutism in gynaecological practice. *Br J Obstet Gynaecol* **105**, 687–96

Considine, R.V., Sinha, M.K., Heiman, M.L. *et al.* (1996) Serum immunoreactive-leptin concentrations in normal-weight and obese humans. *N Engl J Med* **334**, 292–5

Conway, G.S. and Jacobs, H.S. (1990) Acanthosis nigricans in obese women with the polycystic ovary syndrome: disease spectrum not distinct entity. *Postgrad Med J* **66**, 536–8

Conway, G.S., Jacobs, H.S., Holly, J.M. and Wass, J.A. (1990) Effects of luteinising hormone, insulin, insulin-like growth factor I and insulin-like growth factor small binding protein 1 in the polycystic ovary syndrome. *Clin Endocrinol (Oxf)* **33**, 593–603

Conway, G.S., Agrawal, R., Betteridge, D.J. and Jacobs, H.S. (1992) Risk factors for coronary artery disease in lean and obese women with the polycystic ovary syndrome. *Clin Endocrinol (Oxf)* **37**, 119–25

Dahlgren, E., Johansson, S., Lindstedt, G. *et al.* (1992a) Women with polycystic ovary syndrome wedge resected in 1956 to 1965: a long-term follow-up focusing on natural history and circulating hormones. *Fertil Steril* **57**, 505–13

Dahlgren, E., Janson, P.O., Johansson, S., Lapidus, L. and Oden, A. (1992b) Polycystic ovary syndrome and risk for myocardial infarction. Evaluated from a risk factor model based on a prospective population study of women. *Acta Obstet Gynecol Scand* **71**, 599–604

Diamanti-Kandarakis, E., Tolis, G. and Duleba, A.J. (1995) Androgens and therapeutic aspects of antiandrogens in women. *J Soc Gynecol Investig* **2**, 577–92

Donesky, B.W. and Adashi, E.Y. (1995) Surgically induced ovulation in the polycystic ovary syndrome: wedge resection revisited in the age of laparoscopy. *Fertil Steril* **63**, 439–63

Dunaif, A. (1997) Insulin resistance and the polycystic ovary syndrome: mechanism and implications for pathogenesis. *Endocr Rev* **18**, 774–800

Dunaif, A., Segal, K.R., Shelley, D.R., Green, G., Dobrjansky, A. and Licholai, T. (1992) Evidence for distinctive and intrinsic defects in insulin action in polycystic ovary syndrome. *Diabetes* **41**, 1257–66

Dunaif, A., Xia, J., Book, C.B., Schenker, E. and Tang, Z. (1995) Excessive insulin receptor serine phosphorylation in cultured fibroblasts and in skeletal muscle. A potential mechanism for insulin resistance in the polycystic ovary syndrome. *J Clin Invest* **96**, 801–10

Dunaif, A., Scott, D., Finegood, D., Quintana, B. and Whitcomb, R. (1996) The insulin-sensitizing agent troglitazone improves metabolic and reproductive abnormalities in the polycystic ovary syndrome. *J Clin Endocrinol Metab* **81**, 3299–306

Hague, W.M., Adams, J., Reeders, S.T., Peto, T.E. and Jacobs, H.S. (1988) Familial polycystic ovaries: a genetic disease? *Clin Endocrinol (Oxf)* **29**, 593–605

Hague, W.M., Honour, J.W., Adams, J., Vecsei, P. and Jacobs, H.S. (1989) Steroid responses to ACTH in women with polycystic ovaries. *Clin Endocrinol (Oxf)* **30**, 355–65

Halaas, J.L. and Friedman, J.M. (1997) Leptin and its receptor. *J Endocrinol* **155**, 215–16

Havel, P.J., Kasim-Karakas, S., Dubuc, G.R., Mueller, W. and Phinney, S.D. (1996) Gender differences in plasma leptin concentrations. *Nat Med* **2**, 949–50

Holte, J. (1996) Disturbances in insulin secretion and sensitivity in women with the polycystic ovary syndrome. *Baillières Clin Endocrinol Metab* **10**, 221–47

Hube, F., Lietz, U., Igel, M. *et al.* (1996) Difference in leptin mRNA levels between omental and subcutaneous abdominal adipose tissue from obese humans. *Horm Metab Res* **28**, 690–3

Karlsson, C., Lindell, K., Svensson, E. *et al.* (1997) Expression of functional leptin receptors in the human ovary. *J Clin Endocrinol Metab* **82**, 4144–8

Kiddy, D.S., Hamilton-Fairley, D., Bush, A. *et al.* (1992) Improvement in endocrine and ovarian function during dietary treatment of obese women with polycystic ovary syndrome. *Clin Endocrinol (Oxf)* **36**, 105–11

Kotani, K., Tokunaga, K., Fujioka, S. *et al.* (1994) Sexual dimorphism of age-related changes in whole-body fat distribution in the obese. *Int J Obes Relat Metab Disord* **18**, 207–12

Laughlin, G.A., Morales, A.J. and Yen, S.S. (1997) Serum leptin levels in women with polycystic ovary syndrome: the role of insulin resistance/hyperinsulinemia. *J Clin Endocrinol Metab* **82**, 1692–6

Legro, R.S., Finegood, D. and Dunaif, A. (1998) A fasting glucose to insulin ratio is a useful measure of insulin sensitivity in women with polycystic ovary syndrome. *J Clin Endocrinol Metabol* **83**, 2694–8

Mantzoros, C.S., Dunaif, A. and Flier, J.S. (1997) Leptin concentrations in the polycystic ovary syndrome. *J Clin Endocrinol Metab* **82**, 1687–91

Nestler, J.E. (1997) Role of hyperinsulinemia in the pathogenesis of the polycystic ovary syndrome, and its clinical implications. *Semin Reprod Endocrinol* **15**, 111–22

Nestler, J.E., Powers, L.P., Matt, D.W. *et al.* (1991) A direct effect of hyperinsulinemia on serum sex hormone-binding globulin levels in obese women with the polycystic ovary syndrome. *J Clin Endocrinol Metab* **72**, 83–9

Nestler, J.E., Jakubowicz, D.J., Reamer, P., Gunn, R.D. and Allan, G. (1999) Ovulatory and metabolic effects of D-chiro-inositol in the polycystic ovary syndrome. *N Engl J Med* **340**, 1314–20

Norman, R.J. and Clark, A.M. (1998) Obesity and reproductive disorders: a review. *Reprod Fertil Dev* **10**, 55–63

Odunsi, K. and Kidd, K.K. (1999) A paradigm for finding genes for a complex human trait: polycystic ovary syndrome and follistatin. *Proc Natl Acad Sci U S A* **96**, 8315–17

Pierpoint, T., McKeigue, P.M., Isaacs, A.J., Wild, S.H. and Jacobs, H.S. (1998) Mortality of women with polycystic ovary syndrome at long-term follow-up. *J Clin Epidemiol* **51**, 581–6

Plymate, S.R., Matej, L.A., Jones, R.E. and Friedl, K.E. (1988) Inhibition of sex hormone-binding globulin production in the human hepatoma (Hep G2) cell line by insulin and prolactin. *J Clin Endocrinol Metab* **67**, 460–4

Polson, D.W., Adams, J., Wadsworth, J. and Franks, S. (1988) Polycystic ovaries – a common finding in normal women. *Lancet* **i**, 870–2

Poretsky, L., Cataldo, N.A., Rosenwaks, Z. and Giudice, L.C. (1999) The insulin-related ovarian regulatory system in health and disease. *Endocr Rev* **20**, 535–82

Reginato, M.J. and Lazar, M.A. (1999) Mechanisms by which thiazolidinediones enhance insulin action. *Trends in Endocrinology and Metabolism* **10**, 9–13

Rohner-Jeanrenaud, F. and Jeanrenaud, B. (1996) Obesity, leptin and the brain. *N Engl J Med* **334**, 324–5

Rosenbaum, M., Nicolson, M., Hirsch, J. *et al.* (1996) Effects of gender, body composition, and menopause on plasma concentrations of leptin. *J Clin Endocrinol Metab* **81**, 3424–7

Rouru, J., Anttila, L., Koskinen, P. *et al.* (1997) Serum leptin concentrations in women with polycystic ovary syndrome *J Clin Endocrinol Metab* **82**, 1697–700

Shoham, Z., Jacobs, H.S. and Insler, V. (1993) Luteinising hormone: its role, mechanism of action, and detrimental effects when hypersecreted during the follicular phase. *Fertil Steril* **59**, 1153–61

Stein, I.F. and Leventhal, M.L. (1935) Amenorrhea associated with bilateral polycystic ovaries. *Am J Obstet Gynecol* **29**, 181–91

Urbanek, M., Legro, R.S., Driscoll, D.A. *et al.* (1999) Thirty-seven candidate genes for polycystic ovary syndrome: strongest evidence for linkage is with follistatin. *Proc Natl Acad Sci U S A* **96**, 8573–8

Wabitsch, M., Blum, W.F., Muche, R. *et al.* (1997) Contribution of androgens to the gender difference in leptin production in obese children and adolescents. *J Clin Invest* **100**, 808–13

White, D.M., Polson, D.W., Kiddy, D. *et al.* (1996) Induction of ovulation with low-dose gonadotropins in polycystic ovary syndrome: an analysis of 109 pregnancies in 225 women. *J Clin Endocrinol Metab* **81**, 3821–4

Wyne, K.L. and Bradshaw, K.D. (1998) Treatment of insulin resistance in polycystic ovary syndrome. *Current Opinion in Endocrinology and Diabetes* **5**, 321–9

Zachow, R.J. and Magoffin, D.A. (1997) Direct intraovarian effects of leptin: impairment of the synergistic action of insulin-like growth factor-I on follicle-stimulating hormone-dependent estradiol-17β production by rat ovarian granulosa cells. *Endocrinology* **138**, 847–50

26

Evidence-based fertility practice

Allan Templeton and Mark Hamilton

Two major influences have shaped the management of infertility in recent years. One has been the effect of evidence-based medicine and the other has been the availability of *in vitro* fertilisation (IVF) and related techniques. Furthermore, there has been an increasing realisation that the outcome of treatment, whatever the clinical diagnosis, is dependent on certain patient characteristics, particularly female age, the occurrence of previous pregnancies and the duration of infertility. These factors also have a major impact in determining background (treatment-independent) pregnancy rates and, hence, the decision when, if at all, it is appropriate to initiate treatment (Templeton and Morris 1998).

At the same time, many aspects of management from donor insemination, through IVF to surrogacy, have attracted their share of controversy, opprobrium and debate, and in several respects continue to challenge current ethical and legal dogma. The development of effective services has not always been helped by a tendency among a few practitioners to invite controversy and court publicity. Despite these difficulties, infertility is now increasingly accepted as a disease process worthy of investigation and treatment, while the management is increasingly seen to be scientifically and medically sound. However, this was not always so.

HISTORICAL PERSPECTIVE

Many early textbooks of gynaecology and infertility are characterised by extensive descriptions of disease processes, usually anatomically based. In contrast, the sections on therapy tended to be vague and brief. Some texts have been more frank than others in their admission of the difficulties in finding effective remedies for sterility. One of the few successful treatments was artificial insemination and, by the 1950s, heterologous artificial insemination was being discussed and presented in a positive light: '. . . the surgeon who undertakes it must do so only after due consideration and a full sense of responsibility' (Baird 1950). However, not all were so ready to accept the practice, even in 1969. In another textbook, another Scottish professor indicated that there were 'No compassionate grounds . . . to envisage this disgusting practice which is legally questionable, ethically unsound and politically dangerous . . . reducing human reproduction to the status of controlled stock breeding' (Donald 1969).

Against a background of essentially ineffective remedies it is perhaps not so surprising that the practice of infertility treatment came to be characterised by unproven, empirical and occasionally harmful remedies. The difficulty that complicated the issue was the occurrence of spontaneous pregnancies, later to be called treatment-independent pregnancies, which characterised all types of infertility, and would occur more or less frequently after any intervention. Modern practitioners are well used to seeing patients with apparent bilateral tubal occlusion or with failed treatment turn up a year or two later in their antenatal clinics. All practitioners could claim successes from all forms of treatment, even the most unlikely or bizarre. It gradually dawned that only randomised studies could demonstrate efficacy or effectiveness, but even here, as will be seen, there were difficulties because of the overwhelming effects on outcome of female age, parity and duration of infertility.

EVIDENCE-BASED FERTILITY TREATMENT

It has been said that evidence-based medicine has ancient origins but remains a young discipline, whose impact is only now being evaluated (Sackett *et al.* 1996). Some have claimed that the randomised controlled trial is the most important development in medicine this century, although the much-quoted streptomycin trial may have had as much to do with the availability of tiny amounts of streptomycin as with an explicit description of the methods of randomisation (Editorial 1998). Whatever the background, it is now evident that we are in the era of unbiased, relevant and reliable assessments in health care, and that the randomised trial has come of age. The issue is, as far as possible, to control bias in assessing the efficacy and value of new treatments (Chalmers 1998).

This approach has served the management of infertility well. The first published randomised studies in the area of infertility were in the late 1960s and early 1970s and were concerned mainly with the use of clomiphene for anovulation and a variety of drug treatments for male infertility (it turned out that clomiphene was good for women and bad for men). However, it was not until the mid-1980s that the number of randomised studies began to increase dramatically (Vandekerckhove *et al.* 1993). Critical appraisal of the available evidence including systematic review and meta-analysis has helped to clarify many aspects of fertility management. For example, drug treatment for male infertility and endometriosis-related infertility is no longer recommended. However, there is still much work to be done and the evidence-based approach has some way to go, not least in the discipline of reproductive medicine.

At present many wrong, or at least unreliable, answers are being generated by randomised studies that are too small, meta-analyses that are inadequate and statistical analyses that are inappropriate. Even large randomised studies can fall foul of selection biases (Peto and Baigent 1998). There is a need to simplify trial design and data collection, as well as the treatment interventions. Two recent studies of laparoscopic ablation of mild endometriosis have drawn different conclusions in relation to treatment outcome, both of which have significant management and resource implications. The interpretation of the data in relation to the management of varicocoele remains controversial and again invites different conclusions. The value of clomiphene in unexplained infertility is still uncertain: it may be marginally beneficial or possibly harmful.

Finally, it has been said that evidence-based medicine is about integrating individual clinical expertise with the best external evidence. The gathering of evidence is not restricted to randomised studies. The accuracy of a diagnostic test will require proper cross-sectional studies. Assessment of prognosis will need proper follow-up of identified and defined cohorts. Not infrequently, the answer to a particular problem will come straight out of basic science (Sackett *et al.* 1996). Furthermore, both physicians and patients need to understand better the implications and outcomes of the various trials. Odds ratios can be unclear to a patient, who may have a better understanding if she is told how many patients need to be treated to achieve a pregnancy (the NNT or 'number needed to treat' approach).

The next section is based on evidence and makes clinical recommendations for practice in that light.

CURRENT STATUS OF EVIDENCE-BASED FERTILITY PRACTICE

In this section, initially in the context of the preliminary assessment of the infertile couple and subsequently for the management of specific diagnostic categories of infertility, a critically appraised, relevant and contemporary fertility practice will be presented. In keeping with the evidence-based background of this chapter, the recommendations will be graded according to the level of evidence upon which they are based. The grading used here was formulated by the Clinical Outcomes Group of the National Health Service Executive and has been used in all RCOG Guidelines and Study Groups in recent years (Table 1).

Initial assessment of the infertile couple

Referral

In counselling couples experiencing difficulty in achieving pregnancy, account must be taken of what is a realistic expectation of fertility in normal circumstances. Sound epidemiological data would suggest that conception should occur in 75% of women within 12 months of ceasing contraception and in 90% within two years. Thus, it would seem reasonable to define infertility as failure to conceive after at least two years of unprotected intercourse. While this may be based on robust epidemiological principles, there may be particular pressures which, in individual cases, lead to couples seeking advice before two years has elapsed.

The role of the general practitioner (GP) cannot be overemphasised. As a matter of good practice patients should be seen as couples, in appropriate surroundings. Facilities should be made available to permit examination, if appropriate of both male and female, and with sufficient time (usually half an hour) set aside to make an adequate overall assessment of the problem. It is advisable that agreed local guidelines for GP management and referral of couples should be put in place (grade A evidence). There is

Table 1 *Grading of recommendations*

Grade	Recommendation
A	Requires at least one randomised controlled trial as part of the body of literature of overall good quality and consistency addressing the specific recommendation.
B	Requires availability of well-conducted clinical studies but no randomised clinical trials on the topic of recommendation
C	Requires evidence from expert committee reports or opinions and/or clinical experience of respected authorities. Indicates absence of directly applicable studies of good quality

good evidence from a prospective study that where guidelines for appropriate initial assessment in, and referral from, the primary care setting are used, benefits to patient care accrue (Emslie *et al.* 1993).

General advice

Good practice should dictate that, in line with recommendations from the Department of Health (1996), the rubella status of the female partner be checked and, if seronegative, rubella vaccination offered (grade C evidence). Randomised double-blind studies have shown that folic acid supplementation should be recommended (grade A evidence) at a dose of 0.4 mg daily to prevent neural tube defects. The dose should be increased to 4 mg daily in women who have previously given birth to a child with neural tube defects or who have epilepsy and are taking medication (MRC Vitamin Study Research Group 1991). Both women (grade B evidence) and men (grade C evidence) who have problems conceiving should be advised to stop smoking since there is evidence that smoking, as well as being detrimental to health generally, in women reduces fecundity, increases the risk of miscarriage and diminishes the chances of success where assisted conception is required (Hughes and Brennan 1996; RCOG 1997a). A safe amount of alcohol consumption has not yet been determined in couples attempting to conceive but published guidelines would suggest that women should avoid intoxication and drink no more than two units once or twice per week (grade C evidence) (Health Education Authority 1996).

It is recognised that obesity and disturbances of ovulation are often related and, even in ovulatory women, pregnancy rates are reduced both in natural cycles as well as after ovulation induction and IVF. Several randomised studies have shown that weight loss is an important facet of management in women with ovulatory dysfunction (Clark *et al.* 1995) and thus, as a routine, body mass index (BMI) should be calculated in the female partner and a weight-loss programme advised for any woman with a BMI in excess of 30 kg/m^2 (grade A evidence). In contrast, there would appear to be no evidence that obesity *per se* reduces fertility in men, although weight loss in already overweight men will improve general health (grade C evidence) (Garrow 1991).

Testicular hyperthermia may be detrimental to sperm quality and measures to ensure that high scrotal temperatures are avoided can be encouraged (RCOG 1997b), particularly in those individuals who have sub-optimal semen quality (grade B evidence). The use of basal body temperature charts and LH detection kits have not been shown to increase conception rates in infertile couples (grade C evidence). Temperature charts are unreliable in predicting ovulation, kits are expensive and their use may add to the psychological stress which infertile couples already face. Rather, regular intercourse should be encouraged throughout the cycle (grade C evidence) which should ensure that intercourse occurs during the fertile period.

Initial investigations

The ability of a semen analysis to identify the potentially fertile male remains poor. The results of conventional semen analysis do not quantify the number of sperm which have the capacity to fertilise eggs but do provide information on their number, motility and morphology compared with the range of values to be found in normal healthy men. While it has been suggested that a single sample may be sufficient for assessment where the result is normal, in a significant number of cases, analysis of a second specimen will reveal an abnormality (Oehninger 1995). Thus the World Health Organization recommends that, apart from the case where a man may have small-volume testicles and azoospermia, all men should provide two specimens for analysis (grade C evidence). The laboratory to which the specimen is sent by the GP should ideally be the same laboratory that serves the regional fertility clinic and should develop internal quality-control mechanisms and belong to an external quality-control scheme (grade C evidence). In addition, authoritative sources (Barratt 1995) suggest that laboratories reporting results of semen analysis should establish normal ranges for their own populations and report these on the results sheets issued (grade C evidence).

Existing published guidelines suggest that ovulation in the female should be confirmed by measurement of luteal-phase progesterone (grade B evidence) seven days prior to the onset of the expected next menstrual period, even where the menstrual cycle is regular (RCOG 1992). Some debate exists as to the level of progesterone indicative of ovulation but a single value in excess of 30 nmol/l is satisfactory. Levels below this merit further evaluation. Other endocrine tests such as thyroid function and prolactin are unnecessary where the woman has a regular cycle (grade B evidence), unless there are symptoms suggestive of thyroid disease or galactorrhoea is present.

Assessment in the referral centre

Setting

In the hospital setting, infertile couples should be managed at a dedicated clinic (grade C evidence) where the necessary support staff, including nursing, laboratory and counselling personnel, are readily available, to best provide an integrated efficient service. GPs should endeavour to refer patients to such a clinic and patients should request that they be referred to such a clinic. Further management will require close liaison between the clinic and the GP, who should remain closely involved in the couples' continued care.

Further investigations

The female partner should normally have a test of tubal patency at this stage. In many instances, abnormal findings may be encountered in the absence of any suggestive features in the history. In a population where the prevalence of tubal infertility is likely to be low the most appropriate screening test is the hysterosalpingogram (HSG) (grade B evidence). A normal result in this case will virtually exclude the possibility of tubal blockage (Swart *et al.* 1995). However, an abnormal result may, in a low-risk population, be a false positive and this would require verification through laparoscopic evaluation of the pelvis. In women with abnormal physical findings on pelvic examination the chance of tubal blockage will be higher. For these women laparoscopy with dye hydrotubation will be the screening test of choice (grade B evidence) since the HSG may have a high false-negative rate in this group.

It is well recognised that chlamydial infection can lead to tubal-factor infertility, increased risk of ectopic pregnancies and pelvic pain. Since uterine instrumentation can lead to ascending chlamydial infection in the upper genital tract, at-risk infertile women should be screened for *Chlamydia trachomatis* (grade C evidence). Good evidence exists that appropriately targeted antibiotic therapy can reduce infection rates following termination of pregnancy (Templeton 1996). While the population of couples seeking treatment for infertility can be regarded as being at low risk of chlamydia infection, it would be most unfortunate if their fertility status were to be further compromised through acquiring iatrogenic pelvic sepsis, such as might be consequent upon hysterosalpingography, laparoscopy and dye, hysteroscopy or intrauterine insemination (IUI). If chlamydia is detected, treatment with doxycycline 100 mg orally twice a day for seven days or azithromycin 1 g as a single dose have been shown to be effective in achieving a microbiological cure (grade B evidence). Furthermore, sexual partners of screened-positive women should be traced and treated (grade C evidence).

Tests which should not be employed on a routine basis include:

(1) Endometrial biopsy to evaluate the luteal phase (grade B evidence);
(2) The postcoital test (grade B evidence);
(3) Sperm function tests (grade C evidence);
(4) Antisperm antibodies (grade C evidence);
(5) Hysteroscopy (grade C evidence);
(6) Endometrial ultrasound (grade C evidence).

Some of these tests may be of use in special cases in predicting fertility. Their use and interpretation should be restricted to the few centres with relevant expertise (grade C evidence) (RCOG 1997c).

Evidence-based specialist care

Delay in initiating investigations, giving an informed prognosis and instituting appropriate treatment are sources of considerable frustration and disappointment for infertile couples. Through close liaison between referring practitioners and the specialist clinic rapid and efficient patient management can be established to the benefit of all. The next section deals with management issues in respect of specific diagnostic categories. Space does not permit an exhaustive review but some key points are highlighted.

Male infertility

A number of prognostic factors have been shown to be of importance in advising infertile couples of their chances of spontaneous conception (Collins *et al.* 1995). These include the duration of infertility, the age of the female partner and history of any previous pregnancies (grade B evidence). Where male factors, other than azoospermia or extreme oligozoospermia, are identified, these should be taken into account in giving advice. Men with abnormal semen counts are at greater risk of having genital pathology, occasionally of a serious nature. It is good practice to examine males with suboptimal semen parameters (grade C evidence), although it should be borne in mind that the findings may not be predictive of fertility outcome (Honig *et al.* 1994).

Endocrine disorders are infrequent causes of male infertility. Azoospermia may be associated with testicular failure or obstruction. Measurement of serum follicle-stimulating hormone (FSH) may be helpful in discriminating between these causes although, even where the FSH levels are found to be high, islands of spermatogenesis may be found in the testis (Tournaye *et al.* 1997). If there are signs of androgen deficiency, measurement of prolactin and testosterone will be necessary (grade C evidence). In the rare cases of hypogonadotrophic hypogonadism the use of gonadotrophin drugs is an effective fertility treatment (grade B evidence) (Finkel *et al.* 1985). Occasionally, hyperprolactinaemia may be associated with testicular failure and dopamine agonists are effective in such cases. Where high prolactin levels are found in association with oligozoospermia no improvement in semen quality results with treatment, although sexual function, if impaired, may be enhanced (grade A evidence) (Vandekerckhove *et al.* 1998).

Testicular biopsy may be helpful in determining the cause of azoospermia but it has largely been superseded by the use of FSH measurement. Expert opinion would favour combining any such surgical procedures with attempts to retrieve and store sperm (grade C evidence), since there have been reported instances of postoperative testicular compromise which would make future attempts at sperm retrieval less likely to succeed (Schlegel and Su 1997). Thus, it is recommended that surgery on the male genital tract should be carried out only in centres where there are appropriate facilities and trained staff (grade C evidence). Surgical options in other facets of male infertility include vasectomy reversal, which would appear to be more cost effective than initial surgical sperm retrieval and subsequent IVF with intracytoplasmic sperm injection (ICSI) (grade B evidence) (Pavlovich and Schlegel 1997). ICSI should be reserved for failed reversal cases or those cases not amenable to surgery. The role of varicocoele in the genesis of male factor infertility has been controversial. However, a recent systematic review of the literature does not support varicocoele ligation as either an effective prophylaxis against, or treatment for, infertility (grade A evidence) (Evers 1998).

While treatment of infection of the male genital tract accessory glands would seem intuitively to be a wise course of action, there is no evidence that this will improve fertility (grade A evidence). Similarly, empirical treatment of infertile men with antibiotics confers no clinical benefit in terms of pregnancy rates. Other pharmacological interventions which have, as yet, no scientific basis to justify their use in men with seminal fluid abnormalities include the use of anti-oestrogens, androgens, bromocriptine and kinin-enhancing drugs (grade A evidence). Further trials in this area will be helpful. The use of systemic steroids in cases of antisperm antibodies has not been shown to be beneficial in randomised studies (grade C evidence). The potentially serious adverse effects of treatment, together with the advances in assisted conception technology, render this an area of research interest only. Large clinical trials are now unlikely to be carried out in this area (RCOG 1998a).

Systematic review (Cohlen 1998) has demonstrated that IUI in natural and stimulated cycles is more effective than timed intercourse in couples with male-factor infertility although the cycle fecundity remains low (grade A evidence). An alternative option of IVF may be more beneficial, although a randomised trial comparing the cost effectiveness of IUI with or without controlled ovarian stimulation remains to be carried out.

Disorders of ovulation

As a general principle, strategies for successful treatment of ovulatory dysfunction centre around precise diagnosis and delivery of care, minimising the significant risks of multiple pregnancy and ovarian hyperstimulation. These risks should be explained at the outset of treatment (grade C evidence).

The use of clomiphene in appropriately selected women is an effective form of treatment (RCOG 1998b) and, although the Committee on Safety of Medicines has recommended that a maximum of six cycles should be offered, there remains no conclusive evidence to suggest that prolonged use may lead to an increased risk of ovarian cancer in women with up to twelve cycles of clomiphene treatment (grade B evidence). Thus, most practitioners would allow between nine and a maximum of twelve cycles of clomiphene treatment before switching to more complex forms of therapy. In view of the observed increased risk of multiple pregnancy with anti-oestrogen treatment, it is recommended that access to ovarian ultrasound should be available in the first cycle of treatment, in order to allow identification of women at risk through multiple follicular development (grade C evidence). In women with polycystic ovarian syndrome (PCOS) who fail to respond to clomiphene, gonadotrophins are effective second-line drugs (grade A evidence) (Hughes *et al.* 1998a). As yet, there is no convincing evidence to suggest a cost effectiveness advantage in using recombinant FSH over urinary-derived gonadotrophins. The use of adjunctive gonadotrophin-releasing analogues should not be routinely advocated in such women, since pregnancy rates are no better and the incidence of ovarian hyperstimulation may be increased (grade A evidence). The putative risks of ovarian cancer associated with ovulation induction therapy should be explained to all patients (grade C evidence) undertaking treatment, although there is, as yet, no convincing evidence to suggest a link. What is clear, however, is the fact that infertile women who conceive as a result of treatment will reduce their lifetime risk of ovarian cancer. Women may thus conclude that the potential risks of treatment are far outweighed by the chances of conceiving and overcoming their infertility.

Ovarian drilling, either with a laser or with diathermy, is an alternative to gonadotrophins in clomiphene-resistant PCOS (grade A evidence) (Gadir *et al.* 1990). As yet, no trial has been performed comparing laser with diathermy but multiple ovulation rates may be lower with either method. Surgical techniques such as this require high levels of skill and should only be carried out by appropriately trained individuals (grade C evidence).

Hypothalamic anovulation responds well to pulsatile gonadotrophin-releasing hormone treatment (grade B evidence) (Filicori *et al.* 1994). In many cases, such individuals will be underweight. If, through dietary measures, a normal BMI can be achieved, ovulation may resume spontaneously. Women with hyperprolactinaemia-associated anovulation respond well to treatment with dopamine agonists (grade B evidence). Newer preparations with longer biological half-lives than bromocriptine have recently been introduced (Webster *et al.* 1994) and there is evidence that these may be more effective and better tolerated.

Tubal factor

The role of surgery in tubal-factor infertility requires careful evaluation. Patient selection is critical in determining prognosis and factors such as female age and the presence or not of other infertility factors should be taken into account in choosing appropriate management. In common with other high-level fertility treatment, such procedures should only be carried out by highly trained practitioners, with access to appropriate equipment (grade C evidence), including an operating microscope, and in a facility where there is sufficient throughput of patients to maintain a high level of expertise. Isolated proximal tubal obstruction is an infrequent phenomenon but where it is found there is reasonably robust evidence to suggest that selective salpingography and tubal catheterisation is as effective, and potentially less expensive, than surgery or IVF (grade B evidence) (RCOG 1998c). Both simple and complex systems are available to access and attempt to recanalise the cornual portion of the fallopian tube. Where tubal damage is found beyond the cornua the chance of success with surgery is dependent on the degree of tubal damage. Mild distal tubal disease, or cases with filmy peritubal adhesions, may be more effectively treated with surgery than with IVF (Hull and Fleming 1995). If conception has not occurred within 12 months of surgery, IVF should be considered (grade B evidence) (Winston and Margara 1991). There is no evidence to suggest that outcomes are improved through laparoscopic approaches to surgery (grade B evidence) although length of hospital stay and perioperative morbidity may be less. Tubal reanastomosis is without doubt the treatment of choice for women who seek reversal of sterilisation and the best results will be achieved using a microsurgical approach (grade B evidence) (RCOG 1998c). In cases of moderate or severe tubal disease, IVF is the treatment of choice (grade B evidence). Hydrosalpinges have been shown to be associated with reduced embryo implantation rates in IVF (Nackley and Muasher 1998). There is uncertainty at present as to whether removal of the tubes will enhance pregnancy rates with IVF (grade B evidence).

Unexplained infertility

In common with other infertility diagnostic categories the decision to offer treatment in unexplained infertility will depend on the woman's age, the duration of infertility and her past obstetric history (grade B evidence). Spontaneous pregnancy rates through expectant management do not significantly deteriorate until beyond three years of trying. Thus, empirical treatment should not usually be considered until this time (grade C evidence) although, in some cases, where for example female age is greater than 35 years, earlier recourse to intervention may be appropriate.

Empirical treatment options include the use of clomiphene, although there is little evidence to suggest that it has anything other than a marginal effect on fecundity (grade A evidence) (Hughes *et al.* 1998b). Danazol and bromocriptine have no role in the management of unexplained infertility (grade A evidence). Gonadotrophin stimulation combined with timed IUI has been subject to exhaustive systematic review (Hughes 1997) and current evidence would suggest that conception rates are five times higher using this treatment (grade A evidence). However, if an additional male factor is identified, or the female has endometriosis, the benefits of treatment may be less obvious. Gamete intrafallopian transfer is effective in the management of unexplained infertility (grade A evidence) but IVF may be a more desirable choice of treatment (grade C evidence) since it is just as effective and avoids the need for laparoscopy and general anaesthesia. In addition, potentially useful additional information concerning fertilisation may be provided, which may be of help in making an informed decision about future management (RCOG 1998d).

FUTURE DEVELOPMENTS

Clinical trials

It is now timely to develop a new approach to the organisation of clinical trials in the field of infertility. Future studies must be well constructed, methodologically sound and attempt to answer key questions in management. Now that evidence-based practice has come of age in the area of reproductive medicine, the next step is to address how these trials might be put in place. Firstly, there is a need for professional and educational initiatives aimed at greater acceptance of the need for large trials, which will inevitably be multicentre. Secondly, the trials themselves must be of sufficient size and power to assess clearly defined outcomes. They will have to be simple in design, including entry criteria, require minimal data collection and be both flexible and pragmatic. They must be aimed at answering one clear and important question. No one trial is going to answer all the questions relevant to the management of a particular problem, but a clear result will at least inform future discussion. There is optimism about the possibility of developing this approach in the UK. Already the Nordic countries have demonstrated feasibility in this respect. Inevitably, the funding of such trials will be an issue but should not inhibit the approach. The more methodologically sound the trial, the more likely it is to attract Research Council and NHS funding. Pharmaceutical company funding is also important, particularly for pilot work, but direct pharmaceutical involvement may compromise interpretation and creditability of outcomes, as has been seen with recent trials of recombinant gonadotrophin hormones.

The initiative should be taken by the professional societies acting in collaboration with academic centres and well-organised clinics.

In vitro fertilisation

IVF is now accepted as an effective treatment for most forms of infertility, although there is a need for greater clarity and understanding of the situations where IVF is less effective or ineffective. Follow-up studies will no doubt attest to its continuing safety, while the additional risks, if any, of malformation or genetic problems in the next generation, particularly with ICSI treatment, will be quantified by studies currently under way.

However the major contributor to morbidity in children born as a result of IVF is multiple pregnancy and particularly high-order multiple birth. This problem could be diminished or even avoided by a general move to one- and two-embryo replacement. This will inevitably happen, although some countries may be slower than others to move in this direction. It is to be hoped that the UK will not be among these. Once again the lead in Europe has been provided by the Nordic countries. A reduction in the number of embryos replaced will be facilitated by a greater understanding that more embryos do not always mean higher pregnancy rates, but do inevitably mean higher multiple rates. Further developments that may contribute to the avoidance of this problem will include blastocyst culture and transfer and improved chromosome screening of individual embryos using multiple-probe analyses. In due course, it may be possible to screen all available embryos reliably to detect those which are chromosomally abnormal or have limited developmental competence. However, this latter area is yet to be fully evaluated and there are inevitably a number of wider implications, including genetic, resource and ethical issues.

Current work on the cryopreservation of ovarian tissue, including follicles and oocytes, will no doubt be fruitful and increase treatment options in due course. However, the best hope for improving the outcome of IVF treatment will derive from study of the factors inhibiting the implantation of the embryo. This is the step at which most IVF cycles fail and it appears that in many situations the uterus is unreceptive to implantation, no matter how many embryos are returned. Current work at the tissue and molecular levels may indicate avenues for intervention, which can then be tested clinically.

Prevention of infertility

It is likely that the future will see much more emphasis on the prevention of infertility. Awareness of the importance of screening for chlamydial infection of the lower genital tract is growing rapidly in the UK. It is now apparent that upper-tract infection with chlamydia is the major preventable cause of infertility in women, and possibly also in men, although much more work is needed in the male.

Putatively falling sperm counts have received even more publicity, with the speculation that environmental effects, including certain toxins as well as phyto- and xeno-oestrogens may be responsible for deficiencies in male reproductive tract development, including spermatogenesis. Furthermore, intrauterine influences on reproduction extend to include other developmental factors. The relative contributions of genetic, nutritional and environmental factors on reproduction will continue to distract scientists and funding bodies for some time to come.

SUMMARY AND CONCLUSIONS

The development of an evidence-based approach to infertility has improved management. It has helped rationalise many aspects of treatment and this has benefited patients enormously. At the same time it has made the specialty more attractive to serious-minded clinicians and scientists. IVF has developed into a highly effective treatment, which is likely to become even more effective in the light of a number of current developments and particularly if the physiology of implantation is better understood. However, it should not be forgotten that IVF does not overcome the problem, it merely bypasses it and, in the coming years, there must be much more focus on prevention, as well as understanding the pathophysiology of infertility.

References

Baird, D. (1950) 'Sterility' in: D. Baird (Ed.) *Combined Textbook of Obstetrics and Gynaecology*, pp. 1250–81. Edinburgh: Livingstone

Barratt, C.L.R. (1995) On the accuracy and clinical value of semen laboratory tests. *Hum Reprod* **10**, 250–2

Chalmers, I. (1998) Unbiased, relevant, and reliable assessments in health care. *BMJ* **317**, 1167–8

Clark, A.M., Ledger, W., Galletly, C. *et al.* (1995) Weight loss results in significant improvement in pregnancy and ovulation rates in anovulatory obese women. *Hum Reprod* **10**, 2705–12

Cohlen, B.J. (1998) 'Intrauterine insemination and controlled ovarian hyperstimulation' in: A. Templeton, I.D. Cooke and P.M.S. O'Brien (Eds) *Evidence-based Fertility Treatment*, pp. 205–16. London: RCOG Press

Collins, J.A., Burrows, E.A. and Willan, A.R. (1995) The prognosis for live birth among untreated infertile couples. *Fertil Steril* **64**, 22–8

Department of Health (1996) *Immunisation Against Infectious Diseases*, pp. 68–75. London: HMSO

Donald, I. (1969) 'Rh factor' in: I. Donald (Ed.) *Practical Obstetric Problems*, pp. 902–27. London: Lloyd-Luke

Editor's choice (1998) Fifty years of randomised controlled trials. *eBMJ* **317**, 31 October 1998 (available online only at: http://www.bmj.com)

Emslie, C., Grimshaw, J. and Templeton, A. (1993) Do clinical guidelines improve general practice management and referral of infertile couples? *BMJ* **306**, 1728–31

Evers, J.L.H. (1998) 'Varicocele' in: A. Templeton, I.D. Cooke and P.M.S. O'Brien (Eds) *Evidence-based Fertility Treatment*, pp. 109–19. London: RCOG Press

Filicori, M., Flamigni, C., Dellai, P. *et al.* (1994) Treatment of anovulation with pulsatile gonadotropin-releasing hormone: prognostic factors and clinical results in 600 cycles. *J Clin Endocrinol Metab* **79**, 1215–20

Finkel, D.M., Phillips, J.L. and Snyder, P.J. (1985) Stimulation of spermatogenesis by gonadotropins in men with hypogonadotrophic hypogonadism. *N Engl J Med* **313**, 651–5

Gadir, A., Mowafi, R., Alnaser, H. *et al.* (1990) Ovarian electrocautery versus human menopausal gonadotrophins and pure follicle stimulating hormone therapy in the treatment of patients with polycystic ovarian disease. *Clin Endocrinol (Oxf)* **33**, 585–92

Garrow, J.S. (1991) Treating obesity. *BMJ* **302**, 803–4

Health Education Authority (1996) *Think About Drink – There's More to a Drink Than You Think*. London: HEA

Honig, S.C., Lipshultz, L.I. and Jarow, J. (1994) Significant medical pathology uncovered by a comprehensive male infertility evaluation. *Fertil Steril* **62**, 1028–34

Hughes, E.G. (1997) The effectiveness of ovulation induction and intrauterine insemination in the treatment of persistent infertility: a meta-analysis. *Hum Reprod* **12**, 1865–72

Hughes, E.G. and Brennan, B.G. (1996) Does cigarette smoking impair natural or assisted fecundity? *Fertil Steril* **66**, 679–89

Hughes, E., Collins, J. and Vandekerckhove, P. (1998a) Ovulation induction with urinary follicle stimulating hormone versus human menopausal gonadotrophin for clomiphene resistant polycystic ovary syndrome (Cochrane Review). *The Cochrane Library*, Issue 2. Oxford: Update Software

Hughes, E., Collins, J. and Vandekerckhove, P. (1998b) Clomiphene citrate versus placebo or no treatment in unexplained infertility (Cochrane Review). *The Cochrane Library*, Issue 2. Oxford: Update Software

Hull, M.G. and Fleming, C.F. (1995) Tubal surgery versus assisted reproduction: assessing their role in infertility therapy. *Curr Opin Obstet Gynaecol* **7**, 160–7

MRC Vitamin Study Research Group (1991) Prevention of neural tube defects: results of the Medical Research Council Vitamin Study. *Lancet* **338**, 131–7

Nackley, A.C. and Muasher, S.J. (1998) The significance of hydrosalpinx in *in vitro* fertilisation. *Fertil Steril* **69**, 373–84

Oehninger, S. (1995) An update on the laboratory assessment of infertility. *Hum Reprod* **10**, 38–43

Pavlovich, C.P. and Schlegel, P.N. (1997) Fertility options after vasectomy: a cost effectiveness analysis. *Fertil Steril* **67**, 133–41

Peto, R. and Baigent, C. (1998) Trials: the next 50 years. *BMJ* **317**, 1170–1

RCOG (1992) *Infertility – Guidelines for Practice*. London: RCOG Press

RCOG (1997a) *The Initial Investigation and Management of the Infertile Couple*, pp. 26–7. London: RCOG Press (Evidence-based Clinical Guidelines No. 2)

RCOG (1997b) *The Initial Investigation and Management of the Infertile Couple*, pp. 57–77. London: RCOG Press (Evidence-based Clinical Guidelines No. 2)

RCOG (1997c) *The Initial Investigation and Management of the Infertile Couple*, pp. 36–7. London: RCOG Press (Evidence-based Clinical Guidelines No. 2)

RCOG (1998a) *The Management of the Infertility in Secondary Care*, pp. 44–57. London: RCOG Press (Evidence-based Clinical Guidelines No. 3)

RCOG (1998b) *The Management of the Infertility in Secondary Care*, pp. 65–9. London: RCOG Press (Evidence-based Clinical Guidelines No. 3)

RCOG (1998c) *The Management of the Infertility in Secondary Care*, pp. 90–1. London: RCOG Press (Evidence-based Clinical Guidelines No. 3)

RCOG (1998d) *The Management of the Infertility in Secondary Care*, pp. 146–8. London: RCOG Press (Evidence-based Clinical Guidelines No. 3)

Sackett, D.L., Rosenberg, W.M.C., Gray, J.A.M., Haynes, R.B. and Richardson, W.S. (1996) Evidence-based medicine: what it is and what it isn't. *BMJ* **312**, 71–2

Schlegel, P.N. and Su, L.M. (1997) Physiological consequences of testicular sperm extraction. *Hum Reprod* **12**, 1688–92

Swart, P., Mol, B.W.J., van der Veen, F. *et al.* (1995) The accuracy of hysterosalpingo-graphy in the diagnosis of tubal pathology: a meta-analysis. *Fertil Steril* **64**, 486–91

Templeton, A. (Ed.) (1996) *The Prevention of Pelvic Infection*. London: RCOG Press

Templeton, A. and Morris, J.K. (1998) '*In vitro* fertilisation: factors affecting outcome' in: A. Templeton, I. Cooke and P.M.S. O'Brien (Eds) *Evidence-based Fertility Treatment*, pp. 265–73. London: RCOG Press

Tournaye, H., Verheyen, G., Nagy, P. *et al.* (1997) Are there any predictive factors for successful testicular sperm recovery in azoospermic patients? *Hum Reprod* **12**, 80–6

Vandekerckhove, P., O'Donovan, P.A., Lilford, R.J. and Harada, T.W. (1993) Infertility treatment: from cookery to science. The epidemiology of randomised controlled trials. *Br J Obstet Gynaecol* **100**, 1005–36

Vanderkerckhove, P., Lilford, R. and Hughes, E. (1998) The medical treatment of idiopathic oligo/asthenospermia: bromocriptine versus placebo or no treatment (Cochrane Review). *The Cochrane Library*, Issue 2. Oxford: Update Software

Webster, J., Piscitelli, G., Polli, A. *et al.* (1994) A comparison of cabergoline and bromocriptine in the treatment of hyperprolactinaemic amenorrhoea. *N Engl J Med* **331**, 904–9

Winston, R.M. and Margara, R.A. (1991) Microsurgical salpingostomy is not an obsolete procedure. *Br J Obstet Gynaecol* **98**, 637–42

27

Endometriosis

Eric J. Thomas and R. William Stones

HISTORY

Endometriosis has intrigued both clinicians and scientists since it was first reported in the middle of the 19th century (Rokitansky 1980). The late 19th and early 20th centuries saw a number of case reports and discussions that mostly concluded that the disease resulted from peritoneal metaplasia. The classic papers from Sampson in the 1920s (Sampson 1921) first established that implantation of refluxed endometrium could be the likely mechanism and debate has continued between the two main theories ever since. Overall, the balance of probabilities is that implantation is the mechanism of pathogenesis for most endometriosis. There are epidemiological links with degree of exposure to menstruation. The most common sites of pelvic endometriosis can be mapped to the route of tubal menstrual outflow, refluxed menstruum is vital and can be cultured and there are considerable morphological and functional similarities between eutopic and ectopic endometrium both *in vitro* and *in vivo* (Matthews *et al.* 1992). However, implantation cannot explain all cases especially those where there is endometriosis without endometrium being present.

It is clear that menstrual reflux occurs in all women, yet endometriosis does not. Reasearch has attempted to explain this over the last 20 years. It has become increasingly obvious that some implantation of refluxed endometrium occurs to all women but that in most it is a self-limiting phenomenon. Intellectually, the explanations for progress of implantation to established disease in some women must revolve around whether there are abnormalities of proliferation in the refluxed endometrium or that immune surveillance is inadequate. Numerous papers have shown immune abnormalities in women with endometriosis but it is impossible to say whether these are causal or epiphenomena resulting from the inflammatory state the disease precipitates (Hill 1997). There are recent reports showing cytogenetic abnormalities (Shin *et al.* 1997) and molecular genetic damage in endometriosis similar to that which normally occurs in neoplastic disease, suggesting that there is tumour-suppressor gene inactivation which may lead to abnormal proliferation (Jiang *et al.* 1996). While these questions remain unanswered, it is clear that in the establishment of endometriosis there is profound angiogenesis (McLaren *et al.* 1996) and release of cytokines and inflammatory mediators (Pellicer *et al.* 1998) which cause the pain and damage that are closely associated with the disease.

Perhaps the biggest impact on our understanding and treatment of endometriosis over the past 25 years has been the introduction of laparoscopy. This technique provides simple access to the pelvis in both symptomatic and asymptomatic patients. Observations made by laparoscopy have changed the definition of the disease from the classic cysts and blue-brown spots to one which encompasses clear blister-like lesions, haemorraghic and peticheal areas, scarring and peritoneal defects (Jansen and Russell 1986) and even microscopic lesions present in apparently normal peritoneum. We now appreciate that there is an evolution of the disease from the clear and red lesions, through the blue-brown lesions to scarring. However, this has caused difficulties with what represents disease which needs to be treated and when and this will be addressed later in the chapter. The lack of understanding and clarity over treatment algorithms has led to over-treatment of the disease and clinicians are now becoming aware that they need to individualise treatment to each patient. Sufferers are, quite rightly, demanding more involvement in decisions about their treatment as part of the changing social relationship between doctors and patients.

CURRENT STATUS

What to treat?

It may seem surprising in the context of a pathologically well-characterised disease to address the question of what is to be treated. However, real gaps remain in our understanding of the significance of endometriosis in asymptomatic women, those with pain and those with infertility.

Asymptomatic endometriosis

The most likely setting for the detection of asymptomatic endometriosis is at laparoscopic sterilisation. The prevalence in a multiparous group has been identified as 26 in 3384 (3.7%), although endometriosis was minimal in the majority of cases (Sangi-Haghpeykar and Poindexter 1995). Rather than the simple prevalence, the key questions are whether those with 'asymptomatic' disease do prove on closer questioning to have symptoms not present in women without endometriosis and whether they are at risk of developing new symptoms in the longer term. The above study compared 504 negative controls randomly selected from the sterilisation group for a case–control analysis and found those with asymptomatic endometriosis to have a similar profile to that expected for women with symptomatic disease, that is cycle characteristics associated with increased exposure to menstruation. Another case–control study used 522 women admitted as acute emergencies as controls and compared them with 129 women with various stages of endometriosis (Parazzini *et al.* 1995). Factors significantly associated with a reduced risk of endometriosis were an irregular menstrual cycle, two or more births and one or more induced abortions.

These studies do not provide an evidence base from which to recommend treatment of truly asymptomatic disease. Data are required from longitudinal studies but the only longitudinal data are derived from the placebo arms of studies of treatment for endometriosis associated with infertility, where there is evidence of disease progression (Thomas and Cooke 1987a). In the current state of knowledge, it is debatable whether or not to treat incidentally diagnosed endometriosis. A subgroup of asymptomatic patients will present with an adnexal mass and the indications for further investigation and treatment are to prevent the occurrence of cyst complications and, in older women, to exclude ovarian malignancy.

Endometriosis and pain

In women with pain associated with endometriosis, it is essential to be clear as to what is being treated, whether the aim of therapy is symptom relief, disease suppression or both.

Until recently, research studies of endometriosis treatment were focused on 'objective' parameters with end-points such as resolution of deposits seen at second-look laparoscopy, to the neglect of 'subjective' considerations such as pain relief. More recently, pain control in endometriosis has, appropriately, assumed a higher profile in the literature. The medical tendency to deploy psychological explanations when the extent of disease does not obviously correlate with the symptom profile can be unhelpful and is often resented by patients (Ballweg 1995). Pain is, by definition, a subjective experience and the patient's description of their symptoms needs to be taken seriously.

The conundrum of a poor correlation between symptoms and extent of disease seen at laparoscopy remains. However, some careful clinicopathological studies have pointed the way forward. A systematic investigation of the relationship between symptoms in endometriosis and the depth of implantation, the activity of implants and whether implanted endometriosis was in phase with the endometrium was undertaken by Cornillie et al. (1990). In this study, nerve fibres could usually be identified in specimens of deeply invading endometriosis. Pain was present in 17% of those with deposits invading less than 2 mm, 53% of those with 2–4 mm deposits, 37% of those with 5–10 mm deposits and all six women with deep deposits of more than 10 mm.

A second study (Koninckx et al. 1991) of histological findings in relation to symptoms showed that depth of infiltration of endometriosis was the clearest discriminator for pelvic pain compared with other variables describing the lesions that could be included in staging schemes. Depth of infiltration is not a factor in the revised American Fertility Society scoring system, highlighting the limitations of this system where pain is the main complaint. This larger study again showed a preponderance of pain symptoms in women from whom specimens showed deeply infiltrating endometriosis, but the relationship was not total in that the majority of women with pain alone or both pain and infertility had lesions invading 6 mm or less. There is clearly more to be discovered about the importance of the anatomical relations for pain generation.

Pain symptoms associated with endometriosis may include dysmenorrhoea, pelvic pain at other times in the cycle and dyspareunia. These are, of course, common symptoms in women who do not have endometriosis and the assumption of a causal relationship may be inappropriate. With regard to dysmenorrhoea, a case–control study with two different control groups showed odds ratios for dysmenorrhoea in those with laparoscopically proven endometriosis to be 2.5 (95% CI 1.2–6.0) and 2.3 (95% CI 1.1–5.3) (Darrow et al. 1993). A large study including 598 women undergoing laparoscopic sterilisation and those undergoing diagnostic laparoscopy for pain (156), infertility (312) or hysterectomy (134) reported dysmenorrhoea to be the most common symptom in those with endometriosis (Mahmood et al. 1993). Dysmenorrhoea may be an especially important symptom in younger women presenting with endometriosis. In a series of 73 patients aged 25 years or younger, including seven under 20 years of age, menstrual disturbance was rare (Punnonen and Nikkanen 1980) and in this age group a clear clinical distinction between primary and secondary dysmenorrhoea may not be apparent.

Endometriosis and infertility

An intellectual framework for understanding the relationship between endometriosis and subfertility has to some extent evolved in reverse, from observation of the impact of endometriosis treatments on subsequent pregnancy rates. The current status of our understanding of treatment outcomes is discussed below, but some reflection on the mechanisms involved is appropriate and is naturally of great interest to patients. The cause of subfertility in women with endometriosis is likely to involve at least one of the following mechanisms:

(1) Interference with ovum transport, via release of inflammatory mediators such as prostaglandins from endometriosis tissue;
(2) Mechanical disruption of the normal tubo-ovarian anatomical relationship by adhesion formation and tissue damage;
(3) Impaired oocyte quality because of the adverse influence on the developing follicle of nearby ovarian endometriotic deposits, reflected in poor *in vitro* fertilisation (IVF) conception rates;
(4) Iatrogenic factors including suppressive hormonal therapy and destructive surgery.

There is extensive current literature on the immune environment associated with the implantation and invasion of endometriosis, but it is not yet clear whether the reported immune phenomena are directly relevant to endometriosis-associated fertility problems (Hill 1997). In these circumstances recommendations for treatment must inevitably be pragmatic as to date we do not have a definitive means of reversing the underlying pathological process.

When to treat?

The timing of treatment, or a decision to defer therapy, is a matter for discussion between the patient and her gynaecologist and cannot be reduced to a simple formula. A key issue is the extent of functional impairment suffered, which may be reflected in days off work, consumption of analgesia with attendant side effects, negative impact on sexual function and the inevitable emotional distress resulting from long-standing pain and/or failure to conceive. Given that many of the available treatments are associated with important adverse effects, the decision to proceed is likely to involve balancing benefits and risks. Greater insight into the extent of functional impairment in endometriosis may be obtained by using a disease-specific questionnaire instrument (Colwell *et al.* 1998) rather than a generic quality-of-life questionnaire such as SF-36 which measures physical and mental health status using eight subscales.

Bringing the patient into the decision-making process with regard to treatment requires that sufficient information is available to a depth appropriate to the individual patient. The patient support organisations such as the UK Endometriosis Society play an essential role in disseminating information about the disease and highlighting the issues of greatest concern to patients that may not be sufficiently addressed by professionals.

A major determinant of the preferred type of treatment will be the patient's aspirations with regard to reproduction. With the exception of non-steroidal anti-inflammatory drugs, which will be the first-line recommendation for dysmenorrhoea, all medical treatments will impair fertility during their use. More crucially, there is clear evidence that medical treatment does not enhance subsequent fertility. The early experience with gestrinone proved to be characteristic of medical treatments in general, as shown by a review and meta-analysis of the results of randomised controlled trials and cohort studies reporting pregnancies in two or more treatment arms (Hughes *et al.* 1993). This review identified 37 treatment comparisons among 25 studies. The odds ratios for individual studies comparing ovulation suppression with no treatment ranged from 0.4 to 1.33 with 95% confidence intervals including zero. The overall odds ratio was 0.85 (95%

CI 0.95–1.22). Data from six randomised controlled trials comparing ovulation suppression by means of gestrinone, a GnRH analogue or an oral contraceptive with danazol gave an overall odds ratio for pregnancy of 1.07 (95% CI 0.71–1.61). In the terse language of the Cochrane Collaboration, this clearly represents 'evidence of no benefit' as opposed to 'no evidence of benefit'.

There may be some benefit to medical treatment timed as an adjunct to surgery in specific circumstances. In particular, the laparoscopic surgical treatment of ovarian endometriomas is facilitated by preoperative down-regulation with a GnRH agonist to reduce the size of the cyst (Donnez *et al.* 1993).

Treatment with what?

In contrast to the lack of efficacy of medical treatments in endometriosis-associated infertility, recent systematic reviews have substantiated the clinical impression of benefit for pain. Starting at the simple and inexpensive end of the therapeutic spectrum, the combined oral contraceptive pill is as effective as a GnRH analogue for relief of non-menstrual pain and dyspareunia (Moore *et al.* 1999). However, in order to obtain relief of dysmenorrhoea a tri-cycling or continuous regimen would be required. Danazol is effective in relieving all pain-related symptoms but the adverse-effect profile is the major limiting factor (Selak *et al.* 1999). Twenty-six studies of GnRH agonists versus other medications or placebo were available for review (Prentice *et al.* 1999) including five studies including add-back oestrogen as a treatment arm. The overall conclusion was that GnRH agonists are effective, but no more so than other treatments and that adverse effects could be mitigated by add-back therapy without reduced efficacy. Cost effectiveness is clearly a major issue in the choice of first-line therapy and in these comparisons the combined oral contraceptive pill emerges favourably, especially as it is the only hormonal therapy which can be safely and economically continued for many years. Recurrence of symptoms after discontinuation of GnRH agonist or danazol therapy is all too rapid, with median times to recurrence of five to six months (Miller *et al.* 1998).

Laparoscopic surgery has become established as an appropriate treatment modality for endometriosis-associated pain. The costs of surgery are considerably reduced if a definitive procedure is carried out at the time of diagnosis (Stones and Thomas 1995) and the initial promise of laser surgery has been confirmed in a randomised trial (Sutton *et al.* 1994) with a subsequent report presenting one-year outcomes (Sutton *et al.* 1997). Symptom relief was sustained at one year in 90% of initial responders.

In women with infertility, the potential benefits of laparoscopic surgery were indicated in a meta-analysis of five studies, which gave an overall odds ratio for pregnancy of 2.67 (95% CI 2.08–3.45) (Hughes *et al.* 1993). The combination of danazol pretreatment with either laparoscopic surgery or laparotomy did not enhance the results compared to surgery alone. A multicentre study from the Canadian Collaborative Group on Endometriosis (Marcoux *et al.* 1997) reported pregnancy outcomes in 341 women randomised to undergo either diagnostic laparoscopy or ablation of endometriosis at the time of diagnosis. Fifty of 172 women whose endometriosis was ablated carried a pregnancy beyond 20 weeks, compared with 29 of 169 women who underwent diagnostic laparoscopy alone. The fecundity rate ratio was 1.9 (95% CI 1.2–3.1). The comparative cumulative pregnancy probability curves presented in the report of this study appear to show a sustained effect of surgery over the 36-month follow-up period.

Given that women with endometriosis have a relatively poor outcome from IVF when using their own compared to donor oocytes (Simón *et al.* 1994), pretreatment of endometriosis prior to IVF has been evaluated. For example, a prolonged regimen of GnRH agonist down-regulation was found to enhance pregnancy rates (Marcus and Edwards 1994).

'Definitive' surgery remains a necessity for women who have not responded to medical or conservative surgical treatment, or whose symptoms have recurred. The boundaries of appropriate laparoscopic surgical practice are constantly being extended and now include procedures directed towards deeply invading rectovaginal septum disease. However, pelvic clearance by laparotomy is still a necessity for some patients and these procedures are technically difficult even with the benefit of an open abdominal incision (Magos 1993).

FUTURE DEVELOPMENTS

All treatments for endometriosis have powerful effects on the patient either through their invasiveness (surgery) or adverse effects (medical therapy). The most important future development is, therefore, to provide a scientific and clinical foundation to our understanding of the disease that allows a rational therapeutic approach. As long as a woman continues to menstruate, there is recurrence of the disease over time and therefore endometriosis should not be considered as a disease that can be cured but rather one which can be successfully managed through the reproductive years with long periods of remission. This means that neither surgery nor medical therapy is the best and only approach, but that each can be used with maximum efficacy at a particular time for that particular woman with those particular symptoms and disease. Recognition of individualisation of treatment schedules to each patient is an essential development.

New treatments will continue to develop. There are exciting possibilities with anti-oestrogens, aromatase inhibitors and selective oestrogen receptor modulators already being explored. Angiogenesis is an uncommon event in the adult human and it may be possible to use anti-angiogenics to halt the progress of the disease once implantation has occurred. Research is being prosecuted into stopping implantation by either blocking attachment through compounds which interact with integrins or altering invasion by using compounds which change the interactions between the cell and the extracellular matrix. These therapeutic approaches have value in cancer and we can expect significant investment in them by the pharmaceutical industry and endometriosis will benefit as a result.

There will be a continuing refinement of laparoscopic surgery as the instrumentation and visual technology improves resulting in even more complex surgery being performed by this route. Furthermore, there is now a generation of gynaecologists to whom the laparoscopic approach to surgery is second nature and their training and skills will ensure its development. Photodynamic therapy is likely to develop and thus provide an accurate way of destroying the disease with as little damage to normal tissue as possible.

More research will occur into the basic biology of the disease. Key questions surround the inheritability of the disease, the comparability of its pathogenesis with the paradigm of pathogenesis of malignancy, the mechanisms of implantation, invasion and damage, the evolution of the disease once established and the role of the immune system. Researchers will need to progress from associative to mechanistic work, which will require the use of such methodologies as genetic modification in cell cultures, viral vectors and knockout and transgenic models. It will be essential to know about the epidemiology of the disease. Prevention may well be the best approach in the long term and we will need to know what strategies women should use to minimise the possibility of endometriosis at a time when their health and social changes mean they are maximally exposed to menstruation.

After nearly 150 years and at the dawn of the new millennium, there are still huge numbers of unanswered questions about endometriosis. It is a modern disease which results from social change and will continue to provide a major scientific and clinical challenge to both clinicians and patients.

References

Ballweg, M.L. (1995) Psychologizing of endometriosis. *Clinical Consultations in Obstetrics and Gynecology* **7**, 214–221

Colwell, H.H., Mathias, S.D., Pasta, D.J., Henning, J.M. and Steege, J.F. (1998) A health-related quality-of-life instrument for symptomatic patients with endometriosis: a validation study. *Am J Obstet Gynecol* **179**, 47–55

Cornillie, F.J., Oosterlynck, D., Lauweryns, J.M. and Koninckx, P.R. (1990) Deeply infiltrating pelvic endometriosis: histology and clinical significance. *Fertil Steril* **53**, 978–83

Darrow, S.L., Vena, J.E., Batt, R.E., Zielezny, M.A., Michalek, A.M. and Selman, S. (1993) Menstrual cycle characteristics and the risk of endometriosis. *Epidemiology* **4**, 135–42

Donnez, J., Nisolle, M. and Casanas, F. (1993) Endoscopic surgery. *Baillières Clin Obstet Gynaecol* **7**, 839–48

Hill, J.A. (1997) Immunology and endometriosis – fact, artifact or epiphenomenon? *Obstet Gynecol Clin North Am* **24**, 291

Hughes, E.G., Fedorkow, D.M. and Collins, J.A. (1993) A quantitative overview of controlled trials in endometriosis-associated infertility. *Fertil Steril* **59**, 963–70

Jansen, R.P.S. and Russell, P. (1986) Nonpigmented endometriosis – clinical, laparoscopic, and pathological definition. *Am J Obstet Gynecol* **155**, 1154–9

Jiang, X., Hitchcock, A., Thomas, E.J., Watson, R.H. and Campbell, I.G. (1996) Use of microdissection to detect loss of heterozygosity at candidate tumor-suppressor loci on chromosome 9, chromosome 11, and chromosome 22 in endometriosis. *J Pathol* **179**, A43

Koninckx, P.R., Meuleman, C., Demeyere, S., Lesaffre, E. and Cornillie, F.J. (1991) Suggestive evidence that pelvic endometriosis is a progressive disease, whereas deeply infiltrating endometriosis is associated with pelvic pain. *Fertil Steril* **55**, 759–65

Magos, A. (1993) Endometriosis: radical surgery. *Baillières Clin Obstet Gynaecol* **7**, 849–64

Mahmood, T.A., Templeton, A.A., Thomson, L. and Fraser, C. (1991) Menstrual symptoms in women with pelvic endometriosis. *Br J Obstet Gynaecol* **98**, 558–63

Marcoux, S., Maheux, R., Berube, S. *et al.* (1997) Laparoscopic surgery in infertile women with minimal or mild endometriosis. *N Engl J Med* **337**, 217–22

Marcus, S.F. and Edwards, R.G. (1994) High rates of pregnancy after long-term down-regulation of women with severe endometriosis. *Am J Obstet Gynecol* **171**, 812–17

Matthews, C.J., Redfern, C.P.F., Hirst, B.H. and Thomas, E.J. (1992) Characterization of human purified epithelial and stromal cells from endometrium and endometriosis in tissue-culture. *Fertil Steril* **57**, 990–7

McLaren, J., Prentice, A., Charnock-Jones, D.S. *et al.* (1996) Vascular endothelial growth factor is produced by peritoneal fluid macrophages in endometriosis and is regulated by ovarian steroids. *J Clin Invest* **98**, 482–9

Miller, J.D., Shaw, R.W., Casper, R.F.J. *et al.* (1998) Historical prospective cohort study of the recurrence of pain after discontinuation of treatment with danazol or a gonadotropin-releasing hormone agonist. *Fertil Steril* **70**, 293–6

Moore, J., Kennedy, S. and Prentice, A. (1999) Modern combined oral contraceptives for pain associated with endometriosis (Cochrane Review). *The Cochrane Library*, Issue 3. Oxford: Update Software

Parazzini, F., Ferraroni, M., Fedele, L., Bocciolone, L., Rubessa, S. and Riccardi, A. (1995) Pelvic endometriosis: reproductive and menstrual risk factors at different stages in Lombardy, northern Italy. *J Epidemiol Community Health* **49**, 61–4

Pellicer, A., Albert, C., Mercader, A., Bonilla-Musoles, F., Remohi, J. and Simon, C. (1998) The follicular and endocrine environment in women with endometriosis: local and systemic cytokine production. *Fertil Steril* **70**, 425–31

Prentice, A., Deary, A.J., Goldbeck-Wood, S., Farquhar, C. and Smith, S.K. (1999) Gonadotrophin-releasing hormone analogues for pain associated with endometriosis (Cochrane Review). *The Cochrane Library*, Issue 3. Oxford: Update Software

Punnonen, R.H. and Nikkanen, V.P. (1980) Endometriosis in young women. *Infertility* **3**, 1–10

Rokitansky, C. (1980) Ueber uterusdrusen – neubildung in uterus – und ovarial sarcomen. *Gesselschaft der Aertze zu Wien* **37**, 577–81

Sampson, J.A. (1921) Perforating hemorrhagic (chocolate) cysts of the ovary. Their importance and especially their relation to pelvic adenomas of the endometrial type ('adenomyoma' of the uterus, rectovaginal septum, sigmoid etc). *Arch Surg* **3**, 245–323

Sangi-Haghpeykar, H. and Poindexter A.N. III (1995) Epidemiology of endometriosis among parous women. *Obstet Gynecol* **85**, 983–92

Selak, V., Farquhar, C., Prentice, A. and Singla, A. (1999) Danazol for pelvic pain associated with endometriosis (Cochrane Review). *The Cochrane Library*, Issue 3. Oxford: Update Software

Shin, J.C., Ross, H.L., Elias, S. *et al.* (1997) Detection of chromosomal aneuploidy in endometriosis by multi-color fluorescence in situ hybridization (FISH). *Hum Genet* **100**, 401–6

Simón, C., Gutiérrez, A., Vidal, A. *et al.* (1994) Outcome of patients with endometriosis in assisted reproduction: results from *in-vitro* fertilization and oocyte donation. *Hum Reprod* **9**, 725–9

Stones, R.W. and Thomas, E.J. (1995) 'Cost-effective medical treatment of endometriosis' in: J. Bonnar (Ed.) *Recent Advances in Obstetrics and Gynaecology* no. 19, pp. 139–52. Edinburgh: Churchill Livingstone

Sutton, C.J.G., Pooley, A.S., Ewen, S.P. and Haines, P. (1997) Follow-up report on a randomized controlled trial of laser laparoscopy in the treatment of pelvic pain associated with minimal to moderate endometriosis. *Fertil Steril* **68**, 1070–4

Sutton, J.G., Ewen, S.P., Whitelaw, N. and Haines, P. (1994) Prospective, randomized, double-blind, controlled trial of laser laparoscopy in the treatment of pelvic pain associated with minimal, mild and moderate endometriosis. *Fertil Steril* **62**, 696–700

Thomas, E.J. and Cooke, I.D. (1987a) Impact of gestrinone on the course of asymptomatic endometriosis. *BMJ* **294**, 272–4

Thomas, E.J. and Cooke, I.D. (1987b) Successful treatment of asymptomatic endometriosis: Does it benefit infertile women? *BMJ* **294**, 1117–19

28

Medical management of menorrhagia

Iain T. Cameron

INTRODUCTION

It is nearly 120 years since Moricke first used a curette to obtain endometrial samples from living women (Drife 1998). The intervening years, particularly the last 30 years, have seen a remarkable advance in our understanding of reproductive medicine. At the turn of the century, women had fewer menstrual periods than they do today. They had a later menarche, an earlier menopause and, for many, the reproductive years were characterised by pregnancy and lactational amenorrhoea, with the occasional ovulatory menstrual cycle in between (Short 1976). This has changed. The widespread availability of effective contraception has led to the acceptance of the monthly menstrual cycle as the norm and this has led to the evolution of the common disorders of menstruation – menorrhagia, dysmenorrhoea and premenstrual syndrome.

Heavy menstrual bleeding is one of the main reasons for which women in developed societies seek medical advice, as highlighted by the recent Royal College of Obstetricians and Gynaecologists evidence-based clinical guidelines on the initial management of menorrhagia (RCOG 1998). Furthermore, the treatment of menorrhagia, medical or surgical, is a significant burden to National Health Service resources. Hysterectomy, the traditional surgical treatment for menorrhagia, is only suitable for women who have no further wish to conceive. The operation itself is not without risk. The National Confidential Enquiry into Perioperative Deaths 1996–97 reported seven fatalities due to haemorrhage or infection in women who had undergone hysterectomy for benign disease (National Confidential Enquiry into Perioperative Deaths 1998). Concerns about the 'invasiveness' of hysterectomy led to the development of minimal access surgery (Goldrath 1998). But at least one in five women who have these procedures requires further surgery (repeat resection/ablation or hysterectomy) (Sculpher *et al.* 1996). Again, these approaches can be used only for women who have completed their families.

The aetiology of menorrhagia

Menorrhagia may be secondary to underlying pathology such as fibroids, polyps, malignancy, infection or bleeding diatheses. In these instances, treatment can be directed towards the underlying cause. In the majority of cases, there is no demonstrable pathology and the disorder is termed dysfunctional uterine bleeding. Of these cases, 10–20% are associated with anovulation, especially at the extremes of reproductive life.

The precise cause of dysfunctional uterine bleeding is thought to lie at the level of the endometrium. In his 1914 Hunterian Lecture to the Royal College of Surgeons, Beckwith Whitehouse described the phenomenon of fibrinolysis of menstrual blood within the uterine cavity and demonstrated an increase in thrombolysis at the time of menstruation. He reported confirmation of Blair Bell's observations on the production of myometrial contractions by the injection of uterine artery secretions and proposed that 'a portion of the uterine secretion is resorbed and serves as a direct stimulus to uterine contraction, thus diminishing the amount of blood flowing to the endometrium.'

While a haemostatic role for uterine contractility in the non-pregnant state has received limited attention, the importance of active endometrial principles has gained support. Haemostasis during menstruation is now thought to be achieved mainly by vasoconstriction, until the bleeding is definitively checked by repair of the endometrial blood vessels in the first seven days of the cycle (Markee 1940; Campbell and Cameron 1998). Of the factors that are involved in the local control of menstrual bleeding, abnormalities in the prostaglandin and fibrinolytic systems in the endometrium have led to a rational medical approach to the treatment of menorrhagia in some women.

Objective assessment of menstrual blood loss

The definition of menorrhagia as menstrual blood loss greater than 80 ml each month arose from a large population study in Gothenberg (Hallberg et al. 1966). Women with a blood loss greater than 80 ml (in the upper 10th centile of the population) were considered to be at increased risk of iron-deficiency anaemia. This study, and subsequent work from the UK, defined normal mean/median monthly menstrual blood loss as 30–40 ml (Hallberg et al. 1966; Cole et al. 1971).

Assessment of blood loss in these population studies relied on the measurement of haemoglobin using the alkaline haematin method (Hallberg and Nilsson 1964). Later work showed that 'blood' makes up less than half of the fluid loss experienced at menstruation (Fraser et al. 1985). Furthermore, menstrual blood loss is less than 80 ml in over half of women complaining of heavy periods. This is of direct relevance in clinical practice. Firstly, women with heavy periods who undergo surgery, and whose blood loss is normal, do not have the surgical procedure to decrease their risk of iron-deficiency anaemia. Secondly, part of the reason for the perception that medical treatment for menorrhagia is ineffective may be that in 50% of cases the treatment is prescribed for women who do not actually have menorrhagia.

Discrepancy between subjective and objective assessment of menorrhagia also highlights that a reduction in measured menstrual loss may not necessarily be associated with resolution of the woman's symptoms. Most studies that have assessed the use of medical treatments for menorrhagia have focused on measured menstrual blood loss, rather than the effect of the medication on the woman's symptoms or her quality of life. While objective measurement is required to judge whether treatment actually reduces menstrual blood loss, subjective assessment of the woman's symptoms is a crucial determinant of the efficacy and acceptability of treatment in clinical practice.

MEDICAL TREATMENTS FOR MENORRHAGIA

The main classes of drugs used for the medical treatment of menorrhagia are inhibitors of prostaglandin synthesis, antifibrinolytic agents and hormonal therapies (Table 1).

Table 1 *Medical treatments for menorrhagia*

Inhibitors of prostaglandin synthesis	e.g. mefenamic acid
Antifibrinolytic agents	Tranexamic acid
Hormonal treatments	Systemic progestogens (e.g. norethisterone) Intrauterine progestogens (LNG IUS) Oestrogen–progestogen contraceptive pill GnRH analogues, danazol

Table 2 *Systematic reviews of medical treatments for menorrhagia in* The Cochrane Library

Authors	Date	Title	Cochrane Library *Issue*
Augood, C., Duckitt, K. and Lethaby, A.	1998	Danazol for heavy menstrual bleeding (Cochrane Review)	1
Cooke, I., Lethaby, A. and Farquhar, C.	1999	Antifibinolytics for heavy menstrual bleeding (Cochrane Review)	1
Cooke, I., Lethaby, A. and Rees, M.	1996	Progesterone/progestogen releasing intrauterine contraceptive devices for heavy menstrual bleeding (Cochrane Protocol)	4
Iyer, V., Farquhar, C. and Jepson, R.	1997	Oral contraceptive pills for heavy menstrual bleeding (Cochrane Review)	3
Lethaby, A., Augood, C. and Duckitt, K.	1998	Non-steroidal anti-inflammatory drugs for heavy menstrual bleeding (Cochrane Review)	3
Lethaby, A., Irvine, G. and Cameron, I.	1998	Cyclical progestogens for heavy menstrual bleeding (Cochrane Review)	4

Details of evidence-based systematic reviews of the use of these agents for the treatment of menorrhagia are shown in Table 2. Ethamsylate, a medication believed to reduce capillary fragility, has doubtful efficacy (Bonnar and Sheppard 1996).

Inhibitors of prostaglandin synthesis

Non-steroidal anti-inflammatory drugs (NSAIDs) are used widely to treat menorrhagia (Coulter *et al.* 1995a). The main mechanism of action of these drugs is to decrease endometrial prostaglandin (PG) concentrations. The endometrium is a rich source of PGE_2 and $PGF_{2\alpha}$, and studies have shown that PG concentrations are increased in the endometrium of women with menorrhagia.

The NSAID used most often for the treatment of menorrhagia is mefenamic acid. This agent reduces menstrual blood loss by about 25% in three-quarters of women with menorrhagia. Various studies have compared the efficacy of prostaglandin synthase inhibitors with other treatments. For example, menstrual blood loss was reduced by 24% and 20%, respectively, in women with ovulatory dysfunctional uterine bleeding treated with mefenamic acid and norethisterone (Cameron *et al.* 1990). Menstrual blood loss was reduced by 22% and 56% in a study that compared mefenamic acid with danazol, although the investigators concluded that mefenamic acid was a better initial treatment because it was less expensive and caused fewer side effects (Dockeray *et al.* 1989). Similar results to those seen with mefenamic acid have also been reported after the use of other NSAIDs, including flurbiprofen and naproxen (Fraser and McCarron 1991; Milsom *et al.* 1991).

In summary, mefenamic acid and related NSAIDs can be effective first-line medical treatments for some women with menorrhagia. The degree of reduction of menstrual blood loss is modest, but NSAIDs have a low adverse-effect profile in otherwise healthy women. NSAIDs are also valuable if pain is an associated symptom.

Antifibrinolytic agents

The endometrium possesses an active fibrinolytic system. Fibrinolytic activity is greater in the endometrium of women with menorrhagia than it is in the endometrium of women with menstrual blood loss in the normal range. Antifibrinolytic agents such as tranexamic acid provide a rational and effective treatment, reducing menstrual blood loss by about 50%. Comparative studies have shown that tranexamic acid is better at lowering menstrual loss than prostaglandin synthase inhibitors, with reductions of 56% and 44% following tranexamic acid and 21% and 24% after flurbiprofen and diclofenac sodium, respectively (Ylikorkala and Viinikka 1983; Milsom *et al.* 1991). Tranexamic acid was also effective in women with iatrogenic menorrhagia caused by the intrauterine contraceptive device (Nilsson and Rybo 1967; Ylikorkala and Viinikka 1983).

The incidence of adverse effects after the use of antifibrinolytic drugs is dose-related. One-third of women experience adverse gastrointestinal effects following treatment with 3–6 g of tranexamic acid daily. As 90% of menstrual blood is lost in the first three days of full flow, adverse effects can be reduced by limiting the number of days on which the drug is taken to the first three or four days of the period. Serious adverse effects are uncommon. Early reports suggested that antifibrinolytic agents might be implicated in the pathogenesis of thromboembolism. However, histochemical studies failed to show suppression of fibrinolysis in superficial vein walls in women using 3–4 g of tranexamic acid daily for three months (Astedt *et al.* 1987). In addition, no increase in the incidence of thromboembolic disease was observed in women of reproductive age in Scandinavia, where tranexamic acid has been used as first-line treatment for menorrhagia since the early 1970s (Rybo 1991). There is no clear evidence that tranexamic acid increases the risk of thrombosis in women who are not already predisposed because of past history or a family history of thrombophilia.

Hormonal therapies

Systemic progestogens

Systemic progestogens, such as norethisterone and medroxyprogesterone acetate, offer a logical approach to the treatment of anovulatory dysfunctional uterine bleeding. However, most studies have shown that oral administration of these agents is not an effective therapy for the management of ovulatory bleeding, if the drugs are given at low dose for a short duration (five to ten days) in the luteal phase of the cycle (Coulter *et al.* 1995b; Dunphy *et al.* 1998). Norethisterone can be used to treat ovulatory menorrhagia if the drug is given at a higher dose for three weeks out of four (5 mg three times daily from day five to day 26 of the cycle) (Fraser 1990; Irvine *et al.* 1998).

Intrauterine progestogens

While menstrual loss is increased after the insertion of inert or copper-containing intrauterine contraceptive devices, it is reduced if the device is impregnated with progesterone or a progestogen (Berqvist and Rybo 1983; Andersson *et al.* 1994). The most recently described medicated device is the levonorgestrel intrauterine system (LNG IUS; Mirena®, Shering Health). This system delivers 20 μg levonorgestrel every 24 hours in a sustained-release formulation that lasts for up to five years. Direct administration of the progestogen to the uterus results in little systemic absorption. Initial studies in 20 women with menorrhagia showed that menstrual blood loss decreased from a median of 176 ml before treatment to 24 ml at three months and 5 ml at 12 months. Seven (35%) women were amenorrhoeic at the end of the study (Andersson and Rybo 1990).

The efficacy of the LNG IUS for the treatment of menorrhagia has been compared with oral norethisterone and endometrial resection (Crosignani *et al.* 1997; Irvine *et al.* 1998). Forty-four individuals with objectively diagnosed menorrhagia were prescribed norethisterone (5 mg three times daily from day five of the cycle for 21 days) or the LNG IUS (Irvine *et al.* 1998). Menstrual blood loss, measured before treatment and after three cycles, was reduced to the normal range in both groups (Table 3). There was no difference in the adverse-effect profile between the two groups, apart from intermenstrual spotting, which was seen in 53% of women treated with LNG IUS but only 13% of those receiving oral progestogen. However, this was not a major constraint to compliance in these women. Eighty percent of those prescribed the LNG IUS chose to continue with this treatment at the end of the study, as opposed to 20% in the norethisterone group.

In another study, 70 premenopausal women with dysfunctional uterine bleeding were randomised to have the LNG IUS inserted or to undergo endometrial resection (Crosignani *et al.* 1997). Blood loss was assessed semi-objectively and a general health questionnaire was completed after 12 months. Estimated blood loss was reduced by 79% and 89% in the LNG IUS and resection groups, respectively. Satisfaction with treatment was high, at 85% and 94%. The LNG IUS would, therefore, appear to compare well with endometrial resection for the management of dysfunctional uterine bleeding when assessed 12 months after the start of treatment. It has the additional advantage of providing contraception, which endometrial resection does not.

Table 3 *Measured menstrual blood loss (ml) before and after treatment with norethisterone (5 mg three times daily from day five of the cycle for 21 days) or the LNG IUS (n=22 in each group); data represent median (range) blood loss*

	Norethisterone	LNG IUS
Control	120 (82–336)	105 (82–780)
Treatment cycle 1	46 (0–213)	16 (0–62)
Treatment cycle 3	20 (4–137)	6 (0–284[a])

[a] LNG IUS expelled spontaneously; data from Irvine *et al.* (1998)

The LNG IUS might also compare well with hysterectomy. An open, randomised study investigated the use of LNG IUS in women on the waiting list for hysterectomy (Lahteenmaki *et al.* 1998). Patients were invited to have an LNG IUS inserted six months prior to surgery or to continue with the form of medical treatment that they had been using. Sixty-four percent of the women in the LNG IUS group and 14% in the control group chose to remove themselves from the waiting list for hysterectomy. While there was a significant bias in the study, in that the control group was likely to be dissatisfied with a treatment option that had already been considered ineffective for them, the LNG IUS might offer an acceptable alternative to hysterectomy for some women.

The main adverse effect associated with the LNG IUS is irregular breakthrough bleeding and spotting, particularly within the first few months after insertion of the system. Furthermore, 20% of women using the system will become amenorrhoeic within one year. Many women will consider this a positive benefit, whereas others will have the anxiety of pregnancy. These events must be discussed in detail prior to treatment. Nevertheless, intrauterine progestogen treatment is likely to offer a realistic choice for women as an effective and acceptable alternative to surgery, particularly if the problem of irregular breakthrough bleeding can be overcome.

The combined contraceptive pill

The combined oestrogen/progestogen contraceptive pill reduces menstrual blood loss by about 50%. Its main mechanism of action in this regard is thought to be endometrial suppression. It has long been recognised that women using the combined pill for contraception report reduced menstrual blood loss. Despite this, the combined pill was only prescribed by 11% of 518 GPs in a study of the treatment of menorrhagia in primary care (Coulter *et al.* 1995a). It is likely that the combined pill has been unpopular for the treatment of menorrhagia because of concerns about arterial and thromboembolic disease, particularly in women over 35 years of age. However, age alone is not a contraindication to the use of the low-dose combined pill in the absence of smoking, obesity, other predisposing factors or a family history of thromboembolic disease.

Gonadotrophin releasing hormone (GnRH) analogues

GnRH analogues can be used to control menstrual loss by pituitary down-regulation and subsequent inhibition of cyclical ovarian activity. Ovarian suppression and amenorrhoea, with the associated problems of the hypo-oestrogenic state, including hot flushes, vaginal dryness and bone mineral loss (unless oestrogen/progestogen 'add-back' therapy is also prescribed), is not a first-line option, but may have a place for the short-term treatment of women with intractable menorrhagia. Alternatively, GnRH analogues can be prescribed to suppress endometrial growth before transcervical endometrial resection or endometrial ablation. In addition, they can be used for three to four months to reduce the size of fibroids prior to myomectomy or hysterectomy.

Danazol

Danazol is a synthetic androgen with anti-oestrogenic and antiprogestogenic activity. It inhibits the release of pituitary gonadotrophins and has a direct suppressive effect on the endometrium. The drug was initially introduced as a medical treatment for endometriosis. Danazol causes a significant reduction in menstrual blood loss and usually results in amenorrhoea when prescribed at doses of 400 mg daily or greater (Chimbira *et al.* 1980). A high incidence of androgenic side effects has limited the use of danazol as a treatment option for women with gynaecological disease. As with the GnRH analogues, danazol is not a first-line treatment for menorrhagia. Its main use is as a short-term pre-operative adjunct, for example, to make the endometrium atrophic prior to endometrial resection.

FUTURE DEVELOPMENTS

Surgery has offered the definitive approach to the majority of gynaecological disorders since the middle of the 19th century. However, better understanding of the mechanisms underlying pathologies such as dysfunctional uterine bleeding or uterine fibroids has led to the development of a range of effective medical options, particularly for the management of benign disorders (Smith 1996; Lilford 1997).

In addition to this trend towards medical therapies, there is likely to be a progressive move towards locally administered treatments. Local surgical treatment to the endometrial cavity is well established. Patient satisfaction following hysteroscopic endometrial resection or ablation for the treatment of menorrhagia is similar to that following hysterectomy (Garry 1997). A major advantage of these procedures is that they require minimal hospitalisation, although general anaesthesia is usually used. Recent advances have permitted a more widespread approach to endometrial ablation in an outpatient setting (Soderstrom *et al.* 1996). Future developments are likely to include the use of photodynamic therapy, where low-power light is used to destroy the endometrium after local administration of a photosensitising drug (Bown 1998).

Intrauterine devices or systems provide a convenient means of administering medication to the uterine cavity. Indeed, the LNG IUS may offer an acceptable alternative to conventional surgery for medium- to long-term medical treatment of menorrhagia. Such treatment would be even more acceptable if the system could be modified, for example, by the incorporation of an additional active agent to decrease the incidence of breakthrough bleeding and spotting.

In the more distant future, uterine gene transfer might provide another option for local medical treatment for gynaecological disease. Rather than administer an active agent, the gene of interest would be incorporated and then activated as required (Russell 1997). The potential for endometrial gene transfer has already been demonstrated in animal models and in cultured human endometrial epithelial cells *in vitro* (Charnock-Jones *et al.* 1997). The identification of defects in the expression of specific genes involved in the control of endometrial haemostasis and the correction of abnormal gene expression in the endometrium itself could therefore provide a novel strategy for the management of benign gynaecological disease into the next millennium. However, extensive background studies will be required before these new techniques can be considered for everyday clinical practice.

Acknowledgements

I thank Dr C. Jay McGavigan for assistance with the preparation of some of this text, and Ms Sarah Hetrick for providing details of reviews and protocols in *The Cochrane Library*.

References

Andersson, J.K. and Rybo, G. (1990) Levonorgestrel-releasing intrauterine device in the treatment of menorrhagia. *Br J Obstet Gynaecol* **97**, 690–4

Andersson, K., Odlind, V. and Rybo, G. (1994) Levonorgestrel-releasing and copper-releasing (Nova-T®) IUCDs during five years' use: a randomised comparative trial. *Contraception* **49**, 56–72

Astedt, B., Liedholm, P. and Wingerup, L. (1987) The effects of tranexamic acid on the fibrinolytic activity of vein walls. *Ann Chir Gynaecol* **67**, 203–5

Beckwith Whitehouse, H. (1914) The physiology and pathology of uterine haemorrhage. *Lancet* **i**, 877–85, 951–7

Berqvist, A. and Rybo, G. (1983) Treatment of menorrhagia with intrauterine release of progesterone. *Br J Obstet Gynaecol* **90**, 255–8

Bonnar, J. and Sheppard, B.L. (1996) Treatment of menorrhagia during menstruation: randomised controlled trial of ethamsylate, mefenamic acid and tranexamic acid. *BMJ* **313**, 579–82

Bown, S.G. (1998) New techniques in laser therapy. *BMJ* **316**, 754–7

Cameron, I.T., Haining, R., Lumsden, M.A., Reid Thomas, V. and Smith, S.K. (1990) The effects of mefenamic acid and norethisterone on measured menstrual blood loss. *Obstet Gynecol* **76**, 85–8

Campbell, S. and Cameron, I.T. (1998) 'The origins and physiology of menstruation' in: I.T. Cameron, I.S. Fraser and S.K. Smith (Eds) *Clinical Disorders of the Endometrium and Menstrual Cycle*, pp. 13–30. Oxford: Oxford University Press

Charnock-Jones, D.S., Sharkey, A.M., Jaggers, D.C., Yoo, H.J., Heap, R.B. and Smith, S.K. (1997) *In vivo* gene transfer to the uterine endometrium. *Hum Reprod* **12**, 17–20

Chimbira, T.H., Anderson, A.B.M., Naish, C., Cope, E. and Turnbull, A.C. (1980) Reduction of menstrual blood loss by danazol in unexplained menorrhagia: a lack of effect of placebo. *Br J Obstet Gynaecol* **87**, 1152–8

Cole, S.K., Billewicz, W.Z. and Thomson, A.M. (1971) Sources of variation in menstrual blood loss. *J Obstet Gynaecol Br Cwlth* **78**, 933–9

Coulter, A., Kelland, J., Peto, V. *et al.* (1995a) Treating menorrhagia in primary care. An overview of drug trials and a survey of prescribing practice. *Int J Technol Assess Health Care* **11**, 456–70

Coulter, A., Kelland, J. and Long, A. (1995b) *The Management of Menorrhagia*. York: NHS Centre for Reviews and Dissemination (Effective Health Care Bulletin **1**, no. 9)

Crosignani, P.G., Vercellini, P., Mosconi, P., Oldani, S., Cortesi, I. and de Giorgi, O. (1997) Levonorgestrel-releasing intrauterine device versus hysteroscopic endometrial resection in the treatment of dysfunctional uterine bleeding. *Obstet Gynecol* **90**, 257–63

Dockeray, C.J., Sheppard, B.L. and Bonnar, J. (1989) Comparison between mefenamic acid and danazol in the treatment of established menorrhagia. *Br J Obstet Gynaecol* **96**, 840–4

Drife, J.O. (1998) 'Menstruation: a cultural and historical perspective' in: I.T. Cameron, I.S. Fraser and S.K. Smith (Eds) *Clinical Disorders of the Endometrium and Menstrual Cycle*, pp. 3–12. Oxford: Oxford University Press

Dunphy, B.C., Goerzen, J., Greene, C.A., de la Ronde, S., Seidel, J. and Ingelson, B. (1998) A double-blind randomised study comparing danazol and medroxyprogesterone acetate in the management of menorrhagia. *Journal of Obstetrics and Gynaecology* **18**, 553–5

Fraser, I.S. (1990) Treatment of ovulatory and anovulatory dysfunctional uterine bleeding with oral progestogens. *Aust N Z J Obstet Gynaecol* **30**, 353–6

Fraser, I.S. and McCarron, G. (1991) Randomised trial of two hormonal and two prostaglandin-inhibiting agents in women with a complaint of menorrhagia. *Aust N Z J Obstet Gynaecol* **31**, 66–70

Fraser, I.S., McCarron, G., Markham, R. and Resta, T. (1985) Blood and total fluid content of menstrual discharge. *Obstet Gynecol* **65**, 194–8

Garry, R. (1997) Endometrial ablation and resection: validation of a new surgical concept. *Br J Obstet Gynaecol* **104**, 1329–31

Goldrath, M. (1998) 'Hysteroscopic endometrial ablation' in: I.T. Cameron, I.S. Fraser and S.K. Smith (Eds) *Clinical Disorders of the Endometrium and Menstrual Cycle*, pp. 175–91. Oxford: Oxford University Press

Hallberg, L. and Nilsson, L. (1964) Determination of menstrual blood loss. *Scand J Clin Lab Invest* **16**, 244–8

Hallberg, L., Hogdahl, A.M., Nilsson, L. and Rybo, G. (1966) Menstrual blood loss – a population study. *Acta Obstet Gynecol Scand* **45**, 320–51

Irvine, G.A., Campbell-Brown, M.B., Lumsden, M.A., Heikkila, A., Walker, J.J. and Cameron, I.T. (1998) Randomised comparative trial of the levonorgestrel intrauterine system and norethisterone for the treatment of idiopathic menorrhagia. *Br J Obstet Gynaecol* **105**, 592–8

Lahteenmaki, P., Haukkamaa, M., Puolakka, J. *et al.* (1998) Open randomised study of use of levonorgestrel releasing intrauterine system as alternative to hysterectomy. *BMJ* **316**, 1122–6

Lilford, R.J. (1997) Hysterectomy: will it pay the bills in 2007? *BMJ* **314**, 160–1

Markee, J.E. (1940) Menstruation in intraocular endometrial transplants in the rhesus monkey. *Contrib Embryol* **28**, 219–308

Milsom, I., Andersson, J.K., Andersch, B. and Rybo, G. (1991) A comparison of flurbiprofen, tranexamic acid and a levonorgestrel releasing intrauterine contraceptive device in the treatment of idiopathic menorrhagia. *Am J Obstet Gynecol* **164**, 879–83

National Confidential Enquiry into Perioperative Deaths (1998) *National Confidential Enquiry into Perioperative Deaths 1996–97*. London: NCEPOD

Nilsson, L. and Rybo, G. (1967) Treatment of menorrhagia with an antifibrinolytic agent, tranexamic acid. *Acta Obstet Gynecol Scand* **46**, 572–80

RCOG (1998) *The Initial Management of Menorrhagia*. London: RCOG Press (Evidence-Based Clinical Guidelines No. 1)

Russell, S.J. (1997) Gene therapy. *BMJ* **315**, 1289–92

Rybo, G. (1991) Tranexamic acid therapy: effective treatment in heavy menstrual bleeding. Clinical update on safety. *Therapeutic Advances* **4**, 1–8

Sculpher, M.J., Dwyer, N., Byford, S. and Stirratt, G.M. (1996) Randomised trial comparing hysterectomy and transcervical endometrial resection: effect on health related quality of life and costs two years after surgery. *Br J Obstet Gynaecol* **103**, 142–9

Short, R.V. (1976) The evolution of human reproduction. *Proc R Soc Lond* **195**, 3–24

Smith, S.K. (1996) Gynaecology – medical or surgical? *BMJ* **312**, 592–3

Soderstrom, R.M., Brooks, P.G., Corson, S.L. *et al.* (1996) Endometrial ablation using a distensible multielectrode balloon. *J Am Assoc Gynecol Laparosc* **3**, 403–7

Ylikorkala, O. and Viinikka, L. (1983) Comparison between antifibrinolytic and antiprostaglandin treatment in the reduction of increased menstrual blood loss in women with intrauterine contraceptive devices. *Br J Obstet Gynaecol* **90**, 78–83

29

The role of endometrial ablation in modern gynaecological practice

Ian S. Fraser and Raewyn Teirney

Endometrial ablation is an operation designed to treat menorrhagia. The relative simplicity of the concept of endometrial destruction has made it a popular alternative to hysterectomy in certain parts of the world. The common techniques currently used include the neodymium:yttrium-aluminium-garnet (Nd:YAG) laser, hysteroscopic loop resection and rollerball electrocoagulation. These have led to the recent development of new and exciting methods that may simplify the procedure considerably. The aim of all these procedures is to destroy the full thickness of endometrium with some underlying superficial myometrium, leading to a type of Asherman syndrome.

THE PAST

The desire by physicians to destroy the endometrium in women with excessive and life-threatening menstruation is not new. A number of fascinating reports of somewhat barbaric methods exist in the early medical literature, where a variety of toxic substances have been instilled into the uterine cavity with the intention of destroying the endometrium. These have included solutions such as nitric acid, quinacrine, oxalic acid and paraformaldehyde. Other procedures used have been excessive abrasion with vigorous curettage, cryotherapy and intracavity radium (Droegemueller *et al.* 1970; Goldrath *et al.* 1981). Most have been unsuccessful. Intracavity radium had some success, but the risk of causing endometrial cancer prevented its further use for the treatment of menorrhagia.

In the 1940s, Baumann reported a method of treating menorrhagia by thorough diathermy of the endometrium carried out blindly with a steel ball electrode on an intrauterine probe. His ten-year experience involving 387 patients included few failures or complications, but this method fell out of favour with colleagues (Vancaillie 1993).

Droegemueller *et al.* (1971a,b) developed the technique of cryocoagulation of the endometrium using a cylindrical probe (cryoprobe) that was frozen with a cooling agent to below $-40°C$ for a few minutes inside the uterus. The use of the cooling agent Freon had disappointing results, but nitrous oxide was partially successful in some patients. Again, this was a blind procedure and complications of haematometra, full thickness myometrial damage and fistula formation led to its abandonment.

The early history of colposcopic and hysteroscopic examination of the genital tract has been well reviewed by Lindemann (1973) and more recently by LaMorte and DeCherney

(1993). Interested readers are referred to these reviews for more detailed background information. The chronological landmarks in surgical hysteroscopy are listed in Table 1.

An understanding of the living anatomy of the interior of the uterus began after the pioneering efforts of the early endoscopists in the 1800s. Bozzini, in the early 1800s, examined the vagina with a crude speculum-like device using a candle via a concave mirror. In 1860, Desormeaux designed an endoscopic tube for inspecting organs such as the bladder and urethra. Pantaleoni (1869) improved on this device and was the first to carry out a hysteroscopy in a postmenopausal woman with vaginal bleeding. A polyp was found and cauterised with silver nitrate. In 1895, Bumm and colleagues were the first to use an urethroscope and an illuminating headlamp for inspecting the cavity of the uterus. They diagnosed several conditions of the uterus including endometritis and tumours (Lindemann 1973; LaMorte and DeCherney 1993).

Table 1   *Chronological landmarks in surgical hysteroscopy*

1800	Bozzini	Examined vagina and rectum with a tubular speculum
1860	Desormeaux	Designed an endoscopic tube for inspecting bladder
1869	Pantaleoni	Used hysteroscopy tube for inspection of uterine cavity
1877	Nitze	Introduced first urethral and bladder cystoscope with optical lens and illuminator
1895	Bumm	Adapted the urethroscope with a head lamp and light reflector to diagnose conditions of the uterus
1914	Heinenberg	Developed an endoscope with a water irrigation system for uterine inspection
1925	Rubin	Attempted insufflation of cavity with oxygen and carbon dioxide
1926	Seymour	Introduced a hysteroscope with a type of suction tubing to clear away blood
1927	Mikylicz-Radecki	Designed the 'Kurettoskope' with a rinsing device and magnification, capable of removing endometrial biopsy Experimented with hysteroscopic sterilisation
1928	Gauss	Advanced the knowledge of physiology and pathology of uterine conditions with hysteroscopy
1934	Schroeder	Introduced the forward-viewing optic, making it possible to view a larger portion of the uterine cavity
1957	Norment	Developed rubber and plastic balloon to distend the uterine cavity and prevent bleeding
1970	Edstrom and Fernstrom	Experimented with dextran solutions for inspection of the uterine cavity
1976	Neuwirth	Reported the use of the resectoscope for submucus fibroids
1981	Goldrath	First report of ablation of the endometrium with the Nd:YAG laser
1986	DeCherney	First report of endometrium with a loop electrode
1988/ 1989	Lin/ Vancaillie	Independently developed the rollerball technique to coagulate the endometrium

Major problems encountered in the early years were, not unexpectedly, poor visualisation and difficulty with uterine distension. By 1914, Heinenburg had developed a water irrigating system to clear intrauterine blood for better visualisation and, by the1920s, Rubin was using oxygen and later CO_2 to distend the uterine cavity. By the 1970s, varying concentrations of dextran-containing media were introduced to improve distension of the uterus and provide greater clarity of vision (Edstrom and Fernstrom 1970; Levine and Neuwirth 1972).

Schroder, in 1934, helped to develop a hysteroscope with a forward-viewing optic system. The major advantage over earlier instruments was the wider field of view it gave of the uterine cavity. This allowed the development of a more precise approach to the destruction of intrauterine structures. Further advancements in hysteroscopic surgery were due to the introduction of external light sources. The Hopkins rod–lens system for endoscopes and fibre-optic cables contributed to improved visualisation of the uterine cavity.

With the development of laser technology and operative endoscopic equipment, advances in camera and recording technology, safe and effective operative hysteroscopy, including endometrial ablation and resection, became a reality in the mid- to late 1980s.

THE PRESENT

The modern era for endometrial ablation began with Goldrath and the Nd:YAG laser in 1981. Following this, DeCherney and Polan (1983) and DeCherney et al. (1997) reported their impressive experience of endometrial resection using a loop electrode for the emergency treatment of women with life-threatening uterine haemorrhage. The technique of rollerball coagulation of the endometrium was then independently developed by Lin et al. (1988) and Vancaillie (1989).

Goldrath et al. (1981) were the first to report on treatment of excessive uterine bleeding by endometrial ablation using photovaporisation with the Nd:YAG laser. Endometrium was destroyed by laser energy delivered through an optical fibre under direct hysteroscopic vision. Two patients required a repeat procedure, there was one instance of a haematometra, and one uterine perforation. Despite this, 21 of the 22 patients had a successful outcome of amenorrhoea or hypomenorrhoea at two-year follow-up. This was a landmark publication and heralded the start of the present era of simple and effective outpatient endometrial ablation.

Since then a large literature has accumulated on aspects relating to the efficacy, complication rates and conditions of use of the different procedures. These different approaches have meant that several relatively simple and new surgical alternatives have become available for women who do not wish or are unsuitable for hysterectomy.

There is no doubt that endometrial ablation has certain advantages over hysterectomy for some women. The transcervical approach avoids an abdominal incision; operating time and hospital stay are shorter and the reduced morbidity allows an earlier return to normal activities. Hysterectomy, however, guarantees amenorrhoea, usually alleviates associated pelvic pain, can be combined with oophorectomy when indicated and is a once-only procedure.

For safe and effective endometrial ablation, appropriate patient selection, adequate training of the surgeon with meticulous attention to surgical endoscopic principles, a theatre team which understands the instruments and careful monitoring of fluid volume balance is essential. Postoperative follow-up looking at treatment outcomes, including the effect on menstruation, complications, costs and return to normal activity are also important (Garry *et al.* 1995).

No matter what modality is used – resection, rollerball coagulation or vaporisation – the prime principle is to destroy the full thickness of endometrium including all of the basal layer to prevent regeneration. However, the endometrial–myometrial interface is irregular over its entire surface and the normal indentations of the basal endometrium cannot be easily distinguished from abnormal down-growth. This explains the common occurrence of microscopic endometrial regeneration and our inability to guarantee amenorrhoea.

The ablation instrument is inserted through the endocervical canal under direct vision into the uterine cavity, which is carefully inspected for any polyps, fibroids, adhesions or other lesions. Most surgeons use a systematic sequence of destroying the endometrium to ensure no untreated areas are left. The fundus is usually treated first with special care at the cornual region where the myometrium is thinnest. Small submucous fibroids can be removed during the procedure.

PATIENT SELECTION

Most women who present for endometrial ablation have already unsuccessfully tried medical therapy but do not wish to undergo hysterectomy. For a successful outcome by endometrial ablation it is essential that women presenting with clinical menorrhagia are thoroughly investigated and carefully selected. Women most suitable are those with a history of menorrhagia where pathology has been excluded and who have completed their family. Ideally, most women should be over 40 years of age, as women under 35 years of age appear to have a greater chance of gradual regeneration of some endometrium. Women with anovulatory dysfunctional bleeding may be less suitable than ovulatory dysfunctional bleeding because of the increased long-term risks of hyperplasia or endometrial carcinoma. Medically unfit patients, such as those with cardiac or respiratory problems or renal failure, are at risk of complications from fluid absorption and the new balloon ablative techniques may be more suitable in these instances.

Pre-operative assessment of uterine size and any associated pathology is mandatory. Transvaginal ultrasound and diagnostic hysteroscopy with a directed endometrial biopsy may be helpful to assess the uterine cavity more accurately. Uterine cavities greater than 12 cm in length, or with multiple fibroids or deep adenomyosis are associated with a poorer success rate and hysterectomy may be a more appropriate option (Fraser 1994; Pooley *et al.* 1998). Other standard investigations include a full blood count and blood film or other tests to exclude thyroid dysfunction or any blood dyscrasia.

The role of endometrial ablation in irregular or heavy bleeding with postmenopausal hormone replacement therapy remains controversial, although it is highly effective. In such circumstances, it remains mandatory to provide progestogen to prevent endometrial hyperplasia in residual endometrium.

OUTCOMES

The major end-points for endometrial ablation are an absence of or a dramatic reduction in menstruation, plus low rates of failure, recurrence and complication. To patients, of course, these are all of prime importance.

Complications

Randomised trials comparing the safety of endometrial ablation with hysterectomy all agree that hysterectomy is associated with significantly more short-term postoperative morbidity, but serious complications are uncommon with either alternative (Dwyer *et al.* 1993; Pinion *et al.* 1994).

The MISTLETOE survey demonstrated that endometrial ablation has low mortality and morbidity rates. However, it is not without risk and, in relatively unskilled hands, loop resection and laser ablation are potentially dangerous operations. Mistakes are more likely to occur in the first few procedures by an inexperienced operator (Overton *et al.* 1997).

Possible complications that can occur with endometrial ablation are well described in the literature and are listed in Table 2. Haemorrhage and uterine perforation are two serious intra-operative complications that can occur from loop resection or laser vaporisation deep into the myometrium which can be avoided by careful attention to technique. Fluid overload with non-electrolyte solution can complicate 1–3% of resection procedures, with large volumes being rapidly absorbed into uterine vessels. This can be minimised by ensuring low intrauterine operating pressures and observing a strict monitoring of fluid volume balance intra-operatively.

Both haematometra and haematosalpinges in patients with intrauterine adhesions or cervical stenosis have been reported to occur both in the short and long term (Narayansingh *et al.* 1999). The true incidence of this post-ablation complication is unclear but should be investigated in women with persistent cyclical pain.

Other potential late complications related to incomplete removal of endometrium are pregnancy and delay in diagnosis of endometrial cancer.

Table 2   *Complications following endometrial ablation*

Intra-operative		
Uterine perforation	Following loop resection (usually inexperienced operator or myoma resection)	Uncommon
Haemorrhage	From uterine vessels	Uncommon
	From extrauterine vessels after perforation	Rare
	Bowel damage and uterine damage	
	Following uterine perforation	Rare
Fluid overload	Following prolonged procedure or deep resection	Mild overload is common
Postoperative		
Early	Uterine infection	
	Predisposing factors unclear	Uncommon
Later	Haematometra haematosalpinges	
	Residual endometrium or adenomyosis causing cyclical bleeding and pain	Uncommon
Pregnancy	Predisposing factors unclear	Rare
	Delay in diagnosis of endometrial cancer	
	Recognised predisposing factors for endometrial cancer	Rare

Post-ablation pregnancy is a potentially serious complication, because of the risks of miscarriage, ectopic pregnancy, premature labour, antepartum haemorrhage, growth restriction of the fetus and placenta accreta. A small number of normal pregnancy outcomes has been reported (Maher and Hill 1990; Opperman et al. 1998).

Endometrial cancer is a rare but serious diagnosis and, although removal of over 90% of endometrium must reduce the incidence, ablation cannot guarantee the complete removal of endometrium or adenomyosis to prevent its occurrence totally. Intrauterine adhesions and cervical stenosis caused by endometrial ablation could potentially mask abnormal endometrial pathology and cause a delay in diagnosis.

A few cases have been reported of unexpected premalignant endometrial changes diagnosed from endometrial strips removed at endometrial resection, as well as rare cases of malignancy (Sorensen and Colov 1996; Iqbal and Paterson 1997). Valle and Baggish (1998) highlighted the well-known factors in women that may indicate a potential risk for endometrial carcinoma and in whom hysterectomy would be a better option. These factors are:

(1) Diabetes mellitus;
(2) Obesity;
(3) Hypertension;
(4) Prolonged anovulatory dysfunctional bleeding;
(5) Complex endometrial hyperplasia;
(6) Persistent hyperplasia not responsive to progestogen therapy.

This highlights the importance of careful patient selection and thorough investigation of the uterine cavity to detect any endometrial pathology prior to ablation.

EFFICACY

Many thousands of ablations have now been reported with amenorrhoea rates varying from 30% to 60% and hypomenorrhoea from 20% to 40% in the short and medium term, but with few data so far reported on long-term success. Most of these follow-up studies to date have relied on subjective assessments such as questionnaires or semi-objective measurement (pad charts or pictorial blood-loss assessment charts) of menstrual blood loss in assessment of their success rates.

Studies that have objectively measured menstrual blood loss confirm amenorrhoea rates of 62–74% in the short term and hypomenorrhoea around 20% (Fraser et al. 1995) while, in the medium term, rates of 20–25% and 40–58%, respectively, have been reported (Chullapram et al. 1996).

No matter what technique is used, success can be influenced by several factors – operator experience, pre-operative endometrial thinning and patient age of greater than 40 years are associated with greater success rates. Factors such as enlarged uterus, adenomyosis, uterine myomata and anovulatory dysfunctional bleeding have higher failure rates (Chullapram et al. 1996; Donnez et al. 1997; Hart and Magos 1997; Gandhi et al. 1999).

Endometrial thinning with hormonal regimens danazol and gonadotrophin-releasing hormone agonists prior to ablation have been demonstrated in randomised clinical trials to be of great benefit, by improving both the intrauterine operating environment and postoperative outcome. Bleeding during surgery is minimised, improving the visibility within the uterine cavity, producing shorter operating times and increasing the ease of surgery (Vercillini et al. 1996; Donnez et al. 1997).

Goserelin acetate is the most widely studied thinning agent and in randomised placebo-controlled trials is shown to be superior to endometrial ablation alone, in ease of surgery and increased amenorrhoea and hypomenorrhoea rates in the short term. A few randomised trials comparing goserelin acetate with danazol have shown there to be a small but significant increase in amenorrhoea rates. Progestogens are much less effective since the endometrium may be unpredictably decidualised and oedematous (Fraser *et al.* 1995; Garry *et al.* 1996; Donnez *et al.* 1997; Sowter *et al.* 1997).

All studies have shown a gradually increasing failure rate with time, with a plateau in efficacy at three years (Chullapram *et al.* 1996; Hart and Magos 1997; O'Connor *et al.* 1997). The majority of larger scale studies report that 5–10% of patients may require a repeat ablation and up to 10% may require a hysterectomy. Careful review of the pathology from women who undergo hysterectomy not suprisingly demonstrates a high incidence of uterine myomata, adenomyosis or endometriosis (Chullapram *et al.* 1996; Vilos *et al.* 1996; Steffensen and Schuster 1997; Phillips *et al.* 1998).

Pretreatment counselling regarding the short-, medium- and long-term realistic outcomes of success and complications is extremely important in determining patient satisfaction with the procedure. Women need to be counselled that amenorrhoea is not the expected outcome after endometrial ablation but that a dramatic reduction in blood-loss volume is the aim. Overall, in most follow-up studies, patient satisfaction with the outcomes is high and comparable to hysterectomy (Chullapram *et al.* 1996; Bhattacharya *et al.* 1997; Crosignani *et al.* 1997; O'Connor *et al.* 1997).

TRAINING

Most gynaecologists are well trained in the traditional surgical approaches of hysterectomy, either abdominal or vaginal, but many have also taken up the challenge to learn the different skills required to perform endoscopic procedures inside the small and relatively non-distensible uterine cavity. There is a substantial learning curve involved in becoming proficient in these techniques and many find some difficulty in mastering the hand–eye co-ordination of operating from a two-dimensional video screen (which is complicated further by use of a foot pedal for diathermy activation).

Safe and effective operative hysteroscopy requires specialised training. Learning diagnostic hysteroscopy skills is essential, followed by simple operative procedures such as endometrial polypectomy and removal of small submucous myomas, before embarking on the more advanced operations of endometrial ablation. Rollerball ablation is the easiest and safest to master and should be learnt first before laser or endometrial resection with the resectoscope. Attendance at training programmes and workshops, hands-on assisting and other practice sessions are important in achieving these skills.

THE FUTURE

Man's urgency and the desire to apply new technology is pointing the way to a 'Brave New World' with intriguing initiatives for the simplification of endometrial destruction.

These new developments began with Phipps *et al.* (1990), who designed a non-hysteroscopic approach to destroying endometrium with the radio-frequency endometrial ablation (RaFEA) probe. The technique used the principle of capacitative heating, where an electric field is generated around the probe by applying radio-frequency electro-magnetic energy, causing heating and destruction of the endometrium. This method was moderately effective, with early reports of 74% reduction in menstrual loss from pad studies. Uncommon complications such as burns and vesicovaginal fistulas, plus the expense of the equipment, have led to its abandonment.

Recently, a wide range of new technologies has been introduced which utilises simplified and effective delivery of different energy modalities (heating, cooling and laser) to destroy the endometrium.

New techniques such as balloons, microwaves, cryo-ablation and instillation of fluid are under investigation, with preliminary reports in the literature that show promising results. Some key characteristics of these systems are listed in Table 3. These methods appear to be simple to use, easy to master and are associated with a low incidence of complications. The major concern is the temptation for the surgeon to 'cut corners' and not investigate the patients fully prior to surgery, because of the ease of the techniques.

Most are blind non-hysteroscopic procedures that require a disposable handpiece to deliver the energy inside the uterus – at variable cost. All utilise a complex and expensive control box that generates energy and contains a series of fail-safe mechanisms to prevent complications and maximise efficiency. Systems that involve inflatable balloons do not require prethinning of the endometrium, but rely on adequate balloon pressures against the uterine wall to flatten the endometrium. Other techniques involve the use of a probe or free flow of hot saline, and will require endometrial thinning.

The thermal balloons (Thermachoice®, Gynecare; Cavaterm®, Wallsten Medical) consist of a catheter with a latex balloon attached to the distal end, housing the heating elements and temperature sensors, which are inflated to pressures of 100–180 mmHg. When activated, the heater maintains the intra-balloon solution temperature at around 87°C for a heating time of eight minutes (Neuwirth et al. 1994). Amenorrhoea and hypomenorrhoea rates are reported to be 15–30% and 32–48%, respectively (Vilos et al. 1997; Amso et al. 1998; Friberg et al. 1998; Meyer et al. 1998).

The Vesta® (multi-electrode balloon, Valleylab) has six ventral and six dorsal electrode plates covering the surface of the balloon, each with its own thermistor. When the balloon is distended the electrodes are held firmly against the endometrial surface and destruction occurs to a depth of 4–5 mm into the myometrium, with a precisely controlled treatment phase lasting four minutes. Preliminary results to two years post-treatment show an amenorrhoea rate of 40% and hypomenorrhoea of 49% (Soderstrom et al. 1996; Corson et al. 1999).

The main advantages of the balloon systems are that they require minimal skill, they are simple and safe, have no serious complications and have the potential for use in an outpatient setting. The disadvantages are that it is a blind procedure and a normal uterine cavity is needed for contact of the balloon with the endometrium. Therefore, the technique should not be used in the presence of fibroids, polyps or adhesions.

Probe systems work by destroying the endometrium as they move from one cornual area to the other over a period of a few minutes. Microwave endometrial ablation (MEA) uses microwave power to generate temperatures reaching 95°C within a few seconds, with a treatment time of only two or three minutes (Sharp et al. 1995). The Endocryo® (Surgical Technology Group) probe is a system based on similar designs to Droegemueller's that uses CO_2 or nitrous oxide via a probe to freeze a small amount of normal saline, forming an ice mould to freeze the endometrium to temperatures of −40°C (Pittrof et al. 1994).

The Hydrotherm® ablator involves the infusion and circulation within the uterine cavity of externally heated 0.9% normal saline under direct visualisation through a

Table 3 *Characteristics of the different techniques for endometrial ablation*

Technique	Energy source	Energy delivery system	Intrauterine medium	Expensive control box/ generator power source	Endometrial thinning	Operating time (minutes)	Surgical skill required
Laser	Nd:YAG laser	Bare fibre	Saline	Yes	Yes	30–45	+++
Rollerball	Electrosurgery	Retractable ball	Glycine sorbitol	No	Yes	10–30	++
Resection	Electrosurgery	Retractable loop	Glycine sorbitol	No	Yes	10–30	+++
RaFEA	Micro-radio-frequency waves	Probe	–	Yes	Yes	15	++
Vesta®	Electrosurgery	Balloon	–	Yes	No	<15	+
Cavaterm®	Heating element	Balloon	Hot water	Yes	No	<15	+
Hydrotherm ablation	Heating element	Hot saline through handpiece	Hot saline	Yes	No	<15	+
Endocryo® probe	Rapid cooling source	Balloon	Freezing coolant	Yes	No	<15	+
Thermachoice®	Heating source	Balloon	Hot saline	Yes	No	<15	+
MEA	Microwave	Probe	–	Yes	No	<15	++
Photo-dynamic therapy	Laser light	Trifurcated diffusing tip	Photoactive metabolite	Yes	Yes	<15	+

MEA=microwave endometrial ablation; RaFEA=radio-frequency endometrial ablation; +=minimal hysteroscopic skill required; ++=moderate hysteroscopic skill required; +++=experienced hysteroscopic skill required continuous-flow hysteroscope to a temperature of about 90°C for a period of ten minutes (Goldrath *et al.* 1997).

The feasibility and effectiveness of an intrauterine light probe which aims to destroy endometrium by photodynamic laser light therapy looks promising (Tadir *et al.* 1999).

Preliminary short-term results of these new techniques are encouraging, although most have yet to be thoroughly evaluated in an objective manner over the medium to long term. Objective long-term outcomes are needed before we can say that these new techniques will be superior or equal to more conventional methods.

If gynaecologists are no longer performing endometrial ablations in five years' time it will be because of the widespread introduction of the levonorgestrel-releasing intrauterine system (LNG-IUS) (Mirena®, Leiras and Schering). This device dramatically reduces the volume of menstrual blood loss in women with menorrhagia (Andersson and Rybo 1990) and comparative trials have shown no difference in the reduction of blood loss between endometrial ablation and LNG-IUS (Crosignani *et al.* 1997; Kittlesen and Istre 1998).

Uterine arterial embolisation by interventional radiological techniques is currently being assessed and may be appropriate for certain patients, particularly for those with menorrhagia due to fibroids.

CONCLUSION

Endometrial ablation is a simple procedure in principle, but for maximum efficiency and safety it requires careful selection of patients, proper counselling, appropriate pre-operative evaluation and preparation, training of operating-theatre staff and careful attention to technique. There is optimum efficacy in women with ovulatory dysfunctional uterine bleeding, or when combined with hysteroscopic resection of small endometrial polyps or submucous myomata. There is considerable promise that the new endometrial ablative technologies will make the procedure easier and more cost-effective with outpatient surgery under light sedation and local analgesia.

References

Amso, N.N., Stabinsky, S.A., McFaul, P., Blanc, B., Pendley, L. and Neuwirth, R. (1998) Uterine thermal balloon therapy for the treatment of menorrhagia: the first 300 patients from a multicentre study. *Br J Obstet Gynaecol* **105**, 517–23

Andersson, K. and Rybo, G. (1990) Levonorgestrel releasing intrauterine device in the treatment of menorrhagia. *Br J Obstet Gynaecol* **97**, 690–4

Baumann, A. (1948) Ueber die elektrokoagulation des endometrium sowie der zervikalschleimhaut. *Geburtshilfe und Frauenheilkunde* **8**, 221

Bhattacharya, S., Cameron, I. and Parkin, D. (1997) A pragmatic randomised comparison of transcervical resection of the endometrium with endometrial laser ablation for the treatment of menorrhagia. *Br J Obstet Gynaecol* **104**, 601–7

Chullapram, T., Song, J. Y. and Fraser, I. S. (1996) Medium term follow-up of women with menorrhagia treated by rollerball endometrial ablation. *Obstet Gynecol* **88**, 71–6

Corson, S., Brill, A., Brooks, P. *et al.* (1999) Interim results of the American Vesta trial of endometrial ablation. *J Am Assoc Gynecol Laparosc* **6**, 45–9

Crosignani, P.G., Vercellini, P,. Mosconi, P., Oldani, S., Cortesi, I. and De Giorgi, O. (1997) Levonorgestrel-releasing intrauterine device versus hysteroscopic endometrial resection in the treatment of dysfunctional uterine bleeding. *Obstet Gynecol* **90**, 257–63

DeCherney, A. and Polan, M.L. (1983) Hysteroscopic management of intrauterine lesions and intractable uterine bleeding. *Obstet Gynecol* **61**, 392–7

DeCherney, A., Diamond, M., Lavy, G. and Polan, M. (1987) Endometrial ablation for intractable uterine bleeding hysteroscopic resection. *Obstet Gynecol* **70**, 668–70

Donnez, J., Vilos, G., Gannon, M., Stampe-Sorensen, S., Klinte, I. and Miller, R. (1997) Goserelin acetate (Zoladex) plus endometrial ablation for dysfunctional uterine bleeding: a large randomised double blind study. *Fertil Steril* **68**, 29–36

Droegemueller, W., Greer, B.E. and Makowski, E.L. (1970) Preliminary observations of cryocoagulation of the endometrium. *Am J Obstet Gynecol* **107**, 958–61

Droegemueller, W., Greer, B. and Makowski, E. (1971a) Cryosurgery in patients with dysfunctional uterine bleeding. *Obstet Gynecol* **38**, 256–8

Droegemueller, W., Makowski, E. and Macsalka, R. (1971b) Destruction of the endometrium by cryosurgery. *Am J Obstet Gynecol* **110**, 467–9

Dwyer, N., Hutton, J. and Stirrat, G. (1993) Randomised controlled trial comparing endometrial resection with abdominal hysterectomy. *Br J Obstet Gynaecol* **100**, 237–43

Edstrom K. and Fernstrom, J. (1970) The diagnostic possibilities of a modified hysteroscopic technique. *Acta Obstet Gynecol Scand* **49**, 327–30

Fraser, I.S. (1994) Menorrhagia: a pragmatic approach to the understanding of causes and the need for investigations. *Br J Obstet Gynaecol* **101** Suppl 11, 3–7

Fraser, I.S., Healy, D.L., Torode, H., Song, J.Y., Mamers, P. and Wilde, F. (1995) Depot goserelin and danazol pretreatment before rollerball endometrial ablation for menorrhagia. *Obstet Gynecol* **4**, 544–50

Friberg, B., Persson, B.R., Willen, R. and Ahlgren, M. (1998) Endometrial destruction by thermal coagulation for a new form of treatment of menorrhagia. *Gynaecological Endoscopy* **7**, 73–8

Gandhi, S., Fear, K. and Sturdee, D. (1999) Endometrial resection: factors affecting long term success. *Gynaecological Endoscopy* **8**, 41–50

Garry, R., Erian, J., Fraser, I. *et al.* (1995) Good practise with endometrial ablation. *Obstet Gynecol* **86**, 144–51

Garry, R., Khair, A., Mooney, P. and Stuart, M. (1996) A comparison of goserelin and danazol as endometrial thinning agents prior to endometrial laser ablation. *Br J Obstet Gynaecol* **103**, 339–44

Goldrath, M., Fuller, T. and Segal, S. (1981) Laser photovaporization of endometrium for the treatment of menorrhagia. *Am J Obstet Gynecol* **140**, 14–19

Goldrath, M.H., Barrionuero, M. and Husain, M. (1997) Endometrial ablation by hysteroscopic instillation of hot saline solution. *J Am Assoc Gynecol Laparosc* **4**, 235–40

Hart, R. and Magos, A. (1997) Endometrial ablation. *Curr Opin Obstet Gynecol* **9**, 226–32

Iqbal, P.K. and Paterson, M.E.L. (1997) Endometrial carcinoma after endometrial resection for menorrhagia. *Br J Obstet Gynaecol* **104**, 1097–8

Kittelsen, N. and Istre, O. (1998) A randomised study comparing levonorgestrel intrauterine system and transcervical resection of the endometrium in the treatment of menorrhagia: preliminary results. *Gynecological Endoscopy* **7**, 61–5

LaMorte, A. and DeCherney, A. (1993) 'History of operative hysteroscopy' in: A.G. Gordon and V. Lewis (Eds) *Endometrial Ablation*, pp. 1–6. Edinburgh: Churchill Livingstone

Levine, R. and Neuwirth, R. (1972) Evaluation of a method of hysteroscopy with the use of 30% dextran. *Am J Obstet Gynecol* **113**, 696–9

Lin, B., Miyamoto, N. and Tomomatu, M. (1988) The development of a new hysteroscopic resectoscope and its clinical applications for transcervical resection and endometrial ablation. *Jap J Gynecol Obstet Endoscopy* **56**, 56–61

Lindemann, H. (1973) Historical aspects of hysteroscopy. *Fertil Steril* **24**, 240–3

Maher, P.J. and Hill, D.J. (1990) Trancervical endometrial resection for abnormal uterine bleeding: report of 100 cases and review of the literature. *Aust N Z J Obstet Gynaecol* **30**, 357–60

Meyer, W.R., Walsh, B.W., Grangeer D.A., Peacock, L.M., Loffler, F.D. and Steege, J.F. (1998) Thermal balloon and rollerball ablation to treat menorrhagia: a multicentre comparison. *Obstet Gynecol* **92**, 98–103

Narayansingh, G., Parkin, D. and Dillon, P. (1999) Gross bilateral haematosalpinges presenting five years following endometrial resection. *Gynaecological Endoscopy* **8**, 55–7

Neuwirth, R.S., Duran, A.A. and Singer, A. (1994) The endometrial ablator: a new instrument. *Obstet Gynecol* **83**, 792–6

O'Connor, H., Broadbent, J., Magos, A.L. and McPherson, K. (1997) Medical Research Council randomised trial of endometrial resection and hysterectomy in management of menorrhagia. *Lancet* **349**, 897–901

Opperman, J., Child, A., Browning, D. and Fraser, I.S. (1998) Pregnancy following endometrial ablation. *Gynaecological Endoscopy* **7**, 21–4

Overton, C., Hardgraves, J. and Maresh, M. (1997) A national survey of the complications of endometrial destruction for menstrual disorders. The MISTLETOE study. *Br J Obstet Gynaecol* **104**, 1351–9

Pantaleoni, D. (1869) On endoscopic examination of the cavity of the womb. *Medical Press Circular* **8**, 26–7

Phillips, G., Chien, P. and Garry, R. (1998) Risk of hysterectomy after 1000 consecutive endometrial laser ablations. *Br J Obstet Gynaecol* **105**, 897–903

Phipps, J.H., Lewis, B.V., Roberts, T. *et al.* (1990) Treatment of functional menorrhagia with radio frequency endometrial ablation. *Lancet* **335**, 374–6

Pinion, S.B., Parkin, D.E., Abramovich, D.R. *et al.* (1994) Randomised trial of hysterectomy, endometrial laser ablation and transcervical resection for dysfunctional uterine bleeding. *BMJ* **309**, 979–83

Pittrof, R., Majid, S. and Murray, L. (1994) Transcervical endometrial cryoablation (ECA) using 0.9% saline as a uterine distension medium: a safe easy effective minimally invasive treatment for menorrhagia. *Int J Gynaecol Obstet* **4**, 40–5

Pooley, A., Ewan, S. and Sutton, C. (1998) Does transcervical resection of the endometrium for menorrhagia really avoid hysterectomy? Life table analysis of a large series. *J Am Assoc Gynecol Laparosc* **5**, 229–35

Sharp, N.C., Cronin, N., Feldberg, I., Evans, M., Hodgson, D. and Ellis, S. (1995) Microwave for menorrhagia: a new fast technique for endometrial ablation. *Lancet* **346**, 1003–4

Soderstrom, R.M., Brooks, P.G., Corson, S.L. *et al.* (1996) Endometrial ablation using a distensible multi-electrode balloon. *J Am Assoc Gynecol Laparosc* **3**, 403–7

Sorensen, S.S. and Colov, N.P. (1996) Endometrial ablation and potential risk of subsequent malignancy. *Gynaecological Endoscopy* **5**, 97–100

Sowter, M.C., Bidgood, K. and Richardson, J.A. (1997) A perspective randomised trial of the effect of pre-operative endometrial inhibition on the long term outcome of trans-cervical endometrial resection. *Gynaecological Endoscopy* **6**, 33–7

Steffensen, A. and Schuster, M. (1997) Endometrial resection and late re-operation in the treatment of menorrhagia. *J Am Assoc Gynecol Laparosc* **4**, 325–9

Tadir, Y., Hornung, R., Pham, T.H. and Tromberg, B.J. (1999) Intrauterine light probe for photodynamic ablation therapy. *Obstet Gynecol* **93**, 299–303

Valle, R.F. and Baggish, M.S. (1998) Endometrial carcinoma after endometrial ablation: high risk factors predicting its occurrence. *Am J Obstet Gynecol* **179**, 569–72

Vancaillie, T. (1989) Electrocoagulation of the endometrium with the ball-end resectoscope. *Obstet Gynecol* **74**, 425–7

Vancaillie, T. (1993) 'Endometrial electroablation' in: C. Sutton and M. Diamond (Eds) *Endoscopic Surgery for Gynaecologists*, pp. 307–17. London: W.B. Saunders

Vercillini, P., Perino. A., Consonni, R., Trespadi, L., Parazzini, F. and Crosignani, P.G. (1996) Treatment with a gonadotrophin-releasing hormone agonist before endometrial resection: a multicentre, randomised controlled trial. *Br J Obstet Gynaecol* **103**, 562–8

Vilos, G., Vilos, E. and King, J. (1996) Experience with 800 hysteroscopic endometrial ablations. *J Am Assoc Gynecol Laparosc* **4**, 33–8

Vilos, G.A., Fortin, C.A., Sanders, B., Pendley, L. and Stabinsky, S. (1997) Clinical trial of the uterine thermal balloon for treatment of menorrhagia. *J Am Assoc Gynecol Laparosc* **4**, 559–65

30

Endoscopy in the millennium

Oswald M. Petrucco

INTRODUCTION

Endoscopic examination of body cavities began almost a century ago and so it is timely that we appraise our achievements in this field at the end of the 20th century.

The history of laparoscopy has been fully documented by Steptoe (1967). His book, *Laparoscopy in Gynaecology*, describes diagnostic and surgical approaches as well as complications that remain pertinent today. In the book he reports the endoscopy milestones shown in Table 1. It is of interest in relation to culdoscopy that Gordts *et al.* (1997) recently reintroduced this technique describing the office procedure 'transvaginal hydro laparoscopy using the lithotomy position and local anaesthesia', claiming that this technique may eliminate routine laparoscopy in up to 50% of infertile patients. More recent milestones are shown in Table 2.

Table 1 *Endoscopy milestones; adapted from Steptoe (1967)*

Date	Reference	Milestone
1901	Kelling	Endoscopy in the dog
1910	Jacoboeus	First clinical endoscopy
1912	Nordentoeft	Gaseous distension and use of Trendelenburg position
1928	Short	Use of cystoscope via abdominal incision
1937	Ruddock	Biopsy forceps and diathermy coagulation
	Hope	Laparoscopy for diagnosis of ectopic pregnancy
	Hope and Anderson	Suggested laparoscopic diathermy for sterilisation
1938	Veress	Needle for pneumoperitoneum
1944	Decker and Cherry	Vaginal 'culdoscopy' using local anaesthesia, pneumoperitoneum in genupectoral position
	Palmer	Transparietal coelioscopy
1946	Palmer	Culdoscopy – Trendelenburg position with pneumoperitoneum and uterine elevation
1947	Palmer	Operative hysteroscopy
1948	Telinde and Rutledge	Vaginal 'culdoscopy' approach
1951	Kalk and Bruhl	Laparoscopy in Europe
1952	Fourestier, Gladu, Vulmière	Quartz rod cool light illumination
1954	Hopkins and Kapany	Fibre optic laparoscopy

Continuing improvement in the quality of telescopes, camera systems, television monitors and ancillary endoscopic instruments has facilitated the introduction of minimal access surgery (MAS) techniques. The evolution of the medical video camera is summarised in Table 3.

Once introduced to the world of endoscopy, it is readily apparent why endoscopists enjoy endoscopic surgery. The clear, panoramic view currently available via endoscopes of the abdominal, pelvic and uterine cavities has been a prime motivating factor for the rapid expansion of MAS.

ENDOSCOPIC MAS – CURRENT STATUS

MAS utilises endoscopic techniques to perform invasive surgical procedures through smaller entry incisions thus obviating laparotomy. This fundamental difference has led to rapid growth of endoscopic surgery, initially because of the obvious cosmetic and recuperative advantages that include faster recovery, shorter hospitalisation and earlier

Table 2 *Recent endoscopy milestones*

Date	Reference	Milestone
1965	Palmer and Cohen	Electrocautery of polycystic ovaries
1977	Semm	Laparoscopic suture device
1977	Bruhat	Laparoscopic salpingostomy
1986	Nezhat	Video pelviscopy
1990	Kerin	Falloposcopy

Table 3 *Evolution of the medical video camera*

Year	Camera device	Highlights	Resolution (lines)	Light sensitivity (lux)	Signal to noise ratio (dB)
To 1981	Glass vacuum tube – 1 in	Used 1500 volts	250	30	35
1982	Metal oxide silicon chip – $\frac{2}{3}$ in	Solid state one-chip, smaller	260	100	35
1985	Charged coupled device (CCD) – $\frac{2}{3}$ in	Smaller	350	30	42
1992	$\frac{1}{2}$ in CCD	Super VHS brighter one-chip unit	470	10	46
1992	3 chip hyper CCD	3 prism block uses all available light	850	1.5	60
Current	High-definition television	High-definition TV technology improves resolution	1200+	0.1	70

return to full activity. Just as important, however, are the advantages associated with improved visibility within the abdomen and pelvis and improved assessment of pathology. The possibilities of therapy at diagnosis and day-surgery application with potential cost reduction in general health expenditure, make MAS attractive to gynaecologists and healthcare providers.

In most countries endoscopic operations have been introduced by innovative surgeons without clinical validation and with outcome data usually limited to uncontrolled personal series or retrospective comparisons with equivalent open surgery. This contrasts sharply with the legislative requirements for initial evaluation and introduction of new drugs and pharmaceuticals for which there is, in most countries, a strict assessment process involving clinical trials, proof of safety and mechanisms for reporting complications to a central body.

The dissension between proponents of new endoscopic techniques and traditionalists has been heightened by the realisation that endoscopic surgery, while fulfilling expectations of improved outcome is, at times, associated with new complications unexpected in traditional surgery. Added to issues of efficacy and safety, escalating healthcare expenditure has necessitated examination of the cost effectiveness of new surgical techniques, particularly when new technology has been introduced to perform the surgery.

In the obstetric and perinatal subspecialties, the Cochrane Pregnancy and Childbirth Database has provided evidence to systematically review effective obstetric care. The application of epidemiological principles to effective gynaecology and particularly MAS is still in its infancy. The publication of *Effective Procedures in Gynaecology Suitable for Audit* by the RCOG (1999) and the involvement of leading clinicians in the Cochrane Collaboration groups in gynaecology seems timely to correct this anomaly. Evolution of MAS in gynaecological practice should examine:

(1) Efficacy – an ideal situation when a new technique is practised by experts and results are substantiated by controlled clinical trials;
(2) Effectiveness – when a new operation achieves satisfactory results by the majority of surgeons and fulfils most patients' expectations;
(3) Efficiency – to be efficient the new technique has been proven to be cost effective with least complications after adequate comparison with non-surgical and previously available surgical techniques.

Unless proven safe and clinically effective, new MAS procedures must be considered experimental. One explanation why MAS procedures are still under assessment is that, in most countries, many gynaecologists are still learning to perform new endoscopic operations, some of which are undergoing constant modification.

To examine the role of endoscopic MAS in gynaecological practice we should assess not only current clinical applications but also, and more importantly, the available evidence for the epidemiological and scientific validation of specific operations with regard to:

(1) Appropriateness;
(2) Clinical effectiveness;
(3) Performance outcome;
(4) Efficacy and safety;
(5) Cost effectiveness.

Table 4 *Gynaecological conditions – endoscopic minimal access surgery*

Disease process	Endoscopic technique
Menorrhagia	Laparoscopic associated hysterectomy
	Hysteroscopic endometrial ablation/resection
Ectopic pregnancy	Laparoscopic salpingostomy/salpingectomy
	Laparoscopic injection methotrexate/other destructive agents
Urinary stress incontinence	Laparoscopic Burch colposuspension
Benign ovarian tumours	Laparoscopic cystectomy/oophorectomy
Pelvic and rectovaginal, gastrointestinal and bladder endometriosis	Laparoscopic laser/electrosurgical ablation, laparoscopic excision
Vaginal prolapse	Laparoscopic pelvic-floor reconstruction
Pelvic malignancy	Laparoscopic lymphadenectomy
Uterine fibroids	Laparoscopic myomectomy
	Hysteroscopic myoma resection
Congenital uterine abnormalities (recurrent miscarriages)	Hysteroscopic resection uterine septum
Blind uterine horn	Laparoscopic excision
Uterine synechiae	Hysteroscopic division adhesions
Infertility diagnosis adhesions, hydrosalpinx, sterilisation	Falloposcopy, laparoscopic adhesiolysis, salpingostomy, salpingectomy, laparoscopic tubal anastomosis
Polycystic ovarian disease	Laparoscopic laser/electrocautery drilling

The latter should include an assessment of costs incurred in postoperative care of patients discharged from day-surgery centres or following discharge from hospital.

MAS has found application for the management of the majority of surgically treatable gynaecological conditions (summarised in Table 4). Some applications of MAS have been more controversial than others and will be reviewed according to the above guidelines.

LAPAROSCOPY-ASSISTED HYSTERECTOMY (LAH)

Since the introduction of laparoscopic hysterectomy by Reich *et al.* (1989) with the objective of obviating abdominal hysterectomy, diverse views have been expressed in the gynaecological literature as to the role of the operation in modern gynaecological practice. An important sequela has been the reassessment by many gynaecologists of the indications for the abdominal, vaginal and LAH operations.

The type of procedure chosen is usually dependent on the attitude and operative skill of the surgeon in performing vaginal hysterectomy. The presence of a large uterine mass (greater than 12 weeks' gestational size), associated endometriosis, pelvic adhesions, the need to perform oophorectomy, vaginal scarring and nulliparity are usually considered contraindications to the vaginal route. This has resulted in the majority of hysterectomies being performed abdominally, with UK gynaecologists carrying out 19.2% of hysterectomies vaginally in 1993–94 (Nuffield Institute for Health 1995). In 1995, 74% of 15 379 hysterectomies performed for dysfunctional uterine bleeding (normal pelvic findings) were carried out abdominally (Hall *et al.* 1998). It is interesting to note that in some countries the incidence of vaginal hysterectomy began to rise in the early 1990s despite a low (4–8%) incidence of LAH in the UK, USA and Australia (Wood *et al.* 1997) and 7–11% in Finland (Harkki-Siren *et al.* 1998). Between 1990 and 1995 vaginal hysterectomy increased from 22% to 35% in Australia. The impact of LAH on choice of operation has been difficult to assess for several reasons:

(1) Availability of trained gynaecologists, preceptors, training units;
(2) Operator preference for vaginal hysterectomy, despite having advanced endoscopy skills (Querleu *et al.* 1993);
(3) Overall preference for vaginal hysterectomy (Browne and Fraser 1991; Kovac 1995; Richardson *et al.* 1995).

Following the introduction of LAH, important questions remained unanswered unrelated to operator surgical skills, requiring a review of evidence-based data to formulate guidelines for best practice in relation to hysterectomy procedures. Several reviews have been written on this topic (Garry and Phillips 1995, 1998; Kovac 1995; Wood *et al.* 1997; Healy and Petrucco 1998), each reaching different conclusions. The most important reason why it is difficult to reach a consensus decision is the paucity of randomised prospective controlled trials comparing different types of hysterectomies. Other reasons include:

(1) The influence of learning-curve experience;
(2) Difficulty in comparing results of past studies, for example the study of Dicker *et al.* (1982) used unmatched historical controls (Garry 1998);
(3) The lack of agreed criteria as to what pathology may contraindicate vaginal hysterectomy;
(4) The need to carry out laparoscopy to assess pelvic pathology rather than facilitate hysterectomy;
(5) The substantial overlap in the indications to perform abdominal, LAH or vaginal hysterectomy (Bertram *et al.* 1997);

Table 5   *Comparison laparoscopic hysterectomy (LH) versus abdominal hysterectomy (AH) – randomised controlled trials*

	Olsson et al. (1996)		Langebrekke et al. (1996)		Marana et al. (1997)		Petrucco et al. (1999)	
	LH	*AH*	*LH*	*AH*	*LH*	*AH*	*LH*	*AH*
Sample size	71	72	46	54	58	58	63	62
Operating time (minutes)	148	85	100	60.5	91	92	100	75
Analgesia (days)	–	–	2	5	–	–	0.9	1.4
Pain score (visual analogue 48 hours)	3.6	4.2	–	–	–	–	–	–
Hospital stay (median) (days)	2	4	2	5	–	–	2	3
Nurse dependencies (units)	–	–	–	–	–	–	1.1	1.3
Return to work (days)	–	–	19.5	36.5	–	–	21	28
Complications	27%	33%	21%	26%	–	–	11% [a]	9% [a]

[a] Haemorrhage requiring transfusion and unintended major surgery

(6) Lack of agreed terminology and definition for different types of LAH;
(7) Lack of validated evidence-based data to compare vaginal versus abdominal hysterectomy before comparison can be made with LAH procedures (Davies and Magos 1997).

Comparison of clinical results of LAH versus abdominal and vaginal hysterectomy from prospective randomised trials

The earliest studies (Nezhat *et al.* 1992; Phipps *et al.* 1993; Raju and Auld 1994) had small numbers of patients but reached the same clinical conclusions as more recent studies (Table 5). All these studies have tended to indicate that LAH took significantly longer to perform than abdominal hysterectomy but was associated with a significantly shorter stay in hospital and shorter convalescence.

Olsson *et al.* (1996) confirmed a significantly lower blood loss and need for blood transfusion following LAH. Overall, complication rates were similar in most studies for both groups of patients. The study by Marana *et al.* (1997) is particularly important as it included patients with a mean uterine weight of 300 g. They observed the same operating time, with blood loss and postoperative pain in favour of LAH. Urinary-tract injuries were reported in three of the studies (ureteric injuries: Langebrekke *et al.* 1996 and Petrucco *et al.*, unpublished data; vesicovaginal fistula: Olsson *et al.* 1996).

The results of the two small randomised studies comparing vaginal to laparoscopy-assisted vaginal hysterectomy (LAVH) again indicated a longer operating time but otherwise similar clinical outcomes for the two procedures. Assessment of non-randomised prospective and retrospective series with inclusion of meta-analysis have indicated similar (patient outcome) results (Bertram *et al.* 1997; Healy and Petrucco 1998). These reviews found an overall increase in cost for LAH compared to abdominal and vaginal hysterectomy, particularly with the use of disposable instruments and when more extensive use was made of laparoscopic techniques. A more recent Australian study (Tsaltas *et al.* 1997) which examined all resources used in patient care, concluded that there were no significant differences in hospital-related costs between carrying out abdominal and LAVH. Surgical techniques, operating time, hospital stay, analgesic use, complications, return to normal activity, conversion to laparotomy and costs in relation to randomised and non-randomised studies have been summarised by Healy and Petrucco (1998).

Safety and complications of LAH were assessed in a meta-analysis of 20 studies involving skilled laparoscopic surgeons contributing 3189 cases (Garry and Phillips 1995). Compared with abdominal and vaginal hysterectomy (Dicker *et al.* 1982) LAH indicated:

(1) Less febrile morbidity;
(2) Less need for transfusion;
(3) Comparable unintended major surgery, bowel and urinary-tract trauma and incidence of pulmonary embolism.

An audit of complications for a total city population of gynaecologists during their learning-curve experience for the years 1991–94 was carried out in Adelaide, South Australia (O'Shea and Petrucco 1996). In these 760 cases a greater incidence of pelvic haematoma, conversion to laparotomy and urinary tract injury were observed and confirmed that in the 'real world' complication rates are higher than in series from experienced operators.

A prospective quality assurance survey was undertaken by the Royal Australian College of Obstetricians and Gynaecologists and Australian Gynaecological Endoscopy Society. Questionnaires returned by Fellows and patients (546) confirmed that the overall complication rate was not significantly different from abdominal and vaginal hysterectomy cases. Four hundred and fifteen patients (98%) indicated that they would recommend LAH procedure to a relative or friend (Petrucco *et al.* 1996).

The resurgence of subtotal hysterectomy

To improve safety (uterine artery and ureteric injury) and also render the operation easier and faster to perform, several authors have reported on the use of laparoscopic subtotal hysterectomy (LSH) (Donnez and Nisolle 1993; Hasson 1993; Lyons 1993; Semm 1993; Ewen and Sutton 1994). Morcellation of uterine tissue with electronic morcellators and electrocoagulation or resection of the transformation zone and cervical canal of the remaining cervical stump have facilitated and improved subtotal hysterectomy.

The 1990–96 500-case series of Donnez *et al.* (1997) confirmed a favourable operating time and low intra- and postoperative complication rates. Daniell *et al.* (1998), using an electromechanical morcellator, found a mean morcellation time of 12 minutes and mean operating time of 94 minutes (range 60–225 minutes). Thirty-six of 41 patients were discharged within 23 hours and all were discharged within 48 hours of admission.

Retrospective studies compared LSH with LAVH (Lyons 1993; Schwartz 1993; Richards and Simpkins 1995) and abdominal hysterectomy (case–controlled study, Sutton 1995). These series have indicated a statistically significant difference favouring laparoscopic subtotal technique for operating time, blood loss, hospital stay and interval to return to work. The results of these studies, although of interest, indicate a need for more formal randomised studies to be performed, due to the less than ideal comparisons between groups.

The importance of clinical indications for hysterectomy

Garry (1998) makes the important point that 'hysterectomy will alleviate menorrhagia whereas it may not always improve pelvic pain, dyspareunia or general ill health'. A good example is the failure of hysterectomy to cure pelvic pain due to rectovaginal septum endometriosis. This clinical finding requires the resection of all tissues infiltrated by endometriosis for complete cure. Hysterectomy, unless performed with bilateral oophorectomy, is of secondary importance in this clinical setting. The use of guidelines to determine the route of hysterectomy based on pelvic pathology suggested by Kovac (1998) is also of interest in choosing the hysterectomy technique most appropriate for a particular patient. While supporting Magos' (1996) view that vaginal hysterectomy 'remains the optimal route of surgery' randomised trials of different techniques for different pelvic pathology need to be undertaken.

Conclusions

(1) LAH has proven to be a more efficient, acceptable and cost-effective procedure in comparison to abdominal hysterectomy;

(2) Cost effectiveness, acceptability and efficiency versus vaginal hysterectomy has not been proven;
(3) Possible benefits of laparoscopic subtotal or laparoscopic Doderlein procedures versus LAH need further assessment by prospective randomised trials;
(4) Complication rates of LAH, exclusive of 'learning curve' experience, are not higher than for abdominal and vaginal hysterectomy;
(5) Gynaecologists in training should become skilled in vaginal as well as advanced endoscopic surgery.

MAS FOR ECTOPIC GESTATION

Endoscopic management of ectopic gestation commenced in 1973 when laparoscopic salpingectomy was introduced (Shapiro and Adler 1973) and salpingostomy in 1977 (Bruhat et al. 1977). Despite widespread acceptance of these techniques debate still exists on the most cost effective approach to management, so that even in developed countries a substantial number of ectopic pregnancies are managed by laparotomy. Australian Medicare statistics relating to privately insured patients indicate that there has been a steady increase in endoscopically treated cases. However, by the end of 1996 only 59% of ectopic gestations were managed laparoscopically (Molloy and Crosdale 1996).

MAS should be applicable to management of ectopic pregnancies in up to 90% of cases. Tubal diameter greater than 6 cm, difficulty in controlling haemorrhage and haemodynamic instability are the main indications for conversion to laparotomy.

Endoscopic versus laparotomy management of ectopic gestation

Garry (1996), having reviewed six major series of laparoscopic treated patients ($n=951$) reported between 1986–94, concluded that MAS should be 'the gold standard' for the management of ectopic pregnancy. The success rate was 95–100%, operating time 36–62 minutes, hospital stay 0.8–2 days and complications 0–3.6% of cases. Garry (1996) also examined six studies ($n=660$) treated by laparoscopy or laparotomy, finding that in at least one of the studies (Brumsted 1996) the operating time was statistically in favour of laparoscopy. One study (Zouves et al. 1992) reported a 3.8% complication rate for laparoscopy and 1.2% for the laparotomy group, while other studies failed to demonstrate a significant difference in complication rates. Analgesic requirement, hospital stay and return to full activity were statistically significant in favour of laparoscopy. Three of the studies estimated a saving of from $US700 to $US3500 in favour of endoscopic surgery.

In a review of 32 studies (1626 patients) of laparoscopic salpingostomy or fimbrial expression, comprising seven randomised controlled studies, two well designed controlled trials, two cohort studies and 21 case series, 93% had successful treatment (Pisarka et al. 1998). Of the patients who had subsequent tubal assessment 76% had patent tubes. Of the 647 women attempting further pregnancies, 57% had intrauterine and 13% recurrence of ectopic gestation.

Pouly et al. (1995) compared pregnancy outcome following laparoscopic (four series) and laparotomy (six series) salpingostomy and reported similar conclusions. The intrauterine pregnancy rate was 59% for laparoscopy and 61.5% for laparotomy-treated cases while the recurrent ectopic pregnancy rate was 12% following laparoscopy and 16% in the laparotomy group.

One of the studies was a randomised study (Lundorff *et al.* 1992). Among 45 patients in each group the intrauterine pregnancy rate (52.4% for laparotomy and 44.7% for laparoscopy) and recurrent ectopic pregnancy rate (7.1% for laparotomy, 11.1% for laparoscopy) were not significantly different. Second-look laparoscopy 12 weeks following salpingostomy in 65 patients demonstrated significantly fewer adhesions affecting the previously operated fallopian tube when compared with patients treated by laparotomy (Lindblom *et al.* 1997).

Laparoscopic salpingostomy versus salpingectomy

The review of Yao and Tulandi (1997), comprising one case–control, one cohort and seven case series, concluded that subsequent intrauterine and ectopic gestation rates were similar in each group. Comparison of two large pre-*in vitro* fertilisation series of laparoscopic salpingostomy (Pouly *et al.* 1986) and laparoscopic salpingectomy (Dubuisson *et al.* 1987) demonstrated a higher subsequent intrauterine pregnancy rate (83% versus 47%) in favour of the more conservative approach. The recurrent ectopic pregnancy rate was also lower for conservative management (8% versus 19%). The groups were not strictly comparable as the salpingectomy group included cases with long-term infertility and pathological tubes in which conservative management was not possible.

A ten-year review (1983–93) of 375 patients having undergone laparoscopic salpingectomy examined the outcome of 145 patients with a patent contralateral tube (Dubuisson *et al.* 1996). The overall rate of intrauterine pregnancy was 50.3% with a recurrent ectopic pregnancy rate of 15.2%. The authors emphasised the importance of past history and condition of the contralateral tube as the two major factors related to future fertility. The occurrence of ectopic pregnancy in this study in contralateral fallopian tubes that appeared externally normal at initial ectopic intervention indicates that external appearance does not guarantee tubal normality. Assessment by falloposcopy or tuboscopy is required to exclude intraluminal pathology (Kerin *et al.* 1992).

Histologically normal fallopian tubes were found in 17.7% of patients having salpingectomy for ectopic pregnancy (no history of tubal disease) while 32.3% of fallopian tubes were found to have proximal and distal pathology (Dubuisson *et al.* 1997), supporting the proposal for tubal removal for patients with past history or clinical evidence of tubal disease.

Subsequent fertility in patients with ectopic pregnancy in a solitary tube treated by salpingostomy (20 studies) was reviewed by Thornton *et al.* (1991). The intrauterine pregnancy rate of 55% (range 13–100%) supports the advantages of the conservative salpingostomy operation in this clinical setting.

The risks of conservative management must also be taken into account, including:

(1) Failure of complete trophoblast evacuation (at least 5%) (Bruhat *et al.* 1980);
(2) Trophoblast seeding in the peritoneal cavity;
(3) Failure of recognition of underlying tubal disease.

If there is demonstrable extensive tubal disease, tubal rupture, difficulties with uncontrolled haemorrhage, recurrent tubal ectopic in the same tube, no desire for future fertility or wanting sterilisation, there is a clear indication to perform salpingectomy. For patients requiring future fertility there remains a need for objective evidence which can only be derived from randomised prospective trials to confirm whether laparoscopic salpingectomy or salpingostomy is the treatment of choice.

Endoscopy versus non-surgical management

The diagnosis of early stage, unruptured tubal gestations (a common event with improved diagnostic methods) leads to the possibility of non-surgical conservative management including the use of cytotoxic agents, methotrexate or non-intervention.

There have been three randomised trials comparing laparoscopic surgery with laparoscopic administration of methotrexate. The review by Pisarska *et al.* (1998) of 21 non-randomised studies involving direct-injection methotrexate in 660 patients indicated a lower (76%) successful resolution when compared to salpingostomy and systemic methotrexate administration. The use of systemic methotrexate was also reviewed in the study by Pisarska *et al.* (1998). One randomised controlled trial, one cohort study and ten case series comparing laparoscopic salpingostomy and variable dose systemic methotrexate (93% treated successfully) are reported. Tubal patency rates and subsequent fertility were similar with a lower recurrent ectopic pregnancy rate for the methotrexate group.

One trial was aborted because of poor results (Motla *et al.* 1992), the other two finding that laparoscopic salpingostomy and tubal methotrexate tubal injection were equally effective (persistent trophoblastic activity, disappearance of βhCG, subsequent intrauterine pregnancy) in the management of unruptured pregnancies.

The randomised trial (Hajenius *et al.* 1997) found that 82% of the methotrexate treated group (51) required a single treatment, 4% required a second treatment and 14% required surgical intervention for active bleeding or tubal rupture. Of the 49 patients who had laparoscopic salpingostomy, 72% were successfully treated, 8% required salpingectomy and 20% required postoperative methotrexate. This failure rate of laparoscopic salpingostomy seems much higher than other published reports (Bruhat *et al.* 1980). Ipsilateral tubal patency was similar (55% methotrexate and 59% salpingostomy group).

An analysis of 315 ectopic pregnancies treated by outpatient single-dose systemic methotrexate is of interest because of obvious cost savings (Lipscomb *et al.* 1998). Patients were accepted in the study under the following conditions:

(1) Haemodynamic stability;
(2) Not desiring surgery;
(3) Agreement to follow-up;
(4) Size of ectopic 3.5–4.0 cm (without fetal cardiac activity) or 3.5 cm (with fetal cardiac activity).

Excluding withdrawals (six patients requiring surgery within one week of starting therapy) the overall success rate was 92.9% with a reduced success rate of 87.5% for 44 patients with evidence of fetal heart activity.

A second dose of methotrexate was administered to 50 patients (47 successes) while four patients had three (all successful) and one patient four doses (unsuccessful). Five patients had tubal rupture and haemorrhage. This study has demonstrated that fetal cardiac activity is not a contraindication to methotrexate therapy. However, the lower success rate with a viable fetus has to be compared with the risk of failure of conservative laparoscopic surgery.

Quantifying the total cost in France on the basis of a literature review for laparoscopy and methotrexate management of unruptured ectopic pregnancy, Lecuru *et al.* (1996) found a cost saving of 40% in favour of systemic methotrexate. Disadvantages include failure of resolution, persistent pelvic pain and need for hospitalisation to exclude tubal rupture (Stovall and Ling 1993). The adverse effects of methotrexate, although infrequent, must also be considered. These include:

(1) Bone marrow suppression;
(2) Hepatotoxicity;
(3) Stomatitis;
(4) Pulmonary fibrosis;
(5) Alopecia;
(6) Photosensitivity.

Surgical intervention may be required for the late sequelae of haematosalpinx and haematocele which have been diagnosed even months after methotrexate treatment (Zullo *et al.* 1996). Failure of patients to attend for follow-up visits and inadvertent treatment of early intrauterine pregnancies are also concerns.

Non-intervention

Expectant management should be considered in a clinically stable patient when clinical and ultrasound examination fails to locate the site of an early intrauterine or ectopic pregnancy. Spontaneous resolution (88%) is possible when serum βhCG concentrations are below 1000 iu/l (Trio *et al.* 1995). Expectant management was successful in only 60% of 60 women with laparoscopically proven ectopic pregnancy with βhCG concentrations below 2000 iu/l (Shalev *et al.* 1995).

Conclusions

There is good evidence to indicate that endoscopic management of ectopic pregnancy should be the preferred technique when surgery is indicated. MAS offers less pain and need for analgesia, shorter hospital stay and shorter overall convalescence.

To determine whether expectant, methotrexate, conservative or more aggressive endoscopic management is the best choice for treating ectopic pregnancies, there remains a need to carry out randomised, prospective, clinical studies.

LAPAROSCOPIC OVARIAN SURGERY (LOS) FOR POLYCYSTIC OVARY SYNDROME (PCOS)

Comprehensive reviews of this subject (Saravelos *et al.* 1997; Farquhar *et al.* 1999; Balen and Jacobs 2000; Cohen 2000) evaluate currently available evidence for surgical management of PCOS. The consensus of opinion is that LOS should totally replace ovarian wedge resection as a surgical treatment for patients with PCOS unresponsive to ovulation induction with clomiphene. Ovarian diathermy has been suggested to be as effective as gonadotrophin therapy (Abdel Gadir *et al.* 1990) with the added benefits of full pelvic assessment, less need for intensive monitoring and reduced risk of ovarian hyper-stimulation and multiple pregnancy. The most useful predictor of successful outcome (clinical and endocrine response) following LOS is the finding of a high basal luteinising hormone (LH) level pre-operatively (Abdel Gadir *et al.* 1992).

In a prospective randomised study, Balen and Jacobs (1994) demonstrated that unilateral ovarian diathermy restored bilateral ovarian activity with responders having a fall in serum LH concentrations. This finding led to the hypothesis by these authors that ovarian injury changes ovarian–pituitary feedback possibly associated with the release of growth factors which interact with FSH producing follicular growth and the hormone 'gonadotrophin surge attenuating inhibitory factor', causing a fall in serum LH.

In a systematic review of available data on the effectiveness of LOS for ovulation induction in women with PCOS with anovulation, Farquhar et al. (1999) identified 12 trials, seven of which were suitable for inclusion in the review, five of which were randomised. Criteria for inclusion required a comparison of LOS with a concurrent control group of women with PCOS requiring induction of ovulation. The trials were assessed for primary (ovulation and pregnancy rate) and secondary (miscarriage and multiple pregnancy rate, incidence of overstimulation and ovarian hyperstimulation syndrome) quality criteria.

The interventions studied were:

(1) LOS using cautery or laser versus:
   – observation;
   – clomiphene;
(2) Gonadotrophin therapy with or without the use of GnRH analogue;
(3) LOS followed by ovulation induction with clomiphene or gonadotrophins versus gonadotrophins only;
(4) Various modalities of LOS.

This Cochrane Review indicates that the available observational series have inadequacies of quantity, quality and controlled data. The availability of few randomised controlled trials render evaluation of LOS in PCOS difficult. The conclusions reached included:

(1) LOS as a primary treatment for anovulatory PCOS in preference to using clomiphene citrate has not been proven;
(2) The case for LOS as a secondary treatment for patients who are clomiphene resistant, despite possible advantages over gonadotrophin therapy, has not been established;
(3) Different LOS techniques failed to demonstrate a significant difference in results.

In view of the risks and morbidity associated with laparoscopy, postoperative adhesion formation (Greenblatt and Casper 1993), theoretical risk of ovarian failure and undetermined long-term effect on the ovary, LOS for patients with PCOS should remain under review.

Conclusions

The results of well-constructed, controlled randomised clinical trials involving adequate numbers of patients currently being undertaken are necessary to fully assess this MAS technique for this important group of infertile patients.

ENDOSCOPIC MAS – OTHER USES

The role and repercussions of endoscopic MAS for the management of:

(1) Adnexal tumours;
(2) Uterine septa and submucous fibroids;
(3) Tubal disease;
(4) Genital cancer;

_(5) Stress incontinence;
(6) Genital prolapse;

should be similarly discussed and results compared with those of traditional surgery (Cooke 1995; Verhulst and Devroey 1995; Nagele *et al.* 1996; Gates *et al.* 1997; Hamberger and Janson 1997; Hart and Magos 1997).

ENDOSCOPY IN THE NEW MILLENNIUM

It is probable that early in the next century gynaecologists and general surgeons will witness a less apparent division between minimal access and conventional surgery. MAS will expand in parallel with the numerous advances occurring in the applied sciences, particularly bioengineering. To make use of the advances occurring in fibre optics, robotics, ceramics and computer technology, future surgeons will become part of a multidisciplinary team comprising bioengineers, industrial designers, health economists and computer scientists.

In a closer time-frame the introduction of high-definition endocameras and monitors will ensure improvement in image quality and resolution. The incorporation of three-dimensional and stereoscopic imaging (Von Pichler *et al.* 1996) will help to obviate the current physical problems of hand–eye co-ordination and depth perception. Camera manipulation will occur via 'remote tracking' systems responding to head and eyeball movements (Schurr *et al.* 1996). Projection of three-dimensional endoscopic images in space above the operative field may become a reality (Cuschieri 1996).

Ancillary systems integrated to future endoscopy will ensure optical clarity (Flemming *et al.* 1996) and maintenance of clear vision (Bessell *et al.* 1996). Integrated single-unit workstations are already providing pressure-controlled CO_2 insufflation, variable electrocautery, suction- and temperature-controlled irrigation, electronically controlled light source and on-demand video for proximal and telemedicine transmission (Beger 1998; Senft 1998). Networking from such workstations will allow simulation and training to be achieved at a distance from the surgical site.

Three-dimensional imaging provided by virtual-reality displays will facilitate training, not always possible in live situations (Satava 1996). Virtual reality will find application not only in education and training but also for the development of new methods and procedures (Ayache *et al.* 1998; Wapler and Stallkamp 1998). Telemedicine has already expanded beyond teleconsulting with potential for teaching MAS utilising remote guidance of endoscopes (tele-assistance) and surgical instruments (telemanipulation) by a remote expert in another continent (Schurr *et al.* 1998). The challenge for gynaecologists in the new millennium will be to capitalise on these advances and integrate new MAS techniques for more effective and efficient surgery for our patients.

References

Abdel Gadir, A., Mowafi, R.S., Alnaser, H.M.I., Alrashid, A.H., Alonezi, O.M. and Shaw, R.W. (1990) Ovarian electrocautery versus human menopausal gonadotrophins and pure follicle stimulating hormone therapy in the treatment of patients with polycystic ovarian disease. *Clin Endocrinol (Oxf)* **33**, 585–92

Abdel Gadir, A., Alnaser, H.M.I., Mowafi, R.S. and Shaw, R.W. (1992) The response of patients with polycystic ovarian disease to human menopausal gonadotrophin therapy after ovarian electrocautery or a luteinizing hormone-releasing hormone agonist. *Fertil Steril* **57**, 309–13

Anderson, E.T. (1937) Peritoneoscopy. *Am J Surg* **35**, 136

Ayache, N., Cotin, S., Delingette, H., Clément, J.M., Russier, Y. and Marascaux, J. (1998) Simulation of endoscopic surgery. *Minimally Invasive Therapy and Allied Technology* **7**, 71–7

Balen, A.H. and Jacobs, H.S. (1994) A prospective study comparing unilateral and bilateral laparoscopic ovarian diathermy in women with the polycystic ovary syndrome. *Fertil Steril* **62**, 921–5

Balen, A. and Jacobs, H. (2000) 'Polycystic ovary syndrome – ovulation induction' in: G. Kovacs (Ed.) *Polycystic Ovarian Syndrome*. Cambridge: Cambridge University Press (in press)

Beger, F.M. (1998) The surgical workstation: an industrial designer's view. *Minimally Invasive Therapy and Allied Technology* **7**, 427–32

Bertram, D.A., Kovac, S.R. and Cruikshank, S.H. (1997) The role of laparoscopy in hysterectomy. *Journal of Pelvic Surgery* **3**, 147–58

Bessell, J.R., Flemming, E., Kunert, W. and Buess, G. (1996) Maintenance of clear vision during laparoscopic surgery. *Minimally Invasive Therapy and Allied Technology* **5**, 450–5

Browne, D.S. and Fraser, M.L. (1991) Hysterectomy revisited. *Aust N Z J Obstet Gynaecol* **31**, 148-52

Bruhat, M.A., Manhes, H., Choukroun, J. and Essai, S.F. (1977) De traitement per coeleoscopique de la grosesse extra-uterine à propos de 6 observations. *Revue Française de Gynecologie et d'Obstétrique* **72**, 667–9

Bruhat, M.A., Manhes, H., Mage, G. and Pouly, J.L. (1980) Treatment of ectopic pregnancy by means of laparoscopy. *Fertil Steril* **33**, 411–17

Brumsted, J.B. (1996) Managing ectopic pregnancy nonsurgically. *Contemporary Obstetrics and Gynecology* **41**, 43–56

Cohen, J. (2000) 'Laparoscopic surgical treatment of infertility related to PCOS revisited' in: G. Kovacs (Ed.) *Polycystic Ovarian Syndrome*. Cambridge: Cambridge University Press (in press)

Cooke, I.D. (1995) Infertility – the role of minimally invasive surgery. *Current Obstetrics and Gynaecology* **5**, 131–6

Cuschieri, A. (1996) Visual display technology for endoscopic surgery. *Minimally Invasive Therapy and Allied Technology* **5**, 427–34

Daniell, J.F., Channell, C., Lindays, J., Staggs, S. and Henry, T. (1998) Early evaluation of an electromechanical morcellator for laparoscopic supracervical hysterectomy. *Gynaecological Endoscopy* **7**, 295–305

Davies, A. and Magos, A.L. (1997). Indications and alternatives to hysterectomy. *Baillières Clin Obstet Gynecol* **11**, 61–75

Decker, A. and Cherry, T.H. (1944) Culdoscopy – a new method in the diagnosis of pelvic disease – a preliminary report. *Am J Surg* **64**, 40-4

Dicker, R.C., Greenspan, J.R., Strauss, L.T. *et al.* (1982) Complications of abdominal and vaginal hysterectomy among women of reproductive age in the United States. *Am J Obstet Gynecol* **144**, 841–8

Donnez, J. and Nisolle, M. (1993) Laparoscopic subtotal hysterectomy (LASH). *Gynaecological Endoscopy* **2**, 77–8

Donnez, J., Nisolle, M., Smets, M., Polet, R. and Bassil, S. (1997) Laparoscopic supra-cervical (subtotal) hysterectomy: a first series of 500 cases. *Gynaecological Endoscopy* **6**, 73–6

Dubuisson, J.B., Aubriot, F.X. and Cordon, V. (1987) Laparoscopic salpingectomy for ectopic pregnancy. *Fertil Steril* **47**, 225–8

Dubuisson, J.B., Morice, P., Chapron, C., De Gayffier, A. and Mouelhi, T. (1996) Salpingectomy – the laparoscopic surgical choice for ectopic pregnancy. *Hum Reprod* **11**, 1199–203

Dubuisson, J.B., Chapron, C., Morice, P. and Vacher-Lavenu, M.C. (1997) Histological results of salpingectomy for ectopic pregnancy a series of 344 tubal pregnancies. *Gynaecological Endoscopy* **6**, 341–5

Ewen, S.P. and Sutton, C.J.G. (1994). Initial experience with supracervical laparoscopic hysterectomy and removal of the cervical transformation zone. *Br J Obstet Gynaecol* **101**, 225–8

Farquhar, C., Vanderkerckhove, P., Arnot, M. and Lilford, R. (1999) 'Laparoscopic 'drilling' by diathermy or laser for ovulation induction in anovulatory polycystic ovary syndrome (Cochrane Review)' in: *The Cochrane Library*, Issue 1. Oxford: Update Software

Flemming, E., Bessell, J.R., Kunert, W., Eibl, H. and Buess, G. (1996) Principles determining optical clarity in endoscopic surgery. *Minimally Invasive Therapy and Allied Technology* **5**, 440–4

Garry, R. (1996) The laparoscopic treatment of ectopic pregnancy: the long road to acceptance. *Gynaecological Endoscopy* **5**, 65–8

Garry, R. (1998) Towards evidence-based hysterectomy. *Gynaecological Endoscopy* **7**, 225–33

Garry, R. and Phillips, G. (1995) How safe is the laparoscopic approach to hyster-ectomy? *Gynaecological Endoscopy* **4**, 77–9

Gates, E.A., Vontver, L.A., Pillsbury, S.G. Jr., Caillouette, J.C., Kirk, E.P. and Allen, R. (1997) New surgical procedures: can our patients benefit while we learn? *Am J Obstet Gynecol* **176**, 1293–9

Gordts, S., Campo, R., Rombaults, L. and Brosens, I. (1997) The office mini culdoscopy: a new and simple method for the exploration of the female pelvis in infertility. *Gynaecological Endoscopy* **6** Suppl 2, 2

Greenblatt, E.M. and Casper, R.F. (1993) Adhesion formation after laparoscopic ovarian cautery for polycystic ovarian syndrome: lack of correlation with pregnancy rate. *Fertil Steril* **60**, 766–70

Hajenius, P.J., Engelsbel, S., Mobl, B.W.J. *et al.* (1997) Randomised trial of systemic methotrexate versus laparoscopic salpingostomy in tubal pregnancy. *Lancet* **350**, 774–9

Hall, V., Overton, C., Hargreaves, J. and Maresh, M.J.A. (1998) Hysterectomy in the treatment of dysfunctional uterine bleeding. *Br J Obstet Gynaecol* **105** Suppl 17, 60

Hamberger, L. and Janson, P.O. (1997) Global importance of infertility and its treatment: role of fertility technologies. *Int J Gynaecol Obstet* **58**, 149–58

Harkki-Siren, P., Sjoberg, J. and Tiitinen, A. (1998) Urinary tract injuries after hysterectomy. *Obstet Gynecol* **92**, 113–18

Hart, R. and Magos, A. (1997) Endometrial ablation. *Curr Opin Obstet Gynecol* **9**, 226–32

Hasson, H. (1993) Experience with laparoscopic hysterectomy. *J Am Assoc Gynecol Laparosc* **1**, 1–11

Healy, D. and Petrucco, O. (1998) *Effective Gynaecological Day Surgery*. London: Chapman and Hall

Hope, R.B. (1937) The differential diagnosis of ectopic gestation by peritoneoscopy. *Surg Gynecol Obstet* **64**, 229–34

Hopkins, H.H. and Kapany, N.S. (1954) Flexible fiberoscope using static scanning. *Nature* **173**, 39–41

Jacobeaus, H. (1910) Uber die Mögleichkeit die Zystoskopie bei Untersuchunger seröser höhlungen anzuwenden. *Munch Med Wochenschr* **27**, 2090–2

Kalk and Bruhl (1951) *Laparosckopie und Gastroscopie*. Stuttgart: Thieme

Kelling cited in: P. C. Steptoe (1967) *Laparoscopy in Gynaecology*. London: Livingstone

Kerin, J., Daykhovsky, L., Grundfest, W. and Surrey, E. (1990) Falloposcopy: a micro endoscopic trans vaginal technique for diagnosing and treating endotubal disease incorporating guide wire cannulation and direct balloon tuboplasty. *J Reprod Med* **35**, 606–12

Kerin, J.F., Williams, D.B., Sanroman, G.A., Pearlstone, A.C., Grundfest, W.S. and Surrey, E.S. (1992) Falloposcopic classification and treatment of fallopian tube lumen disease. *Fert Steril* **57**, 731–41

Kovac, S.R. (1995) Guidelines to determine the route of hysterectomy. *Obstet Gynecol* **85**, 18–23

Kovac, S.R. (1998) Guidelines to determine the role of laparoscopically assisted vaginal hysterectomy. *Am J Obstet Gynecol* **178**, 1257–63

Langebrekke, A., Eraka, R., Nesheim, B.I., Urnes, A., Busund, B. and Sponland, G. (1996) Abdominal hysterectomy should not be considered as a primary method for uterine removal. A prospective randomised study of 100 patients referred to hysterectomy. *Acta Obstet Gynecol Scand* **75**, 404–7

Lecuru, F., Taurelle, R., Viens-Bitker, C. and Robin, F. (1996) Cost of unruptured tubal pregnancy: comparison of laparoscopy and methotrexate infection. *Gynaecological Endoscopy* **5**, 25–8

Lindblom, B., Lundorff, P. and Thorburn, J. (1997) Second-look laparoscopy after ectopic pregnancy. *Gynaecological Endoscopy* **6** Suppl 2, 1

Lipscomb, G.H., Bran, D., McCord, M.L., Portera, C. and Ling, F.W. (1998) Analysis of three hundred and fifteen ectopic pregnancies treated with single-dose methotrexate. *Am J Obstet Gynecol* **178**, 1354–8

Lundorff, P., Thorburn, J. and Lindblom, B. (1992) Fertility outcome after conservative surgical treatment of ectopic pregnancy evaluated in a randomised trial. *Fertil Steril* **57**, 998–1002

Lyons, T. (1993) Supracervical laparoscopic hysterectomy. A comparison of morbidity and mortality results with LAVH. *J Reprod Med* **38**, 763–7

Magos, A. (1996). Endoscopic surgery: yes, but . . . *Curr Opin Obstet Gynecol* **8**, 243–5

Marana, R., Busacca, M., Garcia, N. *et al.* (1997) LAVH versus AH. *J Am Assoc Gynecol Laparoc* **4**, S5

Molloy, D. and Crosdale, S. (1996) National trends in gynaecological endoscopic surgery. *Aust N Z J Obstet Gynaecol* **36**, 27–31

Mottla, G.L., Rulin, M.C. and Guzick, D.S. (1992) Lack of resolution of ectopic pregnancy by intratubal injection of methotrexate. *Fertil Steril* **57**, 685–7

Nagele, F., Molnar, B.G., O'Connor, H. and Magos, A.L. (1996) Randomized studies in endoscopic surgery – where is the proof? *Curr Opin Obstet Gynecol* **8**, 281–9

Nezhat, C., Crowgey, S.R. and Garrison, C.P. (1986) Surgical treatment of the endometriosis via laser laparoscopy. *Fertil Steril* **45**, 778–83

Nezhat, F., Nezhat, C., Gordon, S. and Wilkins, E. (1992) Laparoscopic versus abdominal hysterectomy. *J Reprod Med* **37**, 247–50

Nordentoeft, S. (1912) *Verh Dtsch Ges Chir* **1**, 78

Nuffield Institute for Health, University of Leeds and NHS Centre for Reviews and Dissemination, University of York (1995). The management of menorrhagia: what are effective ways of treating excessive regular menstrual blood loss in primary and secondary care? *Effective Health Care* **9**, 1–14

Olsson, J.H., Ellstrom, M. and Hahlin, M. (1996) A randomised prospective trial comparing laparoscopic and abdominal hysterectomy. *Br J Obstet Gynaecol* **103**, 345–50

O'Shea, R.T. and Petrucco, O.M. (1996) Laparoscopic hysterectomy – Adelaide audit (1991–1994). Complications in the real world! *Gynaecological Endoscopy* **4**, 261–3

Palmer, R. (1946) *Mém Acad Chir* **72**, 363

Palmer, R. (1947) Instrumentation et technique de la coelioscopie gynecologique. *Gynecologic and Obstetrica* **46**, 422–6

Palmer, R. and Cohen, J. (1965) Biopsies percoelioscopiques. *Minerva Ginecologica* **17**, 238–9

Petrucco, O., Maher, P., Molloy, D. and Ryan, M. (1996) The Laparoscopically Assisted Hysterectomy (LAH) Project. *RACOG Bulletin* **10**, 22–3

Petrucco. O.M., Luke, C., Moss, J. and Healy, D. (1999) 'Abdominal v. laparoscopic hysterectomy – prospective randomised trial.' Paper presented at the *IX Annual Scientific Meeting of the Australian Gynaecological Endoscopy Society*, May 1999, Adelaide, South Australia

Phipps, J.A., John, M. and Nayak, S. (1993) Comparison of laparoscopically assisted vaginal hysterectomy and bilateral salpingo-oophorectomy with conventional abdominal hysterectomy and bilateral salpingo-oophorectomy. *Br J Obstet Gynaecol* **100**, 698–700

Pisarska, M.D., Carson, S.A. and Buster, J.E. (1998) Ectopic pregnancy. *Lancet* **351**, 1115–20

Pouly, J.L., Manhes, H., Mage, G., Canis. M. and Bruhat, M.A. (1986) Conservative laparoscopic treatment of 321 ectopic pregnancies. *Fertil Steril* **46**, 1093–7

Pouly, J.L., Manhes, H., Chapron, C. *et al.* (1995) Laparoscopic treatment of ectopic pregnancy. *Experts Conference – Satellite Symposium, Vichy, September 14–16*. Amsterdam: Excerpta Medica

Querleu, D., Casson, M., Parmenter, D. and Deboinance, P. (1993) The impact of laparoscopic surgery on vaginal hysterectomy. *Gynaecological Endoscopy* **2**, 89–91

Raju, K.S. and Auld, B.J. (1994) A randomised prospective study of laparoscopic vaginal hysterectomy versus abdominal hysterectomy each with bilateral salpingo-oophorectomy. *Br J Obstet Gynaecol* **101**, 1068–71

RCOG Clinical Audit Unit (1999) *Effective Procedures in Gynaecology Suitable for Audit*. London: RCOG Press

Reich, H., Decaprio, J. and McGlynn, F. (1989) Laparoscopic hysterectomy. *Journal of Gynecological Surgery* **5**, 213–17

Richards, S.R. and Simpkins, D.S. (1995). Laparoscopic supracervical hysterectomy versus laparoscopic-assisted vaginal hysterectomy. *J Am Assoc Gynecol Laparosc* **2**, 431–5

Richardson, R.E., Bournas, N. and Magos, A.L. (1995) Is laparoscopic hysterectomy a waste of time? *Lancet* **345**, 36–41

Ruddock, J.C. (1937) Peritoneoscopy. *Surg Gynecol Obstet* **65**, 623–9

Saravelos, H., Li, T-C., Bontis, J., Tarlatzis, B.C. and Cooke, I.D. (1997) Laparoscopic management of polycystic ovarian syndrome. *Gynaecological Endoscopy* **6**, 331–40

Satava, R.M. (1996) Three-dimensional imaging and image displays: surgical application of advanced technologies. *Semin Laparosc Surg* **3**, 193–8

Schurr, M.O., Buess, G., Kunert, W., Flemming, E., Hermeking, H. and Gumb, L. (1996) Human sense of vision: a guide to future endoscopic imaging systems. *Minimally Invasive Therapy and Allied Technology* **5**, 410–18

Schurr, M.L., Kunert, W., Neck, J., Voges, U. and Buess, G.F. (1998) Telematics and telemanipulation in surgery. *Minimally Invasive Therapy and Allied Technology* **7**, 97–103

Schwartz, R.O. (1993) Complications of laparoscopic hysterectomy. *Obstet Gynecol* **81**, 1022–4

Semm, K. (1977) Pelviskopische chirurgie in der gynakologie. *Geburtschilfe und Frauenheilkunde* **37**, 909–16

Semm, K. (1993) 'Hysterectomy by pelviscopy: an alternative approach without colpotomy (CASH)' in: R. Garry and H. Reich (Eds) *Laparoscopic Hysterectomy*, pp. 118–32. Oxford: Blackwell Scientific

Senft, R. (1998). Workstation for endoscopic surgery. *Minimally Invasive Therapy and Allied Technology* **7**, 449–54

Shalev, E., Peleg, D., Tsabari, A., Romano, S. and Bustan, M. (1995) Spontaneous resolution of ectopic tubal pregnancy: natural history. *Fertil Steril* **63**, 15–19

Shapiro H.I. and Adler, D.H. (1973) Excision of an ectopic pregnancy through the laparoscope. *Am J Obstet Gynecol* **117**, 290–1

Short, A.R. (1928) The uses of coelioscopy. *BMJ* **ii**, 254-5

Steptoe, P.C. (1967) *Laparoscopy in Gynaecology*. Edinburgh: Churchill Livingstone

Stovall, T.G. and Ling, F.W. (1993) Single-dose methotrexate: an expanded clinical trial. *Am J Obstet Gynecol* **168**, 1759–65

Sutton, C. (1995) Laparoscopic hysterectomy. *Current Obstetrics and Gynaecology* **5**, 142–6

Telinde, R.W. and Rutledge, F.N. (1948) *Am J Obstet Gynecol* **55**, 102

Thornton, K.L., Diamond, M.P. and De Cherney, A.H. (1991). Linear salpingostomy for ectopic pregnancy. *Obstet Gynecol Clin North Am* **18**, 95–109

Trio, D., Strobelt, N., Picciolo, C., Lapinski, R.H. and Ghidini, A. (1995) Prognostic factors for successful expectant management of ectopic pregnancy. *Fertil Steril* **63**, 469–72

Tsaltas, J., Magnus, A., Mamers, P.M., Lawrence, A.S., Lolatgis, N. and Healy, D.L. (1997) Laparoscopic and abdominal hysterectomy: a cost comparison. *Med J Aust* **166**, 205–7

Veress, J. (1938) Neues instrument zur ausfuhrung von brust-order bauch pumktionen und pneumothorax behandlung. *Dtsch Med Wochenschr* **64**, 1480–2

Verhulst, G. and Devroey, P. (1995) Endoscopic surgery in gynecologic practice. *Int J Gynaecol Obstet* **49**, 107–23

Von Pichler, C., Radermacher, R. and Rau, G. (1996) The state of 3–D technology and evaluation. *Minimally Invasive Therapy and Allied Technology* **5**, 419–26

Wapler, M. and Stallkamp, J. (1998) Virtual reality concepts and their description. *Minimally Invasive Therapy and Allied Technology* **7**, 85–7

Wood, C., Maher, P. and Hill, D. (1997) The declining place of abdominal hysterectomy in Australia. *Gynaecological Endoscopy* **6**, 257–60

Yao, M. and Tulandi, T. (1997) Current status of surgical and nonsurgical management of ectopic pregnancy. *Fertil Steril* **67**, 421–33

Zouves, C., Arman, B. and Gomel, V. (1992) Laparoscopic surgical treatment of tubal pregnancy. A safe effective alternative to laparotomy. *J Reprod Med* **37**, 205–9

Zullo, F., Pellicano, M., Di Carlo, C., De Stefano, R., Trantonio, P. and Nappi, C. (1996) Late complications after systemic methotrexate treatment of unruptured ectopic pregnancies: a report of three cases. *Eur J Obstet Gynecol Reprod Biol* **70**, 213–14

31

Adenocarcinoma of the endometrium

William T. Creasman and Matthew F. Kohler

HISTORY

In the industrialised world, adenocarcinoma of the endometrium is the most common cancer in the female genital pelvis. In the USA, it is more frequent than cancers of the cervix and ovary combined and now represents the fourth most common cancer in women.

Historically, corpus cancer was infrequently seen compared with carcinoma of the cervix. In the first edition of *Operative Gynecology*, TeLinde (1946) stated that in his hospital the incidence of cervical to endometrial cancer was eight to one, although he noted that incidence was dependent upon the hospital population served. In the middle of this century, more women in the USA died from cervical cancer than from any other cancer. Subsequently, the incidence of cervical cancer has decreased remarkably and is now only the twelfth most common cause of cancer deaths. The increased use of the Papanicolaou test has undoubtedly contributed to this dramatic decline in deaths. The Third National Cancer Survey in the USA (Cramer *et al.* 1974) noted no increase in the incidence of endometrial cancer from the time of the previous survey in 1947. In the early 1970s, data suggested a consistent increase in the incidence of endometrial cancer. This increase occurred in all groups over 50 years of age, almost doubling in incidence by the end of that decade, with a subsequent decrease after the end of the decade. Before the mid-1970s, the American Cancer Society (ACS) did not separate incidence figures for cervical cancer and endometrial cancer in their yearly estimate of new cancers, although the reported deaths were compiled separately. In 1975, the ACS estimated 27 000 new corpus cancers. This reached a high of 39 000 estimated cases in 1984, gradually decreasing to 36 000 in 1998 (Landis *et al.* 1998).

It has been suggested that the increased incidence of endometrial cancer over the last two or three decades has been because of the ageing population in the western world. The increasing number of women who are at the age of greatest frequency for this cancer is staggering. In the USA, an estimated 50 million women will be in or past the menopause by the year 2000. As the population increases in age, the vulnerability to a worse prognostic lesion may also become evident. According to the last annual report of FIGO (Pecorelli *et al.* 1998), patients with stage Ia endometrial cancer had a mean age of 59.5 years while for those with stage IV cancer the mean age was approximately 65 years. This age discrimination was also seen with regard to the grade of tumour. Women with tumours with well-differentiated lesions had a mean age of 60.4 years, while those

344

with poorly-differentiated cancers had a mean age of 63.9 years. This was also true when the depth of myometrial invasion was evaluated.

During the last 25 years, data revealed that unopposed oestrogen replacement was associated with adenocarcinoma of the endometrium and this link was suggested as the reason for the increased incidence (Smith *et al.* 1975; Ziel and Finkle 1975). The Connecticut Tumor Registry data (Marrett *et al.* 1978), attempted to correlate increased oestrogen use to increased numbers of endometrial carcinomas and although a trend was suggested it was not conclusive. It should be noted that in countries in which oestrogen is either unavailable or not used for replacement, the incidence of endometrial cancer also increased. The unopposed oestrogen relationship brought further research which noted that when oestrogen was combined with progestin, the incidence of endometrial cancer actually decreased (Hammond *et al.* 1979; Persson *et al.* 1996). Additionally, the cancers that did develop with unopposed oestrogen were well-differentiated, superficially invasive and with survival equal to a similar population which did not take oestrogen or develop endometrial cancer (Chu *et al.* 1982). Combined oral contraceptives actually decrease the risk of developing endometrial cancer and several studies noted a 0.5 risk ratio when compared with women who had never used oral contraceptives. Protection seemed to last for more than ten years and is probably related to the fact that oral contraceptives tend to cause the endometrium to become atrophic (Anonymous 1983).

During the last few decades, risk factors have been identified that increase the possibility of women developing endometrial cancer. For many years, obesity, hypertension and diabetes were felt to be leading risk factors. More recently, the consensus has been that obesity, nulliparity and late menopause are the important risk factors. For decades, the classic definition for someone at risk of endometrial cancer was the white female in her fifties or sixties who was obese, nulliparous or low parity, had a well-differentiated superficially invasive cancer treated with abdominal hysterectomy and bilateral salpingo-oophorectomy with excellent long-term survival. Exceptions were thought to be infrequent. In the early 1980s, Bohkman (1983) classified this as the 'typical' pathogenic type but also noted an 'atypical' pathogenic type. The latter tends to be a black female who is usually thin, multiparous and who has a poorly-differentiated deeply invasive cancer with an overall poor survival. The atypical type also includes the poor histological type such as papillary serous carcinoma. These subgroupings are well appreciated today.

A recent factor that has received a considerable amount of medical as well as lay attention is the possible association of tamoxifen to endometrial cancer. In the mid-1980s the first case report appeared which noted three patients who developed endometrial cancer and who had taken tamoxifen. This was followed by a review of many of the tamoxifen trials in progress, as well as completed, in patients with breast cancer in which placebo was compared with tamoxifen. Of 15 studies, 12 found no increased endometrial cancers, one noted fewer endometrial cancers in the tamoxifen arm compared to the placebo arm and two noted an increased number of endometrial cancers in the tamoxifen arm (Creasman 1997).

All these studies share a common problem – none of the patients had the endometrium evaluated prior to taking tamoxifen. These studies were not designed to evaluate endometrial cancer. It is recognised that tamoxifen can cause an increase in uterine bleeding which leads to investigation and, in some instances, a diagnosis of adenocarcinoma of the endometrium. A recently published study from Japan in which all the patients had their endometrium evaluated prior to taking tamoxifen or a placebo and followed for a median of nine years, had similar low incidence of endometrial cancer in both arms of the study (Katase *et al.* 1998). It is appreciated that women who have had breast cancer have an increased incidence of endometrial cancer and this may explain the slight increase in endometrial cancers in the two studies.

CURRENT STATUS

To review the significant advances in adenocarcinoma of the endometrium during the last century and to look forward to progress in the next millennium is beyond the scope of this presentation. Books have been written on the subject and to attempt a detailed analysis in a few pages would be presumptuous. Important prognostic factors, some known for a century or more, have been better defined, refined and expanded during the recent past and their impact on treatment and on what the future may hold will be briefly reviewed.

PATHOLOGY

Adenocarcinoma is the most common histologic cell type. As a variant, adenosquamous was previously thought to be a poor prognostic factor but two large studies (Zaino *et al.* 1991; Abeler and Kjorstad 1992) reviewed large databases corrected for multiple other factors and found that squamous component *per se*, irrespective of its differentiation, did not affect survival. When a squamous component is present, glandular differentiation is a better predictor of outcome.

One hundred years ago, Cullen was credited with identifying papillary carcinomas of the endometrium (Christopherson *et al.* 1982). Today, uterine papillary serous carcinoma is recognised as a distinct, highly aggressive, carcinoma of the uterus. These histologic types resemble a high-grade serous carcinoma of the ovary that have a propensity for early extrauterine spread. Even when the disease appears limited to the endometrium, a significant number of these patients will have lymph-node metastasis as well as intraperitoneal spread. When disease is limited to the uterus, even after full surgical staging, there is a greater propensity for higher recurrence than in the more common adenocarcinoma. Adjunctive therapy has been suggested by some in order to decrease this recurrence, which usually occurs at distant sites, with varying success (Goff *et al.* 1994). Similarly, clear-cell carcinomas, although infrequent, are considered to be poor prognostic histotypes. Microscopic identification is characteristic, with large polyhedral epithelial cells admixed with typical non-clear-cell adenocarcinoma. Even in early-stage disease, survival is poor.

HISTOLOGICAL GRADE

One of the earliest of all of the prognostic factors described for endometrial cancer was histological grade. Over the decades, several grading symptoms have been used with a correlation of this factor and prognosis. Grading was based mainly on an architectural pattern grade. More recently, it has been recognised that nuclear grading also appears to be important prognostically (Kodama *et al.* 1996). In 1988, when FIGO revised the staging system for this malignancy, it included the World Health Organization (WHO) histopathological classification and grading of the tumour which uses both architectural and nuclear criteria (Pecorelli *et al.* 1998). Architectural pattern was determined by the amount of non-squamous or non-modular solid growth pattern. Architecturally, grade I or grade II cancers should be increased by one grade in the presence of nuclear atypia. Standardisation of histological grading has contributed to less confusion utilising different grading systems and the FIGO/WHO system has now been adopted world-wide. In the last annual report of FIGO (Pecorelli *et al.* 1998), stage I, grade I tumours had a 91.7% estimated five-year survival compared with 73.6% for stage I, grade III tumours. In a multivariate analysis of risk of prognostic factors, histological grade was an independent variable.

Histological grade is not only important prognostically, but it is also an indicator of other poor prognostic indicators. As a generalisation, as the grade becomes more poorly differentiated there is a greater chance of having deep myometrial invasion and extension to the endocervix as well as nodal metastasis (Creasman *et al.* 1987). As noted above (Pecorelli *et al.* 1998), patients with grade I endometrial involvement only have a chance of metastasis to the pelvic nodes of under 1%. This increases to almost 24% if there is deep myometrial involvement and a grade III lesion.

MYOMETRIAL INVASION

Depth of myometrial invasion is an indicator, to a certain degree, of tumour volume, which is important prognostically as well as a predictor of extrauterine disease. Grade and depth of invasion do correlate well, although there are some exceptions. Well-differentiated cancers can have deep myometrial invasion and grade III tumours can be limited to the endometrium. It would appear that the former have a greater propensity for extant disease than the poorly differentiated cancer limited to the endometrium. Depth of myometrial invasion predicts lymph node metastasis. The FIGO annual report (Pecorelli *et al.* 1998) indicates pelvic node metastasis in grade I lesions increased from less than 1% with endometrium only involved, to over 15% if deep myometrial invasion is present. This is true for each of the separate grades.

STAGE OF DISEASE

Tumour volume remains the most important prognostic factor for all cancers. Staging is a gross reflection of tumour volume and correlates with long-term survival. This was also true when clinical staging was used. Endometrial cancer can, and does, metastase to both the pelvic and para-aortic lymph nodes and dictates that these should be surgically evaluated, at least in those patients who have a significant risk of metastasis to the lymph nodes.

Studies with surgically staged patients with endometrial cancer allowed correlation of multiple prognostic factors, particularly with regard to determining whether disease was limited to the uterus as clinically thought, or had extrauterine spread (Boronow *et al.* 1984; Creasman *et al.* 1987). These studies noted a significant staging error when clinically evaluated and, as a result, FIGO, in 1988, changed staging from a clinical to a surgical classification. Knowing the true extent of the disease process allows the opportunity to be more precise in determining optimal therapy for a given patient.

LYMPH NODE METASTASIS

It is now appreciated that endometrial cancer can, and does, metastasise to both pelvic and para-aortic lymph nodes (Boronow *et al.* 1984; Creasman *et al.* 1987). Either or both groups may be involved. As noted, other prognostic factors do correlate with lymph-node metastasis. As a generalisation, both grade and depth of invasion relate to lymph-node involvement. As both grade and depth of invasion increase, lymph-node metastasis also increases. Knowing this correlation and incidence can be helpful in deciding whether a pelvic and para-aortic lymphadenectomy may be indicated.

SURGICAL STAGING

Nowhere has there been a greater input than in the treatment of adenocarcinoma of the endometrium. Thomas Cullen, as early as 1900, stated that treatment of choice in patients with endometrial cancer was abdominal hysterectomy with removal of the adnexae. This remains the mainstay of therapy for this malignancy to this day. For much of this century, relatively large numbers of patients with endometrial cancer were considered inoperable and previously FIGO recognised a subclassification for these patients. As a result and as radium and external irradiation became available, alternative methods of treatment were developed. For example, Kelly (1916) reported a large series of patients treated with radium for uterine cancer. However, he believed that surgical treatment was still an important part of therapy. Heyman, during the 1930s, developed a technique of packing the uterus with multiple capsules of radium before hysterectomy and showed an approximately 60% five-year survival rate in stage I cancer (Heyman 1935).

During the 1940s, renewed interest in radical surgery became apparent. Javert was one of the earliest advocates of radical hysterectomy and pelvic lymphadenectomy for this malignancy (Javert and Douglas 1956). Javert believed that pre-operative radiation added nothing to the surgical procedure. In his excellent review, Rutledge (1974) concluded that in stage I cancer of the uterus, radical hysterectomy and pelvic lymphadenectomy had a limited role and were probably not indicated. Lymph-adenectomy, however, could provide considerable information and this was well-illustrated in the study by Lewis *et al.* (1970) in which a radical hysterectomy and pelvic lymphadenectomy were carried out in over 100 patients with endometrial cancer. They found a significant number of stage I patients with pelvic lymph node metastasis, which was pivotal in changing the concept that endometrial cancer did not metastasise to the pelvic lymph nodes. Previously, it was felt that if metastasis did occur in patients with endometrial cancer, it was to the para-aortic area and not to the pelvic nodes. Although autopsy studies noted para-aortic metastasis, there were few clinical data to support this thesis. During the 1970s and early 1980s, pivotal studies were performed which documented the incidence of both pelvic and para-aortic node metastasis in patients who had clinical stage I carcinoma of the endometrium (Creasman *et al.* 1976, 1987). It became apparent that clinical staging had a large margin of error and, if the full extent of the disease was unknown, optimal therapy could not be applied. In clinical stage I, 25–30% of the patients had more advanced disease when surgical staging was performed. In a recent review of over 100 patients (Creasman *et al.* 1999) with clinical stage II cancer, the margin of error was 75%. These studies led FIGO, in 1988, to designate endometrial cancer to be surgical staged. The more precise prognostic information with surgical staging is evident from the recent annual report of FIGO in which patients with surgical staging in stage I and stage II cancers had much better five-year survival rates (87% and 72%, respectively) compared with clinical stage I and stage II cancers with five-year survival rates of 69% and 48%, respectively (Pecorelli *et al.* 1998). During the

1970s and 1980s, appreciation of the location of recurrent disease has also changed remarkably. For many, the rationale for using local irradiation including only brachy-therapy was that the most common sites of recurrence were the vagina or pelvis. In the 1970s and subsequently, it was appreciated that even in early-stage disease, the most common metastatic site was distant (Onsrud *et al.* 1976). There have been several prospective randomised studies using systemic therapy in an attempt to decrease this recurrence in high-risk patients, but without appreciable success.

MOLECULAR GENETICS

It is now thought that the majority of human cancers result from the stepwise accumulation of DNA damage in multiple cellular genes. These molecular insults commonly lead to the activation of cellular proto-oncogenes or to the inactivation of tumour-suppressor genes. Proto-oncogenes are genes normally found in the cell which are involved in the control of cellular division and differentiation. Their activation, via mutation, deletion, chromosomal rearrangement or amplification can result in exaggerated cellular proliferation and neoplasia. In contrast, the function of the tumour-suppressor gene in normal cells is to suppress the malignant phenotype, a role which is abrogated if both copies of the tumour-suppressor gene are damaged. A model of carcinogenesis that emphasises the accumulation of multiple genetic insults ('hits') has been demonstrated by Vogelstein and Kinzler (1993) in the progression of colonic polyps to invasive colon cancer. While the study of the molecular genetics of endometrial carcinoma is in its infancy, not yet providing a molecular paradigm as compelling as that for cancer of the colon, a great deal of work has been done and this is briefly summarised here.

Perhaps the most intensively studied molecular abnormality in endometrial carcinoma involves the *p53* gene. The *p53* tumour-suppressor gene is located on chromosome 17p and encodes for a nuclear phosphoprotein that appears to regulate critical check-points in the cell cycle. Loss of function of the normal *p53* gene is thought to be a recessive event, requiring mutation, inactivation or deletion of both alleles and it appears to be the most common genetic event in human cancer. The p53 protein normally has a short half-life in the cell but, when mutated, accumulates in the cell nucleus where it can be visualised as immunohistochemical overexpression. We and others (Kohler *et al.* 1992) have shown that approximately 20% of endometrial carcinomas demonstrate *p53* overexpression and mutation, which was found to strongly correlate with advanced stage, high grade and papillary serous histology. Studies of uterine papillary serous carcinoma, for example, have demonstrated that at least 85% of these cancers demonstrate *p53* overexpression (Moll *et al.* 1996). Since *p53* mutation is rarely observed in endometrial hyperplasia, it is thought to represent a late event in endometrial carcinogenesis (Kohler *et al.* 1993).

Another tumour-suppressor gene which has been studied in endometrial carcinoma is the *DCC* tumour suppressor. The *DCC* gene encodes a transmembrane protein similar to neural-cell adhesion molecules and this is possibly important in regulating self proliferation, differentiation and aggregation. The *DCC* gene is located on chromosome 18q with expression absent or decreased in at least 50% of colorectal, pancreatic, breast and prostatic carcinomas. While loss of heterozygosity has been observed in chromosome 18q in some endometrial cancers, initial studies have not demonstrated *DCC* mutations in endometrial carcinoma (Fujino *et al.* 1994).

The E-cadherin gene is a tumour suppressor located on chromosome 16 which encodes the calcium-dependent protein which may behave as a cell adhesion molecule. Loss of E-cadherin function may result in a breakdown of intracellular junctions leading to the malignant phenotype. E-cadherin mutations and down-regulation have been identified in a variety of human cancers, including ovarian and breast cancer. Risinger *et al.* (1994), however, demonstrated only three mutations in 72 cases of endometrial cancer, suggesting that this tumour suppressor is likely to play a minor role in endometrial carcinogenesis.

Recently, the candidate tumour-suppressor gene, *PTEN/MMAC1*, located on chromosome 10q23, has been found to be mutated in several human cancers, most commonly glioblastomas. Since this chromosomal region is known to be abnormal in some endometrial cancers, Risinger *et al.* (1997) recently performed mutational analysis for the *PTEN/MMAC1* gene in 70 endometrial carcinomas. Somatic mutations were detected in 24 cases (34%), including 21 cases that resulted in premature truncation of the protein, which would be expected to have a drastic result on protein function. Cancers harbouring the *PTEN/MMAC1* mutation did not have a particular clinical phenotype and, interestingly, the highest frequency of mutations (86%) was seen in stage Ia well-differentiated cases and not in papillary serous or clear-cell cancers, arguing that this molecular abnormality is more common in type I oestrogen-dependent uterine cancers. These data indicate that mutations in the *PTEN/MMAC1* gene are the most common molecular genetic abnormality so far identified in endometrial carcinoma.

In addition to abnormalities in tumour-suppressor genes, a number of oncogene abnormalities have been investigated in endometrial carcinoma. *HER-2/neu* is a cellular proto-oncogene encoding a transmembrane tyrosine kinase receptor. Overexpression of the *HER-2/neu* gene, often found in association with gene amplification, is found in 15–40% of breast and ovarian cancers. Berchuck *et al.* (1991) demonstrated that overexpression of *HER-2/neu* occurred in 9% of endometrial carcinomas and was associated with metastatic disease (27%) as compared with tumours confined to the uterus (4%). In some studies, but not others, overexpression of *HER-2/neu* has been associated with poor prognosis.

An intensively studied oncogene in endometrial carcinoma is the *RAS* family of genes. The *RAS* oncogenes encode 21 kDa proteins, known as G proteins, which are involved in signal transduction across the plasma membrane. *K-RAS* mutations, in particular, are common in a wide variety of human cancers, including 75–95% of pancreatic cancers. Multiple studies in endometrial carcinoma have demonstrated that *K-RAS* activating mutations are found in 10–37% of endometrial carcinomas, as well as 6–16% of endometrial hyperplasias, suggesting that *K-RAS* mutation can be an early event in endometrial carcinogenesis. *C-MYC*, another cellular oncogene which is amplified in some human cancers, appears to be only infrequently activated in endometrial carcinoma (Bandera and Boyd 1997).

In addition to alterations in specific cellular oncogenes and tumour suppressors, the phenomenon of microsatellite instability has been investigated in endometrial cancer. Microsatellite instability is a molecular genetic phenomenon which is broadly observed in human cancer. Microsatellites are simple sequence repeats which are found throughout the human genome and, since they do not encode for specific proteins, their function is not fully understood. Amplification of DNA segments containing microsatellites by the polymerase chain reaction frequently demonstrates abnormal electrophoretic shifts indicative of the accumulation of abnormal microsatellite lengths in the tumour DNA.

Microsatellite instability was initially identified in the human non-polyposis colorectal cancer syndrome (HNPCC) where it is associated with a high frequency of mutation in DNA mismatch repair genes. Endometrial carcinoma can be a feature of the HNPCC syndrome and 75% of these are associated with microsatellite instability (Risinger et al. 1993). In addition, approximately 20% of sporadic endometrial carcinomas demonstrate microsatellite instability, although these are not necessarily found in association with DNA mismatch repair-gene mutations.

It is hoped that a more complete understanding of the molecular genetic abnormalities in endometrial cancer will result in improved screening and early detection, better selection of patients for postoperative adjuvant treatment based on prognostic risk category and, eventually, in the development of effective targeted immunotherapy or gene therapy for the treatment of patients with advanced or recurrent disease.

Complicating these goals is the fact that no one molecular genetic alteration dominates or appears absolutely crucial for the development of endometrial cancer. Rather, endometrial carcinoma appears to be a heterogeneous disease, with multiple potential molecular genetic pathways. Nonetheless, while most endometrial cancers are localised and highly curable, the more aggressive forms of endometrial carcinoma, including papillary serous and clear-cell variants, are often associated with extrauterine disease at initial diagnosis, which usually heralds a poor prognosis. A screening strategy that precedes the development of symptoms (postmenopausal bleeding) could conceivably lead to earlier detection and improved outcome in these individuals. Since conventional Papanicolaou cytological screening is extremely insensitive for detecting endometrial cancer, molecular diagnostic techniques which can detect, on a Papanicolaou smear, specific genetic abnormalities in an endometrial cell destined to become malignant may show promise. Al-Jehani et al. (1998) recently demonstrated that *K-RAS* mutations could be detected in the endometrial aspirates and cervical smears of patients with endometrial cancer with an apparent sensitivity greater than that of conventional cytology.

At present, the conflicting nature of the data regarding the prognostic impact of various molecular alterations on survival in endometrial cancer means that a decision for postoperative adjuvant treatment, based on the molecular profile of a patient's tumour, cannot be made with confidence, although this should be a goal for future studies. Finally, although no studies have yet been published which target the molecular alterations in endometrial cancer for therapeutic purposes, trials in progress of anti-*HER-2/neu* monoclonal antibody and *p53* gene therapy in ovarian cancer (Gomez-Navarro et al. 1998) suggest that similar approaches may be used in patients with endometrial cancer who have advanced or recurrent disease.

References

Abeler, V.M. and Kjorstad, K.E. (1992) Endometrial adenocarcinoma with squamous cell differentiation. *Cancer* **69**, 488–95

Al-Jehani, R.M., Jeyarajah, A.R., Hagen, B., Hogdall, E.V., Oram, D.H. and Jacobs, J.J. (1998) Model for the molecular genetic diagnosis of endometrial cancer using *K-RAS* mutation analysis. *J Natl Cancer Inst* **90**, 540–2

Anonymous (1983) Oral contraceptive use and the risk of endometrial cancer. The Centers for Disease Control Cancer and Steroid Hormone Study. *JAMA* **249**, 1600–4

Bandera, C.A. and Boyd, J. (1997) The molecular genetics of endometrial carcinoma. *Prog Clin Biol Res* **396**, 185–203

Berchuck, A., Rodriguez, G., Kinney, R.B. *et al.* (1991) Overexpression of *HER-2/neu* in endometrial cancer is associated with advanced stage disease. *Am J Obstet Gynecol* **164**, 15–21

Bohkman, J.V. (1983) Two pathogenetic types of endometrial carcinoma. *Gynecol Oncol* **15**, 10–17

Boronow, R.C., Morrow, C.P., Creasman, W.T. *et al.* (1984) Surgical staging in endometrial cancer: clinical–pathologic findings of a prospective study. *Obstet Gynecol* **63**, 825–32

Christopherson, W.M., Alberhasky, R.C. and Connelly, P.J. (1982) Carcinoma of the endometrium. Papillary adenocarcinomas: a clinical–pathological study, 46 cases. *Am J Clin Pathol* **77**, 534–40

Chu, J., Schweid, A.I. and Weiss, N.S. (1982) Survival among women with endometrial cancer: a comparison of oestrogen users and non-users. *Am J Obstet Gynecol* **143**, 569–73

Cramer, D.W., Cutler, S.J. and Christine, D. (1974) Trends in the incidence of endometrial cancer in the USA. *Gynecol Oncol* **2**, 130–43

Creasman, W.T. (1997) Endometrial cancer: incidence, prognostic factors, diagnosis and treatment. *Semin Oncol* **24**, SI140–50

Creasman, W.T., Boronow, R.C., Morrow, C.P., DiSaia, P.J. and Blessing, J. (1976) Adenocarcinoma of the endometrium: its metastatic lymph node potential. A preliminary report. *Gynecol Oncol* **4**, 239–43

Creasman, W.T., Morrow, C.P., Bundy, B.N. *et al.* (1987) Surgical pathologic spread patterns of endometrial cancer. *Cancer* **60**, 2035–41

Creasman, W.T., De Geest, K., Di Saia, P.J. *et al.* (1999) Significance of true surgical pathologic staging. *Am J Obstet Gynecol* **181**, 31–4

Cullen, T.S. (1990) *Cancer of the Uterus.* Philadelphia, PA: W.B. Saunders

Fujino, T., Risinger, J.I., Collins, N.K. *et al.* (1994) Allelotype of endometrial carcinoma. *Cancer Res* **54**, 4291–8

Goff, B.A., Kato, D.D., Schmidt, R. A. *et al.* (1994) Uterine papillary serous carcinoma: pattern of metastatic spread. *Gynecol Oncol* **54**, 264–8

Gomez-Navarro, J., Siegal, G.P., Alvarez, R.D. and Curiel, D.T. (1998) Gene therapy. Ovarian carcinoma as the paradigm. *Am J Clin Pathol* **109**, 444–67

Hammond, C.B. Jelovsek, F.R., Lee, K.L. *et al.* (1979) Effects of long-term estrogen replacement therapy. II. Neoplasia. *Am J Obstet Gynecol* **133**, 537–47

Heyman, J. (1935) The so-called Stockholm method and the results of treatment of uterine cancer with Radiumhemmet. *Acta Radiol* **16**, 129–43

Javert, C. and Douglas, R. (1956) Treatment of endometrial carcinoma. *Am J Radiol* **75**, 580–95

Katase, K., Sugiyama, Y., Hasumi, K. *et al.* (1998) The incidence of subsequent endometrial carcinoma with tamoxifen use in patients with primary breast carcinoma. *Cancer* **82**, 1698–703

Kelly, H. (1916) Radium therapy and cancer of the uterus. *Trans Am Gynecol Soc* **41**, 532–52

Kodama, S., Kase, H., Tanaka, K. and Matsui, K. (1996) Multivariant analysis of prognostic factors in patients with endometrial cancer. *Int J Gynaecol Obstet* **53**, 23–30

Kohler, M.F., Berchuck, A., Davidoff, A.M. *et al.* (1992) Overexpression and mutation of p53 in endometrial carcinoma. *Cancer Res* **52**, 1622–7

Kohler, M.F., Nishii, H., Humphrey, P.A. *et al.* (1993) Mutation of the p53 tumor-suppressor gene is not a feature of endometrial hyperplasias. *Am J Obstet Gynecol* **169**, 690–4

Landis, S.H., Murray, T., Bolden, S. and Wingo, P.A. (1998) Cancer statistics, 1998. *CA Cancer J Clin* **48**, 6–29

Lewis, B.V., Stallworthy, J.A. and Cowdell, R. (1970) Adenocarcinoma of the body of the uterus. *J Obstet Gynaecol Br Cwlth* **77**, 343–8

Marrett, L.D., Elwood, J.M., Epid, S.M., Meigs, J.W. and Flannery, J.T. (1978) Recent trends in the incidence and mortality of cancer of the uterine corpus in Connecticut. *Gynecol Oncol* **6**, 183–95

Moll, U.M., Chalas, E., Auguste, M., Meaney, D. and Chumas, J. (1996) Uterine papillary serous carcinoma evolves via a p53-driven pathway. *Hum Pathol* **27**, 1295–300

Onsrud, M., Kolstad, P. and Normann, T. (1976) Postoperative external pelvic irradiation in carcinoma of the corpus stage 1: a controlled clinical trial. *Gynecol Oncol* **4**, 222–31

Pecorelli, S., Benedet, L., Creasman, WT. and Shepherd, J.H. on behalf of the 1994–97 FIGO Committee on Gynecologic Oncology (1998) FIGO staging of gynecologic cancer. *Int J Gynaecol Obstet* **64**, 5–10

Persson, I., Yuen, J., Bergkvist, L. and Schairer, C. (1996) Cancer incidence and mortality in women receiving estrogen and estrogen-progestin replacement therapy – long term follow-up of a Swedish cohort. *Int J Cancer* **67**, 327–32

Risinger, J.I., Berchuck, A., Kohler, M.F., Watson, P., Lynch, H.T. and Boyd, J. (1993) Genetic instability of microsatellites in endometrial carcinoma. *Cancer Res* **53**, 1–4

Risinger, J.I., Berchuck, A., Kohler, M. and Boyd, J. (1994) Mutations of the E-cadherin gene in human gynecologic cancers. *Nat Genet* **7**, 98–102

Risinger, J.I., Hayes, A.K., Berchuck, A. and Barrett, J.C. (1997) PTEN/MMAC1 mutations in endometrial cancers. *Cancer Res* **57**, 4736–8

Rutledge, F.N. (1974) The role of radical hysterectomy in adenocarcinoma of the endometrium. *Gynecol Oncol* **2**, 331–47

Smith, D.C., Prentice, R., Thompson, D.J. and Hermann, W.L. (1975) Association of exogenous estrogen and endometrial carcinoma. *N Engl J Med* **293**, 1164–7

TeLinde, R.W. (1946) *Operative Gynecology*. Philadelphia, PA: J.B. Lippincott

Vogelstein, B. and Kinzler, K.W. (1993) The multistep nature of cancer. *Trends Genet* **9**, 138–41

Zaino, R.J., Kurman, R., Herbold, D. *et al.* (1991) The significance of squamous differentiation in endometrial carcinoma. Data from a Gynecologic Oncology Group study. *Cancer* **68**, 2293–302

Ziel, H.K. and Finkle, W.D. (1975) Increased risk of endometrial carcinoma among users of conjugated estrogens. *N Engl J Med* **293**, 1167–70

32

Urogynaecology

Linda D. Cardozo and Vik Khullar

INTRODUCTION

During the past decade urogynaecology has become recognised as one of the four main subspecialties of obstetrics and gynaecology. Urogynaecology encompasses problems of the female lower urinary and genital tracts which, due to their close proximity, often have co-existent disorders. Urinary problems and pelvic floor dysfunction are common in women and clinical assessments have led to inappropriate treatment and disappointing results. Using the wide range of investigations available the appropriate management can be chosen leading to an improvement in a woman's quality of life. Urogynaecology involves not only the assessment and treatment of women with urinary incontinence, but the management of vaginal prolapse, faecal incontinence, urinary tract infections, anatomical abnormalities of the lower urinary tract and dysfunction of the bladder and bowel. This wide remit is impossible to cover within this chapter, which will briefly review a few key areas within urogynaecology. These will include investigation and treatments for urinary dysfunction and vaginal prolapse.

HISTORY

The first historical evidence of urogynaecological pathology was the mummified body of Henhenit, dated back to 2050 BC, who was one of six women attached to the court of Pharaoh Menuhotep II. She was found to have a vesicovaginal fistula (Mahfouz Bey 1929). Hippocrates (400 BC) noted that this condition caused urinary incontinence (Lower 1930). The first recorded conservative treatment for urinary incontinence was by the Egyptians using a golden phallus inserted into the vagina (Edwards 1970). Surgery for incontinence was initiated by Marion Sims who, in 1849, developed a technique of closing vesicovaginal fistulae using silver wire drawn out to be as thin as horse hair, followed by a week of bladder drainage. Success was only achieved after performing thirteen operations on a single female slave, Anarcha. In 1852, Sims reported the cure of 252 fistulas out of 320 attempts.

Howard A. Kelly, who was appointed the first professor of gynaecology at Johns Hopkins Medical School, invented the cystoscope by introducing air into the bladder with the woman in the knee–chest position. Kelly's interest in urogynaecology increased and he co-authored a book in 1919 entitled *Disease of the Kidney, Ureters and Bladder* and in this he wrote 'The list of operations devised to overcome the incontinence is legion; most unsuccessful, but occasionally, temporarily at least, affording some control.' He then described the forerunner of the Kelly plication as a component of the anterior colporrhaphy and reported 16 of 20 women having a successful outcome.

In 1949, Marshall *et al.* wrote about a new operation in which they treated 50 women with stress incontinence, of whom 25 had previously undergone unsuccessful operations for incontinence. They reported an overall success rate of 82%. Burch (1961) described a modified retropubic operation which has achieved great acceptance, fixing the periurethral tissue to Cooper's ligament.

INVESTIGATION

In the 19th century, investigation of urinary disorders began with the technique of cystometry described by Mosso and Pellacani (1882) and using a smoked drum to record changes in bladder pressure. They noted bladder contractions in women with urinary symptoms and, much later, Crabtree *et al.* (1936) studied the control of micturition using fluoroscopy and a contrast-filled bladder. Table 1 shows the range of investigations in urogynaecology.

Imaging has been used as a tool to discriminate between the different causes of incontinence. Jeffcoate and Roberts (1952) used lateral cystourethrography to measure the posterior urethrovesical angle. Loss of the posterior urethrovesical angle was reported in 80% of women complaining of stress incontinence (Jeffcoate and Roberts 1952) but later this feature was shown not to be diagnostic (Green 1968). Hodgkinson *et al.* (1958) introduced lateral bead-chain cystourethrography, but this was also shown to have a marked overlap between continent and incontinent women (Hertogs and Stanton 1985). Currently, the diagnosis of urinary incontinence is based on cystometry, with imaging as a useful but non-essential adjunct.

The need for urodynamic evaluation of all women with incontinence has been questioned but has not been tested in a randomised trial. Women's symptoms do not correlate well with the urodynamic diagnosis (Jarvis *et al.* 1980). Even when women who complain only of stress incontinence and have a normal frequency/volume chart are investigated, 65% have genuine stress incontinence and 8% have detrusor instability (James *et al.* 1997). Thus, it is inappropriate to perform surgical procedures on the basis of urinary symptoms alone. The best utilisation of conservative therapies should involve urodynamic investigation prior to selecting the treatment method (level IV evidence). Levels and grades of evidence are shown in Table 2. Videocystourethrography involves

Table 1 *Range of investigations in urogynaecology*

Simple (nonspecialist investigations)	Mid-stream specimen of urine
	Frequency/volume chart
	Pad test
Complex (specialist investigations)	Uroflowmetry
	Cystometry
	Videocystourethrography
	Ambulatory urodynamics
	Urethral pressure profilometry
	Urethral electrical conductance
	Electromyography
	Micturating cystography
	Ultrasonography
	Cystourethroscopy
	Magnetic resonance imaging

Table 2 *Levels of evidence; source: US Agency for Health Care Policy and Research*

(a)

Level	Type of evidence
Ia	Evidence obtained from meta-analysis of randomised controlled trials
Ib	Evidence obtained from at least one randomised controlled trial
IIa	Evidence obtained from at least one well-designed controlled study without randomisation
IIb	Evidence obtained from at least one other type of well-designed quasi-experimental study
III	Evidence obtained from well-designed non-experimental descriptive studies, such as comparative studies, correlation studies and case–control studies
IV	Evidence obtained from expert committee reports or opinions and clinical experiences of respected authorities

(b)

Grade	Recommendation
A (evidence levels Ia, Ib)	Required: at least one randomised controlled trial as part of the body of literature of overall good quality and consistency addressing the specific recommendation
B (evidence levels IIa, IIb, III)	Required: availability of well-conducted clinical studies but no randomised clinical trials on the topic of recommendation
C (evidence level IV)	Required: evidence obtained from expert committee reports or opinions and clinical experiences of respected authorities Indicates absence of directly applicable clinical studies of good quality

filling the bladder with contrast and is useful to identify morphological abnormalities such as trabeculation, ureteric reflux, bladder and urethral diverticula (Benness *et al.* 1989). Between 7% and 16% of women investigated for lower urinary tract symptoms will have no bladder abnormality detected on standard laboratory urodynamic investigation.

Ambulatory urodynamics has been advocated as an additional investigation of lower urinary tract dysfunction where standard urodynamics has either not provided a diagnosis or the diagnosis is not consistent with the urinary symptoms (Anders *et al.* 1997). The test is more sensitive in detecting detrusor instability but less so for diagnosing genuine stress incontinence (Webb *et al.* 1991; Hill 1995a). Ambulatory urodynamics has been criticised for a reported high prevalence of abnormal detrusor activity in asymptomatic subjects (van Waalwijk van Doorn *et al.* 1992; Robertson *et al.* 1994; Heslington and Hilton 1995) but this may be related to the technique used (Salvatore *et al.* 1998). Ambulatory urodynamics alters management in over 60% of symptomatic women who have shown no abnormality on laboratory urodynamics when compared with treatment based on symptoms (Salvatore *et al.* 1999).

Transvaginal ultrasound measurement of bladder-wall thickness has been found to be a sensitive method of screening for detrusor instability (Khullar *et al.* 1996) and may be a useful second line of investigation if standard urodynamics has not been satisfactory and ambulatory urodynamics is not available (level III evidence).

TREATMENT OF INCONTINENCE

Successful treatment is assessed differently after conservative and surgical therapy. Conservative treatment is considered a 'success' if cure or improvement occur. In contrast, surgical treatment is only considered a success if total continence is demonstrated.

CONSERVATIVE THERAPY

Simple measures

All women with urinary incontinence can be helped even if a 'cure' is not possible. General advice regarding lifestyle should include moderating fluid intake to 1–1.5 litres per day, avoiding caffeine- or alcohol-containing drinks (Creighton and Stanton 1990). Evening fluid intake is thought to be related to nocturia and the nocturnal voided volume. However, evening fluid restriction does not improve nocturia significantly (Hill *et al.* 1995b). There is a weaker relationship between diurnal fluid intake and voiding (Griffiiths *et al.* 1993). Nocturnal polyuria appears to be related to subclinical heart failure (Carter *et al.* 1992) when fluid pools in the limbs during the day and returns to the intravascular space at night to produce a diuresis. Frusemide taken six hours before sleep has been shown to reduce nocturia in a randomised placebo-controlled trial (Reynard *et al.* 1998) (level Ib evidence).

Weight loss is thought to improve urinary incontinence but there are no prospective randomised trials. However, two prospective cohort studies (Deitel *et al.* 1988) have investigated this, one involved using objective tests (Bump *et al.* 1992). Incontinence was found to resolve when massive weight loss occurred in morbidly obese women (level IIb and III evidence) and appears to be an independent risk factor in the prevalence of urinary incontinence, having an increased odds ratio of 1.6 per 5 body mass index units (Brown *et al.* 1996). It may be argued that women who suffer from urinary incontinence cannot exercise and thus they become overweight. Unfortunately, there is no information regarding weight loss in moderately overweight women and the relationship to improvement of urinary incontinence. There is no evidence that strenuous exercise causes incontinence (Nygaard 1997) but exercise does exacerbate it (Davis and Goodman 1996) (level IIb and III evidence).

Pelvic floor exercises

Pelvic floor exercises were first advocated by Kegel (1948) for the treatment of genuine stress incontinence and mixed incontinence. Four prospective randomised studies have compared pelvic floor exercises to no treatment. All these studies have described significant improvements in those groups undergoing pelvic floor exercises compared with the control group (Henalla *et al.* 1989; O'Brien *et al.* 1991; Lagro-Janssen *et al.* 1992; Burns *et al.* 1993). Cure and improvement rates of 68–74% have been reported compared with 3–5% of the control groups. Burns *et al.* (1993) reported a 68% cure/improvement rate compared with 18% of controls. Henalla *et al.* (1989) used an objective outcome measure (pad test) and found that 65% of the treatment group were cured/improved compared with 0% of the control group. O'Brien *et al.* (1991) described 68% of the women being cured/improved after four years. There is level Ib evidence that women with stress, urge and mixed incontinence benefit from pelvic floor exercise compared with no treatment.

Pelvic floor exercises compared with electrical stimulation

Five trials (Henalla *et al.* 1989; Hofbauer *et al.* 1990; Hahn *et al.* 1991; Laycock and Jerwood 1993; Smith 1996) (Table 3) have compared pelvic floor exercises with electrical stimulation for genuine stress incontinence with contradictory findings. This is not surprising as mixed outcome measures (subjective and pad test) were employed at intervals of six weeks to six months. The relative benefits of electrical stimulation and pelvic floor exercises are not clear.

Pelvic floor exercises compared with surgery

There have been two randomised controlled trials comparing continence surgery with pelvic floor exercises and these have found that symptomatic improvement was less in women undergoing pelvic floor exercises and the cure after surgery was sustained for longer (Table 4).

Pelvic floor exercises compared with vaginal cones

No significant differences have been demonstrated between the outcome of vaginal cones and pelvic floor exercises (Peattie and Plevnik 1988; Haken *et al.* 1991; Wise *et al.* 1993). A recent randomised study did show reduced urinary loss using a short provocative pad test in women who had learnt pelvic floor exercises (Bo *et al.* 1999), but this outcome was reversed when a 24-hour pad test was reported in the same group of women (Bo and Talseth 1998).

Devices

Devices are used to control urinary incontinence and are not for treatment. They act by supporting the urethra and bladder neck to improve pressure transmission or increasing the outflow resistance of the urethra through compression or occlusion. The two main categories of devices are intravaginal or intra-urethral.

Table 3   *Cured/improved outcomes for the studies comparing pelvic floor exercises and electrical stimulation*

Author	Pelvic floor exercise outcome (%)	Electrical stimulation outcome (%)
Hahn *et al.* 1991	100	80
Henalla *et al.* 1989	65	32
Hofbauer *et al.* 1990	64	27
Laycock and Jerwood 1993	41	82
Smith 1996	44	66

Table 4   *Outcome after pelvic floor exercises and continence surgery compared (cure only reported)*

Authors	Pelvic floor exercise (%)	Continence surgery (%)	Outcome method
Klarskov *et al.* 1986	71	88	Subjective
Tapp *et al.* 1988	9	75	Objective

Intravaginal devices

Many devices have been used for urinary incontinence such as pessaries and diaphragms, tampons and other intravaginal devices. All these devices have been demonstrated to be effective when used once under direct supervision, with no follow-up. There are few long-term studies. Sanitary tampons have been reported to produce continence rates of 43% and improvement in 14% (Nygaard 1995). Sanitary tampons were used in a small prospective randomised single-blind controlled study during aerobic exercise sessions. There was a reduction in mean loss from 45.3 to 31.0 g. Eight women lost less than 4 g using a tampon (Nygaard 1992).

The Introl® intravaginal device is a flexible ring with two blunt prongs located at one end. When the ring is placed in the vagina, the prongs elevate the bladder neck like a retropubic operation. The Introl® intravaginal device was been found to cure 83% of women and reduce incontinent episodes (Bernier and Harris 1995). The ability of the woman to retain a device was important; the Introl® had an 11% expulsion rate and 10% of women described it as unacceptable (Biswas 1988). Another problem with the device is that there are four prong lengths and six ring diameters to be stocked. Minimal adverse effects have been reported (Biswas et al. 1993) (level IIa and III evidence).

Intra-urethral devices

Intra-urethral devices are reported to have high rates of continence and improvement in the short and long term (Nielsen et al. 1993; Staskin et al. 1996). Unfortunately, these devices are associated with discomfort, urinary tract infection and haematuria (Staskin et al. 1996). In a randomised controlled trial of an external occlusive device (Femassist®) and the Reliance® intra-urethral insert, the latter had a higher rate of continence at the cost of greater morbidity (Boos et al. 1998) (level Ib evidence). Completion rates for the intra-urethral device studies vary between 45% and 66%, indicating the degree of morbidity associated with their use (Neilson et al. 1993; Miller and Bavendam 1996; Peschers et al. 1996; Staskin et al. 1996). The longest period of follow-up for intra-urethral device use has been one year (Staskin et al. 1995).

Electrical stimulation

Electrical stimulation has been used to treat genuine stress incontinence and four randomised controlled trials with sham stimulation have shown significant improvements in the active group alone (Plevnik et al. 1986; Blowman et al. 1991; Laycock and Jerwood 1993; Sand et al. 1995). Two other studies showed no significant difference between electrical stimulation and sham stimulation (Brubaker et al. 1997; Luber and Wolde-Tsadik 19976) (Table 5). The two most robust studies show improvement in one and no change in the other, indicating that more randomised studies are required.

Bladder retraining

Bladder retraining involves patient education, a voiding regimen with increasing intervals between voids, methods of controlling urgency such as relaxation or distraction and self-modification of voiding behaviour. Two trials have compared bladder retraining with an untreated control group (Fantl et al. 1991; Jarvis and Millar 1980). Jarvis and Millar (1980) report that 90% of the treatment group were continent compared with 23% of

Table 5 *Groups comparing electrical stimulation with sham devices (cured/improved rates are quoted)*

Author and assessment method	Electrical stimulation group (%)	Sham device group (%)
Subjective		
Hofbauer *et al.* 1990	27	0
Blowman *et al.* 1991	100	33
Laycock and Jerwood 1993	33	27
Luber and Wolde-Tsadik 1997	25	29
Objective		
Sand *et al.* 1995 (pad test)	56	30
Brubaker *et al.* 1997 (urodynamics)	15	12

Table 6 *Results of randomised trials of anticholinergic drug therapy versus bladder retraining*

Authors	Bladder retraining (%)	Anticholinergics (%)
Jarvis 1981	84	56
Columbo *et al.* 1995	74	42

the control group. Fantl *et al.* (1991) included women with genuine stress incontinence, detrusor instability and mixed incontinence. They found that 12% of the treatment group were continent and 76% had reduced incontinence episodes by 50%. Bladder retraining is an effective treatment for urge, stress and mixed incontinence (grade A, level Ib evidence).

Bladder retraining has been compared with anticholinergic therapy in two randomised controlled trials the first used flavoxate hydrochloride and imipramine (Jarvis 1981) and the second used oxybutynin (Colombo *et al.* 1995) (Table 6). Unfortunately, these women only had six weeks of follow-up.

DRUG THERAPY

Drugs for the treatment of detrusor instability

Many drugs are used to treat detrusor instability, which has a high rate of placebo response, so randomised placebo controlled trials are mandatory to demonstrate efficacy. The drugs which have been shown to be efficacious in randomised trials are shown in Table 7.

There have been few placebo-controlled studies of drugs for genuine stress incontinence. Hilton *et al.* (1990) reported the results of a double-blind, placebo-controlled study using oestrogen (oral or vaginal) alone or with phenylpropanolamine, in 60 postmenopausal women with urodynamically proven genuine stress incontinence. The symptoms of frequency and nocturia improved more with combined treatment than with oestrogen alone and that of stress incontinence improved subjectively in all groups but objectively only in the combined group. It is likely that the effect of phenylpropanolamine

Table 7   *Drugs for the treatment of detrusor instability which have shown efficacy in randomised controlled trials*

Drug	Authors
Propantheline	Thuroff *et al.* 1991
Trospium	Stohrer *et al.* 1991; Madersbacher *et al.* 1995
Emepronium	Stanton 1973; Massey and Abrams 1986
Tolterodine	Appell 1997; Jonas *et al.* 1997; Rentzhog *et al.* 1998
Oxybutynin	Hehir and Fitzpatrick 1985; Cardozo *et al.* 1987; Moore *et al.* 1990; Tapp *et al.* 1990; Thuroff *et al.* 1991
Imipramine	Castleden *et al.* 1981
Desmopressin	Norgaard *et al.* 1989; Kinn and Larsson 1990; Eckford *et al.* 1995

on α-adrenergic receptors in the urethra was potentiated by the concomitant use of oestrogen replacement therapy in postmenopausal women.

Midodrine, an α-adrenergic agonist, has been used to treat women with mild to moderate genuine stress incontinence. There was significant decrease in pad test loss when taking 5–10 mg of midodrine compared with placebo without an increase in blood pressure (Weil *et al.* 1994). This may be a helpful method of treatment in the future.

There are no randomised controlled studies evaluating the use of drugs in the treatment of voiding difficulties causing overflow incontinence.

SURGICAL TREATMENT FOR GENUINE STRESS INCONTINENCE

More than 150 operations have been described for genuine stress incontinence. Blaivas (1987) has stated 'a (subjective) cure rate of at least 90% should be the accepted standard for the treatment of stress incontinence of women'. Most published literature for the surgical treatment of genuine stress incontinence is poor quality as only 2.8% of the studies and 11.5% of women included in studies are in a randomised trial (Jarvis 1994). Additionally, it is important that surgeons should know their own results rather than those quoted in the literature, as there may be great differences (Black *et al.* 1997).

Two randomised controlled trials have compared vaginal to abdominal procedures. Stanton *et al.* (1986) randomised 52 women to colposuspension or anterior colporrhaphy and bladder buttress. Objective assessment with urodynamic testing was performed at three months after surgery. Sixty-five per cent of women who underwent vaginal surgery were continent compared with 85% of the women who underwent colposuspension. Bergman *et al.* (1989) performed a three-arm randomised study allocating women to the Pereyra needle suspension, Burch colposuspension or a bladder buttress procedure. Objective assessment was performed at three months, one year and five years. The results are shown in Table 8. Colposuspension produces significantly superior results to anterior colporrhaphy and needle suspension (grade A, level Ia evidence).

The results of needle suspensions have been evaluated in the short and long term. Jarvis (1994), from a meta-analysis of the literature, quotes a short-term mean continence rate of 79.5% for the Pereyra operation and 77.7% after the Stamey needle suspension. The long-term results of these procedures are poor, with continence rates between 6% and 33% at ten years (Jarvis 1992; Hilton and Mayne 1991; Trockman *et al.* 1995; Mills *et al.* 1996). In randomised studies of bladder buttress compared with needle suspension

Table 8 *Comparative cure rates of women randomised to one of the three procedures*

	n	Bladder buttress (%)	Pereyra (%)	Colposuspension (%)
Three months	127	80	82	92
One year	342	63	65	89
Five years	93	37	43	82

studied at 6–12 months, there is no significant difference between the two techniques (Bergman and Elia 1995).

SUPRAPUBIC PROCEDURES

The Marshall–Marchetti–Krantz operation has been compared with the Burch colposuspension in three randomised controlled trials (Milani *et al.* 1985, 1991; Colombo *et al.* 1994) and the mean objective continence rate at 6–12 months was 89.9% for the Burch colposuspension and 80.3% for the Marshall–Marchetti–Krantz operation. All these studies have come from the same unit with no significant difference between the results, although oseitis pubis has been reported in 2.5% of Marshall–Marchetti–Krantz procedures (grade A, level Ib evidence).

Paravaginal repairs

It has been suggested that anterior vaginal-wall prolapse may be due to lateral detachment of the vagina from the pelvic side wall. Paravaginal repair closes the defect lateral to the vagina in the connective tissue between the pubocervical fascia and the obturator internus at the level of the arcus tendinus (Richardson *et al.* 1976). This operation has been compared to the Burch colposuspension in one randomised study, with small numbers (*n*=18) in each group. At six months, 100% of the women who underwent colposuspension were dry but only 72% of the women with paravaginal defect repairs (Colombo *et al.* 1996). The benefit of repairing defects in the fascia in the treatment of genuine stress incontinence is not yet clear (level Ib evidence).

Suburethral sling

Slings have traditionally been used after primary continence surgery has failed and where the vagina has reduced capacity and mobility. Additionally, slings have been suggested as the treatment of choice in cases of low maximal urethral pressure (<20 cmH$_2$O) although there are few data to support this assertion. A mean continence rate of 93.9% (95% CI 89–99%) may be achieved if a suburethral sling is used as a primary procedure. There has been only one study randomising women undergoing a primary continence procedure to a colposuspension or sling operation (Lalos *et al.* 1993). There was no significant difference between the groups. There have been three other randomised studies comparing colposuspension with sling procedures (Henriksson and Ulmsten 1978; Richmond and Sutherst 1989; Enzelberger *et al.* 1996). These also show no difference between the two procedures. The occurrence after a sling of *de novo* detrusor instability is

16.6% and of postoperative voiding difficulty 10.4% (Jarvis 1994). These compared with 17% and 10.3%, respectively, for colposuspension. There appear to be higher rates of erosion with synthetic graft material compared with organic materials (Leach *et al.* 1997).

Laparoscopic surgery

A laparoscopic approach has been used to perform colposuspensions and has been compared with open procedures in two randomised studies. Burton (1994) randomised 60 women and reported objective continence rates of 97% and 73% at one-year follow-up. After three years the objective continence rate had dropped to 93% and 60%, respectively (Burton 1997). Su *et al.* (1997) reported a 96% open colposuspension objective cure rate compared with 80% after laparoscopic surgery at three months. Laparoscopic colposuspension produces significantly inferior results to open colposuspension (grade A, level Ib evidence). However, both studies did suffer from the operator starting the study while still on their 'learning curve'. A multicentre Medical Research Council funded study is under way and should help to clarify this contentious issue.

Prolapse and genuine stress incontinence

Vaginal prolapse and genuine stress incontinence can co-exist as they have a common aetiology. Continent women sometimes become incontinent once a prolapse has been reduced (Richardson *et al.* 1983; Bump *et al.* 1988, 1996a; Rosenweig *et al.* 1992; Hextall *et al.* 1998). One approach is to repair the prolapse and at the same time perform a continence procedure to treat occult genuine stress incontinence. Thirty women with severe uterovaginal prolapse and occult genuine stress incontinence underwent vaginal repair and a Kelly bladder neck plication. Fifteen women (50%) developed postoperative stress incontinence and this was confirmed as genuine stress incontinence on urodynamics. An additional eleven women (37%) had objective evidence of genuine stress incontinence but no symptoms (Gordon *et al.* 1999). Bump *et al.* (1996a) conducted a prospective randomised trial of 29 women with both severe uterovaginal prolapse and occult genuine stress incontinence who were randomised to needle suspension or bladder neck endopelvic fascia plication. Only 7% of women developed stress incontinence compared with the 67% predicted by preoperative urodynamics. Sze *et al.* (1997) reported the results of sacrospinous ligament fixation with a transvaginal needle suspension. Of 54 women, 18 (33%) developed recurrent prolapse beyond the hymenal ring and five (9%) developed recurrent stress incontinence.

VAGINAL PROLAPSE

The assessment and the evaluation of treatment for vaginal prolapse has been difficult as methods of examination have not been reproducible (Athanasiou *et al.* 1995). The International Continence Society prolapse score is simple to perform and has good inter- and intra-observer variability (Athanasiou *et al.* 1995; Bump *et al.* 1996b). This will allow an accurate assessment of treatment and the outcome of treatment. There is only one randomised study using two different methods of treating recurrent anterior vaginal wall prolapse. This study compared the use of a marlex mesh and a routine fascial defect repair. After two years there were significantly more failures in the fascial repair group (Julian 1996). There are inadequate data in this area and further randomised studies need to be carried out.

Table 9   *Areas of future developments in urogynaecology*

Area	Developments
Vaginal prolapse	Quality of life measurements Objective prolapse measurement (POP-Q)
Imaging	Three-dimensional ultrasound Dynamic magnetic resonance imaging
Urodynamic testing	More sensitive methods of diagnosing detrusor instability Quantifying detrusor instability Measuring urethral instability
Detrusor instability	New drugs, fewer adverse effects New routes of administration
Genuine stress incontinence	Selective α-adrenergic agonists for treatment Less invasive surgical treatments
Bladder pain and detrusor instability	Molecular technology to determine aetiology

FUTURE DEVELOPMENTS

Effective communication and comparison of data by different groups will rely on standardising reporting and the evaluation of outcomes. The range of outcomes must vary between standardised symptom questionnaires, quality-of-life assessment and objective tests such as pad tests and urodynamics. Treatment of urogynaecological conditions will improve with increased understanding of the pathophysiology leading to the symptoms. Table 9 indicates the areas where developments are expected in the next decade.

Urogynaecology is an exciting field in which there will be many changes leading to better treatment of debilitating chronic disease. The aim of treatment is to improve quality of life even if complete cure is not obtainable.

References

Anders, K., Khullar, V., Cardozo, L.D., Salvatore, S. and Toozs-Hobson, P. (1997) Ambulatory urodynamic monitoring in clinical urogynaecological practice. *Neurourol Urodyn* **16**, 510–12

Appell, R.A. (1997) Clinical efficacy and safety of tolterodine in the treatment of the overactive bladder: a pooled analysis. *Urology* **50** Suppl 6A, 90–6

Athanasiou, S., Hill, S., Gleason, C., Anders, K. and Cardozo, L.D. (1995) Validation of the ICS proposed pelvic organ prolapse descriptive system. *Neurourol Urodyn* **14**, 414–15

Benness, C.J., Barnick, C.G. and Cardozo, L.D. (1989) Is there a place for routine videocystourethrography in the assessment of lower urinary tract dysfunction? *Neurourol Urodyn* **8**, 299–300

Bergman, A. and Elia, G. (1995) Three surgical procedures for genuine stress incontinence: five-year follow-up of a prospective randomized study. *Am J Obstet Gynecol* **173**, 66–71

Bergman, A., Ballard, C.A. and Koonings, P.P. (1989) Comparison of three different surgical procedures for genuine stress incontinence: prospective randomized study. *Am J Obstet Gynecol* **160**, 1102–6

Bernier, F. and Harris, L. (1995) Treating stress incontinence with the bladder neck support prosthesis. *Urologic Nursing* **15**, 5–9

Biswas, N.C. (1988) A Silastic vaginal device for the treatment of stress urinary incontinence. *Neurourol Urodyn* **7**, 271–2

Biswas, N.C., Spencer, P. and King, J. (1993) Conservative management of stress incontinence with a bladder neck support prosthesis (BSP). *Neurourol Urodyn* **12**, 311–13

Black, N., Griffiths, J., Pope, C., Bowling, A. and Abel, P. (1997) Impact of surgery for stress incontinence on morbidity: cohort study. *BMJ* **315**, 1493–8

Blaivas, J.G. (1987) A modest proposal for the diagnosis and treatment of urinary incontinence in women. *J Urol* **138**, 597–8

Blowman, C., Pickles, C., Emery, S., Creates, V. and Towell, L. (1991) Prospective double-blind controlled trial of intensive physiotherapy with and without stimulation of the pelvic floor in the treatment of genuine stress incontinence. *Physiotherapy* **77**, 727–9

Bo, K. and Talseth, T. (1998) Single blinded randomized controlled trial on the effect of pelvic floor muscle strength training, electrical stimulation, cones or control on severe genuine stress incontinence. *Neurourol Urodyn* **17**, 421–2

Bo, K., Talseth, T. and Holme, I. (1999) Single blind, randomised controlled trial of pelvic floor exercises, electrical stimulation, vaginal cones, and no treatment in management of genuine stress incontinence in women. *BMJ* **318**, 487–93

Boos, K., Anders, K., Hextall, A., Toozs-Hobson, P. and Cardozo, L. (1998) Randomised trial of Reliance versus Femassist devices in the management of genuine stress incontinence. *Neurourol Urodyn* **17**, 455–6

Brown, J.S., Seeley, D.G., Fong, J., Black, D.M., Enstrud, K.E. and Grady, D. (1996) Urinary incontinence in older women: who is at risk? *Obstet Gynecol* **87**, 715–21

Brubaker, L., Benson, J.T., Bent, A., Clark, A. and Shott, S. (1997) Transvaginal electrical stimulation for female urinary incontinence. *Am J Obstet Gynecol* **177**, 536–40

Bump, R.C., Fantl, J.A. and Hurt, W.G. (1988) The mechanism of urinary continence in women with severe uterovaginal prolapse: results of barrier studies. *Obstet Gynecol* **72**, 291–5

Bump, R.C., Sugerman, J.H., Fantl, J.A. and McClish, D.K. (1992) Obesity and lower urinary tract function in women: effect of surgically induced weight loss. *Am J Obstet Gynecol* **167**, 392–8

Bump, R.C., Hurt, W.G., Theofrastous, J.P. *et al.* (1996a) Randomised prospective comparison of needle colposuspension versus endopelvic fascia plication for potential stress incontinence prophylaxis in women undergoing vaginal reconstruction for stage III or IV pelvic organ prolapse. *Am J Obstet Gynecol* **175**, 326–35

Bump, R.C., Mattiasson, A., Bo, K. *et al.* (1996b) The standardization of terminology of female pelvic organ prolapse and pelvic floor dysfunction. *Am J Obstet Gynecol* **175**, 10–17

Burch, J.C. (1961) Urethrovesical fixation to Cooper's ligament form for correction of stress incontinence, cystocele and prolapse. *Am J Obstet Gynecol* **81**, 281–90

Burns, P.A., Pranikoff, K., Nochajksi, T.H., Hadley, E.C. and Levy, K.J. (1993) A comparison of effectiveness of biofeedback and pelvic muscle exercise treatment of stress incontinence in older community-dwelling women. *J Gerontology* **48**, M167–74

Burton, G. (1994) A randomised comparison of laparoscopic and open colposuspension. *Neurourol Urodyn* **7**, 497–8

Burton, G. (1997) A three-year prospective randomised urodynamic study comparing open and laparoscopic colposuspension. *Neurourol Urodyn* **16**, 353–4

Cardozo, L.D., Cooper, D. and Versi, E. (1987) Oxybutynin chloride in the management of idiopathic detrusor instability. *Neurourol Urodyn* **6**, 256–7

Carter, P.G., McConnell, A.A. and Abrams, P. (1992) The significance of atrial natriuretic peptide in nocturnal urinary symptoms in the elderly. *Neurourol Urodyn* **11**, 420–1

Castleden, C.M., George, C.F., Renwick, A.G. and Asher, M.J. (1981) Imipramine – a possible alternative to current therapy for urinary incontinence in the elderly. *J Urol* **125**, 318–20

Colombo, M., Scalambrino, S., Maggioni, A. and Milani, R. (1994) Burch colposuspension versus modified Marshall–Marchetti–Krantz urethropexy for primary genuine stress urinary incontinence: a prospective, randomized clinical trial. *Am J Obstet Gynecol* **171**, 1573–9

Colombo, M., Zanetta, G., Scalambrino, S. and Milani, R. (1995) Oxybutynin and bladder retraining in the management of female urinary urge incontinence. *Int Urogynecol J* **6**, 63–7

Colombo, M., Milani, R., Vitobello, D. and Maggioni, A. (1996) A randomized comparison of Burch colposuspension and abdominal paravaginal defect repair for female stress urinary incontinence. *Am J Obstet Gynecol* **175**, 78–84

Crabtree, T.G., Brodney, M.L., Kontoff, H.A. and Muellner, S.R. (1936) Roentgenological diagnosis of urological and gynecological diseases of the female bladder. *J Urol* **35**, 52–69

Creighton, S.M. and Stanton, S.L. (1990) Caffeine: does it affect your bladder? *Br J Urol* **66**, 613–14

Davila, G.W. (1996) Introl bladder neck support prosthesis: a nonsurgical urethropexy. *J Endourol* **10**, 293–6

Davis, E.D. and Goodman, M. (1996) Stress urinary incontinence in nulliparous female soldiers in airborne infantry training. *J Pelvic Surg* **2**, 68–71

Deitel, M., Stone, E., Kassam, H.A., Wilk, E.J. and Sutherland, D.J.A. (1988) Gynecologic-obstetric changes after loss of massive excess weight following bariatric surgery. *J Am Coll Nutr* **7**, 147–53

Eckford, S.D., Carter, P.G., Jackson, S.R., Penney, M.D. and Abrams, P. (1995) An open, inpatient incremental safety and efficacy study of desmopressin in women with multiple sclerosis and nocturia. *Br J Urol* **76**, 459–63

Edwards, S.L. (1970) 'Mechanical and other devices' in: K.P.S. Caldwell (Ed.) *Urinary Incontinence*, 1st edn, pp. 115–27. London: Academic Press

Enzelsberger, H., Helmer, H. and Schatten, C. (1996) Comparison of Burch and lyodura sling procedures for repair of unsuccessful incontinence surgery. *Obstet Gynecol* **88**, 251–6

Fantl, J.A., Wyman, J.F., McClish, D.K. *et al.* (1991) Efficacy of bladder training in older women with urinary incontinence. *JAMA* **265**, 609–13

Gordon, D., Groutz, A., Wolman, I., Lessing, J.B. and David, M.P. (1999) Development of postoperative urinary stress incontinence in clinically continent patients undergoing prophylactic Kelly plication during genitourinary prolapse repair. *Neurourol Urodyn* **18**, 193–8

Green, T.H. Jr (1968) The problem of urinary stress incontinence in the female: an appraisal of its current status. *Obstet Gynecol Surv* **23**, 603–34

Griffiths, D.J., McCracken, P.N., Harrison, G.M. and Gormley, E.A. (1993) Relationship of fluid intake to voluntary micturition and urinary incontinence in geriatric patients. *Neurourol Urodyn* **12**, 1–7

Hahn, I., Sommar, S. and Fall, M. (1991) A comparative study of pelvic floor training and electrical stimulation for the treatment of genuine stress urinary incontinence. *Neurourol Urodyn* **10**, 545–54

Haken, J., Benness, C., Cardozo, L. and Cutner, A. (1991) A randomised trial of vaginal cones and pelvic floor exercises in the management of genuine stress incontinence. *Neurourol Urodyn* **10**, 393–4

Hehir, M. and Fitzpatrick, J.M. (1985) Oxybutynin and the prevention of urinary incontinence in spina bifida. *Eur Urol* **11**, 254–6

Henalla, S.M., Hutchins, C.J., Robinson, P. and MacVicar, J. (1989) Non-operative methods in the treatment of female genuine stress incontinence of urine. *Journal of Obstetrics and Gynecology* **9**, 222–5

Henriksson, L. and Ulmsten, U. (1978) A urodynamic evaluation of the effects of abdominal urethrocystopexy and vaginal sling urethroplasty in women with stress incontinence. *Am J Obstet Gynecol* **131**, 77–82

Hertogs, K. and Stanton, S.L. (1985) Lateral bead chain urethrocystography after successful and unsuccessful colposuspension. *Br J Obstet Gynaecol* **92**, 1179–83

Heslington, K. and Hilton, P. (1995) Ambulatory monitoring and conventional cystometry in asymptomatic volunteers. *Br J Obstet Gynaecol* **103**, 434–41

Hextall, A., Boos, K., Cardozo, L.D., Toozs-Hobson, P., Anders, K. and Khullar, V. (1998) Videocystourethrography with a ring *in situ*. A clinically useful preoperative investigation for continent women with urogenital prolapse. *Int Urogynecol J* **9**, 205–9

Hill, S., Khullar, V., Cardozo, L.D., Anders, K. and Yip, A. (1995a) Ambulatory urodynamics versus videocystourethrogram – a test retest analysis. *Neurourol Urodyn* **14**, 528–9

Hill, S., Cardozo, L.D. and Khullar, V. (1995b) Does evening fluid restriction improve nocturia? *Int Urogynecol J* **6**, 242

Hilton, P. and Mayne, C.J. (1991) The Stamey endoscopic bladder neck suspension: a clinical and urodynamic investigation, including actuarial follow-up over four years. *Br J Obstet Gynaecol* **98**, 1141–9

Hilton, P., Tweddel, A.L. and Mayne, C. (1990) Oral and intravaginal estrogens alone and in combination with alpha adrenergic stimulation in genuine stress incontinence. *Int Urogynecol J* **12**, 80–6

Hodgkinson, C.P., Dank, H.P. and Kelly, W.T. (1958) Urethrocystogram: metallic bead chain technique. *Clin Obstet Gynecol* **1**, 668–77

Hofbauer, V.J., Preisinger, F. and Nurnberger, N. (1990) Der stellenwert der physiokotherapie bei der weiblichen genuinen stress-inkontinenz. *Z Urol Nephrol* **83**, 249–4

James, M.C., Jackson, S.L., Shepherd, A.M. and Abrams, P. (1997) Can detrusor instability really be discounted with a history of pure stress urinary incontinence? *Int Urogynecol J* **8**, S53

Jarvis, G.J. (1981) A controlled trial of bladder drill and drug therapy in the management of detrusor instability. *Br J Urol* **53**, 565–7

Jarvis, G.J. (1992) Erosion of buttress following bladder neck suspension (letter comment). *Br J Urol* **70**, 695

Jarvis, G.J. (1994) Surgery for genuine stress incontinence. *Br J Obstet Gynaecol* **101**, 371–4

Jarvis, G.J. and Millar, D.R. (1980) Controlled trial of bladder drill for detrusor instability. *BMJ* **281**, 1322–3

Jarvis, G.J., Hall, S., Stamp, S., Millar, D.R. and Johnson, A. (1980) An assessment of urodynamic examination in incontinent women. *Br J Obstet Gynaecol* **87**, 893–6

Jeffcoate, N. and Roberts, H. (1952) Stress incontinence. *Br J Obstet Gynaecol* **59**, 685–720

Jonas, U., Hofner, K., Madersbacher, H. and Holmdahl, T.H. (1997) Efficacy and safety of two doses of tolterodine versus placebo in patients with detrusor overactivity and symptoms of frequency, urge incontinence, and urgency: urodynamic evaluation. The International Study Group. *World J Urol* **15**, 144–51

Julian, T.M. (1996) The efficacy of Marlex mesh in the repair of severe, recurrent vaginal prolapse of the anterior midvaginal wall. *Am J Obstet Gynecol* **175**, 1472–5

Kegel, A.H. (1948) Progressive resistance exercise in the functional restoration of the perineal muscles. *Am J Obstet Gynecol* **56**, 238–48

Khullar, V., Cardozo, L., Salvatore, S. and Hill, S. (1996) Ultrasound: a noninvasive screening test for detrusor instability. *Br J Obstet Gynaecol* **103**, 904–8

Kinn, A.C. and Larsson, P.O. (1990) Desmopressin: a new principle for symptomatic treatment of urgency and incontinence in patients with multiple sclerosis. *Scand J Urol Nephrol* **24**, 109–14

Klarskov, P., Belving, D., Bischoff, N., Dorph, S. and Gerstenberg, T.C. (1986) Pelvic floor exercise versus surgery for female urinary stress incontinence. *Urol Int* **41**, 129–32

Lagro-Janssen, A.L.M., Debruyne, F.M., Smits, A.J.A. and Van Weel, C. (1992) The effects of treatment of urinary incontinence in general practice. *Fam Pract* **9**, 284–9

Lalos, O., Berglund, A.L. and Bjerle, P. (1993) Urodynamics in women with stress incontinence before and after surgery. *Eur J Obstet Gynecol Reprod Biol* **48**, 197–205

Laycock, J. and Jerwood, D. (1993) Does pre-modulated interferential cure genuine stress incontinence? *Physiotherapy* **79**, 553–60

Leach, G.E., Dmochowski, R.R., Appell, R.A. *et al.* (1997) Female Stress Urinary Incontinence Clinical Guidelines Panel summary report on surgical management of female stress urinary incontinence. *J Urol* **158**, 875–80

Lower, W.E. (1930) Vesico-vaginal fistula. *Ann Surg* **92**, 774–8

Luber, K.M. and Wolde-Tsadik, G. (1997) Efficacy of functional electrical stimulation in treating genuine stress incontinence: a randomized clinical trial. *Neurourol Urodyn* **16**, 254–8

Madersbacher, H., Stohrer, M., Richter, R., Burgdorfer, H., Hachen, H.J. and Murtz, G. (1995) Trospium chloride versus oxybutynin: a randomized, double-blind, multicentre trial in the treatment of detrusor hyper-reflexia. *Br J Urol* **75**, 452–6

Mahfouz Bey, N. (1929) Urinary and rectovaginal fistulae in women. *J Obstet Gynaecol Br Empire* **36**, 581–9

Marshall, V.F., Marchetti, A.A. and Krantz, K.E. (1949) The correction of stress incontinence by simple vesico-urethral suspension. *Surg Gynecol Obstet* **88**, 509–18

Massey, J.A. and Abrams, P. (1986) Dose titration in clinical trials: an example using emepronium carrageeate in detrusor instability. *Br J Urol* **58**, 125–8

Milani, R., Scalambrino, S., Quadri, G., Algeri, M. and Marchesin (1985) Marshall–Marchetti–Krantz procedure and Burch colposuspension in the surgical treatment of female urinary incontinence. *Br J Obstet Gynaecol* **92**, 1050–3

Milani, R., Magsoni, A., Colombo, M., Pisani, G. and Quinto, M. (1991) Burch colposuspension versus modified Marshall–Marchetti–Krantz for stress urinary incontinence. *Neurourol Urodyn* **10**, 454–5

Miller, J.L. and Bavendam, T. (1996) Treatment with the Reliance urinary control insert: one year experience. *J Endourol* **10**, 287–92

Mills, R., Persad, R. and Handley, A.M. (1996) Long-term follow-up results with the Stamey operation for stress incontinence of urine. *Br J Urol* **77**, 86–8

Moore, K.H., Hay, D.M., Imrie, A.E., Watson, A. and Goldstein, M. (1990) Oxybutynin hydrochloride (3 mg) in the treatment of women with idiopathic detrusor instability. *Br J Urol* **66**, 479–85

Mosso, A. and Pellacani, P. (1882) Sur les fonctions de la vessie. *Archives of Italian Biology* **1**, 97–127

Nielsen, K.K., Walter, S., Maegaard, E. and Kromann-Andersen, B. (1993) The urethral plug II: an alternative treatment in women with genuine urinary stress incontinence. *Br J Urol* **72**, 428–32

Norgaard, J.P., Rillig, S. and Djurhuus, J.C. (1989) Nocturnal enuresis: an approach to treatment based on pathogenesis. *J Pediatr* **114**, 705–9

Nygaard, I. (1992) Treatment of exercise incontinence with mechanical devices. *Neurourol Urodyn* **11**, 367–8

Nygaard, I. (1995) Prevention of exercise incontinence with mechanical devices. *J Reprod Med* **40**, 89–94

Nygaard, I.E. (1997) Does prolonged high-impact activity contribute to later urinary incontinence? A retrospective cohort study of female Olympians. *Obstet Gynecol* **90**, 718–22

O'Brien, J., Austin, M., Sethi, P. and O'Boyle, P. (1991) Urinary incontinence: prevalence, need for treatment and effectiveness of intervention by nurse. *BMJ* **303**, 1308–12

Peattie, A.B. and Plevnik, S. (1988) Cones versus physiotherapy as conservative management of genuine stress incontinence. *Neurourol Urodyn* **7**, 165–6

Peschers, U., Zen Ruffinen, F., Schaer, G. and Schussler, B. (1996) The VIVA urethral plug: a sensible expansion of the spectrum for conservative therapy of urinary stress incontinence? *Geburtshilfe und Frauenheilkunde* **56**, 118–23

Plevnik, S., Janez, J., Vrtacnik, P., Trsinar, B. and Vodusek, D.B. (1986) Short-term electrical stimulation: home treatment for urinary incontinence. *World J Urol* **4**, 24–6

Rentzhog, L., Stanton, S.L., Cardozo, L., Nelson, E., Fall, M. and Abrams, P. (1998) Efficacy and safety of tolterodine in patients with detrusor instability: a dose-ranging study. *Br J Urol* **81**, 42–8

Reynard, J.M., Cannon, A., Yang, Q. and Abrams, P. (1998) A novel therapy for nocturnal polyuria: a double-blind randomized trial of frusemide against placebo. *Br J Urol* **81**, 215–18

Richardson, A.C., Lyon, J.B. and Williams, N.L. (1976) A new look at pelvic relaxation. *Am J Obstet Gynecol* **126**, 568–73

Richardson, D.A., Bent, A. and Ostergard, D.R. (1983) The effect of uterovaginal prolapse on urethrovesical pressure dynamics. *Am J Obstet Gynecol* **146**, 901–5

Richmond, D.H. and Sutherst, J.R. (1989) Burch colposuspension or sling for stress incontinence? A prospective study using transrectal ultrasound. *Br J Urol* **64**, 600–3

Robertson, A.S., Griffiths, C.J., Ramsden, P.D. and Neal, D.E. (1994) Bladder function in healthy volunteers: ambulatory monitoring and conventional urodynamic studies. *Br J Urol* **73**, 242–9

Rosenweig, B.A., Pushkin, S., Blumenfeld, D. and Bhatia, N.N. (1992) Prevalence of abnormal urodynamic test results in continent women with severe genitourinary prolapse. *Obstet Gynecol* **79**, 539–42

Salvatore, S., Khullar, V., Anders, K. and Cardozo, L.D. (1998) Reducing artefacts in ambulatory urodynamics. *Br J Urol* **81**, 211–14

Salvatore, S., Khullar, V., Cardozo, L.D., Anders, K., Digesu, G.A. and Bidmead, J. (1999) Ambulatory urodynamics: do we need it? *Neurourol Urodyn* **18**, 257–8

Sand, P.K., Richardson, D.A., Staskin, D.R., Swift, S.E. and Appell, R.A. (1995) Pelvic floor electrical stimulation in the treatment of genuine stress incontinence: a multicenter, placebo-controlled trial. *Am J Obstet Gynecol* **173**, 72–9

Smith, J.J. (1996) Intravaginal stimulation randomized trial. *J Urol* **155**, 127–30

Stanton, S.L. (1973) A comparison of emepronium bromide and flavoxate hydrochloride in the treatment of urinary incontinence. *J Urol* **110**, 529–32

Stanton, S.L., Chamberlain, G.V.P. and Holmes, D.M. (1986) Randomised study of the anterior repair and colposuspension operation in the control of genuine stress incontinence. Paper presented at the 16th International Continence Society meeting

Staskin, D., Sant, G., Sand, P. *et al.* (1995) Use of an expandable urethral insert for GSI – long term results of multicenter trial. *Neurourol Urodyn* **14**, 420–2

Staskin, D., Bavendam, T., Miller, J. *et al.* (1996) Effectiveness of a urinary control insert in the management of stress urinary incontinence: early results of a multicenter study. *Urology* **47**, 629–36

Stohrer, M., Bauer, P., Giannetti, B.M., Richter, R., Burgdorfer, H. and Murtz, G. (1991) Effect of trospium chloride on urodynamic parameters in patients with detrusor hyperreflexia due to spinal cord injuries: a multicenter placebo controlled double-blind trial. *Urol Int* **47**, 138–43

Su, T.H., Wang, K.G., Hsu, C.Y., Wei, H.J. and Hong, B.K. (1997) Prospective comparison of laparoscopic and traditional colposuspensions in the treatment of genuine stress incontinence. *Acta Obstet Gynecol Scand* **76**, 576–82

Sze, E.H.M., Miklos, J.R., Partoli, L., Roat, T.W. and Karam, M.M. (1997) Sacrospinous ligament fixation with transvaginal needle suspension for advanced pelvic organ prolapse and stress incontinence. *Obstet Gynecol* **89**, 94–6

Tapp, A., Hills, B. and Cardozo, L.D. (1988) Randomised study comparing pelvic floor physiotherapy with the Burch colposuspension. *Neurourol Urodyn* **8**, 356–7

Tapp, A.J.S., Cardozo, L.D., Versi, E. and Cooper, D. (1990) The treatment of detrusor instability in postmenopausal women with oxybutynin chloride: a double-blind placebo controlled study. *Br J Obstet Gynaecol* **97**, 521–6

Thuroff, J., Bunke, B., Ebner, A. *et al.* (1991) Randomised double-blind multicentre trial on treatment of frequency, urgency and incontinence related to detrusor hyperactivity: oxybutynin versus propantheline versus placebo. *J Urol* **145**, 813–17

Trockman, B.A., Leach, G.E., Hamilton, J., Sakamoto, M., Santiago and Zimmern, P.E. (1995) Modified Pereyra bladder neck suspension: 10-year mean follow-up using outcomes analysis in 125 patients. *J Urol* **154**, 1841–7

van Waalwijk van Doorn, E.S.C., Remmers, A. and Janknegt, R.A. (1992) Conventional and extramural ambulatory urodynamic testing of the lower urinary tract in female volunteers. *J Urol* **47**, 1319–26

Webb, R.J., Ramsden, P.D. and Neal, D.E. (1991) Ambulatory monitoring and electronic measurement of urinary leakage in the diagnosis of detrusor instability and incontinence. *Br J Urol* **68**, 148–52

Weil, E., Eerdmans, P., van Waalwijk van Doorn, E., Ralph, G. and Janknegt, R. (1994) The effect of the alpha-1-adrenoceptor selective agonist midodrine on mild to moderate female stress incontinence. *Neurourol Urodyn* **13**, 446–7

Wise, B.G., Haken, J., Cardozo, L. and Plevnik, S. (1993) A comparative study of vaginal cone therapy, cones and Kegel exercises and maximal electrical stimulation in the treatment of female genuine stress incontinence. *Neurourol Urodyn* **12**, 436–7

33

Hormone replacement therapy

John Studd and Fred Wadsworth

INTRODUCTION

Oestrogen has been a recognised replacement therapy for the problems of the menopause for 25 years and is so accepted that many hospitals and primary care centres have their own menopause centre. There is no doubt that oestrogen therapy stops the climacteric symptoms of vasomotor instability and the local symptoms of pelvic atrophy as well as preventing osteoporosis, cardiovascular disease and depression. However, there is a problem. If this treatment is so effective, why do only 15–20% of British women take oestrogens and why do about 50% of women who start discontinue within a year? (Barlow *et al.* 1991; Wilkes and Mead 1991; Ryan *et al.* 1992).

It is certain that for patients after hysterectomy and bilateral oophorectomy, the need for oestrogen replacement is clear and uncontroversial. The treatment is straightforward without progestogen or bleeding. The reality is that only 30% of such women are still taking oestrogens after two years (Spector 1989). Is it simply a question of communication between the health care professional and the patient, or is there a more fundamental problem in that the patients may not feel better with the hormones given or the doses used?

SYMPTOMS

Vasomotor instability

The most characteristic symptoms of the menopause are hot flushes, sweats, giddiness, palpitations and headaches. These symptoms usually precede the cessation of periods. They can be most distressing, but should be easy to treat with moderately low doses of oestrogen. These are the symptoms which patients receiving tamoxifen for breast cancer complain of most severely. In these circumstances, if oestrogen is contraindicated (and probably it is not) it is difficult to find a non-hormonal therapy which removes this symptom. Progestogens may help but clonidine and evening primrose oil do not.

Pelvic atrophy

The prolonged oestrogen deficiency of the menopause produces atrophic vaginitis with vaginal dryness and dyspareunia. After the menopause, collagen loss may result in uterine prolapse and symptoms of recurrent 'cystitis'. This bladder atrophy symptom complex, better called the urethral syndrome, is common in the older population. It is often poorly treated, not responding to repeated courses of antibiotics or antispasmodics, although it should respond to fairly long-term systemic oestrogens. Local oestrogens are not helpful unless there is considerable systemic absorption.

Generalised atrophy

After the menopause, women lose large quantities of collagen, which results in the thin translucent skin of old age, brittle nails and hair loss. Apart from cosmetic issues, collagen loss and its replacement by oestrogen therapy is clearly a factor in such diverse pathology as osteoporosis and varicose ulceration. Osteoporosis is essentially a problem of collagen loss and Albright, in his initial description of 1941, made the association with osteoporosis and thin skin. Collagen is lost from the bone matrix, with resulting loss of mineral and bone substance. Brincat *et al.* (1983) showed that oestrogen therapy increases skin thickness, skin collagen content and bone density, with a decrease in hydroxyproline secretion. More recently, Khastgir *et al.* (1998) demonstrated the increase in bone collagen in histomorphometric bone biopsy studies.

Depression

There is much controversy about the role of oestrogen deficiency in the aetiology of depression in women. The majority of psychologists (Hunter 1996) have failed to demonstrate an association, but cross-sectional studies are difficult to interpret because climacteric depression is at its worst in the two or three years before periods stop (Van Keep and Kellerhans 1974). Depressive symptoms may improve after the cessation of periods. Depression is related to the perimenopausal hormonal cycles of oestrogen and progesterone in vulnerable women. There is no doubt that many women have an improvement in mood after menstruation ceases, when they have no bleeding, no dysmenorrhoea, no premenstrual syndrome and no menstrual migraine. These women are at risk of recurrence of these symptoms, including depression, when they begin sequential hormone replacement therapy (HRT) with cyclical progestogens. Herein lies part of the answer to the problem of poor compliance to HRT in women who still have a uterus.

ROUTES OF OESTROGEN THERAPY

Oral

The oral route is the most traditional and the most commonly used. Premarin® remains, for incomprehensible reasons, the most commonly used oestrogen in Europe and North America and it contains oestrone and a mixture of thirteen or more equine oestrogens. Oestradiol, an oestrogen with which the female body is familiar, is the most logical hormone to use. It also has the advantage that plasma oestradiol levels can be measured if there are any problems of inappropriate response or poor absorption. Oral oestradiol passes through the enterohepatic circulation and is partly converted to oestrone.

Percutaneous

The first-pass liver effect is prevented by using transdermal routes of administration. This produces an oestradiol:oestrone ratio of about two to one, rather than the reverse, which is found in oral oestradiol therapy. As oestradiol is the most powerful of oestrogens, it is probable that the higher levels of oestradiol obtained with percutaneous therapy will produce a greater response. Percutaneous oestrogens also decrease triglycerides and low-density lipoprotein (LDL) and increase high-density lipoproteins (HDLs). Theoretically, they have a smaller effect upon the coagulation cascade proteins which are produced in the liver. Transdermal oestrogens can be administered by patch, gel, implant or, most recently, nasal aerosol.

The former alcohol reservoir patch has been mostly superseded by the matrix patch with oestradiol in the adhesive gum. This produces a less severe skin reaction. It is available in doses of 25–100 µg for use twice weekly.

Oestradiol gels are becoming popular and work well with good absorption. They do not produce the skin reactions found with patches, particularly in hot and humid climates.

Vaginal oestrogens are used in patients who do not want systemic medication. This is illogical because any oestrogen which is effective is absorbed through the vagina and can achieve blood levels as high as percutaneous therapy. There is a claim that vaginal oestriol, or the small amount of oestradiol in vaginal rings, has a local action only, with no systemic absorption, but the logic and the evidence of efficacy is not convincing.

Hormone implantation is a convenient way of administering oestrogens and is associated with higher oestradiol levels and a prolonged duration of action. There is a fear that oestrogen implants may produce high oestradiol levels and result in excessive endometrial stimulation. This tachyphylaxis can be avoided by using the correct starting dose (25–50 mg) and repeating every six months. The danger is to start with 100 mg and repeat at 3–4 months.

The value of a new preparation of oestradiol in a nasal aerosol has been reported to be as effective as oral oestrogens. One advantage may be that the high oestradiol levels of up to 2000 pmol/l are found in the first half an hour of administration with low levels two hours later (Studd *et al.* 1999). Twice-daily administration is necessary. This preparation is not yet licensed, but would seem to have a promising future.

LONG-TERM BENEFITS

Osteoporosis

One in three women will sustain an osteoporotic fracture in their lifetime, either in the proximal radius, the vertebral body or the neck of the femur. This is a mostly preventable disease which produces great physical and emotional suffering to women. It costs the exchequer in excess of £800 million pounds per year. Although calcium, vitamin D, bisphosphonates, calcitonin and selective oestrogen receptor modulators (SERMs) all have their place in special cases, the cornerstone of prevention and treatment is oestrogen. Physicians held a stubborn view, until recently, that bone density could be maintained, but not increased on oestrogens. This was a dangerous view in relation to women over 60 years of age. We now know that the osteoporotic bone in this age group has a greater incremental increase in mass than the more normal bone of the 50-year-old woman. There is a clear correlation between this incremental increase in bone density and plasma oestradiol levels. Plasma levels of about 300 pmol/l are required. For 20 years there was no mention of plasma oestradiol levels until Holland *et al.* (1993) showed that there was an increase in bone density using 2 mg oestradiol

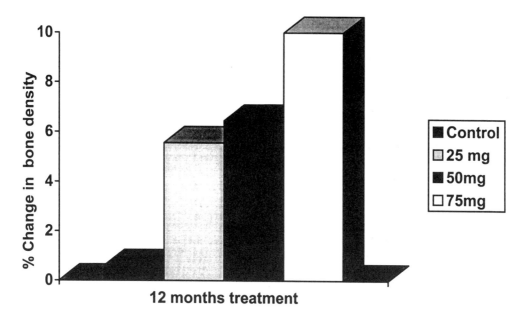

Figure 1 *Changes in bone density at the lumbar spine in treatment (oestradiol implants) and control groups at 12 months. Values are median*

valerate, with a plasma oestradiol level of 300 pmol. It is almost as if there was an extensive literature on diabetes without anybody measuring blood sugar. The reason for this deficiency was that most studies used Premarin® where it is not possible to have meaningful measurements of plasma oestrogens. Later hormone implant studies of 25, 50 and 75 mg doses showed that this produced plasma oestradiol levels of 327, 358 and 518 pmol/l, respectively, and a change in spinal bone density (Figure 1) (Studd *et al.* 1994).

Oestradiol patches of 50 μg and Premarin® 0.625 mg seem to have an equivalent effect upon bone density. Low-dose Premarin® 0.625 mg is generally believed to be the bone-sparing dose based on the early work from Glasgow (Lindsay *et al.* 1976) but in practice about 20% of women on this regimen long term have low bone density. This may be due to poor compliance, an inadequate oestrogen dose or poor absorption.

Cardiovascular disease

There is currently a new debate about the cardioprotective effect of oestrogens. This therapy causes beneficial effects on lipids, reducing LDL and increasing HDL and virtually all of the epidemiological case–control studies indicate a 50% reduction in the incidence of heart attacks (Stampfer *et al.* 1990) and a slightly smaller reduction in the number of strokes (Paganini *et al.* 1988). These population studies may have been open to selection-bias as the results may have been influenced by the choice of healthier low-risk patients who would have fewer contraindications to HRT. In spite of this, Henderson *et al.* (1991) showed that when the data were cross-stratified, looking at risk factors, the benefits were clear even in those patients who were hypertensive, hyperlipidaemic, smoked or had previous coronary disease. The data from the huge Women's Initiative Study in the USA, a primary oestrogen intervention study, will not be ready for another ten years. It was suggested that an easier and quicker way to find the answer would be a secondary interventional study in patients with established coronary disease. This has been reported in the HERS (Heart and Estrogen/progestin Replacement) study (Hulley et al. 1998) using Premarin® 0.625 mg on a group of women with severe coronary heart disease and an average age of 78 years. To the surprise of many workers, there was no clear benefit and even an excess of cardiovascular incidents in the first year. It is probable that this study was stopped prematurely, before the benefits of longer-term therapy became apparent. It was a missed opportunity.

Alzheimer's disease

Alzheimer's disease is characterised by severe progressive cognitive deterioration. It represents one of the most feared consequences of ageing. Its prevalence in the elderly doubles every 4.5 years (Jorm et al. 1987) and it is more common in women than in men (Molsa et al. 1982). It is certain that a number of factors may be responsible for the development and manifestation of Alzheimer's disease (Kukull et al. 1996), but oestrogen deficiency after the menopause may be an endocrine factor that increases a woman's risk of this dementia.

Oestrogen has effects on the brain through steroid receptors regulating specific gene transcription and other non-genomic actions including interactions with growth and neurotrophic factors and its anti-inflammatory and antioxidant properties (Wong et al. 1996). Oestrogen influences neurotransmitters, including acetylcholine, which is involved in interactions between the basal forebrain, the hippocampus and neocortex. These areas are particularly rich in oestrogen receptors and severely affected by Alzheimer's disease (Coyle et al. 1983; Toran-Allerand et al. 1992).

Therapeutic strategies for the treatment of Alzheimer's disease, which are aimed at increasing acetylcholine levels in the brain, may be augmented by concomitant use of oestrogens (Schneider et al. 1996). The antioxidant and anti-inflammatory properties of oestrogen may also be important in retarding the progress of established Alzheimer's disease (Sack et al. 1994). Ischaemic cerebrovascular disease potentiates Alzheimer's disease and oestrogen is known to augment cerebral blood flow (Belfort et al. 1995). In healthy postmenopausal women, cognitive skills are improved by oestrogen therapy, particularly verbal fluency and memory (Phillips and Sherwin 1992; Van Goozen et al. 1995). These effects are independent of oestrogen's influence on mood (Phillips and Sherwin 1992).

Only two double-blind prospective studies have been conducted which looked at oestrogen as a treatment in Alzheimer's (Honjo et al. 1993; Asthana et al. 1999). Both showed significant benefit, but numbers were small in both studies. Strong support for the protective role of oestrogen comes from recent epidemiological studies (Paganini-Hill and Henderson 1996). This Leisure World retirement community cohort contained over 1400 women when it was established by postal survey in the early 1980s. Information was collected prospectively and the women were followed until their deaths. Ever-users of oestrogen had a relative risk of 0.65 for Alzheimer's disease. Trends suggested a lower risk with increasing dose and duration of oestrogen therapy.

Evidence of disease prevention remains observational, with a small number of studies, which lack consistency.

Longevity

Long-term oestrogen therapy is associated with lower all-cause mortality and confers this apparent protection primarily through reduction in cardiovascular disease (Ettinger *et al.* 1996). The Leisure World cohort showed a 20% lower age adjusted, all-cause mortality than lifetime non-users. Current users with more than 15 years of oestrogen use had a 40% reduction in mortality. The prime effect also appeared to be through reducing cardiovascular risk (Henderson *et al.* 1991).

However, the Nurses Health Study from Boston suggested that there was a benefit, but this was reduced in long-term users as the mortality of breast cancer increased. Current users with coronary risk factors had a relative risk of 0.51 (95% CI 0.45–0.57), but women at low risk of coronary disease were seen to benefit less with a relative risk of 0.89 (Grodstein *et al.* 1997).

ADVERSE EFFECTS

Endometrium

Smith *et al.* (1975) reported the first proven problem with oestrogen therapy: a five-fold increase in endometrial carcinoma. This was supported by many other writers. It was clear that this was a result of unopposed oestrogens in patients who developed cystic hyperplasia, atypical complex hyperplasia and some subsequently developed carcinoma. Paterson *et al.* (1980) were the first to show that ten or thirteen days of progestogen would prevent hyperplasia and that the duration of progestogen was more important than the dosage. With adequate progestogenic opposition, Persson *et al.* (1986) have reported a decrease in the incidence of endometrial cancer to baseline levels.

However, analysis of the age–incidence curve for endometrial cancer suggests there will be lifelong effects of even a short duration of exogenous hormones. Five years of exogenous unopposed oestrogen replacement will increase subsequent lifetime risk by 90%. Even five years of 'adequately' opposed oestrogen and progestogen therapy is likely to increase subsequent lifetime risk by at least 50% (Key and Pike 1988).

Experimental evidence suggests overproduction of oestrogen receptor mRNA in endometrial cancers and also the presence, in some tumours, of mutated DNA binding domains for this RNA. Oestrogen may also lead to a disorder in the production of oestrogen-inducible proteins in endometrial tumours, promoting dedifferentiation, division and development of cancer cells (Fujimoto *et al.* 1994). *In vitro* studies have suggested that oestrogen may enhance the migration potential of endometrial carcinoma through the basement membrane (Fujimoto *et al.* 1996).

The study of Beresford *et al.* (1997) suggests that the current belief of the long-term safety of opposed therapy, which is not based on long-term prospective studies, may be falsely reassuring (Table 1).

Continuous combined HRT is now accepted as a safe and effective method of minimising or avoiding vaginal bleeding on HRT. It was introduced to provide progestogenic opposition to oestrogen without the need for vaginal bleeding. It was hypothesised that a lower daily progestogen dose would prevent unacceptable adverse effects and that the endometrial atrophy induced by continuous progestogen would prevent bleeding.

The endometrial shedding produced by cyclical therapy had been hypothesised to discourage the formation of hyperplasia and, therefore, the development of cancer (Gambrell *et al.* 1980). Progestogens revert endometrial hyperplasia and reduce its

Table 1 *Duration of oestrogen and cyclical progestogen therapy and the risk of endometrial cancer in current users and never-users (from Beresford et al. 1997)*

Duration of HRT (months)	Cases (n %)	Controls (n %)	Odds ratio[a]
Never-users	87.3	89	1.0
Current users: <10 days of progestogen per month			
6–59	2.8	1.7	2.2 (0.9–5.2)
>59	3.6	1.2	4.8 (2.0–11.4)
Current users: >10–21 days of progestogen per month			
6–59	3.1	6.2	0.7 (0.4–1.4)
>59	3.1	1.9	2.7 (1.2–6.0)

[a]Adjusted for age, body mass index, county of residence

occurrence on oestrogen therapy, but this does not justify the assumption that progestogens completely prevent endometrial carcinoma or offer continuing protection after treatment is stopped. When there is no regular withdrawal bleed, the long-term protective effect of progestogens may be even more limited. Perhaps shedding of the endometrium is as important as the anti-proliferative effect of progestogens.

Breast cancer

The vast literature on the subject is confused, but the consensus would accept the view that there is a 2.3% increase of breast cancer per year (Beral *et al.* 1997) and that women should consider stopping oestrogen therapy after ten years. There have been more than 30 publications on the subject, but unfortunately none has reviewed the initial pathology. It is quite possible that this apparent excess is due to either surveillance bias or the difficulty in making firm diagnoses of invasive cancer in the hormone-stimulated breast. This grey area of diagnosis occurs in at least 4% of specimens and there is a temptation to over-diagnose a carcinoma both for the safety of the patient and the medico-legal safety of the pathologist.

With the exception of the paper by Colditz *et al.* (1995) from the Nurses Study, other reports show a much reduced mortality from breast cancer in women taking HRT. The mortality data from the breast-cancer studies support the hypothesis that the increase in breast cancer is more apparent than real. Other data show a better survival in colon cancer (Grodstein *et al.* 1998) and 'all malignancies' (Hunt *et al.* 1987) in women who are taking oestrogens. These data suggest that there may be an improved host response in women taking oestrogens. It is probable that fewer oestrogen users die of breast cancer than non-users per unit of population.

Venous thromboembolic disease

HRT has recently been implicated in thromboembolic disease. A long-standing argument suggested that HRT represented 'physiological' doses of 'natural' oestrogens, thereby avoiding the risk of deep vein thrombosis seen with the oral contraceptive pill. The lack of an association was not supported in the literature and evidence either way was lacking. Case–controlled studies started to appear in 1996 showing an increase in the risk of venous thromboembolism by a factor of 2–3.5 (Daly *et al.* 1996; Grodstein *et al.* 1996;

Jick *et al.* 1996). The risk appeared highest in short-term current users and in the first year of use. These studies looked at oral preparations and no clear conclusions can be drawn about the risk of transdermal administration.

The mechanism of action that leads to increased risk may be related to changes in the clotting cascade induced by oestrogens. Both the menopause and exogenous oestrogen replacement lead to changes in clotting factor production. However, if this was the only cause, the increased risk should persist after the first year and a higher frequency of thromboembolism would be expected in case–control studies.

Congenital thrombophilias are a group of conditions where a component of the anticoagulation system is either deficient or defective. They are characterised by a propensity to thromboembolism. The condition is exacerbated in high oestrogen states such as pregnancy (Walker 1991). The most widely recognised defects include protein C deficiency, protein S deficiency, anti-thrombin III deficiency and the factor V von Leiden mutation. The number of identified defects is growing and with it the accepted incidence of thrombophilia in the population. In western European populations the prevalence of thrombophilic defects has been calculated to be in excess of 5% (Greer 1998).

The presence of thrombophilia is likely to identify a patient in a high-risk population, but the aetiology of thromboembolism is multifactorial. It involves genetic, physiological, pathological and pharmacological factors. Oestrogen cannot be seen as the only factor responsible for venous thromboembolism in postmenopausal users of HRT.

Although a thrombophilia represents a high-risk factor for thromboembolic disease, untargeted screening is not helpful, thrombophilic defects are fairly common and thromboembolic disease is uncommon. The association between thrombophilias and thromboembolism on HRT is unproven. The absolute risk of thromboembolism remains low at around 3 in 10 000 (Daly *et al.* 1996; Jick *et al.* 1996). The benefits of HRT, particularly in the cardiovascular and skeletal systems, outweigh the low risk of thromboembolism. Information about the risks should be provided to patients within this context and other readily identified risk factors considered (Lowe *et al.* 1992). Personal history and family history of thromboembolic disease should be actively sought in order to target selective screening.

If a thrombophilia is identified and combined with a good history of previous thromboembolism, HRT should probably be avoided altogether. If a high-risk patient has a particularly pressing need for HRT, concomitant anticoagulation could be considered. This would require expertise in the area and the involvement of a haematologist. Where a previous screening result is known to show thrombophilia (in the absence of previous thromboembolism) the result should be viewed in the context of disease expression in other members of the family.

There are no data to support an increased postoperative risk of thromboembolism in users of HRT, although its use could increase multifactorial risk in someone with an underlying thrombophilia. All women on HRT are likely to justify thromboprophylaxis by guidelines such as those of the THRIFT (Thromboembolic Risk Factors) Consensus Group. Anticoagulation, rather than cessation, of a patient's HRT is probably more appropriate management.

Adverse progestogen symptoms

Unfortunately, many women do not feel well with oestrogen therapy, particularly if it is an inadequate dose or a sequential preparation with more than ten days of progestogen.

They have monthly bleeding, which may be painful, heavy and irregular. They may have symptoms of pre-menstrual syndrome (PMS), menstrual headaches and bloating. They may feel that these symptoms are not worth suffering in order to reduce the risk of osteoporosis in later life.

Weight gain

It is a commonly held belief among patients on HRT that it will cause weight gain. Increased body fat and the resultant gain in weight are affected by numerous mechanisms, some of which may be influenced by sex steroids. In order for body fat to increase, either calorific intake must increase or calorific consumption must fall. If HRT were to act as an appetite stimulant it might account for an increase in weight. However, if mood is lifted and activity increased, weight would be expected to fall. Minor changes in weight could be caused by water retention, via the ability of the sex steroids to mimic aldosterone.

The literature contains no evidence to support this concern. HRT may stimulate a redistribution of fat to a gynaecoid pattern (Kohrt *et al.* 1998). It may attenuate fat accumulation, particularly in the abdominal region, when combined with an exercise program (Kohrt *et al.* 1998). In long-term users, abdominal fat is lower than in matched non-users (Perrone *et al.* 1999). Oestrogen does not appear to influence levels of leptin, a genetic marker for obesity, but in women with high leptin levels it may cause weight loss (Ongphiphadhanakul *et al.* 1998).

NON-BLEEDING REGIMENS

Intact uterus

Continuous combined oestrogen and progestogen preparations

Preparations such as Kliofem® (Novo Nordisk) are valuable in obliterating cycles, bleeding and the adverse effects of progestogen. The newer, lower dose Kliovance® (Novo Nordisk) is probably preferable. This contains 1 mg oestradiol and 0.5 mg norethisterone acetate and should be preferred to the other low-dose preparation, Premique,® which contains Premarin® (see above). This level of dose does not cause breast discomfort and the progestogen dose is adequate to prevent bleeding without causing systemic progestogenic effects. It sometimes takes three months to achieve amenorrhoea but, once established, the treatment is of great benefit. If bleeding occurs after a long period of amenorrhoea, this should be treated as postmenopausal bleeding and investigated accordingly. Leather *et al.* (1991) reviewed 41 patients receiving continuous combined therapy for eight years. Those without bleeding had atrophic endometria but, of the four patients with bleeding, two had polyps and two had adenocarcinoma. There is no suggestion that this therapy caused the carcinomas, because both patients had previously had atypical hyperplasia before therapy, but had refused hysterectomy.

Tibolone

Tibolone is a non-bleeding form of HRT. Tibolone appears to be at least as efficacious for climacteric symptoms as other forms of HRT. When ingested, it is broken down into metabolites, of which the progestogenic metabolite predominates at the level of the endometrium, so that an atrophic endometrium is produced. It does not cause withdrawal bleeding when used in women with at least one year of amenorrhoea. It is, therefore, not indicated in perimenopause because it may cause irregular bleeding. The androgenic action of tibolone may have a two-fold benefit; it may help depression and libido more than some other forms of HRT and it may improve some lipid parameters such as Lp(a), and triglycerides. However, this androgenic action may also be responsible for the reduction of HDL cholesterol, that may thus reduce the beneficial effect of tibolone on lipids.

It is estimated that only 30% of cardiovascular risk protection of HRT is due to improvement of the parameters for classical lipids while a large role is played by the direct effect of oestrogen on vessels. Tibolone, as well as oestrogen, has been shown to induce peripheral vasodilatation and also has a direct effect on vascular reactivity, thus increasing peripheral blood flow with no changes in blood pressure or cardiac output. Tibolone seems to exert a similar effect as other forms of HRT on markers of bone metabolism and bone mass, but no data are yet available on fracture prevention (Albertazzi et al. 1998; Rymer 1998).

Other clinical situations in which tibolone may be useful include women who have had hormone-dependent tumours in the past and women who have had endometriosis. Tibolone may have a protective effect in breast cancer. It appears to maintain lower genital tract epithelium while maintaining the endometrium as inactive.

Intrauterine systems

The levonorgestrel-releasing intrauterine system was initially designed as a long-acting contraceptive device. It is also a promising delivery system for progestogen in opposition to oestrogen in HRT. It renders the endometrium atrophic even with exogenous oestrogens, but avoids unwanted progestogenic side effects.

The current device releases 20 g of levonorgestrel daily. Concentrations are maintained for 78 months after insertion at levels adequate for contraception (Sturridge et al. 1996). The system is highly effective at preventing endometrial proliferation in HRT users (Suhonen et al. 1995; Antoniou et al. 1997). It appears probable that adequate endometrial protection could be provided by a 5 g or 10 g daily dose. This would lead to lower serum levels and less effect on lipids (Wolter-Svenson et al. 1995). The 20-g device is relatively wide for insertion through a postmenopausal cervix and a 5–10 g unit could be more slimline.

A disadvantage of this system other than the need for insertion is initial breakthrough bleeding which may last several months. This is usually followed by amenorrhoea.

Hysterectomy

The most effective way to have non-bleed therapy is for a woman to undergo a hysterectomy and many request this definitive procedure if the adverse effects of cyclical progestogens are intolerable. Without progestogen, these cases are straightforward without PMS-like effects or bleeding. The ideal hormone replacement is with oestradiol implants and, after oophorectomy, testosterone implants to replace the loss of endogenous ovarian androgens. The correct doses are oestradiol 50 mg and testosterone 100 mg. Surgeons should be strongly counselled against using 100 mg oestradiol postsurgery. Unfortunately, this is commonplace and leads to women developing greater expectations and dependence on high plasma oestradiol levels. This problem has been discussed at length by Gangar and Whitehead (1991) and Garnett *et al.* (1990).

SPECIAL CASES

Hysterectomy

This is referred to above but is worthy of a second mention, because these patients are so straightforward, but are often badly treated or not treated at all. Both the gynaecologist and the general practitioner must be vigilant to ensure that these women have long-term hormone replacement therapy. This may be required in many patients, even when the ovaries have been conserved.

Premenopausal

It is sometimes necessary to treat women with various climacteric symptoms, particularly PMS and depression, before their periods have ceased. Climacteric depression responds better in the premenopausal woman than in women after the cessation of periods (Montgomery *et al.* 1987). PMS in this age group can be particularly troublesome, but easy to treat. These women are often intolerant to their own progesterone and to the drop in serum oestradiol or progesterone that occurs in the perimenopausal years. They are the same women who develop postnatal depression and the same women who develop premenstrual depression. They also give a history of feeling well during pregnancy. It is this triad of hormone-responsive mood disorders which responds so well to oestrogen. Gynaecologists and general practitioners are in a superb position to treat these types of depression, which are so often inappropriately treated by psychiatrists.

WOMEN OVER 60 YEARS

Women over 60 years of age are a neglected population in terms of HRT. Numerous studies have demonstrated an increase in bone mass density in this population in response to oestrogen, with increases of 10% at the spine and 5% at the hip. The greatest response was seen in those women furthest from their menopause (Christiansen and Riis 1990; Lindsay and Tohme 1990; Lufkin *et al.* 1992; Holland *et al.* 1995). Schneider *et al.* (1997) showed that the skeletal benefits of HRT diminished after the end of treatment and protection from fracture was greatest among current users. Even current late users have a better bone density than past users. Therefore, the use of HRT in an elderly population should bring the maximum benefit.

SELECTIVE OESTROGEN RECEPTOR MODULATORS (SERMS)

SERMs have been recently marketed for use in postmenopausal osteoporosis. They appear to function as weak oestrogens, with anti-oestrogen effects in the breast and endometrium. They offer no symptom control and even exacerbate symptoms such as hot flushes.

A potential synergistic role could be considered between oestrogen and a selective anti-oestrogen. Full beneficial effects on the central nervous, cardiovascular and skeletal systems could be provided by oestrogen with selective, antagonistic protection of the breast and uterus by SERMs rather than progestogens. This level of receptor selectivity has not been demonstrated in the currently available SERMs.

In respect to their use alone, SERMs will have a useful role in a similar setting to bisphosphonates in the treatment of osteoporosis. Patients who cannot or will not take oestrogen-based HRT may be offered raloxifene for known vertebral osteoporosis. However, it should not be used as an equivalent alternative or as a safer alternative to oestrogen replacement on the basis of the currently published data. The apparent preventative influence of raloxifene on breast cancer is a potential major benefit; further data are awaited (Delmas *et al.* 1997).

COMPLIANCE

Continuation with HRT reflects the more general problem of the prescribing of medication. Up to 30% of patients may not even collect their prescription (Ravnikar 1987). An epidemiological study involving 1400 general practices suggests that although HRT use increased three-fold between 1981 and 1990, only 16% of non-hysterectomised and 36% of hysterectomised women are ever-users of HRT. A mere 9% were classified as current users. However, when we compare HRT use by women doctors with the general population, the difference is significant. Isaacs *et al.* (1995) revealed that 55% of menopausal female doctors aged 45–65 years were ever-users and, of these, 70% were taking it for more than five years. A more recent Swedish study (Andersson *et al.* 1998) found 88% of postmenopausal gynaecologists and 72% of GPs to be currently using HRT. Female doctors may be expected to have a higher uptake of HRT due to their higher socio-economic status, but they are also less likely to be negatively influenced by their caregivers, particularly regarding duration of use.

It is increasingly understood by the lay population that the menopausal transition represents an array of problems. One of the roles of a menopause clinic should be the promotion of general advice on managing the climacteric and the postmenopause in addition to prescribing HRT. The risks and benefits of HRT versus the polypharmacy that may be necessary for the multitude of short- and long-term problems can then be deliberated. The perceptions of doctors and patients may differ towards both the indications and the potential adverse effects. More studies are necessary to analyse the decision-making processes of women when determining their use of medication (Hunter *et al.* 1997). Those who have qualitatively investigated these attitudes appear to suggest that media discourse does not define the attitude of women to the menopause.

The plethora of products available today allow an enthusiastic and motivated physician the opportunity to find a suitable regime for the majority of women. An element of consumer choice will enhance compliance amongst an educated population. Careful follow-up and stabilisation of therapy has been shown to increase continuation amongst non-hysterectomised women (Vestergaard *et al.* 1997). Women who have had a hysterectomy should be the most compliant of users as they are free of the most common adverse effects of bleeding and progestogen intolerance. Even this group of women is not receiving adequate advice and follow-up. A National Osteoporosis Society survey in 1995 suggested that only 37% remembered receiving HRT information at the time of their operation. However, with meticulous counselling, these women can achieve high long-term continuation rates. In the Lister Hospital (London) unit, 86% of a population who had a hysterectomy between 1986 and 1997 were current users of oestrogen replacement therapy. The majority of these were receiving hormone implants (Domoney and Studd 1999).

Targeting women without climacteric symptoms can be more difficult. Although 96% of women in one study had heard of HRT and 96% would consider starting if a bone mineral density scan suggested they were at risk of osteoporosis (Garton *et al.* 1995), in practice significantly lower uptake and continuation rates are achieved (Torgerson *et al.* 1995). Wallace *et al.* (1990) determined that only 23% of women over 69 years of age, targeted in a fracture clinic, were prepared to start HRT. Continuous combined regimes specifically tailored for the older woman who does not want to bleed should encourage healthcare professionals to offer this therapy for those at risk of the long-term consequences of oestrogen deficiency. Doctors are aware of the benefits (Norman and Studd 1994) but may also encourage the reluctance of many women to try a therapy that works.

References

Albertazzi, P., Di Micco, R. and Zanardi, E. (1998) Tibolone: a review. *Maturitas* **16**, 295–305

Albright, F., Smith, P.H. and Richardson, A.M. (1941) Postmenopausal osteoporosis. *JAMA* **116**, 2465–74

Andersson, K., Pedersen, A.T., Mattsson, L.A. and Milsom, I. (1998) Swedish gynecologists' and general practitioners' views on the climacteric period: knowledge, attitudes and management strategies. *Acta Obstet Gynecol Scand* **77**, 909–16

Antoniou, G., Kalogirou, D., Karakitsos, P. *et al.* (1997) Transdermal oestrogen with a levonorgestrel-releasing intrauterine device for climacteric complaints versus oestradiol-releasing ring with a vaginal progesterone suppository: clinical and endometrial responses. *Maturitas* **26**, 103–11

Asthana, S., Craft, S., Baker, L.D. *et al.* (1999) Cognitive and neuroendocrine response to transdermal oestrogen in postmenopausal women with Alzheimer's disease: results of a placebo-controlled, double-blind, pilot study. *Psychoneuroendocrinology* **24**, 657–77

Barlow, D.H., Brockie, J.A. and Rees, C.M.P. (1991) A study of general practice consultations and menopausal symptoms. *BMJ* **302**, 274–6

Belfort, M.A., Saade, G.R., Snabes, M. *et al.* (1995) Hormonal status affects the reactivity of the cerebral vasculature. *Am J Obstet Gynecol* **172**, 1273–8

Beral, V., Bank, E., Reeves, G. and Wallis, M. (1997) Breast cancer and hormone replacement therapy: collaborative re-analysis of data from 51 epidemiological studies of 52 705 women with breast cancer and 108 411 women without breast cancer. *Lancet* **350**, 1047–59

Beresford, S., Weiss, N.S., Voigt, L. and McKnight, B. (1997) Risk of endometrial cancer in relation to use of oestrogen combined with cyclic progestogen therapy in postmenopausal women. *Lancet* **349**, 458–61

Brincat, M., Moniz, C.F., Studd, J.W., Darby, A.J., Magos, A. and Cooper, D. (1983) Sex hormones and skin collagen content in postmenopausal women. *BMJ* **287**, 1337–8

Christiansen, C. and Riis, B.J. (1990) 17 β-estradiol and continuous norethisterone: a unique treatment for established osteoporosis in elderly women. *Baillières Clin Endocrinol Metab* **71**, 836–41

Colditz, G.A., Hankinson, S.E., Hunter, D.J. *et al.* (1995) The use of estrogens and progestins and the risk of breast cancer in postmenopausal women. *N Engl J Med* **332**, 1589–93

Coyle, J.T., Price, D.L. and DeLong, M.R. (1983) Alzheimer's disease: a disorder of cortical cholinergic innervation. *Science* **219**, 1184–90

Daly, E., Vessey, M.P., Hawkins, N.M. *et al.* (1996) Case–control study of venous thrombo-embolism risk in users of hormone replacement therapy. *Lancet* **348**, 977–80

Delmas, P.D., Bjarnson, N.H., Mitlak, B.H. *et al.* (1997) Effects of raloxifene on bone mineral density, serum cholesterol concentrations and the uterine endometrium in postmenopausal women. *N Engl J Med* **337**, 1641–7

Domoney, C.L. and Studd, J.W.W. (1999) 'Long term continuation of hormone replacement therapy in hysterectomised women' in: *The Menopause Annual Review*, pp. 35–49. Carnforth: Parthenon

Ettinger, B., Friedman, G.D., Bush, T. and Quesenberry, C.P. (1996) Reduced mortality associated with long-term postmenopausal estrogen therapy. *Obstet Gynecol* **87**, 6–12

Fujimoto, J., Hori, M., Ichigo, S., Morishita, S. and Tamaya, T. (1996) Oestrogen activates migration potential of endometrial cancer cells through the basement membrane. *Tumour Biol* **17**, 48–57

Fujimoto, J., Hori, M., Ichigo, S., Nishigaki, M., Itoh, T. and Tamaya, T. (1994) Expression of aberrant oestrogen receptor mRNA in endometrial cancers in comparison with normal endometria. *Horm Res* **42**, 116–19

Gambrell, R.D., Massey, F.M., Castaneda, T.A., Ugenas, A.J., Ricci. C. and Wright, S. (1980) Use of the progestogen challenge test to reduce the risk of endometrial cancer. *Journal of Obstetrics and Gynaecology* **55**, 732–8

Gangar, K. and Whitehead, M.I. (1991) Hormone implants and tachyphylaxis. *Br J Obstet Gynaecol* **98**, 607–9

Garnett, T., Studd, J.W., Henderson, A., Watson, N., Savvas, M. and Leather, A. (1990) Hormone implants and tachyphylaxis. *Br J Obstet Gynaecol* **97**, 917–21

Garton, M., Reid, D. and Rennie, E. (1995) The climacteric, osteoporosis and hormone replacement; views of women aged 45–49. *Maturitas* **21**, 7–15

Greer, I.A. (1998) Practical strategies for hormone replacement therapy and risk of thrombo-embolism. *Br J Obstet Gynaecol* **105**, 376–9

Grodstein, F., Stampfer, M.J., Colditz, G.A. *et al.* (1997) Postmenopausal hormone therapy and mortality. *N Engl J Med* **336**, 1769–75

Grodstein, F., Martinez, M.E., Platz, E.A. *et al.* (1998) Postmenopausal hormone use and risk for colorectal cancer and adenoma. *Ann Intern Med* **128**, 705–12

Grodstein, F., Stampfer, M.J., Goldhaber, S.Z. *et al.* (1996) Prospective study of exogenous hormones and risk of pulmonary embolism in women. *Lancet* **348**, 983–7

Henderson, B.E., Paganini-Hill, A. and Ross, R.K. (1991) Decreased mortality in users of estrogen replacement therapy. *Arch Intern Med* **151**, 75–8

Holland, E.F., Leather, A.T. and Studd, J.W. (1995) Increase in bone mass of older postmenopausal women with low mineral bone density after one year of percutaneous oestradiol implants. *Br J Obstet Gynaecol* **102**, 238–42

Holland, E.F., Leather, A.T., Studd, J.W. and Garnett, T.J. (1993) The effect of a new sequential oestradiol valerate and levonorgestrel preparation on the bone mineral density of postmenopausal women. *Br J Obstet Gynaecol* **100**, 966–7

Honjo, H., Ogino, Y., Tanaka, K. *et al.* (1993) An effect of conjugated oestrogen to cognitive impairment in women with senile dementia – Alzheimer's type: a placebo controlled, double blind study. *Journal of the Japanese Menopause Society* **1**, 167–71

Hulley, S., Grady, D., Bush, T. *et al.* (1998) Randomised trial of estrogen plus progestin for secondary prevention of coronary heart disease in postmenopausal women. Heart and Estrogen/progestin Replacement Study (HERS) Research Group. *JAMA* **280**, 605–13

Hunt, K., Vessey, M., McPherson, K. and Coleman, M. (1987) Long-term surveillance of mortality and cancer incidence in women receiving hormone replacement therapy. *Br J Obstet Gynaecol* **94**, 620–35

Hunter, M. (1996) Depression and the menopause. *BMJ* **313**, 1217–18

Hunter, M.S., O'Dea, I. and Britten, N. (1997) Decision making and hormone replacement therapy: a qualitative analysis. *Soc Sci Med* **45**, 1541–8

Isaacs, A.J., Britton, A.R. and McPherson, K. (1995) Utilisation of hormone replacement therapy by women doctors. *BMJ* **311**, 1399–401

Jick, H., Derby, L.E., Myers, M.W., Vasilakis, C. and Newton, K.M. (1996) Risk of hospital admission for idiopathic venous thrombo-embolism among users of postmenopausal oestrogens. *Lancet* **348**, 981–3

Jorm, A.F., Korten, A.E. and Henderson, A.S. (1987) The prevalence of dementia: a quantitative integration of the literature. *Acta Psyciatr Scand* **76**, 465–79

Key, T.J. and Pike, M.C. (1988) The dose–effect relationship between 'unopposed oestrogens and endometrial mitotic rate': its central role in explaining and predicting endometrial cancer risk. *Br J Cancer* **57**, 205–12

Khastgir, G., Studd, J., Holland, N., Zadeh, J., Fox, S. and Chow, J. (1998) Histomorphometric evidence of an anabolic effect of oestrogen on bone in older postmenopausal women. *Br J Obstet Gynaecol* **105** Suppl 17, 6

Kohrt, W.M., Ehsani, A.A. and Birge, S.J. (1998) HRT preserves increase in bone mineral density and reductions in body fat after a supervised exercise program. *J Appl Physiol* **84**, 1506–12

Kukull, W.A., Schellenberg, G.D., Bowen, J.D. *et al.* (1996) Apolipoprotein E in Alzheimer's disease risk and case detection: a case–control study. *J Clin Epidemiol* **49**, 1143–8

Leather, A.T., Savvas, M. and Studd, J.W.W. (1991) Endometrial histology and bleeding patterns after 8 years of continuous combined estrogen and progestogen therapy in postmenopausal women. *Obstet Gynecol* **6**, 1008–10

Lindsay, R., Hart, D.M., Aitken, J.M. *et al.* (1976) Long term prevention of postmenopausal osteoporosis by oestrogen. *Lancet* **i**, 1038–41

Lindsay, R. and Tohme, J.F. (1990) Estrogen treatment of patients with established postmenopausal osteoporosis. *Obstet Gynecol* **76**, 290–5

Lowe, G.D., Greer, I.A., Cooke, T.G. *et al.* (1992) Thromboembolic Risk Factors (THRIFT) Consensus Group. Risk of and prophylaxis for venous thromboembolism in hospital patients. *BMJ* **305**, 567–74

Lufkin, E.G., Wahner, H.W., O'Fallon, W.M. *et al.* (1992) Treatment of postmenopausal osteoporosis with transdermal estrogen. *Ann Intern Med* **117**, 1–9

Molsa, P.K., Marttila, R.J. and Rinne, U.K. (1982) Epidemiology of dementia in a Finnish population. *Acta Neurol Scand* **65**, 541–52

Montgomery, J.C., Appleby, L., Brincat, M. *et al.* (1987) Effect of oestrogen and testosterone implants on psychological disorders in the climacteric. *Lancet* **i**, 297–9

Norman, S.G. and Studd, J.W.W. (1994) A survey of views on hormone replacement therapy. *Br J Obstet Gynaecol* **101**, 879–87

Ongphiphadhanakul, B., Chanprasertyothin, S., Piaseu, N. *et al.* (1998) Change in body weight after hormone replacement therapy is dependent on basal circulating leptin. *Maturitas* **30**, 283–8

Paganini-Hill, A. and Henderson V.W. (1996) Estrogen replacement therapy and risk of Alzheimer's disease. *Arch Intern Med* **156**, 2213–17

Paganini-Hill, A., Ross, R.K. and Henderson, B.E. (1988) Postmenopausal oestrogen treatment and stroke: a prospective study. *BMJ* **297**, 519–22

Paterson, M.E., Wade-Evans, T., Sturdee, D.W., Thom, M.H. and Studd J.W. (1980) Endometrial disease after treatment with oestrogens and progestogens in the climacteric. *BMJ* **280**, 822–4

Perrone, G., Liu, Y., Capri, O. *et al.* (1999) Evaluation of the body composition and fat distribution in long-term users of hormone replacement therapy. *Gynecol Obstet Invest* **48**, 52–5

Persson, I.R., Adami, H.O., Eklund, G., Johansson, E.D., Lindberg, B.S. and Lindgren, A. (1986) The risk of endometrial neoplasia and treatment with estrogens and estrogen–progestogen combinations. First results of a cohort study after one to four completed years of observation. *Acta Obstet Gynecol Scand* **65**, 211–17

Phillips, S.M. and Sherwin, B.B. (1992) Effects of oestrogen on memory function in surgically menopausal women. *Psychoneuroendocinology* **17**, 485–95

Ravnikar, V.A. (1987) Compliance with HRT. *Am J Obstet Gynecol* **156**, 1332–4

Ryan, P.J., Harrison, R., Blake, G. and Fogelman, I. (1992) Compliance with hormone replacement therapy after screening for postmenopausal osteoporosis. *Br J Obstet Gynaecol* **99**, 325–8

Rymer, J.M. (1998) The effects of tibolone. *Gynecol Endocrinol* **12**, 213–20

Sack, M.N., Rader, D.J. and Cannon, R.O.I. (1994) Oestrogen and inhibition of oxidation of low-density lipoproteins in postmenopausal women. *Lancet* **343**, 269–70

Schneider, D.L., Barrett-Connor, E.L. and Morton, D.J. (1997) Timing of postmenopausal estrogen for optimal bone mineral density. The Rancho Bernardo Study. *JAMA* **277**, 543–7

Schneider, L.S., Farlow, M.R., Henderson, V.W. *et al.* (1996) Effects of oestrogen therapy on response to tacrine in patients with Alzheimer's disease. *Neurology* **46**, 1580–4

Smith, D., Pentice, R., Thompson, D. and Herrman, W. (1975) Association of exogenous estrogen and endometrial carcinoma. *N Engl J Med* **293**, 1164–7

Spector, T.D. (1989) Use of oestrogen replacement therapy in high risk groups in the United Kingdom. *BMJ* **299**, 1434–5

Stampfer, M.J., Colditz ,G.A. and Willett, W.C. (1990) Menopause and heart disease. A review. *Ann N Y Acad Sci* **592**, 193–203, 257–62

Studd, J., Pornel, B., Marton, I. *et al.* (1999) Efficacy and acceptability of intranasal 17 β-oestradiol for menopausal symptoms: randomised dose-response study. Aerodiol Study Group. *Lancet* **353**, 1574–8

Studd, J.W., Holland, E.F., Leather, A.T. and Smith, R.N. (1994) The dose-response of percutaneous oestradiol implants on the skeletons of postmenopausal women. *Br J Obstet Gynaecol* **101**, 787–91

Sturridge, F. and Guillebaud, J. (1996) A risk–benefit assessment of the levonorgestrel-releasing intrauterine system. *Drug Safety* **15**, 430–40

Suhonen, S.P., Allonen, H.O. and Lahteenmaki, P. (1995) Sustained release estradiol implants and a levonorgestrel-releasing intrauterine device in hormone replacement therapy. *Am J Obstet Gynecol* **172**, 562–7

Toran-Allerand, C.D., Miranda, R.C., Bentham, W.D. *et al.* (1992) Estrogen receptors co-localise with low affinity nerve growth factor receptors in cholinergic neurones of the basal forebrain. *Proc Natl Acad Sci U S A* **89**, 4468–72

Torgerson, D.J., Donaldson, C., Russell, I.T. *et al.* (1995) Hormone replacement therapy: compliance and cost after screening for osteoporosis. *Eur J Obstet Gynecol Reprod Biol* **59**, 57–60

Van Goozen, S.H.M., Cohen-Kettenis, P.T., Gooren, L.J. *et al.* (1995) Gender differences in behaviour activating effects of cross-sex hormones. *Psychoneuroendocrinology* **20**, 343–63

Van Keep, P. and Kellerhans, J. (1974) The impact of socio-cultural factors on symptom formation. *Psychother Psychosom* **23**, 251–63

Vestergaard, P., Harmann, A.P., Gram, J. *et al.* (1997) Improving compliance with hormone replacement therapy in primary osteoporosis prevention. *Maturitas* **28**, 137–45

Walker, I.D. (1991) Management of thrombophilia in pregnancy. *Blood Rev* **5**, 227–33

Wallace, W.A., Price, V.H., Elliot, C.A. *et al.* (1990) Hormone replacement therapy acceptability to Nottingham postmenopausal women with a risk factor for osteoporosis. *J R Soc Med* **83**, 699–701

Wilkes, H.C. and Meade, T.W. (1991) Hormone replacement therapy in general practice; a survey of doctors in the MRC's general practice framework. *BMJ* **302**, 1317–20

Wolter-Svenson, L.P., Stadberg, E., Andersson, K. *et al.* (1995) Intrauterine administration of levonorgestrel in two doses in HRT. A randomised clinical trial during one year: effects on lipid and lipoprotein metabolism. *Maturitas* **22**, 199–205

Wong, M., Thompson, T.L. and Moss, R.L. (1996) Nongenomic actions of estrogens in the brain: physiological significance and cellular mechanisms. *Crit Rev Nerobiol* **10**, 189–203

ADDITIONAL READING

Studd, J. (Ed.) (1998) *The Management of the Menopause: Annual Review 1998*. London: Parthenon

Studd, J. (Ed.) (1999) *The Management of the Menopause: Annual Review 1999*. London: Parthenon

Studd, J. and Whitehead, M. (1988) *The Menopause*. Oxford: Blackwell Science

34

Osteoporosis and its prevention

David W. Purdie and S. Anthony Beardsworth

HISTORY

The current definition of osteoporosis: 'a progressive systemic skeletal disease character-ised by low bone mass and micro-architectural deterioration of bone tissue, with a consequent increase in bone fragility and susceptibility to fracture' was internationally agreed in 1991 (Consensus Development Conference 1991). However, it was the French pathologist, Jean Georges Chrétien Frédéric Martin Lobstein 'the Younger' (1777–1835) who first used the word 'osteoporose', in the early 1820s to describe a pathological state of bone (Lobstein 1829). The term, which occurred to him in the context of osteitis, is derived linguistically from the Greek οστεον (bone) and ππροξ (passage). Though the term is mentioned in most French and German 19th-century dictionaries it was not until after the turn of the century that it first appeared in English dictionaries with the Latin suffix *osis* (full of), thus osteoporosis depicts a 'bone full of passages'. Perhaps the most interesting aspect of the evolution of the term osteoporosis is presented by its successive definitions. Unlike other scientific notions whose meaning does not change with time, here is a term whose evolving definitions have reflected the progress of research on the subject.

Though the term osteoporosis did not exist prior to 1820, the condition itself has existed since ancient times. Palaeopathologic examinations of old skeletons confirm the presence of vertebral and distal forearm fractures (Berg 1972). The hieroglyphs of ancient Egypt reveal images of old men leaning on walking sticks with spinal deformities that could be due to osteoporosis (Leca 1983). An Attic vase found in an Etruscan tomb in Cerveti illustrates Heracles and an old lady who demonstrates spinal deformities that again could be consequent on osteoporosis. In his third book, *Thalia*, Herodotus (484–425 BC) noted that the skulls of Persian warriors, who wore tiaras (turbans), were much more fragile than those of the shaven headed Egyptians, perhaps the first reference to the role that sunlight plays in protection against osteoporosis.

In more recent history an excellent representation of spinal osteoporosis is to be found in Vittorio Carpaccio's painting 'The Arrival of the English Ambassadors at the Court of the King of Brittany' in the Venice Accademia (painted 1490–95). In this work, an old governess exhibits several features of osteoporosis including Dowager's hump and has a walking aid that is relatively long for her stature. Furthermore, study of her anthropomorphic measurements reveals height loss due to vertebral collapse (Dequeker 1994).

The catalyst for the explosion of research into osteoporosis over the last decades of the 20th century has been our ability to assess bone mass non-invasively and with high precision, resolution and reproducibility. The development of these techniques has its origin in conventional x-rays, discovered in 1895 by Wilhelm Conrad Roentgen (1845–1923). However, this is relatively insensitive since radiographic evidence of bone loss only becomes apparent when mass has decreased by 30–50% (Ardran 1951). It was the development of single energy absorptiometry in the 1960s (Cameron and Sorensen 1963), quantitative computed tomography in the 1970s (Ruegsegger *et al.* 1976) and dual energy absorptiometry in the 1980s (Mazess *et al.* 1989) that resulted in the World Health Organization (1994) defining osteoporosis in terms of bone mineral density (BMD). Thus, an individual with a BMD of more than 2.5 standard deviations below the mean of a normal young adult population is defined as having osteoporosis, even in the absence of a non-traumatic fracture.

OSTEOPOROSIS

The clinical impact of osteoporosis, the most common human metabolic bone disorder, derives exclusively to its associated fractures. Typically, fractures of the proximal femur, the vertebrae and the distal forearm are linked with osteoporosis. However, because bone is lost throughout the skeleton, almost all types of fracture in the elderly are due, in part, to osteoporosis. It has been estimated that in the postmenopausal UK population there are 52 000 hip fractures, 41 000 wrist fractures and 25 000 clinically apparent vertebral fractures every year (Dolan and Torgerson 1998). These fractures may be uncomplicated and followed by full recovery, but many will result in chronic pain, disability and deformity that necessitates increased dependence on others or even nursing-home care. The personal and social cost of osteoporosis is therefore incalculable but the financial cost has been estimated at nearly one billion pounds per annum in the UK alone (Dolan and Torgerson 1998).

As the definition of osteoporosis indicates these fractures are, in part, due to low bone mass. Indeed bone density accounts for 75–85% of the variance in the ultimate strength of bone tissue (Melton *et al.* 1988) and correlates closely with the load-bearing capacity of the skeleton *in vitro* (Mosekilde *et al.* 1989; Courtney *et al.* 1995). The ability to assess BMD non-invasively has led to the disease being defined in practice by an intermediate outcome and not a health outcome. This allows the diagnosis of osteoporosis to be made before a fracture has occurred and more importantly to quantify an individual's risk of developing osteoporosis in the future and thus be able to offer preventative intervention.

Pathogenesis

An individual's bone density in later life reflects the accumulated contribution of peak bone mass attained as a young adult and bone mass lost with ageing. Factors governing the acquisition of bone mineral as a function of normal growth have received far less attention than those related to adult bone loss. The factors most associated with achieving maximal peak bone mass are genetic heritage, physical exercise and mineral content of diet. Factors associated with bone loss also include genetic heritage, diet and exercise, but various medical conditions and corticosteroid use are also implicated. However, the main pathogenetic factor behind osteoporosis is the hormone-dependent increase in bone resorption and accelerated loss of bone that occurs in the first five to ten years after the menopause (Riggs *et al.* 1981; Slemenda *et al.* 1987). That oestrogen deficiency plays a major role in this bone loss is strongly supported by the higher prevalence of osteoporosis in women than men (Nilas and Christiansen 1987), the increase in the rate of bone mineral loss, as measured by bone densitometry, after an artificial or natural menopause (Riggs *et al.* 1981; Genant *et al.* 1982; Slemenda *et al.* 1987) and the existence of a relationship between plasma oestrogen levels and rates of bone loss (Ohta *et al.* 1993). During the reproductive years, oestrogen maintains bone mass by exerting a tonic suppression of cancellous bone remodelling and maintaining the balance between osteoblast and osteoclast activity (Parfitt 1979). Exactly how oestrogen achieves this control is still unclear, but when oestrogen is deficient there is an increase in activation frequency of new bone remodelling units and remodelling balance is lost. This imbalance is the result of increased osteoclastic activity excavating deeper resorption pits and there is some evidence that the ability of osteoblasts to refill them is impaired. Moreover, the deeper resorption pits can result in perforation of trabecular plates and loss of architectural elements. These changes are reversed by the administration of oestrogen (Parfitt 1979).

Conventional hormone replacement therapy (HRT)

In women with or at increased risk of osteoporosis, HRT should be considered early in their management. A large number of controlled clinical trials, well summarised by Grady *et al.* (1992), have shown that HRT maintains bone mass. Most of these trials have been of short duration, usually three years, but a number of studies has shown that HRT also maintains bone mass over longer periods (Garnett *et al.* 1991; Nielson *et al.* 1994; Wahab *et al.* 1997). In addition, several studies have shown that HRT is able to halt or possibly reverse bone loss even if started long after the menopause (Naessen *et al.* 1993; Holland *et al.* 1995). The addition of a progestogen, whether sequentially or continuously, does not appear to adversely affect the effect of oestrogen on bone. Indeed, it is possible that the 19-nortestosterone derivatives may even enhance the effect of oestrogen (Abdalla *et al.* 1985).

Only two small studies have looked prospectively at fracture reduction (Nachtigall *et al.* 1979; Lindsay *et al.* 1980). They both show a reduction in vertebral fractures but were of insufficient power to demonstrate a reduction in hip fracture. Many observational studies have found a lower incidence of hip fractures in oestrogen users compared with non-users. A pooled estimate of the evidence suggests that any use of HRT, usually less than five years, reduces the risk of hip fracture by 25% (Grady *et al.* 1992).

In addition to these skeletal benefits of HRT, the effects of oestrogen on the vaso- and psychomotor symptoms of the menopause and the beneficial effect of oestrogen on the cardiovascular, urogenital, cerebral and immune systems are well documented. Indeed, each year the potential benefits of oestrogen therapy grow. However, when HRT is discontinued some authors have demonstrated that bone loss appears to accelerate, implying that the benefits of HRT lessen with time after cessation of therapy (Lindsay *et al.* 1978; Christiansen *et al.* 1981). We have observed a similar phenomenon after three years of cessation of therapy at lumbar spine but not at femoral neck (Purdie and Steel 1998). Thus, to obtain maximum benefit HRT needs to be continued for many years or at least continued into the ages when fractures are most likely to occur.

However, despite the benefits of HRT, acceptance and then continuation of therapy is poor even in women identified to be as being at risk of osteoporosis by bone densitometry. In 1425 early postmenopausal women identified at risk and suitable for HRT, over 30% did not accept the offer of therapy and of those who did accept the offer, 30% had discontinued therapy at two years. Therefore only 55% of the 1425 will have achieved significant skeletal benefit from their HRT. Reassuringly, there was little discontinuation of therapy after two years in women followed up for five years (Purdie *et al.* 1996).

This poor acceptance and continuation of therapy is, in the main, due to concerns about breast cancer and the unacceptability of cyclical uterine bleeding caused by the monthly addition of a progestin necessary to afford endometrial protection (Purdie *et al.* 1996). Our understanding of the relationship between HRT and breast cancer is based entirely on historical and sometimes contradictory data. However, a recent re-analysis of data from 51 epidemiological studies of 52 705 women with breast cancer and 108 411 women without breast cancer by the Collaborative Group on Hormonal Factors in Breast Cancer (1997) has greatly clarified the evidence. They suggest that for each year of HRT use there is an increase in relative risk of breast cancer. This increase in relative risk is small at 1.023 (95% CI 1.011–1.036) and translates to an estimated cumulative excess of two breast cancers for every 1000 users of HRT for five years, while ten years' use is associated with an excess of six breast cancers. In addition, this overall excess appears to be due to localised disease with its much better prognosis. However, these data appear to be of little comfort to a large proportion of the women in whom HRT is recommended.

'No bleed' HRT

Combined continuous HRT regimens

The continuous combined preparations of HRT have done much to allay the concerns of cyclical uterine bleeding. However, the occurrence of bleeding in the first few months, which is most common when therapy is commenced close to the menopause, does result in discontinuation in some women. Similarly, many women stop treatment due to unscheduled bleeding, in many ways worse than cyclical bleeding, that continues to occur in a small proportion of women after the initial six-month start-up. Clearly, a compound that produced no endometrial stimulation while maintaining its beneficial effects would be preferred.

Fewer data exist for these preparations with regard to skeletal benefit. However, a series of short-term studies has shown a preservation of BMD similar to that seen with sequential HRT (Riis and Christiansen 1988; Grey *et al.* 1994). This is not surprising since they contain the same oestrogen as the sequential preparations. But it is this same oestrogen which causes the increase in the risk of breast cancer.

Tibolone

Even fewer data exist for the gonadomimetic, tibolone. Short-term studies have shown preservation of BMD on a par with HRT (Rymer *et al.* 1994; Prelevic *et al.* 1996; Lippuner *et al.* 1997) but fracture data, both epidemiological and prospective, do not exist. It does provide symptomatic relief from menopausal symptoms and provides what is thought to be a favourable lipid profile that may extrapolate into cardiovascular protection. Tibolone has a much better, although not perfect, bleeding profile than the continuous combined preparations and has the advantage of improving energy and libido. Few data exist with respect to the breast, although it is associated with less breast tenderness than conventional HRT and exciting *in vitro* studies have shown that tibolone significantly inhibits the enzymes involved in the biosynthesis of oestradiol in the MCF-7 and T-47D human breast-cancer cell lines and also inhibits the growth of 7,12-dimethylbenzanthracene (DMBA) induced mammary carcinoma in rats (Kloosterboer *et al.* 1994; Chetrite *et al.* 1997). No data exist for humans.

Selective oestrogen receptor modulators (SERMs)

It is clear that the ideal compound for the prevention or treatment of osteoporosis would be one that is well tolerated and that can be taken for many years and would have all the beneficial effects of oestrogen on bone, brain, heart and immune system without the detrimental effects on uterus and breast. The first suggestion that such a compound might exist was in the late 1970s and early 1980s when it was discovered that the 'anti-oestrogens' clomiphene and tamoxifen, rather than exacerbating, actually prevented bone loss in ovariectomised rats (Beale *et al.* 1984; Jordan *et al.* 1987). These findings were confirmed in humans, as was a degree of cardioprotection similar to that seen in oestrogen users. So the concept of tissue selective oestrogen receptor modulation was born. However, a factor limiting the use of tamoxifen for indications other than the adjuvant chemotherapy of breast cancer proved to be the question of uterine safety. As early as 1985, a link between endometrial carcinoma and tamoxifen was suspected and was borne out by the large National Surgical Adjuvant Breast and Bowel Project, in which the estimated annual risk of endometrial cancer was eight times that seen in non-users (Fischer *et al.* 1994).

This work has led to the first of the second-generation SERMs, raloxifene, recently obtaining a licence for protection against osteoporosis. Published data are scarce. Two short-term studies have shown preservation of bone density with modest gains at lumbar spine and proximal femur, although less than one would have expected with oestrogen (Delmas *et al.* 1997; Lufkin *et al.* 1998). Data from the large phase III trial, involving over 7500 osteoporotic women and of four-years' duration, remain unpublished but have been presented in abstract form. The bone preservation seen in the published studies was confirmed and, more importantly, a 40–60% reduction in new and recurrent vertebral fractures was seen (Ettinger *et al.* 1999). The phase III trial was not powered to demonstrate a reduction in hip fracture incidence.

Raloxifene does not cause endometrial stimulation as measured both by biopsy and ultrasound assessments of endometrial thickness (Draper *et al.* 1996; Delmas *et al.* 1997). This is supported clinically by the rarity of vaginal bleeding seen in raloxifene users in the phase III trial. In addition, raloxifene causes a favourable lipid profile similar to that seen with oestrogen (Walsh *et al.* 1998). Of great interest was the reduction in the incidence of breast cancer seen in raloxifene users. At the 33-month data analysis point this reduction was 70% (RR 0.30; 95% CI 0.16–0.52) due entirely to an 87% reduction in oestrogen-receptor positive tumours (Cummings *et al.* 1998).

Unfortunately, raloxifene has no effect on the common vasomotor symptom of the menopause, hot sweats and flushes, and no data exist as to its effect on the urogenital, immune and central nervous systems. In addition, raloxifene use is associated with an increased incidence of venous thrombotic events similar to that seen with conventional HRT (3–4/10 000). Thus, raloxifene is not yet the ideal SERM and will not replace HRT. However, it provides a useful extension to HRT and should continue the beneficial bone and cardiovascular effects of oestradiol while sparing the patient the effects of breast or uterine stimulation. It also provides an alternative to those unwilling or unable to take conventional HRT, usually due to the return of bleeding or the fear of breast cancer.

Other treatments

Calcium

Calcium is a mineral that plays an essential role in the development and maintenance of a healthy skeleton. On the basis of the most current information available (National Institutes of Health Consensus Development Conference on Optimal Calcium Intake 1994), optimal calcium intake is estimated to be 1000 mg per day for a postmenopausal woman on HRT and 1500 mg for a postmenopausal woman not on HRT. For women older than 65 years this increases to 1500 mg irrespective of HRT status. The preferred source of this calcium is through diet, but clearly supplementation will often be necessary.

Vitamin D

Vitamin D, or more precisely 1,25-dihydroxyvitamin D, promotes active absorption of calcium across the intestinal wall and may play a role in bone mineralisation. The main source of vitamin D is sunlight, though it can also be ingested from some animal and plant sources, most notably cod liver oil. Women who are or suspected to be vitamin D deficient should have vitamin D supplements, though the dose remains uncertain and ranges from 200 to 800 iu per day.

Bisphosphonates

The bisphosphonates are probably too expensive to be considered for prevention, but may be considered in the treatment of osteoporosis in those unwilling or unable to take HRT. There is emerging evidence that a combination of bisphosphonates and HRT is more effective at maintaining BMD than either compound alone, that is, they are synergistic (Ulla et al. 1997).

THE FUTURE

Today we still have difficulty identifying individuals prior to the occurrence of the first fracture. Widespread screening of the female population, at the time of the menopause, has been neither technically nor logistically feasible. In 1994, the UK had the lowest number of bone densitometers in Europe, less than two per million of the population, and we still have no universally accepted long-term intervention that will prevent fracture. The short-term future lies in better targeting of the existing bone densitometry service on those individuals at most risk of developing osteoporosis. This targeting will involve established indications for densitometry based on recognised risk factors. Modern technologies for assessing bone density such as peripheral site densitometry and heel ultrasound could be utilised as an additional screening tool in the primary care setting. Following identification of the individual at risk, the therapeutic options available to us today will need to be better utilised. This will require better education of both healthcare professionals and the general public as to the relative risks and benefits of conventional

HRT, with greater support for women experiencing problems or expressing concerns about treatment.

Better understanding of the factors governing the acquisition of bone mineral as a function of normal growth and better awareness of the problems caused by osteoporosis will allow the development of general healthcare strategies aimed at maximising peak bone mass in adolescence and young adulthood and minimising bone loss after the menopause.

In the longer term, if the early data on oestrogen receptor modulation are confirmed and compounds closer to the ideal therapeutic profile can be developed, then the concept of population screening, whether at the age of 50 years or possibly later, will need to be re-evaluated. Finally, early data on parathyroid hormone administration suggest that it is anabolic on bone with increases in BMD of 13.0% at lumbar spine after three years with a trend towards a reduction in vertebral fracture (Lindsay et al. 1997). If these data are confirmed then we may soon have the first true treatment of established osteoporosis.

It is clear that the gynaecologist has a central role to play in vigilance for women at risk of osteoporosis. Such events as prolonged amenorrhoea, premature and early surgical menopause, or anorexia nervosa should trigger a request for densitometry so that appropriate treatment can be instituted. Similarly, conservation of the normal ovary at hysterectomy and counselling of women to be alert to symptoms of oestrogen deficiency postoperatively will aid the early prevention of bone loss which, if unrestrained, may blight the older age of the very women whose well-being it is our central duty to protect.

References

Abdalla, H.I., Hart, D.M., Lindsay, R. et al. (1985) Prevention of bone mineral loss in postmenopausal women by norethisterone. Obstet Gynecol **66**, 789–92

Ardran, G.M. (1951) Bone destruction not demonstrable by radiography. Br J Radiol **24**, 107–9

Beale, P.T., Misra, L.K., Young, R.L., Spjut, H.J., Evans, H.J. and LeBlanc, A. (1984) Clomiphene protects against osteoporosis in the mature ovariectomized rat. Calcif Tissue Int **36**, 123–5

Berg, E. (1972) Paleopathology: bone lesions in ancient times. Clin Orthop **82**, 263–7

Cameron, J.R. and Sorensen, J. (1963) Measurement of bone mineral in vivo: an improved method. Science **142**, 230–2

Chetrite, G., Kloosterboer, H.J. and Pasqualini, J.R. (1997) Effect of tibolone (Org OD 14) and its metabolites on estrone sulphatase activity in MCF-7 and T-47D mammary cancer cells. Anticancer Res **17**, 135–40

Christiansen, C., Christiansen, M.S. and Transbøl, I.B. (1981) Bone mass in postmenopausal women after withdrawal of oestrogen/gestagen replacement therapy. Lancet **i**, 459–61

Collaborative Group on Hormonal Factors in Breast Cancer (1997) Breast cancer and hormone replacement therapy: collaborative reanalysis of data from 51 epidemiological studies of 52 705 women with breast cancer and 108 411 women without breast cancer. *Lancet* **350**, 1047–59

Consensus Development Conference (1991) Consensus development conference: diagnosis, prophylaxis and treatment of osteoporosis. *Am J Med* **94**, 646–50

Courtney, A.C., Wachtel, E.F., Myers, E.R. and Hayes, W.C. (1995) Age related reductions in the strength of the femur tested in a fall-loading configuration. *J Bone Joint Surg Am* **77**, 387–95

Cummings, S.R., Norton, L., Eckert, S. *et al.* (1998) Raloxifene reduces the risk of breast cancer and may decrease the risk of endometrial cancer in postmenopausal women: two-year findings from the multiple outcomes of raloxifene evaluation trial. *Proceedings of the American Society of Clinical Oncology 34th Annual Meeting, May 1998* **2a**, abstract 3. Philadelphia: W.B. Saunders

Delmas, P.D., Bjarnason, N.H., Mitlak, B.H. *et al.* (1997) Effects of raloxifene on bone mineral density, serum cholesterol concentrations and uterine endometrium in postmenopausal women. *N Engl J Med* **337**, 1641–7

Dequeker, J. (1994) Vertebral osteoporosis as painted by Vittore Carpaccio (1465): reflections on paleopathology of osteoporosis in pictorial art. *Calcif Tissue Int* **55**, 321–3

Dolan, P. and Torgerson, D.J. (1998) The cost of treating osteoporotic fractures in the United Kingdom female population. *Osteoporos Int* **8**, 611–17

Draper, M.W., Flowers, D.E., Huster, W.J., Neild, J.A., Harper, K.D. and Arnaud C.A. (1996) Controlled trial of raloxifene (LY139481) HCl: impact on bone turnover and serum lipid profile in healthy postmenopausal women. *J Bone Miner Res* **11**, 835–42

Ettinger, B., Black, D., Cummings, S.R. *et al.* (1999) Raloxifene reduces the risk of incident vertebral fractures: 24-month interim analyses. *JAMA* **282**, 637–45

Fischer, B., Constantino, J.P. and Redmond, C.K. (1994) Endometrial cancer in tamoxifen treated breast cancer patients: findings NSABP B-14. *J Natl Cancer Inst* **86**, 527–37

Garnett, T., Studd, J., Watson, N. and Savvas, M. (1991) A cross-sectional study of the effects of long term percutaneous hormone replacement therapy on bone mineral density. *Obstet Gynecol* **78**, 1002–7

Genant, H.K., Cann, C.E., Ettinger, B. and Gordan, G.S. (1982) Quantitative computed tomography of vertebral spongiosa: a sensitive method of detecting early bone loss after oophorectomy. *Ann Intern Med* **97**, 699–705

Grady, D., Rubin, S.M., Petitti, D.B. *et al.* (1992) Hormone therapy to prevent disease and prolong life in postmenopausal women. *Ann Intern Med* **117**, 1016–37

Grey, A.B., Cundy, T.F. and Reid, L.R. (1994) Continuous combined oestrogen/progestin therapy is well tolerated and increases bone density at the hip and spine in postmenopausal osteoporosis. *Clin Endocrinol* **40**, 671–7

Holland, E.F.N., Leather, A.T. and Studd, J.W.W. (1995) Increase in bone mass of older postmenopausal women with low mineral bone density after one year of percutaneous oestradiol implants. *Br J Obstet Gynaecol* **102**, 238–4

Jordan, V.C., Phelps, E. and Lindgren, J.U. (1987) Effects of anti-estrogens on bone in castrated and intact female rats. *Breast Cancer Res Treat* **10**, 31–5

Kloosterboer, H.J., Schoonenm, W.G.E.J., Deckers, G.H. and Klijn, J.G.M. (1994) Effects of progestogens and Org OD 14 in *in-vitro* and *in-vivo* tumour models. *J Steroid Biochem Mol Biol* **49**, 311–18

Leca, A-P. (1983) *La Médecine Égyptienne au Temps des Pharaons*, p. 407. Paris: Edition Dacosta

Lindsay, R., Hart, D.M., Maclean, A. *et al.* (1978) Bone response to termination of estrogen treatment. *Lancet* **i**, 1325–7

Lindsay, R., Hart, D.M., Forrest, C. and Baird, C. (1980) Prevention of spinal osteoporosis in oophorectomised women. *Lancet* **ii**, 1151–4

Lindsay, R., Nieves, J., Formica, C. *et al.* (1997) Randomised controlled study of effect of parathyroid hormone on vertebral bone mass and fracture incidence among post-menopausal women on oestrogen with osteoporosis. *Lancet* **350**, 550–5

Lippuner, K., Haenggi, W., Birkhaeuser, M.H. and Jaeger, P. (1997) Prevention of postmenopausal bone loss using tibolone or conventional peroral or transdermal hormone replacement therapy with 17β-oestradiol and dydrogesterone. *J Bone Miner Res* **12**, 806–12

Lobstein, J.G.C.F.M., the Younger (1829) *Traité d'Anatomie Pathologique*. Paris and Strasbourg

Lufkin, E.G., Whitaker, M.D., Nickelsen, T. *et al.* (1998) Treatment of established postmenopausal osteoporosis with raloxifene: a randomized trial. *J Bone Miner Res* **13**, 1747–54

Mazess, R., Collick, B., Trempe, J., Barden, H. and Hanson, J. (1989) Performance evaluation of a dual energy x-ray bone densitometer. *Calcif Tissue Int* **44**, 228–32

Melton, L.J., Chao, E.Y.S. and Lane, J. (1988) 'Biomechanical aspects of fractures' in: B.L. Riggs and L.J. Melton (Eds) *Osteoporosis: Etiology, Diagnosis and Management*, p. 111. New York: Raven Press

Mosekilde, L., Bentzen, S.M., Ortoft, G. and Jorgensen, J. (1989) The predictive value of quantitative computed tomography for vertebral body compressive strength and ash density. *Bone* **10**, 465–70

Nachtigall, L.E., Nachtigall, R.H., Nachtigall, R.D. and Beckmann, E.M. (1979) Estrogen replacement therapy: a 10-year prospective study in the relationship to osteoporosis. *Obstet Gynecol* **53**, 277–81

Naessen, T., Persson, I., Thor, L., Mallmin, H., Ljunghall, S. and Begstrom, R. (1993) Maintained bone density at advanced ages after long term treatment with low dose oestradiol implants. *Br J Obstet Gynaecol* **100**, 454–9

National Institutes of Health Development Consensus Development Conference on Optimal Calcium Intake (1994) Optimal calcium intake. NIH Consensus. *JAMA* **272**, 1942–8

Nielson, S.P., Barenholdt, O., Hermansen, F. and Munk-Jensen, N. (1994) Magnitude and pattern of skeletal response to long term continuous and cyclic sequential oestrogen/progestin treatment. *Br J Obstet Gynaecol* **101**, 319–24

Nilas, L. and Christiansen, C. (1987) Bone mass and its relationship to age and the menopause. *J Clin Endocrinol Metab* **65**, 697–702

Ohta, H., Ikeda, T., Masuzawa, T., Makita, K., Suda, Y. and Nozawa, S. (1993) Differences in axial bone mineral density, serum levels of sex steroids and bone metabolism between postmenopausal age- and body size-matched premenopausal subjects. *Bone* **14**, 111–16

Parfitt, A.M. (1979) Quantum concept of bone remodelling and turnover: implications for the pathogenesis of osteoporosis. *Calcif Tissue Int* **28**, 1–5

Prelevic, G.M., Bartram, C., Wood, J., Okola, S. and Ginsburg, J. (1996) Comparative effects on bone mineral density of tibolone, transdermal oestrogen and oral oestrogen/progestogen therapy in postmenopausal women. *Gynecol Endocrinol* **10**, 413–20

Purdie, D.W. and Steel, S.A. (1998) A five-year prospective study of BMD behaviour in HRT treated and untreated perimenopausal women. Paper presented at the Annual Meeting of the American Society of Bone and Mineral Research, San Francisco, USA, Abstract SA498

Purdie, D.W., Steel, S.A., Howey, S. and Doherty, S.M. (1996) The technical and logistical feasibility of population densitometry using DEXA and directed HRT intervention: a two-year prospective study. *Osteoporosis Int* **6**, S31–6

Riggs, B.L., Wahner, H.W., Dunn, W.L. *et al.* (1981) Differential changes in bone mineral density of the appendicular and axial skeleton with ageing. *J Clin Invest* **67**, 328–35

Riis, B.J. and Christiansen, C. (1988) Continuous oestrogen-progestogen treatment and bone metabolism in postmenopausal woman. *Maturitas* **10**, 51–8

Ruegsegger, P., Elsasser, V., Anliker, M., Grehm, H., Kind, H. and Prader, A. (1976) Quantification of bone mineralisation using computed tomography. *Radiology* **121**, 93–7

Rymer, J., Chapman, M.G. and Fogelman, I. (1994) Effect of tibolone on postmenopausal bone loss. *Osteoporosis Int* **4**, 314–19

Slemenda, C., Hui, S.L., Longcope, C. and Johnston, C.C. (1987) Sex steroids and bone mass: a study of changes about the time of the menopause. *J Clin Invest* **80**, 261–9

Ulla, M.R., Aruajo, G.L., Giglione, F. *et al.* (1997) Effects on bone mass of oral alendronate, hormone replacement therapy and combined regimes in postmenopausal women: preliminary report on a comparative study. *Medecina (B Aires)* **57**, 49–55

Wahab, M., Ballard, P., Purdie, D.W., Cooper, A. and Willson, J.C. (1997) The effect of long term oestradiol implantation on bone mineral density in postmenopausal women who have undergone hysterectomy and bilateral oophorectomy. *Br J Obstet Gynaecol* **104**, 728–31

Walsh, B.W., Kuller, L.H., Wild, R.A. *et al.* (1998) Effects of raloxifene on serum lipids and coagulation factors in healthy postmenopausal women. *JAMA* **279**, 1445–51

World Health Organization (1994) *Assessment of Fracture Risk and its Application to Screening for Postmenopausal Osteoporosis.* Geneva: WHO (Technical Report Series no. 843)

35

Neural networks

Allan M.Z. Chang and Daljit S. Sahota

THE DEVELOPMENTAL HISTORY OF NEURAL NETWORKS

Advances in statistics and mathematics since the Second World War have allowed the study and modelling of human thought in numerical terms and the development of computer technology has allowed these models to be put to practical use. Many of these models have been used successfully in medicine and can roughly be classified into two major approaches. The first approach concerns how the best decision can be logically made under a set of circumstances using many of the established statistical and probability theories. The second concerns the modelling of how human beings process information, acquire concepts and make decisions. Neural networks belong to this second approach.

Neural networks were conceptualised to explain how the brain processes complex information at speed. The basis of this efficiency was thought to be the parallel and simultaneous processing of information by a large number of small units, each of which performed a relatively simple task. The neurone was a basic small unit and the task was to transform input signals from the dendrites into an output signal through the axon. The complexity was achieved by the neurones interlinking with each other. Between these processes, memories and concepts developed. It was thought that if these processes could be simulated, then artificial intelligence could be produced.

Hebb (1949) proposed a mathematical model for the neurone. Numerical inputs to the neurone were weighted and combined through a transfer function, and the neurone produced an output if the result of this function exceeded a defined threshold. Lashley (1950) went on to describe distributed representation, arranging a number of neurones in such a manner that each neurone represented the memory of some pattern. Rosenblatt (1959) described the 'Perceptron' which was able to accept a complex set of data and identify them as one of a number of known patterns. Rosenblatt also established mathematical rules to train the Perceptron using the differences (delta) between the output of the Perceptron and the idealised pattern to change the weighting of the input data. This allowed the Perceptron to adapt to known patterns and thus to simulate memory.

Although early neural networks showed considerable promise, they were found to be capable of handling only patterns where the outputs were linearly separable. For example, they were unable to represent the Exclusive OR (XOR) pattern, where two inputs were used to produce an output with the characteristics shown in Figure 1.

Minsky and Papert (1969) proved mathematically that the Perceptron could not solve this problem and for a time it was thought that there was an insurmountable limitation

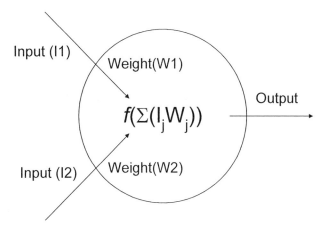

Figure 1 *Schematic representation of a back propagation network indicating the input, output and hidden layers with a typical truth table used during training; the internal architecture of the hidden layer will be dependent on the nature of the neural network being designed and constructed; such an architecture is able to resolve the XOR pattern described in the accompanying truth table used during training. The XOR logic gate operates on two logical inputs (true or false) to produce a single output (false '0' or true '1'). When both inputs are the same then the output is false and when they are different the output is true*

to the further development of neural networks. This pessimism led many to focus on the development of serial and algorithmic approaches often described as the 'von Neumann' computer metaphor, where the output of the system is produced by sequential logical decisions based on probability and statistical theories.

Renaissance in neural network research occurred when Rumelhart *et al.* (1986) demonstrated solutions to overcome the problems where outputs were not linearly separable, using a multiple layered neural network and modifying the manner in which such a network could be trained. Since then, interest and development in neural networks have expanded into many fields of endeavour, including medicine.

WHAT ARE NEURAL NETWORKS?

Neural networks represent more a particular approach to information processing rather than a number of discrete techniques. Their structure consists of a set of processing units formed into layers:

(1) A state of activation;
(2) An output function for each unit;
(3) A pattern of connectivity between the units;
(4) A rule to govern how the activities are propagated amongst the units;
(5) An activation rule to govern how input signals are converted into output signals;
(6) A rule to control network learning;
(7) An environment within which the system works.

As any change to any part of the structure will affect the capabilities and behaviour of the network as a whole, an infinite variety of neural networks can be constructed. The emphasis is therefore to construct networks that are appropriate for the tasks to be performed.

The parallel processing of neural networks confers particular advantages over that of serial processing of logic algorithms. Erroneous information at any point does not have a devastating effect on the results and the system is said to degrade graciously. The system is able to assign default values to missing data. It tends to match input information to memory and so will assign the nearest known answer when presented with ambiguous information. It learns by adapting to patterns in the reference data set, rather than following theoretical assumptions on the nature of the information and so is capable of coping with non-parametric data. This adaptive nature can also handle irregular and non-linear relationships in the data set.

The basic processing unit in a neural network is the neurone (Figure 2), where a number of inputs are weighted, which produces an output through a transfer function. There are two types of neural network in common clinical use. The first consists of variants of the multilayer Perceptron as described by Rumelhart *et al.* (1986), the most common one being the back propagation network (Figure 1). This type of network can be trained to memorise patterns and is used for making diagnoses or predictions. The second type are self-organising maps similar to those described by Kohonen (1984) (Figure 3). These are useful in performing taxonomy and are commonly used to reduce large volumes of data into clusters that are similar (Gabor 1998). A detailed discussion on all neural networks is beyond the scope of this chapter, but the more commonly used ones are listed in Table 1 with a glossary of common terminology listed in Table 2.

THE USE OF NEURAL NETWORKS IN MEDICINE

Neural networks have been used to model many systems, from designing consumer products to predicting the stock market. Their abilities to recognise patterns allow the

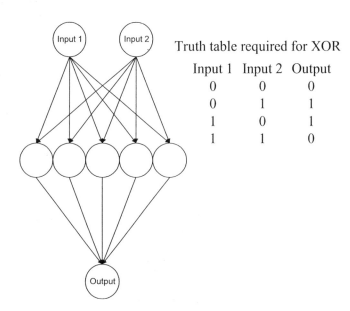

Figure 2   *Schematic mathematical representation of a neurone, the basic processing element in a neural network; inputs (I1, I2) are weighted according to the values of the weights (W1, W2) and then combined mathematically to produce an output*

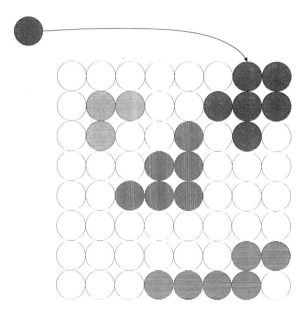

Figure 3   *Schematic representation of a self-organising map neural network such as the Kohonen Map; the different shadings represent clusters or families of neurones which are similar; the number of neurones within a family represent the variation within that family; in a self-organising map an input pattern is matched to all neurones in the map, the neurone with the closest matching memorised pattern to the input being the winner*

Table 1   *More commonly used forms of neural networks with a brief description of their main properties*

Type	Property	Reference
Back propagation networks (BPN) and variants:	Similar to non-parametric multiple regression modelling; commonly used to represent learned patterns of complex associations	
Elman network		Rao and Rao 1995
Jordan network		Rao and Rao 1995
Functional link network		Rao and Rao 1995
Probabilistic network		Skapura 1996; Jirousek and Kushmerick 1997
Self-organising map (SOM)	A form of cluster analysis; commonly used to perform taxonomy	
Kohonen map		Ritter *et al.* 1992
Counter propagation networks (CPN)	Combines the functionality of SOM and BPN	Hecht-Nielsen 1988
Adaptive resonance theory networks (ART)	Similar to BPN; capable of adapting its memory to atypical patterns during use	Grossberg 1975
Recurrent networks and variants:	Incorporates feedback mechanisms between individual processing neurones and layers; used mainly in neuro-modelling and control systems	
Bidirectional associative memory network		Kosko 1988
Multidirectional associative memory network		Hagiwara 1990
Fuzzy associative memory network		Rao and Rao 1995

Table 2 *Glossary of common terminology*

Term	Definition
Algorithm	Set of fixed logical or arithmetic mathematical statements executed in a defined sequence
Fuzzy	Mathematical transformation of a continuous variable into one of a concept, for example pH into acidotic, alkalotic, neither
Neurone	Basic mathematical processing unit in a network
Weights	Mathematical weighting applied to each input variable before being processed at the neurone
Layers	Group of neurones representing the different processing levels within the network; usually described as the input, hidden and output layers
Neural network	Combination of interconnected layers

dynamic modelling and prediction of events. They have been shown to outperform existing statistical methods in some cases (Vineis and Rainoldi 1997; Geddes *et al.* 1998; Winterer *et al.* 1998).

Neural networks are particularly adaptive to medical decision making (Forsstrom and Dalton 1995; Lim *et al.* 1997), as strong similarities exist in the way information is processed. Neural networks can easily handle multivariate data input, simulating clinical situations where large volumes of information are weighted and then considered. Partially erroneous or missing data that commonly exist in clinical situations will cause only a proportionate degradation of the output and this compares favourably with the probabilistic or algorithmic models where errors in input often have a catastrophic effect on output. Computationally, neural networks handle data according to degrees of truth, rather than an absolute true or false. They also make no assumptions as to whether the data used conform to any known probability distribution, or whether measurements in a data set have linear or regular inter-relationships with one another. This 'fuzzy' and adaptive approach is more in keeping with clinical practice, where information is often ambiguous and does not fit into any neat mathematical or probability model.

PUBLICATIONS ON THE USE OF NEURAL NETWORKS IN MEDICINE

These publications began to appear in the late 1980s following publication of Rumelhart's solution. Up to 1998 there were in excess of 2354 publications indexed (Ovid) and this number has continued to increase at a steady rate. Neural networks have been used extensively by neurophysiologists to model brain function and these form a separate discipline of their own. Clinically, neural networks have been used mainly for taxonomy or classification (Bishop *et al.* 1997; Aleynikov and Micheli-Tzanakou 1998; Wang *et al.* 1998) or as a diagnostic (Bellotti *et al.* 1997; Kazi *et al.* 1998) or predictive tool (Dorsey *et al.* 1997; Bagli *et al.* 1998; Nikiforidis and Sakellaropoulos 1998; Pofahl *et al.* 1998). The use of neural networks has been successful in cytology and histopathology but the validity of published results in other areas has often been limited by the small size of the studies and an absence of comparisons with conventional statistical methods (Vineis and Rainoldi 1997).

While other medical disciplines have experimented extensively with neural networks, there are, as yet, few publications relating to their use in obstetrics and gynaecology. It is currently not clear whether this reflects a lack of interest in this technology, or if the methods are unsuitable for the problems of the specialty.

NEURAL NETWORKS IN GYNAECOLOGY

The most published neural network is the PAPNET (Neuromedical Systems Inc., Suffern, NY, USA), an automated cervical cytology screening system (Boon and Kok 1993; Mango 1994, 1996; Spitzer 1998; Walker 1999). This uses a hybrid of algorithms and neural networks to differentiate normal from atypical cells and is able to compensate for inconsistencies in slide preparation, cellular image segmentation and human interpretation. Digital images of stained cells are initially processed to identify possible abnormal regions according to colour and morphological features such as border regularity using mathematical and logical algorithms. These extracted features are then presented to the neural network which makes a diagnosis of normal or suspicious cells by comparing these features against memorised patterns. The PAPNET system has been reported as being used in many different ways. These include auditing of quality control (Cenci *et al.* 1997; Halford *et al.* 1997; Mitchell and Medley 1998), acting as a rescreening tool of negative smears (Doornewaard *et al.* 1997; Mango and Valente 1998; Sturgis *et al.* 1998) and as the primary screening instrument (Ouwerkerk-Noordam *et al.* 1994; Michelow *et al.* 1997).

Neural networks have also been used as an 'artificial nose' in the detection and diagnosis of bacterial vaginosis (Chandiok *et al.* 1997). High vaginal swabs were processed and the amines extracted and presented to an array of conductive polymer sensors. The patterns of the amines, therefore, represented the 'electronic smell' and these were mapped to the nearest memorised odour patterns. This was a promising approach to a difficult problem, but unfortunately the study was a small one and it has not been replicated.

An indirect use of neural networks in gynaecology was to use the self-organising map to distinguish the borders of atheromatous plaques in arteries of rabbits that had been exposed to a high cholesterol diet and oestrogen therapy (Haines *et al.* 1999). This allowed for a more consistent decision on the borders and thereby the area of the damaged arteries.

NEURAL NETWORKS IN OBSTETRICS

Neural networks have been used to interpret fetal heart-rate patterns (Keith *et al.* 1994; Devoe *et al.* 1995, 1996; Kol *et al.* 1995; Ulbricht *et al.* 1998), the prediction of birth weights (Farmer *et al.* 1992; Lapeer *et al.* 1995; Gurgen *et al.* 1997) and the interpretation of fetal blood gas measurements (Mongelli *et al.* 1997). All the studies appear exploratory and there is as yet no widespread use of this technology.

Early attempts to train neural networks using arrays of antenatal and intrapartum cardiotocographic (CTG) data have been unsuccessful (Keith *et al.* 1994). The network has difficulty in distinguishing significant from trivial patterns because of the great variations between patterns presented and the absence of any statistical averaging of the data. Networks precisely trained to make a correct diagnosis on the reference data set therefore had difficulty reproducing the results on an independent data set. More recently, attempts have been made to use mathematical and logical algorithms to first extract features from arrays of CTG data and then present these features to the neural network for diagnosis. The performance of these approaches was claimed to be better, but the usefulness of the networks that were developed remains unproven.

Neural networks have also been developed to predict birth weights, using a number of antenatal features and ultrasound measurements as predictors. The performance of these networks on independent samples has not been found to be better than existing statistical methods if the same set of predictors was used.

A more successful use of neural network is in the interpretation of blood gas results (Mongelli *et al.* 1997). By training the network to memorise how experienced clinicians perform the interpretation, it can be shown that not only can the network reproduce these decisions but that it can also make the nearest 'correct' decision when presented with marginal or ambiguous patterns.

PROBLEMS AND PITFALLS IN THE CLINICAL USE OF NEURAL NETWORKS

Neural networks are essentially a complex set of simultaneous equations, the coefficients of which can be altered during training so that they can produce predictable results from sets of input. Because the processes are arithmetic rather than Boolean (algebraic), neural networks have been labelled as 'black box' technology. A major misconception of a neural network is that, because it is a 'black box', there is no need to understand how it works and that if sufficient data are fed into it, it will in some unknown way produce a good answer.

The earlier work on CTG interpretation reflects this misconception, when large quantities of raw data were used to train neural networks, but only to produce inconsistent answers. The PAPNET was more successful because raw data were firstly subjected to algorithmic interpretation and the neural network was used to make decisions using these features.

Neural networks are highly adaptable and it is possible to train a neural network so that it can accurately identify all data in the reference data set used for training. A neural network will, therefore, also learn trivial and random patterns in the reference set and excessive training will produce a network that is unreliable when presented with data that contain different trivial patterns (Figure 4). A misconception of this adaptability may lead to an unrealistic expectation that neural networks can produce a highly accurate prediction. The study on birth weight exemplified this misconception. The failure of the neural network to perform better can only be expected, since birth-weight measurements have a known distribution pattern and the relationships between birth weight and its predictors tends to be regular and linear. Standard statistical methods, with the advantages of averaging, would therefore be better models. Neural networks have the additional disadvantage that they attempt to separate true from false rather than locating a point on an interval scale and this logistic approach increases the error of estimations, particularly values that are far from the mean.

Neural networks faithfully reflect the manner of their training and are able to match input data sets to the nearest pattern. They are, therefore, particularly useful as objective inference engines, to make consistent decisions unaffected by the vagaries of memory and emotion and to make decisions in the face of marginal or ambiguous data. These abilities are best reflected by studies of PAPNET, those on blood gas interpretation and in the many reports where neural networks have successfully been used to interpret visual input in histology and radiology. This faithfulness and ability to cope with ambiguity has

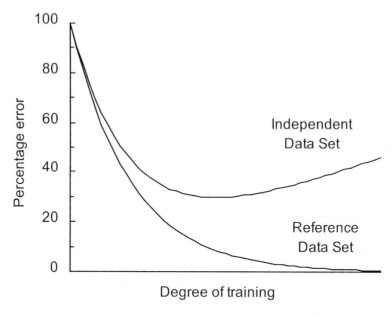

Figure 4 *Graphical demonstration of the effect of overtraining on the ability to predict in an independent data set; increasing training continues to reduce the difference between the expected and actual output for the reference data set, but beyond an optimal point this difference tends to increase in an independent data set as the network adapts and memorises trivial patterns present in the reference data set*

sometimes been mistaken as a greater precision in statistical modelling, as has been shown in the CTG and birth-weight studies. The objective success of any modelling system is based more on the validity of the data used and the soundness of the theoretical model proposed. In many cases, models relying on statistical assumptions and averaging can better be generalised while the faithful adaptability of a trained neural network may work against this.

FUTURE OF NEURAL NETWORKS IN OBSTETRICS AND GYNAECOLOGY

There is currently rapid progress and change in neural network technology and many of these changes will be found to be useful in medicine. Some of their current limitations in medicine may be overcome when better models are developed and it may be possible that neural networks in future will be able to produce analytical tools that are objectively better than those based on statistical methods.

Currently, however, neural networks seem most useful in providing decision support in clinical situations. The feed-forwards networks are best used as memory surrogates, where a trained network represents a known area of expertise and can be used to assist clinical decision making under difficult or ambiguous situations. The self-organising maps, on the other hand, are useful analytical tools and can be used to make classifications and define borders when these cannot be easily separable or defined. The main advantages of neural networks appear to be their invariable response to any given set of input data and their ability to make the 'best possible' decision in the face of ambiguity.

References

Aleynikov, S. and Micheli-Tzanakou, E. (1998) Classification of retinal damage by a neural network based system. *J Med Syst* **22**, 129–36

Bagli, D.J., Agarwal, S.K., Venkateswaran, S. *et al.* (1998) Artificial neural networks in pediatric urology: prediction of sonographic outcome following pyeloplasty. *J Urol* **160**, 980–3

Bellotti, M., Elsner, B., Paez, D.L., Esteva, H. and Marchevsky, A.M. (1997) Neural networks as a prognostic tool for patients with non-small cell carcinoma of the lung. *Mod Pathol* **10**, 1221–7

Bishop, J.B., Szpalski, M., Ananthraman, S.K., McIntyre, D.R. and Pope, M.H. (1997) Classification of low back pain from dynamic motion characteristics using an artificial neural network. *Spine* **22**, 2991–8

Boon, M.E. and Kok, L.P. (1993) Neural network processing can provide means to catch errors that slip through human screening of pap smears. *Diagn Cytopathol* **9**, 411–16

Cenci, M., Nagar, C., Giovagnoli, M.R. and Vecchione, A. (1997) The PAPNET system for quality control of cervical smears: validation and limits. *Anticancer Res* **17**, 4731–4

Chandiok, S., Crawley, B.A., Oppenheim, B.A., Chadwick, P.R., Higgins, S. and Persaud, K.C. (1997) Screening for bacterial vaginosis: a novel application of artificial nose technology. *J Clin Pathol* **50**, 790–1

Devoe, L.D. (1996) Computerized fetal heart rate analysis and neural networks in antepartum fetal surveillance. *Curr Opin Obstet Gynecol* **8**, 119–22

Devoe, L.D., Carlton, E. and Prescott, P. (1995) Neural network prediction of nonstress test results: how often should we perform nonstress tests? *Am J Obstet Gynecol* **173**, 1128–31

Devoe, L.D., Samuel, S., Prescott, P. and Work, B.A. (1996) Predicting the duration of the first stage of spontaneous labor using a neural network. *J Matern Fetal Med* **5**, 256–61

Doornewaard, H., Woudt, J.M., Strubbe, P., van de Seijp, H. and van den Tweel, J.G. (1997) Evaluation of PAPNET-assisted cervical rescreening. *Cytopathology* **8**, 313–21

Dorsey, S.G., Waltz, C.F., Brosch, L., Connerney, I., Schweitzer, E.J. and Bartlett, S.T. (1997) A neural network model for predicting pancreas transplant graft outcome. *Diabetes Care* **20**, 1128–33

Farmer, R.M., Medearis, A.L., Hirata, G.I. and Platt, L.D. (1992) The use of a neural network for the ultrasonographic estimation of fetal weight in the macrosomic fetus. *Am J Obstet Gynecol* **166**, 1467–72

Forsstrom, J.J. and Dalton, K.J. (1995) Artificial neural networks for decision support in clinical medicine. *Ann Med* **27**, 509–17

Gabor, A.J. (1998) Seizure detection using a self-organizing neural network: validation and comparison with other detection strategies. *Electroencephalogr Clin Neurophysiol* **107**, 27–32

Geddes, C.C., Fox, J.G., Allison, M.E., Boulton-Jones, J.M. and Simpson, K. (1998) An artificial neural network can select patients at high risk of developing progressive IgA nephropathy more accurately than experienced nephrologists. *Nephrol Dial Transplant* **13**, 67–71

Grossberg, S. (1975) A neural model of attention, reinforcement and discrimination learning. *Int Rev Neurobiol* **18**, 263–327

Gurgen, F., Onal, E. and Varol, F.G. (1997) IUGR detection by ultrasonographic examinations using neural networks. *IEEE Eng Med Biol Mag* **16**, 55–8

Hagiwara, M. (1990) 'Multidirectional associative memories' in: *Proceedings of the International Joint Conference on Neural Networks, Washington, DC*, pp. 3–9. Washington, DC: Institute of Electrical and Electronic Engineering

Haines, C.J., James, A.E., Panesar, N.S. *et al.* (1999) The effect of percutaneous oestradiol on atheroma formation in ovariectomized cholesterol-fed rabbits. *Atherosclerosis* **143**, 369–75

Halford, J.A., Wright, R.G. and Ditchmen, E.J. (1997) Quality assurance in cervical cytology screening. Comparison of rapid rescreening and the PAPNET testing system. *Acta Cytol* **41**, 79–81

Hebb, D.O. (1949) *The Organisation of Behaviour*. NewYork: John Wiley

Hecht-Nielsen, R. (1988) Applications of counterpropagation network. *Neural Networks* **1**, 131–9

Jirousek, R. and Kushmerick, N. (1997) Constructing probabilistic models. *Int J Med Inf* **45**, 9–18

Kazi, J.I., Furness, P.N. and Nicholson, M. (1998) Diagnosis of early acute renal allograft rejection by evaluation of multiple histological features using a Bayesian belief network. *J Clin Pathol* **51**, 108–13

Keith, R.D., Westgate, J., Ifeachor, E.C. and Greene, K.R. (1994) Suitability of artificial neural networks for feature extraction from cardiotocogram during labour. *Med Biol Eng Comput* **32**, S51–7

Kohonen, T. (1984) *Self Organization and Associative Memory*, 2nd edn. Berlin: Springer-Verlag

Kol, S., Thaler, I., Paz, N. and Shmueli, O. (1995) Interpretation of non-stress tests by an artificial neural network. *Am J Obstet Gynecol* **172**, 1372–9

Kosko, B. (1988) Bidirectional associative memories. *IEEE Transactions on Systems, Man and Cybernetics* **18**, 49–60

Lapeer, R.J., Dalton, K.J., Prager, R.W., Forsstrom, J.J., Selbmann, H.K. and Derom, R. (1995) Application of neural networks to the ranking of perinatal variables influencing birth weight. *Scand J Clin Lab Invest* **222**, 83–93

Lashley, K.S. (1950) 'In search of the engram' in: *Society of Experimental Biology Symposium No. 4: Psychological Mechanisms in Animal Behaviour*, pp. 478–505. London: Cambridge University Press

Lim, C.P., Harrison, R.F. and Kennedy, R.L. (1997) Application of autonomous neural network systems to medical pattern classification tasks. *Artif Intell Med* **11**, 215–39

Mango, L.J. (1994) Computer-assisted cervical cancer screening using neural networks. *Cancer Lett* **77**, 155–62

Mango, L.J. (1996) Reducing false negatives in clinical practice: the role of neural network technology. *Am J Obstet Gynecol* **175**, 1114–19

Mango, L.J. and Valente, P.T. (1998) Neural-network-assisted analysis and microscopic rescreening in presumed negative cervical cytologic smears: a comparison. *Acta Cytol* **42**, 227–32

Michelow, P.M., Hlongwane, N.F. and Leiman, G. (1997) Simulation of primary cervical cancer screening by the PAPNET system in an unscreened, high-risk community. *Acta Cytol* **41**, 88–92

Minsky, M. and Papert, S. (1969) *Perceptrons*. Cambridge, MA: MIT Press

Mitchell, H. and Medley, G. (1998) Detection of laboratory false negative smears by the PAPNET cytologic screening system. *Acta Cytol* **42**, 265–70

Mongelli, M., Chang, A.M.Z. and Sahota, D.S. (1997) The development of a hybrid expert system for the interpretation of fetal acid-base status. *Int J Med Inf* **44**, 135–44

Nikiforidis, G.C. and Sakellaropoulos, G.C. (1998) Expert system support using Bayesian belief networks in the prognosis of head-injured patients of the ICU. *Med Inform (Lond)* **23**, 1–18

Ouwerkerk-Noordam, E., Boon, M.E. and Beck, S. (1994) Computer-assisted primary screening of cervical smears using the PAPNET method: comparison with conventional screening and evaluation of the role of the cytologist. *Cytopathology* **5**, 211–18

Pofahl, W.E., Walczak, S.M., Rhone, E. and Izenberg, S.D. (1998) Use of an artificial neural network to predict length of stay in acute pancreatitis. *Am Surg* **64**, 868–72

Rao, V.B. and Rao, H.V. (1995*) Neural Networks and Fuzzy Logic*. New York: MIS Press

Ritter, H., Martinez, T. and Schulten, K. (1992) *Neural Computation and Self Organizing Maps*. Reading, MA: Addison Wesley

Rosenblatt, F. (1959) 'Two theorems of statistical separability in the Perceptron' in: *Mechanisation of Thought Processes: Proceedings of a Symposium held in the National Physical Laboratory*, pp. 421–56. London: HMSO

Rumelhart, D.E., Hinton, G.E. and Williams, R.J. (1986) 'Learning internal representation by error propagation' in: D.E. Rumelhart, J.L. McClelland and the PDP Research Group (Eds) *Parallel Distributed Processing. Explorations in the Microstructure of Cognition: Foundations* **2**, pp. 318–62. Cambridge, MA: MIT Press

Schechter, C.B. (1996) Cost-effectiveness of rescreening conventionally prepared cervical smears by PAPNET testing. *Acta Cytol* **40**, 1272–82

Skapura, D.M. (1996) *Building Neural Networks*. New York: Addison Wesley

Spitzer, M. (1998) Cervical screening adjuncts: recent advances. *Am J Obstet Gynecol* **179**, 544–56

Sturgis, C.D., Isoe, C., McNeal, N.E., Yu, G.H. and DeFrias, D.V. (1998) PAPNET computer-aided rescreening for detection of benign and malignant glandular elements in cervicovaginal smears: a review of 61 cases. *Diagn Cytopathol* **18**, 307–11

Ulbricht, C., Dorffner, G. and Lee, A. (1998) *Neural networks* for recognizing patterns in cardiotocograms. *Artif Intell Med* **12**, 271–84

Vineis, P. and Rainoldi, A. (1997) Neural networks and logistic regression: analysis of a case–control study on myocardial infarction. *J Clin Epidemiol* **50**, 1309–10

Walker, P. (1999) 'PAPNET and cervical screening' in: P.M.S. O'Brien (Ed.) *Yearbook of Obstetrics and Gynaecology* **7**, pp. 163–9. London: RCOG Press

Wang, H.C., Dopazo, J. and Carazo, J.M. (1998) Self-organizing tree growing network for classifying amino acids. *Bioinformatics* **14**, 376–7

Winterer, G., Ziller, M., Kloppel, B., Heinz, A., Schmidt, L.G. and Herrmann, W.M. (1998) Analysis of quantitative EEG with artificial neural networks and discriminant analysis – a methodological comparison. *Neuropsychobiology* **37**, 41–8

Index